SELLING YOUR COINS & BANKNOTES?

Warwick and Warwick have an expanding requirement for coin and banknote collections, British and worldwide and for coins and notes of individual value. Our customer base is increasing dramatically and we need an ever larger supply of quality material to keep pace with demand. The market has never been stronger and if you are considering the sale of your collection, now is the time to act.

2 6 NOV 2018

FREE VALUATIONS
We will provide a free, professional and without obligation valuation of your collection. Either we will make you a fair, binding private treaty offer, or we will recommend inclusion of your property in our next specialist public auction.

FREE TRANSPORTATION
We can arrange insured transportation of your collection to our Warwick offices completely free of charge. If you decline our offer, we ask you to cover the return carriage costs only.

FREE VISITS
Visits by our valuers are possible anywhere in the country or abroad, usually within 48 hours, in order to value larger collections. Please telephone for details.

VALUATION DAYS
We are staging a series of valuation days and will be visiting all areas of England, Scotland, Wales and Ireland during the coming months. Please visit our website or telephone for further details.

EXCELLENT PRICES
Because of the strength of our customer base we are in a position to offer prices that we feel sure will exceed your expectations.

ACT NOW
Telephone or email Richard Beale today with details of your property.

Warwick & Warwick Ltd.
Auctioneers and Valuers
Chalon House, Scar Bank, Millers Road,
Warwick CV34 5DB
Tel: 01926 499031 Fax: 01926 491906
E-mail: richard.beale@warwickandwarwick.com
www.warwickandwarwick.com

D0293755

Warwick & Warwick

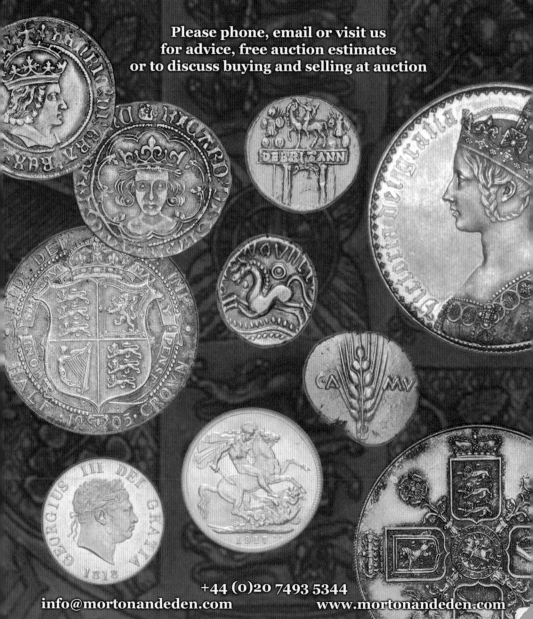

CHARD

— SINCE 1964 —

32-36 Harrowside
Blackpool FY4 1RJ
Tel: 01253 843784
Email: info@chards.co.uk
www.chards.co.uk
Open - Mon to Fri 9am-5pm
First Saturday of each month

COINS MEDALLIONS BARS HAMMERED MILLED BRITISH FOREIGN ANCIENT MODERN MEDALS

As the UK's Bullion Dealer of the Year, we offer a wide selection of coins.

Inform, Educate, Inspire

WE BUY COINS - High Grade Coins Wanted

No matter which coins you have for sale, we will always make you an offer. We are particularly interested in high grade numismatic material, including early sovereigns, British hammered and milled, Roman, Greek and Ancient coins.

No Minimum or Maximum Price or Quantity

Whether you have one coin or thousands, we will make you an offer. We pride ourselves in being fair and competitive with our prices - and that price is guaranteed - no waiting for auctions to end.

Immediate Payment

Payment is usually effected the same day, either by cheque, cash or bank transfer. No commission, no fees, no delay.

We Sell Coins

We have an increasing selection of coins from the world's leading mints and refineries. We sell the latest bullion and commemorative coins, we also have an exceptional range of coins going back to ancient times.

COINS MEDALLIONS BARS HAMMERED MILLED BRITISH FOREIGN ANCIENT MODERN MEDALS

Established Over 50 Years

We have been buying and selling coins since 1964. We have both an online and physical presence and you are welcome to visit our showroom. Whether you want to buy or sell, our team of professionals will be happy to help you.

Voted UK Bullion Dealer of the Year 2016 and 2015!

Visit our showroom

THE

COIN
Yearbook

2017

Edited by
John W. Mussell, FRGS
and the Editorial Team of COIN NEWS

ISBN 978 1 908828 30 9

Published by
TOKEN PUBLISHING LIMITED
40 Southernhay East, Exeter, Devon EX1 1PE
Telephone: 01404 46972
email: info@tokenpublishing.com. Website: www.tokenpublishing.com

Printed in Great Britain by Latimer Trend & Company Ltd., Plymouth

Mark Rasmussen Numismatist Ltd.

Specialising in Coins of Great Britain, Scotland, Ireland and the Islands

A small selection of notable coins handled in recent years

Twenty Pound Piece of James VI of Scotland

Sovereign of Henry VII

Sovereign of Henry VIII

Ryal of Elizabeth I

Triple Unite of Charles I

Five Guineas of Charles II

Countermarked U.S. Dollar of George III

Proof Gold Penny of George III

1933 Penny of George V

1935 Proof Crown in Gold

1937 Penny of Edward VIII

1819 Sovereign of George III

1952 Penny of George VI

1937 Threepence of Edward VIII

P. O. Box 42, Betchworth, Surrey RH3 7YR
Telephone/Fax: 01306 884 880
Mobile: 07798 611006
e-mail: mark.rasmussen@rascoins.com   www.rascoins.com

BNTA

CONTENTS

FOREWORD

WELCOME to the 2017 edition of the COIN YEARBOOK—the best-selling British price guide and collector's handbook for the increasingly popular hobby of coin collecting. If this is your first YEARBOOK then welcome, you will find just about every English, Irish and Scottish coin listed here, as well as the most collected "Island" coins, not to mention a cross section of the early Roman and ancient British coins. The book will prove invaluable when you are trying to work out exactly what you have and how much it is worth! Remember, the prices here are those you can expect to pay at a dealer's table, on-line or at auction, they are not selling prices. Unlike the United States market, which produces two books: red books for buying, blue books for selling, the British market doesn't work that way; the price you might get for your coins depends very much on who you are selling to—different dealers operate on different margins so you may well find that one dealer will offer you one price, another will offer something different, so it's worth "shopping around". Of course, the reality is that if you've picked this book up because you have found granddad's old collection in the attic, then most of the coins you find won't actually appeal to dealers at all, so no matter how much you shop around no-one will offer you anything! This may sound overly negative and you may be wondering why you'd be interested in collecting, in carrying on granddad's hobby if there's nothing exciting to be found. The answer to that is simple: take granddad's collection of pennies. He has them all from 1900 until decimalisation in 1971, you take the album to a dealer and as he flicks through the first pages tells you that they really aren't worth much at all and that he doesn't want them. Then he turns the page and his eyes light up—he reaches for his cheque book and offers you tens of thousands of pounds for it! Why? What's the difference? Well, the first ones he saw were just a drop in the ocean of a huge mintage. Millions of those coins were produced and the collectors who want them already have them— there's no market and so they are not of interest to a dealer. Then his eyes alighted on one coin that was minted in 1933 and is one of just seven known, and that makes it worth a . . . ahem, mint!

That's the attraction of coin collecting, that's the thrill, the buzz, getting a complete set of something, finding that rarity, finding the best example you can (that's very important, always buy the best grade coin you can—even in a mintage of hundreds of thousands the extremely fine or uncirculated coins will appeal); and that's where a book like this will come into its own. You are unlikely to find a 1933 penny (sorry) but this book will tell you which variety of 1983 2p is worth £750, which variety of Olympic 50p is worth a similar amount (yes, even coins you find in your change every day can be worth thousands of times their face value if you know what to look for) and, just as importantly will tell you what you should be paying to add to your collection when you realise you don't actually want to part with granddad's coins at all and instead want to carry on where he left off!

Coin Collecting may have been a little more popular back when granddad was a schoolboy than it is today but that's only because there was a wider variety of coins to look for and the

youngster who found a 1905 shilling in his change was a happy one. Today's decimal coinage has meant a slow-down in those "checking their change" for rarities (although some are still out there), but that doesn't mean coin collecting is dying— far from it. In recent years the hobby has gone from strength to strength, both as a fun pastime and as a great way to invest. The hobby as a whole, and that includes the publishers of this book, doesn't encourage coin collecting for investment , we would rather people collected for the enjoyment of it, but there is no doubt that as interest rates go down and gold goes up in the wake of the Brexit vote, more and more people are looking to put their money into other things. If you're one of those then you're welcome too! We cannot, of course, ever guarantee that your "investment" will go up, but we can guarantee you will enjoy the actual collecting part of it. This hobby is an absorbing one, a fascinating one and the acquisition of that elusive date or die variety piece (see the article on varieties on pages 17–19) is exhilarating and a great deal of fun —but not if it comes at too high a price and that's why you need a book like this!

Naturally there are factors beyond our control, for example the price of gold is volatile at the best of times, so those coins bought just for their metal content rather than numismatic value will be subject to the natural vagaries of market forces. Also, grading is a very subjective issue and a coin that you may consider to be one grade, a dealer may believe is another and that too will affect price. But at least with the COIN YEARBOOK you will have a guide. You will be able to buy and sell with confidence and that is why we take a great deal of care to ensure that the prices contained within these pages reflect the market conditions. We check auction results, dealers lists and on-line auctions too (although that can be a mine-field with some wide swings depending on who is bidding on any given day). However, we also get leading experts in their field to oversee what we are doing and with that in mind we would like to thank the following for their help, guidance and expertise: Chris Rudd and Elizabeth Cottam (Celtic), Mike Vosper (Roman), Stephen Mitchell of Studio Coins (Hammered), Roy Norbury of West Essex Coin Investments (Milled), Nick Swabey (Maundy), Patrick Mackenzie (Decimal) and Charles Riley (Commemorative medals). We also acknowledge the help given by David Stuart (Scottish section), Del Parker (Irish) and the many other dealers and collectors who have given us the benefit of their expertise in the various sections which make this book the leader in its field. In addition we would like to thank the many auction houses who have allowed us to use images from their archives.

Should you have any questions regarding this publication or indeed any aspect of the absorbing hobby of coin or medal collecting, feel free to write or email to the address given on page 9 and we will do our best to help. If you are unfamiliar with our monthly magazine COIN NEWS, or if you need any accessories such as coin holders, trays or albums to help you with your hobby, them visit our website at www.tokenpublishing.com where you will find everything you need. If you would like a free sample copy of the magazine simply email us and we will be happy to send a copy, with our compliments.

On a final note, remember that the prices given for modern gold and many silver coins in this book are subject to variation due to the volatility of the market prices for precious metals. This obviously affects the coin market in many ways, particularly when buying and selling common-date sovereigns and the like, therefore the prices quoted must be seen as a guide only and can change on a daily basis. The current price of gold can be checked on our website which is constantly up-dated.

Variety
is the spice of life

Many collectors become very enthusiastic about varieties. Learned tomes have been written, recording every known variation of every coin issued, such as those by Peck, Freeman, Rayner, Davies, to name just a few. In this introductory article collector CHRIS RIGBY gives us a fascinating insight into the world of varieties. It is not a list of varieties, as it would take a volume the size of this Yearbook to record the milled varieties since 1816 alone! Here we look at the many different causes of such variations, and illustrate each different sort of variety using the "bun penny" series of 1860–94, which encapsulates just about all kinds.

It might be useful to begin with a tentative definition of what should be classed as a "variety". My own would be: "an observable difference between currency coins of the same date and design". That would exclude proofs, for example; there are no official proofs in the bun penny series, but nevertheless some extremely rare specimens of certain dates do exist. However, as a proof is a special strike of the same design as was issued for currency, I would not class it as a variety as such.

The same applies to patterns. Peck records pennies of 1860 where Victoria is crowned rather than wreathed, and another where the date is in Roman numerals. These are also extremely rare, but were never adopted for currency issues, and for the purposes of this article are not considered "varieties". (There are exceptions of course—the 1882 penny struck by the London Mint and not by Heatons and therefore carrying no H mintmark, is so rare one must assume it is a pattern or trial, but the few which exist are widely sought after.)

Finally we should exclude mis-strikes. There is certainly a healthy market for brockages and their like, but as each specimen is unique, other examples of the same thing cannot be hunted down by collectors, and that—after all—is the point of varieties; however rare, more than one example exists and they can be collected.

So what are the different kinds of variety, and what examples of them occur in the bun penny series? We could start with the classic "overdate variety". These are often found throughout the milled series from the 17th to 19th centuries, and are usually the result of an unused die from a previous year being pressed into service for use in a later year. The last digit in the date is re-punched often with a trace of the underlying digit remaining. The 1865/3 penny is a typical example: the mintage for 1863 was very high, and given the similarity between the figures 3 and 5 (especially as the type of 3 used had the same flat top as a 5), it's easy to see why dies would be re-used in 1865. This also occurs on other digits including the 8 over a 6 on the rare 1862 penny illustrated below.

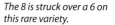

The 8 is struck over a 6 on this rare variety.

The colon dots after the D of F:D: have disappeared from this 1860 penny.

As well as deliberate "overdate" amendments, dies could suffer from accidental damage and wear. A crack would produce a thin raised line on the struck coin, while wear might cause colon dots to gradually disappear. Neither of these effects is particularly remarkable or noted in publications, but occasionally a dramatic effect leads to a notable variety. One such is the 1860 penny that reads "ONF PENNY" on the reverse. This has been caused by the bottom of the "E" becoming clogged on the die, and because of its distinctiveness (leading some collectors to believe it's an error) has led to a very collectable variety.

Speaking of mistakes, the engraving of dies is also subject to human error. For example, lettering errors in the king's name are legion on the copper coins of William III (the Latin for William is GVLIELMVS, not an easy thing to spell!). However, there is also a bun penny dated 1862 where the date numerals have been mistakenly used from a halfpenny punch, and another variety dated 1861 where the 6 has been re-punched over an erroneous 8. These are very rare and noticeable varieties. However, as time goes by human error becomes less and less a factor, and these two penny varieties are both examples of the "exception that proves the rule".

A halfpenny punch was used on some 1862 pennies, giving smaller than normal figures in the date.

The next type of variety might also be considered human error, though it could equally be pragmatism. "Mules" are coins featuring an obverse/reverse combination not designed to be used together. A classic example would be the 1860 pennies where one face has the earlier beaded border, while the other has the later toothed border. As these mules are so rare, they should perhaps be considered an error—noticed early in the strike—as there would be thousands in existence if they had been planned.

Mules with beaded border (left) on one side and toothed border (right) on the other are rare.

Before leaving the subject of varieties that result from features of individual dies, we should mention "die identifiers" which the Mint used often on silver coins during Victoria's reign, but which are also present on some very rare bun pennies too. A few specimens dated 1863 have a small number below the date, "2", "3" or "4". These were probably a trial, as die numbers were introduced very soon afterwards on silver, and although varieties as such, are not widely collected for the number, unlike the 1863 pennies which are collected for their rarity.

The most common cause of varieties, and the most widely reported and collected, are those that result from minor design changes. There are very many of these in the bun penny series, and the range of examples chosen will simply reflect the differing sorts, and how recognisable they are. For further enlightenment, please see the books by Michael Freeman and Michael Gouby which attempt to classify every known variety in the series.

First, we must distinguish between varieties and types. The most obvious example of the latter is the existence of both large copper and smaller bronze pennies, both dated 1860. The copper penny is not a variety. In every possible way, it's different—size, weight, composition, design.

1860 penny with a clear raised dot between E and N of PENNY.

It's the last date of the old series of base metal denominations before the Mint switched from copper to bronze. It's a type.

However, knowing where to draw the line is a bit more difficult. In 1874, the obverse of the bun penny was "aged" subtly (the Queen was no spring chicken by then!); her hair, chin, eyes, and mouth, have all been recut, and experienced collectors have no difficulty in telling the two different obverse types of 1874 apart. But what about inexperienced collectors? To them, the two obverses would look more or less the same, the "bun" design. So what are they—different types, or varieties? This is a matter of judgement for individual collectors, I believe. I would personally think of them as types but I can understand the opposite point of view.

The tiny number 3 can be clearly seen below the date of this 1863 penny.

As stated before, there are a vast number of small design changes in the first few years of bun pennies, almost certainly not all fully discovered or documented even now. Peck, Freeman, Jerraims and Gouby have all produced detailed and illustrated descriptions of their discoveries each adding to what was already known at the time. These range from the recognisable to the microscopic, and those that are CLEARLY RECOGNISABLE and / or RARE are more popular with collectors than those that aren't either.

The list of changes to bun pennies between 1860 and 1863 is too long to deal with in a general article, but to just give an idea of their scope and range they include: the beaded border became toothed; the number and delineation of berries and leaves in Victoria's wreath; features such as her nose, eyes, mouth, strands of hair; the design and curvature of Britannia's shield, trident, helmet; lighthouse and ship; outer circle; the thickness of lettering; the presence and location of designer initials; among others. Nor is it confined to the early years, as the dramatically different date widths between 1875 and 1879 attest. But by 1883, the designs had stabilised, and from then until the end of the series in 1894, there are very few varieties to look out for.

On the reverse of this 1862 penny Britannia definitely has extra plumes to her helmet.

So that's almost it. Varieties come in all shapes and sizes, and have a multiplicity of sources. Almost as varied are the different kinds of "variety collector" who range from the devoted completist to the occasion dabbler in the better known sort. As stated earlier though, the popularity (i.e. fame) and rarity of a particular variety will attract more collectors and ultimately higher catalogue values. This goes a long way to explain why tiny changes that occur on pennies of both 1905 and 1937—none of which is rare—attract little attention, while an equally tiny variation in the exergue line of 1940 pennies has resulted in a now-popular variety, the first issue being so much scarcer than the second.

I hope you've enjoyed reading about the world of varieties, and that if you are, or are inspired to become, a collector of them, you will find what you are looking for and experience a great deal of satisfaction in the search. Good hunting!

Illustrations for this article are from the Laurie Bamford Collection courtesy of DNW.

PUBLIC AUCTIONS
IN THE NORTH OF ENGLAND
Coins, Medals & Banknotes

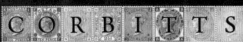

MUSEUM *archive*

Every month in COIN NEWS we are privileged to feature one of the rare items from the Royal Mint's Museum at Llanstrisant. The collection represents one of the most impressive numismatic collections in the world, featuring outstanding rarities alongside the currency we all use in our every day lives. Here we have chosen a few of the items we have featured, as a "snap shot" of the Museum's treasures.

First accession to the Royal Mint Museum

The Royal Mint Museum has recently celebrated its 200th anniversary, an event which has led to some reflection on the origins of the Museum. It all started on February 12, 1816 when William Wellesley Pole wrote a memorandum expressing his deep concern that there was no collection of coins, medals or tools in the Royal Mint. He requested, in reasonably robust terms, that from then on arrangements should be put in place for the establishment of such a collection which would provide for specimens of newly struck coins and medals to be set aside.

The original instruction indicated that accessions registers should be created containing details of the items in question, together with the names of the designers, principal Mint officers, mintages and, importantly, precisely where the items were to be located. The first coin recorded in the first Royal Mint Museum accessions register was a Military Guinea of 1813. In line with Pole's wishes, it is an attractive proof specimen and other early items included, not unexpectedly, coins of the recoinage of 1816–17 as well as very rare gold five-sovereign and double-sovereign pieces from the end of George III's reign. Pole was almost certainly strongly influenced by the famous naturalist Sir Joseph Banks to start the collection and what both men began is still thriving to this day.

23

Coins of Iceland

THE Royal Mint Museum's collection of coins is a reflection of the work undertaken by the Royal Mint, with samples from every order finding their way into the Museum. It should come as no surprise, then, that there are a larger number of coins in the collection from overseas countries than there are from the United Kingdom. Although the work of the Mint has had this international profile for hundreds of years, exporting to the world received a boost in 1922 with the arrival of the energetic Deputy Master Sir Robert Johnson. He actively sought work from wherever it could be found, whether from Albania, Guatemala, the Soviet Union or anywhere else and a long-standing relationship with Iceland has emerged from Johnson's legacy.

The coinage of most counties has a distinctive national character but this is especially true of Iceland. A major reform of the coinage in the early 1980s resulted in a complete re-design of the circulating coins and it was the highly stylised work of Icelandic artist Throstur Magnusson that was chosen for the new obverses. The reverses, with their representations of animals important to the economy and culture of Iceland in the form of dolphins, cod and shrimp, bear more than a passing resemblance to the Irish coinage of the 1920s. It is a symbolically rich coinage, projecting the myths and legends of the country, and it remains one of the most abidingly beautiful of the modern age.

Gold trial plate of 1542

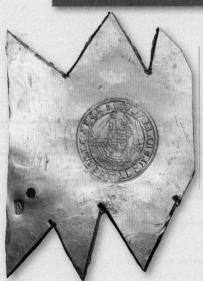

The presence of privy marks on coinage is very familiar. In medieval and early modern times, prior to coins carrying an actual date, they provide a means by which a sequence of production can be established and periods of issue determined. It is much less common to see such marks on trial plates, but there are instances when this happened, one of which being the gold trial plate of 1542.

Precious metal trial plates were used in the testing of gold and silver coins to ensure their composition was correct and Sir Martin Bowes, who at this time was Master of the Royal Mint, chose to have the symbol of a bow punched into the plate as an additional identifying mark. Bowes was a significant figure and was one of the chief architects of the debasement of English coins of the mid 1540s. The presence of the bow might be seen as evidence of the personal authority he exercised over the coinage and it is certainly illustrative of his influence and power that his should be one of the few such marks to appear on trial plates.

Medal of Joseph Edgar Boehm

The name of the sculptor Joseph Edgar Boehm, and in particular his initials J E B, are well known to numismatists, associated as they are with his portrait of Queen Victoria on the Jubilee coinage of 1887. He was a highly regarded artist and evidence of his work is readily to be found in London and elsewhere, such as his statue of Wellington at Hyde Park Corner and of Charles Darwin in the Natural History Museum. But his effigy of Victoria was vilified, surviving for less than a decade before being replaced by the portrait by Thomas Brock.

Less well known are images of Boehm but the Royal Mint Museum recently acquired a handsome bronze medal created by his fellow sculptor Edouard Lanteri. French by birth, Lanteri came to London in 1872 and served as a studio assistant to Boehm, later becoming an influential teacher in his own right and his books on the human form have been standard texts for generations of sculptors. Lanteri exhibited a statuette of Boehm at the Royal Academy in 1885 and the medal dates from 1891, a year after Boehm's death. It has always been something of a tragedy that a sculptor of Boehm's standing should have such a poorly regarded portrait as the chief aspect of his numismatic legacy but he was a man of considerable ability and the inspiration he gave to his fellow sculptors is amply demonstrated in Lanteri's medal.

The Royal Mint Museum in 1904

On February 12 this year the Royal Mint Museum celebrated its 200th anniversary with a conference at the Tower of London. The history of any collection, be it private or public, local or national, will always be influenced by those who are charged with looking after it. Towards the end of the 19th century the Royal Mint Museum was fortunate enough to be in the care of William John Hocking, a senior figure at the Royal Mint who somehow found the time to catalogue and add extensively to the collection. He also arranged for it to be put on public display for the first time.

A large room, with a floor area of more than 1,300 square feet, was identified and, assisted by the London dealer F. W. Lincoln, Hocking classified and put together an exhibition made up of no fewer than 25 show cases. The exhibition opened to the public in October 1904 and presented more than 5,000 items ranging across Ancient British, Anglo-Gallic, Scottish, Irish and colonial coins, as well as a selection of medals and tradesman's tokens. It was a gathering together of rare and beautiful items in bewildering profusion. The image of the Museum from 1904 is well known from sets of Royal Mint postcards but this version is taken direct from a recently unearthed glass negative in the collection and reveals the Museum's public display in a remarkable level of clarity.

THE Royal Mint Museum celebrated its 200th anniversary in 2016 so it was rather appropriate that the UK's mint should open The Royal Mint Experience on this auspicious date. Situated in its vast 35-acre site at Llantrisant in Wales, the purpose-built visitors' centre opened to great acclaim on May 19 and the team from Token Publishing were there for the special preview day, an opportunity to see what all the excitement was about—they were not disappointed. The new centre is sure to prove a big draw and not only to numismatists but also for anyone interested in our history or those who simply want a behind the scenes look at one of the country's oldest institutions. With a large, free car park and restaurant, the only tricky bit is getting there! Above is a "snapshot" of the day the Token Team saw the Royal Mint Experience go live!

To find out more, simply go to www.royalmint.com/experience.

MONARCHS *of England*

Here we list the Kings and Queens from Anglo-Saxon times to the present, with the dates of their rule. Before Eadgar became the King of all England the country had been divided up into small kingdoms, each with their own ruler.

ANGLO-SAXON KINGS

The Anglo-Saxon monarchs ruled over the various kingdoms which existed in England following the withdrawal of the Romans in the 5th century AD. The most prominent kingdoms in the land were Kent, Sussex, Wessex, Mercia and Northumbria. Each kingdom produced its own coinage but in 973 Eadgar introduced a new coinage that became the standard for the whole of the country.

Eadgar (959–975)
Edward the Martyr (975–978)
Aethelred II (978–1016)
Cnut (1016–1035)
Harold I (1035–1040)
Harthacanut (1035–1042)
Edward the Confessor (1042–1066)
Harold II (1066)

NORMAN KINGS

The Normans came to Britain from their native France following the establishment of a kingdom in Sicily and southern Italy. An expedition led by the powerful Duke William of Normandy culminated in the battle of Hastings in 1066 where he defeated Harold II and was proclaimed King of All England. Their influence spread from these new centres to the Crusader States in the Near East and to Scotland and Wales in Great Britain, and to Ireland. Today their influence can be seen in their typical Romanesque style of architecture.

William I (1066–1087)
William II (1087–1100)
Henry I (1100–1135)
Stephen (1135–1154)

PLANTAGENETS

The Plantagenet kings of England were descended from the first House of Anjou who were established as rulers of England through the Treaty of Wallingford, which passed over the claims of Eustace and William, Stephen of Blois's sons, in favour of Henry of Anjou, son of the Empress Matilda and Geoffrey V, Count of Anjou.

Henry II (1154–1189)
Richard I (1189–1199)
John (1199–1216)
Henry III (1216–1272)
Edward I (1272–1307)
Edward II (1307–1327)
Edward III (1327–1377)
Richard II (1377–1399)

HOUSE OF LANCASTER

The House of Lancaster, a branch of the English royal House of Plantagenet, was one of the opposing factions involved in the Wars of the Roses, the civil war which dominated England and Wales during the 15th century. Lancaster provided England with three Kings

Henry IV (1399–1413)
Henry V (1413–1422)
Henry VI (1422–1461) and again 1470

HOUSE OF YORK

The House of York was the other branch of the House of Plantagenet involved in the disastrous Wars of the Roses. Edward IV was descended from Edmund of Langley, 1st Duke of York, the fourth surviving son of Edward III.

Edward IV (1461–1483 and again 1471–83)
Richard III (1483–1485)

TUDORS

The House of Tudor was an English royal dynasty that lasted 118 years, from 1485 to 1603. The family descended from the Welsh courtier Owen Tudor (Tewdwr). Following the defeat of Richard III at Bosworth, the battle that ended the Wars of the Roses, Henry Tudor, 2nd Earl of Richmond, took the throne as Henry VII.

Henry VII (1485–1509)
Henry VIII (1509–1547)
Edward VI (1547–1553)
Mary (1553–1558)
Philip & Mary (1554–1558)
Elizabeth I (1558–1603)

STUARTS

The House of Stuart ruled Scotland for 336 years, between 1371 and 1707. Elizabeth I of England's closest heir was James VI of Scotland via her grandfather Henry VII of England, who was founder of the Tudor dynasty. On Elizabeth's death, James Stuart ascended the thrones of England and Ireland and inherited the English claims to the French throne. The Stuarts styled themselves "Kings and Queens of Great Britain", although there was no parliamentary union until the reign of Queen Anne, the last monarch of the House of Stuart.

James I (1603–1625)
Charles I (1625–1649)
The Commonwealth (1653–1658)
Charles II (1660–1685)
James II (1685–1688)
William III & Mary (1688–1694)
William III (1694–1702)
Anne (1702–1714)

HOUSE OF HANOVER

The House of Hanover was a Germanic royal dynasty which ruled the Duchy of Brunswick-Lüneburg and the Kingdom of Hanover. George Ludwig ascended to the throne of the Kingdom of Great Britain and Ireland through the female line from Princess Elizabeth, sister of Charles I.

George I (1714–1727)
George II (1727–1760)
George III (1760–1820)
George IV (1820–1830)
William IV (1830–1837)
Victoria (1837–1901)

HOUSES OF SAXE-COBURG-GOTHA AND WINDSOR

The name Saxe-Coburg-Gotha was inherited by Edward VII from his father Prince Albert, the second son of the Duke of Saxe-Coburg-Gotha and husband of Victoria. During World War I the name was changed to Windsor to avoid the Germanic connotatiion.

Edward VII (1901–1910)
George V (1910–1936)
Edward VIII (1936)
George VI (1936–1952)
Elizabeth II (1952–)

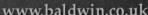

BUYING *on eBay*

Here is some timely advice for those thinking of bidding on-line

When I registered with eBay UK 18 years ago the grand total of items for sale in all categories was 850,000 which I thought at the time was an enormous amount of listings but that now looks tiny. Eighteen years later the "coins" category alone contains over 215,000 items, "banknotes" over 74,000, over 9,500 in "tokens" and almost 10,000 in "historical medals/medallions". This gives a grand total of about 308,500 numismatic items to choose from. At the time of writing the number of British items listed on eBay.co.uk in each category was as follows: coins, over 143,000; banknotes, almost 9,500; more than 6,000 tokens and almost 5,000 in historical medals/medallions. Sellers have moved away from auction type listings with around 75 per cent now preferring to list under "Buy It Now" with a fixed price which is sometimes open to offers, the prices ranged from one penny to £29,000.

When SELLING on eBay make full use of the title rather than putting off potential bidders by just having "coin" in the title as some lazy sellers do. If a seller can't be bothered to write an informative title then why should bidders be bothered to bid? The title of any numismatic item should include as much relevant information as there is space for, i.e. country of origin, denomination, date, metal, size, condition. It's acceptable to have a title in all capitals but not the actual listing, as this might put bidders off—if a bidder is visually impaired they will have adjusted their PC's font size accordingly so a huge font size is unnecessary. Some sellers have minimum information about their item on offer but have several paragraphs of terms and conditions, this is not required as all that happens is the buyer pays and the seller posts the well packed item. It's advisable to search eBay for completed similar items before creating a listing as it is pointless asking £100 for a coin if a similar one sold recently for £9.99. Try to use the most appropriate numismatic category to maximise the selling price and avoid spelling errors in order to appear in the maximum number of search results. If selling an error coin or banknote, have the side with the error as the main picture as potential buyers tend to look at the illustrations rather than the title description.

When BUYING on eBay beware of sellers who sell coins using US grading terms or coins that have been graded by US grading companies and then quoting UK catalogue prices, as the US grade EF is very different from a UK EF. Few collectors would claim to be an expert on coin grading so compare the grading given on eBay with similar coins on offer on the web sites of long established UK dealers before deciding on a maximum bid. A professional dealer's coin priced at £200 and graded VF might be a better buy than a similar coin at priced at £100 and graded as being EF on eBay.

Always read the seller's coin descriptions very carefully, especially when bidding on gold coins. For example, if a coin is described as weighing .2gr, don't misread this as 2gr as sometimes happens—an honest seller will use "0.2" and not ".2" to make it clear.

To snipe or not to snipe is a subject often under consideration by bidders. Not bidding until the final few seconds has advantages as it denies competitors the chance to place any more bids, but it also does likewise for the sniper. Another benefit is that rival collectors who regularly battle for items are prevented from searching for current items bid on by competing collectors if sniping is used, it also prevents drawing attention to that once in a decade eBay super bargain. As most coin dealers seem to recommend not sniping then it's definitely the best tactic for a collector to get an item for the lowest possible price. It also removes the possibility of a bidding war breaking out with the victim of "auction

fever" paying over the odds just to win at all costs and beat the opposition.

eBay listings can be entertaining when looking at silly sellers listing items at silly high prices, many of whom sell just a very small percentage of their overpriced and often over graded offerings. A search for "unknown" or "mystery" can sometimes bring up interesting or valuable items but some sellers sell only "unknown" items regardless of how easy they are to identify. A search using spelling errors can find items that the majority of collectors might miss, e.g. "soveren", "Scotish", etc., or if local tokens are the item of interest try a few town name spelling errors.

Unfortunately, as it now seems possible to fool many of the people most of the time, 100 per cent feedback is no longer a true indication of a seller's honesty. Some unscrupulous eBay sellers will list a penny for sale at one penny with "collection only", with no option to have it posted and of course the penny is never collected, so every time they do this they and each buyer receives a positive feedback. They are in effect selling feedback for 1p and they get to build up a lot of positive feedback for themselves,

presumably to make it easier to defraud buyers later when they have a reasonable amount of feedback.

For young collectors or for those on a limited budget, eBay shops can be worth a browse but the better coins tend to be listed as an auction or a "Buy It Now". The categories are well laid out so finding a specific area of interest is easy. Shop items tend to be low grade and priced at full retail so a bargain buy will require a lot of time-consuming luck to find. A seller can be offering several thousand UK coins with some priced at hundreds of pounds each but a look at their feedback reveals that the majority of their sales are for coins priced at under a tenner. For a seller this is a way of getting a lot of traffic which would be very difficult to achieve otherwise.

As a few banknote collectors might be reading this, a few words of warning will not go amiss There are very large numbers of ironed notes on eBay with some sellers selling only ironed notes to gullible collectors. Some collectors have yet to work out that to be able to offer an unlimited supply of older "uncirculated" notes the seller must be selling ironed notes that they themselves have probably

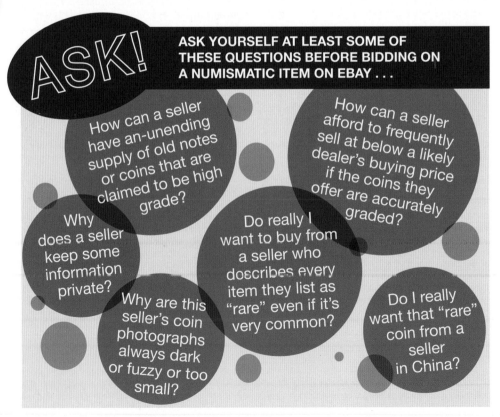

ASK!

ASK YOURSELF AT LEAST SOME OF THESE QUESTIONS BEFORE BIDDING ON A NUMISMATIC ITEM ON EBAY . . .

How can a seller have an-unending supply of old notes or coins that are claimed to be high grade?

How can a seller afford to frequently sell at below a likely dealer's buying price if the coins they offer are accurately graded?

Why does a seller keep some information private?

Do really I want to buy from a seller who describes every item they list as "rare" even if it's very common?

Why are this seller's coin photographs always dark or fuzzy or too small?

Do I really want that "rare" coin from a seller in China?

ironed. Look at a seller's buying feedback as their "unc" note may have been VF if bought a few weeks previously. USA and Canada grading of bank notes is similar to their grading of coins—very optimistic, so look at the pictures very carefully and ignore the claimed grade before bidding. If a note has been slabbed it's probably best to assume that the note will grade in the UK at least one full grade below the grade on the slab. Overgrading of notes is also rife on eBay with many notes that appear from the scans to be in no better than fine condition claimed to be "gVF". If a note arrives in the post that is of lower grade than claimed then send it back and give at least a neutral feedback to warn other collectors. As it's now easier to get unc money for an ironed note than it is to get VF money for a genuine VF note, overgrading can only get worse as more sellers adopt the view "if you can't beat them join them". Unfortunately if a seller claims to grade to IBNS standards this is not a guarantee that they accurately grade their notes, as notes claimed to be "EF" can have many creases. When a banknote has been sold and placed in a sleeve and encased in cardboard it's good practice to place the complete package inside a waterproof bag and seal it with tape before going into the envelope, an unused food bag will do the job cheaply, most of us will have experienced a soggy envelope coming through the letterbox, so a note should be sent in waterproof packaging.

Entering an eBay seller's ID into Google can be a way of avoiding expensive buying mistakes as it can sometimes reveal information that a bad seller would rather have kept quiet. They might have sold forgeries, have a history of selling over-graded coins or have had legal problems for example. Regular readers of *Coin News* are probably savvy enough not to be fooled by bad eBay sellers but the less experienced collector must bid with extreme caution. Due to the huge number of fake ancient coins and antiquities now being listed on eBay it has become essential to perform a Google search for the seller's ID before buying any ancient coin. Some sellers are revealed by a Google search to be sellers of mostly fake ancient coins but they still have hundreds of happy but ignorant repeat buyers. Some major overseas dealers and auction houses have been fooled by very convincing fake ancient coins, so what chance does a collector have of spotting the fakes?

Regular browsing of eBay can be time well spent as a few astute buys can produce a greater short-term profit than twelve months of small time selling with no time consuming scanning and listing to do and no ever increasing eBay and PayPal fees to pay.

In addition to the points raised on the opposite page, here are a few more "rules" to consider before buying on-line:

• Never buy an ancient coin without first Googling the seller's eBay name.

• Always compare the grade of a coin with a similar item on dealers' web sites especially if it's an expensive one.

• If a coin is rare, Google the description with the word "fake" added before buying, e.g. "1934 crown fake", which delivers 1,600,000 results.

• How can a seller afford to frequently sell at below a likely dealer's buying price if the coins they offer are accurately graded?

• Ignore the stated grade and judge from the pictures especially if graded by a USA "slabbing" company as their "EF" can sometimes be a UK fine.

• Avoid sellers whose reply to negative feedback is insults to the giver of the negative feedback.

DATES *on coins*

The vast majority of modern coins bear the date prominently on one side. In most cases dates are expressed in modified Arabic numerals according to the Christian calendar and present no problem in identification. There have been a few notable exceptions to this general rule, however. Morocco, for example, has used European numerals to express dates according to the Moslem calendar, so that a coin dated 1321 actually signifies 1903. Dates are almost invariably written from left to right—even in Arabic script which writes words from right to left. An exception, however, occurred in the Philippines quarto of 1822 where the date appeared as 2281, and the "2"s back to front for good measure.

	ARABIC-TURKISH	CHINESE, JAPANESE KOREAN, ANNAMESE (ORDINARY)	CHINESE, JAPANESE KOREAN, ANNAMESE (OFFICIAL)	INDIAN	SIAMESE	BURMESE
1	۱	一	壹	۹	๑	၁
2	۲	二	貳	২	๒	၂
3	۳	三	叁	৩	๓	၃
4	٤	四	肆	৪	๔	၄
5	٥	五	伍	५	๕	၅
6	٦	六	陸	६	๖	၆
7	٧	七	柒	৩	๗	၇
8	٨	八	捌	৮	๘	၈
9	٩	九	玖	৭	๙	၉
0	٠			০	๐	၀
10	۱۰	十	拾		๙๐	
100	۱۰۰	百			๙๐๐	
1000	۱۰۰۰	千				

Dates in Roman numerals have been used since 1234 when this practice was adopted by the Danish town of Roskilde. Such Roman numerals were used sporadically throughout the Middle Ages and in later centuries and survive fitfully to this day. This was the system used in England for the first dated coins, the gold half-sovereigns of Edward VI struck at Durham House in 1548 (MDXLVIII). This continued till 1550 (MDL) but thereafter Arabic numerals were used, beginning with the half-crown of 1551. Notable exceptions of more recent times include the Gothic coinage of Queen Victoria (1847–87).

The first coin with the date in European numerals was a plappart of St Gallen, Switzerland dated 1424, but this was an isolated case. In 1477 Maria of Burgundy issued a guldiner which bore a date on the reverse, in the form of two pairs of digits flanking the crown at the top. The numerals in this instance were true Gothic, an interesting transition between true Arabic numerals and the modified Arabic figures now used in Europe. The Tyrolese guldengroschen of 1484–6 were the first coins to be regularly dated in European numerals and thereafter this custom spread rapidly.

For the numismatist, the problem arises when coins bear a date in the numerals of a different alphabet or computed according to a different era. Opposite is a table showing the basic numerals used in different scripts. The various eras which may be found in coin dates are as listed and explained opposite.

Hijra

The era used on Moslem coins dates from the flight of Mohammed from Mecca to Medina on July 15, 622 and is often expressed as digits followed by AH (Anno Hegirae). Moslems employ a lunar calendar of twelve months comprising 354 11/30 days. Tipu Sultan of Mysore in 1201 AH (the fifth year of his reign) introduced a new era dating from the birth of Mohammed in AD 570 and using a luni-solar system. Tipu also adopted the Hindu cycle of sixty years (the Tamil Brihaspate Cycle), but changed this two or three years later, from Hijra to Muludi.

Afghan coins used the lunar calendar until 1920 and during 1929–31, but at other times have used the solar calendar. Thus the Democratic Republic began issuing its coins in SH 1358 (1979).

To convert an AH date to the Christian calendar you must translate the Arabic into European numerals. Taking an Arabic coin dated 1320, for example, first deduct 3% (to convert from the Moslem lunar year to our solar year). This gives 39.6 which, rounded up to the nearest whole number, is 40. Deduct 40 from 1320 (1280), then add 622. The answer is 1902.

There have been a few notable exceptions. Thus the Khanian era of Ilkhan Ghazan Mahmud began on 1st Rajab 701 AH (1301). This era used a solar calendar, but was shortlived, being confined to coins of Mahmud and his nephew Abu Said down to year 34 (1333).

The era of Tarikh Ilahi was adopted by the Mughal emperor Akbar in the thirteenth year of his reign (922 AH). This era dated from his accession on 5th Rabi al-Sani 963 AH (February 19, 1556). The calendar had solar months and days but no weeks, so each day of the month had a different name. This system was used by Akbar, Jahangir and Shah Jahan, often with a Hijra date as well.

Saphar

The era of the Caesars began on January 1, 38 BC and dated from the conquest of Spain by Augustus. Its use on coinage, however, seems to have been confined to the marabotins of Alfonso VIII of Castile and was expressed in both Latin and Arabic.

Samvat

The era of Vikramaditya began in 57 BC and was a luni-solar system used in some Indian states. Coins may be found with both Samvat and Hijra dates. Conversion to the Christian date is simple; merely subtract 57 from the Samvat to arrive at the AD date.

Saka

This originated in the southwestern district of Northern India and began in AD 78. As it used the luni-solar system it converts easily by adding 78 to the Saka date.

Nepal

Nepalese coins have used four different date systems. All coins of the Malla kings were dated in Nepal Samvat (NS) era, year 1 beginning in 881. This system was also used briefly by the state of Cooch Behar. Until 1888 all coins of the Gurkha dynasty were dated in the Saka era (SE) which began in AD 78. After 1888 most copper coins were dated in the Vikram Samvat (VS) era from 57 BC. With the exception of some gold coins struck in 1890 and 1892, silver and gold coins only changed to the VS era in 1911, but now this system is used for all coins struck in Nepal. Finally, dates in the Christian era have appeared on some commemorative coins of recent years.

Ethiopian

This era dates from August AD 7, so that EE 1885 is AD 1892. Ethiopian dates are expressed in five digits using Amharic numerals. The first two are the digits of the centuries, the third is the character for 100, while the fourth and fifth are the digits representing the decade and year. On modern coins dates are rendered in-Amharic numerals using the Christian era.

Thailand

Thai coins mainly use the Buddhist era (BE) which dates from 543 BC, but some coins have used dates from the Chula-Sakarat calendar (CS) which began in AD 638, while others use a Ratanakosind Sok (RS) date from the foundation of the Chakri dynasty in AD 1781.

Hebrew

The coins of Israel use the Jewish calendar dating from the beginning of the world (Adam and Eve in the Garden of Eden) in 3760 BC. Thus the year 1993 is rendered as 5753. The five millennia are assumed in dates, so that only the last three digits are expressed. 735 therefore equates with AD 1975. Dates are written in Hebrew letters, reading from right to left. The first two characters signify 400 and 300 respectively, totalling 700. The third letter denotes the decades (lamedh = 30) and the fourth letter, following the separation mark (") represents the final digit (heh = 5). The Jewish year runs from September or October in the Christian calendar.

Dates from the creation of the world

This system was also used in Russia under Ivan IV. The dating system Anno Mundi (AM) was established by the Council of Constantinople in AD 680 which determined that the birth of Christ had occurred in 5508 AM. Ivan's coins expressed the date as 7055 (1447).

Dynastic dates

The system of dating coinage according to regnal years is a feature of Chinese and Japanese coins. Chinese coins normally have an inscription stating that they are coins of such and such a reign period (not the emperor's name), and during the Southern Sung dynasty this was joined by the numeral of the year of the reign. This system was continued under the republic and survives in Taiwan to this day, although the coins of the Chinese Peoples Republic are dated in western numerals using the Christian calendar.

Early Japanese coins bore a reference to the era (the title assumed by each emperor on his accession) but, like Chinese coins, could not be dated accurately. From the beginning of the Meiji era (1867), however, coins have included a regnal number. The Showa era, beginning in 1926 with the accession of Hirohito, eventually ran to sixty-three (expressed in western numerals on some denominations, in Japanese ideograms on others) to denote 1988, although the rest of the inscription was in Japanese characters.

Dynastic dates were used on Korean milled coins introduced in 1888. These bore two characters at the top Kae Kuk (founding of the dynasty) followed by quantitative numerals. The system dated from the founding of the Yi dynasty in 1392. Curiously enough, some Korean banknotes have borne dates from the foundation of the first dynasty in 2333 BC.

Iran adopted a similar system in 1975, celebrating the 15th anniversary of the Pahlavi regime by harking back to the glories of Darius. The new calendar dated from the foundation of the Persian Empire 2535 years earlier, but was abolished only three years later when the Shah was overthrown.

Political eras

France adopted a republican calendar in 1793 when the monarchy was abolished. Coins were then inscribed L'AN (the year) followed by Roman numerals, but later Arabic numerals were substituted. This continued to the year 14 (1806) but in that year the Emperor Napoleon restored the Christian calendar. The French system was emulated by Haiti whose coins dated from the revolution of 1803. The date appeared as AN followed by a number until AN 31 (1834) on some coins; others had both the revolutionary year and the Christian date from 1828 until 1850 (AN 47). Coins with a date in the Christian calendar appeared only in 1807–9 and then from 1850 onwards.

Mussolini introduced the Fascist calendar to Italy, dating from the seizure of power in October 1922. This system was widely employed on documents and memorials, but was first used on silver 20 lire coins of 1927 and then only in addition to the Christian date and appearing discreetly as Roman numerals. Subsequently it was extended to gold 50 lire and 100 lire coins in 1931 and the subsidiary coinage in 1936, being last used in the year XXI (1943).

There must be one that fits!

44

COIN TERMS *glossary*

In this section we list all the terms commonly encountered in numismatics or in the production of coins.

Abbey Coins Medieval coins struck in the abbeys, convents and other great religious houses which were granted coinage rights. These coins were often used also by pilgrims journeying from one monastery to another.

Abschlag (German for "discount") A *restrike* from an original die.

Accolated Synonym for *conjoined* or *jugate* and signifying two or more profiles overlapping.

Acmonital Acronym from *Aciaio Monetario Italiano*, a stainless steel alloy used for Italian coins since 1939.

Adjustment Reduction of metal in a *flan* or *blank* to the specified weight prior to striking, accomplished by filing down the face. Such file marks often survived the coining process and are occasionally met with in coins, especially of the 18th century.

Ae Abbreviation for the Latin *Aes* (bronze), used for coins made of brass, bronze or other copper alloys.

Aes Grave (Latin for heavy bronze) Heavy circular coins first minted at Rome in 269 BC.

Aes Rude (Latin for rough bronze) Irregular lumps of bronze which gradually developed into ingots of uniform shape and were the precursors of coins in Rome.

Aes Signatum (Latin for signed bronze) Bronze ingots of regular size and weight, bearing marks of authority to guarantee their weight (289–269 BC).

Agonistic (Greek) Term for coins issued to commemorate, or pertaining to, sporting events.

Alliance Coinage struck by two or more states acting together and having common features of design or inscription.

Alloy Coinage metal composed of two or more metallic elements.

Altered Deliberately changed, usually unofficially, with the aim of increasing the numismatic value of a coin, medal or note. This applies particularly to dates, where a common date may be altered to a rare date by filing or re-engraving one of the digits.

Aluminium (American *Aluminum*) Silvery lightweight metal, developed commercially in the late 19th century for commemorative medals, but used for tokens and emergency money during the First World War and since 1940 widely used in subsidiary coinage.

A typical aes grave, from Appulia, c. 225 BC.

Aluminium-bronze Alloy of aluminium and copper. Hard-wearing and gold-coloured, it is now widely used in tokens and subsidiary coinage.

Amulet   Coin or medal believed to have talismanic qualities, such as warding off disease and bad luck. Many Chinese and Korean pieces come into this category. See also *Touchpiece*.

Androcephalous   Heraldic term for creatures with a human head.

Anepigraphic   Coins or medals without a legend.

Annealing   Process of heating and cooling applied to metal to relieve stresses and prepare it for striking into coins.

Annulet   Small circle often used as an ornament or spacing device in coin inscriptions.

Antimony   Brittle white metal, chemical symbol *Sb*, virtually impractical as a coinage metal but used for the Chinese 10 cents of Kweichow, 1931. Alloyed with tin, copper or lead, it produces the white metal popular as a medallic medium.

Antoniniani   Silver coins minted in Imperial Rome. The name derives from the Emperor Caracalla (Marcus Aurelius Antoninus) in whose reign they were first struck. The silver content was progressively reduced and by the last issue (AD 295) they were reduced to *billon*.

Ar   Abbreviation for Latin *Argentum* (silver), used for coins struck in this metal.

Assay Mark   Mark applied to a medal struck in precious metal by an assayer or assay office as a guarantee of the fineness of the metal.

Assignat   Type of paper money used in France 1789–96, representing the land assigned to the holders.

Attribution   Identification of a coin by characteristics such as issuing authority, date or reign, mint, denomination, metal, and by a standard reference.

Au   Abbreviation for *aurum* (Latin for gold), denoting coins of this metal.

AU   Abbreviation for "About Uncirculated", often found in catalogues and dealers' lists to describe the condition of a numismatic piece.

Autodollar   Name given to the silver yuan issued by Kweichow, 1928, and having a contemporary motor car as the obverse motif.

Auxiliary Payment Certificate   Form of paper money intended for use by American military personnel stationed in overseas countries. See also *Baf* and *Scrip*.

Babol Noto   Nickname given to the paper money of the Russian Socialist Federated Soviet Republic (1919) because it bore the slogan "workers of the world unite" in seven languages, a reference to the biblical tower of Babel.

Baf   Acronym from British Armed Forces, the popular name for the vouchers which could only be exchanged for goods in service canteens from 1945 onwards.

Bag Mark   Minor scratch or abrasion on an otherwise uncirculated coin, caused by coins in mint bags knocking together.

Banknote   Form of paper money issued by banks and usually promising to pay the bearer on demand in coin of the realm.

Barbarous   Imitation of Greek or Roman coins by the Celtic and Germanic tribes who lived beyond the frontiers of the civilised world.

Base   Non-precious metals or alloys.

Bath Metal   Inferior bronze alloy, named after the English city where it was used for casting cannon. Used by William Wood of Bristol for Irish and American tokens and by Amos Topping for Manx coins of 1733/4.

Beading   Ornamental border found on the raised rim of a coin.

Behalfszahlungsmittel   German term for auxiliary payment certificates used in occupied Europe from 1939 to 1945.

Bell Metal   Alloy of copper and tin normally used for casting bells, but employed for the subsidiary coinage of the French Revolutionary period.

Billon   Silver alloy containing less than 50 per cent fine silver, usually mixed with copper. In Spain this alloy was known as *vellon*.

1997 £2—the UK's first bi-metallic coin.

Bi-metallic   Coins struck in two separate metals or alloys. Patterns for such coins exist from the 19th century but actual coins with a centre of one metal surrounded by a ring of another did not appear till 1982 (Italy, San Marino and Vatican), since then many countries, including Great Britain, have introduced bi-metallic coins. See also *Clad, Plugged* and *Sandwich*.

Bi-metallism   Monetary system in which two metals are in simultaneous use and equally available as legal tender, implying a definite ratio between the two. A double standard of gold and silver, with a ratio of 16:1, existed till the mid-19th century.

Bingle   American term for a trade token, more specifically the US government issue of tokens for the Matacuska, Alaska colonization project, 1935.

Birthday Coins   Coins celebrating the birthday of a ruler originated in Roman Imperial times, notably the reigns of Maximianus (286–305) and

Constantinus I (307–37). Birthday talers were issued by many German states, and among recent examples may be cited coins marking the 70th, 80th and 90th birthdays of Gustaf Adolf VI of Sweden, 80th and 90th birthday coins from Great Britan and the British Commonwealth for Her Majesty the Queen, as well as other members of our Royal Family..

Bit Term denoting fragments of large silver coins, cut up and circulating as fractional values. Spanish dollars were frequently broken up for circulation in the American colonies and the West indies. Long bits and short bits circulated at 15 and 10 cents respectively, but the term came to be equated with the Spanish real or eighth peso, hence the American colloquialism "two-bit" signifying a quarter dollar.

Black Money English term for the debased silver deniers minted in France which circulated freely in England until they were banned by government decree in 1351.

Blank Piece of metal, cut or punched out of a roller bar or strip, and prepared for striking to produce coins. Alternate terms are *flan* and *planchet*.

Blundered Inscription Legend in which the lettering is jumbled or meaningless, indicating the illiteracy of the tribes who copied Greek and Roman coins.

Bonnet Piece Scottish gold coin, minted in 1539–40. The name is derived from the obverse portraying King James V in a large, flat bonnet.

Bon Pour French for "good for", inscribed on Chamber of Commerce brass tokens issued in 1920–7 during a shortage of legal tender coinage.

Bouquet Sou Canadian copper token halfpenny of 1837 deriving its name from the nosegay of heraldic flowers on the obverse.

Box Coin Small container formed by *obverse* and *reverse* of two coins, hollowed out and screwed together.

Bracteate (Latin *bractea*, a thin piece of metal) Coins struck on blanks so thin that the image applied to one side appears in reverse on the other. First minted in Erfurt and Thuringia in the 12th century, and later produced elsewhere in Germany, Switzerland and Poland till the 14th century.

Brass Alloy of copper and zinc, widely used for subsidiary coinage. The term was also formerly used for bronze Roman coins, known numismatically as first, second or third brass.

Breeches Money Derisive term given by the Royalists to the coinage of the Commonwealth, 1651, because the conjoined elongated oval shields on the reverse resembled a pair of breeches.

Brockage Mis-struck coin with only one design, normal on one side and *incuse* on the other. This occurs when a coin previously struck adheres to the die and strikes the next blank to pass through the press.

Broken Bank-note Note issued by a bank which has failed, but this is often applied more generally to banknotes which have actually been demonetised.

Bronze Alloy of copper and tin, first used as a coinage metal by the Chinese c. 1000 BC. Often used synonymously with copper, though it should be noted that bronze only superseded copper as the constituent of the base metal British coins in 1860.

Bull Neck Popular term for the coins of King George III, 1816–17.

Bullet Money Pieces of silver, *globular* in shape, bearing various *countermarks* and used as coins in Siam (Thailand) in the 18th and 19th centuries.

Bullion Precious metal in bars, ingots, strip or scrap (i.e. broken jewellery mounts, watch-cases and plate), its weight reckoned solely by weight and fineness, before being converted into coin.

Bullion Coin A coin struck in platinum, gold or silver, whose value is determined solely by the prevailing market price for the metal as a commodity. Such coins do not generally have a nominal face value, but include in their inscriptions their weight and fineness. Good examples of recent times include the Krugerrand (South Africa), the Britannia (UK), the Maple Leaf (Canada), the Libertad (Mexico), the Nugget (Australia) and the Eagle (USA).

Victoria Young or "Bun" head bronze penny.

Bun Coinage British coins of 1860–94 showing Queen Victoria with her hair in a bun.

Bungtown Coppers Derisive term (from Anglo-American slang *bung*, to swindle or bribe) for halfpence of English or Irish origin, often counterfeit, which circulated in North America towards the end of the colonial period.

Carat (American *Karat*) Originally a unit of weight for precious stones, based on carob seeds (ceratia), it also denotes the fineness or purity

of gold, being 1/24th part of the whole. Thus 9 carat gold is .375 fine and 22 carat, the English sovereign standard, is .916 fine. Abbreviated as ct or kt.

Cartwheel Popular term for the large and cumbersome penny and twopenny pieces of 1797 weighing one and two ounces, struck by Matthew Boulton at the Soho Mint, Birmingham.

Cased Set Set of coins in mint condition, housed in the official case issued by the mint. Formerly leather cases with blue plush or velvet lining were used, but nowadays many sets are encapsulated in plastic to facilitate handling.

Typical Chinese cash coins.

Cash (from Portuguese *caixa*, Hindi *kasu*). Round piece of bronze or brass with a square hole in the centre, used as subsidiary coinage in China for almost 2000 years, till the early 12th century. In Chinese these pieces were known as *Ch'ien* or *Li* and strung together in groups of 1000 were equivalent to a silver tael.

Cast Coins Coins cast from molten metals in moulds. This technique, widespread in the case of early commemorative medals, has been used infrequently in coins, the vast majority of which are struck from *dies*. Examples include the Chinese cash and the Manx coins of 1709.

Check A form of *token* given as a means of identification, or issued for small amounts of money or for services of a specific nature.

Cheque (American *Check*) A written order directing a bank to pay money.

Chop (Hindi, to seal). Countermark, usually consisting of a single character, applied by Chinese merchants to precious metal coins and ingots as a guarantee of their weight and fineness. Coins may be found with a wide variety of chop marks and the presence of several different marks on the same coin enhances its interest and value. See also *Shroff mark*.

Christmas Coins issued as Christmas gifts date from the Middle Ages when the Venetian Doges struck *Osselle* as presents for their courtiers. In modern times, however, the custom has developed only since the late 1970s and several countries having issued them since then.

Cistophori (Greek for chest bearing) a generic term for the coins of Pergamum with an obverse motif of a chest showing a serpent crawling out of the half-opened lid. Cistophori became very popular all over Asia Minor in the 3rd and 2nd centuries BC and were struck also at mints in Ionia, Phrygia, Lydia and Mysia.

Clad Coins Coins with a core of one alloy, covered with a layer or coating of another. US half dollars from 1965 to 1970, for example, had a core of 21 per cent silver and 79 per cent copper, bonded to outer layers of 80 per cent silver and 20 per cent copper. More recently, however, coins usually have a body in a cheap alloy, with only a thin cladding of a more expensive material, such as the British 1p and 2p coins of stainless steel with a copper cladding, introduced late in 1992.

Clash Marks Mirror image traces found on a coin which has been struck from a pair of dies, themselves damaged by having been struck together without a blank between.

Clipped Coins Precious metal coins from which small amounts have been removed by clipping the edges. It was to prevent this that *graining* and *edge inscriptions* were adopted.

Cob Crude, irregularly shaped silver piece, often with little more than a vestige of die impressions, produced in the Spanish American mints in the 16th–18th centuries.

Coin Piece of metal, marked with a device, issued by government authority and intended for use as money.

Collar Retaining ring within which the *dies* for the *obverse* and *reverse* operate. When the *blank* is struck under high pressure between the dies the metal flows sideways and is formed by the collar, taking up the impression of *reeding* or *edge inscription* from it.

Commemorative Coin, medal, token or paper note issued to celebrate a current event or the anniversary of a historic event or personality.

Communion Token Token, cast in lead, but later struck in pewter, brass, bronze or white metal, issued to members of a congregation to permit them to partake of the annual communion service in the Calvinist and Presbyterian churches. John Calvin himself is said to have invented the communion token in 1561 but they were actually referred to in the minutes of the Scottish General Assembly in 1560. Later they were adopted by the Reformed churches in many parts of Europe. They survived in Scotland till the early years of this century. Each parish had its own tokens, often bearing the names or initials of individual ministers, with dates, symbols and biblical texts.

Conjoined Term denoting overlapped profiles of two or more rulers (e.g. William and Mary).

Contorniate (from Italian *contorno*, edge). Late 4th and 5th century Roman bronze piece whose name alludes to the characteristic grooving on the edges.

Contribution Coins Coins struck by Bamberg, Eichstatt, Fulda and other German cities in the 1790s during the First Coalition War against the French Republic. The name alludes to the fact that the bullion used to produce the coins necessary to pay troops was raised by contribution from the Church and the public.

Convention Money Any system of coinage agreed by neighbouring countries for mutual acceptance and interchange. Examples include the Amphictyonic coins of ancient Greece, and the Austrian and Bavarian talers and gulden of 1753–1857 which were copied by other south German states and paved the way for the German Monetary union.

Copper Metallic element, chemical symbol *Cu*, widely used as a coinage medium for 2,500 years. Pure or almost pure copper was used for subsidiary coinage in many countries till the mid-19th century, but has since been superseded by copper alloys which are cheaper and more durable: *bronze* (copper and tin), *brass* (copper and zinc), *Bath metal* or *bell metal* (low-grade copper and tin), *aluminium-bronze* (copper and aluminium), *potin* (copper, tin, lead and silver) or *cupro-nickel* (copper and nickel). Copper is also alloyed with gold to give it its reddish hue, and is normally alloyed with silver in coinage metals. When the copper exceeds the silver content the alloy is known as *billon*.

Copperhead Popular term for a copper *token* about the size and weight of an American cent which circulated in the USA during the Civil War (1861–65) during a shortage of subsidiary coinage. Many different types were produced, often of a political or patriotic nature.

Coppernose Popular name for the debased silver shillings of Henry VIII. Many of them were struck in copper with little more than a silver wash which tended to wear off at the highest point of the obverse, the nose on the full-face portrait of the king.

Counter A piece resembling a coin but intended for use on a medieval accountancy board or in gambling. See also *jeton*.

Counterfeit Imitation of a coin, token or banknote intended for circulation to deceive the public and defraud the state.

Countermark Punch mark applied to a coin some time after its original issue, either to alter its nominal value, or to authorise its circulation in some other country.

Cowrie Small shell (*Cypraea moneta*) circulating as a form of primitive currency from 1000 BC (China) to the present century (East and West Africa) and also used in the islands of the Indian and Pacific Oceans.

Crockard Debased silver imitation of English pennies produced in the Netherlands and imported into England in the late 13th century. Edward I tried to prevent their import then, in 1299, allowed them to pass current as halfpennies. As they contained more than a halfpennyworth of silver this encouraged their trading in to be melted down and they disappeared from circulation within a year. Sometimes known as *pollards*. See also *Lushbourne*.

Crown Gold Gold of 22 carat (.916) fineness, so called on account of its adoption in 1526 for the English gold crown. It has remained the British standard gold fineness ever since.

"Cumberland Jack" or "To Hanover" token marking the Duke of Cumberland's departure from Britain. These pieces were struck through much of the 19th century as whist counters and were sometimes passed as real gold coins to the unwary.

Cumberland Jack Popular name for a counter or medalet of sovereign size, struck unofficially in 1837 in brass. The figure of St George was replaced with the Duke of Cumberland on horseback with the inscription "To Hanover" a reference to the unpopular Duke of Cumberland, uncle of Queen Victoria, who succeeded to the Hanoverian throne since Victoria, as a female, was debarred by Salic law from inheritance.

Cupellation (Latin *cupella*, a little cup). Process by which gold and silver were separated from lead and other impurities in their ores. A cupel is a shallow cup of bone-ash or other absorbent material which, when hot, absorbs any molten material that wets its surface. Lead melts and oxidises with impurities into the cupel, whereas gold and silver remain on the cupel. Cupellation is also used in assaying the fineness of these precious metals.

Cupro-nickel Coinage alloy of 75 per cent copper and 25 per cent nickel, now widely used as a base metal substitute for silver. A small amount of zinc is added to the alloy in modern Russian coins.

Currency Coins, tokens, paper notes and other articles intended to pass current in general circulation as money.

Current Coins and paper money still in circulation.

Cut Money Coins cut into smaller pieces to provide correspondingly smaller denominations. The cross on many medieval coins assisted the division of silver pennies into halfpence and farthings. Spanish dollars were frequently divided into *bits* which themselves became units of currency in America and the West Indies.

Darlehnskassen (German for "state loan notes"). Paper money issued during the First World War in an abortive bid to fill the shortage of coinage in circulation. These low-denomination notes failed to meet demand and were superseded by local issues of small *Notgeld* in 1916.

Debasement The reduction in the precious metal content of the coinage, widely practised since time immemorial by governments for economic reasons. British coins, for example, were debased from sterling (.925 fine) silver to .500 in 1920 and from silver to cupro-nickel in 1947.

Decimalisation A currency system in which the principal unit is subdivided into ten, a hundred, or a thousand fractions. Russia was the first country to decimalise, in 1534 when the rouble of 100 kopeks was introduced, but it was not till 1792 that France adopted the franc of 100 centimes and 1793 when the USA introduced the dollar of 100 cents. Most European countries decimalised their currency in the 19th century. Britain toyed with the idea, introducing the florin or tenth of a pound in 1849 as the first step, but did not complete the process till 1971. The last countries to decimalise were Malta and Nigeria, in 1972 and 1973 respectively.

Demidiated Heraldic term to describe the junction of two armorial devices, in which only half of each is shown.

Domonetisation The withdrawal of coins or paper money from circulation and declaring them to be worthless.

Device Heraldic term for the pattern or emblem on coins or paper notes.

Die Hardened piece of metal bearing a mirror image of the device to be struck on one side of a coin or medal.

Die Proof An impression, usually pulled on soft carton or India paper, of an *intaglio* engraving of a banknote, usually taken during the progress of the engraving to check the detail. Banknote proofs of this nature usually consist of the portrait or some detail of the design, such as the border, rather than the complete motif.

Dodecagonal Twelve-sided, a term applied to the nickel-brass threepence of Great Britain, 1937–67.

Dump Any primitive coin struck on a very thick *flan*, but more specifically applied to the circular pieces cut from the centre of Spanish dollars, countermarked with the name of the colony, a crown and the value, and circulated in New South Wales at 15 pence in 1813. See *Holey Dollar*.

Duodecimal Currency system based on units of twelve, i.e. medieval money of account (12 denarii = 1 soldo) which survived in Britain as 12 pence to the shilling as late as 1971.

Ecclesiastical Coins Coins struck by a religious authority, such as an archbishop, bishop, abbot, prior or the canons of a religious order. Such coins were common in medieval times but survived as late as the early 19th century, the bishops of Breslau (1817) and Gurk (1823) being the last prelates to exercise coinage rights. Coins were always struck by authority of the Pope at Rome till 1870 but since 1929 coinage has been struck at the Italian state mint on behalf of the Vatican.

Edge Inscription Lettering on the edge of a coin or medal to prevent clipping. Alluding to this, the Latin motto *Decus et Tutamen* (an ornament and a safeguard) was applied to the edge of English milled coins in the reign of Charles II.

Edge Ornament An elaboration of the *graining* found on many milled coins to prevent clipping, taking the form of tiny leaves, florets, interlocking rings, pellets and zigzag patterns. In some cases the ornament appears between layers of more conventional reeding.

A die used for striking the reverse of the Great Britain 1991 £1 coin (Image courtesy of the Royal Mint).

EF Abbreviation for Extremely Fine.

Effigy An image or representation of a person, normally the head of state, a historical personage, or an allegorical figure, usually on the *obverse* or "heads" side of a coin or medal.

Electrotype A reproduction of a coin or medal made by an electrolytic process.

Electrum Alloy of gold and silver, sometimes called white gold, used for minting the staters of Lydia, 7th century BC, and other early European coins.

Elongated Coin An oval *medalet* created by passing a coin, such as an American cent, between rollers under pressure with the effect of squeezing it out and impressing on it a souvenir or commemorative motif.

Emergency Money Any form of money used in times of economic and political upheaval, when traditional kinds of currency are not available. Examples include the comparatively crude silver coins issued by the Royalists during the *Civil War* (1642–49), *obsidional* money, issued in time of siege, from Tyre (1122) to Mafeking (1900), the *Notgeld* issued by many German towns (1916–23), *encased money*, *fractional currency, guerrilla notes, invasion, liberation* and *occupation money* from the two World Wars and minor campaigns. Among the more recent examples may be cited the use of sweets and cheques in Italy (1976–77) and the issue of coupons and vouchers in many of the countries of the former Soviet Union pending the introduction of their own coins and notes.

Enamelled Coins Coins decorated by enamelling the obverse and reverse motifs in contrasting colours was an art practised by many jewellers in Birmingham and Paris in the 19th century, and revived in Europe and America in the 1970s.

Encased Money Postage and revenue stamps enclosed in small metal and mica-faced discs, circulated as small change in times of emergency. The practice was invented by John Gault, a Boston sewing-machine salesman, during the American Civil War (1862). The face of the stamp was visible through the transparent window, while the back of the disc was embossed with firms' advertisements. This practice was revived during and after the First World War when there was again a shortage of small coins. Encased stamps have also been recorded from France, Austria, Norway, Germany and Monaco. See also under *Stamp Money*.

Engrailing Technical term for the close serrations or vertical bars round the edge of a coin, applied as a security device.

Engraving The art of cutting lines or grooves in plates, blocks or dies. Numismatically this takes the form of engraving images into the face of the dies used in striking coins, a process which has now been almost completely superseded by *hubbing* and the use of *reducing machinery*. In the production of paper money, *intaglio* engraving is still commonly practised. In this process the engraver cuts the design into a steel die and the printing ink lies in the grooves. The paper is forced under great pressure into the grooves and picks up the ink, and this gives banknotes their characteristic ridged feeling to the touch. Nowadays many banknotes combine traditional intaglio engraving with multicolour lithography or photogravure to defeat the would-be counterfeiter.

Epigraphy The study of inscriptions, involving the classification and interpretation of coin legends, an invaluable adjunct to the study of a coin series, particularly the classical and medieval coins which, in the absence of dates and mintmarks, would otherwise be difficult to arrange in chronological sequence.

Erasion The removal of the title or effigy of a ruler from the coinage issued after his or her death. This process was practised in imperial Rome, and applied to the coins of Caligula, Nero and Geta, as part of the more general practice of *damnatio memoriae* (damnation of the memory) ordered by the Senate.

Error Mistakes on coins and paper money may be either caused at the design or engraving stage, or as a result of a fault in the production processes. In the first category come mis-spellings in legends causing, in extreme cases, *blundered inscriptions*, or anachronisms or inaccuracies in details of the design. In the second, the most glaring error is the mule caused by marrying the wrong dies. Faulty alignment of dies can cause obverse and reverse to be out of true. Although many coins are issued with obverse and reverse upside down in relation to each other, this can also occur as an error in coins where both sides should normally be facing the same way up. Other errors caused at the production stage include striking coins in the wrong metal or with the wrong *collar* thus creating a different edge from the normal.

Essay (From the French *essai*, a trial piece). The term is applied to any piece struck for the purposes of examination, by parliamentary or financial bodies, prior to the authorisation of an issue of coins or paper money. The official nature of these items distinguishes them from *patterns*, which denote trial pieces often produced by mints or even private individuals bidding for coinage contracts.

Evasion Close copy or imitation of a coin, with sufficient deliberate differences in the design or inscription to avoid infringing counterfeit legislation. A good example is the imitation of Sumatran coins by European merchants, inscribed SULTANA instead of SUMATRA.

Exergue Lower segment of a coin or medal, usually divided from the rest of the *field* by a horizontal line, and often containing the date, value, ornament or identification symbols.

Exonumia Generic term for numismatic items not authorised by a government, e.g. *patterns*, *tokens*, *medalets* or *model coins*.

F Abbreviation for Fine.

Face The surface of a coin, medal or token, referred to as the *obverse* or the *reverse*. The corresponding faces of a paper note are more correctly termed *verso* and *recto*, but the coin terms are often used instead.

Facing Term for the portrait, usually on the obverse, which faces to the front instead of to the side (profile).

Fantasy Piece of metal purporting to be the coinage of a country which does not exist. Recent examples include the money of Atlantis and the Hutt River Province which declared its independence of Western Australia.

FDC Abbreviation for *Fleur de Coin*, a term denoting the finest possible condition of a coin.

Fiat Money Paper notes issued by a government but not redeemable in coin or bullion.

Field Flat part of the surface of a coin or medal, between the *legend*, the *effigy* and other raised parts of the design.

Fillet Heraldic term for the ribbon or headband on the effigy of a ruler or allegorical figure.

Find Term applied to an archaeological discovery of one or more coins. A large quantity of such material is described as a *hoard*.

Flan Alternative name for *blank* or *planchet*, the piece of metal struck between dies to produce a coin or medal.

Forgery An unauthorised copy or imitation, made with the intention of deceiving collectors. Forgeries intended to pass current for real coins or banknotes are more properly called *counterfeits*.

Fractional Currency Emergency issue of small-denomonation notes by the USA in 1863–65, following a shortage of coins caused by the Civil War. This issue superseded the *Postage Currency* notes, but bore the inscription "Receivable for all US stamps", alluding to the most popular medium of small change at that time. Denominations ranged from 3c to 50c.

Franklinium Cupro-nickel alloy developed by the Franklin Mint of Philadelphia and used for coins, medals and gaming tokens since 1967.

Freak An *error* or *variety* of a non-recurring type, usually caused accidentally during production.

Frosting Matt surface used for the high relief areas of many proof coins and medals, for greater contrast with the mirrored surface of the field.

Funeral Money Imitations of banknotes, used in China and Latin America in funeral ceremonies.

Geat (Git) Channel through which molten metal is ducted to the mould. Cast coins often show tiny protrusions known as geat marks.

Ghost Faint image of the design on one side of a coin visible on the other. Good examples were the British penny and halfpenny of George V, 1911–27, the ghosting being eliminated by the introduction of a smaller effigy in 1928.

Globular Coins struck on very thick *dumps* with convex faces. Examples include some Byzantine coins, and the *bullet money* of Siam (Thailand)

Godless (or *Graceless*) Epithet applied to any coin which omits the traditional reference to the deity, e.g. the British florin of 1849 which omitted D.G. (*Dei Gratia*, "by the Grace of God").

Gold Precious metal, chemical symbol and numismatic abbreviation *Au*, from the *Latin Aurum*, used as a coinage medium from the 7th century BC till the present day. The purity of gold is reckoned in *carats* or a decimal system. Thus British gold sovereigns are 22 carat or .916 fine. Medieval coins were 23.5 carat or .995 fine, and some modern bullion coins are virtually pure gold, denoted by the inscription .999. Canadian maple leaves are now struck in "four nines" gold and bear the inscription .9999.

Goodfor Popular name for token coins and *emergency money* made of paper or card, from the inscription "Good for" or its equivalent in other languages (e.g. French *Bon pour* or Dutch *Goed voor*) followed by a monetary value. They have been recorded from Europe, Africa and America during times of economic crises or shortage of more traditional coinage.

Gothic Crown Popular name for the silver crown issued by the United Kingdom (1847–53), so-called on account of its script (more properly Old English, rather than Gothic).

Grain The weight of a single grain of wheat was taken as the smallest unit of weight in England. The troy grain was 1/5760 of a pound, while the avoirdupois grain was 1/7000 pound, the former being used in the weighing of precious metals and thus employed by numismatists in weighing coins. A grain is 1/480 troy ounce or 0.066 gram in the metric system.

Graining Term sometimes used as a synonym for the *reeding* on the edge of milled coins.

Gripped Edge   Pattern of indentations found on the majority of American cents of 1797, caused by the milling process. Coins of the same date with a plain edge are rather scarcer.

Guerrilla Money   Money issued in areas under the control of guerrillas and partisans during wartime range from the *veld ponds* of the Boers (1900–2) to the notes issued by the Garibaldi Brigade in Italy and the anti-fascist notes of Tito's forces in Yugoslavia. The most prolific issues are those produced in Luzon, Mindanao and Negros Occidental by the Filipino resistance during the Japanese occupation (1942–5).

Guilloche   French term signifying the intricate pattern of curved lines produced by the rose engine and used as a security feature in the production of banknote, cheques, stocks and share certificates.

An example of gun money—note the month of issue below the crown.

Gun Money   Emergency coinage of Ireland (1689 –91) minted from gunmetal, a type of bronze used in the casting of cannon. All denominations of James II, from the sixpence to the crown, normally struck in silver, were produced in this base metal.

Gutschein   German word for voucher or coupon, denoting the paper money used aboard ships of the Imperial Navy during the First World War. The last issue was made at Scapa Flow, 1918–19, during the internment of the High Seas Fleet.

Hammered   Term denoting coins produce by the traditional method of striking a *flan* laid on an anvil with a hammer. A characteristic of hammered coins is their uneven shape which tended to encourage *clipping*. This abuse was gradually eliminated by the introduction of the screw press in the 15th century and the mechanisation of coining processes in the course of the 16th and 17th centuries.

Hard Times Token   Copper piece the size of the large cent, issued in the USA, 1834–44, during a shortage of coins caused by the collapse of the Bank of the United States, the panic of 1837 and the economic crisis of 1839, the landmarks in the period known as the Hard Times. Banks suspended *specie* payments and the shortage of coinage was filled by tradesmen's tokens. Many of these were more in the nature of satirical *medalets* than circulating pieces.

Hat Piece   Alternative name for the *bonnet piece* of James VI of Scotland, 1591.

Hell Notes   Imitation paper money used in Chinese funeral ceremonies and buried with the dead to pay for services in the next world.

Hoard   Accumulation of coins concealed in times of economic or political upheaval and discovered, often centuries later. Under English common law, such hoards are subject to th law of *treasure trove* if they contain precious metal.

Hog Money   Popular name for the early coinage of Bermuda, issued about 1616. The coins were minted in brass with a silver wash and circulated at various values from twopence to a shilling. They derived their name from the hog depicted on the obverse, an allusion to the pigs introduced to the island in 1515 by Juan Bermudez.

Holed   Term denoting two different categories: (a) coins which have been pierced for suspension as a form of jewellery or talisman, and (b) coins which have a hole as part of their design. In the latter category come the Chinese *cash* with a square hole, and numerous issues of the 19th and 20th centuries from many countries, with the object of reducing weight and metal without sacrificing overall diameter.

Holey Dollar   Spanish silver peso of 8 reales with the centre removed. The resultant ring was counter-marked "New South Wales" and dated 1813, with "Five Shillings" on the reverse, and placed into circulation during a shortage of British coin. The centre, known as a *dump*, was circulated at 15 pence.

Hub   Heavy circular piece of steel on which the *die* for a coin or medal is engraved. The process of cutting the die and transferring the master die, by means of intermediary *punches*, to the die from which the coins will be struck, is known as hubbing. Soft steel is used in the preliminary process, and after the design has been transferred, the hub is hardened by chemical action.

Hybrid   Alternative name for a *mule*.

Imitation Money   Also known as play money or toy money, it consists of coins and notes produced for games of chance (like Monopoly), children's toy shops and post offices, as tourist souvenirs, or for political satire (e.g. the shrinking pound or dollar). See also *funeral money*, *hell notes*, *model coins* and *skit notes*.

Imprint   Inscription on a paper note giving the name of the printer.

Incuse   Impression which cuts into the surface of a coin or medal, as opposed to the more

usual raised relief. Many of the earliest coins, especially those with a device on one side only, bear an incuse impression often in a geometric pattern. An incuse impression appears on one side of the coins, reflecting the image on the other side. Few modern coins have had an incuse design, notable examples being the American half and quarter eagle gold coins of 1908–29 designed by Bela Pratt. Incuse inscriptions on a raised rim, however, are more common, and include the British *Cartwheel* coins of 1797 and the 20p coins since 1982.

Inflation Money   Coins produced as a result of inflation date back to Roman times when bronze minimi, little bigger than a pinhead, circulated as denarii. Nearer the present day inflation has had devastating effects on the coinge and banknotes of Germany (1921–3), Austria (1923), Poland (1923), Hungary (1945–6), Greece (1946) and many Latin American countries since the 1980s. Hungary holds the record for the highest value of any note ever issued — one thousand million adopengos, which is written as 20,000,000,000,000,000, 000,000,000,000 pengos.

Ingot   Piece of precious metal, usually cast in a mould, and stamped with the weight and fineness. A convenient method of storing bullion, ingots have been used as currency in many countries, notably Russia and Japan.

Inlay   Insertion into the surface of a coin or medal of another substance for decorative effect. e.g. Poland Amber Trade Routes 20zl (amber), Isle of Man Queen Mother centenery (pearl) and various coins incorporating rubies or diamonds.

Intaglio   Form of *engraving* in which lines are cut into a steel die for the recess-printing of banknotes.

Intrinsic   The net metallic value of a coin, as distinguished from the nominal or face value.

Iron   Metal, chemical symbol *Fe* (from Latin *Ferrum*), used as a primitive form of currency from classical times onwards. Iron spits (obeliskoi) preceded the obol as the lowest unit of Greek coinage, a handful of six spits being worth a drachma (from *drassomai*, "I grasp"). Cast iron coins were issued in China as a substitute for copper *cash*. Many of the emergency token issues of Germany during the First World War were struck in iron. Iron coins were issued by Bulgaria in 1943. See also *Steel*.

Ithyphallic   (Greek for "erect penis"). Term descriptive of coins of classical Greece showing a satyr.

Janiform   Double profiles back to back, after the Roman god Janus.

Jeton   (From French *jeter*, to throw). Alternative term for *counter*, and used originally on the chequerboard employed by medieval accountants. Nuremberg was the most important centre for the production of medieval jetons, often issued in lengthy portrait series. In modern parlance the term is often synonymous with *token*, though more specifically confined to pieces used in vending equipment, parking meters, laundromats, telephones and urban transport systems in many European countries. Apart from security, removing the temptation of vandals to break into the receptacles, the main advantage of such pieces is that they can be retariffed as charges increase, without any alteration in their design or composition, a method that is far cheaper than altering costly equipment to take larger coins.

Jubilee Head   The effigy of Queen Victoria by Joseph Boehm adopted for British coinage after the 1887 Golden Jubilee.

Jugate   (From Latin *jugum*, a yoke). Alternative to *accolated* or *conjoined* to denote overlapping profiles of rulers.

Key Date   Term describing the rarest in a long-running series of coins with the dates changed at annual intervals.

Kipperzeit   German term meaning the time of clipped money, denoting the period during and

Jeton from Dordrecht 1588: the Armada destroyed.

after the Thirty Years War (1618–48) in which debased and clipped money was in circulation.

Klippe   Rectangular or square pieces of metal bearing the impression of a coin. Coins of this type were first struck in Sweden in the 16th century and were subsequently produced in many of the German states. The idea has been revived in recent years as a medium for striking commemorative pieces.

Knife Money   Cast bronze pieces, with an elongated blade and a ring at one end to facilitate stringing together in bunches, were used as currency in China from the 9th century BC until the 19th century.

Kreditivsedlar   (Swedish for "credit notes"). The name given to the first issue of paper money made in the western world. Paper money of this type was the brainchild of Johan Palmstruch at

Riga in 1652, but nine years elapsed before it was implemented by the Stockholm Bank. The notes were redeemable in copper *platmynt*.

Laureate Heraldic term for a laurel wreath, often framing a state emblem or shown, in the Roman fashion, as a crown on the ruler's forehead.

Leather Money Pieces of leather embossed with an official device have been used as money on various occasions, including the sieges of Faenza and Leiden and in the Isle of Man in the 15th and 16th centuries. Several towns in Austria and Germany produced leather tokens during and after the First World War.

Legal Tender Coins or paper money which are declared by law to be current money and which tradesmen and shopkeers are obliged to accept in payment for goods or services. (See *Money and the Law*).

Legend The inscription on a coin or medal.

Liberation Money Paper money prepared for use in parts of Europe and Asia, formerly under Axis occupation. Liberation notes were used in France, Belgium and the Netherlands in 1944–5, while various different Japanese and Chinese notes were overprinted for use in Hong Kong when it was liberated in 1945. Indian notes overprinted for use in Burma were issued in 1945–6 when that country was freed from Japanese occupation.

Ligature (From Latin *ligatus*, bound together). Term denoting the linking of two letters in a *legend*, e.g. Æ and Œ.

Long Cross Coinage Type of coinage introduced by King Henry III in 1247, deriving its name from the reverse which bore a cross whose arms extended right to the edge to help safeguard the coins against *clipping*. This remained the style of the silver penny, its fractions and multiples, till the reign of Henry VII, and vestiges of the long cross theme is seen in the silver coins throughout the remaining years of the Tudor period.

Love Token A coin which has been altered by smoothing one or both surfaces and engraving initials, dates, scenes, symbols of affection and messages thereon.

Lushbourne English word for base pennies made of inferior silver, said to have emanated from Luxembourg, from which the name derived. These coins were first minted under John the Blind who adopted the curious spelling of his name EIWANES in the hope that illiterate English merchants might confuse it with EDWARDVS and thus be accepted as coin issued in the name of Edward III. Lushbournes were also minted by Robert of Bethune, William I of Namur and the bishops of Toul during the mid-14th century.

Lustre The sheen or bloom on the surface of an uncirculated coin resulting from the centrifugal flow of metal caused by striking.

Magnimat Trade name used by VDM (*Verein Deutscher Metallwerke*) for a high-security alloy containing copper, nickel and magnetised steel. First used for the 5 deutschemark coin of 1975, it has since been adopted for other high-value coins in Germany and other countries.

Manilla Copper, bronze or brass rings, sometimes shaped like horseshoes and sometimes open, with flattened terminals, used as currency in West Africa until recent years.

Matrix Secondary die for a coin or medal, produced from the master die by means of an intermediate punch. In this way dies can be duplicated from the original cut on the reducing machine.

Matt or Matte Finely granulated surface or overall satin finish to proof coins, a style which was briefly fashionable at the turn of the century. The Edward VII proof set of 1902 is a notable example. In more recent years many issues produced by the Franklin Mint have been issued with this finish.

Maundy Money Set of small silver coins, in denominations of 1, 2, 3 and 4 pence, distributed by the reigning British monarch to the poor and needy on Maundy Thursday. The custom dates back to the Middle Ages, but in its present form, of distributing pence to as many men and women as the years in the monarch's age, it dates from 1666. At first ordinary silver pennies and multiples were used but after they went out of everyday use distinctive silver coins were produced specifically for the purpose from the reign of George II (1727–60) onwards. For centuries the ceremony took place in Westminster Abbey but since 1955 other venues have been used in alternate years.

Medal (French *medaille*, Italian *medaglia*, from Latin *metallum*). A piece of metal bearing devices and legends commemorating an event or person, or given as an award. Military medals date from the 16th and 17th centuries, but were not generally awarded to all ranks till the 19th century. Commemora-tive medals can be traced back to Roman times, but in their present form they date from the Italian Renaissance when there was a fashion for large cast portrait medals.

Medalet A small medal, generally 25mm or less in diameter.

Medallion Synonym for medal, but usually confined to those with a diameter of 50mm or more.

Milling Process denoting the mechanical production of coins, as opposed to the handmade technique implied in *hammering*. It alludes to the use of watermills to drive the machinery of the screw presses and blank rollers developed in the 16th century. As the even thickness and diameter of milled coins permitted a security edge, the term milling is popularly, though erroneously, used as a synonym for *graining* or *reeding*.

Mint The place in which coins and medals are produced. Mint condition is a term sometimes used to denote pieces in an uncirculated state.

Mint Set A set of coins or medals in the package or case issued by the mint. See also *year set*.

Mintmark A device appearing on a coin to denote the place of minting. Athenian coins of classical times have been recorded with up to 40 different marks, denoting individual workshops. In the 4th century AD the Romans adopted this system to identify coins struck in provincial mints. This system was widely used in the Middle Ages and survives in France and Germany to this day. Initials and symbols are also used to identify mints, especially where the production of a coin is shared between several different mints. From 1351 onwards symbols were adopted in England to denote periods between trials of the *Pyx*, and thus assist the proper chronological sequence of coins, in an era prior to the adoption of dating. These mintmarks continued into the 17th century, but gradually died out as the use of dates became more widespread. See also *countermark* and *privy mark*.

Mionnet Scale Scale of nineteen diameters covering all sizes of coins belonging to the classical period, devised by the French numismatist, Theodore-Edme Mionnet (1770–1842) during the compilation of his fifteen-volume catalogue of the numismatic collection in the Bibliotheque Nationale in Paris.

Mirror Finish The highly polished surface of proof coins.

Misstrike A coin or medal on which the impression has been struck off-centre.

Model Coin Tiny pieces of metal, either reproducing the designs of existing coins (used as play money by children) or, more specifically, denoting patterns produced by Joseph Moore and Hyam Hyams in their attempts to promote an improved subsidiary coinage in 19th century Britain. These small coins were struck in bronze with a brass or silver centre and were designed to reduce the size of the existing cumbersome range of pence, halfpence and farthings.

Modified Effigy Any coin in which the profile on the obverse has been subtly altered. Examples

Maundy money. in its colourful leather bag.

include minor changes in the Victorian Young Head and Old Head effigies and the George V profile by Sir Bertram Mackennal.

Money Order Certificate for a specified amount of money, which may be transmitted by post and encashed at a money order office or post office. This system was pioneered by Britain and the United States in the early 19th century and is now virtually worldwide. The term is now confined to certificates above a certain value, the terms *postal order* and *postal note* being used for similar certificates covering small amounts.

Mule Coin whose obverse is not matched with its official or regular reverse. Mules include the erroneous combination of dies from different reigns, but in recent years such hybrids have arisen in mints where coins for several countries are struck. Examples include the Coronation Anniversary crowns combining Ascension and Isle of Man dies and the 2 cent coins with Bahamas and New Zealand dies. *Restrikes* of rare American coins have been detected in which the dated die has been paired with the wrong reverse die, e.g. the 1860 restrike of the rare 1804 large cent.

Mute An *anepigraphic* coin, identifiable only by the devices struck on it.

Nail Mark Small indentation on ancient coins. The earliest coins of Asia Minor developed from the electrum *dumps* which merchants marked with a broken nail as their personal guarantee of value, the ancient counterpart of the *chop* marks used in China and Japan.

NCLT Coins Abbreviation for "Non Circulating Legal Tender", a term devised by modern coin catalogues to denote coins which, though declared *legal tender*, are not intended for general circulation on account of their precious metal content or superior finish.

Nicked Coin   Coin bearing a tiny cut or nick in its edge. Silver coins were tested by this method, especially in the reign of Henry I (1100–35) when so many base silver pennies were in circulation. Eventually people refused to accept these nicked coins a problem which was only overcome when the state decreed that all coins should have a nick in them.

Nickel   Metallic element, chemical symbol *Ni*, a hard white metal relatively resistant to tarnish, and extensively used as a cheap substitute for silver. It was first used for the American 5 cent coin in 1866, hence its popular name which has stuck ever since, although nowadays the higher denominations are minted in an alloy of copper and nickel. Although best known as a silver substitute, nickel was widely used in Jamaica (1869–1969) for halfpence and pennies and in British West Africa for the tiny 1/10th pennies (1908–57). Pure nickel was used for French francs and German marks, but usually it is alloyed with copper or zinc to produce *cupronickel* or nickel brass.

Notaphily   Hybrid word from Latin *nota* (note) and Greek philos (love), coined about 1970 to denote the branch of numismatics devoted to the study of paper money.

Notgeld   German word meaning emergency money, applied to the *tokens*, in metals, wood, leather and even ceramic materials, issued during the First World War when coinage disappeared from circulation. These tokens were soon superseded by low-denomination paper money issued by shops and businessmen in denominations from 10 to 50 pfennige and known as *kleine Notgeld* (small emergency money). These notes were prohibited in September 1922 but by that time some 50,000 varieties are thought to have been issued. Inflation raced out of control and the government permitted a second issue of local notes, known as *large Notgeld*, as the denominations were in thousands, and latterly millions, of marks. Some 3,600 types appeared in 1922 and over 60,000 in 1923. These ceased to circulate in 1924 when the currency was reformed.

Numismatics   The study of coins, medals and other related fields, a term derived from the Latin *numisma* and Greek *nomisma* (money).

Obsidional Currency   (From Latin *obsidium*, a siege). Term for *emergency money* produced by the defenders of besieged towns and cities. These usually took the form of pieces of silver plate, commandeered for the purpose, crudely marked with an official device and the value. Instances of such seige coinage have been recorded from the 12th to the 19th centuries.

Obverse   The "heads" side of a coin or medal, generally bearing the effigy of the head of state or an allegorical figure.

Off Metal   Term denoting a piece struck in a metal other than the officially authorisied or issued alloy. This originally applied to *patterns* which were often struck in lead or copper instead of gold and silver as trial pieces or to test the dies; but in recent years it has applied to collectors' versions, e.g. proofs in platinum, gold or silver of coins normally issued in bronze or cupro-nickel.

Overdate   One or more digits in a date altered by superimposing another figure. Alterations of this kind, by means of small hand punches, were made to dated dies so that they could be used in years other than that of the original manufacture. Coins with overdates invariably show traces of the original digit.

Overstrike   Coin, token or medal produced by using a previously struck pieces as a flan. The Bank of England dollar of 1804 was overstruck on Spanish pieces of eight, and examples showing traces of the original coins are worth a good premium.

Paduan   Name given to imitations of medals and bogus coins produced in Italy in the 16th century, and deriving from the city of Padua where forgeries of bronze sculpture were produced for the antique market.

Patina   Oxidation forming on the surface of metallic objects. So far as coins and medals are concerned, this applies mainly to silver, brass, bronze and copper pieces which may acquire oxidation from the atmosphere, or spectacular patination from salts in the ground in which they have been buried. In extreme forms patina leads to verdigris and other forms of rust which corrode the surface, but in uncirculated coins it may be little more than a mellowing of the original *lustre*. Coins preserved in blue velvet presentation cases often acquire a subtle toning from the dyes in the material.

Pattern   Piece resembling a coin or medal, prepared by the mint to the specifications or on the authorisation of the coin-issuing authority, but also applied to pieces produced by mints when tendering for coinage or medal contracts. Patterns may differ from the final coins as issued in the type of alloy used (*off metal*) but more often they differ in details of the design.

Pellet   Raised circular ornament used as a spacing device between words and abbreviations in the *legend* of coins and medals. Groups of pellets were also used as ornaments in the angles of the cross on the reverse of English silver pennies.

Piece de Plaisir   (French for "fancy piece"). Term given to coins struck in a superior precious metal,

or to a superior finish, or on a much thicker flan than usual. See *off metal*, *piedfort* and *proof*.

Piedfort (Piefort) Piece struck with coinage dies on a *flan* of much more than normal thickness. This practice originated in France in the late 16th century and continues to the present day. In recent years it has been adopted by mints in Britain and other countries as a medium for collectors' pieces.

Pile Lower die incorporating the obverse motif, used in striking coins and medals. See also *trussel*.

Planchet French term used as an alternative for *blank* or *flan*.

Plaque or **Plaquette** Terms sometimes used for medals struck on a square or rectangular flan.

Plaster model for an unaccepted florin design by Humphrey Paget—see COIN NEWS, August 2016, p. 28.

Plaster Cast taken from the original model for a coin or medal sculpted by an artist, and used in modern reducing machines in the manufacture of the master *die*.

Plated Coins Coins stuck in base metal but given a wash of silver or some other precious metal. This expedient was adopted in inflationary times, from the Roman Republic (91 BC) till the Tudor period. American cents of 1943 were struck in steel with a zinc coating, and more recently *clad* coins have produced similar results.

Platinum The noblest of all precious metals, platinum has a higher specific gravity than gold and a harder, brighter surface than silver. Until an industrial application was discovered in the mid-19th century, it was regarded as of little value, and was popular with counterfeiters

as a cheap substitute for gold in their forgeries which, with a light gold wash, could be passed off as genuine. It was first used for circulating coins in Russia (the chief source of the metal since 1819) and 3, 6 and 12 rouble coins were mined at various times between 1828 and 1845. In recent years platinum has been a popular metal for limited-edition proof coins.

Platmynt (Swedish for "plate money"). Large copper plates bearing royal cyphers and values from half to ten dalers produced in Sweden between 1643 and 1768. They represented laudable attempts by a country rich in copper to produce a coinage in terms of its silver value, but the net result was far too cumbersome to be practical. The weight of the daler plate, for example, ranged from 766 grams to 1.1kg, and special carts had to be devised to transport them!

Plugged Coins Coins struck predominantly in one metal, but containing a small plug of another. This curious practice may be found in the farthings of Charles II (1684–85) and the halfpence or farthings of James II (1685–87), which were struck in tin, with a copper plug, to defeat forgers.

Porcelain Money Tokens made of porcelain circulated in Thailand from the late 18th century till 1868. The Meissen pottery struck tokens in 1920–22 as a form of small *Notgeld*, using reddish-brown Bottger stoneware and white *bisque* porcelain. These ceramic tokens circulated in various towns of Saxony.

Postage Currency Small paper notes in denominations of 5, 10, 25 and 50 cents, issued by the US federal government in 1862–63, were thus inscribed and had reproductions of postage stamps engraved on them — five 5c stamps on the 25c and five 10c stamps on the 50c notes. The earliest issue even had perforations in the manner of stamps, but this unnecessary device was soon done away with. See also *stamp money*.

Postal Notes or Orders Low-value notes intended for transmission by post and encashable at post offices. Introduced by Britain in 1883, they were an extension of the earlier *money order* system, and are now issued by virtually every country.

Potin (French for pewter). Alloy of copper, tin, lead and silver used as a coinage metal by the Celtic tribes of eastern Gaul at the beginning of the Christian era.

Privy Mark Secret mark incorporated in the design of a coin or medal to identify the minter, or even the particular die used. The term is also used more loosely to denote any small symbol or initials appearing on a coin other than a *mint*

mark, and is sometimes applied to the symbols associated with the trial of the *Pyx* found on English coins.

Prize Coins   Coins of large size and value struck primarily as prizes in sporting contests. this principle dates from the late 5th century BC when Syracuse minted decadrachms as prizes in the Demareteian Games. The most notable example in modern times is the lengthy series of talers and five-franc coins issued by the Swiss cantons since 1842 as prizes in the annual shooting festivals, the last of which honoured the Lucerne contest of 1939.

Profile   A side view of the human face, widely used as a coinage effigy.

Proof   Originally a trial strike testing the *dies*, but now denoting a special collectors' version struck with dies that have been specially polished on *flans* with a mirror finish. Presses operating at a very slow speed, or multi-striking processes, are also used.

Propaganda Notes   Paper money containing a political slogan or a didactic element. During the Second World War forgeries of German and Japanese notes were produced by the Allies and additionally inscribed or overprinted with slogans such as "Co-Prosperity Sphere — What is it worth?" (a reference to the Japanese occupied areas of SE Asia). Forged dollars with anti-American propaganda were airdropped over Sicily by the Germans in 1943 and counterfeit pounds with Arabic propaganda over Egypt in 1942–43. Various anti-communist organisations liberated propaganda forgeries of paper money by balloon over Eastern Europe during the Cold War period.

Provenance Mark   Form of *privy mark* denoting the source of the metal used in coins. Examples include the plumes or roses on English coins denoting silver from Welsh or West of England mines, and the elephant or elephant and castle on gold coins denoting bullion imported by the African Company. Coins inscribed VIGO (1702–03) or LIMA (1745–46) denote bullion seized from the Spaniards by Anglo-Dutch privateers and Admiral Anson respectively. Other provenance marks on English coins include the letters EIC and SSC, denoting bullion imported by the East India Company or the South Sea Company.

Pseudo Coins   Derisory term coined in recent years to signify pieces of precious metal, often struck in *proof* versions only, aimed at the international investment market. Many of these pieces, though bearing a nominal face value, are not *legal tender* in the countries purporting to issue them and in many cases they go straight from the overseas mint where they are produced to coin dealers in America and western Europe, without ever appearing in the so-called country of origin. See also *NCLT coins*.

Punch or Puncheon   Intermediate *die* whereby working dies can be duplicated from the master die, prior to the striking of coins and medals.

Pyx   Box in which a specimen from every 15 pounds troy weight of gold and every 60 pounds of silver minted in England is kept for annual trial by weight and assay. Many of the *mintmarks* on English coins of the 14th–17th centuries were in use from one trial to the next and still exist today and can therefore be used to date them.

Reducing Machinery   Equipment designed on the pantographic principle for transferring the image from a *plaster* to a *hub* and reducing it to the size of the actual coin or medal. The image is transferred by means of a stylus operating rather like a gramophone needle, but working from the centre to the outer edge.

Reeding   Security edging on coins, consisting of close vertical ridges. As a rule, this appears all round the edge but some coins, e.g. New Zealand's 50c (1967) and the Isle of Man's £1 (1978) have segments of reeding alternating with a plain edge, to help blind and partially sighted persons to identify these coins.

Re-issue   A coin or note issued again after an extended lapse of time.

Relief   Raised parts of the *obverse* and *reverse* of coins and medals, the opposite of *incuse*.

Remainder   A note from a bank or issuing authority which has never been circulated, due to inflation, political changes or bank failure. Such notes, some-times in partial or unfinished state (e.g. missing serial numbers or signatures), are generally unloaded on to the numismatic market at a nominal sum and provide a good source of inexpensive material for the beginner.

Restrike   Coin, medal or token produced from *dies* subsequent to the original use. Usually restrikes are made long after the original and can often be identified by marks caused by damage, pitting or corrosion of the dies after they were taken out of service.

Retrograde   Term describing inscriptions running from right to left, or with the letters in a mirror image, thought to arise from unskilled die-cutters failing to realise that inscriptions have to be engraved in negative form to achieve a positive impression. Retrograde inscriptions are common on ancient Greek coins, but also found on Roman and Byzantine coins.

Reverse   The side of a coin or medal regarded as of lesser importance; in colloquial parlance, the "tails" side.

Saltire   Heraldic term for a cross in the shape of an X.

Sandwich Coin *blank* consisting of thin outer layers in one alloy bonded to a core in another. See *clad coins*.

Sceat (Anglo-Saxon for "treasure", or German *Schatz*). Money of account in Kent early in the 7th century as the twelfth part of a shilling or Merovingian gold tremissis. As a silver coin, it dates from about AD 680–700 and weighed about 20 grains, putting it on par with the Merovingian denier or penny. Sceats spread to other parts of England in the 8th century but tended to decline in weight and value, but from about 760 it was gradually superseded by the silver penny minted under Offa and his successors.

Scissel The clippings of metal left after a *blank* has been cut. Occasionally one of these clippings accidentally adheres to the blank during the striking process, producing characteristic crescent-shaped flaws which are present on on the finished coin.

Scrip Paper money of restricted validity or circulation, e.g.*Bafs* and other military scrip used in canteens and post exchanges.

Scyphate (Greek *scypha*, a skiff or small boat). Byzantine coin with a concave *flan*.

Sede Vacante (Latin for "Vacant See"). Coins struck at *ecclesiastical mints* between the death of a prelate and the election of his successor are often thus inscribed. This practice originated at Rome in the 13th century.

Seignorage or Seigneurage Royalty or percentage paid by persons bringing *bullion* to a mint for conversion into coin, but nowadays synonymous with the royalty paid by mints in respect of the precious metal versions of coins sold direct to collectors. It arises from the medieval right of the king to a small portion of the proceeds of a mint, and amounted to a tax on moneying. It has also been applied to the money accruing to the state when the coinage is re-issued in an alloy of lesser fineness, as, for example, the debased sovereigns of Henry VIII in 20 instead of 23 carat gold, the king's treasury collecting the difference.

Series Term applied to sets of medals of a thematic character, which first became fashionable in the early 18th century. Jean Dassier pioneered the medallic series in the 1720s with his set of 72 medals portraying the rulers of France till Louis XV. The idea was developed by J. Kirk, Sir Edward Thomason, J. Mudie and A. J. Stothard in Britain, and by Moritz Fuerst and Amedee Durand in Europe. The fashion died out in the 19th century, but has been revived in America and Europe since 1964.

Serrated Having a notched or toothed edge, rather like a cogwheel. Coins of this type, struck in *electrum,* an alloy of silver and gold, are known from Carthage in the 2nd century BC, and some silver denarii of Rome in the 2nd century AD also come into this category.

Sexagesimal System Monetary system in which the principal unit is divided into 60 parts. The oldest system in the Western world was based on the gold talent of 60 minae and the mina of 60 shekels. In medieval Europe 60 groschen were worth a fine mark; in England from 1551, the silver coinage was based on the crown of 60 pence, and in the south German states till 1873 the gulden was worth 60 kreuzers.

Shin Plasters Derisory term originally applied to the Continental currency notes issued during the American War of Independence, the fractional currency of the Civil War period and also the low-denomination notes of Canada between 1870 and 1935, but often applied indiscriminately to any other low-denomination, small-format notes.

Short cross penny of John (1199–1216).

Short Cross Coinage Term for the silver coinage introduced by Henry II in 1180 and minted till 1247 at which time it was replaced by the *Long Cross* type. The termination of the arms of the cross on the reverse well within the circumference encouraged the dishonest practice of *clipping*.

Shroff Mark A *countermark* applied by Indian bankers or merchants to attest the full weight and purity of coins. See also *chop*.

Siege Money See *Obsidional Currency*

Silver Precious metal, chemical symbol Ag, numismatic abbreviation Ar, from Latin *Argentum*, widely used as a coinage metal from the 6th century BC to the present day.

Sterling silver denotes an alloy of .925 fine silver with .075 copper. Fine silver alloys used over the past 2,500 years have ranged from .880 to .960 fine, but base silver has also been all too common. British coins from 1920 to 1946 were struck in .500 fine silver, while alloys of

lesser fineness are known as *billon* or *vellon*. Silver alloyed with gold produces a metal called *electrum*, used for the earliest coinage of the western world, the staters of Lydia in the 7th century BC. Since 1970 silver as a medium for circulating coinage has almost virtually disappeared, yet the volume of silver coins for sale to collectors has risen considerably in recent years.

Skit Note Piece of paper masquerading as a banknote. It differs from a *counterfeit* in that its design parodies that of a genuine note, often for political, satirical or advertising reasons. Others were produced as April Fools' Day jokes or a form of Valentine (e.g. the Bank of Lovers). In recent years they have been produced as advertising gimmicks, or as coupons permitting a discount off the list price of goods.

Slug Popular name for the $50 gold pieces produced by private mints in California in the mid-19th century. The term is also applied nowadays to *tokens* intended for use in gaming machines.

Spade Guinea Name given to the guineas of George III issued between 1787 and 1799 because the shield on the reverse design resembled the shape of a spade. In Victorian times the spade guinea was extensively copied in brass for gaming counters.

Spade Money Cast bronze pieces resembling miniature spades and other agricultural implements, used as money and derived from the actual implements which had previously been used in barter. Often referred to as *Pu* or *Boo* money.

Specie Financial term denoting money in the form of precious metals (silver and gold), usually struck as coin, as opposed to money in the form of paper notes and bills of exchange. It occurs in the name of some European coins (e.g. *speciedaler*, *speciestaler* and *speciesducat*) to denote the use of fine silver or gold.

Specimen Generally used to denote a single piece, but more specifically applying to a coin in a special finish, less than *proof* in quality but superior to the general circulating version. It also denotes paper notes intended for circulation between banks or for press publicity and distinguished from the generally issued version by zero serial numbers, punch holes or a security endorsement.

Spintriae Metal tokens produced in Roman imperial times, with erotic motifs, thought to have been tickets of admission to brothels.

Spit Copper or iron rod used as a primitive form of currency in the Mediterranean area. The Greek word *belos* meant a spit, dart or bolt, and from

Spade guinea. Reverse of a guinea of George III with the eponymus shield—the famous spade.

this came the word *obolos* used for a coin worth a 6th of a drachma.

Stamp Money Both postage and revenue (fiscal) stamps have circulated as money during shortages of coins, from the American Civil War onwards. *Encased postage stamps* were used in the USA, 1861–62, before they were superseded by *Postage Currency* notes, but the same expedient was adopted by many countries during and immediately after the First World War. Stamps affixed to special cards have circulated as money in Rhodesia (now Zimbabwe) in 1900, the French colonies and Turkey during the First World War, in Spain during the Civil War (1936–39) and the Philippines during the Second World War. Stamps printed on thick card, with an inscription on the reverse signifying their parity with silver coins, were issued in Russia (1917–18) and also in Armenia, the Crimea and the Ukraine (1918–20). During the Second World War Ceylon (now Sri Lanka) and several Indian states issued small money cards with contemporary stamps printed on them.

Steel Refined and tempered from *iron*, and used in chromed or stainless versions as a coinage metal in the 20th century. Zinc-coated steel cents were issued by the USA (1943) but in the form known as *acmonital* (nickel steel) it has been extensively used by Italy since 1939. Other alloys of nickel and steel have been used for coins of the Philippines (1944–45) and Roumania since 1963. Chrome steel was used by France for 5 centime coins in 1961–64. Copper-clad steel is now extensively used for subsidiary coins formerly struck in bronze.

Sterling Word of uncertain origin denoting money of a standard weight and fineness, and hence the more general meaning of recognised worth. The traditionally accepted derivation from the Easterlings, north German merchants who settled in London in the 13th century and

produced silver pennies of uniform fineness, is unlikely as the term has been found in documents a century earlier. A more plausible explanation is from Old English *steorling* ("little coin with a star"), alluding to Viking pennies with this device, or even as a diminutive of *stater*. Sterling silver denotes silver of .925 fineness.

Stone Money   Primitive currency in the form of large stone discs, used in West Africa in the pre-colonial period, and in the Pacific island of Yap (now Micronesia) as recently as 1940.

Striation   A pattern of alternate light and dark parallel marks or minute grooves on the surface of a coin or medal. In the latter case it is sometimes done for textural effect, but in coins it may result from faulty *annealing*. Deliberate ridging of the surface, however, was a distinctive feature of Japanese *koban* and *goryoban* coins of 1736–1862.

Styca   Name given to the debased silver *sceats* of Northumbria in the 8th century.

Tael   Chinese unit of weight corresponding to the European ounce and sometimes referred to as a liang. It was a measure of silver varying between 32 and 39 grams. In the 19th century it served as *money of account*, 100 British or Mexican trade dollars being worth 72 tael. The term has also been loosely applied to the Chinese silver yuan, although this was worth only .72 tael, or 7 mace and 2 candareens (10 candareens = 1 mace; 10 mace = 1 tael).

Thrymsa   Early Anglo-Saxon gold coin based on the Merovingian tremissis or third-solidus, current in Kent, London and York around AD 63–75.

Tical   Unit of weight in Thailand, first appearing as coins in the form of crudely shaped *bullet money* current from the 14th till the late 19th centuries. When European-style coins were introduced in 1860 the word was retained as a denomination (32 solot = 16 atts = 8 peinung or sio = 4 songpy or sik = 2 fuang= 1 salung or quarter-tical. The currency was decimalised in 1909 (100 satangs = 1 tical), and the tical was superseded by the baht about 1950.

Tin   Metallic element, chemical symbol *Sn* (from Latin *Stannum*). Because of its unstable nature and tendency to oxidise badly when exposed to the atmosphere, it is unsatisfactory as a coinage metal, but has been used on several occasions, notably in Malaya, Thailand and the East Indies. In was also used for British halfpence and farthings, 1672–92.

Token   Any piece of money whose nominal value is greater than its intrinsic value is, strictly speaking, a token or promise. Thus most of the coins issued since 1964 can be regarded in this light, but numismatists reserve the term for a piece of limited validity and circulation, produced by tradesmen, chambers of commerce and other organisations during times of a shortage of government coinage. The term is also loosely applied to metal tickets of admission, such as *communion tokens*, or *jetons* and *counters* intended for games of chance. Tokens with a nominal value may be produced for security reasons to lessen the possibility of theft from milk bottles, vending machines, telephones, parking meters and transport facilities. Tokens exchangeable for goods have been issued by co-operative societies and used in prisons and internment camps in wartime. In addition to the traditional coinage alloys, tokens have been produced in ceramics, plastics, wood, stout card, leather and even rubber, in circular, square or polygonal shapes.

Tombac   Type of brass alloy with a high copper content, used in coinage requiring a rich golden colour. It is, in fact, a modern version of the *aurichalcum* used by the Romans. It was used for the Canadian 5-cent coins of 1942–43, while 5- and 10-pfennig coins of Germany have a tombac cladding on a steel core.

Touchpiece   Coin kept as a lucky charm, but more specifically the medieval gold angel of England which was worn round the neck as an antidote to scrofula, otherwise known as king's evil, from the belief that the reigning monarch possessed the power of healing by touch. The ceremony of touching for king's evil involved the suspension of an angel round the victim's neck, hence the prevalence of these coins pierced for suspension.

Trade Coins   Coins widely used as a medium of international trade, often far beyond the boundaries of the country issuing them. The earliest examples were the Aiginetan turtles and Athenian tetrdrachms of the classical period. In the Middle Ages the English *sterling* was widely prized on account of its silver purity. Arab dinars and Italian florins were popular as gold coins in late-medieval times, while the British gold sovereign has been the preferred gold coin of modern times. The Maria Theresa silver thaler of Austria, with its date frozen at 1782, has been minted widely down to the present time for circulation in the Near and Middle East as a trade coin. Trade dollars were minted by Britain, the USA, the Netherlands and Japan to compete with the Spanish, and later the Mexican, peso or 8-reales coins as a trading medium in the Far East.

Transport Tokens   Coin-like pieces of metal, plastic or card, issued by companies and corporations to employees and exchangeable for rides on municipal transport systems, date

from the mid-19th century. In more recent times similar tokens have been used in many countries to activate turnstiles in buses, trams and rapid-transit railway systems.

Treasury Note   Paper money worth 10 shillings or one pound, issued by the British Treasury on the outbreak of the First World War when *specie* payments were suspended, and continuing till 1928 when the Bank of England took over responsibility for note-issuing.

Treasure Trove   Articles of precious metal concealed in times of economic or political upheaval and discovered years (often centuries) later are deemed by law to be treasure trove (from the French word *trouve*, found). For further details see *Money and the Law*.

Trial Plate   Plate of the same metal as the current coinage against which the fineness and quality of the coins produced are compared and tested.

Troy Weight   System of weights derived from the French town of Troyes whose standard pound was adopted in England in 1526. It continued in Britain till 1879 when it was abolished, with the exception of the troy ounce and its decimal parts and multiples, which were retained for gold, silver, platinum and precious stones. The troy ounce of 480 grains is used for weighing coins.

Truncation   Stylised cut at the base of a coinage effigy, sometimes containing a die number, engraver's initials or *mintmark*.

Trussel   Reverse die in *hammered* coinage, the opposite of the *pile*.

Type   Principal motif on a coin or medal, enabling numismatists to identify the issue.

Type Set   A set of coins comprising one of each coin in a particular series, regardless of the actual date of issue.

Uncirculated   Term used in grading coins to denote specimens in perfect condition, with original mint lustre. In recent years the term "Brilliant Uncirculated" has been adopted (abbreviated as BUnc or BU) both to indicate the condition of a coin, and, by The Royal Mint, to indicate the standard to which some coins are minted, being a standard between Circulation and Proof.

Uniface   Coin with a device on one side only.

Vecture   Term (mainly used in the US) for a *transport token*.

Veiled Head   The effigy of Queen Victoria by Thomas Brock adopted for British coinage after 1893—often referred to as the "Old Head" coinage.

Veld Pond   (Dutch for "field pound"). Gold coin struck by the Boer guerrillas at Pilgrims Rest in 1902, in imitation of the British sovereign.

VF   Standard abbreviation for Very Fine, used to describe the state of a coin or medal.

VG   Abbreviation for Very Good, used to describe the state of a coin or medal, however, it is not a standard grade of a coin in the grading scale.

Vignette   Strictly speaking the pictorial element of a paper note shading off into the surrounding unprinted paper rather than having a clearly defined border or frame; but nowadays applied generally to the picture portion of a banknote, as opposed to portrait, armorial or numeral elements.

Vis-à-Vis   (French for "face to face"). Term describing coins with double portraits of rulers, their profiles or busts facing each other. A good example is the English coinage of Philip and Mary, 1554–58.

Wampum   Barter currency of the North American Indians, composed of shells of *Venus mercenaria* strung together to form belts or "fathoms" worth 5 shillings. Wampum were tariffed variously from three to six to the English penny in the American colonies till 1704.

Wire Money   Primitive currency of the Maldive Islands in the form of lengths of silver wire known as lari, from which the modern currency unit *laree* is derived. The term was also applied to English coins of the 18th century in which the numerals of value were exceptionally thin, resembling wire. Many Russian coins of the 17th/18th century were also made from pieces of wire cut from strips which were then roughly flattened, often in an oval shape. These blanks were then struck with round dies which often meant that parts of the wording and design was missed off.

Wooden Coins   Thin pieces of wood used as tokens are known from many parts of China and Africa, and as small *Notgeld* from Austria and Germany during World War I. Wooden nickels is the name given to tokens of a commemorative nature, widely popular in the USA since 1930.

Young Head   Profile of Queen Victoria sculpted by William Wyon for the Guildhall Medal of 1837 and subsequently utilised for British coins struck from 1837 to 1860 (copper) and 1887 (silver and gold).

Zinc   Metallic element, chemical symbol *Zn*, widely used, with copper, as a constituent of brass. Alloyed with copper to form *tombac*, it was used for Canadian 5-cent coins (1942–43) and, coated on steel, it was used for American cents (1943). Zinc was used for *emergency coinage* in Austria, Belgium, Luxembourg and Germany (1915–18) and in Germany and German-occupied countries during World War II. Since then alloys of copper, nickel and zinc have been used for coinage in Eastern Europe.

MINTMARKS *of the world*

The following is a list of the initials and symbols denoting mints. In many cases, notably the Royal Mint, no mintmark was used on either British coins or those struck on behalf of other countries. Conversely many countries have only used one mintmark, that of one or other of the leading private mints.

It should be noted that the mintmarks of the main private mints have been recorded on the coins of the following countries:

H (Heaton, later the Birmingham Mint): Australia, Bolivia, British Honduras, British North Borneo, British West Africa, Bulgaria, Canada, Ceylon, Chile, Colombia, Costa Rica, Cyprus, Dominican Republic, East Africa, Ecuador, Egypt, El Salvador, Finland, French Indochina, Great Britain, Greece, Guatemala, Guernsey, Haiti, Hong Kong, Iran, Israel, Italy, Jamaica, Jersey, Liberia, Malaya and British Borneo, Mauritius, Mombasa, Mozambique, Newfoundland, Nicaragua, Poland, Roumania, Sarawak, Serbia, Siam, Straits Settlements, Uruguay and Venezuela.

FM (Franklin Mint, Philadelphia): Bahamas, Belize, British Virgin Islands, Cayman Islands, Cook Islands, Guyana, Jamaica, Liberia, Malaysia, Malta, Panama, Papua New Guinea, Philippines, Solomon Islands, Trinidad and Tobago.

PM (Pobjoy Mint, Sutton, Surrey): Ascension, Bosnia, Cook Islands, Gibraltar, Isle of Man, Liberia, Macau, Niue, Philippines, St Helena, Senegal, Seychelles, Tonga and Tristan da Cunha.

ALBANIA
L	London
R	Rome
V	Valona

ARGENTINA
BA	Buenos Aires
Bs	Buenos Aires
B.AS	Buenos Aires
JPP	Jose Policarpo Patino
M	Mendoza
PNP	Pedro Nolasco Pizarro
PP	Pedro Nolasco Pizarro
PTS	Potosi
R	Rioja
RA	Rioja
SE	Santiago del Estero
SoEo	Santiago del Estero
TN	Tucuman

AUSTRALIA
A	Perth
D	Denver
H	Heaton (1912–16)
I	Bombay (1942–43)
I	Calcutta (1916–18)
M	Melbourne
P	Perth
PL	Royal Mint, London
S	Sydney
S	San Francisco (1942–43)
Dot before and after PENNY and I on obverse	Bombay (1942–43)
Dot before and after HALFPENNY and I on obverse	Bombay (1942–43)
Dot before and after PENNY	Bombay (1942–43)
Dot after HALFPENNY	Perth
Dot before SHILLING	Perth (1946)
Dot above scroll on reverse	Sydney (1920)
Dot below scroll on reverse	Melbourne (1919–20)
Dot between designer's initials KG	Perth (1940–41)
Dot after AUSTRALIA	Perth (1952–53)

AUSTRIA

A	Vienna (1765–1872)
AH–AG	Carlsburg, Transylvania (1765–76)
AH–GS	Carlsburg (1776–80)
A–S	Hall, Tyrol (1765–74)
AS–IE	Vienna (1745)
AW	Vienna (1764, 1768)
B	Kremnitz (1765–1857)
B–L	Nagybanya (1765–71)
B–V	Nagybanya (1772–80)
C	Carlsburg (1762–64)
C	Prague (1766–1855)
C–A	Carlsburg (1746–66)
C–A	Vienna (1774–80)
CG–AK	Graz (1767–72)
CG–AR	Graz (1767)
C–K	Vienna (1765–73)
CM	Kremnitz (1779)
CVG–AK	Graz (1767–72)
CVG–AR	Graz (1767)
D	Graz (1765–72), Salzburg (1800–09)
E	Carlsburg (1765–1867)
EC–SK	Vienna (1766)
EvM–D	Kremnitz (1765–74)
EvS–AS	Prague (1765–73)
EvS–IK	Prague (1774–80)
F	Hall (1765–1807)
FH	Hall
G	Graz (1761–63)
G	Gunzburg (1764–79)
G	Nagybanya (1766–1851)
G–K	Graz (1767–72)
G–R	Graz (1746–67)
GTK	Vienna (1761)
H	Hall (1760–80)
H	Gunzburg (1765–1805)
H–A	Hall (1746–65)
H–G	Carlsburg (1765–77)
H–S	Carlsburg (1777–80)
IB–FL	Nagybanya (1765–71)
IB–IV	Nagybanya (1772–80)
IC–FA	Vienna (1774–80)
IC–IA	Vienna (1780)
IC–SK	Vienna (1765–73)
I–K	Graz (1765-67)
I–K	Vienna (1767)
IZV	Vienna (1763–65)
K	Kremnitz (1760–63)
K–R	Kremnitz (1619–1765)
K–D	Kremnitz (1765)
K–M	Kremnitz (1763–65)
M	Milan (1780–1859)
N	Nagybanya (1780)
N–B	Nagybanya (1630–1777, 1849)
O	Oravicza (1783–1816)
P	Prague (1760–63)
P–R	Prague (1746–67)
PS–IK	Prague (1774–80)
3	Hall (1705–00), Schmollnitz (1760 1816)
S–C	Gunzburg (1765–74)
SC–G	Gunzburg (1765)

S–F	Gunzburg (1775–80)
S–G	Gunzburg (1764–65)
S–IE	Vienna (1745)
SK–PD	Kremnitz (1774–80)
TS	Gunzburg (1762–88)
V	Venice (1805–66)
VC–S	Hall (1774–80)
VS–K	Prague (1774–80)
VS–S	Prague (1765–73)
W	Vienna (1748–63)
W–I	Vienna (1746–71)

BAHAMAS

FM	Franklin Mint
JP	John Pinches

BELGIUM

A	Vienna
B	Kremnitz
C	Prague
E	Carlsburg
F	Hall
G	Nagybanya
H	Gunzburg
hand	Antwerp
lion	Bruges

BELIZE (British Honduras)

FM	Franklin Mint
H	Heaton (1912–16)

BOLIVIA

H	Heaton (1892–1953)
P, PTR, PTS	Potosi

BRAZIL

A	Berlin (1913)
B	Bahia (1714–1831)
C	Cuiaba (1823–33)
G	Goias (1823–33)
M	Minas Gerais (1823–28)
P	Pernambuco
R	Rio de Janeiro (1703–1834)
RS	Rio de Janeiro (1869)
SP	Sao Paulo (1825–32)

BRITISH NORTH BORNEO (Sabah)

H	Heaton (1882–1941)

BRITISH WEST AFRICA

G	JR Gaunt, Birmingham
H	Heaton, Birmingham (1911–57)
K	King's Norton
KN	King's Norton
SA	Pretoria

BULGARIA

A	Berlin
BP	Budapest
Heaton	Heaton, Birmingham (1881–1923)
KB	Kormoczbanya
cornucopia	Paris
thunderbolt	Poissy

CANADA
C	Ottawa
H	Heaton (1871–1907)
maple leaf	Ottawa (on coins struck after the year inscribed on them)

CENTRAL AMERICAN REPUBLIC
CR	San Jose (Costa Rica)
G	Guatemala
NG	Guatemala
T	Tegucigalpa (Honduras)

CEYLON
H	Heaton (1912)

CHILE
A	Agustin de Infante y Prado (1768–72)
AJ	The above and Jose Maria de Bobadilla (1800–01)
D	Domingo Eizaguirre
DA	Domingo Eizaguirre and Agustin de Infante (1772–99)
BFF	Francisco Rodriguez Brochero
FJJF	Brochero and Jose Maria de Bobadilla (1803–17)
H	Heaton (1851)
J	Jose Larraneta (1749–67)
So	Santiago
VA	Val Distra

COLOMBIA
A	Paris
B	Bogota
BA	Bogota
B.B	Bogota
H	Heaton (1912)
M	Medellin
NR	Nuevo Reino
NoRo	Nuevo Reino
P	Popayan
PN, Pn	Popayan
SM	Santa Marta

COSTA RICA
CR	San Jose (1825–1947)
HBM	Heaton (1889–93)
S	San Domingo
SD	San Domingo

COURLAND
ICS	Justin Carl Schroder
IFS	Johan Friedrich Schmickert

CYPRUS
H	Heaton (1881–2)

DENMARK
FF	Altona
KM	Copenhagen Altona (1842)
crown	Copenhagen
heart	Copenhagen

orb	Altona (1839–48)

Other letters are the initials of mintmasters and moneyers

DOMINICAN REPUBLIC
HH	Heaton (1888–1919)

EAST AFRICA
A	Ackroyd & Best, Morley
H	Heaton (1910–64)
I	Bombay
K	Kynoch (IMI)
KN	King's Norton
SA	Pretoria

ECUADOR
BIRM^{M}H	Heaton (1915)
BIRMING-HAM	Heaton (1899–1900, 1928)
D	Denver
H	Heaton (1890, 1909, 1924–5)
HEATON BIRMING-HAM	Heaton (1872–95)
HF	Le Locle
LIMA	Lima
Mo	Mexico
PHILA	Philadelphia
QUITO	Quito
SANTIAGO	Santiago de Chile

EGYPT
H	Heaton (1904–37)

EL SALVADOR
CAM	Central American Mint, San Salvador
H	Heaton (1889–1913)
Mo	Mexico
S	San Francisco

FIJI
S	San Francisco

FINLAND
H	Heaton (1921)
heart	Copenhagen (1922). Since then coins have been struck at Helsinki without a mintmark.

Initials of mintmasters:
S	August Soldan (1864–85)
L	Johan Lihr (1885–1912)
S	Isaac Sundell (1915–47)
L	V. U. Liuhto (1948)
H	Uolevi Helle (1948–58)
S	Allan Soiniemi (1958–75)
SH	Soiniemi & Heikki Halvaoja (1967–71)
K	Timo Koivuranta (1977, 1979)
KN	Koivuranta and Antti Neuvonen (1978)
KT	Koivuranta and Erja Tielinen (1982)
KM	Koivuranta and Pertti Makinen (1983)
N	Reino Nevalainen (1983)

FRANCE

A	Paris (1768)
AA	Metz (1775–98)
B	Rouen (1786–1857)
B	Beaumont le Roger (1943–58)
BB	Strasbourg (1743–1870)
C	Castelsarrasin (1914, 1942–46)
CC	Genoa (1805)
CL	Genoa (1813–14)
D	Lyons (1771–1857)
G	Geneva (1796–1805)
H	La Rochelle (1770–1837)
L	Limoges (1766–1837)
K	Bordeaux (1759–1878)
L	Bayonne (1761–1837)
M	Toulouse (1766–1837)
MA	Marseilles (1787–1857)
N	Montpellier (1766–93)
O	Riom
P	Dijon
Q	Perpignan (1777–1837)
R	Royal Mint, London (1815)
R	Orleans (1780–92)
T	Nantes (1739–1835)
U	Turin (1814)
V	Troyes
W	Lille (1759–1857)
X	Amiens (1740)
&	Aix en Provence (1775)
9	Rennes
cow	Pau (1746–93)
flag	Utrecht (1811–14)
crowned R	Rome (1811–14)
thunderbolt	Poissy (1922-24)
star	Madrid (1916)

In addition, French coins include symbols denoting the privy marks of Engravers General (Chief Engravers since 1880) and Mint Directors.

GERMANY

The first name gives the location of the mint, and the second the name of the country or state issuing the coins.

A	Amberg, Bavaria (1763–94)
A	Berlin (1850)
A	Clausthal, Hannover (1832–49)
AE	Breslau, Silesia (1743–51)
AGP	Cleve, Rhineland (1742–43)
AK	Dusseldorf, Julich-Berg (1749–66)
ALS	Berlin (1749)
B	Bayreuth, Franconia (1796–1804)
B	Breslau, Silesia (1750–1826)
B	Brunswick, Brunswick (1850–60)
B	Brunswick, Westphalia (1809–13)
B	Dresden, Saxony (1861–72)
B	Hannover, Brunswick (1860–71)
B	Hannover, East Friesland (1823–25)
B	Hannover, Hannover (1821–66)
B	Hannover, Germany (1866-78)
B	Regensburg, Regensburg (1809)
B	Vienna, Germany (1938–45)

BH	Frankfurt (1808)
B–H	Regensburg, Rhenish Confederation (1802–12)
C	Cassel, Westphalia (1810–13)
C	Clausthal, Brunswick
C	Clausthal, Westphalia (1810–11)
C	Dresden, Saxony (1779–1804)
C	Frankfurt, Germany (1866–79)
CHI	Berlin (1749–63)
CLS	Dusseldorf, Julich-Berg (1767–70)
D	Aurich, East Friesland (1750–1806)
D	Dusseldorf, Rhineland (1816–48)
D	Munich, Germany (1872)
E	Dresden, Germany (1872–87)
E	Koenigberg, East Prussia (1750–98)
E	Muldenhutte, Germany (1887–1953)
EC	Leipzig, Saxony (1753–63)
EGN	Berlin (1725–49)
F	Dresden, Saxony (1845–58)
F	Magdeburg, Lower Saxony (1740–1806)
F	Cassel, Hesse-Cassel (1803–07)
F	Stuttgart, Germany (1872)
FW	Dresden, Saxony (1734–63)
G	Dresden, Saxony (1833–44, 1850–54)
G	Glatz, Silesia (1807–09)
G	Karlsruhe, Germany (1872)
G	Stettin, Pomerania (1750–1806)
GK	Cleve (1740–55)
GN	Bamberg, Bamberg
H	Darmstadt, Germany (1872–82)
H	Dresden, Saxony (1804–12)
HK	Rostock, Rostock (1862–64)
I	Hamburg, Germany (1872)
IDB	Dresden, Prussian occupation (1756–59)
IEC	Dresden, Saxony (1779–1804)
IF	Leipzig, Saxony (1763–65)
IGG	Leipzig, Saxony (1716–34, 1813–32)
J	Hamburg, Germany (1873)
J	Paris, Westphalia (1808–09)
L	Leipzig, Saxony (1761–62)
MC	Brunswick, Brunswick (1813–14, 1820)
PM	Dusseldorf, Julich-Berg (1771–83)
PR	Dusseldorf, Julich-Berg (1783–1804)
S	Dresden, Saxony (1813–32)
S	Hannover, Hannover (1839–44)
S	Schwabach, Franconia (1792–94)
SGH	Dresden, Saxony (1804–12)
ST	Strickling, Blomberg (1820–40)

GREAT BRITAIN

A	Ashby (1645)
B	Nicolas Briot (1631–39)
B	Bridgnorth (1646)
B	Bristol (1696)
Br	Bristol (1643–45)
C	Chester (1696)
CARL	Carlisle (1644–45)
CC	Corfe Castle (1644)
CHST	Chester (1644)
CR	Chester (1644)
E	Southwark (1547–49)

E	Exeter (1696)
E	Edinburgh (1707–13)
E*	Edinburgh (1707–09)
H	Heaton, Birmingham (1874–1919)
HC	Hartlebury Castle (1646)
K	London (1547–49)
KN	King's Norton
N	Norwich (1696)
OX	Oxford (1644–45)
OXON	Oxford (1644)
PC	Pontefract (1648–49)
SC	Scarborough (1644–45)
SOHO	Birmingham (1797–1806)
T	Canterbury (1549)
TC	Bristol (1549)
WS	Bristol (1547–49)
Y	Southwark (1551)
boar	Shrewsbury (1643–44)
book	Aberystwyth (1638–42)
bow	Durham House (1548–49)
castle	Exeter (1644–45)
crown	Aberystwyth Furnace (1648–49)
plume	Shrewsbury (1642)
plume	Oxford (1642–46)
plume	Bristol (1643–46)

Other symbols and marks on the hammered coins of Great Britain are usually referred to as Initial Marks. Complete listings of these marks appear in a number of specialist publications.

GREECE
A	Paris
B	Vienna
BB	Strasbourg
H	Heaton (1921)
K	Bordeaux
KN	King's Norton
owl	Aegina (1828–32)
owl	Athens (1838–55)
thunderbolt	Poissy

GUATEMALA
CG	Guatemala City (1733-76)
G	Guatemala City (1776)
H	Heaton (1894–1901)
NG	Nueva Guatemala (1777)

GUERNSEY
H	Heaton (1855–1949)

HAITI
A	Paris
HEATON	Heaton (1863)

HONDURAS
A	Paris (1869–71)
T	Tegucigalpa (1825–62)

HONG KONG
H	Heaton (1872–1971)
KN	King's Norton

HUNGARY
A	Vienna
B	Kremnitz
BP	Budapest
CA	Vienna
G	Nagybanya
GN	Nagybanya
GYF	Carlsburg
HA	Hall
K	Kremnitz
KB	Kremnitz
NB	Nagybanya
S	Schmollnitz
WI	Vienna

INDIA
B	Bombay (1835-1947)
C	Calcutta (1835-1947)
I	Bombay (1918)
L	Lahore (1943-45)
M	Madras (1869)
P	Pretoria (1943-44)
diamond	Bombay
dot in diamond	Hyderabad
split diamond	Hyderabad
star	Hyderabad

IRAN
H	Heaton (1928–29)

IRAQ
I	Bombay

ISRAEL
H	Heaton (1951–52)
star of David	Jerusalem

ITALY AND STATES
B	Bologna
B/I	Birmingham (1893–4)
FIRENZE	Florence
H	Heaton (1866–67)
KB	Berlin
M	Milan
N	Naples
OM	Strasbourg
R	Rome
T	Turin
V	Venice
ZV	Venice
anchor	Genoa
eagle head	Turin

JAMAICA
C	Ottawa
FM	Franklin Mint
H	Heaton (1882–1916)

JERSEY
H	Heaton (1877)

KENYA

C/M	Calcutta
H	Heaton (1911–64)

LIBERIA

B	Berne
FM	Franklin Mint
H	Heaton (1896–1906)
PM	Pobjoy Mint

LIECHTENSTEIN

A	Vienna
B	Berne
M	Munich

LUXEMBOURG

A	Paris
H	Gunzburg
anchor	Paris
angel	Brussels
caduceus	Utrecht
double eagle	Brussels
sword	Utrecht

MALAYSIA

B	Bombay
FM	Franklin Mint
H	Heaton (1955–61)
I	Calcutta (1941)
I	Bombay (1945)
KN	King's Norton
W	James Watt, Birmingham

MAURITIUS

H	Heaton (1877–90)
SA	Pretoria

MEXICO

A, As	Alamos
C, CN	Culiacan
CA, CH	Chihuahua
Ce	Real del Catorce
D, Do	Durango
Eo	Tlalpam
GA	Guadalajara
GC	Guadelupe y Calvo
Go	Guanajuato
Ho	Hermosillo
M, Mo	Mexico City
Mo	Morelos
MX	Mexico City
O, OA, OKA	Oaxaca
Pi	San Luis Potosi
SLPi	San Luis Potosi
TC	Tierra Caliente
Z, Zs	Zacatecas

MONACO

A	Paris
M	Monte Carlo
clasped hands	Cabanis
thunderbolt	Poissy

MOZAMBIQUE

H	Heaton (1894)
R	Rio

NETHERLANDS AND COLONIES
Austrian Netherlands (1700-93)

H	Amsterdam
S	Utrecht
W	Vienna
hand	Antwerp
head	Brussels
lion	Bruges

Kingdom of the Netherlands

B	Brussels (1821–30)
D	Denver (1943–45)
P	Philadelphia (1941–45)
S	Utrecht (1816–36)
S	San Francisco (1944–45)
Sa	Surabaya
caduceus	Utrecht

NICARAGUA

H	Heaton (1880–1916)
NR	Leon de Nicaragua

NORWAY

hammers	Kongsberg

PANAMA

CHI	Valcambi
FM	Franklin Mint

PERU

AREQ, AREQUIPA	Arequipa
AYACUCHO	Ayacucho
CUZCO, Co	Cuzco
L, LM, LR	Lima
LIMAE	Lima
PASCO	Pasco
Paz, Po,	Pasco
P	Lima (1568-70)
P	Philadelphia
S	San Francisco

PHILIPPINES

BSP	Bangko Sentral Pilipinas
D	Denver (1944–45)
FM	Franklin Mint
M, MA	Manila
PM	Pobjoy Mint
S	San Francisco (1903–47)
5 point star	Manila

POLAND

AP	Warsaw (1772–74)
CI	Cracow (1765–68)
EB	Warsaw (1774–92)
EC	Leipzig (1758–63)
FF	Stuttgart (1916–17)
FH	Warsaw (1815–27)
FS	Warsaw (1765–68)
FWoF	Dresden (1734–64)
G	Cracow (1765–72)

H	Heaton (1924)
IB	Warsaw (1811–27)
IGS	Dresden (1716–34)
IP	Warsaw (1834–43)
IS	Warsaw (1768–74)
JGG	Leipzig (1750–53)
JS	Warsaw (1810–11)
KG	Warsaw (1829–34)
MV, MW	Warsaw
arrow	Warsaw (1925–39)
Dot after	
date	Royal Mint (1925)
8 *torches*	Paris (1924)

ROUMANIA

B	Bucharest (1879–85)
C	Bucharest (1886)
H	Heaton (1867–1930)
HUGUENIN	Le Locle
J	Hamburg
KN	King's Norton
V	Vienna
W	Watt, Birmingham
thunderbolt	Poissy

RUSSIA

AM	Annensk (1762–96)
BM	Warsaw (1825–55)
bM	St Petersburg (1796)
C–M	Sestroretsk (1762–96)
CM	Souzan (1825–55)
E–M	Ekaterinburg (1762–1810)
KM	Kolpina (1810)
K–M	Kolyvan (1762–1810)
MM, M–M	Moscow (1730–96)
MMD	Moscow (1730–96)
MW	Warsaw (1842–54)
NM	Izhorsk (1811–21)
SP	St Petersburg (1798–1800)
SPB	St Petersburg (1724–1915)
SPM	St Petersburg (1825–55)
T–M	Feodosia (1762–96)

SAN MARINO

M	Milan
R	Rome
SIAM	
(Thailand)	H Heaton (1898)

SOUTH AFRICA

SA	Pretoria

SPAIN

B	Burgos
B, BA	Barcelona
Bo	Bilbao
C	Catalonia
C	Cuenca
C	Reus
CA	Zaragoza
G	Granada
GNA	Gerona
LD	Lerida

J, JA	Jubia
M, MD	Madrid
P	Palma de Majorca
PpP, PL, PA	Pamplona
S, S/L	Seville
Sr	Santander
T, To, Tole	Toledo
TOR:SA	Tortosa
V, VA, VAL	Valencia
crowned C	Cadiz
crowned M	Madrid
aqueduct	Segovia
crowned shield	Tarragona
pomegranate	Granada
quartered shield	Palma
scallop	Coruna
stars:	
3 *points*	Segovia
4 *points*	Jubia
5 *points*	Manila
6 *points*	Madrid
7 *points*	Seville (1833)
8 *points*	Barcelona (1838)
wavy lines	Valladolid

SURINAM

P	Philadelphia
S	Sydney
caduceus	Utrecht

SWITZERLAND

A	Paris
AB	Strasbourg
B	Berne
B	Brussels (1874)
BA	Basle
BB	Strasbourg
S	Solothurn

URUGUAY

H	Heaton (1869)

UNITED STATES OF AMERICA

C	Charlotte, North Carolina
Cc	Carson City, Nevada
D	Dahlonega, Georgia (1838–61)
D	Denver, Colorado (1906)
O	New Orleans
P	Philadelphia
S	San Francisco
W	West Point

VENEZUELA

A	Paris
H	Heaton (1852)
HEATON	Heaton (1852–63)

YUGOSLAVIA (including former Serbia)

A	Paris
H	Heaton (1883–84)
KOBHNUA, A.D.	Kovnica
V	Vienna
thunderbolt	Poissy

Coincraft

Sell Where the Dealers Sell !

Everyday we have dealers popping into Coincraft to sell their coins and banknotes. Why? Because selling to Coincraft is easy, pleasant and quick. Our experts look at your material and either pay you what you want or make you an attractive offer, 95% of which are accepted on the spot.

We need to buy and have collectors waiting for the latest issue of The Phoenix, which is published 17 times a year, that's every three weeks, so there is not a lot of waiting time to sell what we buy. We also publish a special listing, The BlueCard Flyer, for our more advanced collectors and that goes out 13 times a year. So we need material for our 30+ catalogues that we publish each year. You want to sell and we need to buy!

If you sell at auction, you have to wait for them to have a sale, which can sometimes be six months. Then you have to hope that everything gets sold, otherwise they return the unsold coins or banknotes to you. Then you have to wait until they get paid, because auction houses do not pay you, until they themselves have been paid. Sometimes auctions get more then a dealer is willing to pay and sometimes they get less, it is a gamble But most of the time, auction houses only want the cream and not the milk...

Dealers sell to Coincraft because they know that once we have agreed the price, we pay them out on the spot and that we will make an offer for almost everything. So there are no unsold or returned goods.

For more then 61 years Coincrat has been helping collectors find coins and banknotes for their collections. Let us help each other, you will get more money selling directly to Coincraft and we will be able to help more of our collectors, fill in those gaps in their collection.

COIN *inscriptions*

This alphabetical listing is confined to inscriptions found on coins, mainly in the form of mottoes or of a commemorative nature. Names of rulers are, for the most part, excluded. Where the inscription is in a language other than English a translation is given, followed by the name of the issuing country or authority in parentheses.

A Deo et Caesare From God and the Emperor (Frankfurt).

A Domino Factum est Istud et est Mirabile in Oculis Nostris This is the Lord's doing and it is marvellous in our eyes (England, Mary).

A Solo Iehova Sapientia From God alone comes true wisdom (Wittgenstein).

Ab Inimicis Meis Libera Me Deus Free me from enemies (Burgundy).

Ad Legem Conventionis According to the law of the Convention (Furstenberg).

Ad Normam Conventionis According to the standard of the Convention (Prussia).

Ad Palmam Pressa Laeturo Resurgo Pressed to the palm I rise more joyfully (Wittgenstein).

Ad Usam Luxemburgi CC Vallati For the use of the besieged Luxembourgers (Luxembourg siege coins).

Adiuva Nos Deus Salutaris Noster Help us, O God, our Saviour (Lorraine).

Adventus Optimi Principis The coming of the noblest prince (Papacy).

Aes Usibus Aptius Auro Bronze in its uses is more suitable than gold (Brazil).

Aeternum Meditans Decus An ornament intended for all time (Alencon).

Aliis Inserviendo Consumor I spend my life devoted to others (Brunswick-Wolfenbuttel).

Alles Mit Bedacht All with reflection (Brunswick).

Amor Populi Praesidium Regis The love of the people is the king's protection (England, Charles I).

Ang Fra Dom Hib & Aquit (King) of England and France, Lord of Ireland and Aquitaine (England, Edward III).

Anno Regni Primo In the first year of the reign (Britain, edge inscription on crowns).

Apres les Tenebres la Lumiere After the shadows, the light (Geneva).

Archangelus Michael Archangel Michael (Italy, Grimoald IV).

Ardua ad Gloriam Via Struggles are the way to glory (Waldeck).

Arte Mea Bis Iustus Moneta Lud Iust By my art I am twice the just coin of King Louis (France, 1641).

Aspera Oblectant Wild places delight (Nassau-Weilburg).

Aspice Pisas Sup Omnes Specio Behold the coin of Pisa, superior to all (Pisa).

Audiatur Altera Pars Let the other part be heard (Stavelot).

Auf Gott Trawe Ich In God I trust (Brunswick).

Ausen Gefaesen der Kirchen und Burger From the vessels of the Church and citizens (Frankfurt siege, 1796).

Auspicio Regis et Senatus Angliae By authority of the king and parliament of England (East India Company).

Auxilio fortissimo Dei With the strongest help of God (Mecklenburg).

Auxilium de Sanctio Aid from the sanctuary (Papacy).

Auxilium Meum a Dno Qui Fecit Celum e Terram My help comes from God who made heaven and earth (Portugal).

Beata Tranquillatis Blessed tranquillity (Rome, Licinius II).

Beatus Qui Speravit in dom Blessed is he who has hoped in the Lord (Mansfeld).

Benedic Haereditati Tuae Blessings on your inheritance (Savoy).

Benedicta Sit Sancta Trinitas Blessed be the Holy Trinity (Albon).

Benedictio Domini Divites Facit The blessing of the Lord makes the rich (Teschen).

Benedictus Qui Venit in Nomine Domini Blessed is he who comes in the name of the Lord (Flanders).

Beschaw das Ziel Sage Nicht Viel Consider the matter but say little (Quedlinburg).

Besser Land und Lud Verloren als ein Falscher Aid Geschworn   Better to lose land and wealth than swear a false oath (Hesse).

Bey Gott ist Rath und That   With God is counsel and deed (Mansfeld).

Britanniarum Regina   Queen of the Britains (Britain, Victoria).

Britt Omn Rex   King of all the Britains (i.e. Britain and the overseas dominions) (Britain, 1902–52).

Cal et Car Com de Fugger in Zin et Norn Sen & Adm Fam   Cajetan and Carl, Counts of Fugger in Zinnenberg and Nordendorf, Lords and Administrators of the Family (Empire, Fugger).

Candide et Constanter   Sincerely and steadfastly (Hesse-Cassel).

Candide sed Provide   Clearly but cautiously (Osterwitz).

Candore et Amore   With sincerity and love (Fulda).

Candore et Constantia   With sincerity and constancy (Bavaria).

Capit Cath Ecclesia Monasteriensis   Chapter of the Cathedral Church of Munster (Munster).

Capit Eccle Metropolit Colon   Chapter of the Metropolitan Church of Cologne (Cologne).

Capitulum Regnans Sede Vacante   Chapter governing, the See being vacant (Eichstadt).

Carola Magna Ducissa Feliciter Regnante   Grand Duchess Charlotte, happily reigning (Luxembourg).

Carolus a Carolo   Charles (I) to Charles (II) (England).

Cedunt Prementi Fata   The fates yield to him who presses (Ploen, Hese-Cassel).

Charitate et Candore   With charity and sincerity (East Frisia).

Charta Magna Bavariae   The Great Charter of Bavaria (Bavaria).

Christo Auspice Regno   I reign under the auspices of Christ (England, Charles I).

Christus Spes Una Salutis   Christ is our one hope of salvation (Cleve).

Chur Mainz   Electoral Principality of Mainz (Mainz).

Circumeundo Servat et Ornat   It serves and decorates by going around (Sweden).

Civibus Quorum Pietas Coniuratione Die III Mai MDCCXCI Obrutam et Deletam Libertate Polona Tueri Conabatur Respublica Resurgens   To the citizens whose piety the reourgent commonwealth tried to protect Poland overturned and deprived of liberty by the conspiracy of the third day of May 1791 (Poland).

Civitas Lucemborgiensis Millesimum Ovans Expletannum   Completing the celebration of a thousand years of the city of Luxembourg (Luxembourg).

Civium Industria Floret Civitas   By the industry of its people the state flourishes (Festival of Britain crown, 1951).

Cluniaco Cenobio Petrus et Paulus   Peter and Paul from the Abbey of Cluny (Cluny).

Comes Provincie Fili Regis Francie   Court of Provence and son of the King of France (Provence).

Communitas et Senatus Bonon   City and senate of Bologna (Bologna).

Concordia Fratrum   The harmony of the brothers (Iever).

Concordia Patriae Nutrix   Peace, the nurse of the fatherland (Waldeck).

Concordia Res Parvae Crescunt   Little things increase through harmony (Batavian Republic).

Concordia Res Parvae Crescunt, Discordia Dilabuntur   By harmony little things increase, by discord they fall apart (Lowenstein-Wertheim-Virneburg).

Concordia Stabili   With lasting peace (Hildesheim).

Confidens Dno Non Movetur   He who trusts in God is unmoved (Spanish Netherlands).

Confidentia in Deo et Vigilantia   Trust in God and vigilance (Prussian Asiatic Company).

Confoederato Helvetica   Swiss Confederation (Switzerland)

Conjuncto Felix   Fortunate in his connections (Solms).

Conservator Urbis Suae   Saviour of his city (Rome, 4th century).

Consilio et Aequitate   With deliberation and justice (Fulda).

Consilio et Virtutis   With deliberation and valour (Hesse-Cassel).

Constanter et Sincere   Steadfastly and sincerely (Lautern).

Crescite et Multiplicamini   Increase and multiply (Maryland).

Cristiana Religio   Christian religion (Germany, 11th century).

Crux Benedicat   May the cross bless you (Oldenburg).

Cuius Cruore Sanati Sumus   By His sacrifice are we healed (Reggio).

Cultores Sui Deus Protegit   God protects His followers (England, Charles I).

Cum Deo et Die (Jure)   With God and the day (Wurttemberg).

Cum Deo et Jure   With God and the law (Wurttemberg).

Cum Deo et Labore   With God and work (Wittgenstein).

Cum His Qui Orderant Pacem Eram Pacificus   With those who order peace I was peaceful (Zug).

Curie Bonthon to so Doulo   Protect his servant, o Lord (Byzantine Empire).

Custos Regni Deus   God is the guardian of the kingdom (Naples and Sicily).

Da Gloriam Deo et Eius Genitrici Marie   Give glory to God and His mother Mary (Wurttemberg).

Da Mihi Virtutem Contra Hostes Tuos   Give me valour against mine enemies (Netherlands, Charles V).

Dat Wort is Fleis Gworden   The word is made flesh (Muster).

Date Caesaris Caesari et Quae Sunt Dei Deo   Render unto Caesar the things that are Caesar's and unto God the things that are God's (Stralsund).

De Oficina . . .   From the mint of . . . (France, medieval).

Decreto Reipublicae Nexu Confoederationis Iunctae Die V Xbris MDCCXCII Stanislao Augusto Regnante   By decree of the state in conjunction with the joint federation on the fifth day of December 1792, Stanislaus Augustus ruling (Poland).

Decus et Tutamen   An ornament and a safeguard (Britain, pound).

Deducet Nos Mirabiliter Dextera Tua   Thy right hand will guide us miraculously (Savoy).

Denarium Terrae Mariae   Penny of Maryland (Maryland).

Deo Conservatori Pacis   To God, preserver of peace (Brandenburg-Ansbach).

Deo OM Auspice Suaviter et Fortiter sed Luste nec Sibi sed Suis   Under the auspices of God, greatest and best, pleasantly and bravely but justly, not for himself but for his people (Speyer).

Deo Patriae et Subditio   For God, fatherland and neighbourhood (Mainz).

Der Recht Glaubt In Ewig Lebt   Who believes in right will live in eternity (Linange-Westerburg).

Der Rhein ist Deutschlands Strom Nicht Deutschlands Grenze   The Rhine is Germany's River not Germany's Frontier.

Deum Solum Adorabis   You will venerate God alone (Hesse).

Deus Constituit Regna   God establishes kingdoms (Ni jmegen).

Deus Dat Qui Vult   God gives to him who wishes (Hanau-Munzenberg).

Deus et Dominus   God and Lord (Rome, 3rd century).

Deus in Adiutorium Meum Intende   God stretch out in my assistance (France).

Deus Providebit   God will provide (Lowenstein-Wertheim-Virneburg).

Deus Refugium Meum   God is my refuge (Cleve).

Deus Solatium Meum   God is my comfort (Sweden).

Dextera Domini Exaltavit Me   The right hand of God has raised me up (Modena, Spain).

Dextra Dei Exalta Me   The right hand of God exalts me (Denmark).

Dieu et Mon Droit   God and my right (Britain, George IV).

Dilexit Dns Andream   The Lord delights in St Andrew (Holstein).

Dilexit Dominus Decorem Iustitiae   The Lord is pleased with the beauty of justice (Unterwalden).

Dirige Deus Gressus Meos   O God, direct my steps (Tuscany, Britain, Una £5).

Discerne Causam Meam   Distinguish my cause (Savoy).

Divina Benedictiae et Caesarea Iustitia   Sacrifice of blessings and imperial justice (Coblenz).

Dn Ihs Chs Rex Regnantium   Lord Jesus Christ, King of Kings (Rome, Justinian II).

Dns Ptetor Ms Z Lib'ator Ms   The Lord is my protector and liberator (Scotland, David II).

Dominabitur Gentium et Ipse   He himself will also be lord of the nations (Austrian Netherlands).

Domine Conserva Nos in Pace   O Lord preserve us in peace (Basle, Mulhausen).

Domine Elegisti Lilium Tibi   O Lord Thou hast chosen the lily for Thyself (France, Louis XIV).

Domine ne in Furore Tuo Arguas Me   O Lord rebuke me not in Thine anger (England, Edward III).

Domine Probasti Me et Congnovisti Me   O Lord Thou hast tested me and recognised me (Mantua).

Domini est Regnum   The Kingdom is the Lord's (Austrian Netherlands).

Dominus Deus Omnipotens Rex   Lord God, almighty King (Viking coins).

Dominus Mihi Adiutor   The Lord is my helper (Spanish Netherlands).

Dominus Providebit   The Lord will provide (Berne).

Dominus Spes Populi Sui   The Lord is the hope of his people (Lucerne).

Donum Dei ex Fodinis Vilmariens   A gift of God from the Vilmar mines (Coblenz).

Duce Deo Fide et Justicia   By faith and justice lead us to God (Ragusa).

Dum Praemor Amplior   I increase while I die prematurely (Savoy).

Dum Spiro Spero   While I live, I hope (Pontefract siege coins).

Dum Totum Compleat Orbem   Until it fills the world (France, Henri II).

Dura Pati Virtus   Valour endures hardships (Saxe-Lauenburg).

Durae Necessitatis   Through force of necessity (Bommel siege, 1599).

Durum Telum Necessitas   Hardship is a weapon of necessity (Minden).

Dux et Gubernatores Reip Genu   Duke and governors of the republic of Genoa (Genoa).

E Pluribus Unum   One out of more (USA).

Eccl S. Barbarae Patronae Fodin Kuttenbergensium Duo Flor Arg Puri   The church of St Barbara, patron of the Kuttensberg mines, two florins of pure silver (Hungary).

Een en Ondelbaer Sterk   One and indivisible (Batavian Republic).

Eendracht Mag Macht   Unity makes strength (Belgium, South African Republic).

Einigkeit Recht und Freiheit   Union, right and freedom (Germany).

Electorus Saxoniae Administrator   Elector and administrator of Saxony (Saxony).

Elimosina   Alms (France, Pepin).

Ep Fris & Ratisb Ad Prum Pp Coad Aug   Bishop of Freising and Regensburg, administrator of Pruem, prince-provost, co-adjutant bishop of Augsburg (Trier).

Equa Libertas Deo Gratia Frat Pax in Virtute Tua et in Domino Confido   I believe in equal liberty by the grace of God, brotherly love in Thy valour and in the Lord (Burgundy).

Equitas Iudicia Tua Dom   Equity and Thy judgments O Lord (Gelderland).

Espoir Me Conforte   Hope comforts me (Mansfeld).

Espreuve Faicto Par Lexpres Commandement du Roy   Proof made by the express commandment of the King (France, piedforts).

Et in Minimis Integer   Faithful even in the smallest things (Olmutz).

Ex Auro Argentes Resurgit   From gold it arises, silver again (Sicily).

Ex Auro Sinico   From Chinese gold (Denmark).

Ex Flammis Orior   I arise from the flames (Hohenlohe-Neuenstein-Ohringen).

Ex Fodinis Bipontio Seelbergensibus   From the Seelberg mines of Zweibrucken (Pfalz-Birkenfeld).

Ex Metallo Novo   From new metal (Spain).

Ex Uno Omnis Nostra Salus   From one is all our salvation (Eichstadt, Mulhouse).

Ex Vasis Argent Cleri Mogunt Pro Aris et Focis   From the silver vessels of the clergy of Mainz for altars and for hearths (Mainz).

Ex Visceribus Fodinse Bieber   From the bowels of the Bieber mine (Hanau-Munzenberg).

Exaltabitur in Gloria   He shall be exalted in glory (England, quarter nobles).

Exemplum Probati Numismatis   An example of a proof coin (France, Louis XIII piedforts).

Exemtae Eccle Passau Episc et SRI Princ   Prince Bishop of the freed church of Passau, prince of the Holy Roman Empire (Passau).

Expectate Veni   Come, o expected one (Roman Britain, Carausius).

Extremum Subidium Campen   Kampen under extreme siege (Kampen, 1578).

Exurgat Deus et Dissipentur Inimici Eius   Let God arise and let His enemies be scattered (England, James I).

Faciam Eos in Gentem Unam   I will make them one nation (England, unites and laurels).

Faith and Truth I will Bear unto You   (UK £5, 1993).

Fata Consiliis Potiora   The fates are more powerful than councils (Hesse-Cassel).

Fata Viam Invenient   The fates will find a way (Gelderland).

Fecit Potentiam in Brachio Suo   He put power in your forearm (Lorraine).

Fecunditas   Fertility (Naples and Sicily).

Fel Temp Reparatio   The restoration of lucky times (Rome, AD 348).

Felicitas Perpetua   Everlasting good fortune (Rome, Constantius II).

Felix coniunctio   Happy Union (Brandenburg-Ansbach).

Fiat Misericordia Tua Dne   Let Thy mercy be O Lord (Gelderland).

Fiat Voluntas Domini Perpetuo   Let the goodwill of the Lord last for ever (Fulda).

Fidei Defensor   Defender of the Faith (Britain).

Fidelitate et Fortitudine   With fidelity and fortitude (Batthanyi).

Fideliter et Constanter   Faithfully and steadfastly (Saxe-Coburg-Gotha).

Fidem Servando Patriam Tuendo   By keeping faith and protecting the fatherland (Savoy).

Filius Augustorum   Son of emperors (Rome, 4th century).

Fisci Iudaici Calumnia Sublata   The false accusation of the Jewish tax lifted (Rome, Nerva).

Florent Concordia Regna   Through harmony kingdoms flourish (England, Charles I and II).

Fortitudo et Laus Mea Dominu   Fortitude and my praise in the Lord (Sardinia).

Free Trade to Africa by Act of Parliment *(Sic)*   (Gold Coast).

Friedt Ernehrt Unfriedt Verzehrt   Peace nourishes, unrest wastes (Brunswick).

Fulgent Sic Littora Rheni   Thus shine the banks of the Rhine (Mannheim).

Fundator Pacis   Founder of peace (Rome, Severus).

Gaudium Populi Romani   The joy of the Roman people (Rome, 4th century).

Gen C Mar VI Dim Col USC & RAMAI Cons & S Conf M   General field marshal, colonel of the only dragoon regiment, present privy councillor of both their sacred imperial and royal apostolic majesties, and state conference minister (Batthanyi).

Gerecht und Beharrlich   Just and steadfast (Bavaria).

Germ Hun Boh Rex AAD Loth Ven Sal   King of Germany, Hungary and Bohemia, Archduke of Austria, Duke of Lorraine, Venice and Salzburg (Austria).

Germ Jero Rex Loth Bar Mag Het Dux   King of Germany, Jerusalem, Lorraine and Bar, Grand Duke of Tuscany (Austrian Netherlands).

Germania Voti Compos   Germany sharing the vows (Brandenburg-Ansbach).

Gloria ex Amore Patriae   Glory from love of country (Denmark).

Gloria in Excelsis Deo   Glory to God in the highest (France, Sweden).

Gloria Novi Saeculi   The glory of a new century (Rome, Gratian).

God With Us   (England, Commonwealth).

Godt Met Ons   God with us (Oudewater).

Gottes Freundt der Pfaffen Feindt   God's friend, the Pope's enemy (Brunswick, Christian).

Gratia Dei Sum Id Quod Sum   By the grace of God, I am what I am (Navarre).

Gratia Di Rex   By the grace of God, king (France, 8th century).

Gratitudo Concivibus Exemplum Posteritati   Gratitude to fellow Citizens, an example to posterity (Poland).

Gud och Folket   God and the people (Sweden).

Hac Nitimur Hanc Tuemur   With this we strive, this we shall defend (Batavian Republic).

Hac Sub Tutela   Under this protection (Eichstadt).

Haec Sunt Munera Minerae S Antony Eremitae   These are the rewards of the mine of St Antony the hermit (Hildesheim).

Hanc Deus Dedit   God has given this (Pontefract siege coins).

Hanc Tuemur Hac Nitimur   This we defend, by this we strive (Batavian Republic).

Has Nisi Periturus Mihi Adimat Nemo   Let no one remove these (Letters) from me under penalty of death (Commonwealth, edge inscription).

Henricus Rosas Regna Jacobus   Henry (united) the roses, James the kingdoms (England and Scotland, James VI and I).

Herculeo Vincta Nodo   Bound by a Herculean fetter (Savoy).

Herr Nach Deinem Willen   O Lord Thy will be done (Palatinate, Erbach).

Herre Gott Verleich Uns Gnade   Lord God grant us grace (Brunswick).

Hic Est Qui Multum Orat Pro Populo   Here is he who prays a lot for the people (Paderborn).

Hir Steid te Biscop   Here is represented the bishop (Gittelde).

His Ventis Vela Levantur   By these winds the sails are raised up (Hesse-Cassel).

Hispaniarum Infans   Infante of Spain and its dominions (Spain).

Hispaniarum et Ind Rex   King of Spain and the Indies.

Hispaniarum Rex   King of Spain (Spain).

Hoc Signo Victor Eris   With this sign you will be victor (Rome, Vetranio).

Honeste et Decenter   Honestly and decently (Nassau-Idstein).

Honi Soit Qui Mal y Pense   Evil to him who evil thinks (Britain, George III).

Honni Soit Qui Mal y Pense   (Hesse-Cassel).

Hospitalis et S Sepul Hierusal   Hospital and Holy Sepulchre of Jerusalem (Malta).

Hun Boh Gal Rex AA Lo Wi et in Fr Dux   King of Hungary, Bohemia and Galicia, Archduke of Austria, Dalmatia, Lodomeria, Wurzburg and Duke in Franconia (Austria).

Hung Boh Lomb et Ven Gal Lod III Rex Aa   King of Hungary, Bohemia, Lombardo-Venezia, Galicia, Lodomeria, Illyria, Archduke (Austria).

Ich Dien   I serve (Aberystwyth 2d, UK 2p).

Ich Getrawe Got in Aller Noth   I trust in God in all my needs (Hesse-Marburg).

Ich Habe Nur Ein Vaterland und das Heisst Deutschland   I have only one fatherland and that is called Germany (Germany).

Ielithes Penniae   Penny of Gittelde (Gittelde, 11th century).

Iesus Autem Transiens Per Medium Illorum Ibat   But Jesus, passing through the midst of them, went His way (England, Scotland, Anglo-Gallic).

Iesus Rex Noster et Deus Noster   Jesus is our king and our God (Florence).

Ihs Xs Rex Regnantium   Jesus Christ, King of Kings (Byzantine Empire).

Ihsus Xristus Basileu Baslie   Jesus Christ, King of Kings (Byzantine Empire).

Imago Sanch Regis Illustris Castelle Legionis e Toleto   The image of Sancho the illustrious king of Castile, Leon and Toledo.

In Casus Per Vigil Omnes   In all seasons through vigil (Wertheim).

In Deo Meo Transgrediar Murum   In my God I shall pass through walls (Teschen).

In Deo Spes Mea   In God is my hope (Gelderland).

In Domino Fiducia Nostra   In the Lord is our trust (Iever).

In Equitate Tua Vivificasti Me   In thy equity Thou hast vivified me (Gelderland).

In God We Trust   (USA).

In Hoc Signo Vinces   In this sign shalt thou conquer (Portugal).

In Honore Sci Mavrici Marti   In honour of the martyr St Maurice (St Maurice, 8th century).

In Manibus Domini sortes Meae   In the hands of the Lord are my fates (Mainz siege, 1688–9).

In Memor Vindicatae Libere ac Relig   In memory of the establishment of freedom and religion (Sweden).

In Memoriam Conjunctionis Utriusque Burgraviatus Norice   In memory of the union of both burgraviates in peace (Brandenburg-Ansbach).

In Memorian Connub Feliciaes Inter Princ Her Frider Carol et Dub Sax August Louis Frider Rodas D 28 Nov 1780 Celebrati   In memory of the most happy marriage between the hereditary prince Friedrich Karl and the Duchess of Saxony Augusta Louisa Frederika, celebrated on 28 Nov 1780 (Schwarzburg-Rudolstadt).

In Memorian Felicisssimi Matrimonii   In memory of the most happy marriage (Wied).

In Memoriam Pacis Teschinensis   Commemorating the Treaty of Teschen (Brandenburg-Ansbach).

In Nomine Domini Amen   In the name of the Lord amen (Zaltbommel).

In Omnem Terram Sonus Eorum   In to all the land their shall go sound (Chateau Renault, Papal States).

In Silencio et Spe Fortitudo Mea   In silence and hope is my fortitude (Brandenburg-Kustrin).

In Spe et Silentio Fortitudo Mea   In hope and silence is my fortitude (Vianen).

In Te Domine Confido   In you O Lord I place my trust (Hesse).

In Te Domine Speravi   In You, O Lord, I have hoped (Gurk).

In Terra Pax   Peace in the land (Papacy).

In Via Virtuti Nulla Via   There is no way for virtue on the way. (Veldenz).

Ind Imp, Indiae Imperator, Imperatrix   Emperor (Empress) of India (Britain).

India Tibi Cessit   India has yielded to thee (Portuguese India).

Infestus Infestis   Hostile to the troublesome (Savoy).

Inimicos Eius Induam Confusione   As for his enemies, I shall clothe them in shame (Sardinia, England, Edward VI).

Insignia Capituli Brixensis   The badge of the chapter of Brixen (Brixen).

Isti Sunt Patres Tui Verique Pastores   These are your fathers and true shepherds (Papacy).

Iudicium Melius Posteritatis Erit   Posterity's judgment will be better (Paderborn).

Iure et Tempore   By right and time (Groningen).

Iusques a Sa Plenitude   As far as your plenitude (France, Henri II).

Iuste et Constanter   Justly and constantly (Paderborn).

Iustirt   Adjusted (Hesse-Cassel).

Iustitia et Concordia   Justice and harmony (Zurich).

Iustitia et Mansuetudine   By justice and mildness (Bavaria, Cologne).

Iustitia Regnorum Fundamentum   Justice is the foundation of kingdoms (Austria).

Iustitia Thronum Firmat   Justice strengthens the throne (England, Charles I).

Iustus Non Derelinquitur   The just person is not deserted (Brandenburg-Calenberg).

Iustus Ut Palma Florebit   The just will flourish like the palm (Portugal).

L Mun Planco Rauracorum Illustratori Vetustis-simo   To L Municius Plancus the most ancient and celebrated of the Rauraci (Basle).

Landgr in Cleggov Com in Sulz Dux Crum   Landgrave of Klettgau, count of Sulz, duke of Krumlau (Schwarzburg-Sondershausen).

Latina Emeri Munita   Latin money of Merida (Suevi).

Logo ot Fido   By law and faith (Austria).

Lex Tua Veritas   Thy law is the truth (Tuscany).

Liberta Eguaglianza   Freedom and equality (Venice).

Libertad en la Ley   Freedom within the law (Mexico).

Libertas Carior Auro   Freedom is dearer than gold (St Gall).

Libertas Vita Carior   Freedom is dearer than life (Kulenberg).

Libertas Xpo Firmata   Freedom strengthened by Christ (Genoa).

Liberte, Egalite, Fraternite   Liberty, equality, fraternity (France).

Lucerna Pedibus Meis Verbum Est   Thy word is a lamp unto mine feet (England, Edward VI).

Lumen ad Revelationem Gentium   Light to enlighten the nations (Papacy).

L'Union Fait la Force   The union makes strength (Belgium)

Macula Non Est in Te   There is no sin in Thee (Essen).

Magnus ab Integro Saeculorum Nascitur Ordo   The great order of the centuries is born anew (Bavaria).

Mandavit Dominus Palatie hanc Monetam Fiert   The lord of the Palatine ordained this coin to be made (Balath).

Manibus Ne Laedar Avaris   Lest I be injured by greedy hands (Sweden).

Mar Bran Sac Rom Imp Arcam et Elec Sup Dux Siles   Margrave of Brandenburg, archchamberlain of the Holy Roman Empire and elector, senior duke of Silesia (Prussia).

Maria Mater Domini Xpi   Mary mother of Christ the Lord (Teutonic Knights).

Maria Unxit Pedes Xpisti   Mary washes the feet of Christ (France, Rene d'Anjou).

Mater Castrorum   Mother of fortresses (Rome, Marcus Aurelius).

Matrimonio Conjuncti   Joined wedlock (Austria).

Me Coniunctio Servat Dum Scinditur Frangor   The relationship serves me while I am being torn to pieces (Lowenstein-Wertheim).

Mediolani Dux   Duke of Milan (Milan).

Mediolani et Man   Duke of Mantua and Milan (Milan).

Memor Ero Tui Iustina Virgo   I shall remember you, o maiden Justina (Venice).

Merces Laborum   Wages of work (Wurzburg).

Mirabilia Fecit   He wrought marvels (Viking coinage).

Misericordia Di Rex   King by the mercy of God (France, Louis II).

Mo Arg Ord Foe Belg D Gel & CZ   Silver coin of the order of the Belgian Federation, duchy of Guelder-land, county of Zutphen (Guelderland).

Moneta Abbatis   Coin of the abbey (German ecclesiastical coins, 13th–14th centuries).

Moneta Argentiae Ord Foed Belgii Holl   Silver coin of the federated union of Belgium and Holland (Batavian Republic).

Mo No Arg Con Foe Belg Pro Hol   New silver coin of the Belgian Federation, province of Holland (Holland).

Mo No Arg Pro Confoe Belg Trai Holl   New silver coin of the confederated Belgian provinces, Utrecht and Holland (Batavian Republic).

Mon Lib Reip Bremens   Coin of the free state of Bremen (Bremen).

Mon Nova Arg Duc Curl Ad Norma Tal Alb   New silver coin of the duchy of Courland, according to the standard of the Albert thaler (Courland).

Mon Nov Castri Imp   New coin of the Imperial free city of . . . (Friedberg).

Moneta Bipont   Coin of Zweibrucken (Pfalz-Birkenfeld-Zweibrucken).

Monet Capit Cathedr Fuld Sede Vacante   Coin of the cathedral chapter of Fulda, the see being vacant (Fulda).

Moneta in Obsidione Tornacensi Cusa   Coin struck during the siege of Tournai (Tournai, 1709).

Moneta Livosesthonica   Coin of Livonia (Estonia).

Moneta Nov Arg Regis Daniae   New silver coin of the king of Denmark (Denmark).

Moneta Nova Ad Norman Conventionis   New coin according to the Convention standard (Orsini-Rosenberg).

Moneta Nova Domini Imperatoris   New coin of the lord emperor (Brunswick, 13th century).

Moneta Nova Lubecensis   New coin of Lubeck.

Moneta Nova Reipublicae Halae Suevicae   New coin of the republic of Hall in Swabia.

Moneta Reipublicae Ratisbonensis   Coin of the republic of Regensburg.

Nach Alt Reichs Schrot und Korn   According to the old empire's grits and grain (Hesse).

Nach dem Conventions Fusse   According to the Convention's basis (German Conventionsthalers).

Nach dem Frankf Schlus   According to the Frankfurt standard (Solms).

Nach dem Schlus der V Staend   According to the standard of the union (Hesse).

Navigare Necesse Est   It is necessary to navigate (Germany).

Nec Aspera Terrent   Nor do difficulties terrify (Brunswick).

Nec Cito Nec Temere   Neither hastily nor rashlly (Cambrai).

Nec Numina Desunt   Nor is the divine will absent (Savoy).

Nec Temere Nec Timide   Neither rashly nor timidly (Danzig, Lippe).

Necessitas Legem Non Habet   Necessity has no law (Magdeburg).

Nemo Me Impune Lacessit   No one touches me with impunity (UK, Scottish pound edge inscription).

Nihil Restat Reliqui   No relic remains (Ypres).

Nil Ultra Aras   Nothing beyond the rocks (Franque-mont).

No Nobis Dne Sed Noi Tuo Da Gloriam   Not to us, o Lord but to Thy name be glory given (France, Francis I).

Nobilissimum Dom Ac Com in Lipp & St   Most noble lord and count in Lippe and Sternberg (Schaumburg-Lippe).

Nomen Domini Turris Fortissima   The name of the Lord is the strongest tower (Frankfurt).

Non Aes Sed Fides   Not bronze but trust (Malta).

Non Est Mortale Quod Opto   What I desire is not mortal. (Mecklenburg).

Non Mihi Sed Populo   Not to me but to the people (Bavaria).

Non Relinquam Vos Orphanos   I shall not leave you as orphans (Papacy).

Non Surrexit Major   None greater has arisen (Genoa, Malta).

Nullum Simulatum Diuturnum Tandem   Nothing that is feigned lasts long (Wittgenstein).

Nummorum Famulus   The servant of the coinage (England, tin halfpence and farthings).

Nunquam Retrorsum   Never backwards (Brunswick-Wolfenbuttel).

O Crux Ave Spes Unica   Hail, o Cross, our only hope (England half-angels, France, Rene d'Anjou).

O Maria Ora Pro Me   O Mary pray for me (Bavaria).

Ob Cives Servatos   On account of the rescued citizens (Rome, Augustus).

Oculi Domini Super Iustos   The eyes of the Lord look down on the just (Neuchatel).

Omnia Auxiliante Maria   Mary helping everything (Schwyz).

Omnia Cum Deo   Everything with God (Reuss-Greiz).

Omnia cum Deo et Nihil Sine Eo   Everthing with God and nothing without Him (Erbach).

Omnis Potestas a Deo Est   All power comes from God (Sweden).

Opp & Carn Dux Comm Rittb SCM Cons Int & Compi Mareschal   Duke of Troppau and Carniola, count of Rietberg, privy councillor of his sacred imperial majesty, field marshal (Liechtenstein).

Opp & Carn . . . Aur Velleris Eques   Duke of Troppau . . . knight of the Golden Fleece (Liechtenstein).

Opportune   Conveniently (Savoy).

Optimus Princeps   Best prince (Rome, Trajan).

Opulentia Salerno   Wealthy Salerno (Siculo-Norman kingdom).

Pace et Iustitia   With peace and justice (Spanish Netherlands).

Pacator Orbis   Pacifier of the world (Rome, Aurelian).

Palma Sub Pondere Crescit   The palm grows under its weight (Waldeck).

Pater Noster   Our Father (Flanders, 14th century).

Pater Patriae   Farther of his country (Rome, Caligula).

Patria Si Dreptul Meu   The country and my right (Roumania).

Patrimon Henr Frid Sorte Divisum   The heritage of Heinrich Friedrich divided by lot (Hohenlohe-Langenberg).

Patrimonia Beati Petri   The inheritance of the blessed Peter (Papacy).

Patrona Franconiae   Patron Franconia (Wurzburg).

Pax Aeterna   Eternal peace (Rome, Marcus Aurelius).

Pax et Abundantia   Peace and plenty (Burgundy, Gelderland).

Pax Missa Per Orbem   Peace sent throughout the world (England, Anne).

Pax Petrus   Peace Peter (Trier, 10th century).

Pax Praevalet Armis   May peace prevail by force of arms (Mainz).

Pax Quaeritur Bello   Peace is sought by war (Commonwealth, Cromwell).

Pecunia Totum Circumit Orbem   Money goes round the whole world (Brazil).

Per Aspera Ad Astra   Through difficulties to the stars (Mecklenburg-Schwerin).

Per Angusta ad Augusta   Through precarious times to the majestic (Solms-Roedelheim, a pun on the name of the ruler Johan August).

Per Crucem Tuam Salva Nos Christe Redemptor   By Thy cross save us, O Christ our Redeemer (England, angels).

Per Crucem Tuam Salva Nos Xpe Redemt   By Thy cross save us, O Christ our Redeemer (Portugal, 15th century).

Perdam Babillonis Nomen   May the name of Babylon perish (Naples).

Perennitati Iustissimi Regis   For the duration of the most just king (France, Louis XIII).

Perennitati Principis Galliae Restitutionis   For the duration of the restoration of the prince of the Gauls (France, Henri IV).

Perfer et Obdura Bruxella   Carry on and stick it out, Brussels (Brussels siege, 1579–80).

Perpetuus in Nemet Vivar   Hereditary count in Nemt-Ujvar (Batthanyi).

Pietate et Constantia   By piety and constancy (Fulda).

Pietate et Iustitia   By piety and justice (Denmark).

Plebei Urbanae Frumento Constituto   Free distribu-tion of grain to the urban working-class established (Rome, Nerva).

Pleidio Wyf Im Gwlad   True am I to my country (UK, Welsh pound edge inscription).

Plus Ultra   Beyond (the Pillars of Hercules) (Spanish America).

Point du Couronne sans Peine   Point of the crown without penalty (Coburg).

Pons Civit Castellana   The bridge of the town of Castellana (Papacy).

Populus et Senatus Bonon   The people and conato of Bologna (Bologna).

Post Mortem Patris Pro Filio   For the son after his father's death (Pontefract siege coins).

Post Tenebras Lux   After darkness light (Geneva).

Post Tenebras Opero Lucem   After darkness I hope for light (Geneva).

Posui Deum Adiutorem Meum   I have made God my helper (England, Ireland, 1351–1603).

Praesidium et Decus   Protection and ornament (Bologna).

Prima Sedes Galliarum   First see of the Gauls (Lyon).

Primitiae Fodin Kuttenb ab Aerari Iterum Susceptarum   First results dug from the Kuttenberg mines in a renewed undertaking (Austria).

Princps Iuventutis   Prince of youth (Roman Empire).

Pro Defensione Urbis et Patriae   For the defence of city and country (France, Louis XIV).

Pro Deo et Patria   For God and the fatherland (Fulda).

Pro Deo et Populo   For God and the people (Bavaria).

Pro Ecclesia et Pro Patria   For the church and the fatherland (Constance).

Pro Fausio PP Reitur VS   For happy returns of the princes of the Two Sicilies (Naples and Sicily).

Pro Lege et Grege   For law and the flock (Fulda).

Pro maximo Dei Gloria et Bono Publico   For the greatest glory of God and the good of the people (Wurttemberg).

Pro Patria   For the fatherland (Wurzburg).

Propitio Deo Secura Ago   With God's favour I lead a secure life. (Saxe-Lauenburg).

Protector Literis Literae Nummis Corona et Salus   A protection to the letters (on the face of the coin), the letters (on the edge) are a garland and a safeguard to the coinage (Commonwealth, Cromwell broad).

Protege Virgo Pisas   Protect Pisa, O Virgin (Pisa).

Provide et Constanter   Wisely and firmly (Wurttem-berg).

Providentia et Pactis   Through foresight and pacts (Brandenburg-Ansbach).

Providentia Optimi Principis   With the foresight of the best prince (Naples and Sicily).

Proxima Fisica Finis   Nearest to natural end (Orciano).

Proxima Soli   Nearest to the sun (Modena).

Pulcra Virtutis Imago   The beautiful image of virtue (Genoa).

Pupillum et Viduam Suscipiat   May he support the orphan and the widow (Savoy).

Quae Deus Conjunxit Nemo Separet   What God hath joined let no man put asunder (England, James I).

Quem Quadragesies et Semel Patriae Natum Esse Gratulamur   Whom we congratulate for the forty-first time for being born for the fatherland (Lippe-Detmold).

Qui Dat Pauperi Non Indigebit   Who gives to the poor will never be in need (Munster).

Quid Non Cogit Necessitas   To what does Necessity not drive. (Ypres).

Quin Matrimonii Lustrum Celebrant   They celebrate their silver wedding (Austria, 1879).

Quocunque Gesseris (Jeceris) Stabit   Whichever way you throw it it will stand (Isle of Man).

Quod Deus Vult Hoc Semper Fit   What God wishes always occurs. (Saxe-Weimar).

Reconduntur non Retonduntur   They are laid up in store, not thundered back (Savoy).

Recta Tueri   Defend the right (Austria).

Recte Constanter et Fortiter   Rightly, constantly and bravely (Bavaria).

Recte Faciendo Neminem Timeas   May you fear no one in doing right. (Solms-Laubach).

Rector Orbis   Ruler of the world (Rome, Didius Julianus).

Rectus et Immotus   Right and immovable (Hesse).

Redde Cuique Quod Suum Est   Render to each that which is his own (England, Henry VIII).

Redeunt antiqui Gaudia Moris   There return the joys of ancient custom (Regensburg).

Reg Pr Pol et Lith Saxon Dux   Royal prince of Poland and Lithuania and duke of Saxony (Trier).

Regia Boruss Societas Asiat Embdae   Royal Prussian Asiatic Society of Emden (Prussia).

Regier Mich Her Nach Deinen Wort   Govern me here according to Thy word (Palatinate).

Regnans Capitulum Ecclesiae Cathedralis Ratisbonensis Sede Vacante   Administering the chapter of the cathedral church at Regensburg, the see being vacant (Regensburg).

Regni Utr Sic et Hier   Of the kingdom of the Two Sicilies and of Jerusalem (Naples and Sicily).

Religio Protestantium Leges Angliae Libertas Parliamenti   The religion of the Protestants, the laws of England and the freedom of Parliament (England, Royalists, 1642).

Relinquo Vos Liberos ab Utroque Homine   I leave you as children of each man (San Marino).

Restauracao da Independencia   Restoration of inde-pendence (Portugal, 1990).

Restitutor Exercitus   Restorer of the army (Rome, Aurelian).

Restitutor Galliarum   Restorer of the Gauls (Rome, Gallienus).

Restitutor Generis Humani   Restorer of mankind (Rome, Valerian).

Restitutor Libertatis   Restorer of freedom (Rome, Constantine).

Restitutor Orbis   Restorer of the world (Rome, Valerian).

Restitutor Orientis   Restorer of the east (Rome).

Restitutor Saeculi   Restorer of the century (Rome, Valerian).

Restitutor Urbis   Restorer of the city (Rome, Severus).

Rosa Americana Utile Dulci   The American rose, useful and sweet (American colonies).

Rosa Sine Spina   A rose without a thorn (England, Tudor coins).

Rutilans Rosa Sine Spina   A dazzling rose without a thorn (England, Tudor gold coins).

S Annae Fundgruben Ausb Tha in N Oe   Mining thaler of the St Anne mine in Lower Austria (Austria).

S Ap S Leg Nat Germ Primas   Legate of the Holy Apostolic See, born Primate of Germany (Salzburg).

S Carolus Magnus Fundator   Charlemagne founder (Munster).

S. Gertrudis Virgo Prudens Niviella   St Gertrude the wise virgin of Nivelles (Nivelles).

Sl Aul Reg Her & P Ge H Post Mag   General hereditary postmaster, supreme of the imperial court of the hereditary kingdom and provinces (Paar).

S. Ian Bapt F. Zachari   St John the Baptist, son of Zachary (Florence).

S. Kilianus Cum Sociis Francorum Apostoli   St Kilian and his companions, apostles to the Franks (Wurzburg).

S. Lambertus Patronus Leodiensis   St Lambert, patron of Liege (Liege).

Sac Nupt Celeb Berol   For the holy matrimony celebrated at Berlin (Brandenburg-Ansbach).

Sac Rom Imp   Holy Roman Empire (German states).

Sac Rom Imp Provisor Iterum   Administrator of the Holy Roman Empire for the second time (Saxony).

Salus Generis Humani   Safety of mankind (Rome, Vindex).

Salus Patriae   Safety of the fatherland (Italy).

Salus Populi   The safety of the people (Spain).

Salus Provinciarum   Safety of the provinces (Rome, Postumus).

Salus Publica Salus Mea   Public safety is my safety (Sweden).

Salus Reipublicae   The safety of the republic (Rome, Theodosius II).

Salus Reipublicae Suprema Lex   The safety of the republic is the supreme law (Poland).

Salvam Fac Rempublicam Tuam   Make your state safe (San Marino).

Sanctus Iohannes Innoce   St John the harmless (Gandersheim).

Sans Changer   Without changing (Isle of Man).

Sans Eclat   Without pomp (Bouchain siege, 1711).

Sapiente Diffidentia   Wise distrust (Teschen).

Scutum Fidei Proteget Eum / Eam   The shield of faith shall protect him / her (England, Edward VI and Elizabeth I).

Secundum Voluntatem Tuam Domine   Your favourable will o Lord (Hesse).

Securitati Publicae   For the public safety (Brandenburg-Ansbach).

Sede Vacante   The see being vacant (Papal states, Vatican and ecclesiastical coinage).

Sena Vetus Alpha et W Principum et Finis   Old Siena alpha and omega, the beginning and the end (Siena).

Senatus Populus QR   Senate and people of Rome (Rome, 1188).

Si Deus Nobiscum Quis Contra Nos   If God is with us who can oppose us (Hesse).

Si Deus Pro Nobis Quis Contra Nos   If God is for us who can oppose us (Roemhild).

Sieh Deine Seeligkeit Steht Fest Ins Vaters Liebe   Behold thy salvation stands surely in thy Father's love (Gotha).

Signis Receptis   When the standards had been recovered (Rome, Augustus).

Signum Crucis   The sign of the cross (Groningen).

Sincere et Constanter   Truthfully and steadfastly (Hesse-Darmstadt).

Sit Nomen Domini Benedictum   Blessed be the name of the Lord (Burgundy, Strasbourg).

St T X Adiuto Reg Iste Domba   Let it be to you, o Christ, the assistant to the king of Dombes (Dombes).

Sit Tibi Xpe Dat q'tu Regis Iste Ducat   May this duchy which Thou rulest be given to Thee, O Christ (Venice, ducat).

Sit Unio Haec Perennis   May this union last for ever (Hohenlohe-Langenberg).

Sola Bona Quae Honesta   The only good things are those which are honest (Brunswick).

Sola Facta Deum Sequor   Through deeds alone I strive to follow God (Milan).

Soli Deo Honor et Gloria   To God alone be honour and glory (Nassau).

Soli Reduci   To him, the only one restored (Naples and Sicily).

Solius Virtutis Flos Perpetuus   The flower of Virtue alone is perpetual (Strasbourg).

Spes Confisa Deo Nunquam Confusa Recedit   Hope entrusted in God never retreats in a disorderly fashion (Lippe).

Spes Nr Deus   God is our hope (Oudenarde siege, 1582).

Spes Rei Publicae   The hope of the republic (Rome, Valens).

Strena ex Argyrocopeo Vallis S Christoph   A New Year's gift from the silver-bearing valley of St Christopher (Wurttemberg, 1625).

Sub His Secura Spes Clupeus Omnibus in Te Sperantibus   Under these hope is safe, a shield for all who reside hope in Thee (Bavaria).

Sub Pondere   Under weight (Fulda).

Sub Protectione Caesarea   Under imperial protection (Soragna).

Sub Tuum Praesidium Confug   We flee to Thy protection (Salzburg).

Sub Umbra Alarum Tuarum   Under the shadow of Thy wings (Iever, Scotland, James V).

Subditorum Salus Felicitas Summa   The safety of the subjects is the highest happiness (Lubeck).

Sufficit Mihi Gratia Tua Domine   Sufficient to me is Thy grace, o Lord (Ploen).

Supra Firmam Petram   Upon a firm rock (Papacy).

Susceptor Noster Deus   God is our defence (Tuscany).

Sydera Favent Industriae   The stars favour industry (Furstenberg).

Sylvarum Culturae Praemium   Prize for the culture of the forest (Brandenburg-Ansbach).

Tali Dicata Signo Mens Fluctuari Nequit   Consecrated by such a sign the mind cannot waver (England, Henry VIII George noble).

Tandem Bona Caus Triumphat   A good cause eventually triumphs (Dillenburg).

Tandem Fortuna Obstetrice   With good luck ultimately as the midwife (Wittgenstein).

Te Stante Virebo   With you at my side I shall be strong (Moravia).

Tene Mensuram et Respice Finem   Hold the measure and look to the end (Burgundy).

Tert Ducat Secular   Tercentenary of the duchy (Wurttemberg).

Thu Recht Schev Niemand   Go with right and fear no one (Saxe-Lauenburg).

Tibi Laus et Gloria   To Thee be praise and glory (Venice).

Timor Domini Fons Vitae   The fear of the Lord is a fountain of life (England, Edward VI shillings).

Tout Avec Dieu   Everything with God (Brunswick, 1626).

Traiectum ad Mosam   The crossing of the Maas (Maastricht).

Transvolat Nubila Virtus   Marriageable virtue soon flies past (Grueyeres).

Travail, Famille, Patrie   Work, family, country (Vichy France).

Triumphator Gent Barb   Victor over the barbarian people (Byzantine Empire, Arcadius).

Tueatur Unita Deus   May God guard these united (Kingdoms) (England, James I; Britain, 1847).

Turck Blegert Wien   Vienna besieged by the Turks (Vienna, 1531).

Tut Mar Gab Pr Vid de Lobk Nat Pr Sab Car et Aug Pr de Lobk   Regency of Maria Gabriela, widow of the prince of Lobkowitz, born princess of Savoy-Carignan, and August prince of Lobkowitz (Lobkowitz).

Tutela Italiae   The guardianship of Italy (Rome, Nerva).

Ubi Vult Spirat   He breathes where he will (Papacy).

Ubique Pax   Peace everywhere (Rome, Gallienus).

Union et Force   Union and strength (France).

Urbe Obsessa   The city under siege (Maastricht).

Urbem Virgo Tuam Serva   Protects thy city o virgin (Mary) (Strasbourg).

USC & RAM Cons Int Gen C Mar & Nob Praet H Turmae Capit   Privy councillor of both their holy imperial and royal apostolic majesties, general field marshal and captain of the noble praetorian Hungarian squadrons (Eszterhazy).

Veni Luumen Cordium   Come light of hearts (Vatican).

Veni Sancte Spiritus   Come Holy Ghost (Vatican).

Verbum Domini Manet in Aeternum   The word of the Lord abides forever (Hesse-Darmstadt, Veldenz).

Veritas Lex Tua   The truth is your law (Salzburg).

Veritas Temporis Filia   Truth is the daughter of time (England and Ireland, Mary Tudor).

Veritate et Labore   By truth and work (Wittgenstein).

Veritate et Iustitia   By truth and justice (German states).
Victoria Principum   The victory of princes (Ostrogoths).
Videant Pauperes et Laetentur   Let the poor see and rejoice (Tuscany).
Virgo Maria Protege Civitatem Savonae   Virgin Mary Protect the city of Savona (Savona).
Viribus Unitis   With united strength (Austria).
Virtute et Fidelitate   By virtue and faithfulness (Hesse-Cassel).
Virtute et Prudentia   With virtue and prudence (Auersperg).
Virtute Viam Dimetiar   I shall mark the way with valour (Waldeck).
Virtutis Gloria Merces   Glory is the reward of valour (Holstein-Gottorp).
Vis Unita Concordia Fratrum Fortior   United power is the stronger harmony of brothers (Mansfeld).
Visitavit Nos Oriens ex Alto   He has visited us arising on high (Luneburg).
Vivit Post Funera   He lives after death (Bremen).

Vota Optata Romae Fel   Vows taken for the luck of Rome (Rome, Maxentius).
Vox de Throno   A voice from the throne (Papacy).
Was Got Beschert Bleibet Unerwert   What God hath endowed leave undisturbed
Wider macht und List Mein Fels Gott Ist   Against might and trickery God is my rock (Hesse-Cassel).
Xpc Vincit Xpc Regnat   Christ conquers, Christ reigns (Scotland, Spain).
Xpc Vivet Xpc Regnat Xpc Impat   Christ lives, Christ reigns, Christ commands (Cambrai).
Xpe Resurescit   Christ lives again (Venice).
Xpistiana Religio   Christian religion (Carolingian Empire).
Xps Ihs Elegit me Regem Populo   Jesus Christ chose me as king to the people (Norway).
Zelator Fidei Usque ad Montem   An upholder of the faith through and through (Portugal).
Zum Besten des Vaterlands   To the best of the fatherland (Bamberg).

ABBREVIATIONS COMMONLY USED TO DENOTE METALLIC COMPOSITION

Cu	Copper
Cu/Steel	Copper plated Steel
Ag/Cu	Silver plated copper
Ae	Bronze
Cu-Ni	Cupro-Nickel
Ni-Ag	Nickel Silver (note-does not contain silver)
Brass/Cu-Ni	Brass outer, Cupro-Nickel inner
Ni-Brass	Nickel-Brass
Ag	Silver
Au/Ag	Gold plated silver
Au	Gold
Pl	Platinum

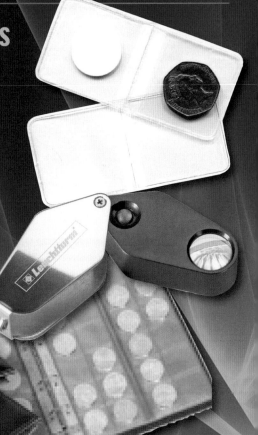

CARE *of coins*

There is no point in going to a great deal of trouble and expense in selecting the best coins you can afford, only to let them deteriorate in value by neglect and mishandling. Unless you give some thought to the proper care of your coins, your collection is unlikely to make a profit for you if and when you come to sell it. Housing your coins is the biggest problem of all, so it is important to give a lot of attention to this.

Storage

The ideal, but admittedly the most expensive, method is the coin cabinet, constructed of air-dried mahogany, walnut or rosewood *(never oak, cedar or any highly resinous timber likely to cause chemical tarnish)*. These cabinets have banks of shallow drawers containing trays made of the same wood, with half-drilled holes of various sizes to accommodate the different denominations of coins. Such cabinets are handsome pieces of furniture but, being largely handmade, tend to be rather expensive. Occasionally good specimens can be picked up in secondhand furniture shops, or at the dispersal of house contents by auction, but the best bet is still to purchase a new cabinet, tailored to your own requirements. These collectors cabinets are hand-made using certified solid mahogany, as specified by leading museums, as mahogany does not contain any chemicals or resins that could result in the discolouration of the collection inside the cabinet. The polish used on the outside of the cabinets is based on natural oils and hand applied then finished with bees wax. The trays are left as untreated mahogany so as not to introduce any harmful contaminants. The coin trays are available as single thickness or double thickness for holding thicker coins, capsules or artifacts.

Peter Nichols Cabinets (telephone 0115 9224149, www.coincabinets.com) was established in 1967. In October 2010 Peter retired and passed the cabinet making business on to Geoff Skinner, Shirley Watts and Ben Skinner-Watts. Now based in Nottingham, the family run business continues to provide specialist and bespoke display and storage systems to suit every need from the seven-tray Pheon all the way up to the massive 40-tray specials supplied to the British Museum. All cabinets are fitted with double doors. Prices start at around £80 and go up to about £350 for the thirty-tray Coronet. They are not cheap, but you have the satisfaction of acquiring exquisite examples of the cabinet maker's craft.

An excellent storage option is provided by a number of firms who manufacture coin trays in durable, felt-lined materials with shallow compartments to suit the various sizes of coins. Most of these trays interlock so that they build up into a cabinet of the desired size, and there are also versions designed as carrying cases, which are ideal for transporting coins.

The Mascle Classic – the ideal "entry-level" coin cabinet for collectors and just one of a range of hand-made pieces for those seeking practical as well as beautiful storage solutions.

The popular and extensive **Lighthouse** range is available from The Duncannon Partnership, 4 Beaufort Road, Reigate, RH2 9DJ (telephone 01737 244222, www.duncannon.co.uk) or Token Publishing Ltd (telephone 01404 46972, www.tokenpublishing.com). This range includes a wide variety of cases and albums for the general collector in basic or de luxe styles as required, as well as printed albums for the specialist. Their cases, including the popular aluminium range, are manufactured to the highest standards, lined with blue plush which displays any coin to its best advantage. The red-lined single trays come in deep or standard size and make an ideal cabinet when stacked together or housed in their attractive aluminium case, which is available separately. The trays themselves come with a variety of compartments for every size of coin. Their complete range can be viewed on-line.

The extensive **Lindner** range is supplied in the UK by Prinz Publications of 3A Hayle Industrial Park, Hayle, Cornwall TR27 5JR (telephone 01736 751914, www.prinz.co.uk) or from Token Publishing Ltd (telephone 01404 46972, www.tokenpublishing.com). Well-known for their wide range of philatelic and numismatic accessories, but these include a full array of coin boxes, capsules, carrying cases and trays. The basic Lindner coin box is, in fact, a shallow tray available in a standard version or a smoked glass version. These trays have a crystal clear frame, red felt inserts and holes for various diameters of coins and medals. A novel feature of these trays is the rounded insert which facilitates the removal of coins from their spaces with the minimum of handling.

Adding on to the stacking Lindner range is easy.

These boxes are designed in such a manner that they interlock and can be built up into banks of trays, each fitted with a draw-handle and sliding in and out easily. Various types of chemically inert plastic capsules and envelopes have been designed for use in combination with plain shallow trays, without holes drilled. Lindner also manufacture a range of luxury cases lined in velvet and Atlas silk with padded covers and gold embossing on the spines, producing a most tasteful and elegant appearance.

Safe Albums of 16 Falcon Business Park, 38 Ivanhoe Road, Finchampstead, Berkshire RG40 4QQ (telephone 0118 932 8976, www.safealbums.co.uk) are the UK agents for the German Stapel-Element, a drawer-stacking system with clear plasticiser-free trays that fit into standard bookshelves. The sliding coin compartments, lined with blue velvet, can be angled for display to best advantage. Stackable drawers can be built up to any height desired. A wide range of drawer sizes is available, with compartments suitable for the smallest coins right up to four-compartment trays designed for very large artefacts such as card-cases or cigarette cases. The Mobel-Element cabinet is a superb specialised cabinet constructed of the finest timber with a steel frame and steel grip bars which can be securely locked. It thus combines elegance with security and is the ideal medium for the most valuable coins and medals.

There are also various storage systems, such as **Coindex**, which operate on the principle of narrow drawers in which the coins are stored in envelopes of chemically-inert plastic. A strip across the top holds a little slip giving a brief description, catalogue number and the price of each coin.

The Sydney Museum in Australia, for example, keeps its coins in manila envelopes stored in plastic lunch-boxes which seems to do the job pretty well!

Coin Albums

When coin collecting became a popular hobby in the 1960s, several firms marketed ranges of coin albums. They had clear plastic sleeves divided into tiny compartments of various sizes and had the merit of being cheap and taking up little room on a bookshelf.

They had several drawbacks, however, not the least being the tendency of the pages to sag with the weight of the coins, or even, in extreme cases, to pull away from the pegs or rings holding them on to the spine. They required very careful handling as the coins could easily fall out of the top row as the pages were turned. The more expensive albums had little flaps that folded over the top of the coin to overcome this problem.

Arguably the worst aspect of these albums was the use of polyvinyl chloride (PVC) in the construction of the sleeves. Collectors soon discovered to their horror that this reacted chemically with their coins, especially those made

of silver, causing a rather disgusting yellow slime to adhere to the coins' surface. I shudder to think how many fine collections were ruined as a result, or of the countless coins that required highly expert treatment in a bid to restore them to as near the original condition as possible.

Fortunately the lesson has been learned and the coin albums now on the market are quite safe. Lighthouse and Lindner offer a wide range of albums designed to house coins, medals or banknotes. The old problem about sagging pages is overcome by the use of a multi-ring binding welded to a very stout spine, while the sleeves contain neither Styrol nor PVC and will not affect any metals at all. In addition to pages with pockets of uniform size, the Karat range of albums operates on a slide principle which enables the user to insert vertical strips of different sizes on the same page, so that the coins of one country or series, or perhaps a thematic display of coins from different countries, can be displayed side by side.

Safe Albums offer a wide range of albums in the Coinholder System and Coin-Combi ranges. These, too, offer the choice of fixed pages with uniform-sized pockets, or interchangeable sliding inserts for different sizes side by side.

In the United States in the past few decades one of the preferred methods for keeping coins in pristine condition is the use of "slabs"—these tough plastic rectangles cannot be easily broken into meaning that the coin inside remains in exactly the same condition as when it was placed in there. This has led to the rise of professional grading and encapsulation companies who not only "slab" your coin but also grade it and guarantee that grade. This allows coins to be bought and sold with both vendor and purchaser knowing exactly what the grade is thus taking out the subjectivity of dealer or collector—an issue that can mean hundreds of pounds difference in the value of the coin. Slabbing in this way is essentially a tool to help a coin maintain a grade and thus more easily guarantee its value, however, many collectors prefer it as a method of protecting their coins as it allows them to be stored or transported easily with no fear of damage. The biggest companies in the United States for the encapsulation of coins are **PCGS** and **NGC**, they have been in business for some years and in America the "slabbed" coin is a common sight. It is less common over here, with many collectors still unsure about the look of the slabs and uncertain whether or not they would prefer to be able to handle their coins directly; British company **CGS** aims to change that and is confident that the benefits of the slab outweigh any disadvantages and they are hoping that the encapsulation and consequent grade guarantee

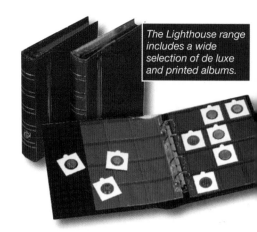

The Lighthouse range includes a wide selection of de luxe and printed albums.

and protection of the coin will soon be as popular in the UK as it is "over the pond".

Token Publishing Ltd stock a varied range of coin accessories from magnifying glasses to coin albums. To find out more, simply log onto www.tokenpublishing.com or call 01404 44166 for an up-to-date illustrated, colour catalogue.

CLEANING *coins*

This is like matrimony—it should not be embarked on lightly. Indeed, the advice given by the magazine *Punch* in regard to marriage is equally sound in this case—don't do it! It is far better to have a dirty coin than an irretrievably damaged one. Every dealer has horror stories of handling coins that previous owners have cleaned, to their detriment. The worst example I ever saw was a display of coins found by a metal detectorist who "improved" his finds by abrading them in the kind of rotary drum used by lapidarists to polish gemstones. If you really must remove the dirt and grease from coins, it is advisable to practise on coins of little value.

Warm water containing a mild household detergent or washing-up liquid will work wonders in removing surface dirt and grease from most coins, but silver is best washed in a weak solution of ammonia and warm water—one part ammonia to ten parts water. Gold coins can be cleaned with diluted citric acid, such as lemon juice. Copper or bronze coins present more of a problem, but patches of verdigris can usually be removed by careful washing in a 20 per cent solution of sodium sesquicarbonate. Wartime coins made of tin, zinc, iron or steel can be cleaned in a 5 per cent solution of caustic soda containing some aluminium or zinc foil or filings, but they must be rinsed afterwards in clean water and carefully dried. Cotton buds are ideal for gently prising dirt out of coin legends and crevices in the designs. Soft brushes (with animal bristles—*never* nylon or other artificial bristles) designed for cleaning silver are most suitable for gently cleaning coins.

Coins recovered from the soil or the sea bed present special problems, due to chemical reaction between the metals and the salts in the earth or sea water. In such cases, the best advice is to take them to the nearest museum and let the professional experts decide on what can or should be done.

Both Lindner and Safe Albums offer a range of coin-cleaning kits and materials suitable for gold, silver, copper and other base alloys respectively. Safe (living up to their name) also provide a stern warning that rubber gloves should be worn and care taken to avoid breathing fumes or getting splashes of liquid in your eyes or on your skin. Obviously, the whole business of cleaning is a matter that should not be entered into without the utmost care and forethought.

POLISHING: A WARNING

If cleaning should only be approached with the greatest trepidation, polishing is definitely OUT! Beginners sometimes fall into the appalling error of thinking that a smart rub with metal polish might improve the appearance of their coins. Short of actually punching a hole through it, there can hardly be a more destructive act. Polishing a coin may improve its superficial appearance for a few days, but such abrasive action will destroy the patina and reduce the fineness of the high points of the surface.

Even if a coin is only polished once, it will never be quite the same again, and an expert can tell this a mile off.

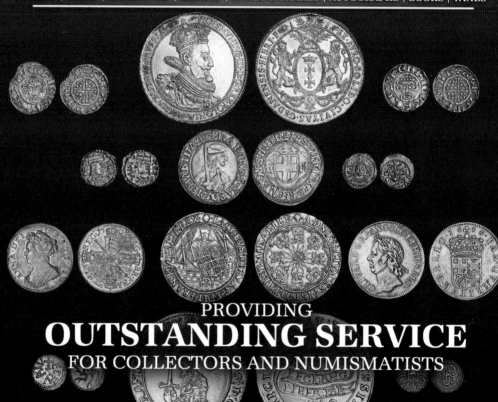

CELTIC *coinage of Britain*

Pritanic coins were the first coins made in Britain. They were issued for a century and a half before the Roman invasion, and possibly a little later in some areas. They were minted by the rulers of thirteen tribal groups or administrative authorities situated on the southeast of a line from the Humber to the Severn. In this short article Pritanic specialist CHRIS RUDD introduces this increasingly popular series.

Most folk call them British Celtic or Celtic coins of Britain. But I'll begin by letting you into a little known secret: most folk may be wrong. You see, there is no ancient textual evidence—none whatsoever—that anyone in iron age Britain called themselves a Celt. Neither is there a hint—not a whisper—that anyone else in the ancient world ever referred to the Brits as Celts. The Greeks didn't, the Gauls didn't, the Romans didn't. The correct name for iron age Britons is Pritani—well formed people or people of the forms. How do we know? Because a sailor from Marseilles said so.

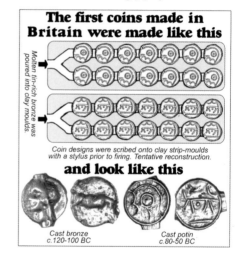

The first coins made in Britain were made like this

Molten tin-rich bronze was poured into clay moulds.

Coin designs were scribed onto clay strip-moulds with a stylus prior to firing. Tentative reconstruction.

and look like this

Cast bronze c. 120-100 BC

Cast potin c. 80-50 BC

Many Gaulish coins were imported to Britain, like this silver stater of the Coriosolites (ABC 70), typical of many in the huge Jersey hoard found in June 2012, containing an estimated 50,000 coins.

Around 330 BC an explorer, Pytheas of Marseilles, sailed to Britain in search of tin. His visit indicates early trade links with southern Gaul and that the Britons were called Pritani. Marseilles inspired Britain's first homemade coinage: potin coins cast in clay strip-moulds, with Apollo on one side and a bull on the other, plus MA for Massalia (Marseilles). Made in Kent c. 120–100 BC, these cast potins circulated alongside gold coins imported from Gaul. During the Gallic Wars (58–51 BC) many other Gaulish coins—gold, silver and bronze—came to Britain, some brought by refugees, others by British mercenaries, others by trade.

The most famous Gallic migrant was Commios "friend", a former ally of Caesar, who became king of the Regini and Atrebates in the south of England c. 50–25 BC. Commios was the first British ruler to place his name on coins. His three sons—Tincomarus (great in peace), Eppillus (little horse) and Verica (the high one), made the Commian dynasty one of the wealthiest and most powerful in Britain. Most of their coins adopted Roman imagery and archaeology indicates that they imported Roman luxury goods, especially Italian wine. Many coins of Verica show grapes, vine leaves and wine cups.

The main rivals of the Regini and Atrebates were the Catuvellauni of Hertfordshire. Their first known ruler was probably Cassivellaunos "bronze commander", leader of the British coalition against Caesar in 54 BC. Many of Britain's earliest gold coins were probably struck to fund resistance to Caesar and then to pay tribute to him. Cassivellaunos may have organised this war money. Addedomaros "great in chariots" (c. 45–25 BC) was the first ruler north of the Thames to inscribe his coins, perhaps copying Commios.

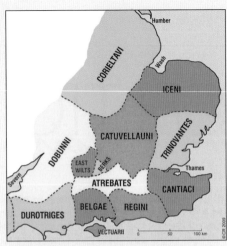

Thirteen possible tribal groups which were producing coins by c.50-40 BC (Cantiaci much earlier). By c.30 BC the Belgae, East Wiltshire and Berkshire group had apparently stopped minting independently.

Gold stater of Commios (ABC 1022) the first British king to place his name on coins. There are two hidden faces on the obverse.

Verica silver minim with wine cup (ABC 1331) and Verica gold stater with vine leaf (ABC 1193)—evidence of Britain's thirst for fine Italian wine and Roman silverware.

Catuvellaunian expansion continued under Tasciovanos "killer of badgers" whose coins became increasingly Roman in style. His son Cunobelinus "hound of Belenus"—Shakespeare's *Cymbeline*) was the most potent tribal king in Atlantic Europe. Suetonius called him "king of the Britons". During his thirty-year reign (c. AD 8–41) Cunobelinus may have minted well over a million gold staters, most of them displaying a corn ear and CAMV— short for *Camulodunon* (Colchester). When his brother Epaticcus "leader of horsemen" and his son Caratacus "the beloved"—both clad as Hercules on their silver coins—crossed the Thames and attacked the Atrebates, Verica fled to Claudius who invaded Britain in AD 43. The minting of tribal coins ceased shortly afterwards.

Other tribes that issued coins included the Cantiaci of Kent, the Belgae of Hampshire, the Durotriges of Dorset, the Dobunni of the West Midlands, the Trinovantes of Essex, the Iceni of East Anglia and the Corieltavi of Lincolnshire. However, only a minority of people in the British Isles used coins regularly—the moneyed minority in southeast England. Cornwall, Devon, Wales, northern England, Scotland and Ireland remained coinless. Which is why ancient British coins are relatively rare. For example, whereas Greek coins

were minted for about 600 years, Roman for about 800 years and Gaulish for about 250 years, ancient British coins were produced for little more than 150 years, and often in much smaller runs.

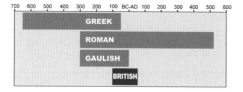

Ancient British coins weren't minted for as long as Greek, Roman or Gaulish coins were. That's one of the reasons they are so scarce.

This century and a half of Pritanic (not Celtic) coin production generated a remarkable flowering of insular creativity and insular technology, unmatched by any other northern European nation of the period. Though initially influenced by Gallic minting techniques and Gallic iconography, ancient British coinage rapidly developed its own denominational systems, its own gold standards and its own highly distinctive coin designs—often inspired by Roman prototypes, but invariably modified to suit local needs. Between c. 110 BC and c. AD 45 around a thousand different coin types were minted in Britain. Many if not most of these thousand types displayed what might loosely be described as "religious" imagery. Not surprising, really, when one recalls that Caesar says that Druidism originated in Britain. Moreover, Tasciovanos struck coins in no fewer than five different denominations, whereas most Gaulish rulers issued no more than two or three.

The history of late iron age Britain, particularly the century prior to the Claudian conquest, has largely been rewritten with the help of ancient British coins. Most of the recent advances in our knowledge of this period have been due to amateur metal detecting. As a direct result of coin finds made by metal detectorists since the 1970s four new coin-issuing groups and maybe ten new rulers, previously unknown or unrecognised, have been identified. Not bad for barely forty years of unfunded, unofficial fieldwork.

Unlike Gaul, most of the British Isles was virtually coinless throughout the late iron age (and later). Coin production was confined to south-east Britain. That's why, overall, ancient British coins are much rarer than Gaulish coins.

What is it about ancient British coins that is making them increasingly popular with collectors all over the world? Having been involved with them for many years (I excavated my first in 1952) I'll tell you why they appeal to me.

I love the *primal antiquity* of Pritanic coins. They were the first coins made in Britain over two thousand years ago. When you see the flamboyant freedom of their designs you realise that they are the most boisterously British coins ever minted, unlike the unsmiling Roman, Anglo-Saxon and Norman series that marched soberly in their dancing footsteps.

I love the *anarchic regality* of Pritanic coins. Like the rumbustious tribal kings that issued them, their personality is wild, strong and highly irregular. These coins were made by the first British rulers known by name to us—unruly, quarrelsome, beer-swilling, tribal warlords such as Cassivellaunos who fought Julius Caesar in 54 BC and Caratacus, the British resistance leader who opposed Claudius in AD 43.

I love the *imaginative imagery* you find on Pritanic coins: all the different gods and goddesses, armed warriors, chariot wheels, hidden faces, decapitated heads, suns, moons, stars, thunderbolts, floral motifs, magic signs and phallic symbols. Plus an amazing menagerie of wild animals, birds and mythical beasts.

I love the *myths, mystery and mysticism* behind Pritanic coins. Look closely at this late iron age money of Albion and you'll catch glimpses

Ancient British denominations

There was no national currency in pre-Roman Britain and little consistency from region to region. Different tribes issued different mixtures of low, medium and high value coins. Here are the most common denominations used by the ancient Brits. The names are ours, not theirs. We've no idea what they called their coins, shown here actual size.

GOLD STATERS
Can also be silver, billon or bronze

Norfolk Wolf, ABC 1393

GOLD QUARTER STATERS
Can also be silver or billon

Irstead Smiler, ABC 1480

SILVER UNITS

Norfolk God, ABC 1567

SILVER HALF UNITS

Aunt Cost Half, ABC 1953

SILVER MINIMS

Verica Sphinx, ABC 1340

BRONZE UNITS

Cunobelinus Centaur, ABC 2957

BRONZE HALF UNITS

Tasciovanos Goat, ABC 2709

CAST POTIN UNITS

Nipples, ABC 174

of long-lost legends and ancient pagan rituals such as head-hunting, bull sacrificing and shape-shifting. You'll marvel at the plethora of occult signs and arcane symbols and you may even feel the secret power of the Druids.

I love the *palpitating unpredictability* of Pritanic coins. Even after sixty years of heart-racing intimacy they are constantly and delightfully surprising me. Attributions, names and dates are always being revised. Not long ago the Coritani were renamed Corieltavi and Tincommios was rechristened Tincomarus. Almost every month exciting new types and new variants keep leaping out of the ground, thanks to metal detectorists. For example, on September 4, 2010 the late

Bronze units of Cunobelinus, son of Tasciovanos, showing a bull being sacrificed (ABC 2972) and a man—perhaps a Druid priest?—carrying a severed human head (ABC 2987).

Danny Baldock discovered the first recorded coin of Anarevitos, a Kentish ruler previously unknown to history.

I love the *uncommon scarcity* of Pritanic coins. Ask any metdet how many so-called Celtic coins he or she has found and you'll immediately realise that they are rarer than Roman coins—at least a thousand times rarer on average—for the reasons stated above.

Finally I love the *galloping good value* of this horsey money (some Pritanic horses have three tails, some breathe fire, others have a human torso). Their greater rarity doesn't mean they are

Silver unit of freedom-fighter Caratacus (ABC 1376) who defied the Roman invaders for eight years until he was betrayed by Cartimandua, queen of the Brigantes.

costlier than other ancient coins. In fact, they are often cheaper because demand determines price and because there are far fewer collectors of ancient British coins than there are, say, of Greek or Roman coins. For example, a very fine British gold stater typically costs less than half the price—sometimes even a third the price of a Roman aureus or English gold noble of comparable quality and rarity. But the disparity is gradually diminishing as more and more canny collectors are appreciating the untamed beauty and undervalued scarcity of Pritanic coins.

Coin Yearbook provides a great guide to current prices of commoner Pritanic types, but because new types keep turning up and because big hoards are sometimes found (causing values to fluctuate temporarily) you'd be well advised to also keep an eye on dealers' catalogues and prices realised at auction. If you're buying in Britain, buy from people who are members of the BNTA (British Numismatic Trade Association). If you're buying overseas, check that your suppliers belong to the IAPN (International Association of Professional Numismatists). And, if you're a beginner, beware of dodgy traders on the internet, or you could end up with a fistful of fakes and no refund.

I'd also counsel you to spend a day at the British Museum. Its collection of almost 7,000 ancient British coins is the most comprehensive, publicly accessible collection of its kind in the world. As their curator, Ian Leins, says: "They're public coins . . . your coins, and they're here for you to see. So come and see them. We'll be pleased to show them to you". Access to the collection is free for everyone. But you'll need to make an appointment before you go, and take some photo ID and proof of address. Email: coins@thebritishmuseum.ac.uk or telephone: 020 7323 8607.

Before you buy coins—any coins of any period—it always pays to read about them first. As an old adman I'm not shy about blowing my own trumpet. The best little introduction to Pritanic coins is *Britain's First Coins* by Chris Rudd (expected late 2012) and the most comprehensive catalogue of the series is *Ancient British Coins* also by Chris Rudd (2010), known in the trade as ABC. If you have even half the fun I've had with ancient British coins (and am still having)—I can promise you that you'll be a very happy person indeed. Never bored, and never with a complete collection.

A unique gold stater of Anarevitos, a previously unknown ruler of the Cantiaci, probably a son of Eppillus, king of Calleva (Silchester). Sold by Elizabeth Cottam of Chris Rudd for £21,000, a record price for an ancient British coin (Coin News, December 2010).

Chris Rudd started studying ancient British coins sixty years ago and has written a hundred articles about them, many published by COIN NEWS. "I've still got a lot to learn" he says.

COLLECTING *ancient coins*

Ancient coins differ from most other series which are collected in Britain in that every piece has spent the major part of the last two thousand years in the ground. As **JOHN CUMMINGS**, dealer in ancient coins and antiquities explains here, the effect that burial has had on the surface of the coin determines more than anything else the value of a particular piece. With more modern coins, the only things which affect price are rarity and grade. There may be a premium for coins exhibiting particularly fine tone, or with outstanding pedigrees, but an 1887 crown in "extremely fine" condition has virtually the same value as every other piece with the same grade and of the same date. With ancient coins the story is very different.

A large number of different criteria affect the price of an ancient coin. Factors affecting prices can be broken down into several categories:

Condition

The most important factor by far in determining price. Ancient coins were struck by hand and can exhibit striking faults. Value suffers if the coin is struck with the designs off-centre, is weakly struck, or if the flan is irregular in shape. Many of the Celtic tribes issued coins of varying fineness and those made from low quality gold or silver are worth less than similar specimens where the metal quality is better. Conversely, coins on exceptional flans, particularly well struck, or with fine patinas command a premium.

Many ancient coins have suffered during their stay in the ground. It must be borne in mind that the prices given in the price guide are for uncorroded, undamaged examples. A Roman denarius should be graded using the same criteria as those used for grading modern coins. The surfaces must be good, and the coin intact. The fact that the coin is 2,000 years old is irrelevant as far as grading is concerned. Coins which are not perfectly preserved are certainly not without value, however, the value for a given grade decreases with the degree of fault.

Rarity

As with all other series, rare coins usually command higher prices than common ones. A unique variety of a small fourth century Roman bronze coin, even in perfect condition, can be worth much less than a more worn and common piece from an earlier part of the empire. In the Celtic series, there is an almost infinite variety of minor types and a unique variety of an uninscribed type will rarely outbid an inscribed issue of a known king.

Historical and local significance

Types which have historical or local interest can command a price far above their scarcity value. Denarii of the emperor Tiberius are believed to have been referred to in the New Testament and command a far higher price than a less interesting piece of similar rarity. Similarly, pieces which have British reverse types such as the "VICT BRIT" reverse of the third century AD are more expensive than their scarcity would indicate. The 12 Caesars remain ever popular especially in the American market and this affects prices throughout the world. In the Celtic series, coins of Cunobelin or Boudicca are far more popular than pieces which have no historical interest but which may be far scarcer.

Reverse types

All Roman emperors who survived for a reasonable time issued coins with many different reverse types. The most common of these usually show various Roman gods. When a coin has an unusual reverse it always enhances the value. Particularly popular are architectural scenes, animals, references to Judaism, and legionary types.

Artistic merit

The Roman coinage is blessed with a large number of bust varieties and these can have a startling effect on price. For example, a common coin with the bust facing left instead of right can be worth several times the price of a normal specimen. Like many of the emperors, the coinage of Hadrian has a large number of bust varieties, some of which are extremely artistic and these, too, can command a premium.

The coinage used in Britain from the time of the invasion in AD 43 was the same as that introduced throughout the Empire by the emperor Augustus around 20 BC. The simple divisions of 2 asses equal to one dupondius, 2 dupondii equal to 1 sestertius, 4 sestertii equal to one denarius and 25 denarii equal to one aureus continued in use until the reformation of the coinage by Caracalla in AD 214.

Aureus (gold)   *Denarius (silver)*

Dupondius (copper)   *Sestertius (bronze)*   *As (copper)*

HAMMERED *coinage*

The hammered currency of medieval Britain is among some of the most interesting coinage in the world. The turbulent history of these islands is reflected in the fascinating changes in size, design, fineness and workmanship, culminating in the many strange examples that emanated from the strife of the Civil War.

The Norman Conquest of England in 1066 and succeeding years had far-reaching effects on all aspects of life. Surprisingly, however, it had little impact on the coinage. William the Conqueror was anxious to emphasise the continuity of his reign, so far as the ordinary people were concerned, and therefore he retained the fabric, size and general design pattern of the silver penny. Almost 70 mints were in operation during this reign, but by the middle of the 12th century the number was reduced to 55 and under Henry II (1154–89) it fell to 30 and latterly to only eleven. By the early 14th century the production of coins had been centralised on London and Canterbury, together with the ecclesiastical mints at York and Canterbury. The silver penny was the principal denomination throughout the Norman period, pieces cut along the lines of the cross on the reverse continuing to serve as halfpence and farthings.

Eight types of penny were struck under William I and five under his son William Rufus, both profiles (left and right) and facing portraits being used in both reigns allied to crosses of various types. Fifteen types were minted under Henry I (1100–35), portraiture having now degenerated to crude caricature, the lines engraved on the coinage dies being built up by means of various punches. Halfpence modelled on the same pattern were also struck, but very sparingly and are very rare.

On Henry's death the succession was contested by his daughter Matilda and his nephew Stephen of Blois. Civil war broke out in 1138 and continued till 1153. Stephen controlled London and its mint, but Matilda and her supporters occupied the West Country and struck their own coins at Bristol. Several of the powerful barons struck their own coins, and there were distinct regional variants of the regal coinage. Of particular interest are the coins

Silver pennies of, from left to right, William I, William Rufus, Henry I and Stephen.

struck from obverse dies with Stephen's portrait erased or defaced, believed to date from 1148 when the usurper was under papal interdict.

Peace was restored in 1153 when it was agreed that Matilda's son Henry should succeed Stephen. On the latter's death the following year, Henry II ascended the throne. Coins of Stephen's last type continued to be minted till 1158, but Henry then took the opportunity to overhaul the coinage which had become irregular and sub-standard during the civil war. The new "Cross Crosslet" coins, usually known as the Tealby coinage (from the hoard of over 5,000 pennies found at Tealby, Lincolnshire in 1807), were produced at 30 mints, but when the recoinage was completed this number was reduced to a dozen. The design of Henry's coins remained virtually the same throughout more than two decades, apart from minor variants. Then, in 1180, a new type, known as the Short Cross coinage, was introduced. This was a vast improvement over the poorly struck Cross Crosslet coins and continued without alteration, not only to the end of the reign of Henry II in 1189, but throughout the reigns of his sons Richard (1189–99) and John (1199–1216) and the first half of the reign of his grandson Henry III (1216–46). Throughout that 66 year period, however, there were minor variations in portraits and lettering which enable numismatists to attribute the HENRICUS coins to specific reigns and periods.

"Tealby" type penny (top), and
"Short Cross" penny of Henry II.

The style and workmanship of the Short Cross coinage deteriorated in the reign of Henry III. By the 1220s coin production was confined to the regal mints at London and Canterbury, the sole exception being the ecclesiastical mint maintained by the Abbot of Bury St Edmunds.

Halfpence and farthings were briefly struck in 1221–30, though halfpence are now extremely rare and so far only a solitary farthing has been discovered.

By the middle of this reign the coinage was in a deplorable state, being poorly struck, badly worn and often ruthlessly clipped. In 1247 Henry ordered a new coinage and in this the arms of the cross on the reverse were extended to the rim as a safeguard against clipping. This established a pattern of facing portrait and long cross on obverse and reverse respectively that was to continue till the beginning of the 16th century. Several provincial mints were re-activated to assist with the recoinage but they were all closed down again by 1250, only the regal mints at London and Canterbury and the ecclesiastical mints at Durham and Bury St Edmunds remaining active.

"Long Cross" pennies of Henry III (top),
and Edward I.

In 1257 Henry tentatively introduced a gold penny (worth 20 silver pence and twice the weight of a silver penny). The coin was undervalued and soon disappeared from circulation.

The Long Cross coinage of Henry III continued under Edward I till 1279 when the king introduced a new coinage in his own name. The penny continued the style of its predecessors, though much better designed and executed; but new denominations were now added. Henceforward halfpence and farthings became a regular issue and, at the same time, a fourpenny coin known as the groat (from French *gros*) was briefly introduced (minting ceased in 1282 and was not revived till 1351). Due to the centralisation of coin production the name of the moneyer was now generally dropped, although it lingered on a few years at Bury St Edmunds. The provincial mints were again revived in 1299–1302 to recoin the lightweight foreign imitations of pennies which had flooded in from the Continent.

The coinage of Edward II (1307–27) differed only in minor respects from that of his father, and a similar pattern prevailed in the first years of Edward III. In 1335 halfpence and farthings below the sterling fineness were struck. More importantly, further attempts were made to introduce gold coins. In 1344 the florin or double

Pre-Treaty Noble of Edward III which contained reference to France in the legend.

leopard of six shillings was introduced, along with its half and quarter. This coinage was not successful and was soon replaced by a heavier series based on the noble of 80 pence (6s. 8d.), half a mark or one third of a pound. The noble originally weighed 138.5 grains but it was successively reduced to120 grains, at which weight it continued from 1351. During this reign the protracted conflict with France known as the Hundred Years' War erupted. Edward III, through his mother, claimed the French throne and inscribed this title on his coins. By the Treaty of Bretigny (1361) Edward temporarily gave up his claim and the reference to France

Noble of Edward IV, issued before he was forced to abandon the throne of England.

was dropped from the coins, but when war was renewed in 1369 the title was resumed, and remained on many English coins until the end of the 18th century. The silver coinage followed the pattern of the previous reign, but in 1351 the groat was re-introduced and with it came the twopence or half-groat. Another innovation was the use of mintmarks at the beginning of the inscriptions. Seven types of cross and one crown were employed from 1334 onwards and their sequence enables numismatists to date coins fairly accurately.

The full range of gold (noble, half-noble and quarter-noble) and silver (groat, half-groat, penny, halfpenny and farthing) continued under Richard II (1377–99). Little attempt was made to alter the facing portrait on the silver coins, by now little more than a stylised caricature anyway.

Noble of Henry IV which was reduced in weight due to the shortage of gold.

Under Henry IV (1399–1413) the pattern of previous reigns prevailed, but in 1412 the weights of the coinage were reduced due to a shortage of bullion. The noble was reduced to 108 grains and its sub-divisions lightened proportionately. The penny was reduced by 3 grains, and its multiples and sub-divisions correspondingly reduced. One interesting change was the reduction of the fleur de lis of France from four to three in the heraldic shield on the reverse of the noble; this change corresponded with the alteration in the arms used in France itself. The Calais mint, opened by Edward III in 1363, was closed in 1411. There was no change in the designs used for the coins of Henry V (1413–22) but greater use was now made of mintmarks to distinguish the various periods of production. Coins were

by now produced mainly at London, although the episcopal mints at Durham and York were permitted to strike pennies.

The supply of gold dwindled early in the reign of Henry VI and few nobles were struck after 1426. The Calais mint was re-opened in 1424 and struck a large amount of gold before closing finally in 1440. A regal mint briefly operated at York in 1423–24. Mintmarks were now much more widely used and tended to correspond more closely to the annual trials of the Pyx. The series of civil upheavals known as the Wars of the Roses erupted in this period.

In 1461 Henry VI was deposed by the Yorkist Earl of March after he defeated the Lancastrians at Mortimer's Cross. The Yorkists advanced on London where the victor was crowned Edward IV. At first he continued the gold series of his predecessor, issuing nobles and quarter-nobles, but in 1464 the weight of the penny was reduced to 12 grains and the value of the noble was raised to 100 pence (8s. 4d.). The ryal or rose-

Groat of Richard III (1483–85).

noble of 120 grains, together with its half and quarter, was introduced in 1465 and tariffed at ten shillings or half a pound. The need for a coin worth a third of a pound, however, led to the issue of the angel of 80 grains, worth 6s. 8d., but this was initially unsucessful and very few examples are now extant. The angel derived its name from the figure of the Archangel Michael on the obverse; a cross surmounting a shield appeared on the reverse.

In 1470 Edward was forced to flee to Holland and Henry VI was briefly restored. During this brief period (to April 1471) the ryal was discontinued but a substantial issue of angels and half-angels was made both at London and Bristol. Silver coins were struck at York as well as London and Bristol, the issues of the provincial mints being identified by the initials B or E (Eboracum, Latin for York). Edward defeated the Lancastrians at Tewkesbury and deposed the luckless Henry once more. In his

second reign Edward struck only angels and half-angels as well as silver from the groat to halfpenny. In addition to the three existing mints, silver coins were struck at Canterbury, Durham and the archiepiscopal mint at York. Mintmarks were now much more frequent and varied. Coins with a mark of a halved sun and rose are usually assigned to the reign of Edward IV, but they were probably also struck in the nominal reign of Edward V, the twelve-year-old prince held in the Tower of London under the protection of his uncle Richard, Duke of Gloucester. Coins with this mark on the reverse had an obverse mark of a boar's head, Richard's personal emblem. The brief reign of Richard III (1483–5) came to an end with his defeat at Bosworth and the relatively scarce coins of this period followed the pattern of the previous reigns, distinguished by the sequence of mint marks and the inscription RICAD or RICARD.

In the early years of Henry VII's reign the coinage likewise followed the previous patterns, but in 1489 the first of several radical changes was effected, with the introduction of the gold sovereign of 20 shillings showing a full-length portrait of the monarch seated on an elaborate throne. For reverse, this coin depicted a Tudor rose surmounted by a heraldic shield. A similar reverse appeared on the ryal of 10 shillings, but the angel and angelet retained previous motifs. The silver coins at first adhered to the medieval pattern, with the stylised facing portrait and long cross, but at the beginning of the 16th century a large silver coin, the testoon or shilling of 12 pence, was introduced and adopted a realistic profile of the king, allied to a reverse showing a cross surmounted by the royal arms. The same design was also used for the later issue of groat and half groat.

First coinage Angel of Henry VIII which retained the traditional 23.5 carat fineness.

This established a pattern which was to continue till the reign of Charles I. In the reign of Henry VIII, however, the coinage was subject to considerable debasement. This led to the eventual introduction of 22 carat (.916 fine) gold for the crown while the traditional 23 1/2 carat gold was retained for the angel and ryal. This dual system continued until the angel was discontinued at the outset of the Civil War in 1642; latterly it had been associated with the ceremony of touching for "King's Evil" or scrofula, a ritual used by the early Stuart monarchs to bolster their belief in the divine right of kings.

Under the Tudors and Stuarts the range and complexity of the gold coinage increased, but it was not until the reign of Edward VI that the silver series was expanded. In 1551 he introduced the silver crown of five shillings, the first English coin to bear a clear date on the obverse. Under Mary dates were extended to the shilling and sixpence.

The mixture of dated and undated coins continued under Elizabeth I, a reign remarkable for the range of denominations—nine gold and

The magnificent second coinage Rose-Ryal of James I (1603–25).

eight silver. The latter included the sixpence, threepence, threehalfpence and threefarthings, distinguished by the rose which appeared behind the Queen's head.

The coinage of James I was even more complex, reflecting the king's attempts to unite his dominions. The first issue bore the legend ANG: SCO (England and Scotland), but from 1604 this was altered to MAG: BRIT (Great Britain). This period witnessed new denominations, such as the rose-ryal and spur-ryal, the unite, the Britain crown and the thistle crown, and finally the laurel of 20 shillings and its sub-divisions.

In the reign of Elizabeth experiments began with milled coinage under Eloi Mestrell. These continued sporadically in the 17th century, culminating in the beautiful coins struck by Nicholas Briot (1631–39). A branch mint was established at Aberystwyth in 1637 to refine and coin silver from the Welsh mines. Relations between King and Parliament deteriorated in the reign of Charles I and led to the Civil War (1642). Parliament controlled London but continued to strike coins in the King's name. The Royalists struck coins, both in pre-war and new types, at Shrewsbury, Oxford, Bristol, Worcester, Exeter, Chester, Hereford and other Royalist strongholds, while curious siege pieces were pressed into service at Newark, Pontefract and Scarborough.

After the execution of Charles I in 1649 the Commonwealth was proclaimed and gold and silver coins were now inscribed in English instead of Latin. Patterns portraying Cromwell and a crowned shield restored Latin in 1656. Plans for milled coinage were already being considered before the Restoration of the monarchy in 1660. Hammered coinage appeared initially, resuming the style of coins under Charles I, but in 1662 the hand-hammering of coins was abandoned in favour of coins struck on the mill and screw press. The hammered coins of 1660–62 were undated and bore a crown mintmark, the last vestiges of medievalism in British coinage.

COIN *grading*

Condition is the secret to the value of virtually anything, whether it be antiques, jewellery, horses or second-hand cars—and coins are certainly no exception. When collecting coins it is vital to understand the recognised standard British system of grading, i.e. accurately assessing a coin's condition or state of wear. Grading is an art which can only be learned by experience and so often it remains one person's opinion against another's, therefore it is important for the beginner or inexperienced collector to seek assistance from a reputable dealer or knowledgeable numismatist when making major purchases.

The standard grades as used in the Price Guide are as follows:

UNC	**Uncirculated** A coin that has never been in circulation, although it may show signs of contact with other coins during the minting process.
EF	**Extremely Fine** A coin in this grade may appear uncirculated to the naked eye but on closer examination will show signs of minor friction on the highest surface.
VF	**Very Fine** A coin that has had very little use, but shows signs of wear on the high surfaces.
F	**Fine** A coin that has been in circulation and shows general signs of wear, but with all legends and date clearly visible.

Other grades used in the normal grading system are:

BU	**Brilliant Uncirculated** As the name implies, a coin retaining its mint lustre.
Fair	A coin extensively worn but still quite recognisable and legends readable.
Poor	A coin very worn and only just recognisable.

Other abbreviations used in the Price Guide are:

Obv	**Obverse**
Rev	**Reverse**

Other abbreviations, mintmarks, etc. can be identified under the appropriate section of this Yearbook.

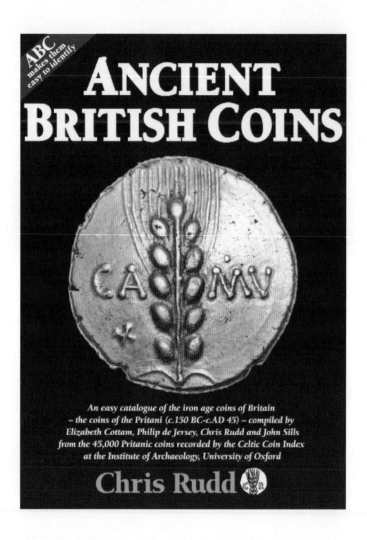

ABC makes them easy to identify

ANCIENT BRITISH COINS

*An easy catalogue of the iron age coins of Britain
– the coins of the Pritani (c.150 BC-c.AD 45) – compiled by
Elizabeth Cottam, Philip de Jersey, Chris Rudd and John Sills
from the 45,000 Pritanic coins recorded by the Celtic Coin Index
at the Institute of Archaeology, University of Oxford*

Chris Rudd

With 2,000 twice-size coin photos *ABC* is the easiest way to identify ancient British coins. *"A great book"* says Professor Sir Barry Cunliffe. *"Superb illustrations"* says Robert Van Arsdell. *"I cannot recommend ABC too highly"* says Dr Daphne Nash Briggs. £75 + postage. Chris Rudd, PO Box 222, Aylsham, Norfolk NR11 6TY. *Tel* 01263 735 007. *Email* liz@celticcoins.com

A SIMPLIFIED PRICE GUIDE TO

ANCIENT COINS
USED IN BRITAIN

PART 1 *Ancient British*

The prices given in this section are those that you would expect to pay from a reputable dealer and not the prices at which you could expect to sell coins.

The list below, which has been generously provided by Celtic coin dealer Elizabeth Cottam of Chris Rudd, contains most of the commonly available types: a fully comprehensive guide is beyond the scope of this book. Prices are for coins with good surfaces which are not weakly struck or struck from worn dies. Examples which are struck from worn or damaged dies can be worth considerably less. Particularly attractive examples of bronze Celtic coins command a very high premium. Where a price is given for an issue of which there are many varieties, the price is for the most common type. The illustrations are representative examples only and are not shown actual size.

UNINSCRIBED COINAGE

	F	VF	EF
GOLD STATERS			
Broad Flan	£700	£1750	£5500
Gallic War Uniface	£225	£300	£650
Remic types	£250	£400	£775
Wonersh types	£250	£450	£1800
Chute	£200	£300	£600
Cheriton	£250	£450	£895
Iceni (various types)	£300	£500	£1300
Norfolk "wolf" type			
fine gold	£250	£450	£1300
brassy gold	£175	£300	£675
very debased	£120	£200	£450
Corieltavi (various types)	£200	£400	£850
Dobunni	£250	£500	£1300
Whaddon Chase types	£275	£450	£1250

Cheriton Smiler gold stater

GOLD QUARTER STATERS			
Gallic Imported Types	£80	£150	£385
Kent types	£200	£300	£500
Southern types	£125	£200	£350
Iceni	£150	£250	£425
Corieltavi	£125	£200	£450
Dobunni	£175	£300	£550
East Wiltshire	£300	£500	£950
Durotriges	£120	£200	£375
North Thames types	£220	£300	£500

SILVER COINAGE			
Armorican billion staters	£80	£150	£425
Kent Types	£150	£300	£650
South Thames types	£120	£175	£350

Cranborne Chase silver stater

	F	VF	EF
Iceni ('crescent' types)	£35	£75	£175
Iceni ('Norfolk God' types)	£60	£100	£275
Corieltavi	£50	£100	£200
Dobunni	£80	£125	£275
Durotriges full stater			
fine silver	£80	£175	£320
base silver	£30	£55	£160
Durotriges quarter silver	£25	£35	£80

(Note—most examples are for base coins as better quality items are appreciably higher)

	F	VF	EF
North Thames types	£110	£185	£350

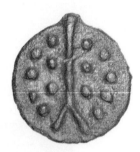

Hengistbury cast bronze

POTIN COINAGE

	F	VF	EF
Kent	£25	£50	£125

BRONZE COINAGE

	F	VF	EF
Durotriges debased stater	£30	£60	£120
Durotriges cast bronze	£65	£125	£220
North Thames types. Various issues from:	£45	£110	£420

INSCRIBED CELTIC COINAGE

CANTIACI

	F	VF	EF
Dubnovellaunos			
stater	£320	£595	£1400
silver unit	£135	£220	£550
bronze unit	£55	£175	£375
Vosenos			
stater	£1100	£2500	£5100
quarter stater	£295	£585	£1200
silver unit	£140	£295	£650
Sam			
stater (unique)	—	—	—
silver unit	£185	£350	£795
bronze unit	£110	£260	£500
Eppillus			
stater	£1100	£2000	£4500
quarter stater	£150	£255	£550
silver unit	£75	£145	£375
bronze unit	£65	£125	£475
bronze minim	£85	£165	£295
Anarevitos			
stater (unique)			—
Touto			
silver unit	£200	£450	£850
Verica			
silver unit	£200	£350	£675
bronze unit	£165	£300	£625
Sego			
stater	£525	£1000	£3200
quarter stater	£220	£500	£1200
silver unit	£150	£350	£650
silver minim	£80	£200	£425
bronze unit	£80	£165	£475
Amminus			
silver unit	£165	£325	£675
silver minim	£110	£215	£450
bronze unit	£85	£160	£525
Solidus			
silver unit	£525	£1100	£2300
silver minim	£525	£1100	£1550

Vosenos gold quarter stater

Verica gold stater

	F	VF	EF
REGINI & ATREBATES			
Commios			
stater	£575	£1550	£3000
silver unit	£80	£160	£325
silver minim	£65	£125	£275
Tincomarus			
stater	£450	£875	£2200
quarter stater	£150	£250	£450
silver unit	£75	£145	£295
silver minim	£65	£125	£195
Eppillus			
quarter stater	£160	£245	£550
silver unit	£80	£145	£320
Verica			
stater	£275	£550	£1250
quarter stater	£155	£275	£425
silver unit	£55	£150	£250
silver minim	£50	£120	£225
Epaticcus			
stater	£1000	£2000	£4200
silver unit	£50	£100	£265
silver minim	£55	£110	£275
Caratacus			
silver unit	£165	£320	£465
silver minim	£110	£220	£325
VECTUARII			
Crab			
silver unit	£165	£325	£675
silver minim	£110	£295	£420
ICENI			
Cani Duro			
silver unit	£115	£275	£575
Antedios			
stater	£425	£1000	£2500
silver unit	£40	£65	£195
silver half unit	£45	£100	£150
Ecen			
stater	£425	£1000	£2500
silver unit	£45	£85	£185
silver half unit	£50	£100	£165
Saenu			
silver unit	£65	£125	£295
Aesu			
silver unit	£65	£125	£295
Ale Scavo			
silver unit	£250	£500	£1200
Esuprasto			
silver unit	£425	£1000	£1900
CORIELTAVI			
Cat			
silver unit	£400	£1000	£2000
silver half unit (unique)			—
VEPO			
stater	£450	£1000	£2500
silver unit	£85	£150	£320
Esuprasu			
stater	£350	£675	£1300
silver unit	£165	£310	£565

Tincomarus gold stater

Ale Scavo silver unit

Vep CorF gold stater

	F	VF	EF
Aunt Cost			
stater	£275	£575	£1300
silver unit	£90	£195	£325
silver half unit	£90	£165	£320
Lat Ison			
stater	£1000	£2000	£4200
silver unit	£165	£425	£1150
silver half unit	£160	£300	£550
Dumnocoveros Tigirseno			
stater	£850	£2000	£3600
silver unit	£100	£195	£500
silver half unit	£100	£200	£600
Volisios Dumnocoveros			
stater	£350	£675	£1300
silver unit	£100	£185	£495
silver half unit	£100	£195	£475
Volisios Cartivellaunos			
stater	£1000	£2000	£4000
silver half unit	£300	£675	£1150
Volisios Dumnovellaunos			
stater	£320	£745	£1600
silver half unit	£150	£325	£650

Catti gold stater

DOBUNNI
	F	VF	EF
Bodvoc			
stater	£1000	£2250	£3200
quarter stater (unique)			—
silver unit	£200	£500	£875
Corio			
stater	£275	£550	£1500
quarter stater	£200	£350	£650
Comux			
stater	£285	£550	£1500
Catti			
stater	£285	£555	£1500
Inamn			
plated stater (unique)			—
silver unit (unique)			—
Anted			
stater	£350	£700	£1500
silver unit	£60	£125	£300
Eisu			
stater	£450	£750	£1575
silver unit	£75	£125	£325

Dumno Tigir Seno gold stater

TRINOVANTES
	F	VF	EF
Dubnovellaunos			
stater	£275	£475	£1300
quarter stater	£175	£350	£600
silver unit	£75	£150	£350
silver half unit	£100	£200	£450
bronze unit	£65	£130	£275

CATUVELLAUNI
	F	VF	EF
Addedomaros			
stater	£300	£450	£1250
quarter stater	£300	£550	£650
silver unit	£100	£200	£400
silver half unit	£100	£200	£450
bronze unit	£35	£75	£275

Addedomaros gold stater

	F	VF	EF
Tasciovanos			
stater	£250	£450	£1500
quarter stater	£165	£250	£495
silver unit	£85	£165	£375
bronze unit	£60	£135	£250
bronze half unit	£60	£135	£275
Andoco			
stater	£350	£550	£1600
quarter stater	£200	£420	£750
silver unit	£155	£400	£750
bronze unit	£85	£220	£350
Dias			
silver unit	£100	£200	£400
bronze unit	£50	£150	£400
Rues			
bronze unit	£50	£150	£400
Cat			
plated silver unit (unique)			—

Tasciovanos gold stater

CATUVELLAUNI & TRINOVANTES

	F	VF	EF
Cunobelinus			
stater	£250	£450	£1600
quarter stater	£150	£250	£475
silver unit	£85	£165	£475
bronze unit	£60	£135	£375
bronze half	£60	£135	£275
Trocc			
bronze unit	£50	£150	£500
Agr			
quarter stater	£125	£250	£850
silver unit	£100	£200	£500
bronze unit (only two)		(too rare to price)	
Dubn			
quarter stater (only three)		(too rare to price)	

Cunobelinus gold stater

Illustrations by courtesy of Chris Rudd

The impressive Chawton hoard of Celtic coins discovered by a metal detectorists at Chawton in Hampshire in 2012 and the subject of a number of articles in Coin News during 2016. The Chawton hoard was originally reported as the "Vine Leaf Hoard".

A SIMPLIFIED PRICE GUIDE TO

ANCIENT COINS USED IN BRITAIN

PART II

Roman Britain

The list below has been generously provided by coin dealer Mike Vosper. These prices are for the most common types unless otherwise noted. In most cases, especially with large bronze coins, the price for coins in extremely fine condition will be <u>much</u> higher than the price for the same coin in very fine condition as early bronze coins are seldom found in hoards and perfect, undamaged examples are rarely available.

The illustrations provided are a representative guide to assist with identification only.

REPUBLICAN COINAGE 280–41 BC

	FROM F	VF	EF
Republican			
Quadrigatus (or Didrachm) (Janus/Quadriga)	£135	£450	£1950
Victoriatus (Jupiter/Victory)	£35	£100	£495
+Denarius (Roma/Biga)	£20	£75	£425
+Denarius (other types)	£30	£85	£495
Denarius (Gallic warrior—L.Hostilius Saserna)	£400	£1100	£6500
Quinarius	£25	£80	£450
Cast Aes Grave, As	£400	£1100	—
Struck As/Semis/Litra	£60	£200	—
Struck Triens/Quadrands	£50	£150	—

Gnaeus Pompey Junior

IMPERATORIAL COINAGE 49–27 BC

Pompey the Great			
Denarius (Hd. of Pompilius/Prow)	£150	£450	£2500
Scipio			
Denarius (Jupiter/Elephant	£100	£295	£1500
Cato Uticensis			
Quinarius (Bacchus/Victory)	£45	£125	£650
Gnaeus Pompey Junior			
Denarius (Roma/Hispania)	£110	£325	£1650
Sextus Pompey			
Denarius (his bust)	£275	£750	£4000
Denarius (other types)	£190	£565	£3000
As	£160	£565	—
Julius Caesar			
Aureus	£1200	£3300	£22,000
Denarius ("elephant" type)	£150	£475	£2200
Denarius (Ceasar portrait)	£450	£1400	£7000
Denarius (heads of godesses)	£115	£375	£1800

Julius Caesar

	FROM F	VF	EF
Brutus			
Denarius (his portrait/EID MAR)........	£25,000	£70,000	£325,000
Denarius (others)..............................	£150	£450	£2500
Cassius			
Denarius...	£125	£400	£1850
Ahenobarbus			
Denarius	£450	£1200	£6000
Mark Antony			
Denarius ("Galley" type)	£75	£265	£1700
Denarius (with portrait)	£100	£375	£2000
Denarius (other types)	£70	£295	£1950
Mark Antony & Lepidus			
AR quinarius	£75	£185	£1000
Mark Antony & Octavian			
AR denarius	£175	£595	£2750
Quninarius	£55	£165	£900
Mark Antony & Lucius Antony			
AR denarius	£345	£850	£4200
Mark Antony & Octavia			
AR Cistophorus	£225	£650	£3200
Cleopatra VII & Mark Antony			
AR denarius	£1400	£4200	£31,000
Fulvia			
AR quinarius	£125	£350	£2000
Octavian (later known as Augustus)			
Gold Aureus	£1200	£4000	£22,000
Denarius	£125	£350	£2200
Quinarius (ASIA RECEPTA)	£50	£125	£750
Octavian & Divos Julius Caesar			
AE sestertius	£275	£1500	—

Brutus

Mark Antony & Octavian

IMPERIAL COINAGE—Julio-Claudian Dynasty 27BC–AD 69

	FROM F	VF	EF
Augustus			
Gold Aureus (Caius & Lucius Caesar)	£1200	£3200	£16500
AR Cistophorus.................................	£200	£650	£3200
Denarius (Caius & Lucius Caesar)	£60	£175	£850
Denarius (other types)	£65	£215	£1200
AR quinarius	£50	£150	£850
Sestertius (large SC)	£135	£395	£1850
Dupondius or as (large SC)..............	£55	£160	£750
Quadrans	£20	£50	£250
Divus Augustus (struck under Tiberius)			
As	£70	£200	£1200
Augustus & Agrippa			
Dupondius (Crocodile rev)	£70	£200	£1200
Livia			
Sestertius or Dupondius	£200	£595	£4000
Gaius Caesar			
AR denarius	£375	£1350	£3950
Tiberius			
Aureus (Tribute penny)	£1000	£2850	£10000
Denarius (Tribute penny)	£85	£225	£1000
Sestertius	£195	£595	£3200
Dupondius	£165	£550	£2750
As	£75	£200	£1000
Drusus			
Sestertius..	£275	£900	£4500
As (Large S C)..................................	£75	£200	£1200
Caligula			
Denarius (rev. portrait)	£450	£1300	£6750
Sestertius (PIETAS & Temple)	£300	£1750	£8500
As (VESTA).......................................	£95	£275	£1450

Augustus

Tiberius

	FROM F	VF	EF
Agrippa (struck under Caligula)			
As..	£65	£170	£1000
Germanicus (struck under Caligula or Claudius)			
As (Large S C)	£65	£190	£1000
Agrippina Senior (struck under Caligula)			
Sestertius (Carpentum)....................	£500	£1450	£9000
Nero & Drusus (struck under Caligula)			
Dupondius (On horseback, galloping)	£185	£650	£3750
Claudius			
Aureus ("DE BRITANN" type)	£1650	£5000	£33000
Denarius as above	£400	£1700	£9000
Didrachm as above	£375	£1100	£6000
Denarius other types	£375	£950	£6000
Sestertius	£165	£500	£3750
Dupondius	£60	£200	£1500
As	£45	£140	£1000
Quadrans	£20	£50	£295
Irregular British Sestertius...............	£30	£85	£495
Irregular British As	£20	£65	£375
Claudius & Agrippina Junior or Nero			
Denarius	£450	£1350	£7250
Nero Cludius Drusus (struck under Claudius)			
Sestertius	£250	£850	£6000
Antonia (struck under Claudius)			
Dupondius	£150	£450	£2750
Britannicus			
Sestertius	£6500	£28000	—
Nero			
Aureus	£1000	£3200	£16000
Denarius	£95	£260	£1750
Sestertius	£135	£550	£3500
Sestertius (Port of Ostia)	£1800	£6000	£50000
Dupondius	£85	£250	£1500
As	£50	£165	£1200
Semis	£45	£125	£625
Quadrans	£20	£75	£325
Civil War			
Denarius	£190	£550	£3000
Galba			
Denarius	£110	£350	£2000
Sestertius	£170	£495	£3000
Dupondius	£180	£500	£2750
As	£110	£325	£1950
Otho			
Denarius	£195	£585	£3500
Vitellius			
Denarius	£100	£265	£1750
Sestertius	£1000	£2800	£18750
Dupondius	£350	£900	£5500
As	£195	£500	£3000

Caligula

Agrippina Senior

Claudius

Nero

IMPERIAL COINAGE—Flavian Dynasty AD 69–96

Vespasian			
Aureus	£850	£2500	£13750
Denarius	£30	£80	£500
Denarius (IVDAEA)	£80	£200	£1250
Sestertius	£195	£595	£4500
Dupondius	£70	£210	£1500
As	£55	£195	£1250
Titus			
Aureus	£900	£2650	£14500
Denarius as Caesar	£40	£115	£750
Denarius as Augustus	£45	£130	£950

Galba

	FROM F	VF	EF
Sestertius	£135	£450	£3500
Dupondius	£50	£175	£1250
As	£45	£160	£1250
As (IVDAEA CAPTA)	£170	£500	£2950
Julia Titi			
Denarious	£190	£565	£3000
Domitian			
Aureus	£950	£2400	£13000
Cistophorus	£125	£400	£2000
Denarius as Caesar	£35	£85	£450
Denarius as Augustus	£25	£75	£395
Sestertius	£95	£340	£1750
Dupondius	£35	£120	£1200
As	£35	£110	£750
Ae Semis	£30	£90	£500
Ae Quadrands...................................	£25	£70	£325
Domitia			
Cistophorus	£235	£695	£3500

Titus

Domitian

IMPERIAL COINAGE — Adoptive Emperors AD 96–138

Nerva			
Aureus	£1850	£5600	£31000
Denarius	£50	£120	£750
Sestertius	£140	£500	£3250
Sestertius (Palm-tree)	£500	£1600	£1000
Dupondius	£70	£225	£1200
As	£65	£160	£1000
Trajan			
Aureus	£950	£2400	£12750
Denarius	£25	£60	£400
Denarius (Trajan's Column)	£40	£130	£795
Sestertius	£65	£225	£1500
Sestertius (Dacian rev.)	£75	£250	£1600
Dupondius or as	£35	£100	£600
Ae Quadrands	£25	£65	£395
Plotina, Marciana or Matidia			
Denarius	£425	£1300	£4250
Hadrian			
Aureus	£950	£2600	£14500
Cistophourus	£120	£450	£1950
Denarius (Provinces)	£45	£135	£800
Denarius other types	£25	£75	£500
Sestertius	£75	£230	£1450
Sestertius (RETITVTORI province types)	£135	£420	£2750
Sestertius (Britannia std)	£3000	£10000	—
Dupondius or As	£35	£120	£675
As (Britannia std)	£210	£650	—
Ae Semiis or Quadrands	£30	£90	£475
Eygpt, Alexandrian Billon Tetradrachm	£30	£85	£495
Sabina			
Denarius	£30	£85	£495
Sestertius	£115	£365	£2200
As or Dupondius	£70	£195	£1100
Aelius Ceasar			
Denarius	£70	£200	£1200
Sestertius	£145	£450	£2750
As or Dupondius	£65	£100	£1200

Nerva

Trajan

Hadrian

	FROM F	VF	EF

IMPERIAL COINAGE — The Antonines AD 138–193

Antoninus Pius

	FROM F	VF	EF
Aureus	£750	£2000	£1000
Denarius	£20	£45	£250
Sestertius Britannia seated	£500	£1400	£12000
Sestertius other types	£40	£135	£950
As - Britannia rev.	£65	£200	£1450
Dupondius or As other types	£25	£75	£395

Antoninus Pius & Marcus Aurelius

Denarius (bust each side)	£30	£100	£550

Diva Faustina Senior

Denarius	£20	£45	£295
Sestertius	£45	£145	£795
As or Dupondius	£25	£80	£450

Marcus Aurelius

Aureus	£850	£2400	£13200
Denarius as Caesar	£22	£65	£350
Denarius as Augustus	£20	£50	£295
Sestertius	£45	£160	£1000
As or Dupondius	£25	£75	£450

Faustina Junior

Denarius	£20	£60	£395
Sestertius	£40	£175	£1200
As or Dupondius	£28	£85	£495

Lucius Verus

Denarius	£25	£75	£450
Sestertius	£45	£200	£1200
As or Dupondius	£30	£100	£575

Lucilla

Denarius	£20	£65	£375
Sestertius	£65	£180	£1200
As or Dupondius	£30	£95	£575

Commodus

Aureus	£1050	£2950	£15500
Denarius as Caesar	£28	£75	£475
Denarius as Augustus	£18	£50	£350
Sestertius	£45	£160	£1000
Sestertius (VICT BRIT)	£150	£500	£3250
As or Dupondius	£25	£85	£495

Crispina

Denarius	£25	£75	£425
Sestertius	£70	£225	£1350
As or Dupondius	£35	£115	£675

IMPERIAL COINAGE — The Severan Dynasty AD 193–235

Pertinax

Denarius	£225	£645	£3750
Sestertius	£500	£1750	£12500

Didius Julianus

Denarius	£395	£1250	£7500
Sestertius or Dupondius	£325	£1000	£7950

Manlia Scantilla or Didia Clara

Denarius	£395	£1250	£8500

Pescennius Niger

Denarius	£270	£750	£4750

Clodius Albinus

Denarius as Caesar	£45	£130	£675
Denarius as Augustus	£85	£265	£1450
Sestertius	£275	£800	£5000
As	£85	£250	£1350

Antoninus Pius

Marcus Aurelius

Faustina Junior

Lucius Verus

Commodus

	FROM F	VF	EF
Septimius Severus			
Aureus	£900	£2500	£13750
Aureus (VICT BRIT)	£1200	£3500	£22000
+Denarius (Mint of Rome)	£15	£35	£205
+Denarius (Mints of Emesa & Laodicea)	£20	£45	£235
Denarius (LEG XIIII)	£30	£85	£475
Denarius (VICT BRIT)	£25	£90	£450
Sestertius other types	£75	£240	£1650
Sestertius (VICT BRIT)....................	£350	£1000	£7000
Dupondius or as	£50	£160	£1000
Dupondius or As (VICT BRIT)	£125	£365	£2200
Julia Domna			
Denarius	£15	£40	£245
Sestertius	£75	£230	£1450
As or Dupondius	£50	£160	£950
Caracalla			
Aureus (VICT BRIT)	£1350	£3500	£22000
Denarius as Caesar	£15	£45	£275
Denarius as Augustus	£15	£40	£250
Denarius (VICT BRIT)	£30	£95	£495
Antoninianus	£25	£75	£450
Sestertius	£100	£295	£1750
Sestertius (VICT BRIT)....................	£300	£860	£6500
Dupondius or As	£50	£165	£950
Dupondius or As (VICT BRIT)	£100	£300	£1750
Plautilla			
Denarius	£25	£75	£450
Geta			
Denarius as Caesar	£15	£45	£275
Denarius as Augustus	£25	£70	£450
Denarius (VICT BRIT)	£30	£95	£595
Sestertius	£125	£350	£2000
Sestertius (VICT BRIT)....................	£250	£770	£4750
Dupondius or as	£75	£230	£1450
As (VICT BRIT)	£120	£340	£2200
Macrinus			
Antoninianus	£90	£275	£1600
Denarius	£40	£125	£750
Sestertius	£175	£400	£3250
Diadumenian			
Denarius	£75	£195	£1000
Dupondius or As	£135	£395	£2500
Elagabalus			
Aureus	£1200	£3500	£17500
Antoninianus	£20	£65	£425
Denarius	£15	£35	£225
Sestertius	£100	£320	£1850
Dupondius or As	£60	£175	£1000
Julia Paula			
Denarius	£30	£110	£575
Aquilia Severa			
Denarius	£55	£185	£1200
Julia Soaemias			
Denarius	£30	£75	£450
Dupondius or As	£65	£225	£1350
Julia Maesa			
Denarius	£15	£45	£275
Sestertius	£80	£250	£1750
Severus Alexander			
Aureus	£900	£2400	£13500
Denarius as Caesar	£65	£200	£1200
Denarius as Augustus	£15	£35	£260
Sestertius	£35	£100	£575
Dupondius or As	£25	£95	£475

Septimus Severus

Julia Domna

Geta

Macrinus

Elagabalus

Julia Maesa

	FROM F	VF	EF
Orbiana			
Denarius	£60	£195	£1200
As	£90	£325	£1850
Julia Mamaea			
Denarius	£15	£40	£225
Sestertius	£35	£110	£595

Orbiana

IMPERIAL COINAGE—Military Anarchy AD 235–270

	FROM F	VF	EF
Maximinus I			
Denarius	£15	£45	£275
Sestertius, Dupondius or As	£35	£125	£695
Diva Paula			
Denarius	£150	£450	£2500
Maximus Caesar			
Denarius	£70	£200	£1200
Sestertius	£65	£165	£1200
Gordian I & II, Africanus			
Denarius	£550	£1500	£6500
Sestertius	£550	£1750	£9000
Balbinus & Pupienus			
Antoninianus	£90	£250	£1375
Denarius	£80	£260	£1500
Gordian III			
Antoninianus	£10	£25	£150
Denarius	£15	£35	£195
Sestertius or As	£25	£85	£495
Tranquillina			
Common Colonial	£30	£110	£595
Philip I			
Antoninianus "Animal"			
Lion, stag, antelope, wolf & twins	£20	£60	£350
Other Antoninianus	£10	£25	£145
Sestertius, Dupondius or As	£25	£80	£475
Otacilla Severa			
Antoninianus	£10	£25	£165
Antoninianus "Hipo"	£25	£80	£475
Sestertius	£25	£85	£465
Philip II			
Antoninianus	£10	£22	£135
Antoninianus "Goat"	£20	£65	£375
Sestertius, Dupondius or As	£30	£85	£495
Pacatian			
Antoninianus	£1500	£4850	—
Trajan Decius			
Antoninianus	£10	£25	£135
Antoninianus (DIVI series Augustus, Trajan etc)	£40	£125	£675
Double Sestertius	£260	£950	£4575
Sestertius, Dupondius or As	£25	£85	£475
Herennius Etruscilla			
Antoninianus	£10	£30	£165
Sestertius, Dupondius or As	£30	£110	£675
Herennius Etruscus			
Antoninianus	£16	£55	£325
Sesterius, Dupondius or As	£55	£185	£1200
Hostilian			
Antoninianus as Caesar	£30	£110	£575
Antoninianus as Augustus	£70	£220	£1225
Trebonianus Gallus			
Antoninianus	£10	£26	£150
Sestertius or As	£30	£100	£565
Volusian			
Antoninianus	£10	£35	£225
Sestertius	£30	£110	£1000

Julia Mamaea

Diva Paula

Gordian III

Trajan Decius

Hostilian

	FROM F	VF	EF
Aemilian			
Antoninianus	£45	£140	£795
Valerian I			
Antoninianus	£10	£25	£150
Sestertius & As..............................	£45	£150	£895
Diva Mariniana			
Antoninianus	£35	£125	£675
Gallienus			
Silver Antoninianus	£10	£22	£120
AE Antoninianus	£5	£18	£100
Ae Antoninianus (Military bust)	£10	£25	£175
AE Antoninianus (Legionary)	£70	£220	—
Ae Sestertius	£40	£140	£1000
Ae Denarius	£45	£125	£750
Saloninus			
Ae Antoninianus	£5	£20	£125
Valerian II			
Billon Antoninianus	£10	£35	£195
Saloninus			
Antoninianus	£15	£45	£245
Macrianus & Quietus			
Billon Antoninianus	£45	£135	£750
Regalianus or Dryantilla			
Billon Antoninianus	£1850	£7200	—
Postumus			
Silver Antoninianus	£10	£22	£145
Ae Antoninianus	£5	£20	£100
Radiated sestertius..........................	£45	£175	£1200
Laelianus			
Ae Antoninianus	£250	£750	£3200
Marius			
Ae Antoninianus	£40	£125	£675
Victorinus			
Ae Antoninianus	£5	£16	£100
Tetricus I & II			
Ae Antoninianus	£5	£20	£120
Claudius II Gothicus			
Ae Antoninianus	£5	£20	£120
Egypt, Alexandrian Billon tetradrachm	£5	£25	£125
DIVO Ae Antoninianus	£5	£25	£145
Quintillus			
Ae Antoninianus	£10	£30	£195

Postumus

Aurelian

Severina

IMPERIAL COINAGE—The Illyrian Emperors—AD 270–285

Aurelian			
Ae Antoninianus	£5	£20	£125
Ae Denarius	£20	£65	£375
Vabalathus & Aurelian			
Ae Antoninianus (bust both sides) ...	£20	£65	£375
Vabalathus			
Ae Antoninianus	£350	£950	—
Severina			
Ae Antoninianus	£15	£35	£220
Ae As..	£35	£100	£595
Zenobia			
Eygpt, Alexandrian Billon Tetradrachm	£700	£2500	—
Tacitus			
Ae Antoninianus	£15	£30	£195
Florian			
Ae Antoninianus	£25	£85	£475
Probus			
Gold Aureus	£1150	£3200	£16500
Ae Antoninianus	£10	£20	£145

Tacitus

Florian

	FROM F	VF	EF
Antoninianus (military or imp. Busts RIC G or H)	£10	£35	£195
Antoninianus (Other military or imp NOT BUSTS G or H)	£20	£65	£375
Antoninianus (VICTOR GERM rev.) ..	£10	£35	£175
Egypt, Alexandrian Billon tetradrachm	£5	£15	£95
Carus			
Ae Antoninianus	£15	£40	£225
Numerian			
Ae Antoninianus	£15	£40	£200
Carinus			
Ae Antoninianus	£10	£35	£195
Magna Urbica			
Ae Antoninianus	£95	£250	£1500
Julian of Pannonia			
Ae Antoninianus	£600	£2500	-

Diocletian

IMPERIAL COINAGE—The Tetrarchy AD 285–307

Diocletian			
Gold Aureus	£1000	£2750	£14,950
AR Argenteus	£90	£275	£1200
Ae Antoninianus & Radiates	£10	£25	£145
Ae Follis (London Mint)	£15	£45	£245
As above with LON mint mark	£100	£300	£1600
Ae Follis (other mints)	£10	£30	£150
Ae Follis (Imperial bust)....................	£25	£75	£395
Maximianus			
AR Argenteus	£90	£275	£1200
Ae Follis (London mint)	£15	£40	£215
Ae Follis (other mints)	£10	£30	£150
Ae Follis (MONETA rev.)	£10	£35	£195
Carausius			
Aureus	£8000	£25500	—
Denarius	£400	£1100	£6500
Ae Antoninianus (PAX)	£25	£85	£475
As above but full silvering	£35	£115	£675
Legionary Antoninianus	£70	£200	£1600
Expectate Veni Antoninianus	£100	£300	—
In the name of Diocletian or Maximian	£35	£120	£750
Allectus			
Aureus	£11000	£32000	—
Ae Antoninianus	£25	£90	£600
As above but full silvering	£45	£145	£900
Quinarius	£25	£90	£650
Constantius I			
AR Argenteus	£95	£285	£1300
Ae Follis (London Mint)	£15	£45	£245
Ae Follis (other mints)	£8	£30	£150
Ae Follis (SALVS rev.)	£15	£40	£220
Ae 4 (Lion or Eagle)	£10	£30	£165
Galerius			
Ae Follis (London mint)	£15	£35	£195
Ae Follis (other mints)	£10	£25	£130
Galeria Valeria			
Ae Follis	£30	£80	£435
Severus II			
Ae Follis (London mint)	£35	£100	£550
Ae Follis (other mints)	£30	£85	£445
Ae Radiate	£15	£50	£245
Ae Denarius	£25	£85	£450
Maximinus II			
Ae Follis (London mint)	£15	£40	£225
Ae Follis (other mints)	£5	£20	£100
Ae Radiate	£10	£30	£150

Maximianus

Carausius

Severus II

Maximinus II

	FROM F	VF	EF
Maxentius			
Ae Follis	£10	£30	£175
Romulus			
Ae Follis	£40	£135	£1300
Licinius I			
Billon Argenteus	£45	£150	£795
Ae Follis (London mint)	£10	£25	£145
Ae Follis (other mints)	£10	£20	£100
AE3	£5	£15	£95
Licinius II			
AE3	£10	£25	£135
Alexander or Martinian			
AE	£1500	£4200	—

Licinius II

IMPERIAL COINAGE—Family of Constantine AD 307–350

Constantine I			
Billon Argenteus	£50	£160	£850
Ae Follis (London mint)	£10	£25	£125
As above—helmeted bust	£15	£45	£250
Ae Follis (other mints) as Caesar ...	£15	£50	£275
Ae Follis (other mints) as Augustus	£5	£15	£95
AE3	£5	£15	£95
AE3 (London mint)	£10	£25	£145
AE3 (SARMATIA rev)	£10	£35	£195
Urbs Roma / Wolf & twins AE3/4..........	£5	£20	£100
Constantinopolis AE3/4	£5	£15	£95
Fausta & Helena			
AE3 (London mint)	£50	£155	£765
AE3 (other mints)	£14	£55	£250
Theodora			
AE4	£10	£25	£145
Crispus			
AE3 (London mint)	£10	£30	£135
AE3	£10	£20	£100
Delmatius			
AE3/4	£15	£40	£195
Hanniballianus Rex			
AE4	£75	£225	£1100
Constantine II			
AE3 (London mint)	£10	£25	£135
AE3	£5	£20	£100
AE3/4	£5	£10	£75
Constans			
AE2 (centenionalis)	£10	£30	£165
AE3 (half centenionalis)	£5	£20	£120
AE4	£5	£10	£75
Constantius II			
Gold Solidus	£300	£750	£3950
Siliqua	£25	£85	£475
AE2 (or centenionalis)	£10	£25	£145
AE3 (or half centenionalis)	£5	£15	£95
AE3 (London mint)........................	£15	£45	£225
AE3..	£5	£10	£45

Constantine I

Constantine II

Magnentius

IMPERIAL COINAGE—Late period to the collapse of the Empire AD 350 to end

Magnentius			
Gold Solidus................................	£800	£2200	£12,000
Silver Siliqua	£250	£790	£3850
Double centenionalis	£45	£185	£1200
Centenionalis	£15	£50	£295
Decentius			
Double centenionalis......................	£70	£225	£1450
Centenionalis	£20	£60	£320
Vetranio			
AE2 (centenionalis)	£40	£125	£675
AE3 (half centenionalis)	£30	£100	£550

Vetranio

	FROM F	VF	EF
Nepotian			
AE2 (centenionalis)	£1950	£6500	—
Constantius Gallus			
AE2 (centenionalis)	£15	£35	£175
AE3 (half centenionalis)	£5	£15	£85
Julian II			
Siliqua	£28	£85	£475
AE1	£40	£125	£695
AE3 (helmeted bust)	£10	£28	£150
Anonymous, Serapis + Jupiter AE3	£195	£550	—
Jovian			
AE1	£65	£210	£1100
AE3	£15	£40	£190
Valentinian I			
Sold Solidus	£200	£525	£2200
Silver Milliarense	£165	£550	£2950
Siliqua	£25	£90	£475
AE3	£5	£15	£85
Valens			
Gold Solidus	£200	£500	£2200
Silver Milliarense	£190	£600	£3250
Siliqua	£25	£85	£475
AE3	£5	£15	£85
Procopius			
AE3	£45	£140	£750
Gratian			
Silver Milliarense	£165	£520	£2200
Siliqua	£25	£80	£450
AE3	£5	£15	£85
AE4	£5	£12	£65
Valentinian II			
Solidus	£220	£550	£2500
Siliqua	£25	£85	£465
AE2	£10	£28	£145
AE4	£2	£10	£60
Theodosius I			
Solidus	£225	£550	£2500
Siliqua	£30	£100	£550
AE2	£10	£35	£175
AE3	£8	£30	£150
Aelia Flaccilla			
AE2	£30	£110	£565
AE4	£15	£50	£275
Magnus Maximus			
Solidus (AVGOB)	£4800	£13000	—
Solidus	£800	£2300	£13000
Siliqua	£40	£125	£725
Siliqua (AVGPS)	£730	£2200	—
AE2	£20	£65	£350
Flavius Victor			
Silver Sliqua	£140	£450	£2200
AE4	£30	£75	£395
Eugenius			
Silver Siliqua	£150	£475	£2250
Arcadius			
Gold Solidus	£200	£500	£2200
Silver Siliqua	£25	£90	£475
Silver Half-siliqua	£150	£450	£2300
AE2	£10	£40	£145
AE4	£2	£10	£60

Julian II

Jovian

Valentinian I

Valens

Theodosius I

Arcadius

123

	FROM F	VF	EF
Eudoxia			
AE3	£25	£70	£395
Honorius			
Gold Solidus	£200	£475	£2000
Silver Siliqua	£30	£95	£495
AE4	£5	£15	£85
Constantine III			
Silver Siliqua	£145	£475	£2300
Theodosius II			
Gold Solidus	£200	£475	£2000
Johannes			
AE4	£115	£450	—
Valentinian III			
Gold Soldius.....................	£200	£495	£2000
AE4	£25	£80	£395

Honorius

Theodosius II

Ae = bronze; AE 1, 2, 3, 4 = bronze coins in descending order of size.

Coin illustrations by courtesy of Classical Numismatic Group/ Seaby Coins.

Recent excavations at Ipplepen near Exeter have revealed that the Romans did indeed settle further afield than originally thought (Exeter was considered their furthest settlement west). An open day held by Exeter University proved popular with visitors while some exhibitors got into the swing of things in period dress! (For the full story see COIN NEWS, News & Views, August 2016).

A SIMPLIFIED PRICE GUIDE TO

ENGLISH
HAMMERED COINS

PART I
959-1485

INTRODUCTION
We have taken our starting point for hammered coin prices back to the Anglo-Saxon reign of Edgar; who could reasonably claim to be the first king of All England. Also it is from this time onwards that we start to get regular "portraits" as well as moneyers and mints on most issues. This gives a total of eight rulers to the list of kings prior to the Norman Conquest and most of these have coin issues that can be purchased quite reasonably. It is also worth pointing out here that of course coins had previously been struck in England for approximately 1000 years prior to our listings by Celtic, Roman and earlier Saxon rulers, details of which can be found in more specific publications.

PRICING
The prices given in the following pages are intended to be used as a "Pocket book guide" to the values of the *most common* coins within any denomination of any one reign. The price quoted is what a collector may expect to pay for such a piece in the condition indicated. For more detailed information we recommend the reader to one of the many specialist publications.

GRADING
The prices quoted are for three different grades of condition: Fine (F), Very Fine (VF) and Extremely Fine (EF). A "Fine" coin is assumed to be a fairly worn, circulated, piece but with all or most of the main features and lettering still clear. "Very Fine" is a middle grade with a small amount of wear and most details fairly clear. For this edition we have included the prices for coins in Extremely Fine condition where appropriate, although very few hammered coins actually turn up in this grade (i.e. nearly mint state with hardly any wear). In some instances the prices quoted are theoretically based and are only included to provide a guide. It is important to note that on all hammered coins the very nature of striking, i.e. individually, by hand, means hammered coinage is rarely a straight grade and when listed by a dealer the overall condition will often be qualified by terms such as: *weak in parts, struck off-centre, cracked or chipped flan, double struck,* etc. When applicable the price should be adjusted accordingly.

HISTORY
Below the heading for each monarch we have given a few historical notes as and when they apply to significant changes in the coinage.

EDGAR (First King of All England)
(959–975)

	F	VF	EF
Edgar Penny, non portrait (2 line inscription)	£275	£550	£1300

EDWARD THE MARTYR
(975–978)

	F	VF	EF
Edward, Penny, Portrait	£1500	£4500	—

AETHELRED II
(978–1016)

	F	VF	EF
Aethelred II, Penny, last small cross type (First hand type illustrated)	£140	£275	£725

CNUT
(1016–1035)

	F	VF	EF
Cnut, Penny (short cross type) (*Quatrefoil type illustrated*)	£125	£250	£600

HAROLD I
(1035–40)

	F	VF	EF
Harold I, Penny	£350	£825	£2100

HARTHACANUTE
(1035–42)

	F	VF	EF
Harthacanute, Penny, English Mint (in his own name)	£1300	£4500	—
Harthacanute, Penny, Danish type	£300	£700	—

Danish type

EDWARD THE CONFESSOR
(1042–66)

	F	VF	EF
Edward the Confessor, Penny	£165	£300	£900

HAROLD II
(1066)

	F	VF	EF
Harold II, Penny	£1500	£3350	—

WILLIAM I
(1066–87)

The Norman Conquest had very little immediate effect on the coinage of England. The Anglo-Saxon standard of minting silver pennies was very high and the practice of the moneyer putting his name and mint town on the reverse continued as before, except with William's portrait of course. It is worth noting here that non-realistic, stylised portraits were used until the reign of Henry VII.
There are eight major types of pennies of which the last, the PAXS type, is by far the commonest.

	F	VF	EF
William I, Penny	£275	£525	£1250

WILLIAM II
(1087–1100)

Very little change from his father's reign except that five new types were issued, most of which were much more crudely designed than previous, all are scarce.

	F	VF	EF
William II, Penny	£850	£2250	—

HENRY I
(1100–35)

There are fifteen different types of penny for this reign of which the last two are the most common. Most issues are of a very poor standard both in workmanship and metal, the prices reflect a poor quality of issue.

	F	VF	EF
Henry I, Penny	£160	£450	—
Halfpenny	£1750	£5500	—

STEPHEN
(1135–54)

This is historically a very complicated time for the coinage, mainly due to civil war and a consequential lack of central control in the country which resulted in very poor quality and deliberately damaged pieces. Coins were struck not only in the name of Stephen and his main rival claimant Matilda but also by their supporters. The commonest issue is the "Watford" type; so named, as are many issues, after the area in which a hoard was found.

	F	VF	EF
Stephen, Penny	£250	£700	—

HENRY II
(1154–89)

There were two distinct issues struck during this reign. The first, Cross and Crosslets or "Tealby" coinage (named after Tealby in Lincolnshire), continued to be very poorly made and lasted 20 years. However, in 1180 the new and superior "Short Cross" issue commenced, being issued from only twelve major towns.

	F	VF	EF
Henry II, Penny, Tealby	£110	£300	—

	F	VF	EF
Henry II, Penny, Short Cross	£40	£135	—

RICHARD I
(1189–1199)

There were no major changes during this reign, in fact pennies continued to be struck with his father Henry's name throughout the reign. The coins struck under Richard tend to be rather crude in style.

	F	VF	EF
Richard I, Penny	£65	£210	—

JOHN
(1199–1216)

As with his brother before him, there were no major changes during the reign of King John, and pennies with his father's name were struck throughout the reign, although they tended to be somewhat neater in style than those struck during the reign of Richard I.

	F	VF	EF
John, Penny	£50	£130	£275

HENRY III
(1216–72)

The coinage during Henry III's reign continued as before with the short cross issue. However, in 1247 a new long cross design was introduced to prevent clipping. This design was to last in one form or another for many centuries. A gold penny is known with a throned monarch on the obverse.

	F	VF	EF
Henry III, Penny, Short Cross	£25	£80	£225
Henry III, Penny, Long Cross	£20	£50	£150

EDWARD I
(1272–1307)

After a few years of issuing similar pieces to his father, in 1279 Edward I ordered a major re-coinage. This consisted of well-made pennies, halfpennies and farthings in relatively large quantities, and for a brief period a groat (four pence) was produced. These were often mounted and gilded, price is for an undamaged peice. The pennies are amongst the most common of all hammered coins.

	F	VF	EF
Edward I (and Edward II)			
Groat (often damaged)	£4000	£9500	—
Penny	£20	£45	—
Halfpenny	£20	£60	—
Farthing	£20	£50	—

Edward I penny

EDWARD II
(1307–1327)

The coinage of Edward II differs in only a very few minor details from that of Edward I and are of similar value for the common types.

EDWARD III
(1327–77)

This was a long reign which saw major changes in the coinage, the most significant being the introduction of a gold coinage (based on the Noble, valued at 6s 8d, and its fractions) and a regular issue of a large silver groat (and half groat). The mints were limited to a few episcopal cities but coins of English type were also struck in the newly-acquired Calais.

	F	VF	EF
Gold			
Noble	£850	£2400	£4750
Half Noble	£550	£1600	£3500
Quarter Noble	£300	£650	£1250
Silver			
Groat	£40	£140	£750
Half Groat	£25	£100	£375
Penny	£20	£85	£300
Half Penny	£20	£70	£250
Farthing	£25	£90	£300

Gold Noble

RICHARD II
(1377–1399)

The denominations continued during this reign much as before. However, coins are quite rare mainly due to the lack of bullion gold and silver going into the mints, mainly because of an inbalance with European weights and fineness.

	F	VF	EF
Gold			
Noble	£1250	£3500	—
Half Noble	£1250	£4300	—
Quarter Noble	£425	£1150	—
Silver			
Groat	£500	£1750	—
Half Groat	£250	£850	—
Penny	£75	£300	—
Half Penny	£30	£110	—
Farthing	£125	£435	—

Gold Noble

HENRY IV
(1399–1413)

Because of the continuing problems with the scarcity of gold and silver the coinage was reduced in weight in 1412, towards the end of the reign. All coins of this reign are quite scarce.

	F	VF
Gold		
Noble	£2000	£7500
Half Noble	£2250	£7500
Quarter Noble	£750	£2200
Silver		
Groat	£3000	£9000
Half Groat	£850	£2500
Penny	£475	£1350
Half Penny	£350	£850
Farthing	£750	£2250

Noble

HENRY V
(1413–22)

Monetary reform introduced towards the end of his father's reign in 1412 improved the supply of bullion and hence coins of Henry V are far more common. All of the main denominations continued as before.

	F	VF	EF
Gold			
Noble	£1050	£3150	£5500
Half Noble	£875	£2800	—
Quarter Noble	£375	£800	£1700
Silver			
Groat	£175	£550	—
Half Groat	£130	£375	—
Penny	£30	£150	—
Half Penny	£25	£85	—
Farthing	£350	£850	—

Groat

HENRY VI
(1422–61 and again 1470–71)

Although there were no new denominations during these reigns (see Edward IV below), Henry's first reign saw eleven different issues, each for a few years and distinguished by privy marks, i.e. crosses, pellets, annulets, etc.

HENRY VI *continued*

Gold	F	VF	EF
First reign—			
Noble	£900	£2850	£5250
Half Noble	£725	£2000	£4250
Quarter Noble	£350	£750	£1400
2nd reign—			
Angel	£1850	£5250	—
Half Angel	£4750	£13750	—

Silver			
Groat	£50	£135	£350
Half Groat	£30	£100	£300
Penny	£25	£80	£350
Half Penny	£20	£60	£185
Farthing	£100	£300	—

Noble

EDWARD IV
(1461–70 and again 1471–83)

The significant changes during these reigns were the replacement of the noble by the rose ryal (and revalued at 10 shillings) and the introduction of the angel at the old noble value. We also start to see mint-marks or initial marks appearing, usually at the top of the coin, they were used to denote the period of issue for dating purposes and often lasted for two to three years.

Gold	F	VF	EF
Ryal	£850	£2600	£4250
Half Ryal	£750	£2150	£3600
Quarter Ryal	£450	£1200	£2100
Angel	£875	£2250	£3750
Half Angel	£750	£2175	—

Silver			
Groat	£50	£125	£450
Half Groat	£40	£130	£400
Penny	£25	£110	£350
Half Penny	£20	£80	—
Farthing	£225	£800	—

Angel

RICHARD III
(1483–85)

The close of the Yorkist Plantagenet and Medieval period come together at this time. There are no new significant numismatic changes but most coins of Richard whilst not really rare, continue to be very popular and priced quite high.

Gold	F	VF	EF
Angel	£5650	£17000	—
Half Angel	£8000	£25000	—

Silver			
Groat	£850	£2200	—
Half Groat	£1500	£4350	—
Penny	£450	£1200	—
Half Penny	£350	£1000	—
Farthing	£1650	£4750	—

Groat

PART II
1485–1663

Among the more significant features of the post-Renaissance period as it affected coinage is the introduction of realistic portraiture during the reign of Henry VII. We also have a much wider and varied number of new and revised denominations, for example eleven different gold denominations of Henry VIII and the same number of silver for Elizabeth I. Here we only mention the introduction or changes in the main denominations, giving a value for all of them, once again listing the commonest type.

HENRY VII
(1485–1509)

The gold sovereign of 20 shillings makes its first appearance in 1489 as does the testoon (later shilling) in about 1500. The silver penny was re-designed to a rather crude likeness of the sovereign.

	F	VF	EF
Gold			
Sovereign	£30000	£90,000	—
Ryal	£35000	£135,000	—
Angel	£750	£2000	—
Half Angel	£675	£1800	—
Silver			
Testoon 1/-	£18000	£40,000	—
Groat	£65	£200	£650
Half Groat	£25	£100	£325
Penny	£25	£100	£300
Half Penny	£20	£70	—
Farthing	£450	£1350	—

Profile Groat

HENRY VIII
(1509–47)

After a long initial period of very little change in the coinage, in 1526 there were many, with an attempt to bring the gold/silver ratio in line with the continental currencies. Some gold coins only lasted a short time and are very rare. The crown (in gold) makes its first appearance. Towards the end of the reign we see large issues of debased silver coins (with a high copper content) bearing the well-known facing portrait of the ageing King. These tend to turn up in poor condition.

Gold			
Sovereign	£6000	£22000	—
Half Sovereign	£900	£3000	—
Angel	£750	£1900	£3400
Half Angel	£700	£1000	£2050
Quarter Angel	£775	£2250	—
George Noble	£11000	£36000	—
Half George Noble	£10000	£32000	—
Crown of the rose	£7250	£26500	—
Crown of the double rose	£750	£2400	—
Half Crown of the double rose	£575	£1500	—
Silver			
Testoon 1/-	£900	£4500	—
Groat	£85	£250	£1000
Half Groat	£50	£170	£650
Penny	£35	£110	£425
Half Penny	£25	£85	—
Farthing	£325	£900	—

Gold Sovereign

EDWARD VI
(1547–53)

Some of the coins struck in the first few years of this short reign could really be called Henry VIII posthumous issues as there is continuity in both name and style from his father's last issue. However, overlapping this period are portrait issues of the boy King, particularly shillings (usually poor quality coins). This period also sees the first dated English coin (shown in Roman numerals). In 1551 however, a new coinage was introduced with a restored silver quality from the Crown (dated 1551) down to the new sixpence and threepence.

	F	VF	EF
Gold			
Sovereign (30s)	£7000	£26500	—
Half Sovereign	£1650	£6250	—
Crown	£1900	£6600	—
Half Crown	£1600	£5250	—
Angel	£14000	£40000	—
Half Angel	—	£45000	—
Sovereign (20s)	£5250	£16500	—
Silver			
Crown	£900	£2750	—
Half Crown	£700	£1850	—
Shilling	£115	£400	—
Sixpence	£120	£475	—
Groat	£775	£3750	—
Threepence	£225	£1100	—
Half Groat	£375	£1250	—
Penny	£50	£200	—
Half Penny	£200	£825	—
Farthing	£1250	£4000	—

Crowned bust half sovereign

MARY
(1553–54)

The early coins of Mary's sole reign are limited and continue to use the same denominations as Edward, except that the gold ryal was reintroduced.

	F	VF
Gold		
Sovereign (30s)	£7500	£25000
Ryal	£35000	—
Angel	£2250	£7000
Half Angel	£5500	£15000
Silver		
Groat	£160	£500
Half Groat	£700	£2350
Penny	£600	£2150

Groat

PHILIP & MARY
(1554–58)

After a very short reign alone, Mary married Philip of Spain and they technically ruled jointly (although not for very long in practise) until her death. After her marriage we see both her and Philip on the shillings and sixpences.

	F	VF
Gold		
Angel	£6500	£20000
Half Angel	£14000	—
Silver		
Shilling	£500	£2000
Sixpence	£425	£1650
Groat	£180	£600
Half Groat	£500	£1800
Penny	£60	£220

Shilling

ELIZABETH I
(1558–1603)

As might be expected with a long reign there are a number of significant changes in the coinage which include several new denominations—so many in silver that every value from the shilling downwards was marked and dated to distinguish them. Early on we have old base Edward VI shillings countermarked to a new reduced value (not priced here). Also due to a lack of small change and the expense of making a miniscule farthing we have a new threehalfpence and threefarthings. Finally we see the beginnings of a milled (machine produced) coinage for a brief period from 1561–71.

	F	VF	EF
Gold			
Sovereign (30s)	£6250	£19000	—
Ryal (15s)	£25000	£80000	—
Angel	£1200	£3300	—
Half Angel	£1000	£3000	—
Quarter Angel	£900	£2800	—
Pound (20s)	£3000	£10000	—
Half Pound	£1500	£4750	—
Crown	£1150	£3500	—
Half Crown	£1150	£3400	—
Silver			
Crown	£1500	£4750	—
Half Crown	£1050	£2650	—
Shilling	£90	£425	£1500
Sixpence	£45	£185	£850
Groat	£65	£265	£750
Threepence	£35	£165	£475
Half Groat	£30	£100	£260
Threehalfpence	£40	£170	—
Penny	£20	£75	£215
Threefarthings	£70	£220	—
Half Penny	£30	£100	£165

Shilling

JAMES I
(1603–25)

Although the size of the gold coinage remains much the same as Elizabeth's reign, the name and weight or value of the denominations have several changes, i.e. Pound = Sovereign = Unite = Laurel. A new four shilling gold coin (thistle crown) was introduced. A number of the silver coins now have their value in Roman numerals on the coin. Relatively few angels were made from this period onwards and they are usually found pierced.

	F	VF	EF
Gold			
Sovereign (20s)	£2700	£11500	—
Unite	£675	£1650	£3750
Double crown/half unite	£450	£1100	£2750
Crown	£275	£650	£1750
Thistle Crown	£310	£700	£1750
Half Crown	£240	£500	—
Rose Ryal (30s)	£3250	£12000	—
Spur Ryal (15s)	£7750	£30000	—
Angel (pierced)	£725	£2150	—
Half Angel (Unpierced)	£3500	£12500	—
Laurel	£675	£1700	£3600
Half Laurel	£475	£1400	£3000
Quarter Laurel	£260	£675	£1600
Silver			
Crown	£725	£1900	—
Half Crown	£300	£750	—
Shilling	£65	£250	—
Sixpence	£55	£200	—
Half Groat	£15	£55	£120
Penny	£15	£45	£110
Half Penny	£10	£30	£90

*Gold Unite,
second bust*

Silver Halfcrown

139

CHARLES I
(1625–49)

This reign is probably the most difficult to simplify as there are so many different issues and whole books have been produced on this period alone. From the beginning of the King's reign and throughout the Civil War, a number of mints operated for varying lengths of time, producing both regular and irregular issues. The Tower mint was taken over by Parliament in 1642 but before this a small quantity of milled coinage was produced alongside the regular hammered issues. The Court then moved to Oxford from where, for the next three years, large quantities of gold and silver were struck (including rare triple unites and large silver pounds). The most prolific of the provincial mints were those situated at Aberystwyth, York, Oxford, Shrewsbury, Bristol, Exeter, Truro, Chester and Worcester as well as some smaller mints mainly situated in the West Country. Among the more interesting coins of the period are the pieces struck on unusually-shaped flans at Newark and Pontefract whilst those towns were under siege. As many of the coins struck during the Civil War were crudely struck on hastily gathered bullion and plate, they provide a fascinating area of study. The prices indicated below are the minimum for the commonest examples of each denomination irrespective of town of origin.

	F	VF	EF
Gold			
Triple Unite (£3)	£15000	£42500	—
Unite	£675	£1750	—
Double crown/Half unite	£475	£1350	—
Crown	£275	£625	—
Angel (pierced)	£800	£2750	—
Angel (unpierced)	£2750	£8500	—
Silver			
Pound (20 shillings—Oxford)	£3000	£8500	—
Half Pound (Shrewsbury)	£1350	£3600	—
Crown (Truro, Exeter)	£475	£1200	—
Half Crown	£50	£200	—
Shilling	£40	£160	£900
Sixpence	£35	£150	£800
Groat (Aberystwyth)	£60	£200	£550
Threepence (Aberystwyth)	£50	£185	£475
Half Groat	£20	£60	£160
Penny	£20	£60	£150
Half Penny	£15	£30	£60

Triple unite

Oxford Halfcrown

Above: Newark siege shilling.

THE COMMONWEALTH
(1649–60)

After the execution of Charles I, Parliament changed the design of the coinage. They are simple non- portrait pieces with an English legend.

	F	VF	EF
Gold			
Unite	£2300	£5250	—
Double crown/Half unite	£1500	£4000	—
Crown	£1200	£3500	—
Silver			
Crown	£1000	£2500	£6750
Half Crown	£365	£800	£3500
Shilling	£240	£625	£2350
Sixpence	£225	£550	£1750
Half Groat	£45	£125	£350
Penny	£40	£130	£350
Halfpenny	£30	£80	£175

Crown

CHARLES II
(1660–85)

Although milled coins had been produced for Oliver Cromwell in 1656–58, after the Restoration of the monarchy hammered coins continued to be produced until 1663, when the machinery was ready to manufacture large quantities of good milled pieces.

	F	VF	EF
Gold			
Unite	£1800	£5000	—
Double crown/Half unite	£1400	£4250	—
Crown	£1750	£5250	—
Silver			
Half Crown	£250	£800	—
Shilling	£150	£575	—
Sixpence	£125	£450	—
Fourpence	£35	£120	£275
Threepence	£30	£100	£225
Twopence	£20	£55	£160
Penny	£25	£65	£175

Halfcrown

A COMPREHENSIVE PRICE GUIDE
TO THE COINS OF

THE
UNITED KINGDOM
1656–2015
including

*England, Scotland,
Isle of Man,
Guernsey, Jersey, Alderney,
also Ireland*

When referring to this price guide one must bear a number of important points in mind. The points listed here have been taken into consideration during the preparation of this guide and we hope that the prices given will provide a true reflection of the market at the time of going to press. Nevertheless, the publishers can accept no liability for the accuracy of the prices quoted.

1. "As struck" examples with flaws will be worth less than the indicated price.
2. Any coin which is particularly outstanding, with an attractive natural toning or in superb state will command a much *higher* price than that shown.
3. These prices refer strictly to the British market, and do not reflect outside opinions.
4. Some prices given for coins not seen in recent years are estimates based on a knowledge of the market.
5. In the case of coins of high rarity, prices are not generally given.
6. In the listing, "—" indicates, where applicable, one of the following:
    a. Metal or bullion value only
    b. Not usually found in this grade
    c. Not collected in this condition
7. Proof coins are listed in FDC under the UNC column.
8. All prices are quoted in £ sterling, exclusive of VAT (where applicable).

FIFTY SHILLINGS

	F	VF	EF

OLIVER CROMWELL (1656–58)

	F	VF	EF
1656	£18,000	£45,000	£130,000

Opinions differ as to whether the portrait coinage of Oliver Cromwell was ever meant for circulation but for the sake of completeness it has been decided to include it in this Yearbook. The fifty shillings gold coin is unique as it was only struck during Cromwell's time using the same dies that were used for the broad or 20 shillings coin but with a weight of approximately 2.5 times that of the broad.

FIVE GUINEAS

CHARLES II (1660–85)

	F	VF	EF
1668 First bust	£3000	£7000	£22000
1668 — Elephant below bust	£2750	£6000	£22000
1669 —	£2750	£6775	—
1669 — Elephant	£3300	£7000	—
1670 —	£2750	£7000	£22000
1670 Proof	—	—	£135000
1671 —	£3000	£7000	£24000
1672 —	£2750	£7000	£22000
1673 —	£2750	£7000	£22000
1674 —	£3500	£7500	£25000
1675 —	£3000	£7000	£24000
1675 — Elephant	£3200	£8000	—
1675 — Elephant & Castle below bust...	£3750	£8000	£30000
1676 —	£3000	£6500	£22000
1676 — Elephant & Castle	£3000	£7500	£25000
1677 —	£3200	£7000	£24500
1677/5 — Elephant	£3500	£8000	£27500
1677 — Elephant & Castle	£3200	£7000	£24000
1678/7 — 8 over 7	£2700	£7000	£22000
1678/7 — Elephant & Castle	£3250	£7500	£24000
1678/7 Second Bust	£3000	£7000	£22000
1679 —	£2700	£7000	£22000
1680 —	£2750	£7000	£22000
1680 — Elephant & Castle	£3250	£7000	£24000
1681 —	£3000	£6750	£24000
1681 — Elephant & Castle	£3000	£7000	£24000
1682 —	£2700	£6500	£22000
1682 — Elephant & Castle	£2750	£7000	£22500
1683 —	£3000	£7000	£24000
1683 — Elephant & Castle	£3000	£7500	£25000
1684 —	£2600	£6500	£22000
1684 — Elephant & Castle	£2750	£7000	£22500

Charles II

JAMES II (1685–88)

	F	VF	EF
1686	£3500	£8000	£28000
1687	£3250	£8000	£25000
1687 Elephant & Castle	£3300	£7750	£25000
1688	£3300	£7500	£24000
1688 Elephant & Castle	£3500	£8000	£26500

	F	VF	EF

WILLIAM AND MARY (1688–94)

	F	VF	EF
1691	£2750	£6750	£20000
1691 Elephant & Castle	£2800	£6750	£20000
1692	£2900	£6500	£20000
1692 Elephant & Castle	£3000	£6500	£21000
1693	£2800	£6500	£20000
1693 Elephant & Castle	£2800	£6750	£21000
1694	£2800	£6500	£20000
1694 Elephant & Castle	£2800	£6500	£21000

WILLIAM III (1694–1702)

	F	VF	EF
1699 First bust	£3000	£8000	£26000
1699 — Elephant & Castle	£3250	£8500	£27500
1700 —	£3000	£8000	£26500
1701 Second bust "fine work"	£3000	£7500	£25000

(1701 "fine work"—beware recent forgeries)

ANNE (1702–14)

Pre-Union with Scotland

	F	VF	EF
1703 VIGO below bust	£35000	£90000	£275000
1705	£4750	£12000	£40000
1706	£4500	£11000	£37500

Post-Union (different shields)

	F	VF	EF
1706	£3200	£7000	£24000
1709 Narrow shields	£3500	£7000	£24000
1711 Broader shields	£3500	£7500	£25000
1713 —	£3500	£7000	£23500
1714 —	£3700	£7750	£26000
1714/3	£3750	£7750	£27000

William & Mary

GEORGE I (1714–27)

	F	VF	EF
1716	£4000	£10000	£32000
1717	£4000	£10500	£30000
1720	£4100	£9000	£30000
1726	£3700	£9500	£28000

GEORGE II (1727–60)

	F	VF	EF
1729 Young head	£2750	£6200	£21000
1729 — E.I.C. below head	£2700	£6000	£18500
1731 —	£3250	£7000	£25000
1735 —	£2800	£7200	£25000
1738 —	£2750	£6000	£22000
1741	£2650	£6000	£21000
1741/38 41 over 38	£2750	£6200	£22000
1746 Old head, LIMA	£2750	£6000	£21000
1748 —	£2750	£6000	£20000
1753 —	£2750	£6250	£20000

GEORGE III (1760–1820)

	F	VF	EF
1770 Patterns	—	—	£222000
1773	—	—	£200000
1777	—	—	£185000

Anne

TWO GUINEAS

	F	VF	EF

CHARLES II (1660–85)

	F	VF	EF
1664 First bust	£1700	£4250	£11000
1664 — Elephant	£1600	£3700	£9500
1665 —		Extremely rare	
1669 —		Extremely rare	
1671 —	£2200	£5500	£16000
1673 First bust		Extremely rare	
1675 Second bust	£1700	£4000	£10000
1676 —	£1650	£4000	£10000
1676 — Elephant & Castle	£1700	£4000	£10000
1677 —	£1650	£3750	£9000
1677 — Elephant & Castle		Extremely rare	
1678/7 —	£1500	£3500	£9500
1678 — Elephant		Extremely rare	
1678 — Elephant & Castle	£1750	£4000	£10000
1679 —	£1600	£4000	£9500
1680 —	£1800	£4500	£12000
1681 —	£1600	£3250	£9000
1682 — Elephant & Castle	£1750	£3750	£11000
1683 —	£1600	£3500	£9500
1683 — Elephant & Castle	£1800	£4500	£12000
1684 —	£1600	£3750	£9750
1684 — Elephant & Castle	£1750	£4500	£12000

Charles II

JAMES II (1685–88)

	F	VF	EF
1687	£2200	£4750	£15000
1688/7	£2400	£5500	£15000

WILLIAM AND MARY (1688–94)

	F	VF	EF
1691 Elephant & Castle		Extremely rare	
1693	£1800	£4500	£12000
1693 Elephant & Castle	£2000	£4750	£15000
1694 — 4 over 3	£1750	£4500	£12000
1694/3 Elephant & Castle	£1700	£4500	£12500

James II

WILLIAM III (1694–1702)

	F	VF	EF
1701 "fine work"	£1850	£4250	£12500

ANNE (1702–14)

	F	VF	EF
1709 Post Union	£1600	£3500	£10000
1711	£1500	£3500	£9750
1713	£1400	£3250	£9000
1714/3	£1600	£3750	£11000

GEORGE I (1714–27)

	F	VF	EF
1717	£1400	£2750	£8000
1720	£1400	£2750	£8200
1720/17	£1500	£3000	£8250
1726	£1350	£2750	£7500

Anne

	F	VF	EF

GEORGE II (1727–60)

	F	VF	EF
1733 Proof only FDC		Extremely Rare	
1734 Young head 4 over 3	£1700	£4200	—
1735 —	£1100	£2250	£7000
1738 —	£850	£1600	£3500
1739 —	£850	£1600	£3500
1739 Intermediate head	£850	£1600	£3200
1740 —	£850	£1600	£3500
1748 Old head	£900	£1800	£4350
1753 —	£950	£1850	£5250

GEORGE III (1760–1820)

	F	VF	EF
1768 Patterns only	—	Extremely Rare	
1773 Patterns only	—	Extremely Rare	
1777 Patterns only	—	Extremely Rare	

George II

GUINEAS

	F	VF	EF

CHARLES II (1660–85)

	F	VF	EF
1663 First bust	£3000	£10000	£37500
1663 — Elephant below	£2500	£8000	—
1664 Second bust	£3000	£8500	—
1664 — Elephant	£3600	£10000	£35000
1664 Third bust	£900	£3000	£12000
1664 — Elephant	£1500	£4500	£15000
1665 —	£900	£3000	£11000
1665 — Elephant	£1500	£5000	£17500
1666 —	£850	£3000	£11000
1667 —	£850	£3000	£11000
1668 —	£850	£3000	£11000
1668 — Elephant		Extremely rare	
1669 —	£850	£2850	£10000
1670 —	£850	£2500	£11000
1671 —	£850	£2500	£11000
1672 —	£850	£3000	£11000
1672 Fourth bust	£800	£2200	£6750
1673 Third bust	£900	£3000	£12000
1673 Fourth bust	£700	£2000	£7000
1674 —	£700	£2000	£7000
1674 — Elephant & Castle		Extremely rare	
1675 —	£700	£2200	£7000
1675 — CRAOLVS Error		Extremely rare	
1675 — Elephant & Castle	£850	£2500	£10000
1676 —	£700	£2200	£7000
1676 — Elephant & Castle	£800	£2500	£9500
1677 —	£675	£2100	£7000
1677/5 — Elephant 7 over 5		Extremely rare	
1677 — Elephant & Castle	£800	£2200	£9000
1678 —	£750	£2000	£7000
1678 — Elephant		Extremely rare	
1678 — Elephant & Castle	£800	£2500	£10000

Charles II, third bust

Charles II, fourth bust, elephant & castle below

	F	VF	EF
1679 —	£750	£2000	£7000
1679 — Elephant & Castle	£800	£2500	£10500
1680 —	£700	£1900	£7000
1680 — Elephant & Castle	£800	£2500	£10000
1681 —	£750	£2100	£7000
1681 — Elephant & Castle	£750	£2500	£9000
1682 —	£700	£2000	£7000
1682 — Elephant & Castle	£850	£2800	£10000
1683 —	£650	£2100	£7000
1683 — Elephant & Castle	£800	£2500	£10000
1684 —	£700	£2200	£7000
1684 — Elephant & Castle	£850	£2600	£11000

James II, first bust, elephant & castle below

JAMES II (1685–1688)

	F	VF	EF
1685 First bust	£700	£2500	£9000
1685 — Elephant & Castle	£800	£2600	£9500
1686 —	£800	£2600	£9000
1686 — Elephant & Castle		Extremely rare	
1686 Second bust	£700	£2300	£7500
1686 — Elephant & Castle	£800	£2500	£9500
1687 —	£700	£2300	£7500
1687 —Elephant & Castle	£800	£2500	£9500
1688 —	£650	£2400	£7500
1688 — Elephant & Castle	£750	£2500	£8750

James II, second bust

WILLIAM AND MARY (1688–94)

	F	VF	EF
1689..	£650	£2000	£8000
1689 Elephant & Castle	£650	£2200	£8000
1690..	£700	£2200	£8000
1690 GVLIFLMVS..............................	£800	£2200	£8000
1690 Elephant & Castle	£800	£2400	£8800
1691..	£650	£2200	£7500
1691 Elephant & Castle	£700	£2200	£7500
1692..	£650	£2000	£7500
1692 Elephant	£900	£3000	£9750
1692 Elephant & Castle	£700	£2500	£8250
1693..	£650	£2000	£7500
1693 Elephant		Extremely rare	
1693 Elephant & Castle		Extremely rare	
1694..	£700	£2000	£7000
1694/3	£700	£2000	£7000
1694 Elephant & Castle	£700	£2200	£7000
1694/3 Elephant & Castle...................	£750	£2400	£7500

WILLIAM III (1694–1702)

	F	VF	EF
1695 First bust	£600	£2000	£6250
1695 — Elephant & Castle	£1000	£3000	£12000
1696 —	£600	£2000	£7000
1696 — Elephant & Castle		Extremely rare	
1697 —	£650	£2000	£6500
1697 Second bust	£600	£2000	£7500
1697 — Elephant & Castle	£1400	£4500	—
1698 —	£600	£1900	£6000
1698 — Elephant & Castle	£600	£2000	£6000
1699 —	£600	£1900	£6500
1699 — Elephant & Castle		Extremely rare	
1700 —	£600	£1800	£6000
1700 — Elephant & Castle	£1200	£4500	—
1701 —	£600	£1800	£5500
1701 — Elephant & Castle		Extremely rare	
1701 Third bust "fine work"...............	£1050	£3500	£11500

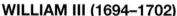

William III, second bust

	F	VF	EF

ANNE (1702–1714)

	F	VF	EF
1702 (Pre-Union) First bust	£1000	£3250	£11000
1703 — VIGO below	£15000	£35000	£90000
1705 —	£1100	£3000	£10000
1706 —	£1100	£3000	£10000
1707 —	£1100	£3000	£10000
1707 — (Post-Union)	£725	£2500	£8500
1707 — Elephant & Castle	£800	£3000	£10000
1707 Second bust	£625	£2200	£7500
1708 First bust	£675	£2500	£8500
1708 Second bust	£600	£1950	£6500
1708 — Elephant & Castle	£800	£3000	£10000
1709 —	£600	£1800	£6000
1709 — Elephant & Castle	£800	£2800	£8500
1710 Third bust	£625	£1500	£4600
1711 —	£625	£1500	£4600
1712 —	£600	£1500	£4500
1713 —	£550	£1400	£4200
1714 —	£550	£1400	£4200
1714 GRΛTIΛ	£700	£1700	£4000

Anne, second bust

GEORGE I (1714–27)

	F	VF	EF
1714 First bust (Prince Elector)	£1350	£3400	£10000
1715 Second bust	£600	£1500	£3500
1715 Third bust	£500	£1500	£4000
1716 —	£525	£1500	£3750
1716 Fourth bust	£525	£1400	£3700
1717 —	£525	£1400	£3700
1718 —		Extremely rare	
1719 —	£500	£1400	£3750
1720 —	£500	£1400	£3800
1721 —	£500	£1400	£3800
1721 — Elephant & Castle		Extremely rare	
1722 —	£500	£1350	£3750
1722 — Elephant & Castle		Extremely rare	
1723 —	£525	£1400	£3750
1723 Fifth bust	£525	£1400	£3800
1724 —	£525	£1350	£3750
1725 —	£525	£1350	£3750
1726 —	£500	£1350	£3500
1726 — Elephant & Castle	£1750	£5200	£17000
1727 —	£600	£1800	£5000

George I, third bust

GEORGE II (1727–60)

	F	VF	EF
1727 First young head, early large shield	£900	£2600	£8000
1727 — Larger lettering, early small shield	£800	£2500	£8000
1728 — —	£900	£2800	£8500
1729 2nd young head E.I.C. below	£1100	£3500	£11000
1729 — Proof		Very Rare	
1730 —	£625	£1500	£5000
1731 —	£550	£1600	£4500
1731 — E.I.C. below	£900	£2750	£8000
1732 —	£700	£2500	£7500
1732 — E.I.C. below	£800	£2500	£8000
1732 — Larger lettering obverse	£650	£1600	£4600
1732 — — E.I.C. below	£900	£1800	£8000
1733 — —	£550	£1400	£3500
1734 — —	£550	£1400	£3500
1735 — —	£550	£1400	£3500
1736 — —	£550	£1500	£3250
1737 — —	£550	£1500	£3250

George II, 1759, old head, larger lettering

	F	VF	EF
1738 — —	£550	£1400	£3500
1739 Intermediate head	£500	£1100	£3000
1739 — E.I.C. below...	£1100	£2900	£9000
1740 —	£550	£1400	£5000
1741/39 —	£800	£2400	£6250
1743 —	£800	£2400	£6250
1745 — Larger lettering obv. Older bust	£500	£1350	£4500
1745 — LIMA below.....................................	£1500	£4500	£12000
1746 — (GEORGIVS) Larger lettering obv........	£500	£1500	£3800
1747 Old head, large lettering	£400	£1000	£3200
1748 —	£400	£1000	£3300
1749 —	£450	£1100	£3400
1750 —	£400	£1000	£3500
1751 — small lettering...................................	£400	£1000	£3500
1753 —	£400	£1000	£3500
1755 —	£400	£1000	£3300
1756 —	£400	£1000	£3400
1758 —	£400	£1000	£3400
1759 —	£400	£1000	£3300
1760 —	£400	£1000	£3000

George III first head

GEORGE III (1760–1820)

	F	VF	EF
1761 First head..	£1900	£5000	£9500
1763 Second head	£1500	£4000	£9000
1764 —	£1300	£3700	£8500
1765 Third head	£400	£750	£1750
1766 —	£400	£750	£1750
1767 —	£500	£800	£2200
1768 —	£400	£700	£1900
1769 —	£400	£700	£2000
1770 —	£1000	£2000	£4500
1771 —	£400	£500	£1250
1772 —	£400	£500	£1250
1773 —	£400	£550	£1500
1774 Fourth head	£375	£575	£1000
1775 —	£375	£600	£975
1776 —	£350	£550	£950
1777 —	£350	£550	£950
1778 —	£500	£900	£2500
1779 —	£400	£700	£1250
1781 —	£350	£550	£1100
1782 —	£350	£550	£1100
1783 —	£350	£550	£1100
1784 —	£350	£600	£1150
1785 —	£350	£600	£1100
1786 —	£400	£650	£1150
1787 Fifth head, "Spade" reverse	£340	£550	£1000
1788 —	£340	£550	£1000
1789 —	£340	£550	£1000
1790 —	£340	£550	£1000
1791 —	£340	£550	£1000
1792 —	£340	£550	£1000
1793 —	£340	£550	£1050
1794 —	£340	£550	£1000
1795 —	£340	£550	£1000
1796 —	£340	£550	£1000
1797 —	£340	£550	£1000
1798 —	£340	£550	£1000
1799 —	£400	£700	£1400
1813 Sixth head, "Military" reverse	£850	£1900	£4400

(Beware of counterfeits of this series—many dangerous copies exist)

Fourth head

Fifth head, Spade reverse

Sixth "Military" head

HALF GUINEAS

	F	VF	EF

CHARLES II (1660–85)

	F	VF	EF
1669 First bust	£375	£1250	£4000
1670 —	£375	£1250	£3500
1671 —	£475	£1400	£5000
1672 —	£400	£1150	£4250
1672 Second bust	£400	£1000	£3750
1673 —	£450	£1350	£4250
1674 —	£500	£1600	£4400
1675 —	£500	£1650	£4400
1676 —	£400	£1150	£3750
1676 — Elephant & Castle	£725	£3000	—
1677 —	£375	£1150	£3500
1677 — Elephant & Castle	£600	£2000	—
1678 —	£400	£1250	£3650
1678 — Elephant & Castle	£500	£1650	£5500
1679 —	£400	£1250	£3500
1680 —	£400	£2000	—
1680 — Elephant & Castle	£600	£2000	£5750
1681 —	£400	£1600	—
1682 —	£400	£1350	£3750
1682 — Elephant & Castle	£600	£2000	—
1683 —	£375	£1150	£3750
1683 — Elephant & Castle		Extremely rare	
1684 —	£350	£1000	£3750
1684 — Elephant & Castle	£600	£2000	£6000

Charles II, first bust

JAMES II (1685–88)

	F	VF	EF
1686	£475	£1150	£4000
1686 Elephant & Castle	£850	£3750	£7000
1687	£450	£1500	£4250
1688	£450	£1500	£4250

WILLIAM AND MARY (1688–94)

	F	VF	EF
1689 First busts	£500	£1850	£4250
1690 Second busts	£500	£2000	£4300
1691 —	£500	£1850	£4250
1691 — Elephant & Castle	£500	£1750	£4400
1692 —	£450	£1600	£3500
1692 — Elephant		Extremely rare	
1692 — Elephant & Castle	£450	£1600	£4000
1693 —		Extremely rare	
1694 —	£450	£1600	£4000

William & Mary, first busts

WILLIAM III (1694–1702)

	F	VF	EF
1695	£350	£850	£3250
1695 Elephant & Castle	£600	£1500	£4550
1696 —	£400	£1000	£3500
1697 Larger Harp rev.	£500	£1500	£4500
1698	£500	£1250	£4150
1698 Elephant & Castle	£600	£1500	£3500
1699		Extremely rare	
1700	£325	£850	£3250
1701	£300	£800	£3200

William III, elephant & castle below bust

	F	VF	EF

ANNE (1702–14)

	F	VF	EF
1702 (Pre-Union)	£700	£2250	£6500
1703 VIGO below bust	£5000	£14000	£32000
1705	£600	£2000	£6000
1707 (Post-Union)	£300	£1000	£2500
1708	£350	£1000	£2500
1709	£350	£1100	£2500
1710	£325	£850	£2350
1711	£325	£850	£2350
1712	£350	£875	£2750
1713	£300	£850	£2300
1714	£300	£850	£2300

Anne

GEORGE I (1714–27)

	F	VF	EF
1715 First bust	£750	£1500	£4500
1717 —	£350	£750	£2750
1718 —	£350	£750	£2750
1719 —	£325	£750	£2750
1720 —	£350	£750	£3000
1721 —		Extremely rare	
1721 — Elephant & Castle		Extremely rare	
1722 —	£350	£750	£2750
1723 —	£425	£850	£3000
1724 —	£350	£850	£3000
1725 Second bust	£350	£750	£2600
1726 —	£350	£750	£2800
1727 —	£350	£750	£3000

George I, second bust

GEORGE II (1727–60)

	F	VF	EF
1728 Young head	£550	£1350	£4000
1729 —	£550	£1400	£3750
1729 — E.I.C.	£650	£1500	£4750
1730 —	£750	£2000	—
1730 — E.I.C.	£700	£2000	—
1731 —	£350	£1000	£3250
1731 — E.I.C.		Extremely rare	
1732 —	£350	£1000	£3250
1732 — E.I.C.		Extremely rare	
1733 —			Unknown
1734 —	£350	£850	£2750
1735 —		Extremely rare	
1736 —	£350	£850	£3250
1737 —	£450	£850	£3500
1738 —	£350	£800	£3000
1739 —	£350	£800	£2750
1739 — E.I.C.		Extremely rare	
1740 Intermediate head	£400	£1000	£3250
1743 —		Extremely rare	
1745 —	£350	£1000	£3250
1745 — LIMA	£1250	£3750	£7500
1746 —	£300	£750	£2250
1747 Old head	£350	£750	£2250
1748 —	£300	£750	£2200
1749 —	£350	£850	£2000
1751 —	£300	£750	£2000
1752 —	£300	£750	£2000
1753 —	£300	£750	£2000
1755 —	£300	£650	£2000
1756 —	£375	£800	£2300
1758 —	£350	£750	£2500
1759 —	£275	£700	£2000
1760 —	£275	£700	£2000

George II, young head

George II, old head

GEORGE III (1760–1820)

	F	VF	EF
1762 First head	£700	£1900	£4500
1763 —	£750	£2250	£4000
1764 Second head	£275	£525	£1100
1765 —	£500	£1225	£3250
1766 —	£275	£500	£1350
1768 —	£275	£550	£1350
1769 —	£325	£550	£1500
1772 —		Extremely rare	
1773 —	£325	£600	£1600
1774 —	£350	£700	£1900
1774 Third head		Extremely rare	
1775 —	£1000	£2500	£6500
1775 Fourth head	£225	£350	£600
1775 — Proof		Extremely rare	
1776 —	£250	£500	£1250
1777 —	£250	£450	£900
1778 —	£250	£450	£900
1779 —	£250	£450	£1000
1781 —	£250	£450	£1050
1783 —	£500	£1800	—
1784 —	£225	£375	£850
1785 —	£225	£375	£750
1786 —	£225	£375	£750
1787 Fifth head, "Spade" rev.	£225	£375	£750
1788 —	£225	£375	£750
1789 —	£225	£375	£750
1790 —	£225	£375	£675
1791 —	£225	£375	£675
1792 —	£1200	£3250	—
1793 —	£225	£450	£750
1794 —	£225	£450	£750
1795 —	£225	£500	£850
1796 —	£225	£450	£750
1797 —	£225	£450	£750
1798 —	£225	£450	£750
1800 —	£325	£900	£2250
1801 Sixth head, Shield in Garter rev.	£225	£325	£600
1802 —	£225	£325	£600
1803 —	£225	£325	£600
1804 Seventh head	£225	£325	£600
1805		Extremely rare	
1806 —	£225	£375	£700
1808 —	£225	£375	£700
1899 —	£225	£375	£700
1810 —	£225	£400	£700
1811 —	£325	£600	£1400
1813 —	£325	£600	£1000

George III, second head

George III, fifth head, "spade" reverse

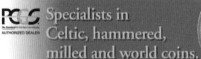

THIRD GUINEAS

DATE	F	VF	EF
GEORGE III (1760–1820)			
1797 First head, date in legend	£150	£250	£525
1798 — —	£150	£250	£525
1799 — —	£150	£275	£525
1800 — —	£150	£250	£525
1801 Date under crown	£150	£250	£525
1802 —	£150	£250	£525
1803 —	£150	£250	£525
1804 Second head	£140	£225	£550
1806 —	£140	£250	£525
1808 —	£140	£300	£525
1809 —	£140	£300	£525
1810 —	£140	£300	£525
1811 —	£500	£1300	£2600
1813 —	£300	£550	£1100

George III, date in legend

George III, date under crown

QUARTER GUINEAS

GEORGE I (1714–27)

	F	VF	EF
1718	£150	£275	£650

GEORGE III (1760–1820)

	F	VF	EF
1762	£225	£425	£750

George I

FIVE POUNDS

DATE	Mintage	F	VF	EF	UNC
GEORGE III (1760–1820)					
1820 (pattern only)	—			Extremely rare	
GEORGE IV (1820–30)					
1826 proof only	—	—	—	£26,500	
VICTORIA (1837–1901)					
1839 Proof Only (Una & The Lion) Many Varieties FDC £60,000 upwards					
1887	53,844	£1400	£1900	£2400	£3250
1887 Proof	797	—	—	—	£5000
1887 S on ground on rev. (Sydney Mint)				Excessively rare	
1893	20,405	£1800	£2500	£3750	£5000
1893 Proof	773	—	—	—	£6800
EDWARD VII (1902–10)					
1902	34,910	£1500	£2000	£2600	£3500
1902 Matt proof	8,066	—	—	—	£2850

154

DATE	MINTAGE	F	VF	EF	UNC

GEORGE V (1911–36)
1911 Proof only 2,812   —   —   —   £5000

GEORGE VI (1937–52)
1937 Proof only 5,501   —   —   —   £2750

Later issues are listed in the Decimal section.

TWO POUNDS

GEORGE III (1760–1820)
1820 (pattern only).............   —   —   —   Extremely rare

GEORGE IV (1820–30)
1823 St George reverse.....   —   £750   £1000   £2000   £2800
1826 Proof only, shield reverse   —   —   —   Extremely rare

WILLIAM IV (1830–37)
1831 Proof only 225   —   —   —   £11000

VICTORIA (1837–1901)
1887.................................. 91,345   £600   £800   £1000   £1100
1887 Proof........................ 797   —   —   —   £2000
1887 S on ground of rev. (Sydney Mint)   Excessively rare
1893.................................. 52,212   £700   £900   £1600   £2200
1893 Proof........................ 773   —   —   —   £3000

EDWARD VII (1902–10)
1902.................................. 45,807   £500   £650   £850   £1300
1902 Matt proof................ 8,066   —   —   —   £1250

GEORGE V (1911–36)
1911 Proof only 2,812   —   —   —   £2000

GEORGE VI (1937–52)
1937 Proof only 5,501   —   —   —   £1400
Later issues are listed in the Decimal section.

CROMWELL GOLD

	F	VF	EF

OLIVER CROMWELL (1656–58)
1656 Fifty Shillings £17,500   £40,000   £120,000
1656 Twenty Shillings............................. £5,500   £13,500   £28,000

SOVEREIGNS

DATE	MINTAGE	F	VF	EF	UNC

GEORGE III (1760–1820)

DATE	MINTAGE	F	VF	EF	UNC
1817..	3,235,239	£500	£850	£2000	£3800
1818..	2,347,230	£600	£900	£2200	£4000
1819..	3,574		Exceedingly rare		
1820..	931,994	£500	£775	£1750	£3400

George III

GEORGE IV (1820–30)

	MINTAGE	F	VF	EF	UNC
1821 First bust, St George reverse	9,405,114	£450	£750	£1700	£2600
1821 — Proof	incl. above	—	—	—	£6500
1822 —	5,356,787	£450	£750	£1650	£3000
1823 —	616,770	£1000	£2750	£7000	—
1824 —	3,767,904	£500	£900	£2000	£3500
1825 —	4,200,343	£700	£2000	£5000	£8500
1825 Second bust, shield reverse	incl. above	£425	£700	£1200	£2500
1826 —	5,724,046	£425	£700	£1200	£2500
1826 — Proof	—	—	—	—	£5500
1827 —	2,266,629	£475	£750	£1500	£3200
1828 —	386,182	£6000	£15000	£27000	—
1829 —	2,444,652	£475	£800	£1800	£3000
1830 —	2,387,881	£475	£800	£1800	£3000

WILLIAM IV (1830–37)

	MINTAGE	F	VF	EF	UNC
1831..	598,547	£600	£1000	£2400	£4250
1831 Proof, plain edge	—	—	—	—	£6500
1832..	3,737,065	£500	£900	£2000	£3750
1833..	1,225,269	£500	£900	£2000	£3750
1835..	723,441	£500	£900	£2000	£3750
1836..	1,714,349	£500	£900	£2000	£3750
1837..	1,172,984	£525	£950	£2000	£3850

George IV, shield reverse

Note—from the Victoria reign onwards, the prices of coins in lower grade will be subject to the bullion price of gold.

VICTORIA (1837–1901)

Many of the gold coins struck at the colonial mints found their way into circulation in Britain, for the sake of completeness these coins are listed here. These can easily be identified by a tiny initial letter for the appropriate mint which can be found below the base of the reverse shield or, in the case of the St George reverse, below the bust on the obverse of the Young Head issues, or on the "ground" below the horse's hoof on the later issues.

William IV

YOUNG HEAD ISSUES

Shield reverse

(Note—Shield back sovereigns in Fine/VF condition, common dates, are normally traded as bullion + a percentage)

	MINTAGE	F	VF	EF	UNC
1838	2,718,694	£700	£1200	£2750	£5000
1839	503,695	£1000	£2750	£5000	£6500
1839 Proof, plain edge	—	—	—	—	£7000
1841..	124,054	£4750	£9500	£20000	—
1842	4,865,375	£300	£400	£700	£1500
1843..	5,981,968	£300	£400	£700	£1500
1843 "Narrow shield" variety......	incl. above	£5000	£10000		
1843 Roman I in date not 1841 ...	—	£750	£1500	—	—
1844	3,000,445	£300	£400	£750	£1400
1845	3,800,845	£300	£400	£750	£1500
1846	3,802,947	£300	£400	£750	£1500

PAUL DAVIES

DATE	MINTAGE	F	VF	EF	UNC
1847	4,667,126	£275	£325	£650	£1300
1848	2,246,701	£275	£325	£650	£1300
1849	1,755,399	£275	£325	£650	£1300
1850	1,402,039	£275	£325	£650	£1200
1851	4,013,624	£275	£325	£650	£1300
1852	8,053,435	£275	£325	£650	£1300
1853	10,597,993	£275	£325	£650	£1200
1853 Proof	—	—	—	—	£16000
1854 Incuse WW	3,589,611	£275	£325	£625	£1200
1854 Surface raised WW	3,589,611	£275	£325	£625	£1800
1855	4,806,160	£275	£325	£625	£1100
1856	8,448,482	£275	£325	£625	£1100
1857	4,495,748	£275	£325	£625	£1100
1858	803,234	£275	£325	£625	£1100
1859	1,547,603	£275	£325	£625	£1100
1859 "Ansell" (additional line on lower part of hair ribbon)	—	£750	£1700	£8000	—
1860	2,555,958	£225	£250	£500	£1100
1861	7,624,736	£225	£250	£500	£1100
1862	7,836,413	£225	£250	£500	£1100
1863	5,921,669	£225	£250	£500	£1100
1863 Die No 827 on Truncation				Extremely rare	
1863 with Die number below shield	incl. above	£225	£250	£500	£1100
1864 —	8,656,352	£225	£250	£500	£1100
1865 —	1,450,238	£225	£250	£500	£1100
1866 —	4,047,288	£225	£250	£500	£1100
1868 —	1,653,384	£225	£250	£500	£1100
1869 —	6,441,322	£225	£250	£500	£1000
1870 —	2,189,960	£225	£250	£500	£1100
1871 —	8,767,250	£225	£250	£500	£1100
1872 —	8,767,250	£225	£250	£500	£1000
1872 no Die number	incl. above	£225	£250	£500	£1000
1873 with Die number	2,368,215	£225	£250	£500	£1000
1874 —	520,713	£2000	£4000	£9500	—

M below reverse shield (Melbourne Mint)

1872	748,180	£225	£250	£500	£1150
1873	—			Extremely rare	
1874	1,373,298	£225	£250	£500	£1200
1879				Extremely rare	
1880	3,053,454	£700	£1650	£3500	£10000
1881	2,325,303	£225	£250	£500	£1500
1882	2,465,781	£225	£250	£500	£1000
1883	2,050,450	£225	£250	£500	£3000
1884	2,942,630	£225	£250	£500	£900
1885	2,967,143	£225	£250	£500	£900
1886	2,902,131	£1800	£4000	£6000	£22000
1887	1,916,424	£600	£1350	£4500	£12000

S below reverse shield (Sydney Mint)

1871	2,814,000	£230	£250	£500	£1300
1072	1,815,000	£230	£250	£500	£1600
1873	1,478,000	£230	£250	£500	£1000
1875	2,122,000	£230	£250	£500	£1300
1877	1,590,000	£230	£250	£500	£1300
1878	1,259,000	£230	£250	£500	£1400
1879	1,366,000	£230	£250	£500	£1300
1880	1,459,000	£230	£250	£500	£2000
1881	1,360,000	£230	£250	£500	£1800
1882	1,298,000	£230	£250	£500	£1500
1883	1,108,000	£230	£250	£500	£1100
1884	1,595,000	£230	£250	£500	£1100
1885	1,486,000	£230	£250	£500	£1100
1886	1,667,000	£230	£250	£500	£1100
1887	1,000,000	£230	£250	£500	£1500

The mint initial appears below the shield, i.e. "S" indicates that the coin was struck at the Sydney Mint

IMPORTANT NOTE:
The prices quoted in this guide are set at August 2016 with the price of 22ct gold at £900 per ounce and silver £12 per ounce—market fluctuations can have a marked effect on the values of modern precious metal coins.

"M" below the horse's hoof above the date indicates that the coin was struck at the Melbourne Mint

DATE	MINTAGE	F	VF	EF	UNC
St George & Dragon reverse					
1871	incl. above	£200	£220	£240	£500
1872	incl. above	£200	£220	£240	£500
1873	incl. above	£200	£220	£240	£500
1874	incl. above	£200	£220	£240	£500
1876	3,318,866	£200	£220	£240	£500
1878	1,091,275	£200	£220	£240	£500
1879	20,013	£550	£1100	£4250	—
1880	3,650,080	£200	£220	£240	£500
1884	1,769,635	£200	£220	£240	£500
1885	717,723	£200	£220	£240	£500
M below bust on obverse (Melbourne Mint)					
1872	incl. above	£250	£500	£1100	£4000
1873	752,199	£200	£220	£240	£500
1874	incl. above	£200	£220	£240	£500
1875	incl. above	£200	£220	£240	£500
1876	2,124,445	£200	£220	£240	£550
1877	1,487,316	£200	£220	£240	£500
1878	2,171,457	£200	£220	£240	£500
1879	2,740,594	£200	£220	£240	£500
1880	incl. above	£200	£220	£240	£500
1881	incl. above	£200	£220	£240	£500
1882	incl. above	£200	£220	£240	£500
1883	incl. above	£200	£220	£240	£500
1884	incl. above	£200	£220	£240	£500
1885	incl. above	£200	£220	£240	£500
1886	incl. above	£200	£220	£240	£500
1887	incl. above	£200	£220	£240	£500
S below bust on obverse (Sydney Mint)					
1871	2,814,000	£200	£220	£240	£500
1872	incl. above	£200	£220	£240	£700
1873	incl. above	£200	£220	£240	£500
1874	1,899,000	£200	£220	£240	£500
1875	inc above	£200	£220	£240	£500
1876	1,613,000	£200	£220	£240	£500
1877	—				Unknown
1879	incl. above	£200	£220	£240	£500
1880	incl. above	£200	£220	£240	£500
1881	incl. above	£200	£220	£240	£500
1882	incl. above	£200	£220	£240	£550
1883	incl. above	£200	£220	£240	£500
1884	incl. above	£200	£220	£240	£500
1885	incl. above	£200	£220	£240	£500
1886	incl. above	£200	£220	£240	£500
1887	incl. above	£200	£220	£240	£500
JUBILEE HEAD ISSUES					
1887	1,111,280	£200	£220	£240	£350
1887 Proof	797	—	—	—	£2200
1888	2,717,424	£200	£220	£240	£350
1889	7,257,455	£200	£220	£240	£350
1890	6,529.887	£200	£220	£240	£350
1891	6,329,476	£200	£220	£240	£350
1892	7,104,720	£200	£220	£240	£350
M on ground on reverse (Melbourne Mint)					
1887	940,000	£200	£220	£240	£350
1888	2,830,612	£200	£220	£240	£350
1889	2,732,590	£200	£220	£240	£350
1890	2,473,537	£200	£220	£240	£350
1891	2,749,592	£200	£220	£240	£350
1892	3,488,750	£200	£220	£240	£350
1893	1,649,352	£200	£220	£240	£350

Jubilee head type

DATE	MINTAGE	F	VF	EF	UNC
S on ground on reverse (Sydney Mint)					
1887	1,002,000	£250	£400	£1000	£2500
1888	2,187,000	£200	£220	£240	£300
1889	3,262,000	£200	£220	£240	£300
1890	2,808,000	£200	£220	£240	£300
1891	2,596,000	£200	£220	£240	£300
1892	2,837,000	£200	£220	£240	£300
1893	1,498,000	£200	£220	£240	£300

OLD HEAD ISSUES

DATE	MINTAGE	F	VF	EF	UNC
1893	6,898,260	£200	£220	£240	£300
1893 Proof	773	—	—	—	£2200
1894	3,782,611	£200	£220	£240	£300
1895	2,285,317	£200	£220	£240	£300
1896	3,334,065	£200	£220	£240	£300
1898	4,361,347	£200	£220	£240	£300
1899	7,515,978	£200	£220	£240	£300
1900	10,846,741	£200	£220	£240	£300
1901	1,578,948	£200	£220	£240	£300
M on ground on reverse (Melbourne Mint)					
1893	1,914,000	£200	£220	£240	£300
1894	4,166,874	£200	£220	£240	£300
1895	4,165,869	£200	£220	£240	£300
1896	4,456,932	£200	£220	£240	£300
1897	5,130,565	£200	£220	£240	£300
1898	5,509,138	£200	£220	£240	£300
1899	5,579,157	£200	£220	£240	£300
1900	4,305,904	£200	£220	£240	£300
1901	3,987,701	£200	£220	£240	£300

DATE	MINTAGE	F	VF	EF	UNC
P on ground on reverse (Perth Mint)					
1899	690,992	£250	£275	£500	£2500
1900	1,886,089	£200	£220	£240	£300
1901	2,889,333	£200	£220	£240	£300
S on ground on reverse (Sydney Mint)					
1893	1,346,000	£220	£250	£300	£450
1894	3,067,000	£200	£220	£240	£300
1895	2,758,000	£200	£220	£240	£300
1896	2,544,000	£200	£220	£240	£300
1897	2,532,000	£200	£220	£240	£300
1898	2,548,000	£200	£220	£240	£300
1899	3,259,000	£200	£220	£240	£300
1900	3,586,000	£200	£220	£240	£300
1901	3,012,000	£200	£220	£240	£300

Old head type

EDWARD VII (1902–10)

DATE	MINTAGE	F	VF	EF	UNC
1902	4,737,796	£200	£220	£240	£300
1902 Matt proof	15,123	—	—	—	£625
1903	8,888,627	£200	£220	£240	£300
1904	10,041,369	£200	£220	£240	£000
1905	5,910,403	£200	£220	£240	£300
1906	10,466,981	£200	£220	£240	£300
1907	18,458,663	£200	£220	£240	£300
1908	11,729,006	£200	£220	£240	£300
1909	12,157,099	£200	£220	£240	£300
1910	22,379,624	£200	£220	£240	£300
C on ground on reverse (Ottawa Mint)					
1908 Satin finish Proof only	633			Extremely rare	
1909	16,300	£240	£275	£375	£675
1910	28,020	£240	£275	£375	£675

DATE	MINTAGE	F	VF	EF	UNC
M on ground on reverse (Melbourne Mint)					
1902	4,267,157	£200	£220	£240	£300
1903	3,521,780	£200	£220	£240	£300
1904	3,743,897	£200	£220	£240	£300
1905	3,633,838	£200	£220	£240	£300
1906	3,657,853	£200	£220	£240	£300
1907	3,332,691	£200	£220	£240	£300
1908	3,080,148	£200	£220	£240	£300
1909	3,029,538	£200	£220	£240	£300
1910	3,054,547	£200	£220	£240	£300
P on ground on reverse (Perth Mint)					
1902	3,289,122	£200	£220	£240	£300
1903	4,674,783	£200	£220	£240	£300
1904	4,506,756	£200	£220	£240	£300
1905	4,876,193	£200	£220	£240	£300
1906	4,829,817	£200	£220	£240	£300
1907	4,972,289	£200	£220	£240	£300
1908	4,875,617	£200	£220	£240	£300
1909	4,524,241	£200	£220	£240	£300
1910	4,690,625	£200	£220	£240	£300
S on ground on reverse (Sydney Mint)					
1902	2,813,000	£200	£220	£240	£280
1902 Proof	incl. above		Extremely rare		
1903	2,806,000	£200	£220	£240	£300
1904	2,986,000	£200	£220	£240	£300
1905	2,778,000	£200	£220	£240	£300
1906	2,792,000	£200	£220	£240	£300
1907	2,539,000	£200	£220	£240	£300
1908	2,017,000	£200	£220	£240	£300
1909	2,057,000	£200	£220	£240	£300
1910	2,135,000	£200	£220	£240	£300

> **IMPORTANT NOTE:** The prices quoted in this guide are set at August 2016 with the price of 22ct gold at £900 per ounce and silver £12 per ounce—market fluctuations can have a marked effect on the values of modern precious metal coins.

GEORGE V (1911–36)

(Extra care should be exercised when purchasing as good quality forgeries exist of virtually all dates and mintmarks)

DATE	MINTAGE	F	VF	EF	UNC
1911	30,044,105	£200	£220	£240	£300
1911 Proof	3,764	—	—	—	£900
1912	30,317,921	£200	£220	£240	£300
1913	24,539,672	£200	£220	£240	£300
1914	11,501,117	£200	£220	£240	£300
1915	20,295,280	£200	£220	£240	£300
1916	1,554,120	£200	£220	£240	£300
1917	1,014,714	£1500	£5000	£14000	—
1925	4,406,431	£200	£220	£240	£300
C on ground on reverse (Ottawa Mint)					
1911	256,946	£200	£220	£240	£400
1913	3,715	£285	£375	£1600	—
1914	14,891	£200	£220	£700	—
1916	6,111		Extremely rare		
1917	58,845	£200	£220	£240	£400
1918	106,516	£200	£220	£240	£400
1919	135,889	£200	£220	£240	£400
I on ground on reverse (Bombay Mint)					
1918	1,295,372	£200	£220	£240	—
M on ground on reverse (Melbourne Mint)					
1911	2,851,451	£200	£220	£240	£300
1912	2,469,257	£200	£220	£240	£300
1913	2,323,180	£200	£220	£240	£300
1914	2,012,029	£200	£220	£240	£300
1915	1,637,839	£200	£220	£240	£300
1916	1,273,643	£200	£220	£240	£300
1917	934,469	£200	£220	£240	£300
1918	4,969,493	£200	£220	£240	£300
1919	514,257	£200	£220	£240	£425

DATE	MINTAGE	F	VF	EF	UNC
1920	530,266	£1350	£2500	£4000	£6500
1921	240,121	£4000	£7000	£10000	£22000
1922	608,306	£4000	£7000	£10000	£20000
1923	510,870	£200	£220	£240	£300
1924	278,140	£200	£220	£240	£300
1925	3,311,622	£200	£220	£240	£300
1926	211,107	£200	£220	£240	£300
1928	413,208	£500	£900	£1500	£3000
1929	436,719	£900	£1500	£2500	£4750
1930	77,547	£200	£220	£240	£300
1931	57,779	£200	£220	£400	£700

P on ground on reverse (Perth Mint)

DATE	MINTAGE	F	VF	EF	UNC
1911	4,373,165	£200	£220	£240	£300
1912	4,278,144	£200	£220	£240	£300
1913	4,635,287	£200	£220	£240	£300
1914	4,815,996	£200	£220	£240	£300
1915	4,373,596	£200	£220	£240	£300
1916	4,096,771	£200	£220	£240	£300
1917	4,110,286	£200	£220	£240	£300
1918	3,812,884	£200	£220	£240	£300
1919	2,995,216	£200	£220	£240	£300
1920	2,421,196	£200	£220	£240	£300
1921	2,134,360	£200	£220	£240	£300
1922	2,298,884	£200	£220	£240	£300
1923	2,124,154	£200	£220	£240	£300
1924	1,464,416	£200	£220	£240	£300
1925	1,837,901	£200	£220	£400	£600
1926	1,313,578	£500	£900	£1500	£3200
1927	1,383,544	£200	£220	£240	£500
1928	1,333,417	£200	£220	£240	£375
1929	1,606,625	£200	£220	£240	£375
1930	1,915,352	£200	£220	£240	£375
1931	1,173,568	£200	£220	£240	£375

S on ground on reverse (Sydney Mint)

DATE	MINTAGE	F	VF	EF	UNC
1911	2,519,000	£200	£220	£240	£300
1912	2,227,000	£200	£220	£240	£300
1913	2,249,000	£200	£220	£240	£300
1914	1,774,000	£200	£220	£240	£300
1915	1,346,000	£200	£220	£240	£300
1916	1,242,000	£200	£220	£240	£300
1917	1,666,000	£200	£220	£240	£300
1918	3,716,000	£200	£220	£240	£300
1919	1,835,000	£200	£220	£240	£300

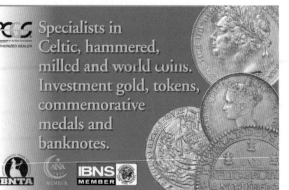

DATE	MINTAGE	F	VF	EF	UNC
1920	—			Excessively rare	
1921	839,000	£600	£900	£1850	£2750
1922	578,000			Extremely rare	
1923	416,000			Extremely rare	
1924	394,000	£600	£1100	£1600	£2750
1925	5,632,000	£185	£200	£240	£300
1926	1,031,050			Extremely rare	
SA on ground on reverse (Pretoria Mint)					
1923	719	£800	£1850	£4000	£7000
1923 Proof	655			Extremely rare	
1924	3,184	—	£3000	£7000	—
1925	6,086,264	£200	£220	£240	£300
1926	11,107,611	£200	£220	£240	£300
1927	16,379,704	£200	£220	£240	£300
1928	18,235,057	£200	£220	£240	£300
1929	12,024,107	£200	£220	£240	£300
1930	10,027,756	£200	£220	£240	£300
1931	8,511,792	£200	£220	£240	£300
1932	1,066,680	£200	£220	£240	£300

GEORGE VI (1937–52)

	MINTAGE	F	VF	EF	UNC
1937 Proof only	5,501	—	—	£1800	£2250

ELIZABETH II (1952–)

Pre Decimal Issues

	MINTAGE	F	VF	EF	UNC
1957	2,072,000	£200	£220	£240	£300
1958	8,700,140	£200	£220	£240	£300
1959	1,358,228	£200	£220	£240	£300
1962	3,000,000	£200	£220	£240	£300
1963	7,400,000	£200	£220	£240	£300
1964	3,000,000	£200	£220	£240	£300
1965	3,800,000	£200	£220	£240	£300
1966	7,050,000	£200	£220	£240	£300
1967	5,000,000	£200	£220	£240	£300
1968	4,203,000	£200	£220	£240	£300

Later issues are included in the Decimal section.

HALF SOVEREIGNS

GEORGE III (1760–1820)

	MINTAGE	F	VF	EF	UNC
1817	2,080,197	£200	£370	£600	£1000
1818	1,030,286	£220	£400	£700	£1200
1820	35,043	£220	£400	£650	£1200

GEORGE IV (1820–30)

	MINTAGE	F	VF	EF	UNC
1821 First bust, ornate shield reverse	231,288	£600	£1600	£3200	£5000
1821 — Proof	unrecorded	—	—	—	£6250
1823 First bust, Plain shield rev.	224,280	£200	£280	£700	£1100
1824 —	591,538	£200	£280	£700	£1100
1825 —	761,150	£200	£280	£700	£1000
1826 bare head, shield with full legend reverse	344,830	£200	£320	£700	£1000
1826 — Proof	unrecorded	—	—	—	£2800
1827 —	492,014	£200	£340	£750	£1000
1828 —	1,224,754	£200	£350	£750	£1200

DATE	MINTAGE	F	VF	EF	UNC

WILLIAM IV (1830–37)

DATE	MINTAGE	F	VF	EF	UNC
1831 Proof only	unrecorded	—	—	—	£3250
1834	133,899	£275	£550	£1100	£1800
1835	772,554	£225	£550	£800	£1500
1836	146,865	£200	£400	£800	£1600
1836 obverse from 6d die	incl. above	£1600	£3500	£7000	—
1837	160,207	£220	£475	£850	£1500

VICTORIA (1837–1901)

YOUNG HEAD ISSUES

Shield reverse

DATE	MINTAGE	F	VF	EF	UNC
1838	273,341	£130	£190	£700	£1500
1839 Proof only	1,230	—	—	—	£3250
1841	508,835	£140	£225	£700	£1750
1842	2,223,352	£130	£180	£600	£950
1843	1,251,762	£130	£180	£600	£1000
1844	1,127,007	£130	£180	£600	£950
1845	887,526	£300	£600	£1800	£3500
1846	1,063,928	£140	£180	£600	£900
1847	982,636	£140	£180	£600	£900
1848	410,595	£140	£180	£600	£900
1849	845,112	£140	£180	£600	£900
1850	179,595	£180	£400	£1100	£2750
1851	773,573	£140	£180	£600	£700
1852	1,377,671	£140	£180	£600	£700
1853	2,708,796	£140	£180	£600	£700
1853 Proof	unrecorded	—	—	—	£8250
1854	1,125,144		Extremely rare		
1855	1,120,362	£140	£180	£600	£850
1856	2,391,909	£140	£180	£600	£850
1857	728,223	£140	£180	£600	£850
1858	855,578	£140	£180	£600	£850
1859	2,203,813	£140	£180	£600	£850
1860	1,131,500	£140	£180	£600	£850
1861	1,130,867	£140	£180	£600	£850
1862	unrecorded	£750	£2000	£8000	—
1863	1,571,574	£140	£180	£600	£800
1863 with Die number	incl. above	£140	£180	£600	£850
1864 —	1,758,490	£140	£180	£600	£850
1865 —	1,834,750	£140	£180	£600	£850
1866 —	2,058,776	£140	£180	£600	£850
1867 —	992,795	£140	£180	£600	£750
1869 —	1,861,764	£140	£180	£600	£850
1870 —	1,159,544	£140	£180	£600	£700
1871 —	2,062,970	£140	£180	£600	£850
1872 —	3,248,627	£140	£180	£600	£850
1873 —	1,927,050	£140	£180	£600	£850
1874 —	1,884,432	£140	£180	£600	£850
1875 —	516,240	£140	£180	£600	£850
1876 —	2,785,187	£140	£180	£600	£850
1877 —	2,197,482	£140	£180	£600	£850
1878 —	2,081,941	£140	£180	£600	£850
1879 —	35,201	£140	£180	£600	£850
1880 —	1,009,049	£140	£180	£600	£850
1880 no Die number	incl. above	£140	£180	£600	£600
1883 —	2,870,457	£140	£180	£600	£600
1884 —	1,113,756	£140	£180	£600	£850
1885 —	4,468,871	£140	£180	£600	£850

M below shield (Melbourne Mint)

DATE	MINTAGE	F	VF	EF	UNC
1873	165,034	£120	£195	£1000	—
1877	80,016	£120	£195	£900	—
1881	42,009	£120	£300	£950	—
1882	107,522	£120	£195	£950	—
1884	48,009	£120	£195	£900	—

Date	Mintage	F	VF	EF	UNC
1885	11,003	£120	£300	£1500	—
1886	38,008	£120	£140	£1500	—
1887	64,013	£120	£400	£1500	£5000

S below shield (Sydney Mint)

1871	180,000 (?)	£120	£140	£700	—
1872	356,000	£120	£140	£700	—
1875	unrecorded	£120	£140	£700	—
1879	94,000	£120	£140	£1150	—
1880	80,000	£120	£400	£1150	—
1881	62,000	£120	£140	£1150	—
1882	52,000			Extremely rare	
1883	220,000	£120	£140	£900	—
1886	82,000	£120	£140	£900	—
1887	134,000	£120	£140	£1100	£4000

JUBILEE HEAD ISSUES

1887	871,770	£120	£130	£150	£175
1887 Proof	797	£120	£130	—	£1150
1890	2.266,023	£120	£130	£150	£175
1891	1,079,286	£120	£130	£150	£175
1892	13,680,486	£120	£130	£150	£175
1893	4,426,625	£120	£130	£150	£175

M below shield (Melbourne Mint)

1887	incl. above	£120	£130	£300	£600
1893	110,024	£120	£130	£550	—

S below shield (Sydney Mint)

1887	incl. above	£120	£130	£280	£500
1889	64,000	£120	£130	£280	—
1891	154,000	£120	£130	£280	—

OLD HEAD ISSUES

1893	incl. above	£120	£130	£150	£175
1893 Proof	773	—	—	—	£1200
1894	3,794,591	£120	£130	£150	£175
1895	2,869,183	£120	£130	£150	£175
1896	2,946,605	£120	£130	£150	£175
1897	3,568,156	£120	£130	£150	£175
1898	2,868,527	£120	£130	£150	£175
1899	3,361,881	£120	£130	£150	£175
1900	4,307,372	£120	£130	£150	£175
1901	2,037,664	£120	£130	£150	£175

M on ground on reverse (Melbourne Mint)

1893	unrecorded			Extremely rare	
1896	218,946	£120	£130	£450	—
1899	97,221	£120	£130	£450	—
1900	112,920	£120	£130	£450	—

P on ground on reverse (Perth Mint)

1899				Proof Unique	
1900	119,376	£120	£300	£550	—

S on ground on reverse (Sydney Mint)

1893	250,000	£120	£130	£375	—
1897	unrecorded	£120	£130	£350	—
1900	260,00	£120	£130	£350	—

EDWARD VII (1902–10)

1902	4,244,457	£115	£120	£140	£150
1902 Matt proof	15,123	—	—	—	£500
1903	2,522,057	£115	£120	£140	£150
1904	1,717,440	£115	£120	£140	£150
1905	3,023,993	£115	£120	£140	£150
1906	4,245,437	£115	£120	£140	£150
1907	4,233,421	£115	£120	£140	£150
1908	3,996,992	£115	£120	£140	£150
1909	4,010,715	£115	£120	£140	£150
1910	5,023,881	£115	£120	£140	£150

DATE		F	VF	EF	UNC
M on ground on reverse (Melbourne Mint)					
1906	82,042	£115	£120	£150	£350
1907	405,034	£115	£120	£150	£325
1908	incl. above	£115	£120	£150	£350
1909	186,094	£115	£120	£150	£325
P on ground on reverse (Perth Mint)					
1904	60,030	£115	£120	£500	—
1908	24,668	£115	£120	£500	—
1909	44,022	£115	£120	£500	—
S on ground on reverse (Sydney Mint)					
1902	84,000	£115	£120	£140	£325
1902 Proof			Extremely rare		
1903	231,000				£300
1906	308,00	£115	£120	£140	£300
1908	538,000	£115	£120	£140	£300
1910	474,000	£115	£120	£140	£300

GEORGE V (1911–36)

		F	VF	EF	UNC
1911	6,104,106	£115	£120	£140	£150
1911 Proof	3,764	—	—	—	£575
1912	6,224,316	£115	£120	£140	£150
1913	6,094,290	£115	£120	£140	£150
1914	7,251,124	£115	£120	£140	£150
1915	2,042,747	£115	£120	£140	£150
M on ground on reverse (Melbourne Mint)					
1915	125,664	£115	£120	£140	£150
P on ground on reverse (Perth Mint)					
1911	130,373	£115	£120	£140	£225
1915	136,219	£115	£120	£140	£225
1918	unrecorded	£175	£500	£1150	£3000
S on ground on reverse (Sydney Mint)					
1911	252,000	£115	£120	£140	£150
1912	278,000	£115	£120	£140	£150
1914	322,000	£115	£120	£140	£150
1915	892,000	£115	£120	£140	£150
1916	448,000	£115	£120	£140	£150
SA on ground on reverse (Pretoria Mint)					
1923 Proof only	655	—	—	—	£1150
1925	946,615	£115	£120	£140	£150
1926	806,540	£115	£120	£140	£150

GEORGE VI (1937–52)

		F	VF	EF	UNC
1937 Proof only	5,501	—	—	—	£650

Later issues are included in the Decimal section.

CROWNS

DATE	F	VF	EF	UNC

OLIVER CROMWELL

	F	VF	EF	UNC
1658 8 over 7 (always)..............................	£1900	£3500	£6750	—
1658 Dutch Copy		Extremely rare		
1658 Patterns. In Various Metals................		Extremely rare		

CHARLES II (1660–85)

	F	VF	EF	UNC
1662 First bust, rose (2 varieties)	£250	£800	£4500	—
1662 — no rose (2 varieties)......................	£250	£800	£4500	—
1663 —	£250	£800	£4400	—
1664 Second bust	£200	£800	£4000	—
1665 —	£1500	£4000	—	—
1666 —	£300	£900	£4750	—
1666 — error RE.X for REX		Extremely rare		
1666 — Elephant below bust	£750	£2750	£15000	—
1667 —	£160	£500	£3000	—
1668/7 — 8 over 7	£170	£550	—	—
1668 —	£170	£550	£3500	—
1669/8 — 9 over 8	£350	£800	—	—
1669 —	£300	£1000	£4750	—
1670/69 — 70 over 69	£200	£1000	—	—
1670 —	£175	£600	£3500	—
1671..	£170	£600	£3000	—
1671 Third bust	£170	£600	£3000	—
1672 —	£170	£500	£3000	—
1673 —	£170	£500	£3000	—
1674 —		Extremely rare		
1675 —	£700	£2200	—	—
1675/3 —	£700	£2200	—	—
1676 —	£175	£550	£3000	—
1677 —	£190	£600	£3250	—
1677/6 — 7 over 6	£200	£900	—	—
1678/7 —	£200	£900	—	—
1678/7 — 8 over 7	£275	£900	—	—
1679 —	£180	£600	£3000	—
1679 Fourth bust	£180	£600	£3000	—
1680 Third bust	£180	£800	£3500	—
1680/79 — 80 over 79	£200	£800	—	—
1680 Fourth bust	£180	£750	£4000	—
1680/79 — 80 over 79	£200	£1000	—	—
1681 —	£180	£600	£3500	—
1681 — Elephant & Castle below bust.......	£3200	£11000	—	—
1682/1 —	£180	£700	£3250	—
1682 — edge error QVRRTO for QVARTO .	£400	—	—	—
1683 —	£400	£1000	£4000	—
1684 —	£400	£1300	—	—

JAMES II (1685–88)

	F	VF	EF	UNC
1686 First bust	£325	£1000	£5000	—
1686 — No stops on obv	£400	£1500	—	—
1687 Second bust	£300	£700	£3500	—
1688/7 — 8 over 7	£320	£850	—	—
1688 —	£280	£800	£3500	—

WILLIAM AND MARY (1688–94)

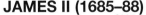

	F	VF	EF	UNC
1691	£700	£1600	£4900	—
1692	£700	£1600	£4800	—
1692 2 over upside down 2	£700	£1600	£4800	—

DATE	F	VF	EF	UNC

WILLIAM III (1694–1702)

DATE	F	VF	EF	UNC
1695 First bust	£100	£300	£1900	—
1696 —	£90	£275	£1750	—
1696 — no stops on obv.	£225	£400	—	—
1996 — no stops obv./rev.	£250	£400	—	—
1696 — GEI for DEI	£750	£1800	—	—
1696 Second bust				Unique
1696 Third bust	£90	£275	£1800	—
1697 —	£1500	£5000	£18500	—
1700 Third bust variety edge year DUODECIMO	£140	£550	£1800	—
1700 — edge year DUODECIMO TERTIO..	£140	£550	£1800	—

ANNE (1702–14)

DATE	F	VF	EF	UNC
1703 First bust, VIGO	£350	£1000	£4000	—
1705 — Plumes in angles on rev.	£500	£1500	£6250	—
1706 — Roses & Plumes in angles on rev...	£160	£600	£2200	—
1707 — —	£160	£600	£2200	—
1707 Second bust, E below	£160	£500	£2100	—
1707 — Plain	£160	£500	£2100	—
1708 — E below	£160	£500	£2100	—
1708/7 — 8 over 7	£160	£800	—	—
1708 — Plain	£160	£650	£2100	—
1708 — — error BR for BRI			Extremely rare	
1708 — Plumes in angles on rev.	£180	£700	£2500	—
1713 Third bust, Roses & Plumes in angles on rev.	£180	£700	£2500	—

GEORGE I (1714–27)

DATE	F	VF	EF	UNC
1716	£650	£1700	£6000	—
1718 8 over 6	£650	£1700	£5250	—
1720 20 over 18	£650	£1700	£5250	—
1723 SSC in angles on rev. (South Sea Co.)	£650	£1700	£5250	—
1726	£650	£1700	£5750	—

GEORGE II (1727–60)

DATE	F	VF	EF	UNC
1732 Young head, Plain, Proof	—	—	£12,500	
1732 — Roses & Plumes in angles on rev ..	£325	£700	£2750	—
1734 — —	£325	£700	£2750	—
1735 — —	£325	£700	£2750	—
1736 — —	£325	£700	£2750	—
1739 — Roses in angles on rev	£325	£600	£2750	—
1741 — —	£325	£600	£2600	—
1743 Old head, Roses in angles on rev	£225	£600	£2250	—
1746 — — LIMA below bust	£225	£600	£2250	—
1746 — Plain, Proof	—	—	£8000	—
1750 — —	£450	£1200	£3750	—
1751 — —	£550	£1600	£4200	—

GEORGE III (1760–1820)

DATE	F	VF	EF	UNC
Dollar with oval counterstamp	£175	£650	£1000	—
Dollar with octagonal counterstamp	£200	£600	£850	—
1804 Bank of England Dollar, Britannia rev.	£120	£275	£550	—
1818 LVIII	£40	£100	£300	£800
1818 LIX	£40	£100	£300	£800
1819 LIX	£40	£100	£300	£800
1819 LIX 9 over 8	£45	£150	£425	—
1819 LIX no stops on edge	£60	£150	£400	£1000
1819 LX	£40	£100	£325	£900
1820 LX	£35	£100	£300	£800
1820 LX 20 over 19	£35	£200	£500	—

DATE	MINTAGE	F	VF	EF	UNC

GEORGE IV (1820–30)

1821 First bust, St George rev.

	MINTAGE	F	VF	EF	UNC
SECUNDO on edge	437,976	£40	£180	£700	£1500
1821 — — Proof	Incl. above	£40	£180	—	£5500
1821 — — Proof TERTIO (error edge)	Incl above	£40	£180	—	£5000
1822 — — SECUNDO	124,929	£40	£180	£700	£1500
1822 — — TERTIO	Incl above	£40	£180	£700	£1500
1823 — — Proof only				Extremely rare	
1826 Second bust, shield rev, SEPTIMO					
Proof only		—	—	£2400	£9000

WILLIAM IV (1830–37)

			UNC
1831 Proof only W.W. on truncation	—	—	£15000
1831 Proof only W. WYON on truncation	—	—	£17500
1834 Proof only	—	—	—£30000

VICTORIA (1837–1901)

YOUNG HEAD ISSUES

	MINTAGE	F	VF	EF	UNC
1839 Proof only	—	—	—	—£12000	
1844 Star stops on edge	94,248	£50	£260	£1200	£3000
1844 Cinquefoil stops on edge	incl. above	£50	£260	£1200	£3000
1845 Star stops on edge	159,192	£50	£260	£1200	£3000
1845 Cinquefoil stops on edge	incl. above	£50	£260	£1200	£3000
1847	140,976	£65	£300	£1400	£4200

GOTHIC HEAD ISSUES (Proof only)

	MINTAGE	F	VF	EF	UNC
1847 mdcccxlvii UNDECIMO on edge	8,000	£800	£1400	£2200	£3500
1847 — Plain edge	—	—	—	—	£4200
1853 mdcccliii SEPTIMO on edge	460	—	—	—£10000	
1853 — Plain edge	—	—	—	—£15000	

JUBILEE HEAD ISSUES

	MINTAGE	F	VF	EF	UNC
1887	173,581	£20	£30	£60	£160
1887 Proof	1,084	—	—	—	£1200
1888 Narrow date	131,899	£20	£35	£90	£250
1888 Wide date	incl above	£25	£60	£300	—
1889	1,807,224	£20	£30	£60	£150
1890	997,862	£20	£30	£70	£240
1891	556,394	£20	£30	£70	£240
1892	451,334	£20	£30	£80	£260

OLD HEAD ISSUES (Regnal date on edge in Roman numerals)

	MINTAGE	F	VF	EF	UNC
1893 LVI	497,845	£20	£45	£150	£375
1893 LVII	incl. above	£20	£45	£200	£425
1893 Proof	1,312	—	—	—	£1400
1894 LVII	144,906	£20	£45	£175	£400
1894 LVIII	incl. above	£20	£45	£175	£400
1895 LVIII	252,862	£20	£45	£175	£400
1895 LIX	incl. above	£20	£45	£175	£400
1896 LIX	317,599	£20	£45	£175	£450
1896 LX	incl. above	£20	£45	£175	£400
1897 LX	262,118	£20	£45	£175	£400
1897 LXI	incl. above	£20	£45	£175	£450
1898 LXI	166,150	£20	£45	£175	£500
1898 LXII	incl. above	£20	£45	£175	£400
1899 LXII	166,300	£20	£45	£175	£400
1899 LXIII	incl. above	£20	£45	£175	£400
1900 LXIII	353,356	£20	£45	£175	£400
1900 LXIV	incl. above	£20	£45	£175	£400

Victoria, Jubilee head

DATE	MINTAGE	F	VF	EF	UNC

EDWARD VII (1901–10)

1902..	256,020	£70	£130	£200	£290
1902 "Matt Proof"	15,123	—	—	—	£300

GEORGE V (1910–36)

1927 Proof only	15,030	—	£100	£170	£350
1928..	9,034	£110	£160	£300	£500
1929..	4,994	£110	£160	£300	£500
1930..	4,847	£110	£160	£300	£525
1931..	4,056	£110	£160	£300	£500
1932..	2,395	£200	£400	£800	£1250
1933..	7,132	£110	£160	£300	£525
1934..	932	£800	£1600	£3500	£5500
1935 Jubilee issue. Incuse edge inscription	714,769	£15	£20	£30	£45
1935 — — error edge inscription	incl. above	—	—	—	£1500
1935 — Specimen in box	incl. above	—	—	—	£60
1935 — Proof	incl. above	—	—	—	£200
1935 — Proof. Raised edge inscription	2,500	—	—	£275	£550
1935 — — fine lettering...............	incl. above	—	—	—	£1000
1935 — — error edge inscription	incl. above	—	—	—	£1500
1935 — Gold proof.....................	30	—	—	Extremely rare	
1936..	2,473	£180	£350	£600	£1000

GEORGE VI (1936–52)

1937 Coronation..........................	418,699	£18	£24	£38	£55
1937 Proof..................................	26,402	—	—	—	£65
1951 Festival of Britain, Proof-like	1,983,540	—	—	£4	£7

ELIZABETH II (1952–   )

Pre-Decimal issues (Five Shillings)

1953	5,962,621	—	—	£3	£6
1953 Proof.................................	40,000	—	—	—	£25
1960..	1,024,038	—	—	£3	£6
1960 Polished dies	70,000	—	—	—	£9
1965 Churchill	19,640,000	—	—	—	£1

Later issues are listed in the Decimal section.

DOUBLE FLORINS

VICTORIA (1837–1901)

1887 Roman I.............................	483,347	£15	£30	£50	£115
1887 Roman I Proof	incl. above	—	—	—	£600
1887 Arabic 1	incl. above	£15	£30	£50	£115
1887 Arabic 1 Proof....................	incl. above	—	—	—	£550
1888..	243,340	£15	£40	£80	£150
1888 Second I in VICTORIA an inverted 1	incl. above	£25	£50	£100	£375
1889..	1,185,111	£18	£30	£45	£140
1889 inverted 1...........................	incl. above	£25	£50	£100	£400
1890..	782,146	£15	£40	£60	£130

Patterns were also produced in 1911, 1914 and 1950 and are all extremely rare.

HALFCROWNS

DATE	MINTAGE	F	VF	EF	UNC

OLIVER CROMWELL

1656				Extremely rare	
1658		£1350	£2500	£5000	—
1658 Proof in Gold				Extremely rare	

CHARLES II (1660–1685)

1663 First bust		£170	£600	£3500	—
1663 — no stops on obv.		£200	£800	—	—
1664 Second bust		£250	£1200	£5000	—
1666 Third bust		£900	—	—	—
1666 — Elephant		£800	£3300	—	—
1667/4 — 7 over 4				Extremely rare	
1668/4 — 8 over 4		£300	£1500	—	—
1669 —		£400	£1600	—	—
1669/4 — 9 over 4		£250	£900	—	—
1670 —		£125	£500	£2500	—
1670 — MRG for MAG		£300	£1000	—	—
1671 —		£150	£500	£2500	—
1671/0 — 1 over 0		£160	£600	£3000	—
1672 — Third bust				Extremely rare	
1672 Fourth bust		£150	£500	£2750	—
1673 —		£150	£500	£2500	—
1673 — Plumes both sides				Extremely rare	
1673 — Plume below bust		£6500	£18,000	—	—
1674 —		£150	£650	—	—
1675 —		£145	£400	£2000	—
1676 —		£145	£400	£2000	—
1676 — inverted 1 in date		£145	£400	£2000	—
1677 —		£145	£400	£1800	—
1678 —		£200	£800	—	—
1679 — GRATTA error				Extremely rare	
1679 —		£150	£420	£1800	—
1680 —		£175	£750	—	—
1681/0 — 1 over 0		£250	—	—	—
1681 —		£145	£500	£2350	—
1681 — Elephant & Castle		£3500	£10000	—	—
1682 —		£150	£500	£3000	—
1683 —		£150	£500	£2750	—
1683 — Plume below bust				Extremely rare	
1684/3 — 4 over 3		£325	£900	£4200	—

JAMES II (1685–1688)

1685 First bust		£220	£650	£3200	—
1686 —		£220	£650	£3500	—
1686/5 — 6 over 5		£220	£700	—	—
1686 — V over S		£225	£750	—	—
1687 —		£220	£675	£3300	—
1687/6 — 7 over 6		£300	£850	—	—
1687 Second bust		£200	£600	£3200	—
1688 —		£200	£600	£3000	—

WILLIAM AND MARY (1688–1694)

1689 First busts; first shield		£100	£350	£1600	—
1689 — — no pearls in crown		£100	£350	£1600	—
1689 — — FRA for FR		£160	£600	£2000	—
1689 — — No stop on obv		£100	£500	£1850	—
1689 — Second shield		£100	£350	£1600	—
1689 — — no pearls in crown		£100	£350	£1600	—
1690 — —		£160	£700	£2600	—
1690 — — error GRETIA for GRATIA		£550	£1600	£5250	—
1691 Second busts		£150	£450	£2200	—
1692 —		£150	£450	£2200	—

DATE	MINTAGE	F	VF	EF	UNC
1693 —		£170	£475	£2200	—
1693 — 3 over inverted 3		£180	£650	£2750	—

WILLIAM III (1694–1702)

1696 First bust, large shields, early harp		£70	£240	£900	—
1696 — — — B (Bristol) below bust		£70	£240	£1000	—
1696 — — — C (Chester)................................		£80	£325	£1100	—
1696 — — — E (Exeter) —		£100	£400	£1300	—
1696 — — — N (Norwich)..............................		£90	£400	£1300	—
1696 — — — y (York)...................................		£80	£350	£1500	—
1696 — — — — Scottish arms at date............				Extremely rare	
1696 — — ordinary harp		£80	£275	£1400	—
1696 — — — C..		£110	£500	£1200	
1696 — — — E..		£100	£500	£1200	—
1696 — — — N...		£150	£600	£2250	—
1696 — Small shields, ordinary harp		£70	£250	£1000	—
1696 — — — B..		£90	£300	£1100	—
1696 — — — C..		£90	£300	£1100	—
1696 — — — E..		£100	£450	£2000	—
1696 — — — N...		£110	£450	£1500	—
1696 — — — y..		£100	£500	£1600	—
1696 Second bust..				Only one known	
1697 First bust, large shields, ordinary harp		£75	£300	£1150	—
1697 — — — GRR for GRA				Extremely rare	
1697 — — — B..		£80	£300	£1250	—
1697 — — — C..		£80	£350	£1300	—
1697 — — — E..		£90	£350	£1300	—
1697 — — — N...		£100	£350	£1300	—
1697 — — — y..		£90	£350	£1350	—
1698 — —		£100	£350	£1350	—
1698/7 — — 8 over 7				Extremely rare	
1699 — —		£150	£475	£1950	—
1699 — — Scottish arms at date.....................				Extremely rare	
1700 — —		£140	£400	£1750	—
1701 — —		£145	£450	£1800	—
1701 — — No stops on rev.............................		£160	£625	—	—
1701 — — Elephant & Castle below .... Fair £2200					
1701 — — Plumes in angles on rev.		£230	£650	£3000	—

ANNE (1702–1714)

1703 Plain (pre-Union)...................................		£600	£2300	—	—
1703 VIGO below bust		£100	£340	£1100	—
1704 Plumes in angles on rev............................		£150	£500	£1600	—
1705 —		£120	£500	£1750	—
1706 Roses & Plumes in angles on rev.		£90	£350	£1400	—
1707 —		£80	£300	£1100	—
1707 Plain (post-Union)..................................		£80	£200	£900	—
1707 E below bust...		£80	£200	£900	—
1707 — SEPTIMO edge				Extremely rare	
1708 Plain..		£80	£250	£1000	—
1708 E below bust...		£80	£250	£1000	—
1708 Plumes in angles on rev.........................		£90	£275	£1100	—
1709 Plain..		£75	£275	£900	—
1709 E below bust...		£220	£900	—	—
1710 Roses & Plumes in angles on rev. ,,,,,,,,,,		£80	£325	£1000	—
1712 —		£80	£325	£1000	—
1713 Plain...		£80	£325	£1000	—
1713 Roses & Plumes in angles on rev.		£80	£325	£1000	—
1714 —		£80	£325	£1000	—
1714/3 4 over 3		£125	£500	—	—

GEORGE I (1714–1727)

1715 Roses & Plumes in angles on rev.		£475	£950	£3200	—
1715 Plain edge..				Extremely rare	
1717 —		£475	£950	£3200	—
1720 —		£450	£950	£3200	—
1720/17 20 over 17		£425	£850	£3000	—
1723 SSC in angles on rev.		£425	£850	£2800	—
1726 Small Roses & Plumes in angles on rev...		£4400	£12,000	—	—

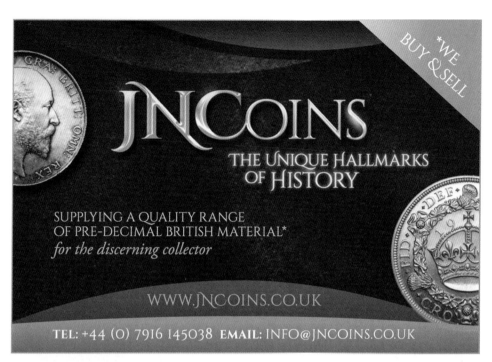

DATE	MINTAGE	F	VF	EF	UNC

GEORGE II (1727–1760)

DATE	MINTAGE	F	VF	EF	UNC
1731 Young head, Plain, proof only	—	—	£6000	—
1731 — Roses & Plumes in angles on rev.	£160	£400	£1600	—
1732 — —	£160	£400	£1600	—
1734 — —	£160	£400	£1650	—
1735 — —	£160	£400	£1650	—
1736 — —	£160	£400	£1650	—
1739 — Roses in angles on rev.	£150	£400	£1500	—
1741/39 — — 41 over 30	£160	£550	—	—
1741 — —	£150	£400	£1500	—
1743 Old head, Roses in angles on rev.	£85	£225	£1000	—
1745 — —	£85	£225	£1000	—
1745 — LIMA below bust	£70	£175	£650	—
1746 — —	£70	£175	£650	—
1746/5 — — 6 over 5	£80	£220	£800	—
1746 — Plain, Proof	—	—	£3500	—
1750 — —	£225	£550	£1900	—
1751 — —	£250	£750	£2100	—

GEORGE III (1760–1820)

DATE	MINTAGE	F	VF	EF	UNC
1816 "Bull head"	—	£25	£80	£250	£500
1817 —	8,092,656	£25	£80	£250	£500
1817 "Small head"	incl. above	£25	£80	£250	£500
1818 —	2,905,056	£25	£80	£250	£500
1819/8 — 9 over 8	incl. above			Extremely rare	
1819 —	4,790,016	£25	£80	£250	£525
1820 —	2,396,592	£50	£140	£500	£1000

GEORGE IV (1820–30)

DATE	MINTAGE	F	VF	EF	UNC
1820 First bust, first reverse	incl. above	£30	£80	£300	£600
1821 — —	1,435,104	£30	£80	£300	£600
1821 — — Proof	incl. above	—	—	—	£2700
1823 — —	2,003,760	£1000	£3200	—	—
1823 — Second reverse	incl. above	£30	£80	£300	£600
1824 — —	465,696	£30	£90	£275	£650
1824 Second bust, third reverse	incl. above			Extremely rare	
1825 — —	2,258,784	£30	£80	£200	£450
1826 — —	2,189,088	£30	£80	£200	£450
1826 — — Proof	incl. above	—	—	—	£1600
1828 — —	49,890	£80	£200	£600	£1200
1829 — —	508,464	£60	£150	£450	£900

WILLIAM IV (1830–37)

DATE	MINTAGE	F	VF	EF	UNC
1831	—			Extremely rare	
1831 Proof (W.W. in script & block)	—	—	—	—	£2200
1834 W.W. in block	993,168	£30	£80	£300	£700
1834 W.W. in script	incl. above	£30	£80	£300	£700
1835	281,952	£35	£90	£300	£750
1836	1,588,752	£30	£70	£300	£675
1836/5 6 over 5	incl. above	£60	£125	£600	—
1837	150,526	£45	£160	£600	£1200

VICTORIA (1837–1901)

YOUNG HEAD ISSUES

DATE	MINTAGE	F	VF	EF	UNC
1839 (two varieties)	—	£1200	£3750	£9000	—
1839 Proof	—	—	—	—	£5000
1840	386,496	£60	£200	£700	£1800
1841	42,768	£900	£2000	£4000	£7500
1842	486,288	£55	£150	£700	£1500
1843	454,608	£140	£450	£1100	£3200
1844	1,999,008	£45	£110	£550	£1500
1845	2,231,856	£45	£110	£550	£1500
1846	1,539,668	£55	£140	£600	£1500
1848 Plain 8	367,488	£150	£450	£1400	£3750
1848/6	incl. above	£120	£300	£800	£2800
1849	261,360	£70	£160	£600	£1600
1849 Small date	incl. above	£90	£220	£850	£1900

DATE	MINTAGE	F	VF	EF	UNC
1850..	484,613	£70	£200	£600	£2000
1853 Proof only	—	—	—	—	£5000
1874..	2,188,599	£25	£70	£260	£600
1875..	1,113,483	£25	£70	£260	£550
1876..	633,221	£30	£80	£280	£650
1876/5 6 over 5	incl. above	£35	£80	£280	£650
1877..	447,059	£25	£70	£250	£550
1878..	1,466,323	£25	£70	£250	£550
1879..	901,356	£35	£80	£280	£650
1880	1,346,350	£25	£70	£250	£500
1881..	2,301,495	£25	£70	£250	£475
1882..	808,227	£30	£70	£250	£475
1883..	2,982,779	£25	£70	£250	£450
1884..	1,569,175	£25	£70	£250	£450
1885..	1,628,438	£25	£70	£250	£440
1886..	891,767	£25	£70	£250	£440
1887..	1,438,046	£25	£65	£260	£450
JUBILEE HEAD ISSUES					
1887	incl. above	£8	£14	£30	£75
1887 Proof.................................	1,084	—	—	—	£400
1888..	1,428,787	£12	£25	£50	£180
1889..	4,811,954	£10	£20	£50	£160
1890..	3,228,111	£12	£22	£70	£180
1891..	2,284,632	£12	£22	£70	£180
1892..	1,710,946	£12	£22	£75	£200
OLD HEAD ISSUES					
1893..	1,792,600	£12	£25	£60	£110
1893 Proof.................................	1,312	—	—	—	£600
1894..	1,524,960	£15	£35	£90	£250
1895..	1,772,662	£12	£30	£70	£190
1896..	2,148,505	£12	£22	£65	£190
1897..	1,678,643	£12	£22	£65	£175
1898..	1,870,055	£12	£22	£65	£175
1899..	2,865,872	£12	£22	£65	£175
1900..	4,479,128	£12	£22	£65	£175
1901..	1,516,570	£12	£22	£65	£175

DATE	MINTAGE	F	VF	EF	UNC

EDWARD VII (1901–10)

DATE	MINTAGE	F	VF	EF	UNC
1902	1,316,008	£12	£30	£80	£170
1902 "Matt Proof"	15,123	—	—	—	£250
1903	274,840	£175	£550	£2200	£4500
1904	709,652	£60	£225	£500	£1500
1905	166,008	£500	£1400	£5000	£9000
1906	2,886,206	£12	£50	£200	£900
1907	3,693,930	£12	£50	£200	£900
1908	1,758,889	£20	£80	£400	£1300
1909	3,051,592	£12	£60	£340	£800
1910	2,557,685	£12	£45	£130	£475

GEORGE V (1910–36)

First issue

DATE	MINTAGE	F	VF	EF	UNC
1911	2,914,573	£12	£30	£75	£200
1911 Proof	6,007	—	—	—	£260
1912	4,700,789	£10	£22	£50	£185
1913	4,090,169	£10	£24	£75	£200
1914	18,333,003	£7	£12	£40	£70
1915	32,433,066	£7	£12	£35	£65
1916	29,530,020	£7	£12	£35	£65
1917	11,172,052	£8	£15	£45	£100
1918	29,079,592	£7	£12	£35	£70
1919	10,266,737	£7	£15	£45	£100

Second issue—debased silver

DATE	MINTAGE	F	VF	EF	UNC
1920	17,982,077	£4	£8	£22	£70
1921	23,677,889	£4	£8	£30	£65
1922	16,396,724	£5	£9	£24	£70
1923	26,308,526	£6	£8	£20	£45
1924	5,866,294	£15	£35	£90	£220
1925	1,413,461	£30	£75	£300	£900
1926	4,473,516	£10	£25	£45	£175

Third issue —Modified effigy

DATE	MINTAGE	F	VF	EF	UNC
1926	incl. above	£6	£14	£40	£100
1927	6,837,872	£6	£12	£35	£75

Fourth issue—New shield reverse

DATE	MINTAGE	F	VF	EF	UNC
1927 Proof	15,000	—	—	—	£100
1928	18,762,727	£5	£8	£20	£35
1929	17,632,636	£5	£8	£20	£35
1930	809,051	£15	£60	£325	£900
1931	11,264,468	£5	£8	£20	£35
1932	4,793,643	£6	£10	£25	£90
1933	10,311,494	£5	£8	£20	£40
1934	2,422,399	£7	£12	£65	£185
1935	7,022,216	£5	£8	£18	£25
1936	7,039,423	£5	£8	£18	£20

George V, fourth issue, new shield reverse

GEORGE VI (1936–52)

DATE	MINTAGE	F	VF	EF	UNC
1937	9,106,440	—	£6	£9	£14
1937 Proof	26,402	—	—	—	£20
1938	6,426,478	£5	£6	£15	£25
1939	15,478,635	£5	£6	£9	£10
1940	17,948,439	£5	£6	£9	£10
1941	15,773,984	£5	£6	£0	£10
1942	31,220,090	£5	£6	£9	£10
1943	15,462,875	£5	£6	£9	£10
1944	15,255,165	£5	£6	£9	£10
1945	19,849,242	£5	£6	£9	£10
1946	22,724,873	£5	£6	£9	£10

Cupro-nickel

DATE	MINTAGE	F	VF	EF	UNC
1947	21,911,484	—	£1	£2	£4
1948	71,164,703	—	£1	£2	£4
1949	28,272,512	—	£1	£2	£6
1950	28,335,500	—	£1	£2	£6
1950 Proof	17,513	—	—	—	£35
1951	9,003,520	—	£1	£2	£6
1951 Proof	20,000	—	—	—	£10
1952			Only one known		

DATE	MINTAGE	F	VF	EF	UNC

ELIZABETH II (1952–)

1953	4,333,214	—	—	£1	£3
1953 Proof	40,000	—	—	—	£8
1954	11,614,953	—	£1	£6	£35
1955	23,628,726	—	—	£1	£6
1956	33,934,909	—	—	£1	£6
1957	34,200,563	—	—	£1	£6
1958	15,745,668	—	£1	£6	£28
1959	9,028,844	—	£1	£9	£32
1960	19,929,191	—	—	£1	£2
1961	25,887,897	—	—	—	£2
1961 Polished dies	incl. above	—	—	£1	£2
1962	24,013,312	—	—	—	£1
1963	17,625,200	—	—	—	£1
1964	5,973,600	—	—	—	£1
1965	9,778,440	—	—	—	£1
1966	13,375,200	—	—	—	£1
1967	33,058,400	—	—	—	£1
1970 Proof	—	—	—	—	£8

FLORINS

VICTORIA (1837–1901)

YOUNG (CROWNED) HEAD ISSUES
"Godless" type (without D.G.—"Dei Gratia")

1848 "Godless" Pattern only plain edge	—			Very rare	
1848 "Godless" Pattern only milled edge	—			Extremely rare	
1849	413,820	£25	£60	£200	£400

(Beware of recent forgeries)
"Gothic" type i.e. date in Roman numerals in obverse legend
"brit." in legend. No die no.

1851 mdcccli Proof	1,540			Extremely rare	
1852 mdccclii	1,014,552	£22	£60	£220	£600
1853 mdcccliii	3,919,950	£22	£55	£220	£575
1853 — Proof	incl. above	—	—	—	£3500
1854 mdcccliv	550,413	£500	£1500	—	—
1855 mdccclv	831,017	£25	£70	£240	£600
1856 mdccclvi	2,201,760	£25	£70	£240	£600
1857 mdccclvii	1,671,120	£25	£55	£240	£600
1858 mdccclviii	2,239,380	£25	£55	£240	£600
1859 mdccclix	2,568,060	£25	£55	£240	£600
1860 mdccclx	1,475,100	£35	£80	£250	£750
1862 mdccclxii	594,000	£240	£600	£1200	£3200
1863 mdccclxiii	938,520	£900	£1800	£3500	£7000

"brit" in legend. Die no. below bust

"Gothic" florin

1864 mdccclxiv	1,861,200	£25	£60	£240	£600
1864 Gothic Piedfort flan	incl. above			Extremely rare	
1865 mdccclxv	1,580,044	£35	£70	£275	£650
1866 mdccclxvi	914,760	£35	£70	£275	£600
1867 mdccclxvii	423,720	£40	£100	£350	£800
1867 — only 42 arcs in border	incl. above			Extremely rare	

"britt" in legend. Die no. below bust

1868 mdccclxviii	896,940	£30	£75	£320	£700
1869 mdccclxix	297,000	£30	£75	£320	£800
1870 mdccclxx	1,080,648	£20	£55	£230	£500
1871 mdccclxxi	3,425,605	£22	£55	£230	£500
1872 mdccclxxii	7,199,690	£22	£55	£210	£450
1873 mdccclxxiii	5,921,839	£22	£55	£220	£450
1874 mdccclxxiv	1,642,630	£22	£55	£220	£450
1874 — iv over iii in date	incl. above	£30	£70	£300	£625
1875 mdccclxxv	1,117,030	£20	£60	£210	£500
1876 mdccclxxvi	580,034	£40	£110	£425	£850
1877 mdccclxxvii	682,292	£25	£60	£220	£475
1877 — 48 arcs in border no W.W.	incl. above	£25	£60	£220	£475
1877 — 42 arcs	incl. above	£25	£60	£220	£475
1877 — — no die number	incl. above			Extremely rare	
1878 mdccclxxviii with die number	1,786,680	£22	£60	£220	£450

DATE	MINTAGE	F	VF	EF	UNC
1879 mdcccixxxix no die no	1,512,247			Extremely rare	
1879 — 48 arcs in border	incl. above	£25	£60	£220	£450
1879 — no die number	incl. above			Extremely rare	
1879 — 38 arcs, no W.W..	incl. above	£22	£55	£210	£450
1880 mdccclxxx Younger portrait	—			Extremely rare	
1880 — 34 arcs, Older portrait ...	2,167,170	£25	£60	£200	£425
1881 mdccclxxxi — —...............	2,570,337	£20	£55	£200	£425
1881 — xxI'i broken puncheon...	incl. above	£30	£70	£200	£480
1883 mdccclxxxiii — —	3,555,667	£20	£50	£190	£400
1884 mdccclxxxiv — —	1,447,379	£20	£50	£190	£400
1885 mdccclxxxv — —	1,758,210	£20	£50	£190	£400
1886 mdccclxxxvi — —	591,773	£20	£50	£190	£400
1887 mdccclxxxvii — —	1,776,903	£50	£120	£300	£675
1887 — 46 arcs......................	incl. above	£50	£120	£350	£725
JUBILEE HEAD ISSUES					
1887	incl. above	£6	£15	£30	£55
1887 Proof	1,084	—	—	—	£300
1888	1,547,540	£7	£15	£45	£120
1889	2,973,561	£8	£18	£50	£140
1890	1,684,737	£10	£25	£80	£260
1891	836,439	£20	£60	£200	£525
1892	283,401	£30	£100	£325	£850
VICTORIA—OLD HEAD ISSUES					
1893	1,666,103	£7	£16	£40	£85
1893 Proof	1,312	—	—	—	£350
1894	1,952,842	£10	£20	£70	£220
1895	2,182,968	£9	£25	£70	£200
1896	2,944,416	£7	£20	£55	£160
1897	1,699,921	£7	£20	£55	£150
1898	3,061,343	£7	£20	£55	£150
1899	3,966,953	£7	£20	£55	£150
1900	5,528,630	£7	£20	£55	£150
1901	2,648,870	£7	£20	£55	£150

EDWARD VII (1901–10)

DATE	MINTAGE	F	VF	EF	UNC
1902	2,189,575	£10	£22	£60	£110
1902 "Matt Proof"	15,123	—	—	—	£160
1903	1,995,298	£10	£35	£120	£550
1904	2,769,932	£12	£40	£150	£500
1905	1,187,596	£65	£175	£600	£1600
1906	6,910,128	£10	£35	£130	£525
1907	5,947,895	£11	£35	£130	£525
1908	3,280,010	£18	£55	£350	£900
1909	3,482,829	£15	£50	£240	£700
1910	5,650,713	£14	£35	£100	£320

GEORGE V (1910–36)

First issue

DATE	MINTAGE	F	VF	EF	UNC
1911	5,951,284	£6	£12	£40	£90
1911 Proof	6,007	—	—	—	£170
1912	8,571,731	£6	£15	£35	£130
1913	4,545,278	£10	£25	£50	£180
1914	21,252,701	£6	£18	£28	£60
1915	12,367,939	£7	£18	£26	£60
1916	21,064,337	£6	£18	£25	£60
1917	11,181,617	£7	£22	£35	£90
1918	29,211,792	£6	£18	£28	£80
1919	9,469,292	£8	£20	£40	£90

Second issue — debased silver

DATE	MINTAGE	F	VF	EF	UNC
1920	15,387,833	£4	£12	£40	£85
1921	34,863,895	£4	£12	£40	£65
1922	23,861,044	£4	£12	£40	£65
1923	21,546,533	£4	£10	£30	£60
1924	4,582,372	£12	£35	£95	£250
1925	1,404,136	£30	£75	£300	£800
1926	5,125,410	£7	£22	£50	£150

Fourth issue—new reverse

DATE	MINTAGE	F	VF	EF	UNC
1927 Proof only..........................	101,497	—	—	—	£110
1928	11,087,186	£4	£7	£15	£40

DATE	MINTAGE	F	VF	EF	UNC
1929	16,397,279	£4	£7	£16	£35
1930	5,753,568	£4	£7	£20	£50
1931	6,556,331	£4	£7	£18	£35
1932	717,041	£12	£30	£225	£600
1933	8,685,303	£4	£7	£18	£40
1935	7,540,546	£4	£7	£14	£30
1936	9,897,448	£4	£7	£14	£30

GEORGE VI (1936–52)

DATE	MINTAGE	F	VF	EF	UNC
1937	13,006,781	£4	£5	£7	£12
1937 Proof	26,402	–	–	–	£18
1938	7,909,388	£6	£8	£15	£30
1939	20,850,607	£4	£5	£8	£10
1940	18,700,338	£4	£5	£7	£12
1941	24,451,079	£4	£5	£7	£9
1942	39,895,243	£4	£5	£7	£9
1943	26,711,987	£4	£5	£7	£9
1944	27,560,005	£4	£5	£7	£9
1945	25,858,049	£4	£5	£7	£9
1946	22,300,254	£4	£5	£7	£9

Cupro-nickel

DATE	MINTAGE	F	VF	EF	UNC
1947	22,910,085	–	–	£1	£3
1948	67,553,636	–	–	£1	£3
1949	28,614,939	–	–	£1	£5
1950	24,357,490	–	–	£2	£7
1950 Proof	17,513	–	–	£1	£9
1951	27,411,747	–	–	£2	£8
1951 Proof	20,000	–	–	–	£9

ELIZABETH II (1952–)

DATE	MINTAGE	F	VF	EF	UNC
1953	11,958,710	–	–	–	£2
1953 Proof	40,000	–	–	–	£6
1954	13,085,422	–	–	£6	£30
1955	25,887,253	–	–	£1	£3
1956	47,824,500	–	–	£1	£3
1957	33,071,282	–	–	£4	£25
1958	9,564,580	–	–	£3	£28
1959	14,080,319	–	–	£4	£30
1960	13,831,782	–	–	£1	£4
1961	37,735,315	–	–	£1	£2
1962	35,147,903	–	–	£1	£2
1963	26,471,000	–	–	£1	£2
1964	16,539,000	–	–	£1	£2
1965	48,163,000	–	–	–	£1.50
1966	83,999,000	–	–	–	£1.50
1967	39,718,000	–	–	–	£1.50
1970 Proof	–	–	–	–	£10

SHILLINGS

OLIVER CROMWELL

1658	£850	£1900	£4000	–
1658 Dutch Copy			Extremely rare	

CHARLES II (1660–85)

1663 First bust	£125	£500	£1500	–
1663 — GARTIA error			Extremely rare	
1663 — Irish & Scottish shields transposed	£270	£800	–	–
1666 — Elephant below bust	£500	£1500	£6000	–
1666 "Guinea" head, elephant	£1800	£4500	–	–
1666 Second bust			Extremely rare	
1668 —	£120	£400	£1400	–
1668/3 — 8 over 3	£150	£500	–	–
1668 Second bust	£120	£450	£1400	–
1669/6 First bust variety			Extremely rare	
1669			Extremely rare	

DATE	F	VF	EF	UNC
1669 Second bust			Extremely rare	
1670 —	£150	£500	£1800	—
1671 —	£150	£500	£1800	—
1671 — Plume below, plume in centre rev.	£400	£1000	£4000	—
1672 —	£150	£550	£1800	—
1673 —	£150	£550	£1800	—
1673 — Plume below, plume in centre rev.	£450	£1200	£5000	—
1673/2 — 3 over 2..................................	£175	£600	—	—
1674/3 — 4 over 3..................................	£150	£550	—	—
1674 —	£150	£500	£2000	—
1674 — Plume below bust, plume in centre rev.	£350	£1200	£4500	—
1674 — Plume rev. only..............................	£700	£2000	£4600	—
1674 Third bust	£450	£1600	—	—
1675 Second bust	£200	£800	—	—
1675/4 — 5 over 4..................................	£220	£850	—	—
1675 — Plume below bust, plume in centre rev.	£400	£1100	£5000	—
1675 Third bust	£350	£1300	—	—
1675/3 — 5 over 3..................................	£300	£1100	—	—
1676 Second bust	£125	£450	£1700	—
1676/5 — 6 over 5..................................	£160	£550	—	—
1676 — Plume below bust, plume in centre rev.	£400	£1500	£5000	—
1677 —	£120	£500	£1900	—
1677 — Plume below bust	£1000	£2500	£8000	—
1678 —	£140	£500	£1750	—
1678/7 — 8 over 7..................................	£160	£700	—	—
1679 —	£140	£500	£2000	—
1679 — Plume below bust, plume in centre rev.	£400	£1100	£4800	—
1679 — Plume below bust	£700	£2500	£5800	—
1679 — 9 over 7......................................	£160	£600	—	—
1680 —			Extremely rare	
1680 — Plume below bust, plume in centre rev.	£900	£2500	£5500	—
1680/79 — — 80 over 79	£850	£2500	—	—
1681 —	£300	£850	£3000	—
1681 — 1 over 0......................................	£375	£900	£3250	—
1681/0 Elephant & Castle below bust	£3000	£9000	—	—
1682/1 — 2 over 1...................................	£1000	£3300	—	—
1683 —			Extremely rare	
1683 Fourth (Larger) bust	£220	£700	£2300	—
1684 —	£220	£700	£2300	—

JAMES II (1685–88)

	F	VF	EF	UNC
1685..	£200	£500	£2000	—
1685 Plume in centre rev. rev			Extremely rare	
1685 No stops on rev.	£220	£650	—	—
1686..	£220	£550	£2300	—
1686/5 6 over 5	£225	£600	£2250	—
1687..	£200	£600	£2200	—
1687/6 7 over 6	£200	£550	£2300	—
1688..	£200	£600	£2300	—
1688/7 last 8 over 7.................................	£220	£550	£2250	—

WILLIAM & MARY (1688–94)

	F	VF	EF	UNC
1692	£180	£500	£2250	—
1692 inverted 1......................................	£210	£550	£2300	—
1600..	£180	£500	£2250	—

WILLIAM III (1694–1702)

Provincially produced shillings carry privy marks or initials below the bust:
B: Bristol. C: Chester. E: Exeter. N: Norwich. Y or y: York.

	F	VF	EF	UNC
1695 First bust	£40	£120	£600	—
1696 —	£40	£100	£450	—
1696 — no stops on rev.	£60	£140	£750	—
1696 — MAB for MAG................................			Extremely rare	
1696 — 1669 error			Extremely rare	
1696 — 1669 various GVLELMVS errors			Extremely rare	
1696 — B below bust	£60	£150	£850	—
1696 — C..	£55	£150	£850	—
1696 — E...	£60	£160	£900	—

DATE	F	VF	EF	UNC
1696 — N	£55	£150	£800	—
1696 — y	£55	£150	£800	—
1696 — Y	£50	£150	£800	—
1696 Second bust		Only one known		
1696 Third bust C below	£160	£400	£1500	—
1696 — Y		Extremely rare		
1697 First bust	£50	£110	£400	—
1697 — GRI for GRA error		Extremely rare		
1697 — Scottish & Irish shields transposed		Extremely rare		
1697 — Irish arms at date		Extremely rare		
1697 — no stops on rev	£60	£180	£700	—
1697 — GVLELMVS error		Extremely rare		
1697 — B	£60	£150	£850	—
1697 — C	£60	£150	£850	—
1697 — E	£60	£150	£850	—
1697 — N	£60	£140	£800	—
1697 — — no stops on obv.		Extremely rare		
1697 — y	£60	£150	£750	—
1697 — — arms of France & Ireland transposed		Extremely rare		
1697 — Y	£50	£150	£650	—
1697 Third bust	£50	£125	£550	—
1697 — B	£60	£150	£650	—
1697 — C	£60	£150	£750	—
1697 — — Fr.a error	£150	£500	—	—
1697 — — no stops on obv.	£90	£300	—	—
1697 — — arms of Scotland at date		Extremely rare		
1697 — E	£60	£150	£750	—
1697 — N	£60	£150	£800	—
1697 — y	£60	£150	£775	—
1697 Third bust variety	£60	£140	£575	—
1697 — B	£60	£150	£900	—
1697 — C	£120	£600	—	—
1698 —	£80	£250	£950	—
1698 — Plumes in angles of rev.	£200	£500	£2000	—
1698 Fourth bust "Flaming hair"	£150	£500	£2000	—
1699 —	£110	£400	£1400	—
1699 Fifth bust	£100	£300	£1100	—
1699 — Plumes in angles on rev.	£150	£450	£1800	—
1699 — Roses in angles on rev.	£160	£500	£1800	—
1700 —	£65	£120	£550	—
1700 — Small round oo in date	£65	£120	£550	—
1700 — no stop after DEI		Extremely rare		
1700 — Plume below bust	£2500	£9500	—	—
1701 —	£80	£250	£900	—
1701 — Plumes in angles on rev.	£160	£600	£1800	—

William III First bust

ANNE (1702–14)

	F	VF	EF	UNC
1702 First bust (pre-Union with Scotland)	£80	£300	£700	—
1702 — Plumes in angles on rev.	£90	£275	£800	—
1702 — VIGO below bust	£70	£220	£650	—
1702 — — colon before ANNA		Extremely rare		
1703 Second bust, VIGO below	£65	£180	£700	—
1704 — Plain	£500	£1800	—	—
1704 — Plumes in angles on rev.	£80	£200	£800	—
1705 — Plain	£75	£200	£700	—
1705 — Plumes in angles on rev.	£70	£200	£725	—
1705 — Roses & Plumes in angles on rev.	£70	£200	£675	—
1707 — —	£60	£180	£625	—
1707 Second bust (post-Union) E below bust	£50	£125	£550	—
1707 — E* below bust	£70	£200	£750	—
1707 Third bust, Plain	£35	£100	£450	—
1707 — Plumes in angles on rev.	£50	£160	£750	—
1707 — E below bust	£40	£90	£500	—
1707 "Edinburgh" bust, E* below		Extremely rare		
1708 Second bust, E below	£50	£100	£450	—
1708 — E* below bust	£55	£165	£700	—
1708/7 — — 8 over 7		Extremely rare		

Anne, VIGO below bust

DATE	MINTAGE	F	VF	EF	UNC
1708 — Roses & Plumes in angles on rev.........		£80	£275	£650	—
1708 Third bust, Plain		£40	£120	£425	—
1708 — Plumes in angles on rev.		£70	£200	£600	—
1708 Third bust, E below bust		£60	£175	£650	—
1708/7 — — 8 over 7		£200	£450	—	—
1708 — Roses & Plumes in angles on rev.........		£70	£180	£575	—
1708 "Edinburgh" bust, E* below.....................		£60	£170	£525	—
1709 Third bust, Plain		£50	£140	£500	—
1709 "Edinburgh" bust, E* below.....................		£50	£170	£650	—
1709 — E no star (filled in die?)......................		£70	£160	£550	—
1710 Third bust, Roses & Plumes in angles......		£60	£140	£650	—
1710 Fourth bust, Roses & Plumes in angles ...		£60	£150	£625	—
1711 Third bust, Plain		£70	£160	£450	—
1711 Fourth bust, Plain		£30	£75	£250	—
1712 — Roses & Plumes in angles on rev.........		£60	£120	£425	—
1713 — —		£60	£120	£400	—
1713/2 — 3 over 2..		£60	£200	—	—
1714 — —		£60	£100	£340	—
1714/3 —				Extremely rare	

GEORGE I (1714–27)

1715 First bust, Roses & Plumes in angles on rev.	£80	£200	£850	—
1716 — —	£150	£500	£2000	—
1717 — —	£90	£300	£1350	—
1718 — —	£70	£225	£800	—
1719 — —	£120	£400	£2000	—
1720 — —	£70	£175	£450	—
1720/18 — —	£150	£500	£1450	—
1720 — Plain	£40	£100	£450	—
1721 — Roses & Plumes in angles on rev.	£100	£350	£1500	—
1721/0 — — 1 over 0	£70	£220	£900	—
1721 — Plain	£120	£450	£1400	—
1721/19 — — 21 over 19	£125	£400	—	—
1721/18 21 over 18 error, Plumes & Roses	£500	£1800	—	—
1722 — Roses & Plumes in angles on rev.	£80	£220	£950	—
1723 — —	£90	£240	£1000	—
1723 — SSC rev., Arms of France at date	£100	£275	£750	—
1723 — SSC in angles on rev	£35	£110	£275	—
1723 Second bust, SSC in angles on rev.	£50	£160	£525	—
1723 — Roses & Plumes in angles	£90	£240	£1000	—
1723 — WCC (Welsh Copper Co) below bust ..	£600	£1800	£6000	—
1724 — Roses & Plumes in angles on rev.	£80	£200	£750	—
1724 — WCC below bust	£600	£1800	£6000	—
1725 — Roses & Plumes in angles on rev.	£80	£200	£1000	—
1725 — — no stops on obv.	£90	£225	£1100	—
1725 — WCC below bust	£650	£2000	£6500	—
1726 — Roses & Plumes	£650	£1750	£6500	—
1726 — WCC below bust	£650	£2000	£6500	—
1727 — —			Extremely rare	
1727 — — no stops on obv.			Extremely rare	

GEORGE II (1727–60)

1727 Young head, Plumes in angles on rev.	£75	£300	£950	—
1727 — Roses & Plumes in angles on rev.	£60	£180	£650	—
1728 — —	£65	£180	£650	—
1728 — Plain	£75	£220	£700	—
1729 — Roses & Plumes in angles on rev.	£60	£200	£700	—
1731 — —	£70	£200	£700	—
1731 — Plumes in angles on rev.	£100	£400	£1250	—
1732 — Roses & Plumes in angles on rev.	£65	£200	£750	—
1734 — —	£65	£200	£700	—
1735 — —	£65	£200	£700	—
1736 — —	£65	£200	£700	—
1736/5 — — 6 over 5	£70	£200	£800	—
1737 — —	£65	£200	£650	—
1739 — Roses in angles on rev.	£50	£160	£450	—
1739/7 — — 9 over 7			Extremely rare	
1741 — —	£50	£160	£450	—
1741/39 — — 41 over 39			Extremely rare	
1743 Old head, Roses in angles on rev.	£30	£80	£325	—
1745 — —	£30	£80	£325	—

George II Young head

DATE	MINTAGE	F	VF	EF	UNC
1745 — — LIMA below bust		£35	£90	£325	—
1745/3 — — — 5 over 3..................................		£60	£175	£400	—
1746 — — ..		£50	£175	£650	—
1746/5 — — — 6 over 5................................		£100	£300	—	—
1746 — Plain, Proof	—	—	£3200	—	
1747 — Roses in angles on rev.		£45	£100	£375	—
1750 — Plain		£40	£140	£400	—
1750/6 — — 0 over 6		£60	£150	£500	—
1751 — — ..		£125	£400	£1200	—
1758 — — ..		£20	£50	£140	—

George II Old head

GEORGE III (1760–1820)

	MINTAGE	F	VF	EF	UNC
1763 "Northumberland" bust		£450	£800	£1600	—
(Beware recent counterfeits)					
1787 rev. no semée of hearts in 4th shield........		£20	£35	£100	—
1787 — No stop over head		£25	£40	£120	—
1787 — No stop at date..................................		£45	£75	£150	—
1787 — No stops on obv		£100	£250	£850	—
1787 rev. with semée of hearts in shield		£35	£65	£125	—
1798 "Dorrien Magens" bust...........................	—	—	—£25,000		

NEW COINAGE—shield in garter reverse

	MINTAGE	F	VF	EF	UNC
1816...	—	£12	£25	£75	£150
1817...	3,031,360	£12	£35	£85	£175
1817 GEOE for GEOR	incl. above	£120	£250	£625	—
1818...	1,342,440	£25	£45	£150	£400
1819...	7,595,280	£15	£35	£100	£200
1819/8 9 over 8	incl. above	£20	£50	£150	—
1820...	7,975,440	£12	£25	£100	£200

GEORGE IV (1820–30)

	MINTAGE	F	VF	EF	UNC
1821 First bust, first reverse	2,463,120	£15	£40	£150	£475
1821 — — Proof..........................	incl. above	—	—	—	£1300
1823 — Second reverse.............	693,000	£50	£90	£250	£600
1824 — —	4,158,000	£12	£40	£150	£400
1825 — —	2,459,160	£20	£50	£150	£525
1825/3 — — 5 over 3	incl. above			Extremely rare	
1825 Second bust, third reverse .	incl. above	£10	£25	£60	£200
1825 — — Roman I.....................	incl. above			Extremely rare	
1826 — —	6,351,840	£10	£25	£60	£200
1826 — — Proof.........................	incl. above	—	—	—	£650
1827 — —	574,200	£30	£70	£200	£475
1829 — —	879,120	£20	£60	£175	£425

WILLIAM IV (1830–37)

	MINTAGE	F	VF	EF	UNC
1831 Proof only	—	—	—	—	£1100
1834...	3,223,440	£15	£35	£170	£400
1835...	1,449,360	£15	£35	£170	£400
1836...	3,567,960	£15	£35	£170	£400
1837...	478,160	£20	£60	£200	£550

VICTORIA (1837–1901)

YOUNG HEAD ISSUES
First head

	MINTAGE	F	VF	EF	UNC
1838 WW on truncation...............	1,956,240	£20	£50	£200	£450
1839 —	5,666,760	£20	£50	£200	£450

Second head

	MINTAGE	F	VF	EF	UNC
1839 WW on truncation, Proof only	incl. above	—	—	—	£1100
1839 no WW...............................	incl. above	£20	£50	£180	£450
1840...	1,639,440	£20	£50	£180	£450
1841	875,160	£22	£50	£180	£450
1842...	2,094,840	£20	£45	£170	£475
1843...	1,465,200	£20	£50	£180	£475
1844	4,466,880	£15	£40	£150	£400
1845...	4,082,760	£15	£40	£150	£400
1846...	4,031,280	£15	£40	£150	£400
1848 last 8 of date over 6...........	1,041,480	£80	£160	£600	£1200

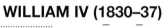

DATE	MINTAGE	F	VF	EF	UNC
1849	845,480	£25	£60	£200	£625
1850	685,080	£800	£1500	£3000	£6500
1850/49	incl. above	£800	£1500	£4500	—
1851	470,071	£40	£110	£400	£850
1852	1,306,574	£15	£35	£125	£400
1853	4,256,188	£15	£35	£125	£400
1853 Proof	incl. above	—	—	—	£1600
1854	552,414	£200	£550	£1200	£3200
1854/1 4 over 1	incl. above	£200	£900	—	—
1855	1,368,400	£12	£30	£110	£300
1856	3,168,000	£12	£30	£110	£300
1857	2,562,120	£12	£30	£110	£300
1857 error F:G with inverted G	incl. above	£200	£600	—	—
1858	3,108,600	£12	£30	£110	£300
1859	4,561,920	£12	£30	£110	£300
1860	1,671,120	£12	£30	£110	£350
1861	1,382,040	£14	£40	£150	£500
1862	954,360	£60	£160	£450	£1350
1863	859,320	£125	£375	£850	£1800
1863/1 3 over 1				Extremely rare	

Die no. added above date up to 1879

1864	4,518,360	£10	£30	£110	£250
1865	5,619,240	£10	£30	£110	£250
1866	4,984,600	£10	£30	£110	£250
1866 error BBITANNIAR	incl. above	£80	£250	£800	—
1867	2,166,120	£10	£35	£110	£275

Third head—with die no

1867	incl. above	£100	£450	—	—
1868	3,330,360	£12	£40	£110	£275
1869	736,560	£18	£50	£120	£350
1870	1,467,471	£12	£40	£100	£275
1871	4,910,010	£10	£40	£100	£250
1872	8,897,781	£10	£40	£100	£250
1873	6,489,598	£10	£40	£100	£250
1874	5,503,747	£12	£40	£100	£250
1875	4,353,983	£10	£40	£100	£250
1876	1,057,487	£12	£45	£110	£400
1877	2,989,703	£10	£40	£100	£275
1878	3,127,131	£10	£40	£100	£275
1879	3,611,507	£20	£60	£200	£550

Fourth head—no die no

1879 no Die no.	incl. above	£10	£28	£75	£190
1880	4,842,786	£10	£28	£75	£190
1881	5,255,332	£10	£28	£75	£190
1882	1,611,786	£22	£75	£200	£450
1883	7,281,450	£10	£28	£65	£180
1884	3,923,993	£10	£28	£65	£180
1885	3,336,526	£10	£28	£65	£180
1886	2,086,819	£10	£28	£65	£180
1887	4,034,133	£10	£28	£65	£180

JUBILEE HEAD ISSUES

1887	incl. above	£4	£8	£15	£40
1887 Proof	1,084	—	—	—	£250
1888	4,526,856	£6	£10	£25	£70
1889	7,039,628	£35	£90	£300	—
1889 Large bust (until 1892)	incl. above	£6	£12	£45	£80
1890	8,794,042	£6	£12	£45	£80
1891	5,665,348	£6	£12	£45	£85
1892	4,591,622	£6	£12	£45	£110

OLD HEAD ISSUES

1893	7,039,074	£5	£10	£30	£65
1893 small lettering	incl. above	£5	£10	£30	£65
1893 Proof	1,312	—	—	—	£220
1894	5,953,152	£9	£25	£60	£160
1895	8,880,651	£9	£25	£55	£150
1896	9,264,551	£7	£15	£40	£80
1897	6,270,364	£7	£12	£40	£75
1898	9,768,703	£7	£12	£40	£70
1899	10,965,382	£7	£12	£40	£70
1900	10,937,590	£7	£12	£40	£75
1901	3,426,294	£7	£12	£40	£70

Victoria Jubilee head

Victoria Old or Veiled head

DATE	MINTAGE	F	VF	EF	UNC

EDWARD VII (1901–10)

DATE	MINTAGE	F	VF	EF	UNC
1902	7,809,481	£5	£15	£45	£80
1902 Proof matt	13,123	—	—	—	£110
1903	2,061,823	£10	£35	£140	£475
1904	2,040,161	£8	£35	£130	£460
1905	488,390	£110	£300	£1100	£3500
1906	10,791,025	£5	£12	£40	£120
1907	14,083,418	£5	£12	£40	£130
1908	3,806,969	£10	£25	£150	£500
1909	5,664,982	£9	£22	£110	£375
1910	26,547,236	£5	£10	£45	£100

GEORGE V (1910–36)

First issue

DATE	MINTAGE	F	VF	EF	UNC
1911	20,065,901	£4	£8	£20	£55
1911 Proof	6,007	—	—	—	£125
1912	15,594,009	£5	£10	£25	£80
1913	9,011,509	£7	£20	£50	£150
1914	23,415,843	£4	£7	£25	£55
1915	39,279,024	£4	£7	£25	£55
1916	35,862,015	£4	£7	£25	£55
1917	22,202,608	£4	£7	£25	£60
1918	34,915,934	£4	£7	£25	£55
1919	10,823,824	£5	£8	£30	£65

Second issue—debased silver

DATE	MINTAGE	F	VF	EF	UNC
1920	22,825,142	£2	£4	£20	£45
1921	22,648,763	£2	£4	£20	£45
1922	27,215,738	£2	£4	£20	£45
1923	14,575,243	£2	£4	£20	£45
1924	9,250,095	£7	£15	£50	£150
1925	5,418,764	£6	£10	£40	£110
1926	22,516,453	£3	£8	£30	£110

George V First obverse

Third issue—Modified bust

DATE	MINTAGE	F	VF	EF	UNC
1926	incl. above	£2	£4	£25	£55
1927 —	9,247,344	£2	£4	£25	£55

Fourth issue—large lion and crown on rev., date in legend

DATE	MINTAGE	F	VF	EF	UNC
1927	incl. above	£2	£4	£20	£40
1927 Proof	15,000	—	—	—	£60
1928	18,136,778	£2	£4	£15	£40
1929	19,343,006	£2	£4	£15	£40
1930	3,172,092	£2	£4	£20	£50
1931	6,993,926	£2	£4	£15	£40
1932	12,168,101	£2	£4	£15	£45
1933	11,511,624	£2	£4	£15	£35
1934	6,138,463	£2	£4	£18	£50
1935	9,183,462	—	£4	£10	£22
1936	11,910,613	—	£4	£9	£20

GEORGE VI (1936–52)

George V Second obverse

E = England rev. (lion standing on large crown). S = Scotland rev. (lion seated on small crown holding sword and mace)

DATE	MINTAGE	F	VF	EF	UNC
1937 E	8,359,122	—	£2	£4	£6
1937 E Proof	26,402	—	—	—	£18
1937 S	6,748,875	—	£2	£4	£6
1937 S Proof	26,402	—	—	—	£18
1938 E	4,833,436	—	£3	£10	£20
1938 S	4,797,852	—	£3	£10	£20
1939 E	11,052,677	—	£2	£4	£6
1939 S	10,263,892	—	£2	£4	£6
1940 E	11,099,126	—	—	£4	£7
1940 S	9,913,089	—	—	£4	£7

DATE	MINTAGE	F	VF	EF	UNC
1941 E	11,391,883	—	—	£4	£6
1941 S	8,086,030	—	—	£4	£5
1942 E	17,453,643	—	—	£4	£5
1942 S	13,676,759	—	—	£4	£5
1943 E	11,404,213	—	—	£4	£6
1943 S	9,824,214	—	—	£4	£5
1944 E	11,586,751	—	—	£4	£5
1944 S	10,990,167	—	—	£4	£5
1945 E	15,143,404	—	—	£4	£6
1945 S	15,106,270	—	—	£4	£5
1946 E	16,663,797	—	—	£4	£5
1946 S	16,381,501	—	—	£4	£5
Cupro-nickel					
1947 E	12,120,611	—	—	—	£2
1947 S	12,283,223	—	—	—	£2
1948 E	45,576,923	—	—	—	£2
1948 S	45,351,937	—	—	—	£2
1949 E	19,328,405	—	—	—	£5
1949 S	21,243,074	—	—	—	£5
1950 E	19,243,872	—	—	—	£5
1950 E Proof	17,513	—	—	—	£20
1950 S	14,299,601	—	—	—	£5
1950 S Proof	17,513	—	—	—	£20
1951 E	9,956,930	—	—	—	£5
1951 E Proof	20,000	—	—	—	£20
1951 S	10,961,174	—	—	—	£6
1951 S Proof	20,000	—	—	—	£20

English reverse

Scottish reverse

ELIZABETH II (1952–)

E = England rev. (shield with three lions). S = Scotland rev. (shield with one lion).

	MINTAGE	F	VF	EF	UNC
1953 E	41,942,894	—	—	—	£1
1953 E Proof	40,000	—	—	—	£4
1953 S	20,663,528	—	—	—	£1
1953 S Proof	40,000	—	—	—	£4
1954 E	30,262,032	—	—	—	£2
1954 S	26,771,735	—	—	—	£2
1955 E	45,259,908	—	—	—	£2
1955 S	27,950,906	—	—	—	£2
1956 E	44,907,008	—	—	—	£10
1956 S	42,853,639	—	—	—	£10
1957 E	42,774,217	—	—	—	£1
1957 S	17,959,988	—	—	—	£10
1958 E	14,392,305	—	—	—	£10
1958 S	40,822,557	—	—	—	£1
1959 E	19,442,778	—	—	—	£1
1959 S	1,012,988	£1	£3	£10	£40
1960 E	27,027,914	—	—	—	£1
1960 S	14,376,932	—	—	—	£1
1961 E	39,816,907	—	—	—	£1
1961 S	2,762,558	—	—	—	£3
1962 E	36,704,379	—	—	—	£1
1962 S	17,475,010	—	—	—	£1
1963 E	49,433,607	—	—	—	£1
1963 S	32,300,000	—	—	—	£1
1964 E	8,590,900	—	—	—	£1
1964 S	5,239,100	—	—	—	£1
1965 E	9,216,000	—	—	—	£1
1965 S	2,774,000	—	—	—	£2
1966 E	15,002,000	—	—	—	£1
1966 S	15,604,000	—	—	—	£1
1970 E Proof	—				£10
1970 S Proof	—				£10

English reverse

Scottish reverse

SIXPENCES

DATE		F	VF	EF	UNC

OLIVER CROMWELL

1658 Patterns by Thos. Simon & Tanner
Four varieties .... Extremely rare

CHARLES II (1660–85)

	F	VF	EF	UNC
1674..	£70	£300	£900	—
1675..	£70	£300	£900	—
1675/4 5 over 4	£80	£300	£950	—
1676..	£80	£300	£900	—
1676/5 6 over 5	£85	£300	£900	—
1677..	£70	£300	£900	—
1678/7..	£70	£300	£950	—
1679..	£75	£300	£900	—
1680..	£90	£500	£1000	—
1681..	£80	£300	£900	—
1682/1	£80	£300	£1000	—
1682..	£100	£320	£1100	—
1683..	£70	£300	£925	—
1684..	£80	£300	£900	—

JAMES II (1685–88)

	F	VF	EF	UNC
1686 Early shields	£140	£425	£1000	—
1687 Ealy Shields..	£150	£475	£1200	—
1687/6 — 7 over 6..	£150	£450	£1100	—
1687 Late shields..	£150	£450	£1300	—
1687/6 — 7 over 6	£150	£475	£1150	—
1688 —	£150	£450	£1150	—

WILLIAM & MARY (1688–94)

	F	VF	EF	UNC
1693	£130	£425	£1000	—
1693 error inverted 3	£200	£500	£1350	—
1694..	£130	£450	£1100	—

WILLIAM III (1694–1702)

Provincially produced sixpences carry privy marks or initials below the bust:
B: Bristol. C: Chester. E: Exeter. N: Norwich. Y or y: York.

	F	VF	EF	UNC
1695 First bust, early harp in 4th shield on rev.	£35	£100	£400	—
1696 — —	£35	£100	£325	—
1696 — — French arms at date		Extremely rare		
1696 — — Scottish arms at date.....................		Extremely rare		
1696 — — DFI for DEI.....................................		Extremely rare		
1696 — — No stops on obv.	£50	£140	£500	—
1696 — — B..	£40	£100	£400	—
1696 — — — B over E.....................................		Extremely rare		
1696 — — C..	£40	£100	£450	—
1696 — — E...	£50	£110	£450	—
1696 — — N...	£45	£100	£450	—
1696 — — y...	£40	£110	£520	—
1696 — — Y...	£50	£200	£525	—
1696 — Later harp	£50	£175	£400	—
1696 — — B..	£70	£225	£600	—
1696 — — — no stops on obv..........................	£80	£275	£550	—
1696 — — C..	£80	£350	£850	—
1696 — — N...	£70	£325	—	—
1696 Second bust..	£300	£800	£2200	—
1697 First bust, later harp	£30	£75	£300	—
1697 — — Arms of France & Ireland transposed		Extremely rare		

DATE	MINTAGE	F	VF	EF	UNC
1697 — — B..............................		£50	£110	£450	—
1697 — — C..............................		£70	£200	£500	—
1697 — — — Irish shield at date			Extremely rare		
1697 — — E..............................		£70	£200	£475	—
1697 — — — error GVLIEMVS......................			Extremely rare		
1697 — — y..............................		£60	£125	£475	—
1697 — — — Irish shield at date			Extremely rare		
1697 Second bust		£175	£500	£1500	—
1697 Third bust		£25	£70	£275	—
1697 — error GVLIEIMVS......................			Extremely rare		
1697 — B..............................		£50	£110	£450	—
1697 — — IRA for FRA			Extremely rare		
1697 — C..............................		£75	£220	£525	—
1697 — E..............................		£75	£200	£550	—
1697 — Y..............................		£60	£200	£525	—
1698 —		£60	£190	£500	—
1698 — Plumes in angles on rev.		£75	£200	£700	—
1699 —		£90	£250	£800	—
1699 — Plumes in angles on rev.		£70	£250	£750	—
1699 — Roses in angles on rev.		£70	£250	£750	—
1699 — — error GVLIELMVS			Extremely rare		
1700 —		£45	£110	£400	—
1700 — Plume below bust		£2000	—	—	—
1701 —		£65	£160	£500	—

ANNE (1702–14)

1703 VIGO below bust Before Union with Scotland	£40	£130	£400	—	
1705 Plain..............................		£60	£170	£500	—
1705 Plumes in angles on rev.		£45	£150	£450	—
1705 Roses & Plumes in angles on rev.		£60	£150	£450	—
1707 Roses & Plumes in angles on rev.		£50	£150	£425	—
1707 (Post-Union), Plain..............		£40	£85	£320	—
1707 E (Edinburgh) below bust		£40	£85	£320	—
1707 Plumes in angles on rev........		£45	£120	£330	—
1708 Plain..............................		£45	£100	£400	—
1708 E below bust		£50	£100	£350	—
1708 E* below bust		£60	£140	£400	—
1708 "Edinburgh" bust E* below		£50	£140	£400	—
1708 Plumes in angles on rev.		£55	£140	£450	—
1710 Roses & Plumes in angles on rev.		£35	£110	£450	—
1711 Plain..............................		£25	£70	£240	—

GEORGE I (1714–27)

1717 Roses & Plumes in angles on rev.		£90	£270	£750	—
1717 Plain edge.......................			Extremely rare		
1720 —		£90	£270	£675	—
1723 SSC in angles on rev.		£30	£70	£200	—
1723 Larger lettering		£30	£70	£200	—
1726 Small Roses & Plumes in angles on rev. ..		£80	£225	£650	—

GEORGE II (1727–60)

1728 Young head, Plain................		£70	£240	£525	—
1728 — Proof..........................		—	—	£3500	—
1728 — Plumes in angles on rev.		£40	£140	£400	—
1728 — Roses & Plumes in angles on rev........		£35	£125	£350	—
1731 — —		£40	£140	£375	—
1732 — —		£35	£125	£350	—
1734 — —		£40	£140	£375	—
1735 — —		£35	£140	£375	—
1735/4 5 over 4		£45	£150	£425	—
1736 — —		£45	£150	£400	—
1739 — Roses in angles on rev.		£30	£100	£320	—
1741 —		£30	£100	£300	—
1743 Old head, Roses in angles on rev...........		£25	£75	£250	—
1745 — —		£25	£75	£250	—

DATE	MINTAGE	F	VF	EF	UNC
1745 — — 5 over 3		£30	£85	£275	—
1745 — Plain, LIMA below bust		£30	£80	£275	—
1746 — — —		£30	£80	£275	—
1746 — — Proof		—	—	£1600	—
1750 — —		£30	£120	£325	—
1751 — —		£35	£150	£350	—
1757 — —		£15	£30	£85	—
1758 — —		£15	£30	£85	—

GEORGE III (1760–1820)

	MINTAGE	F	VF	EF	UNC
1787 rev. no semée of hearts on 4th shield		£15	£35	£80	£110
1787 rev. with semée of hearts		£15	£35	£80	£110

NEW COINAGE

	MINTAGE	F	VF	EF	UNC
1816	—	£7	£15	£40	£100
1817	10,921,680	£7	£15	£40	£100
1818	4,284,720	£10	£25	£80	£175
1819	4,712,400	£8	£15	£40	£90
1819 very small 8 in date	incl. above	£12	£22	£60	£140
1820	1,488,960	£8	£15	£50	£120

GEORGE IV (1820–30)

	MINTAGE	F	VF	EF	UNC
1821 First bust, first reverse	863,280	£12	£30	£120	£350
1821 error BBRITANNIAR		£100	£300	£950	—
1821 — — Proof	incl. above	—	—	—	£900
1824 — Second (garter) reverse..	633,600	£10	£30	£100	£325
1825 —	483,120	£12	£30	£100	£300
1826 — —	689,040	£40	£100	£250	£550
1826 Second bust, third (lion on crown) reverse	incl. above	£10	£30	£100	£220
1826 — — Proof	incl. above	—	—	—	£550
1827 — —	166,320	£40	£100	£300	£650
1828 — —	15,840	£20	£50	£150	£325
1829 — —	403,290	£15	£45	£125	£350

WILLIAM IV (1830–37)

	MINTAGE	F	VF	EF	UNC
1831	1,340,195	£15	£40	£125	£300
1831 Proof, milled edge	incl. above	—	—	—	£650
1834	5,892,480	£15	£40	£125	£300
1835	1,552,320	£15	£40	£125	£300
1836	1,987,920	£15	£45	£250	£350
1837	506,880	£20	£45	£220	£500

VICTORIA (1837–1901)

YOUNG HEAD ISSUES
First head

	MINTAGE	F	VF	EF	UNC
1838	1,607,760	£15	£40	£130	£350
1839	3,310,560	£15	£40	£130	£350
1839 Proof	incl. above	—	—	—	£1000
1840	2,098,800	£15	£40	£130	£350
1841	1,386,000	£18	£40	£130	£375
1842	601,920	£15	£40	£130	£350
1843	3,160,080	£15	£40	£130	£350
1844	3,975,840	£15	£30	£140	£350
1844 Large 44 in date	incl. above	£18	£40	£130	£400
1845	3,714,480	£15	£35	£90	£350
1846	4,226,880	£15	£35	£90	£350
1848	586,080	£50	£100	£300	£450
1848/6 final 8 over 6	incl. above	£50	£120	£400	—
1850	498,960	£12	£35	£100	£370
1850/3 0 over 3	incl. above	£18	£40	£110	£400
1851	2,288,107	£10	£30	£100	£360
1852	904,586	£10	£30	£150	£370
1853	3,837,930	£10	£30	£150	£370

DATE	MINTAGE	F	VF	EF	UNC
1853 Proof	incl above	—	—	—	£1100
1854	840,116	£175	£500	£1000	£2750
1855	1,129,684	£10	£30	£120	£250
1855/3 last 5 over 3	incl. above	£15	£45	£140	£300
1856	2,779,920	£10	£40	£120	£280
1857	2,233,440	£10	£40	£120	£280
1858	1,932,480	£10	£40	£120	£280
1859	4,688,640	£10	£40	£120	£280
1859/8 9 over 8	incl. above	£12	£40	£120	£400
1860	1,100,880	£10	£35	£120	£300
1862	990,000	£100	£200	£600	£1600
1863	491,040	£70	£150	£475	£1200

Die no. added above date from 1864 to 1879

1864	4,253,040	£10	£25	£110	£250
1865	1,631,520	£10	£25	£100	£250
1866	4,140,080	£10	£25	£100	£250
1866 no Die no.	incl. above			Extremely Rare	

Second head

1867	1,362,240	£10	£30	£120	£300
1868	1,069,200	£10	£30	£110	£270
1869	388,080	£10	£30	£110	£280
1870	479,613	£10	£30	£110	£270
1871	3,662,684	£8	£30	£75	£200
1871 no Die no.	incl. above	£8	£30	£75	£220
1872	3,382,048	£8	£30	£75	£200
1873	4,594,733	£8	£30	£75	£200
1874	4,225,726	£8	£30	£75	£230
1875	3,256,545	£8	£30	£75	£220
1876	841,435	£8	£30	£75	£220
1877	4,066,486	£8	£30	£75	£220
1877 no Die no	incl. above	£8	£30	£75	£220
1878	2,624,525	£8	£30	£75	£230
1878 Dritanniar Error	incl. above	£125	£300	£1000	—
1879	3,326,313	£8	£25	£80	£220
1879 no Die no	incl. above	£8	£25	£80	£220
1880 no Die no	3,892,501	£8	£25	£75	£220

Third head

1880	incl above	£8	£20	£80	£175
1881	6,239,447	£8	£20	£80	£175
1882	759,809	£15	£50	£150	£440
1883	4,986,558	£8	£20	£70	£150
1884	3,422,565	£8	£20	£70	£150
1885	4,652,771	£8	£20	£70	£150
1886	2,728,249	£8	£20	£70	£140
1887	3,675,607	£8	£20	£70	£150

JUBILEE HEAD ISSUES

1887 Shield reverse	incl. above	£6	£10	£15	£30
1887 — Proof	incl. above	—	—	—	£175
1887 Six Pence in wreath reverse	incl. above	£6	£8	£18	£35
1888 —	4,197,698	£8	£12	£35	£60
1889 —	8,738,928	£8	£12	£35	£70
1890 —	9,386,955	£8	£12	£35	£70
1891 —	7,022,734	£8	£12	£35	£70
1892 —	6,245,746	£8	£12	£35	£80
1893 —	7,350,619	£700	£1350	£4000	—

OLD HEAD ISSUES

1893	incl. above	£7	£12	£22	£50
1893 Proof	1,312	—	—	—	£200
1894	3,467,704	£8	£18	£50	£130
1895	7,024,631	£8	£18	£45	£100
1896	6,651,699	£7	£15	£35	£65
1897	5,031,498	£7	£15	£35	£65
1898	5,914,100	£7	£15	£35	£65
1899	7,996,80	£7	£15	£35	£55
1900	8,984,354	£7	£15	£35	£55
1901	5,108,757	£7	£15	£35	£55

Jubilee head, shield reverse

Jubilee head, wreath reverse

DATE	MINTAGE	F	VF	EF	UNC

EDWARD VII (1901–10)

DATE	MINTAGE	F	VF	EF	UNC
1902	6,367,378	£10	£30	£60	
1902 "Matt Proof"	15,123	—	—	—	£120
1903	5,410,096	£7	£20	£50	£170
1904	4,487,098	£15	£50	£175	£500
1905	4,235,556	£8	£20	£70	£220
1906	7,641,146	£7	£12	£40	£110
1907	8,733,673	£7	£12	£45	£120
1908	6,739,491	£10	£30	£110	£350
1909	6,584,017	£7	£18	£50	£175
1910	12,490,724	£5	£8	£25	£50

Edward VII

GEORGE V (1910–36)

First issue

	MINTAGE	F	VF	EF	UNC
1911	9,155,310	£3	£7	£15	£40
1911 Proof	6,007	—	—	—	£90
1912	10,984,129	£3	£7	£20	£65
1913	7,499,833	£3	£8	£22	£75
1914	22,714,602	£3	£7	£10	£35
1915	15,694,597	£3	£7	£12	£45
1916	22,207,178	£3	£7	£10	£35
1917	7,725,475	£8	£24	£60	£140
1918	27,553,743	£3	£7	£12	£30
1919	13,375,447	£3	£7	£12	£40
1920	14,136,287	£3	£7	£10	£35

Second issue — debased silver

	MINTAGE	F	VF	EF	UNC
1920	incl. above	£1	£3	£10	£40
1921	30,339,741	£1	£3	£10	£40
1922	16,878,890	£1	£3	£10	£30
1923	6,382,793	£4	£10	£45	£110
1924	17,444,218	£1	£5	£10	£35
1925	12,720,558	£1	£3	£10	£35
1925 Broad rim	incl. above	£1	£3	£10	£35
1926 —	21,809,621	£1	£3	£10	£35

*George V,
first reverse
above and
second reverse
below*

Third issue — Modified bust

	MINTAGE	F	VF	EF	UNC
1926	incl. above	£1	£2	£10	£35
1927	8,924,873	—	£2	£10	£35

Fourth issue — New design (oakleaves)

	MINTAGE	F	VF	EF	UNC
1927 Proof only	15,000	£1	£2	£10	£35
1928	23,123,384	£1	£2	£8	£25
1929	28,319,326	£1	£2	£8	£25
1930	16,990,289	£1	£2	£8	£30
1931	16,873,268	£1	£2	£8	£30
1932	9,406,117	£1	£2	£8	£40
1933	22,185,083	£1	£2	£8	£25
1934	9,304,009	£1	£2	£12	£35
1935	13,995,621	£1	£2	£6	£15
1936	24,380,171	£1	£2	£6	£15

GEORGE VI (1936–52)

First type

	MINTAGE	F	VF	EF	UNC
1937	22,302,524	—	—	£1	£5
1937 Proof	26,402	—	—	—	£10
1938	13,402,701	—	£2	£5	£18
1939	28,670,304	—	—	£1	£5
1940	20,875,196	—	—	£1	£5
1941	23,086,616	—	—	£1	£5
1942	44,942,785	—	—	£1	£4
1943	46,927,111	—	—	£1	£4
1944	36,952,600	—	—	£1	£4
1945	39,939,259	—	—	£1	£3
1946	43,466,407	—	—	£1	£3

George VI first reverse

Cupro-nickel

	MINTAGE	F	VF	EF	UNC
1947	29,993,263	—	—	£1	£3
1948	88,323,540	—	—	£1	£3

Second type — new cypher on rev.

	MINTAGE	F	VF	EF	UNC
1949	41,335,515	—	—	£1	£3

George VI second reverse

DATE	MINTAGE	F	VF	EF	UNC
1950	32,741,955	—	—	£1	£3
1950 Proof	17,513	—	—	—	£7
1951	40,399,491	—	—	£1	£3
1951 Proof	20,000	—	—	—	£7
1952	1,013,477	£5	£20	£45	£120

ELIZABETH II (1952–   )

1953	70,323,876	—	—	—	£2
1953 Proof	40,000	—	—	—	£4
1954	105,241,150	—	—	—	£3
1955	109,929,554	—	—	—	£1
1956	109,841,555	—	—	—	£1
1957	105,654,290	—	—	—	£1
1958	123,518,527	—	—	—	£3
1959	93,089,441	—	—	—	£1
1960	103,283,346	—	—	—	£3
1961	115,052,017	—	—	—	£3
1962	166,483,637	—	—	—	25p
1963	120,056,000	—	—	—	25p
1964	152,336,000	—	—	—	25p
1965	129,644,000	—	—	—	25p
1966	175,676,000	—	—	—	25p
1967	240,788,000	—	—	—	25p
1970 Proof	—				£8

GROATS OR FOURPENCES

DATE	MINTAGE	F	VF	EF	UNC

The earlier fourpences are included in the Maundy oddments section as they are generally considered to have been issued for the Maundy ceremony.

WILLIAM IV (1831–37)

1836	—	£8	£18	£40	£90
1837	962,280	£8	£18	£40	£95

VICTORIA (1838–1901)

1837	Extremely Rare Proofs or Patterns only				
1838	2,150,280	£7	£15	£40	£90
1838 over last 8 on its side		£10	£20	£60	£120
1839	1,461,240	£7	£16	£50	£100
1839 Proof	incl. above				Rare
1840	1,496,880	£7	£15	£50	£100
1840 Small 0 in date	incl. above	£7	£15	£50	£100
1841	344,520	£7	£15	£50	£100
1842/1 2 over 1	incl. above	£7	£15	£45	£100
1842	724,680	£7	£15	£50	£100
1843	1,817640	£8	£16	£50	£120
1843 4 over 5	incl. above	£7	£15	£50	£120
1844	855,360	£7	£15	£50	£110
1845	914,760	£7	£15	£50	£110
1846	1,366,200	£7	£15	£50	£100
1847 7 over 6	225,720	£15	£35	£125	—
1848	712,800	£7	£15	£50	£90
1848/6 8 over 6	incl. above	£30	£110	—	—
1848/7 8 over 7	incl. above	£8	£20	£60	£110
1849	380,160	£7	£15	£50	£100
1849/8 9 over 8	incl. above	£8	£20	£70	£135
1851	594,000	£35	£80	£250	£425
1852	31,300	£55	£130	£400	—
1853	11,880	£80	£170	£550	—
1853 Proof Milled Rim	incl. above	—	—	—	£1000
1853 Plain edge Proof				Extremely rare	
1854	1,096,613	£7	£15	£40	£90
1855	646,041	£7	£15	£40	£90
1857 Proofs only				Extremely rare	
1862 Proofs only				Extremely rare	
1888 Jubilee Head	—	£12	£22	£50	£110

THREEPENCES

DATE	MINTAGE	F	VF	EF	UNC

The earlier threepences are included in the Maundy oddments section.

WILLIAM IV (1830–37)
(issued for use in the West Indies)

DATE	MINTAGE	F	VF	EF	UNC
1834		£8	£20	£80	£200
1835		£8	£20	£80	£200
1836		£8	£20	£80	£200
1837		£8	£25	£100	£230

VICTORIA (1837–1901)

Victoria first type

DATE	MINTAGE	F	VF	EF	UNC
1838 BRITANNIAB error				Extremely rare	
1838	—	£10	£25	£80	£200
1839	—	£10	£25	£80	£200
1840	—	£10	£25	£80	£200
1841	—	£10	£25	£70	£210
1842	—	£10	£25	£70	£200
1843	—	£10	£25	£60	£180
1843/34 43 over 34	—	£10	£25	£90	£220
1844	—	£12	£25	£80	£190
1845	1,319,208	£12	£25	£70	£180
1846	52,008	£15	£35	£150	£350
1847	4,488			Extremely rare	
1848	incl. above			Extremely rare	
1849	131,208	£12	£25	£80	£220
1850	954,888	£12	£25	£50	£175
1851	479,065	£12	£30	£70	£200
1851 5 over 8	incl. above	£25	£50	£200	—
1852	4,488			Extremely rare	
1853	36,168	£40	£110	£250	£600
1854	1,467,246	£8	£22	£60	£175
1855	383,350	£12	£26	£60	£175
1856	1,013,760	£8	£22	£60	£170
1857	1,758,240	£8	£22	£70	£180
1858	1,441,440	£8	£22	£60	£170
1858 BRITANNIAB error	incl. above			Extremely rare	
1858/6 final 8 over 6	incl. above	£10	£30	£125	—
1858/5 final 8 over 5	incl. above	£10	£30	£125	—
1859	3,579,840	£7	£20	£50	£150
1860	3,405,600	£8	£22	£50	£170
1861	3,294,720	£8	£22	£50	£150
1862	1,156,320	£8	£22	£50	£150
1863	950,400	£25	£65	£125	£275
1864	1,330,560	£7	£22	£50	£150
1865	1,742,400	£7	£22	£50	£150
1866	1,900,800	£7	£22	£50	£150
1867	712,800	£7	£22	£50	£150
1868	1,457,280	£7	£22	£50	£150
1868 RRITANNIAR error	incl. above			Extremely rare	
1869	—	£50	£95	£200	£400
1870	1,283,218	£5	£16	£45	£95
1871	999,633	£5	£16	£40	£90
1872	1,293,271	£5	£16	£40	£90
1873	4,055,550	£5	£16	£40	£90
1874	4,427,031	£5	£16	£40	£90
1875	3,306,500	£5	£16	£40	£90
1876	1,834,389	£5	£16	£40	£90
1877	2,622,393	£5	£16	£40	£90
1878	2,419,975	£5	£16	£40	£110
1879	3,140,265	£5	£16	£40	£90
1880	1,610,069	£5	£16	£40	£80
1881	3,248,265	£5	£16	£40	£80
1882	472,965	£8	£25	£70	£170
1883	4,369,971	£5	£10	£30	£60

DATE	MINTAGE	F	VF	EF	UNC
1884............................	3,322,424	£5	£12	£30	£60
1885............................	5,183,653	£5	£12	£30	£60
1886............................	6,152,669	£5	£12	£30	£60
1887............................	2,780,761	£5	£12	£30	£60
JUBILEE HEAD ISSUES					
1887	incl. above	£2	£4	£12	£25
1887 Proof....................	incl. above	—	—	—	£130
1888............................	518,199	£2	£5	£20	£40
1889............................	4,587,010	£2	£5	£20	£45
1890............................	4,465,834	£2	£5	£20	£45
1891............................	6,323,027	£2	£5	£20	£45
1892............................	2,578,226	£2	£5	£20	£45
1893............................	3,067,243	£10	£40	£125	£280
OLD HEAD ISSUES					
1893............................	incl. above	£2	£4	£15	£30
1893 Proof....................	incl. above	—	—	—	£80
1894............................	1,608,603	£3	£6	£25	£60
1895............................	4,788,609	£2	£5	£22	£50
1896............................	4,598,442	£2	£5	£18	£35
1897............................	4,541,294	£2	£5	£18	£35
1898............................	4,567,177	£2	£5	£18	£35
1899............................	6,246,281	£2	£5	£18	£35
1900............................	10,644,480	£2	£5	£18	£35
1901............................	6,098,400	£2	£5	£14	£30

Victoria
Jubilee head

Victoria
Old or Veiled
head

EDWARD VII (1901–10)

	MINTAGE	F	VF	EF	UNC
1902............................	8,268,480	£2	£2	£7	£15
1902 "Matt Proof"	incl. above	—	—	—	£40
1903............................	5,227,200	£2	£4	£20	£50
1904............................	3,627,360	£3	£10	£45	£100
1905............................	3,548,160	£2	£4	£25	£60
1906............................	3,152,160	£2	£6	£25	£65
1907............................	4,831,200	£2	£4	£20	£50
1908............................	8,157,600	£2	£3	£20	£50
1909............................	4,055,040	£2	£4	£20	£50
1910............................	4,563,380	£2	£4	£18	£35

GEORGE V (1910–36)

First issue

	MINTAGE	F	VF	EF	UNC
1911............................	5,841,084	—	—	£3	£10
1911 Proof....................	incl. above	—	—	—	£50
1912............................	8,932,825	—	—	£3	£12
1913............................	7,143,242	—	—	£3	£12
1914............................	6,733,584	—	—	£3	£12
1915............................	5,450,617	—	—	£3	£15
1916............................	18,555,201	—	—	£3	£10
1917............................	21,662,490	—	—	£3	£10
1918............................	20,630,909	—	—	£3	£10
1919	16,845,687	—	—	£3	£10
1920	16,703,597	—	—	£3	£10
Second issue—debased silver					
1920............................	incl. above	—	—	£3	£12
1921............................	8,749,301	—	—	£3	£12
1922............................	7,979,998	—	—	£3	£40
1925	3,731,859	—	—	£5	£25
1926	4,107,910	—	—	£7	£30
Third issue—Modified bust					
1926............................	incl. above	—	—	£8	£22
Fourth issue—new design (oakleaves)					
1927 Proof only	15,022	—	—	—	£100
1928............................	1,302,106	£4	£10	£30	£65
1930............................	1,319,412	£2	£4	£10	£40
1931............................	6,251,936	—	—	£2	£7
1932............................	5,887,325	—	—	£2	£7
1933............................	5,578,541	—	—	£2	£7
1934............................	7,405,954	—	—	£2	£7
1935............................	7,027,654	—	—	£2	£7
1936............................	3,328,670	—	—	£2	£7

George V
second issue

George V,
fourth issue
oak leaves
design reverse

DATE	MINTAGE	F	VF	EF	UNC

GEORGE VI (1936–52)

Silver

DATE	MINTAGE	F	VF	EF	UNC
1937	8,148,156	—	—	£1	£4
1937 Proof	26,402	—	—	—	£15
1938	6,402,473	—	—	£1	£4
1939	1,355,860	—	—	£4	£15
1940	7,914,401	—	—	£1	£3
1941	7,979,411	—	—	£1	£3
1942	4,144,051	£2	£5	£12	£35
1943	1,397,220	£2	£5	£12	£35
1944	2,005,553	£7	£15	£40	£90
1945				Only one known	

Nickel brass

DATE	MINTAGE	F	VF	EF	UNC
1937	45,707,957	—	—	£1	£4
1937 Proof	26,402	—	—	—	£10
1938	14,532,332	—	—	£1	£18
1939	5,603,021	—	—	£3	£40
1940	12,636,018	—	—	£3	£30
1941	60,239,489	—	—	£1	£8
1942	103,214,400	—	—	£1	£8
1943	101,702,400	—	—	£1	£8
1944	69,760,000	—	—	£1	£8
1945	33,942,466	—	—	£3	£20
1946	620,734	£6	£25	£200	£700
1948	4,230,400	—	—	£7	£50
1949	464,000	£5	£25	£225	£750
1950	1,600,000	—	£2	£20	£110
1950 Proof	17,513	—	—	—	£15
1951	1,184,000	—	£2	£25	£110
1951 Proof	20,000	—	—	—	£20
1952	25,494,400	—	—	—	£10

George VI "Thrift" design of the brass 3d

ELIZABETH II (1952–   )

DATE	MINTAGE	F	VF	EF	UNC
1953	30,618,000	—	—	—	£1
1953 Proof	40,000	—	—	—	£6
1954	41,720,000	—	—	—	£5
1955	41,075,200	—	—	—	£5
1956	36,801,600	—	—	—	£6
1957	24,294,500	—	—	—	£6
1958	20,504,000	—	—	—	£9
1959	28,499,200	—	—	—	£6
1960	83,078,400	—	—	—	£2
1961	41,102,400	—	—	—	£1
1962	51,545,600	—	—	—	£1
1963	39,482,866	—	—	—	£1
1964	44,867,200	—	—	—	—
1965	27,160,000	—	—	—	—
1966	53,160,000	—	—	—	—
1967	151,780,800	—	—	—	—
1970 Proof	—				£8

TWO PENCES

GEORGE III (1760–1820)

		F	VF	EF	UNC
1797 "Cartwheel"		£30	£60	£350	£900
1797 Copper Proofs		Many types from £500+			

VICTORIA (1837–1901)

For use in the Colonies

		F	VF	EF	UNC
1838		£4	£10	£18	£35
1848		£4	£12	£20	£40

Earlier issues of the small silver two pences are listed in the Maundy section.

THREE-HALFPENCES

DATE		F	VF	EF	UNC

WILLIAM IV (1830–37)
For use in the Colonies

DATE		F	VF	EF	UNC
1834		£6	£16	£35	£80
1835		£10	£25	£75	£200
1835 over 4		£6	£16	£40	£90
1836		£8	£18	£40	£95
1837		£15	£35	£110	£300

VICTORIA (1837–1901)
For use in the Colonies

DATE		F	VF	EF	UNC
1838		£6	£15	£35	£75
1839		£6	£15	£35	£75
1840		£8	£20	£60	£125
1841		£6	£15	£35	£80
1842		£6	£18	£40	£90
1843		£6	£15	£30	£70
1860		£10	£24	£75	£160
1862		£12	£28	£80	£175

PENNIES

DATE	MINTAGE	F	VF	EF	UNC

The earlier small silver pennies are included in the Maundy oddments section.

GEORGE III (1760–1820)

DATE	MINTAGE	F	VF	EF	UNC
1797 "Cartwheel", 10 laurel leaves	8,601,600	£25	£60	£300	£900
1797 — 11 laurel leaves	incl. above	£25	£60	£300	£900
1806 Third type	—	£7	£18	£70	£300
1807	—	£7	£18	£70	£300
1808					Unique

GEORGE IV (1820–30)

DATE	MINTAGE	F	VF	EF	UNC
1825	1,075,200	£12	£45	£250	£620
1826 (varieties)	5,913,600	£12	£45	£250	£620
1826 Proof	—	—	—	—	£700
1827	1,451,520	£220	£800	£3000	—

WILLIAM IV (1830–37)

DATE	MINTAGE	F	VF	EF	UNC
1831 (varieties)	806,400	£25	£70	£425	£1100
1831 Proof	—	—	—	—	£900
1834	322,560	£30	£70	£400	£1250
1837	174,720	£65	£200	£800	£3000

George III "Cartwheel" penny

VICTORIA (1837–1901)

YOUNG HEAD ISSUES
Copper

DATE	MINTAGE	F	VF	EF	UNC
1839 Proof	unrecorded	—	—	—	£1800
1841	913,920	£10	£50	£300	£750
1841 No colon after REG	incl. above	£8	£20	£175	£550
1843	483,840	£90	£350	£2000	£5000
1844	215,040	£12	£25	£160	£550
1845	322,560	£15	£35	£220	£750
1846	483,840	£15	£25	£200	£700
1846 FID: DEF colon spaced	incl. above	£15	£25	£200	£700
1846 FID:DEF colon close	incl. above	£16	£28	£210	£725
1847	430,080	£12	£25	£180	£550
1848	161,280	£10	£25	£160	£500
1848/7 final 8 over 7	incl. above	£8	£20	£150	£450

DATE	MINTAGE	F	VF	EF	UNC
1848/6 final 8 over 6	incl. above £20	£120	£525	—
1849	268,800 £225	£600	£2300	—
1851	268,800 £15	£45	£200	£800
1853	1,021,440 £7	£15	£100	£180
1853 Proof	— —	—	—	£2000
1854	6,720,000 £8	£20	£100	£190
1854/3 4 over 3	incl. above £14	£45	£180	—
1855	5,273,856 £8	£20	£100	£250
1856	1,212,288 £100	£250	£700	£2700
1857 Plain trident	752,640 £7	£18	£80	£280
1857 Ornamental trident	incl. above £6	£18	£70	£280
1858/7 final 8 over 7	incl. above £7	£18	£80	£300
1858/6 final 8 over 6	— £40	£120	£500	—
1858/3 final 8 over 3	incl. above £25	£90	£400	—
1858	1,599,040 £7	£16	£90	£250
1859	1,075,200 £8	£25	£150	£350
1860/59	32,256 £600	£1500	£3750	£6500

Bronze

Prices of bronze Victoria Young "bun" head pennies are for the common types.
There are many known varieties which are listed in detail in other more specialised
publications. Prices for coins in mint with full lustre will be considerably higher.

1860 Beaded border	5,053,440 £25	£50	£170	£700
1860 Toothed border	incl. above £6	£20	£60	£3000
1860 — Piedfort flan	—	Extremely rare		
1861	36,449,280 £5	£12	£50	£290
1862	50,534,400 £5	£12	£50	£280
1862 8 over 6	incl. above	Extremely rare		
1863	28,062,720 £5	£12	£45	£250
1863 Die no below date	incl. above	Extremely rare		
1864 Plain 4	3,440,640 £25	£140	£600	£3000
1864 Crosslet 4	incl. above £30	£150	£600	£3200
1865	8,601,600 £7	£16	£55	£350
1865/3 5 over 3	incl. above £40	£125	£450	—
1866	9,999,360 £6	£20	£80	£475
1867	5,483,520 £7	£20	£95	£800
1868	1,182,720 £15	£70	£200	£1800
1869	2,580,480 £130	£450	£1800	£5750
1870	5,695,022 £12	£40	£150	£750
1871	1,290,318 £35	£120	£450	£2000
1872	8,494,572 £6	£20	£60	£270
1873	8,494,200 £6	£20	£60	£270
1874	5,621,865 £7	£20	£60	£270
1874 H	6,666,240 £7	£22	£65	£280
1874 Later (older) bust	incl. above £14	£35	£90	£450

Victoria copper penny

Victoria Young or "Bun" head bronze penny

DATE	MINTAGE	F	VF	EF	UNC
1875	10,691,040	£7	£22	£75	£325
1875 H	752,640	£35	£120	£800	£2500
1876 H	11,074,560	£5	£12	£60	£275
1877	9,624,747	£5	£14	£55	£275
1878	2,764,470	£5	£14	£55	£275
1879	7,666,476	£4	£15	£55	£275
1880	3,000,831	£4	£15	£55	£290
1881	2,302,362	£5	£15	£55	£275
1881 H	3,763,200	£5	£15	£55	£275
1882 H	7,526,400	£5	£15	£55	£275
1882 no H	—		Extremely Rare		
1883	6,237,438	£5	£15	£55	£250
1884	11,702,802	£5	£15	£55	£250
1885	7,145,862	£5	£15	£55	£250
1886	6,087,759	£5	£15	£55	£250
1887	5,315,085	£5	£15	£55	£250
1888	5,125,020	£5	£15	£60	£260
1889	12,559,737	£5	£15	£50	£325
1890	15,330,840	£5	£15	£50	£200
1891	17,885,961	£5	£12	£50	£200
1892	10,501,671	£6	£15	£70	£250
1893	8,161,737	£5	£12	£55	£240
1894	3,883,452	£10	£35	£140	£440

OLD HEAD ISSUES

DATE	MINTAGE	F	VF	EF	UNC
1895 Trident 2mm from P(ENNY)	5,395,830	£20	£90	£280	£800
1895 Trident 1mm from P	incl. above	—	£2	£18	£75
1896	24,147,156	—	£2	£18	£65
1897	20,756,620	—	£2	£15	£60
1897 Raised dot after One (O·NE)		£140	£250	£850	—
1898	14,296,836	—	£3	£18	£60
1899	26,441,069	—	£3	£16	£50
1900	31,778,109	—	£3	£16	£40
1901	22,205,568	—	£3	£10	£30

EDWARD VII (1901–10)

DATE	MINTAGE	F	VF	EF	UNC
1902	26,976,768	—	£1	£8	£30
1902 "Low tide" to sea line	incl. above	£4	£15	£60	£200
1903	21,415,296	—	£3	£15	£80
1904	12,913,152	—	£4	£25	£190
1905	17,783,808	—	£3	£15	£80
1906	37,989,504	—	£3	£15	£70
1907	47,322,240	—	£3	£15	£70
1908	31,506,048	—	£3	£18	£125
1909	19,617,024	—	£3	£20	£150
1910	29,549,184	—	£3	£15	£60

GEORGE V (1910–36)

DATE	MINTAGE	F	VF	EF	UNC
1911	23,079,168	—	£3	£12	£65
1912	48,306,048	—	£3	£12	£55
1912 H	16,800,000	—	£4	£40	£220
1913	65,497,812	—	£3	£15	£75
1914	50,820,997	—	£3	£18	£75
1915	47,310,807	—	£3	£20	£85
1916	86,411,165	—	£3	£15	£65
1917	107,905,436	—	£3	£15	£60
1918	84,227,372	—	£3	£12	£55
1918 H	3,660,800	£1	£15	£100	£500
1918 KN	incl. above	£8	£80	£550	£2200
1919	113,761,090	—	£2	£15	£55
1919 H	5,209,600	£1	£15	£200	£700
1919 KN	incl. above	£15	£110	£750	£2850
1920	124,693,485	—	£2	£12	£30
1921	129,717,693	—	£2	£12	£40
1922	16,346,711	—	£3	£25	£150
1922 with reverse of 1927		£1000	£2500	—	—
1926	4,498,519	—	£6	£25	£140
1926 Modified effigy	incl above	£25	£150	£800	£2500
1927	60,989,561	—	£2	£10	£40

DATE	MINTAGE	F	VF	EF	UNC
1928	50,178,00	—	£2	£10	£35
1929	49,132,800	—	£2	£10	£40
1930	29,097,600	—	£2	£20	£70
1931	19,843,200	—	£2	£10	£50
1932	8,277,600	—	£2	£15	£100
1933			Only 7 examples known		
1934	13,965,600	—	£2	£25	£100
1935	56,070,000	—	—	£2	£14
1936	154,296,000	—	—	£2	£12

GEORGE VI (1936–52)

1937	88,896,000	—	—	—	£4
1937 Proof	26,402	—	—	—	£14
1938	121,560,000	—	—	—	£6
1939	55,560,000	—	—	—	£15
1940	42,284,400	—	—	£8	£25
1944 Mint Dark	42,600,000	—	—	—	£8
1945 Mint Dark	79,531,200	—	—	—	£8
1946 Mint Dark	66,855,600	—	—	—	£8
1947	52,220,400	—	—	—	£5
1948	63,961,200	—	—	—	£5
1949	14,324,400	—	—	—	£8
1950	240,000	£7	£15	£30	£50
1950 Proof	17,513	—	—	—	£25
1951	120,000	£20	£26	£50	£75
1951 Proof	20,000	—	—	—	£40

ELIZABETH II (1952–   )

1953	1,308,400	—	—	£1	£4
1953 Proof	40,000	—	—	—	£7
1954			Only one known		
1961	48,313,400	—	—	—	£2
1962	143,308,600	—	—	—	50p
1963	125,235,600	—	—	—	50p
1964	153,294,000	—	—	—	50p
1965	121,310,400	—	—	—	50p
1966	165,739,200	—	—	—	50p
1967	654,564,000	—	—	—	—
1970 Proof	—				£8

Later issues are included in the Decimal section.

HALFPENNIES

CHARLES II (1660–85)

1672		£70	£300	£1300	—
1672 CRAOLVS error			Extremely rare		
1673		£70	£300	£1300	—
1673 CRAOLVS error			Extremely rare		
1673 No rev. stop		£100	£600	—	—
1673 No stops on obv.			Extremely rare		
1675		£60	£500	£1500	—
1675 No stops on obv.		£80	£550	—	—
1675/3 5 over 3		£175	£625	—	—

JAMES II (1685–88)

1685 (tin)	£250	£750	£4000	—
1686 (tin)	£280	£750	£4200	—
1687 (tin)	£320	£800	£4000	—

WILLIAM & MARY (1688–94)

Tin

1689 Small draped busts, edge dated		Extremely rare		
1690 Large cuirassed busts, edge dated	£200	£750	£3400	—
1691 — date on edge and in exergue	£180	£700	£3200	—
1692 — —	£200	£750	£3200	—

DATE	F	VF	EF	UNC

Copper

1694 Large cuirassed busts, date in exergue	£80	£300	£1200	—
1694 — — GVLIEMVS error		Extremely rare		
1694 — — MΛRIΛ error		Extremely rare		
1694 — — No stops on rev.		Extremely rare		

WILLIAM III (1694–1702)

1695 First issue (date in exergue)	£50	£200	£1100	—
1695 — No stop after BRITANNIA on rev.		Extremely rare		
1696 —	£40	£180	£1000	—
1696 — TERTVS error		Extremely rare		
1697 —	£45	£170	£1000	—
1697 — No stop after TERTIVS on obv.	£50	£300	—	—
1698 —	£50	£200	£1000	—
1698 Second issue (date in legend)	£50	£180	—	—
1698 — No stop after date	£50	£180	—	—
1699 —	£55	£210	£1100	—
1699 — No stop after date	£225	—	—	—
1699 Third issue (date in exergue) (Britannia with right hand on knee)	£40	£175	£900	—
1699 — No stop after date		Extremely rare		
1699 — BRITΛNNIΛ error	£200	—	—	—
1699 — TERTVS error		Extremely rare		
1699 — No stop on rev.		Extremely rare		
1699 — No stops on obv.	£90	£375	—	—
1700 —	£45	£190	£950	—
1700 — No stops on obv.	£100	£350	—	—
1700 — No stops after GVLIELMUS	£100	£350	—	—
1700 — BRITVANNIA error		Extremely rare		
1700 — GVIELMS error	£100	£350	—	—
1700 — GVLIEEMVS error	£100	£350	—	—
1701 —	£40	£175	£900	—
1701 — BRITΛNNIΛ error	£80	£300	—	—
1701 — No stops on obv.		Extremely rare		
1701 — inverted As for Vs	£80	£320	—	—

GEORGE I (1714–27)

1717 "Dump" issue	£45	£250	£800	
1718 —	£35	£225	£775	—
1719 "Dump" issue. Patterns				Rare
1719 Second issue	£40	£200	£800	—
1720 —	£35	£160	£600	—
1721 —	£35	£150	£600	—
1721 — Stop after date	£45	£150	—	—
1722 —	£35	£140	£650	—
1722 — inverted A for V on obv.		Extremely rare		
1723 —	£35	£150	£625	—
1723 — No stop on rev.	£110	£500	—	—
1724 —	£35	£150	£625	—

GEORGE II (1727–60)

1729 Young head	£28	£90	£400	—
1729 — No stop on rev.	£28	£80	£400	—
1730 —	£22	£90	£400	—
1730 — GEOGIVS error	£70	£225	£650	—
1730 — Stop after date	£28	£120	£425	—
1730 — No stop after REX on obv.	£32	£150	£450	—
1731 —	£22	£110	£400	—
1731 — No rev. stop	£26	£125	£425	—
1732 —	£22	£100	£400	—
1732 — No rev. stop	£26	£125	£450	—
1733 —	£22	£90	£400	—
1734/3 — 4 over 3	£35	£210	—	—
1734 — No stop on obv.	£35	£210	—	—

DATE	MINTAGE	F	VF	EF	UNC
1735 —		£22	£80	£400	—
1736 —		£22	£80	£400	—
1737 —		£22	£85	£420	—
1738 —		£22	£80	£350	—
1739 —		£20	£70	£350	—
1740 Old head		£17	£70	£320	—
1742 —		£17	£70	£320	—
1742/0 — 2 over 0		£25	£150	£450	—
1743 —		£17	£70	£320	—
1744 —		£17	£70	£330	—
1745 —		£17	£70	£340	—
1746 —		£17	£70	£320	—
1747 —		£17	£70	£320	—
1748 —		£17	£70	£330	—
1749 —		£17	£70	£330	—
1750 —		£17	£70	£330	—
1751 —		£17	£70	£330	—
1752 —		£17	£70	£330	—
1753 —		£17	£70	£330	—
1754 —		£17	£70	£330	—

GEORGE III (1760–1820)

First type—Royal Mint

		F	VF	EF	UNC
1770		£18	£50	£300	—
1770 No stop on rev.		£25	£65	£350	—
1771		£12	£50	£280	—
1771 No stop on rev.		£20	£65	£300	—
1772 Error GEORIVS		£80	£240	£700	
1772		£12	£50	£225	—
1772 No stop on rev		£20	£65	£280	—
1773		£10	£45	£280	—
1773 No stop after REX		£30	£80	£400	—
1773 No stop on rev.		£20	£70	£300	—
1774		£12	£40	£220	—
1775		£12	£40	£220	—

Second type—Soho Mint

		F	VF	EF	UNC
1799		£5	£12	£55	£120

Third type

		F	VF	EF	UNC
1806		£5	£11	£60	£110
1807		£5	£11	£60	£110

George III second type

GEORGE IV (1820–30)

	MINTAGE	F	VF	EF	UNC
1825	215,040	£12	£45	£190	£380
1826 (varieties)	9,031,630	£12	£45	£190	£380
1826 Proof	—	—	—	—	£550
1827	5,376,000	£12	£45	£160	£340

WILLIAM IV (1830–37)

	MINTAGE	F	VF	EF	UNC
1831	806,400	£12	£30	£130	£325
1831 Proof	—	—	—	—	£500
1834	537,600	£12	£30	£130	£325
1837	349,440	£12	£30	£130	£325

VICTORIA (1837–1901)

Copper

	MINTAGE	F	VF	EF	UNC
1838	456,960	£8	£18	£80	£320
1839 Proof	268,800	—	—	—	£500
1841	1,075,200	£6	£16	£60	£220
1843	967,680	£35	£55	£200	£750
1844	1,075,200	£12	£40	£180	£375

DATE	MINTAGE	F	VF	EF	UNC
1845	1,075,200	£200	£450	£1800	—
1846	860,160	£12	£25	£85	£250
1847	725,640	£12	£22	£85	£250
1848	322,560	£12	£22	£80	£250
1848/7 final 8 OVER 7	incl. above	£14	£35	£100	£275
1851	215,040	£7	£18	£75	£250
1852	637,056	£10	£22	£80	£250
1853	1,559,040	£5	£10	£40	£120
1853/2 3 over 2	incl. above	£15	£30	£60	£240
1853 Proof	—	—	—	—	£775
1854	12,354,048	£5	£9	£40	£130
1855	1,455,837	£5	£9	£40	£130
1856	1,942,080	£10	£24	£80	£300
1857	1,820,720	£6	£18	£50	£140
1858	2,472,960	£5	£12	£50	£130
1858/7 final 8 over 7	incl. above	£5	£12	£50	£130
1858/6 final 8 over 6	incl. above	£5	£12	£50	£130
1859	1,290,240	£7	£22	£70	£230
1859/8 9 over 8	incl. above	£8	£25	£70	£275
1860	unrecorded	£1400	£3500	£7000	£12000

Victoria copper halfpenny

Bronze

1860 Beaded border	6,630,400	£3	£10	£50	£190
1860 Toothed border		£4	£12	£60	£270
1861	54,118,400	£4	£10	£40	£185
1862 Die letter A, B or C to left of lighthouse				Extremely rare	
1862	61,107,200	£3	£9	£40	£160
1863	15,948,800	£3	£9	£75	£160
1864	537,600	£3	£10	£45	£175
1865	8,064,000	£4	£18	£75	£300
1865/3 5 over 3	incl. above	£50	£120	£450	—
1866	2,508,800	£5	£15	£70	£240
1867	2,508,800	£5	£15	£60	£220
1868	3,046,400	£5	£15	£70	£260
1869	3,225,600	£30	£100	£250	£1500
1870	4,350,739	£5	£15	£60	£250
1871	1,075,280	£75	£100	£500	£1500
1872	4,659,410	£4	£10	£50	£180
1873	3,404,880	£4	£10	£50	£200
1874	1,347,655	£6	£25	£110	£300
1874 H	5,017,600	£3	£10	£60	£230
1875	5,430,815	£3	£8	£60	£200
1875 H	1,254,400	£5	£12	£60	£200
1876 H	5,809,600	£4	£10	£60	£230
1877	5,209,505	£3	£10	£60	£180
1878	1,425,535	£6	£20	£100	£350
1878 Wide date		£100	£200	£550	—
1879	3,582,545	£3	£10	£40	£200
1880	2,423,465	£4	£12	£60	£210
1881	2,007,515	£4	£12	£50	£180
1881 H	1,792,000	£3	£10	£50	£200
1882 H	4,480,000	£3	£10	£50	£220
1883	3,000,725	£3	£12	£60	£225
1884	6,989,580	£3	£10	£45	£160
1885	8,600,574	£3	£10	£45	£160
1886	8,586,155	£3	£10	£45	£160
1887	10,701,305	£3	£10	£45	£160
1888	6,814,670	£3	£10	£45	£160
1889	7,748,234	£3	£10	£45	£160
1889/8 9 over 8	incl. above	£30	£60	£250	—
1890	11,254,235	£3	£10	£40	£120
1891	13,192,260	£3	£10	£35	£120
1892	2,478,335	£3	£10	£45	£140

Victoria bronze halfpenny

DATE	MINTAGE	F	VF	EF	UNC
1893	7,229,344	£3	£10	£35	£130
1894	1,767,635	£5	£12	£70	£275

OLD HEAD ISSUES

1895	3,032,154	£2	£7	£20	£65
1896	9,142,500	£1	£4	£10	£45
1897	8,690,315	£1	£4	£10	£45
1898	8,595,180	£1	£5	£12	£55
1899	12,108,001	£1	£4	£10	£45
1900	13,805,190	£1	£4	£10	£35
1901	11,127,360	£1	£3	£8	£25

EDWARD VII (1901–10)

1902	13,672,960	£2	£4	£8	£30
1902 "Low tide"	incl. above	£22	£90	£180	£450
1903	11,450,880	£2	£5	£20	£60
1904	8,131,200	£2	£6	£25	£80
1905	10,124,800	£2	£5	£20	£55
1906	16,849,280	£2	£5	£25	£70
1907	16,849,280	£2	£5	£20	£70
1908	16,620,800	£2	£5	£20	£70
1909	8,279,040	£2	£5	£20	£70
1910	10,769,920	£2	£5	£20	£50

GEORGE V (1910–36)

1911	12,570,880	£1	£4	£15	£40
1912	21,185,920	£1	£3	£15	£35
1913	17,476,480	£1	£3	£15	£40
1914	20,289,111	£1	£3	£15	£40
1915	21,563,040	£2	£3	£20	£55
1916	39,386,143	£1	£2	£15	£40
1917	38,245,436	£1	£2	£15	£35
1918	22,321,072	£1	£2	£15	£35
1919	28,104,001	£1	£2	£15	£35
1920	35,146,793	£1	£2	£15	£40
1921	28,027,293	£1	£2	£15	£40
1922	10,734,964	£1	£4	£25	£45
1923	12,266,282	£1	£2	£15	£35
1924	13,971,038	£1	£2	£15	£30
1925	12,216,123	—	£2	£15	£30
1925 Modified effigy	incl. above	£4	£10	£50	£90
1926	6,172,306	—	£2	£10	£40
1927	15,589,622	—	£2	£10	£40
1928	20,935,200	—	£2	£8	£35
1929	25,680,000	—	£2	£8	£35
1930	12,532,800	—	£2	£8	£35
1931	16,137,600	—	£2	£8	£35
1932	14,448,000	—	£2	£8	£35
1933	10,560,000	—	£2	£8	£35
1934	7,704,000	—	£2	£12	£45
1935	12,180,000	—	£1	£6	£20
936	23,008,800	—	£1	£5	£15

GEORGE VI (1936–52)

1937	24,504,000	—	—	£1	£5
1937 Proof	26,402	—	—	—	£18
1938	40,320,000	—	—	£1	£6
1939	28,924,800	—	—	£1	£5
1940	32,162,400	—	—	£2	£10

DATE	MINTAGE	F	VF	EF	UNC
1941	45,120,000	—	—	£1	£8
1942	71,908,800	—	—	£1	£5
1943	76,200,000	—	—	£1	£5
1944	81,840,000	—	—	£1	£5
1945	57,000,000	—	—	£1	£5
1946	22,725,600	—	—	£1	£6
1947	21,266,400	—	—	£1	£6
1948	26,947,200	—	—	£1	£4
1949	24,744,000	—	—	£1	£4
1950	24,153,600	—	—	£1	£5
1950 Proof	17,513	—	—	—	£18
1951	14,868,000	—	—	£1	£6
1951 Proof	20,000	—	—	—	£18
1952	33,784,000	—	—	£1	£4

ELIZABETH II (1952–   )

1953	8,926,366	—	—	—	£1
1953 Proof	40,000	—	—	—	£4
1954	19,375,000	—	—	—	£3
1955	18,799,200	—	—	—	£3
1956	21,799,200	—	—	—	£3
1957	43,684,800	—	—	—	£1
1957 Calm sea	incl. above	—	—	£10	£30
1958	62,318,400	—	—	—	£1
1959	79,176,000	—	—	—	£1
1960	41,340,000	—	—	—	£1
1962	41,779,200	—	—	—	£1
1963	45,036,000	—	—	—	20p
1964	78,583,200	—	—	—	20p
1965	98,083,200	—	—	—	20p
1966	95,289,600	—	—	—	20p
1967	146,491,200	—	—	—	10p
1970 Proof	—				£5

Later issues are included in the Decimal section.

FARTHINGS

DATE		F	VF	EF	UNC

OLIVER CROMWELL

Undated (copper) Draped bust, shield rev. Variations   Extremely rare

CHARLES II (1660–85)

Copper

		F	VF	EF	UNC
1672		£40	£225	£750	—
1673		£45	£240	£775	—
1673 CAROLA for CAROLO error		£125	£500	—	—
1673 No stops on obv.				Extremely rare	
1673 No stop on rev.				Extremely rare	
1674		£45	£250	£800	—
1675		£40	£220	£750	—
1675 No stop after CAROLVS				Extremely rare	
1679		£55	£275	£900	—
1679 No stop on rev.		£60	£300	—	—
Tin					
1684 with date on edge		£250	£800	—	—
1685 —				Extremely rare	

DATE	F	VF	EF	UNC

JAMES II (1685–88)

1684 (tin) Cuirassed bust		Extremely rare		
1685 (tin) —	£180	£625	£2250	—
1686 (tin) —	£190	£625	£2250	—
1687 (tin) —		Extremely rare		
1687 (tin) Draped bust	£230	£850	—	—

WILLIAM & MARY (1688–94)

1689 (tin) Small draped busts	£650	—	—	—
1689 (tin) — with edge date 1690		Extremely rare		
1690 (tin) Large cuirassed busts	£170	£625	£2750	—
1690 (tin) — with edge date 1689		Extremely rare		
1691 (tin) —	£175	£625		—
1692 (tin) —	£185	£650	£2750	—
1694 (copper) —	£70	£250	£900	—
1694 No stop after MARIΛ		Extremely rare		
1694 No stop on obv.		Extremely rare		
1694 No stop on rev.		Extremely rare		
1694 Unbarred As in BRITANNIA		Extremely rare		

WILLIAM III (1694–1702)

1695 First issue (date in exergue)	£40	£200	£800	—
1695 — GVLIELMV error		Extremely rare		
1696 —	£40	£200	£850	—
1697 —	£40	£200	£850	—
1697 — GVLIELMS error		Extremely rare		
1698 —	£200	£750	—	—
1698 Second issue (date in legend)	£50	£250	£850	—
1699 First issue	£40	£200	£800	—
1699 Second issue	£40	£200	£800	—
1699 — No stop after date	£50	£300	—	—
1700 First issue	£35	£140	£675	—
1700 — error RRITANNIA		Extremely rare		

ANNE (1702–14)

1714	£425	£675	£1500	—

GEORGE I (1714–27)

1717 First small "Dump" issue	£200	£600	£1200	—
1718 1 Known				—
1719 Second issue	£30	£140	£450	—
1719 — No stop on rev.	£70	£350	—	—
1719 — No stops on obv.	£70	£300	—	—
1720 —	£30	£140	£500	—
1721 —	£25	£140	£500	—
1721/0 — Last 1 over 0	£40	£160	—	—
1722 —	£35	£125	£475	—
1723 —	£35	£125	£500	—
1723 — R over sideways R in REX		Extremely rare		
1724 —	£35	£140	£500	—

George I, first type

GEORGE II (1727–60)

1730 Young head	£15	£60	£325	—
1731 —	£15	£60	£325	—
1732 —	£15	£75	£375	—
1733 —	£15	£70	£375	—
1734 —	£15	£65	£375	—
1734 — No stop on obv.	£30	£110	£425	—

George I second type

DATE	MINTAGE	F	VF	EF	UNC
1735 —		£15	£60	£350	—
1735 — 3 over 5		£20	£100	£425	—
1736 —		£12	£60	£340	—
1737 —		£12	£60	£320	—
1739 —		£12	£60	£320	—
1741 Old Head		£12	£50	£300	—
1744 —		£12	£50	£300	—
1746 —		£12	£50	£300	—
1746 — V over LL in GEORGIVS..............				Extremely rare	
1749 —		£15	£60	£300	—
1750 —		£15	£55	£285	—
1754 —		£10	£30	£200	—
1754 — 4 over 0		£25	£100	£325	—

GEORGE III (1760–1820)

DATE	MINTAGE	F	VF	EF	UNC
1771 First (London) issue		£20	£60	£250	—
1773 —		£12	£40	£200	—
1773 — No stop on rev........................		£18	£60	£230	—
1773 — No stop after REX		£25	£75	£250	
1774 —		£10	£40	£190	—
1775 —		£10	£40	£190	—
1797 Second (Soho Mint) issue				Patterns only	
1799 Third (Soho Mint) issue................		£2	£8	£40	£100
1806 Fourth (Soho Mint) issue		£2	£8	£40	£100
1807 —		£2	£8	£40	£100

George III, third (Soho Mint) issue

GEORGE IV (1820–30)

DATE	MINTAGE	F	VF	EF	UNC
1821 First bust (laureate, draped), first reverse (date in exergue)...	2,688,000	£3	£10	£60	£110
1822 —	5,924,350	£3	£10	£60	£110
1823 —	2,365,440	£4	£10	£60	£110
1823 I for 1 in date	incl. above	£20	£70	£300	£600
1825 —	4,300.800	£4	£10	£60	£130
1826 —	6,666,240	£4	£10	£60	£110
1826 Second bust (couped, date below), second reverse (ornament in exergue)	incl. above	£4	£10	£60	£110
1826 — Proof	—	—	—	—	£375
1827 —	2,365,440	£4	£10	£60	£140
1828 —	2,365,440	£4	£12	£60	£140
1829 —	1,505,280	£4	£12	£60	£140
1830 —	2,365,440	£4	£12	£60	£140

George III, fourth (Soho Mint) issue

WILLIAM IV (1830–37)

DATE	MINTAGE	F	VF	EF	UNC
1831..	2,688,000	£5	£12	£45	£125
1831 Proof....................................	—	—	—	—	£425
1834..	1,935,360	£5	£12	£50	£120
1835,,,,.......................................	1.720,320	£5	£12	£50	£120
1836..	1,290.240	£5	£12	£55	£120
1837..	3.010,560	£5	£12	£55	£150

VICTORIA (1837–1901)

FIRST YOUNG HEAD (COPPER) ISSUES

DATE	MINTAGE	F	VF	EF	UNC
1838..	591,360	£5	£15	£45	£170
1839..	4,300,800	£5	£15	£45	£170
1839 Proof....................................	—	—	—	—	£500
1840..	3,010,560	£4	£15	£40	£150
1841..	1,720,320	£4	£15	£40	£150
1841 Proof....................................				Extremely rare	
1842..	1,290,240	£10	£35	£100	£350
1843..	4,085,760	£5	£14	£40	£175

DATE	MINTAGE	F	VF	EF	UNC
1843 I for 1 in date		£90	£425	—	—
1844	430,080	£80	£220	£800	£2200
1845	3,225,600	£6	£10	£40	£150
1846	2,580,480	£7	£20	£55	£200
1847	3,879,720	£5	£12	£50	£150
1848	1,290,240	£5	£12	£50	£150
1849	645,120	£50	£100	£300	£900
1850	430,080	£5	£10	£40	£140
1851	1,935,360	£8	£20	£80	£240
1851 D over sideways D in DEI	incl. above	£80	£110	£450	—
1852	822,528	£10	£20	£70	£220
1853	1,028,628	£4	£7	£30	£65
1853 Proof	—	—	—	—	£900
1854	6,504,960	£4	£10	£35	£70
1855	3,440,640	£4	£10	£35	£70
1856	1,771,392	£10	£22	£70	£250
1856 R over E in VICTORIA	incl. above	£20	£50	£250	—
1857	1,075,200	£4	£10	£35	£80
1858	1,720,320	£4	£10	£35	£80
1859	1,290,240	£10	£25	£75	£320
1860	unrecorded	£1500	£3750	£6750	—

Victoria Young Head first (copper) issue

SECOND YOUNG OR "BUN" HEAD (BRONZE) ISSUES

DATE	MINTAGE	F	VF	EF	UNC
1860 Toothed border	2,867,200	£2	£5	£40	£100
1860 Beaded border	incl. above	£3	£7	£40	£110
1860 Toothed/Beaded border mule	incl. above			Extremely rare	
1861	8,601,600	£2	£5	£35	£100
1862	14,336,000	£1	£5	£35	£100
1862 Large 8 in date	incl. above			Extremely rare	
1863	1,433,600	£40	£75	£300	£650
1864	2,508,800	£1	£5	£30	£100
1865	4,659,200	£1	£5	£30	£90
1865 5 over 2	incl. above	£10	£20	£65	—
1866	3,584,000	£1	£5	£25	£90
1867	5,017,600	£1	£5	£25	£90
1868	4,851,210	£1	£5	£25	£90
1869	3,225,600	£2	£10	£45	£160
1872	2,150,400	£1	£5	£25	£80
1873	3,225,620	£1	£5	£25	£80
1874 H	3,584,000	£1	£5	£25	£100
1874 H both Gs over sideways G	incl. above	£150	£350	£1000	—
1875	712,760	£4	£12	£40	£130
1875 H	6,092,800	£1	£5	£20	£80
1876 H	1,175,200	£3	£12	£50	£150
1878	4,008,540	£1	£4	£20	£75
1879	3,977,180	£1	£4	£20	£75
1880	1,842,710	£1	£4	£20	£75
1881	3,494,670	£1	£4	£20	£75
1881 H	1,792,000	£1	£4	£20	£75
1882 H	1,792,000	£1	£5	£22	£80
1883	1,128,680	£5	£18	£60	£150
1884	5,782,000	£1	£4	£20	£40
1885	5,442,308	£1	£4	£20	£40
1886	7.707,790	£1	£4	£20	£40
1887	1,340,800	£1	£4	£20	£40
1888	1,887,250	£1	£4	£20	£40
1890	2,133,070	£1	£4	£20	£40
1891	4,959,690	£1	£4	£20	£40
1892	887,240	£3	£12	£50	£140
1893	3,904,320	£1	£4	£20	£40
1894	2,396,770	£1	£4	£20	£40
1895	2,852,852	£10	£25	£80	£225

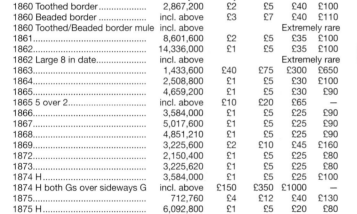

Victoria Young Head second (bronze) issue

DATE	MINTAGE	F	VF	EF	UNC
OLD HEAD ISSUES					
1895 Bright finish	incl. above	£1	£2	£16	£35
1896 —	3,668,610	£1	£2	£16	£25
1897 —	4,579,800	£1	£2	£16	£25
1897 Dark finish	incl. above	£1	£2	£16	£25
1898 —	4,010,080	£1	£2	£16	£25
1899 —	3,864,616	£1	£2	£16	£25
1900 —	5,969,317	£1	£2	£16	£25
1901 —	8,016,460	£1	£2	£10	£20

EDWARD VII (1901–10)

1902..	5,125,120	50p	£1	£10	£15
1903..	5,331,200	50p	£1	£12	£20
1904..	3,628,800	£2	£5	£20	£45
1905..	4,076,800	£1	£2	£12	£30
1906..	5,340,160	50p	£1	£12	£25
1907..	4,399,360	50p	£1	£10	£20
1908..	4,264,960	50p	£1	£10	£20
1909..	8,852,480	50p	£1	£10	£20
1910..	2,298,400	£4	£9	£28	£70

GEORGE V (1910–36)

1911..	5,196,800	50p	£1	£6	£14
1912..	7,669,760	50p	£1	£8	£14
1913..	4,184,320	50p	£1	£6	£14
1914..	6,126,988	50p	£1	£5	£14
1915..	7,129,255	50p	£1	£5	£16
1916..	10,993,325	50p	£1	£5	£14
1917..	21,434,844	25p	50p	£4	£10
1918..	19,362,818	25p	50p	£4	£10
1919..	15,089,425	25p	50p	£4	£10
1920..	11,480,536	25p	50p	£4	£8
1921..	9,469,097	25p	50p	£4	£8
1922..	9,956,983	25p	50p	£4	£8
1923..	8,034,457	25p	50p	£4	£8
1924..	8,733,414	25p	50p	£4	£8
1925..	12,634,697	25p	50p	£4	£8
1926 Modified effigy..................	9,792,397	25p	50p	£4	£8
1927	7,868,355	25p	50p	£4	£8
1928	11,625,600	25p	50p	£4	£8
1929	8,419,200	25p	50p	£4	£8
1930	4,195,200	25p	50p	£4	£8
1931	6,595,200	25p	50p	£4	£8
1932	9,292,800	25p	50p	£4	£8
1933	4,560,000	25p	50p	£4	£8
1934	3,052,800	25p	50p	£4	£8
1935	2.227,200	£1	£3	£10	£25
1936	9,734,400	25p	50p	£3	£6

GEORGE VI (1936–52)

1937..	8,131,200	—	—	50p	£1
1937 Proof..............................	26,402	—	—	—	£7
1938..	7,449,600	—	—	£1	£6
1939..	31,440,000	—	—	50p	£1
1940..	18,360,000	—	—	50p	£1
1941..	27,312,000	—	—	50p	£1
1942..	28,857,600	—	—	50p	£1
1943..	33,345,600	—	—	50p	£1
1944..	25,137,600	—	—	50p	£1
1945..	23,736,000	—	—	50p	£1

DATE	MINTAGE	F	VF	EF	UNC
1946	24,364,800	—	—	50p	£1
1947	14,745,600	—	—	50p	£1
1948	16,622,400	—	—	50p	£1
1949	8,424,000	—	—	50p	£1
1950	10,324,800	—	—	50p	£1
1950 Proof	17,513	—	—	50p	£8
1951	14,016,000	—	—	50p	£1
1951 Proof	20,000	—	—	50p	£8
1952	5,251,200	—	—	50p	£1

ELIZABETH II (1952–)

1953	6,131,037	—	—	—	£1
1953 Proof	40,000	—	—	—	£7
1954	6,566,400	—	—	—	£2
1955	5,779,200	—	—	—	£1.50
1956	1,996,800	—	£1	£2	£6

HALF FARTHINGS

DATE	MINTAGE	F	VF	EF	UNC

GEORGE IV (1820–30)

1828 (two different obverses) (issued for Ceylon)	7,680,000	£10	£20	£50	£150
1830 (large or small date) (issued for Ceylon)	8,766,320	£10	£20	£50	£140

WILLIAM IV (1830–37)

1837 (issued for Ceylon)	1,935,360	£20	£55	£140	£250

VICTORIA (1837–1901)

1839	2,042,880	£5	£10	£30	£85
1842	unrecorded	£4	£8	£25	£85
1843	3,440,640	£3	£6	£20	£50
1844	6,451,200	£3	£6	£15	£50
1844 E over N in REGINA	incl. above	£10	£45	£100	—
1847	3,010,560	£6	£12	£35	£80
1851	unrecorded	£6	£12	£35	£110
1851 5 over 0	unrecorded	£8	£20	£60	£150
1852	989,184	£6	£12	£40	£120
1853	955,224	£6	£15	£50	£130
1853 Proof	incl. above	—	—	—	£500
1854	677,376	£9	£25	£75	£185
1856	913,920	£9	£25	£75	£185
1868 Proof	unrecorded				£1000

THIRD FARTHINGS

DATE	MINTAGE	F	VF	EF	UNC

GEORGE IV (1820–30)

DATE	MINTAGE	F	VF	EF	UNC
1827 (issued for Malta)	unrecorded	£8	£18	£50	£125

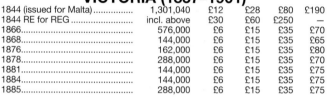

WILLIAM IV (1830–37)

DATE	MINTAGE	F	VF	EF	UNC
1835 (issued for Malta)	unrecorded	£8	£18	£50	£150

VICTORIA (1837–1901)

DATE	MINTAGE	F	VF	EF	UNC
1844 (issued for Malta)	1,301,040	£12	£28	£80	£190
1844 RE for REG	incl. above	£30	£60	£250	—
1866	576,000	£6	£15	£35	£70
1868	144,000	£6	£15	£35	£65
1876	162,000	£6	£15	£35	£80
1878	288,000	£6	£15	£35	£70
1881	144,000	£6	£15	£35	£75
1884	144,000	£6	£15	£35	£75
1885	288,000	£6	£15	£35	£75

EDWARD VII (1902–10)

DATE	MINTAGE	F	VF	EF	UNC
1902 (issued for Malta)	288,000	£5	£10	£25	£45

GEORGE V (1911–36)

DATE	MINTAGE	F	VF	EF	UNC
1913 (issued for Malta)	288,000	£5	£10	£25	£45

QUARTER FARTHINGS

DATE	MINTAGE	F	VF	EF	UNC

VICTORIA (1837–1901)

DATE	MINTAGE	F	VF	EF	UNC
1839 (issued for Ceylon)	3,840,000	£40	£65	£120	£240
1851 (issued for Ceylon)	2,215,680	£40	£65	£120	£240
1852 (issued for Ceylon)	incl. above	£40	£65	£120	£250
1853 (issued for Ceylon)	incl. above	£40	£65	£120	£240
1853 Proof	—	—	—	—	£900

EMERGENCY ISSUES

DATE	F	VF	EF	UNC

GEORGE III (1760–1820)

To alleviate the shortage of circulating coinage during the Napoleonic Wars the Bank of England firstly authorised the countermarking of other countries' coins, enabling them to pass as English currency. The coins, countermarked with punches depicting the head of George III, were mostly Spanish American 8 reales of Charles III. Although this had limited success it was later decided to completely overstrike the coins with a new English design on both sides—specimens that still show traces of the original host coin's date are avidly sought after by collectors. This overstriking continued for a number of years although all the known coins are dated 1804. Finally, in 1811 the Bank of England issued silver tokens which continued up to 1816 when a completely new regal coinage was introduced.

DOLLAR
Oval countermark of George III

	F	VF	EF	UNC
On "Pillar" type 8 reales	£175	£650	£1000	—
*On "Portrait" type.............	£200	£350	£800	—

Octagonal countermark of George III

	F	VF	EF	UNC
On "Portrait" type..............	£200	£600	£850	—

HALF DOLLAR
Oval countermark of George III

	F	VF	EF	UNC
On "Portrait" type 4 reales	£200	£400	£900	—

FIVE SHILLINGS OR ONE DOLLAR
These coins were overstruck on Spanish-American coins

	F	VF	EF	UNC
1804..................................	£120	£275	£550	—

— With details of original coin still visible add from 10%.

BANK OF ENGLAND TOKENS

THREE SHILLINGS

	F	VF	EF	UNC
1811 Draped bust.............	£35	£60	£200	—
1812 —	£35	£60	£220	—
1812 Laureate bust	£35	£60	£150	—
1813 —	£35	£60	£150	—
1814 —	£35	£60	£150	—
1815 —	£35	£60	£150	—
1816 —	£200	£400	£1250	—

ONE SHILLING AND SIXPENCE

	F	VF	EF	UNC
1811 Draped bust.............	£20	£45	£100	£175
1812 —	£20	£45	£100	£175
1812 Laureate bust	£20	£45	£100	£175
1812 Proof in platinum				Unique
1813 —	£20	£40	£75	£175
1813 Proof in platinum				Unique
1814 —	£20	£35	£75	£160
1815 —	£20	£35	£75	£160
1816 —	£20	£35	£75	£160

NINEPENCE

	F	VF	EF	UNC
1812 Pattern only	—	—		Very Rare

MAUNDY SETS

DATE	F	VF	EF	UNC

CHARLES II (1660–85)

DATE	F	VF	EF	UNC
Undated	£240	£370	£800	—
1670	£225	£370	£750	—
1671	£235	£385	£850	—
1672	£215	£350	£735	—
1673	£215	£330	£720	—
1674	£225	£340	£735	—
1675	£210	£325	£715	—
1676	£230	£365	£755	—
1677	£195	£310	£690	—
1678	£270	£460	£850	—
1679	£225	£360	£750	—
1680	£215	£345	£710	—
1681	£240	£355	£750	—
1682	£230	£360	£715	—
1683	£230	£360	£725	—
1684	£250	£415	£775	—

JAMES II (1685–88)

1686	£230	£365	£725	—
1687	£230	£370	£750	—
1688	£240	£400	£775	—

WILLIAM & MARY (1688–94)

1689	£855	£1250	£2100	—
1691	£715	£915	£1850	—
1692	£710	£925	£1725	—
1693	£625	£1000	£1900	—
1694	£485	£735	£1300	—

WILLIAM III (1694–1702)

1698	£245	£480	£900	—
1699	£540	£725	£1650	—
1700	£265	£490	£925	—
1701	£245	£440	£875	—

ANNE (1702–14)

1703	£225	£440	£775	—
1705	£230	£435	£750	—
1706	£200	£375	£675	—
1708	£600	£900	£2100	—
1709	£250	£475	£850	—
1710	£265	£460	£825	—
1713	£240	£435	£725	—

Sets in contemporary dated boxes are usually worth a higher premium. For example approximately £30 can be added to sets from Victoria to George VI in contemporary undated boxes and above £40 for dated boxes.

GEORGE I (1714–27)

1723	£250	£450	£785	—
1727	£225	£435	£765	—

GEORGE II (1727–60)

1729	£195	£325	£675	—
1731	£195	£335	£675	—
1732	£190	£320	£650	—
1735	£190	£320	£650	—
1737	£190	£325	£640	—
1739	£190	£320	£625	—
1740	£175	£300	£585	—
1743	£300	£445	£875	—
1746	£170	£300	£565	—
1760	£185	£325	£595	—

GEORGE III (1760–1820)

1763	£170	£290	£480	—
1763 Proof	—	Extremely rare		
1766	£200	£300	£525	—
1772	£185	£300	£525	—
1780	£225	£325	£575	—
1784	£190	£320	£500	—
1786	£195	£310	£515	—
1792 Wire	£260	£450	£625	£810
1795	£115	£200	£325	£405
1800	£115	£200	£300	£395
New Coinage				
1817	£135	£210	£290	£425
1818	£135	£205	£280	£415
1820	£140	£215	£285	£420

GEORGE IV (1820–30)

1822	—	£160	£245	£415
1823	—	£155	£255	£400
1824	—	£160	£260	£405
1825	—	£150	£250	£380
1826	—	£145	£245	£380
1827	—	£145	£255	£385
1828	—	£150	£250	£400
1828 Proof	—	—	—£3650	
1829	—	£150	£250	£385
1830	—	£150	£240	£375

WILLIAM IV (1830–37)

1831	—	£170	£280	£450
1831 Proof	—	—	—£1700	
1831 Proof Gold	—	—	£37000	
1832	—	£180	£285	£450
1833	—	£170	£275	£410
1834	—	£175	£280	£410
1835	—	£160	£265	£400
1836	—	£175	£285	£425
1837	—	£190	£300	£445

VICTORIA (1837–1901)

YOUNG HEAD ISSUES

DATE	MINTAGE	EF	UNC
1838	4,158	£240	£425
1838 Proof	unrecorded		£3200
1838 Proof Gold			£37000
1839	4,125	£285	£475
1839 Proof	unrecorded	£650	£1500
1840	4,125	£300	£445
1841	2,574	£395	£625
1842	4,125	£395	£600
1843	4,158	£260	£410
1844	4,158	£345	£535
1845	4,158	£225	£400
1846	4,158	£550	£875
1847	4,158	£575	£925
1848	4,158	£525	£875
1849	4,158	£365	£535
1850	4,158	£250	£415
1851	4,158	£295	£445
1852	4,158	£600	£900
1853	4,158	£625	£1000
1853 Proof	unrecorded		£1850
1854	4,158	£260	£420
1855	4,158	£300	£475
1856	4,158	£235	£375
1857	4,158	£265	£425
1858	4,158	£240	£375
1859	4,158	£215	£325
1860	4,158	£240	£375
1861	4,158	£205	£375
1862	4,158	£245	£390
1863	4,158	£260	£445
1864	4,158	£240	£345
1865	4,158	£240	£350
1866	4,158	£225	£340
1867	4,158	£220	£345
1867 Proof	unrecorded	−	£3000
1868	4,158	£200	£315
1869	4,158	£240	£405
1870	4,458	£190	£290
1871	4,488	£185	£280
1871 Proof	unrecorded	−	£2550
1872	4,328	£180	£280
1873	4,162	£180	£270
1874	4,488	£185	£275
1875	4,154	£180	£265
1876	4,488	£190	£270
1877	4,488	£180	£255
1878	4,488	£185	£255
1878 Proof	unrecorded	−	£2500
1879	4,488	£190	£245
1879 Proof	unrecorded	−	£2850
1880	4,488	£185	£240
1881	4,488	£180	£240
1881 Proof	unrecorded	−	£2350
1882	4,146	£215	£285
1882 Proof	unrecorded	−	£2550
1883	4,488	£160	£225
1884	4,488	£160	£225
1885	4,488	£160	£225
1886	4,488	£165	£225
1887	4,488	£180	£255

JUBILEE HEAD ISSUES

DATE	MINTAGE	EF	UNC
1888	4,488	£160	£230
1888 Proof	unrecorded	−	£2100
1889	4,488	£155	£220
1890	4,488	£160	£230
1891	4,488	£160	£230
1892	4,488	£170	£245

OLD HEAD ISSUES

DATE	MINTAGE	EF	UNC
1893	8,976	£100	£200
1894	8,976	£130	£215
1895	8,976	£115	£190
1896	8,976	£115	£195
1897	8,976	£115	£200
1898	8,976	£115	£205
1899	8,976	£115	£205
1900	8,976	£100	£195
1901	8,976	£100	£195

EDWARD VII (1902–110)

DATE	MINTAGE	EF	UNC
1902	8,976	£95	£180
1902 Matt proof	15,123	−	£200
1903	8,976	£100	£190
1904	8,976	£110	£200
1905	8,976	£110	£190
1906	8,800	£100	£180
1907	8,760	£100	£185
1908	8,769	£90	£180
1909	1,983	£165	£275
1910	1,440	£190	£300

GEORGE V (1911–136)

DATE	MINTAGE	EF	UNC
1911	1,786	£150	£240
1911 Proof	6,007	−	£275
1912	1,246	£160	£250
1913	1,228	£155	£250
1914	982	£185	£275
1915	1,293	£165	£265
1916	1,128	£160	£250
1917	1,237	£160	£250
1918	1,375	£165	£255
1919	1,258	£160	£250
1920	1,399	£160	£250
1921	1,386	£160	£255
1922	1,373	£165	£260
1923	1,430	£165	£260
1924	1,515	£165	£260
1925	1,438	£150	£245
1926	1,504	£150	£245
1927	1,647	£155	£255
1928	1,642	£155	£250
1929	1,761	£160	£255
1930	1,724	£150	£240
1931	1,759	£150	£240
1932	1,835	£145	£245
1933	1,872	£140	£240
1934	1,887	£140	£240
1935	1,928	£155	£255
1936	1,323	£200	£300

GEORGE VI (1936–52)

DATE	MINTAGE	EF	UNC
1937	1,325	£140	£200
1937 Proof	20,900	£140	£200
1938	1,275	£170	£255
1939	1,234	£175	£260
1940	1,277	£170	£255
1941	1,253	£180	£260
1942	1,231	£170	£255
1943	1,239	£175	£260
1944	1,259	£170	£255

DATE	MINTAGE	EF	UNC
1945	1,355	£170	£255
1946	1,365	£175	£255
1947	1,375	£180	£275
1948	1,385	£180	£280
1949	1,395	£185	£280
1950	1,405	£185	£285
1951	1,468	£190	£290
1952	1,012	£200	£305
1952 Proof (copper)			£10,200

ELIZABETH II (1952–   )

DATE AND PLACE OF ISSUE	MINTAGE		UNC
1953 St. Paul's Cathedral	1,025	—	£950
1953 Proof in gold	unrecorded		Ex. rare
1953 Proof Matt			Very rare
1954 Westminster Abbey	1,020	—	£200
1955 Southwark Cathedral	1,036	—	£200
1955 Proof Matt		—	£3250
1956 Westminster Abbey	1,088	—	£205
1957 St. Albans Cathedral	1,094	—	£205
1958 Westminster Abbey	1,100	—	£205
1959 St. George's Chapel, Windsor	1,106	—	£205
1960 Westminster Abbey	1,112	—	£205
1961 Rochester Cathedral	1,118	—	£205
1962 Westminster Abbey	1,125	—	£205
1963 Chelmsford Cathedral	1,131	—	£205
1964 Westminster Abbey	1,137	—	£205
1965 Canterbury Cathedral	1,143	—	£205
1966 Westminster Abbey	1,206	—	£205
1967 Durham Cathedral	986	—	£220
1968 Westminster Abbey	964	—	£225
1969 Selby Cathedral	1,002	—	£220
1970 Westminster Abbey	980	—	£220
1971 Tewkesbury Abbey	1,018		£215
1972 York Minster	1,026		£220
1973 Westminster Abbey	1,004		£215
1974 Salisbury Cathedral	1,042		£215
1975 Peterborough Cathedral	1,050		£215
1976 Hereford Cathedral	1,158		£220
1977 Westminster Abbey	1,138		£225
1978 Carlisle Cathedral	1,178		£215

DATE AND PLACE OF ISSUE	MINTAGE	UNC
1979 Winchester Cathedral	1,188	£215
1980 Worcester Cathedral	1,198	£215
1981 Westminster Abbey	1,178	£215
1982 St David's Cathedral	1,218	£220
1983 Exeter Cathedral	1,228	£215
1984 Southwell Minster	1,238	£215
1985 Ripon Cathedral	1,248	£215
1986 Chichester Cathedral	1,378	£225
1987 Ely Cathedral	1,390	£225
1988 Lichfield Cathedral	1,402	£220
1989 Birmingham Cathedral	1,353	£220
1990 Newcastle Cathedral	1,523	£220
1991 Westminster Abbey	1,384	£220
1992 Chester Cathedral	1,424	£225
1993 Wells Cathedral	1,440	£225
1994 Truro Cathedral	1,433	£225
1995 Coventry Cathedral	1,466	£225
1996 Norwich Cathedral	1,629	£230
1997 Birmingham Cathedral	1,786	£230
1998 Portsmouth Cathedral	1,654	£230
1999 Bristol Cathedral	1,676	£230
2000 Lincoln Cathedral	1,686	£220
2000 Silver Proof	13,180	£195
2001 Westminster Abbey	1,132	£250
2002 Canterbury Cathedral	1,681	£215
2002 Gold Proof	2,002	£2250
2003 Gloucester Cathedral	1,608	£235
2004 Liverpool Cathedral	1,613	£240
2005 Wakefield Cathedral	1,685	£240
2006 Guildford Cathedral	1,937	£240
2006 Silver Proof	6,394	£195
2007 Manchester Cathedral	1,822	£275
2008 St Patrick's Cathedral (Armagh)	1,833	£750
2009 St. Edmundsbury Cathedral	1,602	£675
2010 Derby Cathedral	1,617	£650
2011 Westminster Abbey	1,734	£550
2012 York Minster	1,633	£650
2013 Christ Church Cathedral Oxford	1,627	£600
2014 Blackburn Cathedral	1,693	£625
2015 Sheffield Cathedral	1,721	£625
2016 St. George's Chapel, Windsor	1,940	£650

Despite the decimalisation of the coinage in 1971, in keeping with ancient tradition the Royal Maundy sets are still made up of four silver coins (4p, 3p, 2p and 1p). The designs for the reverse of the coins are a crowned numeral in a wreath of oak leaves—basically the same design that has been used for Maundy coins since Charles II.

MAUNDY ODDMENTS
SINGLE COINS

DATE	F	VF	EF

FOUR PENCE
CHARLES II (1660–85)

DATE	F	VF	EF
Undated	£70	£115	£185
1670	£70	£120	£195
1671	£80	£125	£210
1672/1	£65	£105	£175
1673	£75	£110	£180
1674	£70	£105	£170
1674 7 over 6	£75	£130	£205
1675	£60	£100	£165
1675/4	£70	£115	£190
1676	£65	£100	£185
1676 7 over 6	£80	£120	£200
1677	£55	£95	£165
1678	£55	£95	£160
1678 8 over 7	£65	£115	£175
1679	£55	£85	£150
1680	£60	£95	£170
1681	£55	£100	£180
1682	£60	£90	£180
1682/1	£65	£95	£190
1683	£60	£90	£180
1684	£70	£110	£200
1684 4 over 3	£85	£120	£225

JAMES II (1685–88)

DATE	F	VF	EF
1686	£65	£110	£200
1686 Date over crown	£75	£125	£215
1687	£60	£100	£180
1687 7 over 6	£75	£115	£190
1688	£80	£120	£210
1688 1 over 8	£90	£135	£225

WILLIAM & MARY (1688–94)

DATE	F	VF	EF
1689	£60	£110	£175
1689 GV below bust	£70	£120	£190
1689 GVLEELMVS	£135	£225	£325
1690	£60	£115	£210
1690 6 over 5	£90	£130	£230
1691	£80	£130	£225
1691 1 over 0	£90	£150	£230
1692	£120	£170	£275
1692 Maria	£200	£245	£350
1692 2 over 1	£130	£160	£260
1693	£110	£215	£350
1693 3 over 2	£125	£225	£375
1694	£80	£135	£225

WILLIAM III (1694–1702)

DATE	F	VF	EF
1698	£80	£135	£215
1699	£70	£120	£210
1700	£90	£150	£240
1701	£85	£135	£225
1702	£80	£130	£225

ANNE (1702–14)

DATE	F	VF	EF
1703	£75	£125	£210
1704	£60	£105	£185
1705	£110	£175	£260

It is nowadays considered that the early small denomination silver coins 4d–1d were originally struck for the Maundy ceremony although undoubtedly many subsequently circulated as small change—therefore they are listed here under "Maundy silver single coins".

Charles II

William & Mary

Queen Anne

DATE	F	VF	EF	UNC
1706	£70	£115	£175	—
1708	£75	£120	£205	—
1709	£80	£120	£195	—
1710	£60	£100	£165	—
1713	£70	£120	£190	—

GEORGE I (1714–27)

1717	£65	£110	£180	—
1721	£65	£110	£185	—
1723	£85	£135	£205	—
1727	£80	£125	£200	—

GEORGE II (1727–60)

1729	£75	£115	£170	—
1731	£60	£105	£160	—
1732	£65	£110	£160	—
1735	£55	£95	£150	—
1737	£70	£115	£170	—
1739	£55	£100	£155	—
1740	£50	£95	£140	—
1743	£130	£180	£290	—
1743 3 over 0	£140	£205	£300	
1746	£55	£85	£135	—
1760	£65	£115	£160	—

George II

GEORGE III (1760–1820)

1763 Young head	£50	£95	£135	—
1763 Proof	—	—	Extremely rare	
1765	£450	£680	£1175	—
1766	£65	£100	£140	—
1770	£155	£230	£360	—
1772	£80	£130	£190	—
1776	£65	£120	£170	—
1780	£50	£95	£135	—
1784	£50	£95	£130	—
1786	£65	£120	£170	—
1792 Older head, Thin 4	£90	£155	£220	£325
1795	—	£55	£100	£140
1800	—	£50	£90	£125
1817 New coinage	—	£50	£80	£130
1818	—	£50	£80	£125
1820	—	£50	£80	£130

George III

GEORGE IV (1820–30)

1822	—	—	£75	£140
1823	—	—	£70	£130
1824	—	—	£70	£135
1826	—	—	£65	£120
1827	—	—	£70	£130
1828	—	—	£65	£120
1829	—	—	£60	£115
1830	—	—	£60	£115

WILLIAM IV (1830–37)

1831–37	—	—	£70	£145
1831 Proof	—	—	£250	£400

VICTORIA (1837–1901)

1838 Proof	—	—	—	£725
1839 Proof	—	—	—	£450
1853 Proof	—	—	—	£500
1838–87 (Young Head)	—	—	£40	£65
1841	—	—	£50	£75
1888–92 (Jubilee Head)	—	—	£35	£60
1893–1901 (Old Head)	—	—	£30	£50

Victoria

DATE	F	VF	EF	UNC

EDWARD VII (1901–10)

DATE	F	VF	EF	UNC
1902–08	—	—	£30	£50
1909 & 1910	—	—	£60	£90
1902 Proof	—	—	£35	£55

GEORGE V (1910–36)

1911–36	—	—	£50	£65
1911 Proof	—	—	£55	£75

GEORGE VI (1936–52)

1937–52	—	—	£55	£75
1937 Proof	—	—	£40	£60

ELIZABETH II (1952–   )

1953	—	—	£180	£235
1954–85	—	—	£45	£75
1986–2007	—	—	£60	£85
2002 in Gold Proof	—	—	£500	£750
2008	—	—	—	£190
2009	—	—	—	£180
2010	—	—	—	£170
2011	—	—	—	£145
2012	—	—	—	£170
2013	—	—	—	£165
2014	—	—	—	£160
2015	—	—	—	£160

Elizabeth II

THREEPENCE

CHARLES II (1660–85)

	F	VF	EF	UNC
Undated	£65	£105	£195	—
1670	£75	£120	£185	—
1671	£55	£100	£165	—
1671 GRVTIA	£75	£115	£230	—
1672	£70	£120	£185	—
1673	£60	£95	£160	—
1674	£70	£110	£175	—
1675	£70	£110	£180	—
1676	£70	£115	£210	—
1676 ERA for FRA	£90	£135	£225	—
1677	£65	£90	£165	—
1678	£50	£80	£135	—
1679	£50	£80	£135	—
1679 O/A in CAROLVS	£105	£140	£240	—
1680	£60	£100	£175	—
1681	£70	£110	£190	—
1682	£60	£100	£170	—
1683	£60	£105	£170	—
1684	£60	£105	£175	—
1684/3	£70	£110	£180	—

James II

JAMES II (1685–88)

	F	VF	EF	UNC
1685	£65	£105	£190	—
1685 Struck on fourpence flan	£130	£175	£290	—
1686	£65	£95	£175	—
1687	£60	£90	£170	—
1687 7 over 6	£65	£95	£175	—
1688	£65	£120	£195	—
1688 8 over 7	£70	£130	£215	—

WILLIAM & MARY (1688–94)

	F	VF	EF	UNC
1689	£55	£100	£180	—
1689 No stop on reverse	£65	£115	£195	—
1689 LMV over MVS (obverse)	£100	£145	£240	—
1690	£75	£120	£195	—
1690 6 over 5	£85	£135	£210	—
1691 First bust	£390	£590	£850	—
1691 Second bust	£260	£420	£570	—

William & Mary

DATE	F	VF	EF	UNC
1692	£85	£140	£240	—
1692 G below bust	£90	£150	£230	—
1692 GV below bust	£90	£140	£225	—
1692 GVL below bust	£90	£145	£235	—
1693	£120	£195	£270	—
1693 3 over 2	£125	£210	£280	—
1694	£80	£115	£200	—
1694 MARIΛ	£130	£170	£265	—

WILLIAM III (1694–1702)

1698	£75	£125	£210	—
1699	£60	£110	£180	—
1700	£70	£135	£210	—
1701	£65	£110	£180	—
1701 GBA instead of GRA	£80	£140	£205	—

ANNE (1702–14)

1703	£70	£100	£195	—
1703 7 of date above crown	£80	£130	£210	—
1704	£60	£90	£160	—
1705	£80	£130	£200	—
1706	£65	£100	£170	—
1707	£55	£100	£155	—
1708	£60	£115	£180	—
1709	£65	£120	£180	—
1710	£50	£95	£145	—
1713	£65	£125	£180	—

GEORGE I (1714–27)

1717	£60	£100	£160	—
1721	£60	£100	£165	—
1723	£75	£115	£190	—
1727	£70	£110	£185	—

Queen Anne

GEORGE II (1727–60)

1729	£55	£95	£145	—
1731	£55	£95	£150	—
1731 Small lettering	£70	£115	£170	—
1732	£55	£95	£145	—
1732 Stop over head	£65	£110	£165	—
1735	£70	£110	£175	—
1737	£55	£95	£165	—
1739	£65	£100	£175	—
1740	£55	£90	£145	—
1743 Small and large lettering	£65	£90	£155	—
1743 Stop over head	£65	£95	£160	—
1746	£45	£80	£140	—
1746 6 over 3	£50	£85	£150	—
1760	£60	£90	£155	—

GEORGE III (1760–1820)

George II

1762	£30	£50	£70	—
1763	£30	£50	£75	—
1763 Proof	—	—	Extremely rare	
1765	£350	£500	£750	—
1766	£70	£110	£180	—
1770	£70	£110	£190	—
1772	£55	£85	£120	—
1780	£55	£85	£120	—
1784	£80	£115	£190	—
1786	£80	£110	£180	—
1792	£95	£135	£215	£325
1795	—	£40	£80	£120
1800	—	£45	£85	£130
1817	—	£50	£90	£155
1818	—	£50	£90	£155
1820	—	£45	£90	£155

DATE	F	VF	EF	UNC
GEORGE IV (1820–30)				
1822	–	–	£85	£165
1823	–	–	£75	£155
1824	–	–	£75	£160
1825–30	–	–	£75	£155
WILLIAM IV (1830–37)				
1831 Proof	–	–	£225	£425
1831–1832	–	–	£125	£250
1833–1836	–	–	£80	£170
1837	–	–	£105	£190
VICTORIA (1837–1901)				
1838	–	–	£115	£200
1838 Proof	–	–	–	£1650
1839	–	–	£215	£375
1839 Proof	–	–	–	£450
1840	–	–	£160	£275
1841	–	–	£300	£500
1842	–	–	£275	£425
1843	–	–	£125	£225
1844	–	–	£200	£325
1845	–	–	£85	£165
1846	–	–	£400	£700
1847	–	–	£425	£800
1848	–	–	£375	£750
1849	–	–	£215	£365
1850	–	–	£115	£225
1851	–	–	£160	£280
1852	–	–	£450	£775
1853	–	–	£475	£825
1853 Proof	–	–	–	£850
1854	–	–	£155	£275
1855	–	–	£170	£300
1856	–	–	£100	£220
1857	–	–	£150	£275
1858	–	–	£120	£225
1859	–	–	£100	£195
1860	–	–	£135	£240
1861	–	–	£130	£235
1862	–	–	£135	£255
1863	–	–	£175	£300
1864	–	–	£125	£235
1865	–	–	£130	£250
1866	–	–	£120	£240
1867	–	–	£125	£235
1868	–	–	£115	£215
1869	–	–	£155	£275
1870	–	–	£105	£195
1871	–	–	£100	£185
1872	–	–	£95	£180
1873	–	–	£90	£170
1874	–	–	£90	£175
1875	–	–	£85	£165
1876	–	–	£85	£165
1877	F	–	£80	£160
1878	–	–	£85	£165
1879	–	–	£85	£160
1880	–	–	£80	£150
1881	–	–	£80	£150
1882	–	–	£130	£225
1883	–	–	£75	£145
1884	–	–	£75	£145
1885	–	–	£70	£130
1886	–	–	£70	£125
1887	–	–	£80	£170
1888–1892 (Jubilee Head)	–	–	£50	£110
1893–1901 (Old Head)	–	–	£40	£65

Victoria Jubilee Head

DATE	F	VF	EF	UNC
EDWARD VII (1901–10)				
1902	—	—	£30	£50
1902 Proof	—	—	—	£55
1903	—	—	£40	£85
1904	—	—	£55	£105
1905	—	—	£55	£95
1906	—	—	£45	£90
1907	—	—	£45	£90
1908	—	—	£40	£80
1909	—	—	£70	£120
1910	—	—	£80	£150
GEORGE V (1910–36)				
1911–34	—	—	£55	£85
1911 Proof	—	—	—	£95
1935	—	—	£65	£100
1936	—	—	£75	£135
GEORGE VI (1936–52)				
1937–52	—	—	£55	£100
1937 Proof	—	—	—	£70
ELIZABETH II (1952–)				
1953	—	—	£160	£285
1954–85	—	—	£45	£80
1986–2007	—	—	£55	£85
2002 In gold (proof)	—	—	—	£615
2008	—	—	—	£170
2009	—	—	—	£160
2010	—	—	—	£150
2011	—	—	—	£130
2012	—	—	—	£140
2013	—	—	—	£140
2014	—	—	—	£140
2015	—	—	—	£130
2016	—	—	—	£140

TWOPENCE

DATE	F	VF	EF	UNC
CHARLES II (1660–85)				
Undated	£55	£90	£155	—
1668	£65	£90	£170	—
1670	£50	£80	£150	—
1671	£50	£85	£150	—
1672	£50	£85	£150	—
1672/1	£65	£100	£160	—
1673	£50	£85	£155	—
1674	£55	£90	£150	—
1675	£50	£90	£140	—
1676	£55	£95	£155	—
1677	£45	£85	£135	—
1678	£35	£75	£130	—
1679	£40	£70	£125	—
1680	£50	£85	£135	—
1681	£55	£80	£135	—
1682	£65	£90	£165	—
1682/1 ERA for FRA	£75	£110	£210	—
1683	£60	£100	£160	—
1684	£55	£95	£155	—
JAMES II (1685–88)				
1686	£60	£95	£160	—
1686 reads IACOBVS	£75	£120	£215	—
1687	£65	£95	£165	—
1687 ERA for FRA	£75	£130	£215	—
1688	£50	£85	£150	—
1688/7	£65	£90	£170	—

Charles II

James II

DATE	F	VF	EF	UNC
WILLIAM & MARY (1688–94)				
1689......................................	£60	£100	£175	—
1691......................................	£55	£85	£140	—
1692......................................	£75	£130	£200	—
1693......................................	£65	£110	£185	—
1693 GV below bust..............	£75	£115	£185	—
1693/2	£65	£100	£170	—
1694......................................	£50	£85	£140	—
1694 MARLA error.................	£80	£130	£250	—
1694 HI for HIB.....................	£75	£120	£210	—
1694 GVLI under bust	£60	£100	£185	—
1694 GVL under bust.............	£55	£95	£185	—
WILLIAM III (1694–1702)				
1698......................................	£60	£115	£175	—
1699......................................	£50	£90	£145	—
1700......................................	£65	£115	£185	—
1701......................................	£60	£100	£165	—
ANNE (1702–14)				
1703......................................	£65	£100	£180	—
1704......................................	£50	£80	£135	—
1704 No stops on obverse.....	£60	£90	£170	—
1705......................................	£60	£100	£160	—
1706......................................	£80	£115	£185	—
1707......................................	£50	£85	£150	—
1708......................................	£70	£100	£175	—
1709......................................	£85	£125	£215	—
1710......................................	£45	£80	£115	—
1713......................................	£70	£110	£195	—
GEORGE I (1714–27)				
1717......................................	£45	£80	£130	—
1721......................................	£50	£85	£125	—
1723......................................	£65	£95	£160	—
1726......................................	£50	£80	£135	—
1727......................................	£60	£85	£150	—
GEORGE II (1727–60)				
1729......................................	£40	£75	£115	—
1731......................................	£40	£80	£125	—
1732......................................	£40	£80	£115	—
1735......................................	£45	£75	£110	—
1737......................................	£40	£80	£115	·
1739......................................	£45	£80	£120	·
1740......................................	£40	£70	£115	·
1743......................................	£35	£65	£105	·
1743/0	£45	£80	£115	·
1746......................................	£35	£70	£95	·
1756......................................	£35	£65	£95	·
1759......................................	£35	£70	£95	·
1760......................................	£50	£75	£100	·
GEORGE III (1760–1820)				
1763......................................	£40	£70	£95	·
1763 Proof............................			Extremely rai ౨	
1765......................................	£345	£525	£725	—
1766......................................	£45	£75	£95	—
1772......................................	£35	£70	£90	—
1780......................................	£35	£70	£90	—
1784......................................	£40	£70	£90	—
1786......................................	£50	£80	£95	—
1792......................................	—	£80	£125	£190
1795......................................	—	£30	£60	£85
1800......................................	—	£30	£70	£85
1817......................................	—	£35	£70	£90
1818......................................	—	£35	£70	£90
1820......................................	—	£45	£80	£100

Queen Anne

George II

DATE	F	VF	EF	UNC

GEORGE IV (1820–30)

DATE	F	VF	EF	UNC
1822–30	–	–	£40	£70
1825 TRITANNIAR	–	–	£60	£115

WILLIAM IV (1830–37)

DATE	F	VF	EF	UNC
1831–37	–	–	£45	£80
1831 Proof	–	–	£95	£225

VICTORIA (1837–1901)

DATE	F	VF	EF	UNC
1838–87 (Young Head)	–	–	£30	£60
1859 BEITANNIAR	–	–	£75	£135
1861 6 over 1	–	–	£40	£80
1888–92 (Jubilee Head)	–	–	£30	£60
1893–1901 (Old Head)	–	–	£25	£50
1838 Proof	–	–	–	£425
1839 Proof	–	–	–	£235
1853 Proof	–	–	–	£250

Victoria

EDWARD VII (1901–10)

DATE	F	VF	EF	UNC
1902–08	–	–	£25	£35
1909	–	–	£45	£80
1910	–	–	£50	£90
1902 Proof	–	–	£30	£50

GEORGE V (1910–36)

DATE	F	VF	EF	UNC
1911–34	–	–	£35	£65
1911 Proof	–	–	£40	£70
1935	–	–	£40	£65
1936	–	–	£50	£75

GEORGE VI (1936–52)

DATE	F	VF	EF	UNC
1937–47	–	–	£40	£60
1948–52	–	–	£45	£70
1937 Proof	–	–	£35	£60

ELIZABETH II (1952–)

DATE	F	VF	EF	UNC
1953	–	–	£140	£225
1954–85	–	–	£40	£65
1986–2007	–	–	£40	£70
2002 Gold Proof	–	–	–	£450
2008	–	–	–	£125
2009	–	–	–	£115
2010	–	–	–	£110
2011	–	–	–	£85
2012	–	–	–	£100
2013	–	–	–	£110
2014	–	–	–	£105
2015	–	–	–	£100
2016	–	–	–	£125

PENNY

CHARLES II (1660–85)

DATE	F	VF	EF	UNC
Undated	£70	£110	£200	–
1670	£65	£110	£175	–
1671	£65	£110	£170	–
1672/1	£70	£110	£175	–
1673	£65	£110	£170	–
1674	£70	£110	£175	–
1674 Gratia (error)	£100	£160	£250	–
1675	£65	£115	£170	–
1675 Gratia (error)	£100	£165	£260	–
1676	£80	£120	£185	–
1676 Gratia (error)	£110	£170	£275	–
1677	£60	£100	£165	–
1677 Gratia (error)	£95	£135	£230	–
1678	£150	£265	£380	–
1678 Gratia (error)	£180	£280	£400	–
1679	£85	£125	£210	–
1680	£80	£115	£200	–
1681	£110	£155	£230	–
1682	£75	£125	£195	–
1682 ERA for FRA	£90	£150	£245	–

Charles II

DATE	F	VF	EF	UNC
1683	£85	£115	£195	—
1683/1	£85	£150	£225	—
1684	£170	£250	£320	—
1684/3	£180	£265	£330	—

JAMES II (1685–88)

James II

1685	£65	£100	£165	—
1686	£80	£110	£175	—
1687	£80	£120	£180	—
1687/8	£85	£130	£190	—
1688	£65	£90	£165	—
1688/7	£70	£105	£185	—

WILLIAM & MARY (1688–94)

1689	£450	£675	£950	—
1689 MΛRIΛ	£470	£685	£950	
1689 GVIELMVS (Error)	£450	£700	£975	—
1690	£75	£145	£230	—
1691	£75	£150	£225	—
1692	£240	£340	£550	—
1692/1	£250	£355	£570	—
1693	£95	£160	£245	—
1694	£75	£130	£230	—
1694 HI for HIB	£110	£170	£275	—
1694 No stops on obverse	£90	£150	£240	—

WILLIAM III (1694–1702)

1698	£85	£135	£200	—
1698 HI. BREX (Error)	£100	£165	£270	—
1699	£290	£425	£650	—
1700	£95	£150	£225	—
1701	£85	£130	£205	—

ANNE (1702–14)

1703	£75	£125	£195	—
1705	£65	£110	£180	—
1706	£70	£95	£165	—
1708	£475	£600	£850	—
1709	£60	£95	£150	—
1710	£135	£200	£325	—
1713/0	£85	£120	£180	—

GEORGE I (1714–27)

1716	£45	£90	£115	—
1718	£45	£90	£115	—
1720	£50	£95	£125	—
1720 HIPEX (Error)	£75	£115	£205	—
1723	£70	£120	£175	—
1725	£50	£85	£130	—
1726	£50	£85	£125	—
1727	£60	£115	£165	—

GEORGE II (1727–60)

George II

1729	£40	£90	£120	—
1731	£45	£90	£125	—
1732	£50	£80	£120	—
1735	£40	£70	£100	—
1737	£40	£70	£105	—
1739	£40	£70	£100	—
1740	£40	£65	£100	—
1743	£35	£70	£95	—
1746	£45	£80	£115	—
1746/3	£50	£80	£120	—
1750	£30	£55	£85	—
1752	£30	£55	£85	—
1753	£30	£55	£85	—
1754	£30	£55	£85	—
1755	£30	£55	£85	—
1756	£30	£55	£80	—
1757	£30	£55	£80	—
1757 No colon after Gratia	£45	£80	£100	—

DATE	F	VF	EF	UNC
1758	£30	£60	£85	—
1759	£35	£60	£80	—
1760	£40	£75	£95	—

GEORGE III (1760–1820)

1763	£45	£70	£100	—
1763 Proof	—	—	Extremely rare	
1766	£40	£70	£90	—
1772	£40	£70	£85	—
1780	£85	£125	£185	—
1781	£35	£60	£85	—
1784	£45	£65	£90	—
1786	£35	£60	£90	—
1792	£35	£70	£90	£120
1795	—	£25	£50	£70
1800	—	£25	£50	£70
1817	—	£25	£50	£70
1818	—	£25	£50	£70
1820	—	£30	£55	£75

George III

GEORGE IV (1820–30)

1822–30	—	—	£35	£60

WILLIAM IV (1830–37)

1831–37	—	—	£45	£70
1831 Proof	—	—	—	£205

VICTORIA (1837–1901)

1838–87 (Young Head)	—	—	£30	£55
1888–92 (Jubilee Head)	—	—	£30	£50
1893–1901 (Old Head)	—	—	£25	£40
1838 Proof	—	—	—	£265
1839 Proof	—	—	—	£175
1853 Proof	—	—	—	£215

EDWARD VII (1901–10)

1902–08	—	—	£20	£35
1909	—	—	£40	£75
1910	—	—	£50	£90
1902 Proof	—	—	£25	£40

GEORGE V (1910–36)

1911–14	—	—	£45	£80
1915	—	—	£50	£85
1916–19	—	—	£45	£80
1920	—	—	£45	£80
1921–28	—	—	£45	£75
1929	—	—	£45	£80
1930–34	—	—	£40	£75
1935	—	—	£45	£80
1936	—	—	£55	£85
1911 Proof	—	—	£45	£80

GEORGE VI (1936–52)

1937–40	—	—	£50	£80
1941	—	—	£55	£90
1942–47	—	—	£50	£85
1948–52	—	—	£60	£95
1937 Proof	—	—	£45	£80

ELIZABETH II (1952–)

1953	—	—	£285	£400
1965–85	—	—	£45	£80
1986–2007	—	—	£45	£85
2002 Proof in gold	—	—	—	£485
2008	—	—	—	£145
2009	—	—	—	£140
2010	—	—	—	£130
2011	—	—	—	£105
2012	—	—	—	£120
2013	—	—	—	£125
2014	—	—	—	£120
2015	—	—	—	£110
2016	—	—	—	£135

Elizabeth II

DECIMAL COINAGE

Since the introduction of the Decimal system in the UK, many coins have been issued for circulation purposes in vast quantities. In addition, from 1982 sets of coins to non-proof standard, and including examples of each denomination found in circulation, have been issued each year. For 1982 and 1983 they were to "circulation" standard and described as "Uncirculated". Individual coins from these sets are annotated "Unc" on the lists that follow. From 1984 to the present day they were described as "Brilliant Uncirculated" (BU on the lists), and from around 1986 these coins are generally distinguishable from coins intended for circulation. They were from then produced by the Proof Coin Division of the Royal Mint (rather than by the Coin Production Room which produces circulation-standard coins). For completeness however, we have included the annotations Unc and BU back to 1982, the start year for these sets.

It is emphasised that the abbreviations Unc and BU in the left-hand columns adjacent to the date refer to an advertising description or to an engineering production standard, not the preservation condition or grade of the coin concerned. Where no such annotation appears adjacent to the date, the coin is circulation-standard for issue as such.

We have included the "mintage" figures for circulation coins down to Half Penny. The figure given for the 1997 Two Pounds, is considerably less than the actual quantity struck, because many were scrapped before issue due to failing an electrical conductivity test. Where a coin is available in uncirculated grade at, or just above, face value no price has been quoted.

Base metal Proof issues of circulation coinage (£2 or £1 to one or half penny) of the decimal series were only issued, as with Unc or BU, as part of Year Sets, but many of these sets have been broken down into individual coins, hence the appearance of the latter on the market.

The lists do not attempt to give details of die varieties, except where there was an obvious intention to change the appearance of a coin, e.g. 1992 20p.

2008 saw new reverses and modified obverses for all circulation denominations from the One Pound to the One Penny. All seven denominations were put into circulation dated 2008, all with both the old and the new reverses.

The circulation standard mintage figures have mainly been kindly supplied by courtesy of the Head of Historical Services and the Department of UK Circulation Coin Sales, both at the Royal Mint.

KILO COINS
(gold and silver)

The UK's first-ever Kilo coins were struck to commemorate the 2012 Olympic Games in 0.999 fine gold and 0.999 fine silver. These and subsequent issues are listed in detail below, and all were struck to proof standard and to similar metallic standards.

DATE	FACE VALUE	AUTH ISSUE QTY.	ISSUE PRICE

2012 Olympic Gold;
    obverse: 1998 Ian Rank-Broadley's Royal Portrait
    reverse: Sir Anthony Caro's "Individual Endeavour" £1,000
		60	£100,000

2012 Olympic Silver;
    obverse: 1998 Rank-Broadley Royal Portrait
    reverse: Tom Phillip's "Team Endeavour" £500
		2012	£3,000

2012 Diamond Jubilee Gold;
    obverse: Queen in Garter Robes (Rank-Broadley)
    reverse: Royal Arms (Buckingham Palace Gates) £1,000
		60	£60,000

2012 Diamond Jubilee Silver;
    obverse: Queen in Garter Robes (Rank-Broadley)
    reverse: Royal Arms (Buckingham Palace Gates) £500
		1250	£2,600

2013 Coronation Anniversary Gold;
    obverse: 1998 Rank-Broadley Royal Portrait
    reverse: John Bergdahl's Coronation Regalia £1,000
		27	£50,000

2013 Coronation Anniversary Silver;
    obverse: 1998 Rank-Broadley Royal Portrait
    reverse: John Bergdahl's Coronation Regalia £500
		400	£2,600

2013 Royal Christening Gold;
    obverse: 1998 Rank-Broadley Royal Portrait
    reverse: John Bergdahl's Lily Font £1,000
		22	£48,000

2013 Royal Christening Silver;
    obverse: 1998 Rank-Broadley Royal Portrait
    reverse: John Bergdahl's Lily Font £500
		500	£2,600

2014 First World War Outbreak Gold;
    obverse: 1998 Rank-Broadley Royal Portrait
    reverse: Sandle's Hostile Environment £1,000
		25	£45,000

2014 First World War Outbreak Silver;
    obverse: 1998 Rank-Broadley Royal Portrait
    reverse: Sandle's Hostile Environment £500
		430	£2,000

2015 50th Anniversary of Death of Sir Winston Churchill Gold;
    obverse: 1998 Rank-Broadley Royal Portrait
    reverse: Millner's image of Churchill.. £1,000
		15	£45,000

2015 50th Anniversary of Death of Sir Winston Churchill Silver;
    obverse: 1998 Rank-Broadley Royal Portrait
    reverse: Milner's image of Churchill £500
		170	£2,000

2015 The Longest Reign Gold;
    obverse. Butler Royal Portrait
    reverse: Stephen Taylor Queen's Portraits £1,000
		15	£42,500

2016 The Longest Reign Silver;
    obverse: Butler Royal Portrait
    reverse: Stephen Taylor Queen's Portraits £500
		320	£2,000

2016 Year of the Monkey Gold;
    obverse: Clark Royal Portrait
    reverse: Wuon-Gean Ho's rhesus monkey.................................... £1,000
		8	£42,500

2016 Year of the Monkey Silver;
    obverse: Butler Royal Portrait
    reverse: Stephen Taylor Queen's Portraits £500
		88	£2,000

DATE	FACE VALUE	AUTH ISSUE QTY.	ISSUE PRICE
2016 Queen's 90th Birthday Gold; obverse: Clark Royal Portrait reverse: Christopher Hobbs Floral design.. —		25	—
2016 Queen's 90th Birthday Silver; obverse: Clark Royal Portrait reverse: Christopher Hobbs Floral design.. —		450	£2,000

2012 Olympic Silver

2012 Diamond Jubilee Gold

2013 Royal Christening Gold

2015 Anniversary of Death of Sir Winston Churchill Silver

2016 Queen's 90th Birthday Gold

Illustrations on this page are not shown to scale.

2016 Year of the Monkey

FIVE-OUNCE COINS
(gold and silver, including Britannia Coins)

Also appearing for the first time in 2012 were Five-Ounce coins, minted in the same metals and standards as the Kilo Coins. Included here also are Five-Ounce Britannia coins, both gold and silver proofs, which appeared first in 2013. It should be noted that the reverses of these coins, in common with other denominations of Britannias, have a different design from those minted to BU ("bullion") standard.

DATE	FACE VALUE	AUTH ISSUE QTY.	ISSUE PRICE
2012 Olympic Gold; obverse: 1998 Rank-Broadley Royal Portrait reverse: Pegasus (C. Le Brun) £10		500	£11,500
2012 Olympic Silver; obverse: 1998 Rank-Broadley Royal Portrait reverse: Pegasus (C. Le Brun) £10		7500	£525
2012 Diamond Jubilee Gold; obverse: Queen in Garter Robes (Rank-Broadley) reverse: Queen seated (facing) £10		250	£9,500
2012 Diamond Jubilee Silver; obverse: Queen in Garter Robes (Rank-Broadley) reverse: Queen seated (facing) £10		1952	£450
2013 Coronation Anniversary Gold; obverse: 1998 Rank-Broadley Royal Portrait reverse: Regalia in Westminster Abbey (J. Olliffe) £10		129	£9,500
2013 Coronation Anniversary Silver; obverse: 1998 Rank-Broadley Royal Portrait reverse: Regalia in Westminster Abbey (J. Olliffe) £10		1,953	£450
2013 Britannia Gold; obverse: 1998 Rank-Broadley Royal Portrait reverse: Britannia seated with owl (R. Hunt) £500		125	£8,200

DATE	FACE VALUE	AUTH ISSUE QTY.	ISSUE PRICE
2013 Britannia Silver; obverse: 1998 Rank-Broadley Royal Portrait reverse: Britannia seated with owl (R. Hunt).....................£10		4,655	£450
2013 Royal Christening Gold; obverse: 1998 Rank-Broadley Royal Portrait reverse: Bergdahl's Lily Font £10		150	£8,200
2013 Royal Christening Silver; obverse: 1998 Rank-Broadley Royal Portrait reverse: Bergdahl's Lily Font £10		1,660	£450
2014 Britannia Gold; obverse: 1998 Rank-Broadley Royal Portrait reverse: Clark's portrayal of Britannia £500		75	£7,500
2014 Britannia Silver; obverse: 1998 Rank-Broadley Royal Portrait reverse: Clark's portrayal of Britannia £10		1,350	£395
2014 First World War Outbreak Gold; obverse: 1998 Rank-Broadley Royal Portrait reverse: Bergdahl's Britannia..............£10		110	£7,500
2014 First World War Outbreak Silver; obverse: 1998 Rank-Broadley Royal Portrait reverse: Bergdahl's Britannia..............£10		1,300	£395
2015 Year of the Sheep Gold; obverse: 1998 Rank-Broadley Royal Portrait reverse: Wuon-Gean Ho's Swaledale Sheep £500		38	£7,500
2015 Year of the Sheep Silver; obverse: 1998 Rank-Broadley Royal Portrait reverse: Wuon-Gean Ho's Swaledale Sheep £10		1,088	£395
2015 Britannia Gold; obverse: Clark Royal Portrait reverse: Dufort's Britannia..............£500		50	£7,500
2015 Britannia Silver; obverse: Clark Royal Portrait reverse: Dufort's Britannia..............£10		1,150	£395
2015 50th Anniversary of Death of Sir Winston Churchill Gold; obverse: Clark Royal Portrait reverse: Millner's image of Churchill..............£10		60	£7,500
2015 50th Anniversary of Death of Sir Winston Churchill Silver; obverse: Clark Royal Portrait reverse: Millner's image of Churchill..............£10		500	£395
2015 First World War Gold; obverse: Clark Royal Portrait reverse: James Butler Devastation of War		50	£6,950
2015 First World War Silver; obverse: Clark Royal Portrait reverse: James Butler Devastation of War £10		500	£395
2015 The Longest Reign Gold; obverse: Butler Royal Portrait reverse: Stephen Taylor Queen's Portrait..............—		180	£6,950
2015 The Longest Reign Silver; obverse: Butler Royal Portrait reverse: Stephen Taylor Queen's Portrait..............—		1,500	£395
2016 Year of the Monkey Gold; obverse: Clark Royal Portrait reverse: Wuon-Gean Ho's rhesus monkey..............—		38	£7,500
2016 Year of the Monkey Silver; obverse: Butler Royal Portrait reverse: Wuon-Gean Ho's rhesus monkey..............—		588	£395
2016 Queen's 90th Birthday Gold; obverse: Clark Royal Portrait reverse: Christopher Hobbs Floral design..............—		170	£7,500

DATE	FACE VALUE	AUTH ISSUE QTY.	ISSUE PRICE
2016 Queen's 90th Birthday Silver; obverse: Clark Royal Portrait reverse: Christopher Hobbs Floral design... —		1,750	£395
2016 Britannia Gold obverse: Clark Royal Portrait; reverse: Suzie Zamit Britannia.. —		75	£7,500
2016 Britannia Silver obverse: Clark Royal Portrait; reverse: Suzie Zamit Britannia.. —		800	£395
2016 Shakespeare Gold obverse: Clark Royal Portrait; reverse: Tom Phillips Shakespeare Portrait .... —		—	—
2016 Shakespeare Silver obverse: Clark Royal Portrait; reverse: Tom Phillips Shakespeare Portrait .... —		750	£395

5 ounce silver coins
shown actual size
(65mm)

NOTE: As the BRITANNIA series of coins are essentially bullion pieces, their values are usually related to the current price of gold and silver, therefore no attempt has been made in this publication to give values for the series. To ascertain the value of a piece it is necessary to check with the prevailing price of precious metals.

HUNDRED POUNDS AND BELOW
(including Britannia and Olympic Gold series)

In 1987 the gold £100 coin was introduced, known as the Britannia. It contained one Troy ounce of fine gold, alloyed to 22 carat, and this has continued to the present day. At the same time, and also continuing, coins of face value £50, £25 and £10 appeared, containing a half ounce, quarter ounce and one tenth of an ounce of fine gold respectively. From 1987 to 1989 the alloy was of copper (Red Gold), whereas from 1990 to the present day the alloy has been of silver and copper (yellow gold).

Proof sets of these coins are listed in the "Proof and Specimen Sets" section. In addition, non-proof coins have been minted, it is believed for each of the four coins for every year. The one ounce £100 Britannia is primarily issued as a bullion coin in the non-proof standard, originally in competition with the South African Krugerrand. Its price is quoted daily on the financial pages of some newspapers.

There were five reverse designs by Philip Nathan:- 1987-1996 Standing Britannia, 1997 Chariot, 1998-2000 Standing Britannia, 2001 Una and the Lion, 2002 Standing Britannia, 2003 Britannia's Helmeted Head, 2004 Standing Britannia, 2005 Britannia seated, 2006 Standing Britannia. For 2007 the design is a Seated Britannia with lion at her feet, by Christopher Le Brun. The 2008 design is of Britannia standing and facing left, by John Bergdahl. The 2009 reverse is similar to that of 1997, Britannia on a chariot, while 2010 has Suzie Zamit's Britannia potrait with a Corinthian style helmet. The 2011 design is by David Mach, and portrays a seated Britannia with trident and shield, replicating the design on a 1937 penny, superimposed on a Union Flag. The rotation of the coin from left to right, or vice-versa, creates an illusion of Britannia moving with the ripple of the flag.

In general the proof coins have reverse features frosted, The proofs with Standing Britannia and Una and the Lion reverses include P NATHAN on the reverse, whereas the equivalent bullion coins include NATHAN. The other three reverses have PN on both proofs and bullion coins.

The issue of the second series of three coins in the Olympic Games gold proof coin was in 2011, with the completion of the 9-coin series in 2012. The obverses all have the 1998 Ian Rank-Broadley portrait of the Queen, but a few 2011 £100 coins were issued without his initials IRB under her portrait. Reverses are summarised below:

DATE	FACE VALUE	FINE GOLD WEIGHT	FEATURED GOD	FEATURED PART OF OLYMPIC MOTTO
2010	£100 £25 £25	1 Troy oz 1/4 Troy oz 1/4 Troy oz	Neptune Diana Mercury	CITIUS
2011	£100 £25 £25	1 Troy oz 1/4 Troy oz 1/4 Troy oz	Jupiter Juno Apollo	ALTIUS
2012	£100 £25 £25	1 Troy oz 1/4 Troy oz 1/4 Troy oz	Mars Vulcan Minerva	FORTIUS

2012 was also the 25th anniversary of the Gold Britannia coin series, and the reverse design chosen was that of the 1987 coins, standing Britannia, by Philip Nathan. This was repeated in 2013, but only for Brilliant Uncirculated "Bullion" coins. A separate new series was introduced for Proof coins, a seated Britannia with an owl was featured, the artist being Robert Hunt. The range of Britannia Proofs was increased from 4 to 6, with the addition of a Five-ounce coin (qv) and a one-twentieth of an ounce, curiously denominated at One Pound and with a diameter of 12mm, just larger than a Maundy One Penny. All 2013 Gold Britannias are minted in 0.999 Au alloy.

2014 and 2015 each saw three Reverse designs. The Nathan outstretched arm of Britannia continued as the bullion coin. The Shengxiào Collection by Wuon-Gean Ho saw the Year of the Horse (2014) and the Year of the Sheep (2015). The series by new artists of Britannia designs were of a standing Britannia facing left with lion (2014) by Jody Clark, and a "head and shoulders" Britannia holding the trident on her right shoulder, by Antony Dufont, the latter coin included the Clark portrayal of the Queen on the obverse.

A further new denomination appeared in 2014, the gold one-fortieth of an ounce, diameter 8mm and face value 50 pence.

HUNDRED POUNDS AND BELOW
(Britannia Platinum series)

2007 saw the issue of four-coin proof sets in platinum, 0.9995 fine. The denomination and designs are similar to those of the Gold series of the same year. The issue was repeated in 2008, and again in 2009, above rule applies. It is understood that no bullion coins have been issued.

HUNDRED POUNDS

Following on from the late 2013 introduction of the Twenty Pounds (see below) a "Hundred Pounds for £100" appeared, again a 0.999 Fine Silver coin, of two ounces weight, in early 2015.

DATE	Mintage	UNC
2015 Big Ben, BU	50,000	£100
2015 New Portrait, Buckingham Palace, BU	50,000	£100
2016 Trafalgar Square	45,000	£100

FIFTY POUNDS

A new denomination introduced in 2015, with the slogan "Fifty Pounds for £50". A double first for Jody Clark, minted in 99.99 silver, diameter 34mm.

DATE	Mintage	UNC
2015 Britannia BU	100,000	£50

TWENTY POUNDS

Another new denomination was added in late 2013. Marketed by the Royal Mint under the slogan "Twenty Pounds for £20", it is a 27mm diameter 0.999 Fine silver coin.

DATE	UNC
2013 Pistrucci St George & Dragon BU	£24
2014 Centenary of the outbreak of the First World War	£24
2015 Sir Winston Churchill	£20
2015 The Longest Reigning Monarch, New Portrait	£20
2016 The 90th Birthday of Her Majesty the Queen	£20
2016 The Welsh Dragon	£20

FIVE POUNDS (Sovereign series)

This series is all minted in gold, and, except where stated, have the Pistrucci St George and Dragon reverse. BU coins up to 2001 bear a U in a circle. From 2009 the initials B.P. in the exergue are replaced by PISTRUCCI in small letters on the left. From 2014 the denomination is called the "Five-Sovereign" piece by the Royal Mint in their marketing publications.

DATE	Mintage	UNC
1980 Proof	10,000	£1000
1981 Proof	5,400	£1000
1982 Proof	2,500	£1000

DATE	Mintage	UNC
1984 BU	15,104	£1000
1984 Proof	8,000	£1100
1985 New portrait BU	13,626	£1000
1985 — Proof	6,130	£1000
1986 BU	7,723	£1000
1987 Uncouped portrait BU	5,694	£1000
1988 BU	3,315	£1000
1989 500th Anniversary of the Sovereign. Enthroned portrayal obverse and		
Crowned shield reverse BU	2,937	£1400
1989 — Proof	5,000	£1500
1990 Reverts to couped portrait BU	1,226	£1000
1990 Proof	1,721	£1000
1991 BU	976	£1000
1991 Proof	1,336	£1000
1992 BU	797	£1000
1992 Proof	1,165	£1000
1993 BU	906	£1000
1993 Proof	1,078	£1000
1994 BU	1,000	£1000
1994 Proof	918	£1000
1995 BU	1,000	£1000
1995 Proof	1,250	£1000
1996 BU	901	£1000
1996 Proof	742	£1150
1997 BU	802	£1000
1997 Proof	860	£1000
1998 New portrait BU	825	£1100
1998 Proof	789	£1200
1999 BU	991	£1000
1999 Proof	1,000	£1100
2000 ("Bullion")	10,000	£1000
2000 BU	994	£1150
2000 Proof	3,000	£1200
2001 BU	1,000	£1000
2001 Proof	3,500	£1100
2002 Shield rev. ("Bullion")	—	£1000
2002 BU	—	£1100
2002 Proof	3,000	£1150
2003 BU	—	£1000
2003 Proof	—	£1200
2004 BU	—	£1000
2004 Proof	—	£1100
2005 Noad's heraldic St George and Dragon BU	—	£1150
2005 — Proof	—	£1400
2006 BU	—	£1000
2006 Proof	—	£1100
2007 BU	—	£1000
2007 Proof	—	£1100
2008 BU	—	£1000
2008 Proof	—	£1100
2009 BU	—	£1000
2009 Proof	—	£1150
2010 BU	—	£1000
2010 Proof	—	£1150
2011 BU	—	£1000
2011 Proof	—	£1150
2012 Day's St George and Dragon BU	1,250	£1150
2012 — Proof	—	£1450
2013 BU	—	£1000
2013 Proof	—	£1200
2014 BU	—	£1000
2014 Proof	—	£1200
2015 Proof	—	—
2015 New Portrait BU	—	£1450
2015 — Proof	—	—
2016 BU	—	—
2016 Butler Portrait Proof	—	—

> **NOTE: The prices quoted in this guide are set at August 2016 with the price of gold at £900 per ounce and silver £12 per ounce — market fluctuations will have a marked effect on the values of modern precious metal coins.**

The obverse of the 1989 gold coins portray HM the Queen enthroned.

Pistrucci's famous rendering of St George and the Dragon.

FIVE POUNDS (Crown series)

This series commenced in 1990 when the "Crown" was declared legal tender at £5, instead of 25p as all previous issues continued to be. Mintage is in cupro-nickel unless otherwise stated. BU includes those in individual presentation folders, and those in sets sold with stamp covers and/or banknotes.

DATE	Mintage	UNC
1990 Queen Mother's 90th Birthday.	2,761,431	£8
1990 — BU	48,477	£10
1990 — Silver Proof	56,800	£40
1990 — Gold Proof	2,500	£1400
1993 Coronation 40th Anniversary	1,834,655	£8
1993 — BU	—	£10
1993 — Proof	—	£15
1993 — Silver Proof	58,877	£45
1993 — Gold Proof	2,500	£1400
1996 HM the Queen's 70th Birthday	2,396,100	£8
1996 — BU	—	£10
1996 — Proof	—	£15
1996 — Silver Proof	39,336	£45
1996 — Gold Proof	2,127	£1400
1997 Royal Golden Wedding	1,733,000	£8
1997 — BU	—	£10
1997 — — with £5 note	5,000	£75
1997 — Proof	—	£20
1997 — Silver Proof	33,689	£45
1997 — Gold Proof	2,750	£1400
1998 Prince of Wales 50th Birthday	1,407,300	£9
1998 — BU	—	£12
1998 — Proof	—	£20
1998 — Silver Proof	13,379	£50
1998 — Gold Proof	—	£1400
1999 Princess of Wales Memorial.	1,600,000	£10
1999 — BU	—	£14
1999 — Proof	—	£20
1999 — Silver Proof	49,545	£50
1999 — Gold Proof	7,500	£1500
1999 Millennium	3,796,300	£8
1999 — BU	—	£12
1999 — Proof	—	£20
1999 — Silver Proof	49,057	£45
1999 — Gold Proof	2,500	£1400
2000 —	3,147,092*	£12
2000 — BU	—	£20
2000 — — with special Millennium Dome mintmark	—	£30
2000 — Proof	—	£25
2000 — Silver Proof with gold highlight	14,255	£50
2000 — Gold Proof	2,500	£1400
2000 Queen Mother's 100th Birthday	incl. above*	£8
2000 — BU	—	£12
2000 — Silver Proof	31,316	£45
2000 — — — Piedfort	14,850	£60
2000 — Gold Proof	3,000	£1400
2001 Victorian Era	851,491	£10
2001 — BU	—	£12
2001 — Proof	—	£20
2001 — Silver Proof	19,216	£50
2001 — — with frosted relief	596	£150
2001 — Gold Proof	3,000	£1400
2001 — — with frosted relief	733	£1500
2002 Golden Jubilee	3,687,882*	£9
2002 — BU	—	£12
2002 — Proof	—	£20
2002 — Silver Proof	54,012	£45
2002 — Gold Proof	5,502	£1400

DATE	Mintage	UNC
2002 Queen Mother Memorial.. *incl. above**		£9
2002 — BU...	—	£12
2002 — Silver Proof	16,117	£45
2002 — Gold Proof..	3,000	£1100
2003 Coronation Jubilee	1,307,147	£10
2003 — BU...	—	£13
2003 — Proof	—	£20
2003 — Silver Proof	28,758	£45
2003 — Gold Proof..	—	£1150
2004 Entente Cordiale Centenary	1,205,594	£10
2004 — Proof Reverse Frosting		£15
2004 — Silver Proof	11,295	£50
2004 — — Piedfort	2,500	£125
2004 — Gold Proof..	—	£1150
2004 — Platinum Proof Piedfort..............................	501	£4000
2005 Trafalgar Bicentenary..................................	1,075 516	£12
2005 — BU...	—	£14
2005 — Proof	—	£25
2005 — Silver Proof	21,448	£50
2005 — — Piedfort	2,818	£75
2005 — Gold Proof..	—	£1150
2005 Bicentenary of the Death of Nelson ....*incl. above**		£12
2005 — BU...	—	£14
2005 — Proof	—	£25
2005 — Silver Proof	12,852	£50
2005 — — Piedfort	2,818	£75
2005 — Gold Proof..	—	£1150
2005 — Platinum Proof Piedfort..............................	200	£4000
2006 Queen's 80th Birthday....................................	—	£10
2006 — BU...	—	£14
2006 — Proof	—	£20
2006 — Silver Proof	20,790	£50
2006 — — Piedfort, selective gold plating on reverse	5,000	£75
2006 — Gold Proof..	—	£1150
2006 — Platinum Proof Piedfort..............................	250	£4000
2007 Queen's Diamond Wedding	—	£10
2007 — BU...	—	£15
2007 — Proof	—	£20
2007 — Silver Proof	15,186	£50
2007 — — Piedfort	2,000	£80
2007 — Gold Proof..	—	£1150
2007 — Platinum Proof Piedfort..............................	—	£4000
2008 Prince of Wales 60th Birthday	—	£12
2008 — BU...	—	£15
2008 — Proof	—	£20
2008 — Silver Proof	7,446	£55
2008 — — Piedfort	2,000	£90
2008 — Gold Proof..	—	£1150
2008 Elizabeth I 450th Anniversary of Accession	—	£12
2008 — BU...	—	£15
2008 — Proof	—	£20
2008 — Silver Proof	10,398	£50
2008 — — Piedfort	2,000	£90
2008 — Gold Proof..	—	£1150
2008 — Platinum Proof Piedfort..............................	—	£4000
2009 500th Anniversary of Henry VIII accession.....................	30,000	£12
2009 — BU...	—	£15
2009 — Proof	—	£25
2009 — Silver Proof	10,419	£50
2009 — — Piedfort	3,580	£90
2009 — Gold Proof..	1,509	£1150
2009 — Platinum Proof Piedfort..............................	100	£4250
2009 Olympic Countdown (3 years) BU	—	£12
2009 — Silver Proof	26,645	£55
2009 — — Piedfort	4,874	£90
2009 — Gold Proof..	—	£1250
2009 Olympic Celebration of Britain "The Mind" series (incl. green logo):		
Stonehenge Silver Proof	—	£60

DATE	Mintage	UNC
Palace of Westminster/Big Ben Silver Proof	—	£60
— Cu Ni Proof...	—	£20
Angel of the North Silver Proof	—	£60
Flying Scotsman Silver Proof...	—	£60
Globe Theatre Silver Proof..	—	£60
Sir Isaac Newton Silver Proof	—	£60
2010 350th Anniversary of the Restoration of the Monarchy ...	15,000	£12
2010 — BU	—	£15
2010 — Proof	—	£25
2010 — Silver Proof	6,518	£50
2010 — — Piedfort...	4,435	£100
2010 — Gold Proof..	—	£1250
2010 — Platinum Proof Piedfort..	—	£4000
2010 Olympic Countdown (2 years) BU	—	£12
2010 — Silver Proof	20,159	£55
2010 — — Piedfort...	2,197	£150
2010 — Gold Proof..	—	£1250
2010 Olympic Celebration of Britain, "The Body" series (incl. red logo):		
Coastline of Britain (Rhossili Bay) Silver Proof..............	—	£60
Giants Causeway Silver Proof..	—	£60
River Thames Silver Proof...	—	£60
British Fauna (Barn Owl) Silver Proof............................	—	£60
British Flora (Oak Leaves and Acorn) Silver Proof	—	£60
Weather Vane Silver Proof...	—	£60
2010 Olympic Celebration of Britain "The Spirit" series (incl. blue logo):		
Churchill Silver Proof..	—	£60
— CuNi Proof..	—	£20
Spirit of London (Kind Hearts etc.) Silver Proof	—	£60
— CuNi Proof..	—	£20
Humour Silver Proof..	—	£60
Unity (Floral emblems of Britain) Silver Proof.................	—	£60
Music Silver Proof	—	£60
Anti-slavery Silver Proof..	—	£60
2011 90th Birthday of the Duke of Edinburgh BU....................	—	£12
2011 — Silver Proof	4,599	£60
2011 — — Piedfort...	2,659	£115
2011 — Gold Proof..	—	£1250
2011 — Platinum Proof Piedfort..	—	£6000
2011 Royal Wedding of Prince William and Catherine Middleton		
BU	—	£12
2011 — Silver Proof	26,069	£60
2011 — Gold-plated Silver Proof	—	£80
2011 — Silver Proof Piedfort...	2,991	£95
2011 — Gold Proof..	—	£1250
2011 — Platinum Proof Piedfort..	—	£5500
2011 Olympic Countdown (1 year) BU..................................	—	£12
2011 — Silver Proof	25,877	£55
2011 — — Piedfort...	4,000	£100
2011 — Gold Proof..	—	£1250
2012 Diamond Jubilee BU..	—	£15
2012 — Proof	—	£25
2012 — Silver Proof	—	£65
2012 — Gold-plated silver proof	—	£205
2012 — Silver Piedfort Proof...	—	£100
2012 — Gold proof..	—	£1250
2012 — Platinum Piedford Proof..	—	£5500
2012 Olympic Countdown (Games Time) BU	—	£13
2012 — Silver Proof	—	£65
2012 — Silver Piedfort Proof...	—	£120
2012 — Gold proof..	—	£1450
2012 Official Olympic BU	—	£15
2012 — Silver Proof	—	£70
2012 — Gold Plated Silver Proof	—	£90
2012 — Silver Piedfort Proof...	—	£125
2012 — Gold proof..	—	£1450
2012 Official Paralympic BU	—	£15

DATE	Mintage	UNC
2012 — Silver Proof	—	£70
2012 — Silver Piedfort Proof	—	£125
2012 — Gold proof	—	£1750
2013 60th Anniversary of the Queen's Coronation BU	—	£15
2013 — Proof	—	£35
2013 — Silver Proof	—	£80
2013 — Silver Piedfort Proof	—	£125
2013 — Gold-plated silver proof	—	£100
2013 — Gold proof	—	£1750
2013 — Platinum Piedfort Proof	100	£6000

2013 Queen's Portraits, 4 coins each with one of the four portraits, paired with James Butler's Royal Arms. Issued only as sets of 4 in precious metals (see under Proof and Specimen Set section) .... — £300

2013 Royal Birth of Prince George (St George & Dragon), Silver Proof ... — £80

2013 Christening of Prince George BU	—	£15
2013 — Silver Proof	—	£80
2013 — — Piedfort	—	£160
2013 — Gold Proof	—	£1750
2013 — Platinum Proof Piedfort	—	£6000
2014 300th Anniversary of the death of Queen Anne BU	—	£15
2014 — Proof	—	£35
2014 — Silver Proof	—	£80
2014 — — Piedfort	—	£160
2014 — Gold-plated Silver Proof	—	£100
2014 — Gold Proof	—	£1800
2014 First Birthday of Prince George Silver Proof	—	£80

2014 100th Anniversary of the First World War Outbreak, issued only as sets of the 6 Coins (see under Proof and Specimen Sets section) — —

2014 Portrait of Britain, issued only as sets of the 4 coins, incorporating trichromatic colour-printing (see under Proof and Specimen Sets section) — —

2015 50th Anniversary of death of Sir Winston Churchill BU	—	£15
2015 — Silver Proof	—	£80
2015 — — Piedfort	—	£160
2015 — Gold Proof	—	£1800
2015 — Platinum Proof Piedfort	65	£5000
2015 200th Anniversary of the Battle of Waterloo, BU	—	£15
2015 — Gold Proof	100	—

2015 First World War 100th Anniversary, continued, issued only as sets of 6 coins — —

2015 New Portrait, Second Birthday of Prince George, Silver Proof — £80

2015 — Birth of Second Child to the Duke & Duchess of Cambridge, BU	—	£15
2015 — — Silver Proof	—	£80
2015 — — Gold Proof	500	£1800
2015 — Christening of Princess Charlotte, Silver Proof	—	£80
2015 — 200th Anniversary of the Battle of Waterloo, Silver Proof	—	£160
2015 — — Silver Proof Piedfort	—	£160
2015 — — Gold Proof	—	£1650
2015 The Longest Reign BU	—	£15
2015 — Silver Proof	—	£80
2015 — — — Piedfort	—	£160
2015 — Gold Proof	—	£1650
2015 — Platinum Proof Piedfort	—	£5000
2016 Queen's 90th Birthday BU	—	£15
2016 — Proof	—	—
2016 — Silver Proof	—	£80
2016 — — — Piedfort	—	£160
2016 — Gold Proof	—	£1800
2016 — Platinum Piedfort Proof	—	£4500

2016 First World War 100th Anniversary, continued, issued only as set of 6 silver proof coins .... —

DOUBLE SOVEREIGN

As with the Sovereign series Five Pound coins, those listed under this heading bear the Pistrucci St George and Dragon reverse, except where otherwise stated, and are minted in gold. They are, and always have been, legal tender at £2, and have a diameter indentical to that of the base metal Two Pound coins listed further below under a different heading. The denomination does not appear on Double Sovereigns.

DATE	Mintage	UNC
1980 Proof	10,000	£525
1982 Proof	2,500	£525
1983 Proof	12,500	£525
1985 New Portrait Proof	5,849	£525
1987 Proof	14,301	£525
1988 Proof	12,743	£525
1989 525th Anniversary of the Sovereign. Enthroned portrayal obverse and Crowned shield reverse Proof	14,936	£800
1990 Proof	4,374	£525
1991 Proof	3,108	£525
1992 Proof	2,608	£525
1993 Proof	2,155	£525
1996 Proof	3,167	£525
1998 New Portrait Proof	4,500	£525
2000 Proof	2,250	£525
2002 Shield reverse Proof	8,000	£550
2003 Proof	2,250	£525
2004 Proof	—	£525
2005 Noad's heraldic St George and Dragon Proof	—	£650
2006 Proof	—	£525
2007 Proof	—	£525
2008 Proof	—	£525
2009 Proof	—	£525
2010 Proof	—	£525
2011 Proof	—	£525
2012 Day's St George and Dragon BU	—	£500
2012 — Proof	—	£650
2013 BU	—	£650
2013 Proof	—	£650
2014 BU	—	£550
2014 Proof	—	£650
2015 Proof	—	£650
2015 New Portrait Proof	—	£750
2016 Butler Portrait Proof	—	£750

ABBREVIATIONS COMMONLY USED TO DENOTE METALLIC COMPOSITION	
Cu	Copper
Cu/Steel	Copper plated steel
Ag/Cu	Silver plated copper
Ae	Bronze
Cu-Ni	Cupro-nickel
Ni-Ag	Nickel silver (note—does not contain silver)
Brass/Cu-Ni	Brass outer, cupro-nickel inner
Ni-Brass	Nickel-brass
Ag	Silver
Au/Ag	Gold plated silver
Au	Gold
Pl	Platinum

TWO POUNDS AND BELOW
(including Britannia Silver Series)

This series commenced in 1997, and, as with the Gold Britannia series, sets of the coins are listed in the "Proof and Specimen Sets" section. Coins contain one Troy ounce of fine silver (£2) alloyed to Britannia standard, i.e. 95.8 per cent fine silver, or fractions of one ounce as follows: half ounce (£1), quarter ounce (50 pence) and one tenth of an ounce (20 pence). Reverses change anually, all four coins of any particular date being of the same design. The reverses by Philip Nathan appear as follows:

1997 Chariot, 1998 Standing Britannia, 1999 Chariot, 2000 Standing Britannia, 2001 Una and the Lion, 2002 Standing Britannia, 2003 Britannia's Helmeted Head, 2004 Standing Britannia, 2005 Britannia Seated, 2006 Standing Britannia, 2009 Chariot.

The 2007 design is by Christopher Le Brun, and features a seated Britannia with Lion at her feet. The 2008 is by John Bergdahl, and features a standing Britannia facing left.

Two pounds Britannia coins to BU or "bullion" standard have been issued as individual coins for each year from 1998 onwards. 2010 features Suzie Zamit's Britannia with a portrait with a Corinthian style helmet.

The 2011 coins feature a seated Britannia and Union Flag, as described in the Britannia gold series above.

2012 saw the 15th anniversary of the Silver Series, but the reverse chosen was that of the Standing Britannia by Philip Nathan, which also marked the 25th Gold series. In addition, there is a 9-coin proof set of Half-Ounce silver coins dated 2012 featuring each of the Reverses used in the past, a 25th Anniversary collection. The story of the 2013 silver Britannia coins closely parallels that of the gold coins. The silver one-twentieth of an ounce has the logical face value of 10 pence.

The 2014 Silver Britannias closely follow the pattern of the three designs of 2014 Gold. This included the introduction of the silver one-fortieth of an ounce, with a face value of 5 pence. The Nathan Britannia has crenellated borders on both the obverse and the reverse, while the Year of the Horse has plain borders on both. Examples exist, however, of both One ounce silver bullion coins having the Other's obverse, thus producing two error coins, or "mules". 2014 also saw the SS Gairsoppa Quarter-ounce silver Britannia bullion coin with the edge inscription SS GAIRSOPPA. These coins have the Nathan Britannia reverse, and are struck from metal recovered from the vessel which was sunk by enemy action in 1941.

Both 2013 and 2014 one-ounce BU bullion Nathan Britannia coins exists with snakes or horses (respectively) on a plain edge. These were the result of a contract between the Royal Mint and the bullion dealers A-mark of Santa Monica, California, and commemorate Chinese Lunar years.

A new metal combination was the Gold-plated Silver Proof One-ounce coin for the Year of the Sheep.

NOTE: As the BRITANNIA series of coins are essentially bullion pieces, their values are usually related to the current price of gold and silver, therefore no attempt has been made in this publication to give values for the series. To ascertain the value of a piece it is necessary to check with the prevailing price of precious metals.

TWO POUNDS

This series commenced in 1986 with nickel-brass commemorative coins, with their associated base metal and precious metal BU and proof coins. From 1997 (actually issued in 1998) a thinner bi-metal version commenced with a reverse theme of the advance of technology, and from this date the coin was specifically intended to circulate. This is true also for the parallel issues of anniversary and commemorative Two Pound issues in 1999 and onwards. All have their BU and proof versions, as listed below.

In the case of Gold Proofs, a few have Certificates of Authenticity and/or green boxes of issue describing the coin as a Double Sovereign. All Gold Proofs since 1997 are of bi-metallic gold except for 2001 (red gold with the inner circle coated in yellow gold) and 2002 (Technology issue, uncoated red gold).

A new definitive design was introduced during 2015 incorporating the Jody Clark portrait and Britannia by Antony Dufort

NOTE: The counterfeiting of circulation £2 coins has been around for several years but 2015 saw the introduction of proof-like base metal designs. Five types are known at present: 2011 (Mary Rose) and 2015 (all four designs).

DATE	Mintage	UNC
1986 Commonwealth Games	8,212,184	£4
1986 — BU	—	£8
1986 — Proof	59,779	£15
1986 — Silver BU	—	£25
1986 — — Proof	—	£35
1986 — Gold Proof	—	£525
1989 Tercentenary of Bill of Rights.	4,392,825	£8
1989 — BU (issued in folder with Claim of Right)	—	£25
1989 — BU folder	—	£8
1989 — Proof	—	£15
1989 — Silver Proof	—	£35
1989 — — Piedfort	—	£50
1989 Tercentenary of Claim of Right (issued in Scotland)	381,400	£12
1989 — BU (see above)	—	£12
1989 — Proof	—	£25
1989 — Silver Proof	—	£35
1989 — — Piedfort	—	£50
1994 Tercentenary of the Bank of England	1,443,116	£5
1994 — BU	—	£8
1994 — Proof	—	£12
1994 — Silver Proof	27,957	£35
1994 — — Piedfort	9,569	£60
1994 — Gold Proof	—	£550
1994 — — with Double Sovereign obverse (no denomination)	—	£900
1995 50th Anniversary of End of WWII.	4,394,566	£5
1995 — BU	—	£8
1995 — Proof	—	£12
1995 — Silver Proof	35,751	£35
1995 — — Piedfort	—	£60
1995 — Gold Proof	—	£525
1995 50th Anniversary of The United Nations	1,668,575	£6
1995 — BU	—	£9
1995 — Proof	—	£12
1995 — Silver Proof	—	£40
1995 — — Piedfort	—	£60
1995 — Gold Proof	—	£525
1996 European Football Championships.	5,195,350	£6
1996 — BU	—	£8
1996 — Proof	—	£10
1996 — Silver Proof	25,163	£40
1996 — — Piedfort	7,634	£60
1996 — Gold Proof	—	£525
1997	13,734,625	£4
1997 BU	—	£8
1997 Proof	—	£12
1997 Silver Proof	29,910	£35
1997 — — Piedfort	16,000	£60
1997 Gold Proof (red (outer) and yellow (inner) 22ct)..	—	£525

DATE	Mintage	UNC
1998 **New Portrait**	—	£3
1998 BU	91,110,375	£8
1998 Proof	—	£12
1998 Silver Proof	19,978	£35
1998 — — Piedfort	7,646	£60
1999	33,719,000	£3
1999 Rugby World Cup	4,933,000	£6
1999 — BU	—	£10
1999 — Silver Proof (gold plated ring)	9,665	£45
1999 — — — Piedfort (Hologram)	10,000	£85
1999 — Gold Proof	—	£525
2000	25,770,000	£3
2000 BU	—	£6
2000 Proof	—	£10
2000 Silver Proof	—	£40
2001	34,984,750	£3
2001 BU	—	£4
2001 Proof	—	£10
2001 Marconi	4,558,000	£4
2001 — BU	—	£8
2001 — Proof	—	£10
2001 — Silver Proof (gold plated ring)	11,488	£40
2001 — — — Reverse Frosting (issued in set with Canada $5)	—	£65
2001 — — — Piedfort	6,759	£60
2001 — Gold Proof	—	£525
2002	13,024,750	£3
2002 BU	—	£6
2002 Proof	—	£10
2002 Gold Proof (red 22ct)	—	£525
2002 Commonwealth Games, Scotland	771,750	£8
2002 — Wales	558,500	£8
2002 — Northern Ireland	485,500	£8
2002 — England	650,500	£8
2002 — BU (issued in set of 4)	—	£40
2002 — Proof (issued in set of 4)	—	£50
2002 — Silver Proof (issued in set of 4)	—	£150
2002 — — — Piedfort (painted) (issued in set of 4)	—	£275
2002 — Gold Proof (issued in set of 4)	—	£2300
2003	17,531,250	£4
2003 BU	—	£8
2003 Proof	—	£12
2003 DNA Double Helix	4,299,000	£3
2003 — BU	—	£6
2003 — Proof	—	£10
2003 — Silver Proof (Gold-plated ring)	11,204	£40
2003 — — — Piedfort	8,728	£60
2003 — Gold Proof	—	£525
2004	11,981,500	£3
2004 BU	—	£6
2004 Proof	—	£12
2004 Trevithick Steam Locomotive	5,004,500	£4
2004 — BU	—	£8
2004 — Proof	—	£30
2004 — Silver BU	—	£25
2004 — — Proof (Gold-plated ring)	10,233	£45
2004 — — — Piedfort	5,303	£60
2004 — Gold Proof	—	£525
2005	3,837,250	£3
2005 BU	—	£6
2005 Proof	—	£8
2005 Gunpowder Plot	5,140,500	£4
2005 — BU	—	£8
2005 — Proof	—	£6
2005 Silver Proof	4,394	£40
2005 — — — Piedfort	4,585	£65
2005 — Gold Proof	—	£525

DATE	Mintage	UNC
2005 End of World War II...	10,191,000	£4
2005 — BU...	—	£8
2005 — Silver Proof	21,734	£40
2005 — — — Piedfort...	4,798	£65
2005 — Gold Proof...	—	£525
2006	16,715,000	£3
2006 Proof...	—	£6
2006 Brunel, The Man (Portrait)	7,928,250	£4
2006 — BU...	—	£6
2006 — Proof	—	£10
2006 — Silver Proof	—	£40
2006 — — — Piedfort...	—	£65
2006 —Gold Proof..	—	£525
2006 Brunel, His Achievements (Paddington Station)	7,452,250	£4
2006 — BU...	—	£6
2006 — Proof	—	£10
2006 — Silver Proof	—	£40
2006 — — — Piedfort...	—	£65
2006 —Gold Proof..	—	£525
2007	10,270,000	£3
2007 Proof...	—	£8
2007 Tercentenary of the Act of Union........................	7,545,000	£4
2007 BU	—	£6
2007 — Proof	—	£8
2007 — Silver Proof	8,310	£40
2007 — — — Piedfort...	4,000	£65
2007 — Gold Proof..	—	£525
2007 Bicentenary of the Abolition of the Slave Trade .	8,445,000	£4
2007 — BU...	—	£6
2007 — Proof	—	£10
2007 — Silver Proof	7,095	£40
2007 — — — Piedfort...	3,990	£65
2007 — Gold Proof..	—	£500
2008..	15,346,000	£3
2008 BU	—	£6
2008 Proof...	—	£12
2008 Centenary of 4th Olympiad, London	910,000	£4
2008 — BU...	—	£6
2008 — Proof	—	£12
2008 — Silver Proof	8,023	£40
2008 — — — Piedfort...	2,000	£70
2008 — Gold Proof..	—	£500
2008 Olympic Games Handover Ceremony................	853,000	£4
2008 — BU...	—	£7
2008 — Silver Proof	30,000	£45
2008 — — — Piedfort...	3,000	£75
2008 — Gold Proof..	—	£500
2009	8,775,000	£3
2009 BU	—	£4
2009 Proof...	—	£10
2009 Silver Proof	—	£45
2009 250th Anniversary of birth of Robert Burns........	3,253,000	£3
2009 — BU...	—	£8
2009 — Proof	—	£12
2009 — Silver Proof	9,188	£40
2009 — — — Piedfort...	3,500	£70
2009 — Gold Proof..	—	£500
2009 200th Anniversary of birth of Charles Darwin.....	3,903,000	£3
2009 — BU...	—	£8
2009 — Proof	—	£12
2009 — Silver Proof	9,357	£40
2009 — — — Piedfort...	3,282	£70
2009 Gold Proof	—	£500
2010...	6,890,000	£3
2010 BU	—	£8
2010 Proof...	—	£12

DATE	Mintage	UNC
2010 Silver Proof	—	£40
2010 Florence Nightingale 150 Years of Nursing	6,175,000	£4
2010 — BU	—	£10
2010 — Proof	—	£12
2010 — Silver Proof	5,117	£40
2010 – – – Piedfort	2,770	£70
2010 — Gold Proof	—	£500
2011	24,375,000	£4
2011 BU	—	£5
2011 Proof	—	£12
2011 Silver Proof	—	£35
2011 500th Anniversary of the Mary Rose	1,040,000	£4
2011 — BU	—	£9
2011 — Proof	—	£12
2011 — Silver Proof	6,618	£40
2011 — — Piedfort	2,680	£75
2011 — Gold Proof	—	£500
2011 400th Anniversary of the King James Bible	975,000	£4
2011 — BU	—	£9
2011 — Proof	—	£15
2011 — Silver Proof	4,494	£45
2011 — — Piedfort	2,394	£75
2011 — Gold Proof	—	£500
2012	3,900,000	£3
2012 BU	—	£6
2012 Proof	—	£12
2012 Silver Proof	—	£30
2012 Gold Proof	—	£550
2012 200th Anniversary of birth of Charles Dickens	8,190,000	£4
2012 — BU	—	£9
2012 — Proof	—	£12
2012 — Silver Proof	—	£45
2012 — — — Piedfort	—	£75
2012 — Gold Proof	—	£500
2012 Olympic Handover to Rio	845,000	£5
2012 — BU	—	£12
2012 — Silver Proof	—	£50
2012 — — — Piedfort	—	£100
2012 — Gold Proof	—	£500
2013	15,860,250	£3
2013 BU	—	£6
2013 Proof	—	£12
2013 Silver Proof	—	£65
2013 Gold Proof	—	£550
2013 150th Anniversary of the London Underground, Roundel design	1,560,000	£4
2013 — BU	—	£12
2013 — Proof	—	£18
2013 — Silver Proof	—	£50
2013 — — — Piedfort	—	£100
2013 — Gold Proof	—	£550
2013 150th Anniversary of the London Underground, Train design	1,690,000	£4
2013 — BU	—	£10
2013 — Proof	—	£15
2013 — Silver Proof	—	£50
2013 — — — Piedfort	—	£100
2013 — Gold Proof	—	£550
2013 350th Anniversary of the Guinea	2,990,000	£4
2013 — BU	—	£10
2013 — Proof	—	£15
2013 — Silver Proof	—	£50
2013 — — — Piedfort	—	£100
2013 — Gold Proof	—	£600
2014	—	£5
2014 BU	—	£10

DATE	Mintage	UNC
2014 Proof..	—	£25
2014 Silver Proof	—	£55
2014 100th Anniversary of First World War Outbreak .	—	£3
2014 — BU...	—	£10
2014 — Proof	—	£20
2014 — Silver Proof	—	£50
2014 — — Piedfort	—	£100
2014 — Gold Proof..	—	£750
2014 500th Anniversary of Trinity House....................	—	£3
2014 — BU...	—	£10
2014 — Proof	—	£20
2014 — Silver Proof	—	£50
2014 — — Piedfort	—	£100
2014 — Gold Proof..	—	£750
2015	—	£3
2015 BU	—	£10
2015 Proof..	—	£20
2015 Silver Proof	—	£50
2015 Gold Proof	—	£750
2015 Royal Navy First World War.............................	—	£3
2015 — BU...	—	£10
2015 — Proof	—	£20
2015 — Silver Proof	—	£50
2015 — — Piedfort	—	£100
2015 — Gold Proof..	—	£750
2015 800th Anniversary of Magna Carta....................	—	£3
2015 — BU...	—	£10
2015 — Proof	—	£20
2015 — Silver Proof	—	£50
2015 — — Piedfort	—	£100
2015 — Gold Proof..	—	£695
2015 New Portrait, new Reverse..............................	—	£3
2015 — BU...	—	£10
2015 — Proof	—	£20
2015 — Silver Proof	—	£50
2015 — Gold Proof..	—	£750
2015 — Platinum Proof	—	£900
2015 — 800th Anniversary of Magna Carta	—	£3
2015 — — BU	—	£10
2015 — — Silver Proof..	—	£50
2015 — — — Piedfort..	—	£100
2015 — — Gold Proof	—	£695
2016..	—	£3
2016 BU	—	£10
2016 Proof..	—	£20
2016 Silver Proof	—	£50
2016 40th Anniversary of Shakespeare"s death, Comedies	—	—
2016 — — BU	—	—
2016 — — Proof...	—	—
2016 — — Silver Proof..	—	—
2016 — — — Piedfort..	—	—
2016 — — Gold Proof	—	—
2016 — Tragedies	—	—
2016 — — BU	—	—
2016 — — Proof...	—	—
2016 — — Silver Proof..	—	—
2016 — — — Piedfort..	—	—
2016 — — Gold Proof	—	—
2016 — Histories..	—	—
2016 — — BU	—	—
2016 — — Proof...	—	—
2016 — — Silver Proof..	—	—
2016 — — — Piedfort..	—	—
2016 — — Gold Proof	—	—
2016 350th Anniversary of Great Fire of London	—	—
2016 — — BU	—	—
2016 — — Proof...	—	—

DATE	Mintage	UNC
2016 — — Silver Proof	—	—
2016 — — — — Piedfort	—	—
2016 — — Gold Proof	—	—
2016 Army First World War	—	—
2016 — — BU	—	—
2016 — — Proof	—	—
2016 — — Silver Proof	—	—
2016 — — — — Piedfort	—	—
2016 — — Gold Proof	—	—

SOVEREIGN

All are minted in gold, bear the Pistrucci St George and Dragon reverse except where stated, and are legal tender at one pound. From 2009 there is no streamer behind St George's Helmet in the Pistrucci design.

DATE	Mintage	UNC
1974	5,002,566	£200
1976	4,150,000	£200
1978	6,550,000	£200
1979	9,100,000	£200
1979 Proof	50,000	£250
1980	5,100,000	£200
1980 Proof	91,200	£250
1981	5,000,000	£250
1981 Proof	32,960	£250
1982	2,950,000	£200
1982 Proof	22,500	£250
1983 Proof	21,250	£250
1984 Proof	19,975	£250
1985 New portrait Proof	17,242	£250
1986 Proof	17,579	£250
1987 Proof	22,479	£250
1988 Proof	18,862	£250
1989 500th Anniversary of the Sovereign—details as Five Pounds (Sov. Series). Proof	23,471	£750
1990 Proof	8,425	£250
1991 Proof	7,201	£250
1992 Proof	6,854	£250
1993 Proof	6,090	£250
1994 Proof	7,165	£250
1995 Proof	9,500	£250
1996 Proof	9,110	£250
1997 Proof	9,177	£250
1998 New Portrait Proof	11,349	£250
1999 Proof	11,903	£275
2000 (first Unc issue since 1982)	129,069	£225
2000 Proof	12,159	£250
2001	49,462	£200
2001 Proof	10,000	£250
2002 Shield Rev. ("bullion")	74,263	£200
2002 Proof	20,500	£250
2003 ("bullion")	43,208	£200
2003 Proof	—	£250
2004 ("bullion")	28,821	£200
2004 Proof	—	£250
2005 Noad heraldic St George and Dragon	—	£300
2005 — Proof	—	£350
2006 ("bullion")	—	£200
2006 Proof	—	£300
2007 ("bullion")	—	£200
2007 Proof	—	£250

DATE	Mintage	UNC
2008 ("bullion")	—	£200
2008 Proof	—	£250
2009 ("bullion")	—	£200
2009 Proof	—	£250
2010 ("bullion")	—	£200
2010 Proof	—	£250
2011 ("bullion")	—	£200
2011 Proof	—	£300
2012 Day's St George and Dragon BU "bullion"	—	£250
2012 — Proof	—	£300
2013 BU "bullion"	—	£200
2013 — with "I" mintmark, minted by MMTC-PAMP, Haryana, India, under Licence from, and the supervision of, the Royal Mint	—	£250
2013 Proof	—	£350
2014 BU "bullion"	—	£225
2014 Proof	—	£300
2014 BU "bullion" with "I" mintmark	—	£250
2015 BU "bullion"	—	£325
2015 Proof	—	£360
2015 New Portrait, Proof	—	£360
2016 BU "bullion"	—	£360
2016 Butler Portrait Proof	—	£395

> **IMPORTANT NOTE:**
> The prices quoted in this guide are set at August 2016 with the price of gold at £900 per ounce and silver £12 per ounce—market fluctuations can have a marked effect on the values of modern precious metal coins.

The Sovereign's war effort

At the outbreak of the First World War, Britain needed money to finance her war effort by any means possible. Posters were produced appealing to the patriotism of the great British public urging them to donate their gold coins for the war effort. Production of the sovereign as a circulation coin stopped completely in 1917.

HALF SOVEREIGN

Legal Tender at 50 pence, otherwise the notes for the Sovereign apply. From 2009 the exergue in the Pistrucci design is larger in area, and the initials B.P. are absent. From 2011, however, the initials were restored.

DATE	Mintage	UNC
1980 Proof only	86,700	£125
1982	2,500,000	£120
1982 Proof	21,590	£125
1983 Proof	19,710	£135
1984 Proof	19,505	£135
1985 New portrait Proof	15,800	£135
1986 Proof	17,075	£135
1987 Proof	20,687	£135
1988 Proof	18,266	£135
1989 500th Anniversary of the Sovereign—details as Five Pounds (Sov. Series) Proof	21,824	£400
1990 Proof	7,889	£135
1991 Proof	6,076	£135
1992 Proof	5,915	£135
1993 Proof	4,651	£135
1994 Proof	7,167	£135
1995 Proof	7,500	£135
1996 New Portrait Proof	7,340	£150
1997 Proof	9,177	£135
1998 Proof	7,496	£135

DATE	Mintage	UNC
1999 Proof	9,403	£135
2000	146,822	£120
2000 Proof	9,708	£135
2001	98,763	£120
2001 Proof	7,500	£135
2002 Shield reverse ("bullion")	61,347	£120
2002 Proof	—	£135
2003 ("bullion")	47,805	£120
2003 Proof	—	£135
2004 ("bullion")	32,479	£120
2004 Proof	—	£135
2005 Noad heraldic St George and Dragon	—	£185
2005 — Proof	—	£200
2006 ("bullion")	—	£125
2006 Proof	—	£150
2006 ("bullion")	—	£125
2007 Proof	—	£150
2008 ("bullion")	—	£125
2008 Proof	—	£150
2009 ("bullion")	—	£125
2009 Proof	—	£150
2010 ("bullion")	—	£125
2010 Proof	—	£150
2011 ("bullion")	—	£125
2011 Proof	—	£175
2012 Day's St George and Dragon "bullion" or BU	—	£125
2012 — Proof	—	£175
2013 BU "bullion"	—	£125
2013 Proof	—	£170
2014 BU "bullion"	—	£150
2014 Proof	—	£175
2014 BU "bullion" with "I" mintmark	—	£200
2015 BU "bullion"	—	£170
2015 Proof	—	£190
2015 New Portrait, Proof	—	£190
2016 BU "bullion"	—	£195
2016 Butler Portrait Proof	—	—

QUARTER SOVEREIGN

Minted in 22ct Gold, this new denomination was introduced in 2009, and follows on from two different patterns of 1853.

DATE	Mintage	UNC
2009 ("bullion")	—	£65
2009 Proof	—	£85
2010 ("bullion")	—	£65
2010 Proof	—	£85
2011 ("bullion")	—	£65
2011 Proof	—	£85
2012 Day's St George and Dragon BU "bullion"	—	£75
2012 — Proof	—	£85
2013 ("bullion")	—	£65
2013 Proof	—	£85
2014 ("bullion")	—	£75
2014 Proof	—	£110
2015 Proof	—	£110
2016 Butler Portrait Proof	—	—

ONE POUND

Introduced into circulation in 1983 to replace the £1 note, all are minted in nickel-brass unless otherwise stated. The reverse changed yearly until 2008, and until 2008 the Royal Arms was the "definitive" version. 2008 also saw the introduction of the Matthew Dent Uncrowned Shield of the Royal Arms, a new "definitive", and this reverse appeared in 2008 and every year since then. A Capital Cities Series of two coins each year for two years commenced in 2010. From 2013 a further 4-coin series over two years was issued, portraying two floral emblems associated with each of the four countries making up the United Kingdom. Collectors and others should be aware of the many different counterfeit £1 coin versions in circulation, a high proportion of which do not have matching obverses and reverses although many do.

A 12-sided bi-metallic coin will replace the current £1 coin in 2017, and will incorporate several security features to help defeat the counterfeiters.

1983, 1993, 1998, 2003
EDGE: DECUS ET TUTAMEN

DATE	Mintage	UNC
1983 Royal Arms	443,053,510	£3
1983 — BU	1,134,000	£5
1983 — Proof	107,800	£8
1983 — Silver Proof	50,000	£32
1983 — — — Piedfort	10,000	£85
1984 Scottish Thistle	146,256,501	£3
1984 — BU	199,430	£6
1984 — Proof	106,520	£8
1984 — Silver Proof	44,855	£35
1984 — — — Piedfort	15,000	£50
1985 *New portrait.* Welsh Leek	228,430,749	£3
1985 — BU	213,679	£5
1985 — Proof	102,015	£6
1985 — Silver Proof	50,000	£35
1985 — — — Piedfort	15,000	£50
1986 Northern Ireland Flax	10,409,501	£3
1986 — BU	—	£6
1986 — Proof	—	£7
1986 — Silver Proof	37,958	£35
1986 — — — Piedfort	15,000	£50
1987 English Oak	39,298,502	£3
1987 — BU	—	£5
1987 — Proof	—	£8
1987 — Silver Proof	50,000	£35
1987 — — — Piedfort	15,000	£50
1988 Crowned Shield Of The Royal Arms	7,118,825	£4
1988 — BU	—	£6
1988 — Proof	—	£8
1988 — Silver Proof	50,000	£35
1988 — — — Piedfort	10,000	£60
1989 Scottish Thistle	70,580,501	£4
1989 — BU	—	£6
1989 — Proof	—	£9
1989 — Silver Proof	22,275	£35
1989 — — — Piedfort	10,000	£50
1990 Welsh Leek	—	£4
1990 — BU	97,269,302	£6
1990 — Proof	—	£7
1990 — Silver Proof	23,277	£35
1991 Northern Ireland Flax	38,443,575	£3
1991 — BU	—	£6
1991 — Proof	—	£9
1991 — Silver Proof	22,922	£35
1992 English Oak	36,320,487	£2
1992 — BU	—	£6
1992 — Proof	—	£7
1992 — Silver Proof	13,065	£35
1993 Royal Arms	114,744,500	£3
1993 — BU	—	£6

1984, 1989
NEMO ME IMPUNE LACESSIT

1985, 1990
PLEIDIOL WYF I'M GWLAD

1986, 1991
DECUS ET TUTAMEN

1987, 1992
DECUS ET TUTAMEN

DATE	Mintage	UNC
1993 — Proof	—	£7
1993 — Silver Proof	16,526	£35
1993 — — — Piedfort	12,500	£55
1994 Scottish Lion	29,752,525	£4
1994 — BU...	—	£6
1994 — Proof	—	£8
1994 — Silver Proof	25,000	£35
1994 — — — Piedfort	11,722	£55
1995 Welsh Dragon	34,503,501	£3
1995 — BU...	—	£6
1995 — — (Welsh)	—	£7
1995 — Proof	—	£10
1995 — Silver Proof	27,445	£35
1995 — — — Piedfort	8,458	£65
1996 Northern Ireland Celtic Cross	89,886,000	£4
1996 — BU...	—	£6
1996 — Proof	—	£7
1996 — Silver Proof	25,000	£35
1996 — — — Piedfort	10,000	£55
1997 English Lions	57,117,450	£4
1997 — BU...	—	£6
1997 — Proof	—	£7
1997 — Silver Proof	20,137	£35
1997 — — — Piedfort	10,000	£55
1998 **New portrait.** Royal Arms. BU........................	—	£12
1998 — Proof	—	£15
1998 — Silver Proof	13,863	£35
1998 — — — Piedfort	7,894	£50
1999 Scottish Lion. BU	—	£12
1999 — Proof	—	£15
1999 — Silver Proof	16,328	£35
1999 — — — Reverse Frosting..............................	—	£45
1999 — — — Piedfort	9,975	£60
2000 Welsh Dragon	109,496,500	£3
2000 — BU...	—	£6
2000 — Proof	—	£8
2000 — Silver Proof	15,913	£35
2000 — — — Reverse Frosting..............................	—	£45
2000 — — — Piedfort	9,994	£55
2001 Northern Ireland Celtic Cross.	63,968,065	£3
2001 — BU...	58,093,731	£6
2001 — Proof	—	£8
2001 — Silver Proof	11,697	£35
2001 — — — Reverse Frosting..............................	—	£45
2001 — — — Piedfort	8,464	£50
2002 English Lions	77,818,000	£3
2002 — BU...	—	£5
2002 — Proof	—	£8
2002 — Silver Proof	17,693	£35
2002 — — — Reverse Frosting..............................	—	£45
2002 — — — Piedfort	6,599	£50
2002 — Gold Proof...	—	£425
2003 Royal Arms	61,596,500	£4
2003 — BU...	—	£6
2003 — Proof	—	£10
2000 — Silver Proof	15,830	£35
2003 — — — Piedfort	9,871	£50
2004 Forth Railway Bridge	39,162,000	£4
2004 — BU...	—	£6
2004 — Proof	—	£10
2004 — Silver Proof	11,470	£35
2004 — — — Piedfort	7,013	£50
2004 — Gold Proof...	—	£425
2005 Menai Bridge	99,429,500	£4
2005 — BU...	—	£6
2005 — Proof	—	£10
2005 — Silver Proof	8,371	£35

1988
DECUS ET TUTAMEN

1994, 1999
NEMO ME IMPUNE LACESSIT

1995, 2000
PLEIDIOL WYF I'M GWLAD

1996, 2001
DECUS ET TUTAMEN

1997, 2002
DECUS ET TUTAMEN

2004
PATTERNED EDGE

DATE	Mintage	UNC
2005 — — — Piedfort	6,007	£50
2005 — Gold Proof	—	£425
2006 Egyptian Arch	38,938,000	£4
2006 — BU	—	£6
2006 — Proof	—	£10
2006 — Silver Proof	14,765	£35
2006 — — — Piedfort	5,129	£50
2006 — Gold Proof	—	£425
2007 Gateshead Millennium Bridge	26,180,160	£4
2007 — BU	—	£6
2007 — Proof	—	£10
2007 — Silver Proof	10,110	£40
2007 — — — Piedfort	5,739	£50
2007 — Gold Proof	—	£425
2008 Royal Arms	3,910,000	£4
2008 — BU	—	£6
2008 — Proof	—	£8
2008 — Silver Proof	8,441	£35
2008 — Gold Proof	—	£425
2008 — Platinum Proof	—	£500
2008 A series of 14 different reverses, the 25th Anniversary of the modern £1 coin, Silver Proof with selected gold highlighting on the reverses. the latter being all those used since 1983, the coins being with appropriate edge lettering	—	£400
2008 The same as above, Gold Proof (the 2008 Royal Arms being already listed above)	—	£5800
2008 **New Rev.,** Shield of the Royal Arms, no border beads on Obv.	29,518,000	£3
2008 BU	—	£5
2008 Proof	—	£6
2008 Silver Proof	5,000	£35
2008 Silver Proof Piedfort	4,202	£55
2008 Gold Proof	—	£450
2008 Platinum Proof	—	£575
2009	7,820,000	£4
2009 BU	—	£5
2009 Proof	—	£6
2009 Silver Proof	8,508	£35
2009 Gold Proof	—	£595
2010	38,505,000	£4
2010 BU	—	£5
2010 Proof	—	£6
2010 Silver BU	—	£30
2010 — Proof	—	£40
2010 City Series (London)	2,635,000	£4
2010 — BU	—	£5
2010 — Proof	—	£6
2010 — Silver Proof	7,693	£40
2010 — — — Piedfort	3,682	£55
2010 — Gold Proof	—	£450
2010 City Series (Belfast)	6,205,000	£3
2010 — BU	—	£5
2010 — Proof	—	£6
2010 — Silver Proof	5,805	£35
2010 — — — Piedfort	3,503	£55
2010 — Gold Proof	—	£500
2011	25,415,000	£2
2011 BU	—	£3
2011 Proof	—	£8
2011 Silver BU (in 21st and 18th Birthday cards)	—	£45
2011 — Proof	—	£55
2011 City Series (Cardiff)	1,615,000	£4

2005
PATTERNED EDGE

2006
PATTERNED EDGE

2007
PATTERNED EDGE

2008 (proof sets—silver and gold)
DECUS ET TUTAMEN

2008, 2009, 2010, 2011
DECUS ET TUTAMEN

2011
**Y DDRAIG GOCH
DDYRY CYCHWYN**

DATE	Mintage	UNC
2011 — BU	—	£5
2011 — Proof	—	£7
2011 — Silver Proof	5,553	£40
2011 — — — Piedfort	1,615	£60
2011 — Gold Proof	—	£500
2011 City Series (Edinburgh)	935,000	£4
2011 — BU	—	£5
2011 — Proof	—	£8
2011 — Silver Proof	4,973	£45
2011 — — — Piedfort	2,696	£60
2011 — Gold Proof	—	£500
2012	35,700,030	£3
2012 BU	—	£5
2012 Proof	—	£8
2012 Silver BU (in Silver Baby Gift)	—	£75
2012 Silver Proof	—	£50
2012 — with selective gold plating	—	£35
2012 Gold Proof	—	£450
2013	13,690,500	£3
2013 BU	—	£6
2013 Proof	—	£8
2013 Silver BU	—	£60
2013 Silver Proof	—	£45
2013 Gold Proof	—	£450
2013 Floral Series (England)	5,270,000	£3
2013 — BU	—	£6
2013 — Proof	—	£10
2013 — Silver Proof	—	£45
2013 — — — Piedfort	—	£60
2013 — Gold Proof	—	£500
2013 Floral Series (Wales)	5,270,000	£3
2013 — BU	—	£6
2013 — Proof	—	£10
2013 — Silver Proof	—	£45
2013 — — — Piedfort	—	£60
2013 — Gold Proof	—	£500
2013 Royal Coat of Arms (Sewell), Gold Proof	—	£500
2013 Crowned Royal Arms (Gorringe), Gold Proof	—	£500

(The above two coins are part of a set of three, along with the 2013 gold proof, with definitive reverse with Uncrowned Royal Arms (Dent)).

2014	—	£3
2014 BU	—	£6
2014 Proof	—	£10
2014 Silver BU	—	£50
2014 Silver Proof	—	£55
2014 Floral Series (Scotland)	—	£3
2014 — BU	—	£6
2014 — Proof	—	£10
2014 — Silver Proof	—	£45
2014 — — — Piedfort	—	£60
2014 — Gold Proof	—	£850
2014 Floral Series (Northern Ireland)	£0	
2014 — BU	—	£6
2014 — Proof	—	£10
2014 — Silver Proof	—	£45
2014 — — — Piedfort	—	£60
2014 — Gold Proof	—	£850
2015	—	£3
2015 BU	—	£6
2015 Proof	—	£10
2015 Silver Proof	—	£50
2015 Gold Proof	—	£450
2015 Platinum Proof	—	—
2015 New Portrait BU	—	£3

2011
NISI DOMINUS FRUSTRA

2013 Wales £1 Floral gold proof.

Most £1 coins are also available in precious metals.

2014 Scotland £1 Floral gold proof.

2015

DATE	Mintage	UNC
2015 — Proof	—	£10
2015 — Silver Proof	—	£50
2015 — Gold Proof	—	£450
2015 — Platinum Proof	—	£650
2015 — Heraldic Royal Arms	—	£3
2015 — — BU	—	£6
2015 — — Silver Proof	—	£50
2015 — — — —Piedfort	—	£100
2015 — — Gold Proof	—	£450
2016 BU	—	£4
2016 Proof	—	£8
2016 Silver Proof	—	£45
2016 The Last Round Pound BU	—	—
2016 — Proof	—	—
2016 — Silver Proof	—	—
2016 — — — Piedfort	—	—
2016 — Gold Proof	—	—

2016 The last round pound

FIFTY PENCE

Introduced as legal tender for 10 shillings to replace the banknote of that value prior to decimalisation, coins of the original size are no longer legal tender. Unless otherwise stated, i.e. for commemoratives, the reverse design is of Britannia. The reverse legend of NEW PENCE became FIFTY PENCE from 1982.

The description of "Unc" has been used against some 50 pence pieces dated 2009 and 2011 (for Olympic and Paralympic sports) to distinguish them from coins minted to circulation standard and BU standard, being a standard between the latter two. The uncirculated standard coins have a more even rim than the circulation standard examples, particularly observable on the obverse.

All 29 sports coins dated 2011 have now been issued to circulation, a million or more of each (below). There is no limit to each of the uncirculated versions, while there is a 30,000 limit to each silver BU version.

DATE	Mintage	UNC
1969	188,400,000	£6
1970	19,461,500	£5
1971 Proof	—	£8
1972 Proof	—	£7
1973 Accession to EEC	89,775,000	£3
1973 — Proof	—	£5
1973 — Silver Proof Piedfort	—	£3000
1974 Proof	—	£7
1975 Proof	—	£8
1976	43,746,500	£5
1976 Proof	—	£7
1977	49,536,000	£5
1977 Proof	—	£6
1978	72,005,000	£5
1978 Proof	—	£6
1979	58,680,000	£5
1979 Proof	—	£6
1980	89,086,000	£5
1980 Proof	—	£6
1981	74,002,000	£6
1981 Proof	—	£8
1982	51,312,000	£5
1982 Unc	—	£6
1982 Proof	—	£8
1983	62,824,000	£5
1983 Unc	—	£6
1983 Proof	—	£8
1984 BU	—	£6
1984 Proof	—	£8
1985 *New portrait* estimated approx	3,400,000	£3
1985 BU	—	£5
1985 Proof	—	£6
1986 BU	—	£5
1986 Proof	—	£12

New reverses.

Accession to the EEC 1973.

DATE	Mintage	UNC
1987 BU	—	£4
1987 Proof	—	£12
1988 BU	—	£4
1988 Proof	—	£12
1989 BU	—	£4
1989 Proof	—	£12
1990 BU	—	£4
1990 Proof	—	£12
1991 BU	—	£5
1991 Proof	—	£12
1992 BU	—	£7
1992 Proof	—	£12
1992 Presidency of EC Council and EC accession 20th anniversary (includes 1993 date)	109,000	£12
1992 — BU	—	£12
1992 — Proof	—	£14
1992 — Silver Proof	26,890	£35
1992 — — — Piedfort	10,993	£55
1992 — Gold Proof	—	£500
1993 BU	—	£5
1993 Proof	—	£12
1994 50th Anniversary of the Normandy Landings	6,705,520	£3
1994 — BU (also in presentation folder)	—	£5
1994 — Proof	—	£12
1994 — Silver Proof	40,000	£35
1994 — — — Piedfort	10,000	£60
1994 — Gold Proof	—	£500
1995 BU	—	£8
1995 Proof	—	£12
1996 BU	—	£8
1996 Proof	—	£12
1996 Silver Proof	—	£25
1997 BU	—	£8
1997 Proof	—	£10
1997 Silver Proof	—	£25
1997 **New reduced size**	456,364,100	£4
1997 BU	—	£5
1997 Proof	—	£6
1997 Silver Proof	—	£25
1997 — — Piedfort	—	£35
1998 **New portrait**	64,306,500	£3
1998 BU	—	£5
1998 Proof	—	£8
1998 Presidency and 25th anniversary of EU entry	5,043,000	£4
1998 — BU	—	£5
1998 — Proof	—	£8
1998 — Silver Proof	8,859	£30
1998 — — — Piedfort	8,440	£45
1998 — Gold Proof	—	£450
1998 50th Anniversary of the National Health Service	5,001,000	£3
1998 — BU	—	£5
1998 — Silver Proof	9,032	£30
1998 — — — Piedfort	5,117	£45
1998 — Gold Proof	—	£450
1999	24,905,000	£2
1999 BU	—	£5
1999 Proof	—	£10
2000	27,915,500	£2
2000 BU	—	£5
2000 Proof	—	£7
2000 150th Anniversary of Public Libraries	11,263,000	£5
2000 — BU	—	£6
2000 — Proof	—	£9
2000 — Silver Proof	7,634	£30
2000 — — — Piedfort	5,721	£45
2000 — Gold proof	—	£400
2001	84,998,500	£2
2001 BU	—	£5
2001 Proof	—	£7

Presidency of the EC Council 1992.

1994

1998 EU Presidency

1998 NHS

2000 Public Libraries

DATE	Mintage	UNC
2002..	23,907,500	£2
2002 BU	—	£5
2002 Proof......................................	—	£7
2002 Gold Proof	—	£375
2003..	23,583,000	£2
2003 BU	—	£5
2003 Proof......................................	—	£6
2003 Suffragette............................	3,124,030	£2
2003 — BU	—	£6
2003 — Proof	—	£7
2003 — Silver Proof	6,267	£30
2003 — — — Piedfort	6,795	£45
2003 — Gold Proof.........................	—	£350
2004..	35,315,500	£1
2004 BU	—	£5
2004 Proof......................................	—	£8
2004 Roger Bannister....................	9,032,500	£5
2004 — BU	—	£6
2004 — Proof	—	£8
2004 — Silver Proof	4,924	£30
2004 — — — Piedfort	4,054	£45
2004 — Gold Proof.........................	—	£350
2005..	25,363,500	£3
2005 BU	—	£6
2005 Proof......................................	—	£8
2005 Samuel Johnson....................	17,649,000	£3
2005 — BU	—	£5
2005 — Proof	—	£8
2005 — Silver Proof	4,029	£30
2005 — — — Piedfort	3,808	£45
2005 — Gold Proof.........................	—	£350
2006..	24,567,000	£2
2006 Proof......................................	—	£8
2006 Silver Proof............................	—	£30
2006 Victoria Cross, The Award.....	12,087,000	£3
2006 — BU	—	£5
2006 — Proof	—	£8
2006 — Silver Proof	6,310	£30
2006 — — — — Piedfort.................	3,532	£50
2006 — Gold Proof.........................	—	£350
2006 Victoria Cross, Heroic Acts....	10,000,500	£2
2006 — BU	—	£5
2006 — Proof	—	£8
2006 — Silver Proof	6,872	£30
2006 — — — — Piedfort.................	3,415	£50
2006 — Gold Proof.........................	—	£350
2007	5,300,000	£2
2007 BU	—	£6
2007 Proof......................................	—	£8
2007 Centenary of Scout Movement	7,710,750	£5
2007 — BU	—	£8
2007 — Proof	—	£12
2007 — Silver Proof	10,895	£30
2007 — — — Piedfort	1,555	£65
2007 — Gold Proof.........................	—	£400
2008	700,000	£2
2008 — BU	—	£5
2008 — Proof	—	£6
2008 — Silver Proof	—	£25
2008 — Gold Proof.........................	—	£400
2008 — Platinum Proof	—	£1550
2008 **New Shield Rev.** Obv. rotated by approx. 26 degrees	12,320,000	£5
2008 BU	—	£6
2008 Proof......................................	—	£8
2008 Silver Proof............................	—	£25
2008 Silver Proof Piedfort	—	£45
2008 Gold Proof..............................	—	£400
2008 Platinum Proof.......................	—	£1550

DATE	Mintage	UNC
2009 BU	—	£4
2009 Proof	—	£6
2009 Silver Proof	—	£20
2009 250th Anniversary of Kew Gardens	210,000	£30
2009 — BU	—	£75
2009 — Proof	—	£85
2009 — Silver Proof	7,575	£125
2009 — — Piedfort	2,967	£150
2009 — Gold Proof	—	£500
2009 Olympic and Paralympic Sports (Track & Field Athletics) Unc (Blue Peter Pack)	—	£10
2009 16 different reverses from the past marking the 40th Anniversary of the 50p coin. Proof	1,039	£300
2009 — Silver Proof	1,163	£650
2009 — Gold Proof	125	£8000
2009 — — Piedfort	40	£20,950
2010 BU	—	£4
2010 Proof	—	£25
2010 Silver Proof	—	£35
2010 100 years of Girl Guiding UK	7,410,090	£2
2010 — BU	—	£7
2010 — Proof	—	£20
2010 — Silver Proof	5,271	£35
2010 — — Piedfort	2,879	£55
2010 — Gold Proof	—	£575
2011 BU	—	£2
2011 Proof	—	£8
2011 Silver Proof	—	£45
2011 50th Anniversary of the WWF	3,400,000	£2
2011 — BU	—	£5
2011 — Proof	—	£25
2011 — Silver Proof	24,870	£45
2011 — — Piedfort	2,244	£65
2011 — Gold Proof	—	£675
2011 Olympic & Paralympic Sports Issues:		
Aquatics Unc, head clear of lines	2,179,000	£2
— Head with lines BU (as illustrated top right)	—	£750
— Head clear of lines. BU	—	£4
— Silver BU	30,000	£25
Archery Unc	3,345,000	£2
— BU	—	£3
— Silver BU	30,000	£25
Athletics Unc	2,224,000	£2
— BU	—	£3
— Silver BU	30,000	£25
Badminton Unc	2,133,000	£2
— BU	—	£3
— Silver BU	30,000	£25
Basketball Unc	1,748,000	£2
— BU	—	£3
— Silver BU	30,000	£25

For the rest of the Olympic series see overleaf and page 268.

DATE	Mintage	UNC
2011 Olympic & Paralympic issues continued		
Boccia Unc	2,166,000	£2
— BU	—	£3
— Silver BU	30,000	£25
Boxing Unc	2,148,000	£2
— BU	—	£3
— Silver BU	30,000	£25
Canoeing Unc	2,166,000	£2
— BU	—	£3
— Silver BU	30,000	£25
Cycling Unc	2,090,000	£2
— BU	—	£3
— Silver BU	30,000	£25
Equestrian Unc	2,142,000	£2
— BU	—	£3
— Silver BU	30,000	£25
Fencing Unc	2,115,000	£2
— BU	—	£3
— Silver BU	30,000	£25
Football Unc	1,125,000	£2
— BU	—	£3
— Silver Bu	30,000	£25
Goalball Unc	1,615,000	£2
— BU	—	£3
— Silver BU	30,000	£25
Gymnastics Unc	1,720,000	£1
— BU	—	£3
— Silver BU	30,000	£25
Handball Unc	1,676,000	£2
— BU	—	£3
— Silver BU	30,000	£25
Hockey Unc	1,773,000	£2
— BU	—	£3
— Silver BU	30,000	£25
Judo Unc	1,161,000	£2
— BU	—	£3
— Silver BU	30,000	£25
Modern Pentathlon Unc	1,689,000	£2
— BU	—	£3
— Silver BU	30,000	£25
Rowing Unc	1,717,000	£2
— BU	—	£3
— Silver BU	30,000	£25
Sailing Unc	1,749,000	£2
— BU	—	£3
— Silver BU	30,000	£25
Shooting Unc	1,656,000	£2
— BU	—	£3
— Silver BU	30,000	£25
Table Tennis Unc	1,737,000	£2
— BU	—	£3
— Silver BU	30,000	£25
Taekwondo Unc	1,664,000	£2
— BU	—	£3
— Silver BU	30,000	£25
Tennis Unc	1,454,000	£2
— BU	—	£3
— Silver BU	30,000	£25
Triathlon Unc	1,163,000	£2
— BU	—	£3
— Silver BU	30,000	£25
Volleyball Unc	2,133,000	£2
— BU	—	£3
— Silver BU	30,000	£25
Weightlifting Unc	1,879,000	£2
— BU	—	£3
— Silver BU	30,000	£25

DATE	Mintage	UNC
2011 Olympic & Paralympic issues continued		
Wheelchair Rugby Unc	1,765,000	£2
— BU...	—	£3
— Silver BU	30,000	£25
Wrestling Unc..	1,129,000	£2
— BU...	—	£3
— Silver BU	30,000	£25

Note—Each of the artists of the 29 Olympic sports above was presented with a gold proof coin with their own design. The Track & Field Athletics design coin was dated 2009, the Cycling was dated 2010, and the remaining 2011. No other examples of these coins were issued.

2012	32,300,030	£2
2012 BU	—	£5
2012 Proof...	—	£10
2012 Silver Proof with selective gold plating	—	£20
2012 Gold Proof..	—	£500
2012 Gold Proof Piedfort. The 11 Olympic sports in which the United Kingdom Team GB achieved a Gold Medal was celebrated with an issue of 29 Piedfort coins for each sport, some in sets, some as individual coins (see under Proof and Specimen sets)	—	—
2013	10,301,000	£2
2013 BU	—	£5
2013 Proof...	—	£10
2013 Silver Proof...	—	£55
2013 Gold Proof..	—	£450
2013 100th anniversary of birth of Christopher Ironside	7,000,000	£2
2013 — BU...	—	£5
2013 — Proof..	—	£12
2013 — Silver Proof	—	£45
2013 — — — Piedfort..	—	£90
2013 — Gold Proof..	—	£450
2013 Centenary of the Birth of Benjamin Britten	5,300,000	£2
2013 — BU...	—	£5
2013 — Silver Proof	—	£55
2013 — — — Piedfort..	—	£90
2013 — Gold Proof..	—	£450
2014	—	£2
2014 BU	—	£5
2014 Proof...	—	£12
2014 Silver Proof...	—	£55
2014 XX Commonwealth Games	—	£2
2014 — BU...	—	£5
2014 — Proof	—	£12
2014 — Silver Proof	—	£45
2014 — — — Piedfort..	—	£100
2014 — Gold Proof..	—	£450
2015	—	£2
2015 BU	—	£5
2015 Proof...	—	£10
2015 Silver Proof...	—	£30
2015 Gold Proof..	—	£350
2015 Platinum Proof..	—	—
2015 Battle of Britain 75th Anniversary BU...............	—	£2
2015 — Proof	—	£12
2015 — Silver Proof	—	£30
2015 — — — Piedfort..	—	£80
2015 — Gold Proof..	—	£350
2015 New Portrait..	—	£2
2015 — BU...	—	£5
2015 — Proof	—	£12
2015 — Silver Proof	—	£30
2015 — Gold Proof..	—	£350
2015 — Platinum Proof	—	—
2016	—	—
2016 BU	—	—

For the remainder of the 29 coins in the 2011 Olympic and Paralympic series see page 268.

DATE	Mintage	UNC
2016 Proof...	—	—
2016 Silver Proof...	—	—
2016 Battle of Hastings 950th Anniversary...............	—	—
2016 — BU...	—	—
2016 — Proof...	—	—
2016 — Silver Proof.......................................	—	—
2016 — — — Piedfort......................................	—	—
2016 — Gold Proof...	—	—
2016 Beatrix Potter 150th Anniversary...................	—	—
2016 — BU...	—	—
2016 — Proof...	—	—
2016 — Silver Proof.......................................	—	—
2016 — — — Piedfort......................................	—	—
2016 — Gold Proof...	—	—
2016 Peter Rabbit..	—	—
2016 — BU...	—	—
2016 — Silver Proof.......................................	—	—
2016 Jemima Puddle-Duck..................................	—	—
2016 — BU...	—	—
2016 — Silver Proof.......................................	—	—
2016 Mrs. Tiggy-Winkle....................................	—	—
2016 — BU...	—	—
2016 — Silver Proof.......................................	—	—
2016 Squirrel Nutkin.......................................	—	—
2016 Team GB for Olympics...............................	—	—
2016 — BU...	—	—
2016 — Silver Proof.......................................	—	—
2016 — — Piedfort...	—	—
2016 — Gold Proof...	—	—

TWENTY-FIVE PENCE (CROWN)

This series is a continuation of the pre-decimal series, there having been four crowns to the pound. The coins below have a legal tender face value of 25p to this day, and are minted in cupro-nickel except where stated otherwise.

DATE	Mintage	UNC
1972 Royal Silver Wedding.............................	7,452,100	£2
1972 — Proof...	150,000	£8
1972 — Silver Proof.....................................	100,000	£30
1977 Silver Jubilee......................................	37,061,160	£2
1977 — in Presentation folder..........................	Incl. above	£3
1977 — Proof...	193,000	£8
1977 — Silver Proof.....................................	377,000	£25
1980 Queen Mother 80th Birthday......................	9,306,000	£2
1980 — in Presentation folder..........................	Incl. above	£3
1980 — Silver Proof.....................................	83,670	£30
1981 Royal Wedding.....................................	26,773,600	£2
1981 — in Presentation folder..........................	Incl. above	£3
1981 — Silver Proof.....................................	218,140	£30

TWENTY PENCE

The series commenced in 1982, some 11 years after the introduction of decimal coinage. Its presence from introduction date meant that there was no requirement for ten pence circulation-standard coins until the latter's size was reduced in 1992. Its alloy is uniquely 84% copper and 16% nickel, unlike the 75/25 of the fifty pence.

DATE	Mintage	UNC	DATE	Mintage	UNC
1982......................	740,815,000	£2	1982 Proof.....................................	—	£7
1982 Unc.................	—	£3	1982 Silver Proof Piedfort....................	—	£35

DATE	Mintage	UNC
1983	158,463,000	£1
1983 Unc	—	£3
1983 Proof	—	£6
1984	65,350,000	£1
1984 BU	—	£3
1984 Proof	—	£6
1985 **New portrait**	74,273,699	£2
1985 BU	—	£4
1985 Proof	—	£6
1986 BU	—	£5
1986 Proof	—	£8
1987	137,450,000	£1
1987 BU	—	£3
1987 Proof	—	£5
1988	38,038,344	£1
1988 BU	—	£3
1988 Proof	—	£5
1989	132,013,890	£1
1989 BU	—	£3
1989 Proof	—	£5
1990	88,097,500	£1
1990 BU	—	£3
1990 Proof	—	£6
1991	35,901,250	£1
1991 BU	—	£3
1991 Proof	—	£6
1992	Est. approx. 1,500,000	£4
1992 BU	—	£5
1992 **Enhanced effigy**		
	Est. approx. 29,705,000	£4
1992 — BU	—	£5
1992 — Proof	—	£8
1993	123,123,750	£1
1993 BU	—	£3
1993 Proof	—	£5
1994	67,131,250	£1
1994 BU	—	£3
1994 Proof	—	£5
1995	102,005,000	£1
1995 BU	—	£3
1995 Proof	—	£5
1996	83,163,750	£2
1996 BU	—	£3
1996 Proof	—	£5
1996 Silver Proof	—	£25
1997	89,518,750	£2
1997 BU	—	£3
1997 Proof	—	£5
1998 **New portrait**	76,965,000	£2
1998 BU	—	£4
1998 Proof	—	£5
1999	73,478,750	£2
1999 BU	—	£3
1999 Proof	—	£5
2000	136,428,750	£2
2000 BU	—	£3
2000 Proof	—	£5
2000 Silver Proof	—	£25
2001	148,122,500	£2
2001 BU	—	£3
2001 Proof	—	£5
2002	93,360,000	£2
2002 BU	—	£3
2002 Proof	—	£5
2002 Gold Proof	—	£225
2003	153,383,750	£2
2003 BU	—	£4
2003 Proof	—	£6
2004	120,212,500	£2
2004 BU	—	£4
2004 Proof	—	£6

DATE	Mintage	UNC
2005	124,488,750	£2
2005 BU	—	£4
2005 Proof	—	£6
2006	114,800,000	£2
2006 BU	—	£6
2006 Proof	—	£7
2006 Silver Proof	—	£25
2007	117,075,000	£2
2007 BU	—	£4
2007 Proof	—	£6
2008	11,900,000	£2
2008 BU	—	£4
2008 Proof	—	£7
2008 Silver Proof	—	£25
2008 Gold Proof	—	£250
2008 Platinum Proof	—	£750
2008 **New Rev.,** date on Obv.	81,920,000	£2
2008 — paired with old Obv. (thus no date)..		
Est. approx. 120,000 (?) .		£50
2008 BU	—	£3
2008 Proof	—	£6
2008 Silver Proof	—	£25
2008 — — Piedfort	—	£30
2008 Gold Proof	—	£250
2008 Platinum Proof	—	£750
2009	94,500,300	£2
2009 BU	—	£5
2009 Proof	—	£7
2009 Silver Proof	—	£25
2010	91,700,500	£2
2010 BU	—	£5
2010 Proof	—	£7
2010 Silver Proof	—	£25
2011	39,550,000	£2
2011 BU	—	£5
2011 Proof	—	£8
2011 Silver Proof	—	£25
2012	—	£2
2012 BU	—	£5
2012 Proof	—	£8
2012 Silver Proof (issued in set with Victorian		
4 Shilling piece)	—	£25
2012 — — with selective gold plating	—	£35
2012 Gold Proof	—	£300
2013	—	£2
2013 BU	—	£5
2013 Proof	—	£20
2013 Silver Proof	—	£20
2013 Gold Proof	—	£300
2014	—	£2
2014 BU	—	£5
2014 Proof	—	£10
2014 Silver Proof	—	£25
2015	—	—
2015 BU	—	—
2015 Proof	—	—
2015 Silver Proof	—	—
2015 Gold Proof	—	—
2015 Platinum Proof	—	—
2015 New Portrait	—	—
2015 — BU	—	—
2015 — Proof	—	—
2015 — Silver Proof	—	—
2015 — Gold Proof	—	—
2015 — Platinum Proof	—	—
2016	—	—
2016 BU	—	—
2016 Proof	—	—
2016 Silver Proof	—	—

TEN PENCE

The series commenced before decimalisation with the legend NEW PENCE, this changed to TEN PENCE from 1982. These "florin-sized" coins up to 1992 are no longer legal tender. Cupro-nickel was replaced by nickel-plated steel from 2011.

DATE	Mintage	UNC	DATE	Mintage	UNC
1968	336,143,250	£3	1994 Proof	—	£7
1969	314,008,000	£4	1995	43,259,000	£1
1970	133,571,000	£3	1995 BU	—	£5
1971	63,205,000	£3	1995 Proof	—	£7
1971 Proof	—	£4	1996	118,738,000	£2
1972 Proof only	—	£5	1996 BU	—	£4
1973	152,174,000	£3	1996 Proof	—	£7
1973 Proof	—	£4	1996 Silver Proof	—	£25
1974	92,741,000	£3	1997	99,196,000	£2
1974 Proof	—	£4	1997 BU	—	£4
1975	181,559,000	£3	1997 Proof	—	£4
1975 Proof	—	£4	1998 *New portrait* BU	—	£8
1976	228,220,000	£3	1998 Proof	—	£10
1976 Proof	—	£4	1999 BU	—	£4
1977	59,323,000	£6	1999 Proof	—	£11
1977 Proof	—	£8	2000	134,733,000	£1
1978 Proof	—	£6	2000 BU	—	£4
1979	115,457,000	£2	2000 Proof	—	£7
1979 Proof	—	£4	2000 Silver Proof	—	£15
1980	88,650,000	£3	2001	129,281,000	£1
1980 Proof	—	£4	2001 BU	—	£3
1981	3,487,000	£8	2001 Proof	—	£4
1981 Proof	—	£15	2002	80,934,000	£2
1982 BU	—	£4	2002 BU	—	£3
1982 Proof	—	£6	2002 Proof	—	£5
1983 BU	—	£3	2002 Gold Proof	—	£250
1983 Proof	—	£4	2003	88,118,000	£2
1984 BU	—	£4	2003 BU	—	£3
1984 Proof	—	£6	2003 Proof	—	£5
1985 *New portrait* BU	—	£5	2004	99,602,000	£1
1985 Proof	—	£7	2004 BU	—	£3
1986 BU	—	£4	2004 Proof	—	£5
1986 Proof	—	£6	2005	69,604,000	£1
1987 BU	—	£4	2005 BU	—	£2
1987 Proof	—	£7	2005 Proof	—	£4
1988 BU	—	£5	2006	118,803,000	£1
1988 Proof	—	£7	2006 BU	—	£3
1989 BU	—	£6	2006 Proof	—	£7
1989 Proof	—	£9	2006 Silver Proof	—	£25
1990 BU	—	£6	2007	72,720,000	£1
1990 Proof	—	£9	2007 BU	—	£4
1991 DU	—	£6	2007 Proof	—	£7
1991 Proof	—	£9	2008	9,720,000	£1
1992 BU	—	£5	2008 BU	—	£4
1992 Proof	—	£7	2008 Proof	—	£5
1992 Silver Proof	—	£12	2008 Silver Proof	—	£25
1992 *Size reduced (24.5mm)*	1,413,455,170	£3	2008 Gold Proof	—	£250
1992 BU	—	£4	2008 Platinum Proof	—	£450
1992 Proof	—	£5	2008 *New Rev.*, no border beads		
1992 Silver Proof	—	£12	on Obv.	53,900,000	£1
1992 — — Piedfort	—	£35	2008 BU	—	£4
1993 BU	—	£2	2008 Proof	—	£5
1993 Proof	—	£7	2008 Silver Proof	—	£25
1994 BU	—	£2	2008 — — Piedfort	—	£45

DATE	Mintage	UNC	DATE	Mintage	UNC
2008 Gold Proof	—	£250	2013 Silver Proof	—	£25
2008 Platinum Proof	—	£450	2013 Gold Proof	—	£250
2009	60,000,000	£1	2014	—	£1
2009 BU	—	£3	2014 BU	—	£5
2009 Proof	—	£5	2014 Proof	—	£12
2009 Silver Proof	—	£25	2014 Silver Proof	—	£25
2010	25,320,500	£1	2015	—	—
2010 BU	—	£5	2015 BU	—	—
2010 Proof	—	£7	2015 Proof	—	—
2010 Silver Proof	—	£25	2015 Silver Proof	—	—
2011 Nickel-plated steel	40,601,850	£1	2015 Gold Proof	—	—
2011 — BU	—	£5	2015 Platinum Proof	—	—
2011 — Proof	—	£10	2015 New Portrait	—	—
2011 Silver Proof	—	£25	2015 — BU	—	—
2012	—	£1	2015 — Proof	—	—
2012 BU	—	£5	2015 — Silver Proof	—	—
2012 Proof	—	£10	2015 — Gold Proof	—	—
2012 Silver proof with selective gold plating	—	£30	2015 — Platinum Proof	—	—
2012 Gold Proof	—	£250	2016	—	—
2013	—	£1	2016 BU	—	—
2013 BU	—	£5	2016 Proof	—	—
2013 Proof	—	£10	2016 Silver Proof	—	—

SIX PENCE

This new denomination has been struck, dated 2016, as part of the Royal Mint's gifting range. They are of Sterling silver to BU standard, and of diameter 19.41mm. Being similar in size to the pre-decimal 6d (or latterly 2 1/2p) they have also been marketed as part of a 3-coin set along with two old sixpences (£50), the 2016 6p being £30 on its own.

FIVE PENCE

This series commenced simultaneously with the Ten Pence (qv). They were the same size and weight as their predecessor, the shilling, and such coins up to 1990 are no longer legal tender. As with the Ten Pence, cupro-nickel was replaced by nickel-plated steel from 2011.

DATE	Mintage	UNC	DATE	Mintage	UNC
1968	98,868,250	£3	1981 Proof	—	£7
1969	120,270,000	£3	1982 BU	—	£7
1970	225,948,525	£3	1982 Proof	—	£9
1971	81,783,475	£3	1983 BU	—	£5
1971 Proof	—	£3	1983 Proof	—	£6
1972 Proof	—	£7	1984 BU	—	£4
1973 Proof	—	£8	1984 Proof	—	£6
1974 Proof	—	£8	1985 *New Portrait*. BU	—	£2
1975	141,539,000	£3	1985 Proof	—	£7
1975 Proof	—	£6	1986 BU	—	£2
1976 Proof	—	£7	1986 Proof	—	£7
1977	24,308,000	£8	1987	48,220,000	£1
1977 Proof	—	£9	1987 BU	—	£3
1978	61,094,000	£4	1987 Proof	—	£5
1978 Proof	—	£4	1988	120,744,610	£1
1979	155,456,000	£4	1988 BU	—	£3
1979 Proof	—	£4	1988 Proof		£5
1980	220,566,000	£3	1989	101,406,000	£1
1980 Proof	—	£4	1989 BU	—	£4

DATE	Mintage	UNC
1989 Proof	—	£5
1990 BU	—	£2
1990 Proof	—	£5
1990 Silver Proof	—	£15
1990 *Size reduced (18mm)*	1,634,976,005	£2
1990 BU	—	£3
1990 Proof	—	£4
1990 Silver Proof	—	£20
1990 — — Piedfort	—	£25
1991	724,979000	£1
1991 BU	—	£3
1991 Proof	—	£5
1992	453,173,500	£1
1992 BU	—	£3
1992 Proof	—	£7
1993 BU	—	£3
1993 Proof	—	£5
1994	93,602,000	£1
1994 BU	—	£5
1994 Proof	—	£7
1995	183,384,000	£1
1995 BU	—	£5
1995 Proof	—	£7
1996	302,902,000	£1
1996 BU	—	£4
1996 Proof	—	£7
1996 Silver proof	—	£25
1997	236,596,000	£1
1997 BU	—	£4
1997 Proof	—	£7
1998 *New portrait*	217,376,000	£1
1998 BU	—	£4
1998 Proof	—	£7
1999	195,490,000	£1
1999 BU	—	£4
1999 Proof	—	£7
2000	388,512,000	£1
2000 BU	—	£4
2000 Proof	—	£7
2000 Silver Proof	—	£25
2001	337,930,000	£1
2001 BU	—	£3
2001 Proof	—	£5
2002	219,258,000	£1
2002 BU	—	£3
2002 Proof	—	£5
2002 Gold Proof	—	£150
2003	333,230,000	£1
2003 BU	—	£3
2003 Proof	—	£5
2004	271,010,000	£1
2004 BU	—	£3
2004 Proof	—	£5
2005	236,212,000	£1
2005 BU	—	£3
2005 Proof	—	£5
2006	317,697,000	£1
2006 BU	—	£3
2006 Proof	—	£7
2006 Silver Proof	—	£25

DATE	Mintage	UNC
2007	246,720,000	£1
2007 BU	—	£5
2007 Proof	—	£7
2008	86,400,000	£1
2008 BU	—	£3
2008 Proof	—	£5
2008 Silver Proof	—	£20
2008 Gold Proof	—	£150
2008 Platinum Proof	—	£250
2008 *New Rev.,* no border beads on Obv	109,460,000	£1
2008 BU	—	£4
2008 Proof	—	£5
2008 Silver Proof	—	£15
2008 — — Piedfort	—	£35
2008 Gold Proof	—	£150
2008 Platinum Proof	—	£250
2009	125,520,300	£1
2009 BU	—	£6
2009 Proof	—	£7
2009 Silver Proof	—	£15
2010	180,250,500	£1
2010 BU	—	£4
2010 Proof	—	£5
2010 Silver Proof	—	£15
2011 Nickel-plated steel	50,400,000	£1
2011 — BU	—	£4
2011 — Proof	—	£6
2011 Silver Proof	—	£15
2012	—	£1
2012 BU	—	£5
2012 Proof	—	£8
2012 Silver Proof with selective gold plating	—	£15
2012 Gold Proof	—	£150
2013	—	£1
2013 BU	—	£5
2013 Proof	—	£8
2013 Silver Proof	—	£20
2013 Gold Proof	—	£150
2014	—	£1
2014 BU	—	£5
2014 Proof	—	£8
2014 Silver Proof	—	£20
2015	—	—
2015 BU	—	—
2015 Proof	—	—
2015 Silver Proof	—	—
2015 Gold Proof	—	—
2015 Platinum Proof	—	—
2015 New Portrait	—	—
2015 — BU	—	—
2015 — Proof	—	—
2015 — Silver Proof	—	—
2015 — Gold Proof	—	—
2015 — Platinum Proof	—	—
2016	—	—
2016 BU	—	—
2016 Proof	—	—
2016 Silver Proof	—	—

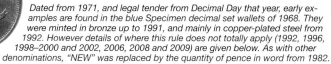

TWO PENCE

*Dated from 1971, and legal tender from Decimal Day that year, early ex-
amples are found in the blue Specimen decimal set wallets of 1968. They
were minted in bronze up to 1991, and mainly in copper-plated steel from
1992. However details of where this rule does not totally apply (1992, 1996,
1998–2000 and 2002, 2006, 2008 and 2009) are given below. As with other
denominations, "NEW" was replaced by the quantity of pence in word from 1982.*

DATE	Mintage	UNC	DATE	Mintage	UNC
1971	1,454,856,250	£2	1993	235,674,000	£1
1971 Proof	—	£3	1993 BU	—	£2
1972 Proof	—	£5	1993 Proof	—	£3
1973 Proof	—	£6	1994	531,628,000	£1
1974 Proof	—	£6	1994 BU	—	£2
1975	Est. approx. 273,145,000	£2	1994 Proof	—	£5
1975 Proof	—	£2	1995	124,482,000	£1
1976	Est. approx. 53,779,000	£2	1995 BU	—	£2
1976 Proof	—	£2	1995 Proof	—	£5
1977	109,281,000	£2	1996	296,278,000	£1
1977 Proof	—	£2	1996 BU	—	£2
1978	189,658,000	£3	1996 Proof	—	£5
1978 Proof	—	£2	1996 Silver Proof	—	£25
1979	260,200,000	£2	1997	496,116,000	£1
1979 Proof	408,527,000	£2	1997 BU	—	£2
1980	—	£1	1997 Proof	—	£5
1980 Proof	—	£2	1998 *New portrait*	Est. approx. 120,243,000	£1
1981	353,191,000	£4	1998 BU	—	£2
1981 Proof	—	£4	1998 Proof	—	£4
1982 Legend changed to TWO PENCE	—	£4	1998 Bronze	Est. approx. 93,587,000	£1
1982 Proof	—	£5	1999	353,816,000	£1
1983	—	£2	1999 Bronze BU	—	£2
1983 Error NEW instead of TWO	—	£850	1999 — Proof	—	£4
1983 Proof	—	£4	2000	536,659,000	£1
1984	—	£2	2000 BU	—	£3
1984 Proof	—	£4	2000 Proof	—	£5
1985 *New portrait*	107,113,000	£2	2000 Silver Proof	—	£22
1985 BU	—	£2	2001	551,880,000	£1
1985 Proof	—	£4	2001 BU	—	£2
1986	168,967,500	£1	2001 Proof	—	£4
1986 BU	—	£2	2002	168,556,000	£1
1986 Proof	—	£4	2002 BU	—	£3
1987	218,100,750	£1	2002 Proof	—	£4
1987 BU	—	£2	2002 Gold Proof	—	£275
1987 Proof	—	£4	2003	260,225,000	£1
1988	419,889,000	£1	2003 BU	—	£2
1988 BU	—	£2	2003 Proof	—	£4
1988 Proof	—	£4	2004	356,396,000	£1
1989	359,226,000	£1	2004 BU	—	£2
1989 BU	—	£2	2004 Proof	—	£4
1989 Proof	—	£4	2005	280,396,000	£1
1990	204,499,700	£1	2005 BU	—	£2
1990 BU	—	£2	2005 Proof	—	£3
1990 Proof	—	£3	2006	170,637,000	£1
1991	86,625,250	£1	2006 BU	—	£3
1991 BU	—	£2	2006 Proof	—	£4
1991 Proof	—	£5	2006 Silver Proof	—	£15
1992 Copper plated steel	102,247,000	£1	2007	254,500,000	£2
1992 Bronze BU	—	£2	2007 BU	—	£3
1992 — Proof	—	£5	2007 Proof	—	£5

DATE	Mintage	UNC	DATE	Mintage	UNC
2008	10,600,000	£2	2012 Proof	—	£8
2008 BU	—	£3	2012 Silver Proof with selective gold plating	—	£45
2008 Proof	—	£5	2012 Gold Proof	—	£250
2008 Silver Proof	—	£25	2013	—	£2
2008 Gold Proof	—	£275	2013 BU	—	£3
2008 Platinum Proof	—	£450	2013 Proof	—	£8
2008 New Rev.,			2013 Silver Proof	—	£25
no border beads on Obv	129,530,000	£2	2013 Gold Proof	—	£250
2008 — BU	—	£3	2014	—	£2
2008 — Proof	—	£5	2014 BU	—	£3
2008 — Silver Proof	—	£20	2014 Proof	—	£8
2008 — Silver Proof Piedfort	—	£45	2014 Silver Proof	—	£45
2008 — Gold Proof	—	£300	2015	—	—
2008 — Platinum Proof	—	£500	2015 BU	—	—
2009	65,200,000	£2	2015 Proof	—	—
2009 BU	—	£3	2015 Silver Proof	—	—
2009 Proof	—	£5	2015 Gold Proof	—	—
2009 Silver Proof	—	£25	2015 Platinum Proof	—	—
2010	38,000,000	£2	2015 New Portrait	—	—
2010 BU	—	£3	2015 — BU	—	—
2010 Proof	—	£6	2015 — Proof	—	—
2010 Silver Proof	—	£25	2015 — Silver Proof	—	—
2011	93,900,000	£2	2015 — Gold Proof	—	—
2011 BU	—	£3	2015 — Platinum Proof	—	—
2011 Proof	—	£6	2016	—	—
2011 Silver Proof	—	£25	2016 BU	—	—
2012	—	£2	2016 Proof	—	—
2012 BU	—	£3	2016 Silver Proof	—	—

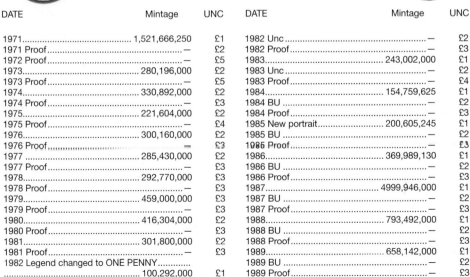

ONE PENNY

The history of this coin is very similar to that of the Two Pence coin (qv) except that all 1998 examples were of copper-plated steel.

DATE	Mintage	UNC	DATE	Mintage	UNC
1971	1,521,666,250	£1	1982 Unc	—	£2
1971 Proof	—	£2	1982 Proof	—	£3
1972 Proof	—	£5	1983	243,002,000	£1
1973	280,196,000	£2	1983 Unc	—	£2
1973 Proof	—	£5	1983 Proof	—	£4
1974	330,892,000	£2	1984	154,759,625	£1
1974 Proof	—	£3	1984 BU	—	£2
1975	221,604,000	£2	1984 Proof	—	£3
1975 Proof	—	£4	1985 New portrait	200,605,245	£1
1976	300,160,000	£2	1985 BU	—	£2
1976 Proof	—	£3	1986 Proof	—	£3
1977	285,430,000	£2	1986	369,989,130	£1
1977 Proof	—	£3	1986 BU	—	£2
1978	292,770,000	£3	1986 Proof	—	£3
1978 Proof	—	£3	1987	4999,946,000	£1
1979	459,000,000	£3	1987 BU	—	£2
1979 Proof	—	£3	1987 Proof	—	£3
1980	416,304,000	£2	1988	793,492,000	£1
1980 Proof	—	£3	1988 BU	—	£2
1981	301,800,000	£2	1988 Proof	—	£3
1981 Proof	—	£3	1989	658,142,000	£1
1982 Legend changed to ONE PENNY			1989 BU	—	£2
	100,292,000	£1	1989 Proof	—	£3

DATE	Mintage	UNC	DATE	Mintage	UNC
1990	529,047,500	£2	2008 Silver Proof	—	£15
1990 BU	—	£3	2008 Gold Proof	—	£150
1990 Proof	—	£4	2008 Platinum Proof	—	£200
1991	206,457,000	£1	2008 New Rev,		
1991 BU	—	£2	no border beads on Obv	386,830,000	£1
1991 Proof	—	£4	2008 — BU	—	£2
1992 Copper-plated steel	253,867,000	£3	2008 — Proof	—	£3
1992 Bronze BU	—	£6	2008 — Silver Proof	—	£15
1992 — Proof	—	£4	2008 — Silver Proof Piedfort	—	£25
1993	602,590,000	£1	2008 — Gold Proof	—	£150
1993 BU	—	£2	2008 — Platinum Proof	—	£200
1993 Proof	—	£5	2009	469,207,800	£1
1994	843,834,000	£1	2009 BU	—	£3
1994 BU	—	£2	2009 Proof	—	£4
1994 Proof	—	£5	2009 Silver BU, in "Lucky Baby Gift Pack"	—	£15
1995	303,314,000	£1	2009 — Proof	—	£15
1995 BU	—	£3	2010	402,602,000	£1
1995 Proof	—	£5	2010 BU	—	£3
1996	723,840,060	£1	2010 Proof	—	£4
1996 BU	—	£2	2010 Silver BU, in "Lucky Baby Gift Card"	—	£15
1996 Proof	—	£5	2010 — Proof	—	£15
1996 Silver Proof	—	£28	2011	210,404,000	£1
1997	396,874,000	£1	2011 BU	—	£2
1997 BU	—	£2	2011 Proof	—	£3
1997 Proof	—	£4	2011 Silver BU in "Lucky Baby Pack"	—	£18
1998 New portrait	739,770,000	£1	2011 – Proof	—	£15
1998 — BU	—	£3	2012	—	£1
1998 Proof	—	£4	2012 BU	—	£2
1999	891,392,000	£2	2012 Proof	—	£4
1999 Bronze BU	—	£4	2012 Silver BU (three different packagings)	—	£15
1999 Bronze Proof	—	£8	2012 Silver Proof with selective gold plating	—	£18
2000	1,060,420,000	£1	2012 Gold Proof	—	£175
2000 BU	—	£2	2013	—	£1
2000 Proof	—	£4	2013 BU	—	£2
2000 Silver Proof	—	£25	2013 Proof	—	£5
2001	928,698,000	£1	2013 Silver BU	—	£25
2001 BU	—	£2	2013 — Proof	—	£30
2001 Proof	—	£4	2013 Gold Proof	—	£175
2002	601,446,000	£1	2014	—	£1
2002 BU	—	£2	2014 BU	—	£2
2002 Proof	—	£4	2014 Proof	—	£5
2002 Gold Proof	—	£175	2014 Silver BU	—	£20
2003	539,436,000	£1	2014 Silver Proof	—	£25
2003 BU	—	£2	2015	—	—
2003 Proof	—	£3	2015 BU	—	—
2004	739,764,000	£1	2015 Proof	—	—
2004 BU	—	£2	2015 Silver BU	—	—
2004 Proof	—	£4	2015 — Proof	—	—
2005	536,318,000	£1	2015 Gold Proof	—	—
2005 BU	—	£2	2015 Platinum Proof	—	—
2005 Proof	—	£3	2015 New Portrait	—	—
2006	524,605,000	£1	2015 — BU	—	—
2006 BU	—	£2	2015 — Proof	—	—
2006 Proof	—	£4	2015 — Silver Proof	—	—
2006 Silver Proof	—	£15	2015 — Gold Proof	—	—
2007	548,002,000	£1	2015 — Platinum Proof	—	—
2007 BU	—	£4	2016	—	—
2007 Proof	—	£7	2016 BU	—	—
2008	180,600,000	£1	2016 Proof	—	—
2008 BU	—	£3	2016 Silver BU	—	—
2008 Proof	—	£5	2016 Silver Proof	—	—

HALF PENNY

No longer legal tender, its history tracks that of the Two Pence and One Penny.

1971	1,394,188,250	£2
1971 Proof	—	£3
1972 Proof	—	£15
1973	365,680,000	£2
1973 Proof	—	£3
1974	365,448,000	£2
1974 Proof	—	£3
1975	197,600,000	£2
1975 Proof	—	£3
1976	412,172,000	£2
1976 Proof	—	£3
1977	66,368,000	£1
1977 Proof	—	£3
1978	59,532,000	£1
1978 Proof	—	£4
1979	219,1322,000	£2
1979 Proof	—	£4
1980	202,788,000	£2
1980 Proof	—	£3
1981	46,748,000	£2
1981 Proof	—	£4
1982 Legend changed to HALF PENNY	190,752,000	50p
1982 Unc	—	£2
1982 Proof	—	£3
1983	7,600,000	50p
1983 Unc	—	£1
1983 Proof	—	£4
1984	40,000	£4
1984 BU	—	£5
1984 Proof	—	£6

For the other 9 coins in the 29-coin 2011 Olympic and Paralympic series see pages 257–259.

PROOF AND SPECIMEN SETS

NOTE: The prices quoted in this guide were set at August *2016* with the price of gold around £900 per ounce and silver £12 per ounce—market fluctuations will have a marked effect on the values of modern precious metal coins. However, the prices quoted here for the *recently issued* sets are the original Royal Mint retail prices.

The following listings are an attempt to include all officially marketed products from the Royal Mint of two coins or more, but excluding those which included non-UK coins. It is appreciated that not all have been advertised as new to the public, but it is assumed that at some time they have been, or will be, available. In a few cases, therefore, the prices may be conjectural but are, nevertheless, attempts at listing realistic values, in some instances based on an original retail price. In the case of Elizabeth II sets, if no metal is stated in the listing, the coins in the sets are of the same metal as the circulation coin equivalent. In addition to the above we have excluded historical gold coin sets, such as sets of sovereigns from different mints, where the dates of the coins vary from one set to another.

DATE	FDC

GEORGE IV
1826 £5–farthing (11 coins) ....From £45,000

WILLIAM IV
1831 Coronation £2–farthing (14 coins) ....From £35,000

VICTORIA
1839 "Una and the Lion" £5–farthing (15 coins)...From £75,000
1853 Sovereign–quarter farthing, including "Gothic"crown (16 coins) .... From £50,000
1887 Golden Jubilee £5–3d (11 coins)..£30,000
1887 Golden Jubilee Crown–3d (7 coins)...£3500
1893 £5–3d (10 coins)...£28,000
1893 Crown–3d (6 coins)..£5000

EDWARD VII
1902 Coronation £5–Maundy penny, matt proofs (13 coins) £6500
1902 Coronation Sovereign–Maundy penny, matt proofs (11 coins) £3500

GEORGE V
1911 Coronation £5–Maundy penny (12 coins)..£8000
1911 Sovereign–Maundy penny (10 coins) £3500
1911 Coronation Halfcrown–Maundy penny (8 coins) £1500
1927 New types Crown–3d (6 coins)...£850

GEORGE VI
1937 Coronation £5–half sovereign (4 coins) £6500
1937 Coronation Crown–farthing including Maundy money (15 coins) £550
1950 Mid-century Halfcrown–farthing (9 coins) £200
1951 Festival of Britain, Crown–farthing (10 coins)...£250

ELIZABETH II
1953 Proof Coronation Crown–farthing (10 coins) £125
1953 Currency (plastic) set halfcrown–farthing (9 coins)..£15
1968 Specimen decimal set 10p, 5p and 1971-dated bronze in blue wallet (5 coins)..£3
1970 Proof Last £sd coins (issued from 1972) Halfcrown–halfpenny (8 coins)..£20
1971 Proof (issued 1973) 50p–half penny (6 coins)..£18
1972 Proof (issued 1976) 50p–half penny (7 coins including Silver Wedding crown) £24
1973 Proof (issued 1976) 50p–half penny (6 coins)...£16
1974 Proof (issued 1976) 50p–half penny (6 coins)...£18
1975 Proof (issued 1976) 50p–half penny (6 coins)...£18

DATE	FDC
1976 Proof 50p–half penny (6 coins)	£18
1977 Proof 50p–half penny (7 coins including Silver Jubilee crown)	£22
1978 Proof 50p–half penny (6 coins)	£16
1979 Proof 50p–half penny (6 coins)	£18
1980 Proof gold sovereign series (4 coins)	£2500
1980 — 50p–half penny (6 coins)	£16
1981 Proof £5, sovereign, Royal Wedding Silver crown, 50p–half penny (9 coins)	£800
1981 — 50p–half penny (6 coins)	£18
1982 Proof gold sovereign series (4 coins)	£2500
1982 — 50p–half penny (7 coins)	£20
1982 Uncirculated 50p–half penny (7 coins)	£15
1983 Proof gold double-sovereign to half sovereign (3 coins)	£1000
1983 — £1–half penny (8 coins) (includes H. J. Heinz sets)	£25
1983 Uncirculated £1–half penny (8 coins) (includes Benson & Hedges and Martini sets)	£30
1983 — — (8 coins) (only Benson & Hedges and Martini sets) with "2 NEW PENCE" legend	£1000
1983 — 50p–half penny (7 coins) (H. J. Heinz sets)	£16
1983 — — (7 coins) (H. J. Heinz set) with "2 NEW PENCE" legend	£1000
1984 Proof gold five pounds, sovereign and half-sovereigns (3 coins)	£1000
1984 — £1 (Scottish rev.)–half penny (8 coins)	£20
1984 BU £1 (Scottish rev.)–half penny (8 coins)	£16
1985 New portrait proof gold sovereign series (4 coins)	£1250
1985 Proof £1–1p in de luxe case (7 coins)	£25
1985 — in standard case	£20
1985 BU £1–1p (7 coins) in folder	£15
1986 Proof gold Commonwealth Games £2, sovereign and half sovereign (3 coins)	£1000
1986 — Commonwealth Games £2–1p, de luxe case (8 coins)	£30
1986 — — in standard case (8 coins)	£25
1986 BU £2–1p in folder (8 coins)	£20
1987 Proof gold Britannia set (4 coins)	£2000
1987 — — — £25 and £10 (2 coins)	£450
1987 — — double- to half sovereign (3 coins)	£1000
1987 — £1–1p in de luxe case (7 coins)	£35
1987 — £1–1p in standard case (7 coins)	£25
1987 BU £1–1p in folder (7 coins)	£20
1988 Proof gold Britannia set (4 coins)	£2000
1988 — — — £25 and £10 (2 coins)	£450
1988 — — double- to half sovereign (3 coins)	£1000
1988 — £1–1p in de luxe case (7 coins)	£35
1988 — £1–1p in standard case (7 coins)	£30
1988 BU £1–1p in folder (7 coins) (includes Bradford & Bingley sets)	£18
1989 Proof gold Britannia set (4 coins)	£2000
1989 — — — £25 and £10 (2 coins)	£450
1989 — — 500th anniversary of the sovereign series set (4 coins)	£4000
1989 — — double- to half sovereign (3 coins)	£2000
1989 — Silver Bill of Rights £2, Claim of Right £2 (2 coins)	£65
1989 — — Piedfort as above (2 coins)	£100
1989 BU £2 in folder (2 coins)	£25
1989 Proof £2 (both)–1p in de luxe case (9 coins)	£35
1989 — in standard case (9 coins)	£30
1989 BU £1–1p in folder (7 coins)	£25
1990 Proof gold Britannia set (4 coins)	£2000
1990 — — sovereign series set (4 coins)	£2000
1990 — — double- to half sovereign (3 coins)	£1000
1990 — silver 5p, 2 sizes (2 coins)	£28
1990 — £1–1p in de luxe case (8 coins)	£35
1990 — £1–1p standard case (8 coins)	£30
1990 BU £1–1p in folder (8 coins)	£20
1991 Proof gold Britannia set (4 coins)	£2000
1991 — — sovereign series set (4 coins)	£2000
1991 — — double- to half sovereign (3 coins)	£1000
1991 — £1–1p in de luxe case (7 coins)	£35
1991 — £1–1p in standard case (7 coins)	£28
1991 BU £1–1p in folder (7 coins)	£18

DATE	FDC
1992 Proof gold Britannia set (4 coins)	£2000
1992 — — sovereign series set (4 coins)	£2000
1992 — — double- to half sovereign (3 coins)	£1000
1992 — £1–1p including two each 50p and 10p in de luxe case (9 coins)	£38
1992 — £1–1p as above in standard case (9 coins)	£32
1992 BU £1–1p as above in folder (9 coins)	£16
1992 — with Enhanced Effigy on obverse of 20p	£25
1992 Proof silver 10p, two sizes (2 coins)	£25
1993 Proof gold Britannia set (4 coins)	£2000
1993 — — sovereign series set (4 coins plus silver Pistrucci medal)	£2000
1993 — — double- to half sovereign (3 coins)	£1000
1993 — Coronation anniversary £5–1p in de luxe case (8 coins)	£38
1993 — — in standard case (8 coins)	£35
1993 BU £1–1p including 1992 EU 50p (8 coins)	£15
1994 Proof gold Britannia set (4 coins)	£2000
1994 — — sovereign series set (4 coins)	£2000
1994 — — £2 to half sovereign (3 coins)	£1000
1994 — Bank of England Tercentenary £2–1p in de luxe case (8 coins)	£38
1994 — — in standard case (8 coins)	£35
1994 BU £1–1p in folder (7 coins)	£18
1994 Proof gold 1992 and 1994 50p (2 coins)	£350
1994 — "Family silver" set £2–50p (3 coins)	£65
1995 Proof gold Britannia set (4 coins)	£2000
1995 — — sovereign series (4 coins)	£2000
1995 — — £2 to half sovereign (3 coins)	£850
1995 — 50th Anniversary of WWII £2–1p in de luxe case (8 coins)	£40
1995 — — as above in standard case (8 coins)	£35
1995 BU as above in folder (8 coins)	£16
1995 Proof "Family Silver" set £2 (two) and £1 (3 coins)	£90
1996 Proof gold Britannia set (4 coins)	£2000
1996 — — sovereign series set (4 coins)	£2000
1996 — — double- to half sovereign (3 coins)	£1000
1996 — Royal 70th Birthday £5–1p in de luxe case (9 coins)	£50
1996 — — as above in standard case (9 coins)	£45
1996 BU Football £2–1p in folder (8 coins)	£20
1996 Proof gold Britannia £10 and half-sovereign (2 coins)	£550
1996 — sovereign and silver £1 (2 coins)	£250
1996 — — "Family silver" set £5–£1 (3 coins)	£85
1996 — silver 25th Anniversary of Decimal currency £1–1p (7 coins)	£150
1996 Circulation and BU 25th Anniversary of Decimalisation 2s 6d–halfpenny (misc.) and £1–1p in folder (14 coins)	£25
1997 Proof gold Britannia set (4 coins)	£2000
1997 — — sovereign series set (4 coins)	£2000
1997 — — — £2 to half sovereign (3 coins)	£1000
1997 — — Silver Britannia set (4 coins)	£150
1997 — Golden Wedding £5–1p in red leather case	£45
1997 — — as above in standard case (10 coins)	£35
1997 BU £2 to 1p in folder (9 coins)	£25
1997 Proof silver 50p set, two sizes (2 coins)	£45
1997/1998 Proof silver £2 set, both dates (2 coins)	£70
1998 Proof gold Britannia set (4 coins)	£2000
1998 — — sovereign series set (4 coins)	£2000
1998 — — — double- to half sovereign (3 coins)	£1000
1998 Proof silver Britannia set (4 coins)	£185
1998 — Prince of Wales £5–1p (10 coins) in red leather case	£45
1998 — — as above in standard case (10 coins)	£38
1998 BU £2–1p in folder (9 coins)	£16
1998 Proof silver European/NHS 50p set (2 coins)	£60
1998 BU Britannia/EU 50p set (2 coins)	£8
1999 Proof gold Britannia set (4 coins)	£2000
1999 — — Sovereign series set (4 coins)	£2000
1999 — — — £2 to half sovereign (3 coins)	£1000
1999 — Princess Diana £5–1p in red leather case (9 coins)	£65
1999 — — as above in standard case (9 coins)	£45

DATE	FDC
1999 BU £2–1p (8 coins) in folder	£20
1999 Proof "Family Silver" set. Both £5, £2 and £1 (4 coins)	£150
1999 Britannia Millennium set. Bullion £2 and BU £5 (2 coins)	£30
1999/2000 Reverse frosted proof set, two x £1 (2 coins)	£75
2000 Proof gold Britannia set (4 coins)	£2000
2000 — — Sovereign series set (4 coins)	£2000
2000 — — — double- to half sovereign (3 coins)	£1000
2000 Millennium £5–1p in de luxe case (10 coins)	£50
2000 — — as above in standard case (10 coins)	£45
2000 — Silver set Millennium £5 to 1p plus Maundy (13 coins)	£225
2000 BU £2–1p set in folder (9 coins)	£20
2000 Millennium "Time Capsule" BU £5 to 1p (9 coins)	£30
2001 Proof gold Britannia set (4 coins)	£2000
2001 — — Sovereign series set (4 coins)	£2000
2001 — — — £2–half sovereign (3 coins)	£1000
2001 — Silver Britannia set (4 coins)	£150
2001 — Victoria £5–1p in Executive case (10 coins)	£100
2001 — — as above in red leather case (10 coins)	£75
2001 — — as above in "Gift" case (10 coins)	£48
2001 — — as above in standard case (10 coins)	£40
2001 BU £2–1p in folder (9 coins)	£18
2002 Proof gold Britannia set (4 coins)	£2000
2002 — — Sovereign series set, all Shield rev. (4 coins)	£2000
2002 — — — double- to half sovereign (3 coins)	£1000
2002 — Golden Jubilee set £5–1p plus Maundy (13 coins)	£4500
2002 — Golden Jubilee £5–1p in Executive case (9 coins)	£75
2002 — — as above in red leather de luxe case (9 coins)	£50
2002 — — as above in "Gift" case (9 coins)	£42
2002 — — as above in standard case (9 coins)	£40
2002 BU £2–1p (8 coins) in folder	£16
2002 Proof Gold Commonwealth Games £2 set (4 coins)	£2000
2002 — Silver Piedfort Commonwealth Games £2 set (4 coins)	£250
2002 — — Commonwealth Games £2 set (4 coins)	£125
2002 — Commonwealth Games £2 set (4 coins)	£30
2002 BU Commonwealth Games £2 set (4 coins) in folder	£25
2003 Proof gold Britannia set (4 coins)	£2000
2003 — — — £50–£10 (3 coins)	£1000
2003 — — — type set, one of each £100 reverse (4 coins)	£2500
2003 — — Sovereign series set (4 coins)	£2000
2003 — — — series £2–half sovereign (3 coins)	£1000
2003 — Silver Britannia set (4 coins)	£45
2003 — — type set (one of each £2 reverse) (4 coins)	£85
2003 — £5 to 1p, two of each £2 and 50p in Executive case (11 coins)	£80
2003 — — as above in red leather case (11 coins)	£55
2003 — — as above in standard case (11 coins)	£48
2003 BU £2 (two)–1p in folder (10 coins)	£22
2003 Proof silver Piedfort set. DNA £2, £1 and Suffragette 50p (3 coins)	£150
2003 Proof "Family Silver" set £5, Britannia and DNA £2, £1 and Suffragette 50p (5 coins)	£175
2003 Circ & BU "God Save the Queen" Coronation anniversary set 5s/0d to farthing (1953) and £5 to 1p (2003) in folder (19 coins)	£55
£000 Circulation or bullion "Royal Sovereign" collection, example of each Elizabeth II date (21 coins)	£3500
2004 Proof gold Britannia set (4 coins)	£2000
2004 — — — £50 to £10 (3 coins)	£1000
2004 — — Sovereign series set (4 coins)	£2000
2004 — — — Series £2-half sovereign (3 coins)	£1000
2004 (Issue date) Royal Portrait gold sovereign set, all proof except the first: Gillick, Machin, Maklouf and Rank-Broadley sovereigns, and the 2nd, 3rd and 4th of above half-sovereigns, various dates (7 coins)	£1500
2004 Proof silver Britannia set (4 coins)	£150
2004 — "Family Silver" set £5, Britannia and Trevithick £2, £1 and Bannister 50p (5 coins)	£165
2004 — Silver Piedfort set, Trevithick £2, £1 and Bannister 50p (3 coins)	£175
2004 — £2 to 1p, two each of £2 and 50p in Executive case (10 coins)	£75

DATE	FDC
2004 — — as above in red leather case (10 coins)	£45
2004 — — as above in standard case (10 coins)	£40
2004 BU £2 to 1p in folder (10 coins)	£22
2004 — "New Coinage" set, Trevithick £2, £1 and Bannister 50p (3 coins)	£10
2004 BU "Season's Greetings" £2 to 1p and Royal Mint Christmas medal in folder (8 coins)	£18
2005 Proof Gold Britannia set (4 coins)	£2000
2005 — — — £50 to £10 (3 coins)	£1000
2005 — — Sovereign series set (4 coins)	£2000
2005 — — series, double to half sovereign (3 coins)	£1000
2005 — Silver Britannia (4 coins)	£135
2005 — Gold Trafalgar and Nelson £5 crowns (2 coins)	£2000
2005 — Silver, as above (2 coins)	£85
2005 — Piedfort, as above (2 coins)	£135
2005 — Silver Piedfort set, Gunpowder Plot and World War II £2, £1 and Johnson 50p (4 coins)	£200
2005 — £5 to 1p, two of each of £5, £2 and 50p in Executive case (12 coins)	£80
2005 — — as above in red leather case (12 coins)	£60
2005 — — as above in standard case (12 coins)	£45
2005 BU Trafalgar and Nelson £5 crowns in pack (2 coins)	£25
2005 — £2 (two) to 1p in folder (10 coins)	£25
2005 — "New Coinage" set, Gunpowder Plot £2, £1 and Johnson 50p (3 coins)	£10
2005 — "Merry Xmas" £2 to 1p and Royal Mint Christmas medal in folder (8 coins)	£20
2006 Proof Gold Britannia set (4 coins)	£2000
2006 — — Sovereign Series set (4 coins)	£2000
2006 — — — series, double to half sovereign (3 coins)	£1000
2006 — Silver Britannia (4 coins)	£145
2006 — Silver Brunel £2 coin set (2 coins)	£75
2006 — — Piedfort Brunel £2 coin set (2 coins)	£125
2006 — Gold Brunel £2 coin set (2 coins)	£950
2006 — Silver VC 50p coin set (2 coins)	£58
2006 — Silver Piedfort VC 50p coin set (2 coins)	£115
2006 — Gold VC 50p coin set (2 coins)	£675
2006 — Silver proof set, £5 to 1p plus Maundy coins (13 coins)	£325
2006 — — — Piedfort collection £5, with trumpets enhanced with 23 carat gold, both Brunel £2, £1, both VC 50p (6 coins)	£350
2006 — — Britannia £2 "Golden Silhouette" collection, five different reverses, all dated 2006 (5 coins)	£350
2006 — Britannia £25 Gold "Portrait" collection, five different reverses, all dated 2006 (5 coins)	£1550
2006 — £5 to 1p, three of each £2 and 50p in Executive case (13 coins)	£80
2006 — as above in red leather case (13 coins)	£55
2006 — as above in standard case (13 coins)	£45
2006 BU £2 (two), £1, 50p (two) and to 1p in folder (10 coins)	£18
2006 Proof Brunel £2 in folder (2 coins)	£15
2006 — VC 50p in folder (2 coins)	£15
2006 — Gold Half-Sovereign set dated 2005 Noad and 2006 Pistrucci St George and the Dragon (2 coins)	£250
2007 — Gold Britannia set (4 coins)	£2500
2007 — — Sovereign Series set (4 coins)	£2000
2007 — — series, double to half sovereign (3 coins)	£1000
2007 — — Sovereign and half-sovereign (2 coins)	£375
2007 — "Family Silver" set, Britannia, £5 crown, Union and Slavery £2, Gateshead £1 and Scouting 50p (6 coins)	£225
2007 Proof Silver Piedfort Collection, as "Family Silver" above but excluding a Britannia (5 coins)	£300
2007 — Silver £1 Bridge series coins, dated 2004 to 2007 (4 coins)	£135
2007 — Silver Proof Piedfort £1 Bridge Series, dated 2004 to 2007 (4 coins)	£275
2007 — Gold £1 Bridge series coins, dated as above (4 coins)	£2000
2007 — £5 to 1p, three £2 and two 50p in Executive case (12 coins)	£85
2007 — as above, Deluxe in red leather case (12 coins)	£65
2007 — as above, in standard case (12 coins)	£50
2007 BU £2 (two) to 1p (9 coins)	£18
2007 Proof Silver Britannia (four coins)	£145
2007 — Platinum Britannia (4 coins)	£5000
2007 Satin Proof Silver Britannia, 20th Anniversary Collection, six different reverses, all dated 2007 (6 coins)	£300
2007 50th Anniversary Sovereign set, 1957 circulation standard and 2007 Proof (2 coins)	£450
2008 Proof Gold Britannia set (4 coins)	£2000
2008 — Platinum Britannia set (4 coins)	£5000

DATE	FDC
2008 — Silver Britannia set (4 coins)	£150
2008 — Gold Sovereign series set (4 coins)	£2000
2008 — — — double to half-sovereign (3 coins)	£1000
2008 — — Sovereign and half-sovereign (2 coins)	£500
2008 — "Family silver" set, 2x £5, Britannia £2, Olympiad £2 and Royal Arms £1 (5 coins)	£200
2008 — Silver Piedfort Collection, 2x £5, Olympiad £2 and Shield of Royal Arms £1 (4 coins)	£285
2008 — 2 x £5, 2 x £2, £1 to 1p in Executive case (11 coins)	£85
2008 — as above, Deluxe in black leather case (11 coins)	£55
2008 — as above, in standard back case (11 coins)	£60
2008 BU 2 x £2, Royal Arms £1 to 1p (9 coins)	£20
2008 — "Emblems of Britain" ("old" Revs) Royal Arms £1 to 1p (7 coins)	£15
2008 — "Royal Shield of Arms" ("new" Revs) Shield of Royal Arms £1 to 1p (7 coins)	£15
2008 — Above two sets housed in one sleeve	£28
2008 Proof Base Metal "Royal Shield of Arms" set, £1 to 1p (7 coins)	£40
2008 — Silver "Emblems of Britain" set, £1 to 1p (7 coins)	£160
2008 — — "Royal Shield of Arms" set, £1 to 1p (7 coins)	£160
2008 — — Above two sets in one black case	£325
2008 — Gold "Emblems of Britain" set, £1 to 1p (7 coins)	£3500
2008 — — "Royal Shield of Arms" set, £1 to 1p (7 coins)	£3500
2008 — — Above two sets in one oak-veneer case	£6750
2008 — Platinum "Emblems of Britain" set, £1 to 1p (7 coins)	£8500
2008 — — "Royal Shield of Arms" set, £1 to 1p (7 coins)	£8500
2008 — — Above two sets in one walnut veneer case	£15,750
2008 — Silver Piedfort "Royal Shield of Arms" set, £1 to 1p (7 coins)	£325
2008 — Gold set of 14 £1 coins, one of each Rev used since 1983, all dated 2008 (25th anniversary) (14 coins)	£9500
2008 — Silver with gold Rev highlighting as above (14 coins)	£500
2008 — 2 x £2, Royal Arms £1 to 1p (9 coins) Christmas Coin Sets, two different outer sleeves, Father Christmas or Three Wise men	£20
2009 Proof Gold Britannia set (4 coins)	£2200
2009 — Platinum Britannia set (4 coins)	£4000
2009 — Silver Britannia set (4 coins)	£150
2009 — Gold Sovereign series set (5 coins)	£2700
2009 — — double to half-sovereign (3 coins)	£1000
2009 — — sovereign and half-sovereign (2 coins)	£450
2009 — "Family Silver" set, Henry VIII £5, Britannia £2, Darwin and Burns £2, £1 and Kew 50p (6 coins)	£225
2009 — Silver Piedfort collection, Henry VIII £5, Darwin and Burns £2 and Kew Gardens 50p (4 coins)	£275
2009 — Silver Set, £5 to 1p (12 coins)	£275
2009 — Base metal Executive set, £5 to 1p (12 coins)	£80
2009 — — — Deluxe set, £5 to 1p (12 coins)	£55
2009 — — — Standard set, £5 to 1p (12 coins)	£45
2009 BU Base metal set, £2 to 1p (11 coins)	£22
2009 — — —, £1 to 1p "Royal Shield of Arms" set (7 coins)	£12
2009 — — —, £2 to 1p (8 coins)	£15
2009 Proof set of 50p coins as detailed in FIFTY PENCE section, CuNi (16 coins)	£195
2009 — Silver (16 coins)	£425
2009 — Gold (16 coins)	£8500
2009 — Gold Piedfort (16 coins)	£20,000
2009 "Mind" set of £5 coins, silver (6 coins)	£350
2010 Gold Britannia set (4 coins)	£2750
2010 — — —, £50 to £10 (3 coins)	£1500
2010 — Silver Britannia set (4 coins)	£140
2010 — Gold Olympic Series "Faster", £100 and £25 (2), (3 coins)	£2000
2010 — — Sovereign series set (5 coins)	£2750
2010 — — — double to half (3 coins)	£1250
2010 — — — sovereign to quarter (3 coins)	£550
2010 — "Silver Celebration" set, Restoration £5, Nightingale £2, London and Belfast £1 and Girlguiding 50p (5 coins)	£185
2010 Silver Piedfort set, coins as in "Silver Celebration" set (5 coins)	£300
2010 — Silver Collection, £5 to 1p (13 coins)	£300
2010 — Base Metal Executive Set, £5 to 1p (13 coins)	£80

DATE	FDC
2010 — — Deluxe set	£50
2010 — — Standard set	£40
2010 BU — Capital Cities £1 (2 coins)	£15
2010 — — Set, £2 to 1p (12 coins)	£35
2010 — — Definitive pack, £2 to 1p (8 coins)	£20
2010 Proof "Body" Collection of £5 coins, silver (6 coins)	£300
2010 Proof "Spirit" Collection of £5 coins, silver (6 coins)	£300
2011 Proof Gold Britannia set (4 coins)	£2750
2011 — — Premium set (3 coins)	£1500
2011 — Sovereign set (5 coins)	£3000
2011 — — double to half (3 coins)	£1200
2011 — — sovereign to quarter (3 coins)	£650
2011 — Silver Britannia set (4 coins)	£180
2011 — Olympic gold "Higher" set (3 coins)	£2650
2011 — — — "Faster" (2010) and "Higher" set (6 coins) in 9-coin case	£5300
2011 — Silver Collection, £5 to 1p (14 coins)	£400
2011 — — Celebration set, Duke of Edinburgh £5, Mary Rose and King James bible	
Cardiff and Edinburgh £1 and WWF 50p (6 coins)	£250
2011 — — — Piedfort, as above (6 coins)	£395
2011 Executive Proof Base metal set (14 coins)	£85
2011 De-luxe Proof Base metal set (14 coins)	£50
2011 Standard Proof Base metal set (14 coins)	£40
2011 BU set including £2, £1 and 50p commemoratives (13 coins)	£26
2011 BU set of Definitives (8 coins)	£25
2012 Proof Gold Britannia Set (4 coins)	£3600
2012 — — — £50 down (3 coins)	£1900
2012 — — — Half-ounce anniversary(9coins)	£9500
2012 — Sovereign set (5 coins)	£4000
2012 — — Double to Half (3 coins)	£1650
2012 — — Sovereign to Quarter (3 coins)	£825
2012 — Silver Britannia set (4 coins)	£195
2012 — Silver Britannia Half-Ounce Anniversary (9 coins)	£500
2012 BU Sovereign set Double to Half (3 coins)	£1550
2012 Proof Olympic gold Stronger set (3 coins)	£3500
2012 — — — 2x £25 (2 coins)	£1200
2010, 2011, 2012 Proof Olympic gold complete set (9 coins)	£10,500
2009, 2010, 2011, 2012 Complete Countdown sets:	
Gold Proof (4 coins)	£11,500
Silver Proof Piedport (4 coins)	£850
Silver Proof (4 coins)	£325
CuNi BU (4 coins)	£45
2012 Proof Gold set, Diamond Jubilee £5, Dickens & Technology £2, £1 to 1p (10 coins)	£8500
2012 — Silver set, as above with Selective Gold plating on £1 to 1p coins (10 coins)	£490
2012 — set (Premium) (10 coins)	£100
2012 — set (Collector) (10 coins)	£55
2012 BU set, include Diamond Jubilee £5 (10 coins)	£40
2012 — set, Technology £2 to 1p (8 coins)	£21
2012 Proof Gold, Diamond Jubilee £5 and Double Sovereign (2 coins)	£3200
2012 — Olympic and Paralympic £5 (2 coins)	£5500
2012 — Gold Piedfort 50p set, one each of the coins of Olympic sports in which Team GB gained gold	
medals (11 coins)	£25,000
2013 Proof Gold Britannia set, £100 to £1 (5 coins)	£3100
2013 — — — £50 to £10 (3 coins)	£1375
2013 — — —.£25 to £1 (3 coins)	£675
2013 — Silver Britannia set, £2 to 10p (5 coins)	£195
2013 — — — 20p and 10p (2 coins)	£39
2013 — Sovereign set (5 coins)	£4000
2013 — — Double to Half (3 coins)	£1650
2013 — — One to Quarter (3 coins)	£825
2013 — Gold £5 Portraits set (4 coins)	£9500
2013 — Silver Portraits set (4 coins)	£400
2013 — Silver Piedfort Portraits set (4 coins)	£800
2013 — Gold set, £5 Coronation anniversary to 1p (15 coins)	£12,500

DATE	FDC
2013 — Gold set of both London Underground £2 (2 coins)	£2000
2013 — Silver Piedfort set, as above (2 coins)	£200
2013 — Silver set, as above (2 coins)	£100
2013 BU set, as above (2 coins)	£20
2013 — Gold set, 30th anniversary of the One Pound coin, reverses from 1983 (Sewell), 1988 (Gorringe) and 2013 (Dent). (3 coins)	£3600
2013 — Silver, as above (3 coins)	£150
2013 BU Sovereign set, Double to Half (3 coins), struck June 2, 2013	£1550
2013 Proof Silver annual set, £5 Coronation anniv to 1p (15 coins)	£600
2013 — — Piedfort commemorative set (7 coins)	£650
2013 — "Premium" set (15 coins plus a "Latent Image" item)	£150
2013 — "Collector" set (15 coins)	£110
2013 — Commemorative set (7 coins)	£65
2013 BU annual set (15 coins)	£50
2013 — Definitive Set (8 coins)	£25
2014 Proof Gold Britannia (Clark) set £100 to 50p (6 coins)	£2600
2014 — — — £50 to £10 (3 coins)	£1175
2014 — — — £25 to £1 (3 coins)	£595
2014 — Silver Britannia (Clark) set £2 to 5p (6 coins)	£200
2014 — — — 20p to 5p (3 coins)	£45
2014 — Sovereign set (5 coins)	£3300
2014 — — Double to half (3 coins)	£1300
2014 — — One to quarter (3 coins)	£625
2014 — Gold Commemorative set, £5 Queen Anne, 2 x £2, 2 x £1, 50p (6 coins)	£5500
2014 — Silver Piedfort set, as above (6 coins)	£570
2014 — — set as above (6 coins)	£295
2014 — — all major coins of 2014 (14 coins)	£560
2014 — Premium set (14 coins and a premium medal)	£155
2014 — Collector set (14 coins)	£110
2014 — Commemorative set (6 coins)	£65
2014 BU annual set (14 coins)	£50
2014 — definitive set (8 coins)	£25
2014 — Floral £1 set, Scotland and Northern Ireland (2 coins)	£18
2014 Proof Silver Outbreak of First World War set of £5 (6 coins)	£450
2014 — Gold set as above (6 coins)	—
2014 — Silver Portrait of Britain £5 Silver collection (4 coins)	£36
2015 Proof Gold Britannia (Dufort) set £100 to 50p, Clark portrait (6 coins)	£2,600
2015 — — — — £50 to £10 (3 coins)	£1,175
2015 — — — — £10 to 50p (3 coins)	£350
2015 — Silver Britannia (Dufort) set £2 to 5p, Clark portrait (6 coins)	£200
2015 — Sovereign set, Rank-Broadley portrait (5 coins)	£2700
2015 — — Double to half, Rank-Broadley portrait (3 coins)	£1300
2015 — — One to quarter, Rank-Broadley portrait (3 coins)	£625
2015 — Gold Commemorative set, 2 x £5, 2 x £2, 2 x £1, 50p, Rank-Broadley portrait (5 coins)	£5500
2015 — Silver Piedfort set, as above (5 coins)	£570
2015 — — set as above (5 coins)	£295
2015 — Base metal set as above (5 coins)	£65
2015 — Platinum definitive set £2 to 1p, Rank-Broadley portrait plus £2 to 1p Clark portrait (16 coins)	£12,500
2015 — Gold ditto	£7,600
2015 — Silver ditto	£480
2015 — Base metal ditto	£120
2015 BU definitive set as per Platinum set above (16 coins)	£50
The above four entries are also available as 8-coin sets with either the Rank-Broadley ("Final Edition") or the Clark ("First Edition" portrait. These are issued at half the prices quoted above.	
2015 Proof Silver set of definitive and commemorative coins, Rank-Broadley portrait (13 coins)	£560
2015 — Premium set as above (13 coins and a Premium medal)	£155
2015 BU Collector set as above (13 coins and medal)	£110
2015 Proof Double to half sovereign, Clark portrait (3 coins)	£1,200
2015 — Silver commemorative set, Anniversary of First World War (6 coins)	£450
2016 Proof Gold Britannia (Zamit) set (6 coins)	£2,895
2016 — — — £50 to £10 (3 coins)	£1,350
2016 — Silver Britannia (Zamit) set (6 coins)	£200

```
2016 — Sovereign set, Butler Portrait (5 coins) ............................................................................... £2,700
2016 — — Double to half, Butler Portrait (3 coins) ........................................................................... £1,200
2016— — One to quarter, Butler Portrait (3 coins) ............................................................................ £625
2016 — Gold Commemorative set, £5, 5x £2, £1, 50p (8 coins) ..................................................... £6,100
2016 — Silver Piedfort set, as above (8 coins) ................................................................................... £595
2016 — — set as above (8 coins) ....................................................................................................... £395
2016 — Base metal set as above (8 coins) .......................................................................................... £95
2016 — silver set, commemoratives and definitives (16 coins) ........................................................... £595
2016 — Base metal set as above, Premium plus Medal (16 coins) ..................................................... £195
2016 — — Collector set (16 coins) ..................................................................................................... £145
2016 BU Annual set including commemoratives (16 coins) .................................................................. £55
2016 — Definitive set (8 coins) ............................................................................................................ £30
2016 Proof Silver set of £5 coins, Anniversary of First World War (6 coins) ........................................ £450
```

In addition to the above the Royal Mint produce the BU sets detailed above in Wedding and in Baby gift packs each year. Also the following patterns have been made available:

```
1999 (dated 1994) Bi-metal £2, plus three unprocessed or part-processed elements................................ —
2003 Set of patterns of £1 coins with bridges designs, in gold, hall-marked on edges (4 coins) ............ —
2003 — silver £1 as above (4 coins) .................................................................................................. £150
2004 — gold £1 featuring heraldic animal heads, hall-marked on edge (4 coins) .............................. £1000
2004 — silver £1 featuring heraldic animal heads, hall-marked on edge (4 coins) .............................. £350
```

IMPORTANT NOTE:

In this section the prices quoted were set at August 2016 with the price of gold at around £900 per ounce and silver £12 per ounce. As the market for precious metals is notoriously volatile and unpredictable any price fluctuations have a marked effect on the values of modern precious metal coins, therefore it is important to seek professional advice when requiring a valuation for any of the precious metal sets listed. *The prices quoted here are for guidance only whereas the prices quoted for the recently issued sets are the original Royal Mint retail prices.*

ABC Coins and Tokens

We stock a large selection of Scottish coins, tokens & communion tokens and also offer a wide range of hammered & milled British & World coins, tokens and numismatic books.

We are always keen to purchase new material at competitive prices.

Alnwick British and Colonial
Coins and Tokens
P. O. Box 52, Alnwick,
Northumberland, NE66 1YE
United Kingdom

Website: www.abccoinsandtokens.com
E-mail: d-stuart@d-stuart.demon.co.uk
Telephone: 01665 603851

SCOTLAND

The coins illustrated are pennies representative of the reign, unless otherwise stated.

	F	VF

DAVID I (1124–53)

Berwick, Carlisle, Edinburgh and Roxburgh Mints

	F	VF
Penny in the name of David	£1500	£5500
Cut Halfpenny	Extremely rare	
Penny in name of Stephen	£1000	£4000

David I

HENRY (1136–52)

Bamborough, Carlisle and Corbridge Mints for the Earl of Huntingdon and Northumberland

	F	VF
Penny	£2000	£7500
Cut Halfpenny	Extremely rare	

MALCOLM IV (1153–65)

Berwick and Roxburgh Mints

Penny (5 different types)	Extremely rare	

Henry

WILLIAM THE LION (1165–1214)

Berwick, Edinburgh, Dun (Dunbar?), Perth and Roxburgh Mints

		F	VF
Penny - cross pattee early issue	from	£2500	£7000
Penny – pellet & crescent	from	£175	£500
Penny – short cross & stars – mint & moneyer	from	£150	£425
Penny – short cross & stars HVE WALTER & var	from	£100	£225

William the Lion

ALEXANDER II (1214–49)

Berwick and Roxburgh Mints

		F	VF
Penny – in the name of William the Lion	from	£300	£750
Penny – in own name	from	£550	£1450

Alexander II

ALEXANDER III (1249–86)

FIRST COINAGE (1250–80)

Pennies struck at the Mints at

		F	VF
Aberdeen	from	£150	£350
Ayr	from	£225	£600
Berwick	from	£80	£200
Dun (Dumfries / Dunfermline? / Dundee?)	from	£175	£450
Edinburgh	from	£150	£350
Forfar	from	£295	£800
Fres (Dumfries)	from	£300	£700
Glasgow	from	£300	£750
Inverness	from	£275	£600
Kinghorn	from	£295	£775
Lanark	from	£260	£665
Montrose	from	£550	£1000
Perth	from	£110	£285
Roxburgh	from	£120	£310
St Andrews	from	£275	£600
Stirling	from	£200	£550

Alexander III First Coinage

SECOND COINAGE (1280–86)

	F	VF
Penny	£70	£160
Halfpenny	£90	£325
Farthing	£275	£825

Alexander III Second Coinage

F   VF

JOHN BALIOL (1292–1306)

FIRST COINAGE *(Rough Surface issue)*

		F	VF
Penny .... from		£125	£275
Halfpenny .... from		£650	Ex. rare
Penny – St. Andrews .... from		£175	£475
Halfpenny – St. Andrews .... from		£800	Ex. rare

SECOND COINAGE *(Smooth Surface issue)*

Penny .... from		£200	£475
Halfpenny .... from		£150	£425
Farthing		Extremely rare	
Penny – St. Andrews .... from		£350	£950
Halfpenny – St. Andrews		Extremely rare	

John Baliol

ROBERT BRUCE (1306–29)

Berwick Mint

Penny .... from		£600	£1500
Halfpenny .... from		£750	£2000
Farthing .... from		£850	£2250

Robert Bruce

DAVID II (1329–71)

Aberdeen and Edinburgh Mints

Noble		Extremely Rare	
Groat (Edinburgh) .... from		£115	£300
Groat (Aberdeen) .... from		£750	£1750
Halfgroat (Edinburgh)................................... from		£100	£275
Halfgroat (Aberdeen) .... from		£525	£1250
Penny 1st Coinage 2nd Issue....................... from		£65	£195
Penny 2nd Coinage (Edinburgh)................... from		£100	£275
Penny 2nd Coinage (Aberdeen).................... from		£450	£1100
Halfpenny .... from		£250	£725
Farthing .... from		£450	£1250

David II

ROBERT II (1371–90)

Dundee, Edinburgh and Perth Mints

Groat.. from		£100	£275
Halfgroat .... from		£135	£395
Penny .... from		£85	£215
Halfpenny .... from		£95	£275

Robert II

ROBERT III (1390–1406)

Aberdeen, Dumbarton, Edinburgh, Perth Mints

Lion or crown.. from		£1750	£5750
Demy lion or halfcrown.................................. from		£1250	£4500
Groat.. from		£90	£225
Halfgroat .... from		£175	£350
Penny .... from		£250	£725
Halfpenny .... from		£275	£850

JAMES I (1406–37)

Aberdeen, Edinburgh, Inverness, Linlithgow, Perth, Stirling Mints

Demy .... from		£850	£2500
Half demy .... from		£750	£2250
Groat Edinburgh .... from		£175	£395
Groat Other Mints... from		£300	£850
Penny .... from		£250	£650
Halfpenny		Extremely rare	

Robert III Lion

	F	VF

JAMES II (1437–60)

Aberdeen, Edinburgh, Linlithgow, Perth, Roxburgh, Stirling Mints

	F	VF
Demy .... from	£1050	£2950
Lion .... from	£1250	£4500
Half lion	Extremely rare	
Early groats (fleur-de-lis) Edinburgh .... from	£195	£550
Early groats (fleur-de-lis) Other Mints................................	Extremely rare	
Later groats (crown) Edinburgh................................ from	£225	£650
Later groats (crown) Other Mints............................ from	£450	£1250
Later Halfgroats (crown) Edinburgh......................... from	£600	£1650
Later Halfgroats (crown) Other Mints	Extremely rare	
Penny (billon) .... from	£250	£650

JAMES III (1460–88)

Aberdeen, Berwick and Edinburgh Mints

	F	VF
Rider..	£1750	£4500
Half rider	£1750	£4500
Quarter rider...	£2500	£7000
Unicorn...	£2750	£7500
Groat (facing bust) Edinburgh .... from	£130	£375
Groat (facing bust) Berwick............................... from	£500	£1450
Groat (thistle & mullet) Edinburgh..................... from	£250	£650
Groat (threequarter bust) Aberdeen .... from	£550	£1650
Halfgroat .... from	£450	£1250
Penny (silver) .... from	£325	£950
Plack (billon) .... from	£175	£450
Half plack)... from	£195	£525
Penny (billon) .... from	£150	£425
Farthing (copper)..	£200	£650
Penny – ecclesiastical issue............................... from	£70	£185
Farthing – ecclesiastical issue........................... from	£125	£350

James III Groat, Berwick Mint

JAMES IV (1488–1513)

Edinburgh Mint

	F	VF
Unicorn...	£1500	£4250
Half unicorn	£1250	£3500
Lion or crown...	Extremely rare	
Half lion	Extremely rare	
Groat...	£400	£1375
Halfgroat.. from	£700	£2000
Penny (silver) .... from	£150	£400
Plack.. from	£40	£100
Half plack	Extremely rare	
Penny (billon) .... from	£55	£135

James IV Unicorn

JAMES V (1513–42)

Edinburgh Mint

	F	VF
Unicorn	£2050	£5125
Half Unicorn	Extremely rare	
Crown...	£1350	£4250
Ducat or Bonnet piece .... from	£1250	£5000
Two-thirds ducat..	£2500	£6500
One-third ducat	£3500	£9500
Groat... from	£175	£500
One-third groat.. from	£275	£775
Plack .... from	£50	£125
Bawbee .... from	£60	£165
Half bawbee .... from	£140	£325
Quarter bawbee...	Extremely rare	

James V Ducat or Bonnet Piece

	F	VF

MARY (1542–67)

Edinburgh and Stirling Mints

FIRST PERIOD (1542–58)

	F	VF
Crown	£1500	£4250
Twenty shillings	Extremely rare	
Lion (Forty-four shillings)	£1350	£4000
Half lion (Twenty-two shillings)	£1500	£4250
Ryals (Three pounds)	£4000	£11500
Half ryal	£4500	£12500
Portrait testoon	£5000	£14500
Non-portrait testoon .... from	£275	£800
Half testoon .... from	£250	£750
Bawbee .... from	£65	£180
Half bawbee .... from	£125	£325
Bawbee - Stirling	£150	£425
Penny (facing bust) .... from	£325	£900
Penny (no bust) .... from	£225	£650
Lion .... from	£50	£145
Plack .... from	£70	£195

Mary Lion or Forty-Four Shillings

SECOND PERIOD (Francis and Mary, 1558–60)

	F	VF
Ducat (Sixty shillings)	Extremely rare	
Non-portrait testoon .... from	£350	£1000
Half testoon .... from	£400	£1150
12 penny groat .... from	£80	£225
Lion .... from	£55	£135

THIRD PERIOD (Widowhood, 1560–65)

	F	VF
Portrait testoon	£3250	£9500
Half testoon.	£3000	£8500

FOURTH PERIOD (Henry and Mary, 1565–67)

	F	VF
Portrait ryal.	£45000	£125000
Non-portrait ryal .... from	£900	£1850
Two-third ryal .... from	£650	£1550
One-third ryal .... from	£850	£2550

FIFTH PERIOD (Second widowhood, 1567)

	F	VF
Non-portrait ryal .... from	£850	£2250
Two thirds ryal .... from	£475	£1350
One-third ryal .... from	£650	£1550

JAMES VI (1567–1603)

(Before accession to the English throne)

FIRST COINAGE (1567–71)

	F	VF
Ryal .... from	£450	£1100
Two-thirds ryal .... from	£350	£900
One-third ryal .... from	£350	£900

SECOND COINAGE (1571–80)

	F	VF
Twenty pounds	£25,000	£75,000
Noble (or half merk) .... from	£125	£300
Half noble (or quarter merk) .... from	£125	£300
Two merks or Thistle dollar .... from	£1500	£3750
Merk .... from	£2500	£7250

*James VI Fourth coinage
Ten Shillings*

THIRD COINAGE (1580–81)

	F	VF
Ducat	£5000	£14500
Sixteen shillings	£2500	£7250
Eight shillings	£1950	£5750

	F	VF
Four shillings	£4000	£9500
Two shillings	Extremely rare	

FOURTH COINAGE (1582–88)
	F	VF
Lion noble	£5500	£15000
Two-third lion noble	£4750	£13500
One-third lion noble	Extremely rare	
Forty shillings	£5000	£14500
Thirty shillings	£800	£2500
Twenty shillings	£425	£1250
Ten shillings	£425	£1250

FIFTH COINAGE (1588)
	F	VF
Thistle noble	£1700	£5250

James VI Seventh Coinage Rider

SIXTH COINAGE (1591–93)
	F	VF
"Hat" piece	£3500	£10000
"Balance" half merk ...... from	£300	£895
"Balance" quarter merk ...... from	£725	£2000

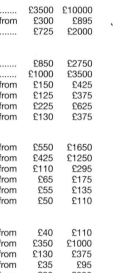

SEVENTH COINAGE (1594–1601)
	F	VF
Rider	£850	£2750
Half rider	£1000	£3500
Ten shillings ...... from	£150	£425
Five shillings ...... from	£125	£375
Thirty pence ...... from	£225	£625
Twelve pence ...... from	£130	£375

EIGHTH COINAGE (1601–04)
	F	VF
Sword and sceptre piece ...... from	£550	£1650
Half sword and sceptre piece ...... from	£425	£1250
Thistle-merk ...... from	£110	£295
Half thistle-merk ...... from	£65	£175
Quarter thistle-merk ...... from	£55	£135
Eighth thistle-merk ...... from	£50	£110

BILLON AND COPPER ISSUES
	F	VF
Eightpenny groat ...... from	£40	£110
Fourpenny groat ...... from	£350	£1000
Twopenny plack ...... from	£130	£375
Hardhead ...... from	£35	£95
Twopence ...... from	£80	£230
Penny plack ...... from	£160	£750
Penny ...... from	£500	£1250

*James VI Seventh Coinage
10 Shillings*

JAMES VI (1603–25)
(After accession to the English throne)
	F	VF
Unit ...... from	£850	£2350
Double crown ...... from	£1100	£3250
British crown ...... from	£550	£1550
Halfcrown ...... from	£750	£2150
Thistle crown ...... from	£650	£2050
Sixty shillings ...... from	£350	£1000
Thirty shillings ...... from	£150	£425
Twelve shillings ...... from	£175	£575
Six shillings ...... from	£500	Ex. rare
Two shillings ...... from	£50	£140
One shilling ...... from	£125	£350
Copper twopence ...... from	£25	£70
Copper penny ...... from	£85	£250

*James VI after accession thirty
shillings*

	F	VF

CHARLES I (1625–49)

FIRST COINAGE (1625–36)

	F	VF
Unit	£1250	£3500
Double crown	£1000	£3150
British crown	Extremely rare	
Sixty shillings	£800	£2500
Thirty shillings	£150	£425
Twelve shillings	£150	£425
Six shillings .... from	£350	£1000
Two shillings	£45	£110
One shilling	£150	£495

SECOND COINAGE (1636)

	F	VF
Half merk	£90	£260
Forty penny piece	£75	£210
Twenty penny piece	£70	£200

THIRD COINAGE (1637–42)

	F	VF
Unit .... from	£1250	£4250
Half unit .... from	£950	£2950
British crown .... from	£600	£1750
British half crown .... from	£525	£1500
Sixty shillings	£775	£1850
Thirty shillings .... from	£125	£400
Twelve shillings .... from	£100	£325
Six shillings .... from	£80	£225
Half merk .... from	£120	£395
Forty pence .... from	£40	£110
Twenty pence .... from	£25	£70

FOURTH COINAGE (1642)

	F	VF
Three shillings thistle	£60	£150
Two shillings large II	£40	£110
Two shillings small II	£60	£155
Two shillings no value	£80	£225

COPPER ISSUES
(1629 Issue)

	F	VF
Twopence (triple thistle	£25	£70
Penny	£175	£500

(1632-39 Issue)

	F	VF
Twopence (Stirling turner .... from	£25	£70

(1642-50 ISSUE)

	F	VF
Twopence (CR crowned	£20	£55

Charles I Third Coinage
Sixty Shillings

Charles I Fourth Coinage
Two Shillings

CHARLES II (1660–85)

FIRST COINAGE

Four merks

	F	VF
1664 Thistle above bust	£1250	£4000
1664 Thistle below bust	£2500	£7250
1665	Extremely rare	
1670 .... varieties from	£1550	£6950
1673 .... varieties from	£1550	£6950
1674 F below bust .... varieties from	£1250	£4000
1675	£950	£2750

Two merks

	F	VF
1664 Thistle above bust	£1000	£2500
1664 Thistle below bust	£2500	£7250

Charles II two merks

	F	VF
1670	£1200	£3000
1673	£750	£1950
1673 F below bust	£1350	£3250
1674	£1200	£3000
1674 F below bust	£1200	£3000
1675	£750	£1950

Merk

1664 .... varieties from	£250	£715
1665	£275	£780
1666	£325	£850
1668	£325	Ex. rare
1669 .... varieties from	£115	£325
1670	£160	£425
1671	£125	£350
1672 .... varieties from	£115	£325
1673 .... varieties from	£125	£350
1674	£250	£715
1674 F below bust	£225	£650
1675 F below bust	£200	£550
1675	£210	£585

Charles II Dollar

Half merk

1664	£275	£725
1665 .... varieties from	£325	£600
1666 .... varieties from	£300	£750
1667	£325	£600
1668	£150	£400
1669 .... varieties from	£105	£285
1670 .... varieties from	£150	£400
1671 .... varieties from	£105	£285
1672	£150	£400
1673	£175	£475
1675 F below bust	£175	£475
1675	£195	£550

SECOND COINAGE
Dollar

1676	£850	£2225
1679	£750	£1925
1680	£850	£1950
1681	£650	£1625
1682	£575	£1550

Charles II Sixteenth Dollar

Half Dollar

1675	£650	£1500
1676	£750	£1950
1681	£400	£1100

Quarter Dollar

1675	£195	£550
1676 .... varieties from	£100	£275
1677 .... varieties from	£145	£400
1678	£165	£450
1679	£185	£500
1680	£150	£375
1681	£120	£325
1682 .... varieties from	£145	£400

Eighth Dollar

1676 .... varieties from	£85	£210
1677	£125	£300

Charles II Bawbee

285

	F	VF
1678/7	£195	£495
1679...	Extremely rare	
1680.. varieties from	£150	£345
1682.. varieties from	£225	£495

Sixteenth Dollar

	F	VF
1677...	£85	£210
1678/7 .... varieties from	£120	£320
1679/7	£135	£360
1680.. varieties from	£135	£360
1681...	£85	£210

Copper Issues

	F	VF
Twopence CR crowned .... varieties from	£25	£70
Bawbees 1677-79 .... varieties from	£65	£195
Turners 1677-79 .... varieties from	£45	£125

JAMES VII (1685–89)

Sixty shillings

	F	VF
1688 proof only .... varieties from	—	£3250

Forty shillings

	F	VF
1687.. varieties from	£400	£950
1688.. varieties from	£400	£950

Ten shillings

	F	VF
1687...	£150	£425
1688.. varieties from	£250	£700

James VII ten shillings

WILLIAM & MARY (1689–94)

Sixty shillings

	F	VF
1691...	£295	£1100
1692...	£475	£1750

Forty shillings

	F	VF
1689.. varieties from	£295	£850
1690.. varieties from	£185	£525
1691.. varieties from	£195	£550
1692.. varieties from	£225	£600
1693.. varieties from	£195	£550
1694.. varieties from	£225	£775

Twenty shillings

	F	VF
1693...	£450	£1500
1694...	Extremely rare	

Ten shillings

	F	VF
1689...	Extremely rare	
1690.. varieties from	£295	£750
1691.. varieties from	£195	£000
1692.. varieties from	£195	£600
1694.. varieties from	£250	£700

Five shillings

	F	VF
1691...	£200	£575
1694.. varieties from	£120	£350

Copper Issues

	F	VF
Bawbees 1691–94.......................... varieties from	£100	£275
Bodle (Turners) 1691–94................. varieties from	£55	£180

William & Mary ten shillings

	F	VF

WILLIAM II (1694–1702)

	F	VF
Pistole	£3000	£7500
Half pistole	£3750	£8500

Forty shillings

		F	VF
1695	varieties from	£175	£550
1696		£200	£525
1697		£250	£550
1698		£200	£495
1699		£325	£650
1700		Extremely rare	

Twenty shillings

		F	VF
1695		£200	£625
1696		£200	£625
1697	varieties from	£250	£700
1698	varieties from	£175	£650
1699		£225	£625

William II ten shillings

Ten shillings

		F	VF
1695		£150	£375
1696		£150	£375
1697	varieties from	£150	£375
1698	varieties from	£150	£375
1699		£295	£750

Five shillings

		F	VF
1695		£70	£195
1696		£65	£180
1697	varieties from	£75	£225
1699		£95	£275
1700		£85	£230
1701		£125	£350
1702		£125	£350

Anne five shillings

Copper Issues

		F	VF
Bawbee 1695–97	varieties from	£85	£325
Bodle (Turners) 1695–97	varieties from	£50	£150

ANNE (1702–14)

Pre -Union 1702–7
Ten shillings

		F	VF
1705		£175	£450
1706	varieties from	£225	£650

Five shillings

		F	VF
1705	varieties from	£85	£225
1706		£85	£225

POST-UNION 1707–14
See listing in English section.

JAMES VIII (The Old Pretender) (1688–1766)

A number of Guineas and Crowns in various metals were struck in 1828 using original dies prepared by Norbert Roettiers, all bearing the date 1716. These coins are extremely rare and are keenly sought after.

Crown

1716	Generally EF+	£2500

Our grateful thanks go to David Stuart of ABC Coins & Tokens who has spent many hours updating the Scottish section for 2017.

ISLE OF MAN

DATE	F	VF	EF	UNC

PENNY

	F	VF	EF	UNC
1709 Cast	£50	£175	£350	—
1709 Silver cast Proof	—	—	—	£2000
1709 Brass	£50	£175	£350	—
1733 "Quocunque"	£40	£75	£275	£400
1733 "Ouocunoue"	£45	£85	£300	£750
1733 Bath metal "Quocunque"	£30	£75	£300	—
1733 Silver Proof	—	—	—	£850
1733 Bronze Proof	—	—	—	£500
1733 Proof	—	—	—	£675
1733 Cap frosted	£35	£75	£300	£500
1733 Brass, cap frosted	£40	£75	£325	£650
1733 Silver Proof cap frosted	—	—	—	£650
1733 Bronze annulets instead of pellets	£50	£100	£400	£500
1758	£30	£50	£250	£450
1758 Proof	—	—	—	£650
1758 Silver Proof	—	—	—	£1000
1786 Engrailed edge	£35	£65	£275	£450
1786 Engrailed edge Proof	—	—	—	£600
1786 Plain edge Proof	—	—	—	£1000
1786 Pellet below bust	£35	£65	£275	£550
1798	£35	£65	£250	£500
1798 Proof	—	—	—	£450
1798 Bronze Proof	—	—	—	£450
1798 Copper-gilt Proof	—	—	—	£2000
1798 Silver Proof	—	—	—	£2500
1813	£40	£75	£300	£500
1813 Proof	—	—	—	£650
1813 Bronze Proof	—	—	—	£650
1813 Copper-gilt Proof	—	—	—	£2500
1839	£35	£75	£200	£450
1839 Proof	—	—	—	£500

HALF PENCE

	F	VF	EF	UNC
1709 Cast	£50	£125	£250	—
1709 Brass	£55	£185	£490	—
1723 Silver	£725	£1250	£3500	—
1723 Copper	£300	£600	£1750	£2500
1733 Copper	£35	£55	£225	£450
1733 Bronze	£35	£55	£225	£450
1733 Silver Proof plain cap	—	—	—	£700
1733 Silver Proof frosted cap	—	—	—	—
1733 Bronze Proof	—	—	—	£500
1733 Bath metal plain cap	£40	£50	£215	—
1733 Bath metal frosted cap	£40	£50	£215	—
1758	£40	£50	£215	£450
1758 Proof	—	—	—	£800
1786 Engrailed edge	£30	£45	£120	£350
1786 Proof engrailed edge	—	—	—	£450
1786 Plain edge	£40	£65	£250	£350
1786 Proof plain edge	—	—	—	£650
1786 Bronze Proof	—	—	—	£450
1798	£35	£45	£150	£350
1798 Proof	—	—	—	£450
1798 Bronze Proof	—	—	—	£400

DATE	F	VF	EF	UNC
1798 Copper-gilt Proof...............................	—	—	—	£1500
1798 Silver Proof.......................................	—	—	—	£1500
1813	£30	£45	£150	£300
1813 Proof..	—	—	—	£375
1813 Bronze Proof....................................	—	—	—	£350
1813 Copper-gilt Proof..............................	—	—	—	£1250
1839	£30	£45	£150	£300
1839 Bronze Proof....................................	—	—	—	£450

FARTHING

	F	VF	EF	UNC
1839 Copper	£30	£45	£150	£300
1839 Bronze Proof	—	—	—	£450
1839 Copper-gilt Proof	—	—	—	£2500

The last issue of coins made in the Isle of Man had been in 1839 but in 1970 Spink & Son Ltd was commissioned to produce a modern coinage for the Isle of Man Government which was struck at the Royal Mint. From 1973 onwards the Pobjoy Mint took over the contract and has been a very prolific producer of definitive and commemorative issues. It is not proposed to give a complete listing of all these coins but the Crown and 25p, which from the collector's point of view are the most interesting in the series, are listed below. However, as the prices for these items vary dramatically according to the source it has been decided not to price them. Additionally a special 50p coin is issued to celebrate Christmas each year.

The listings that follow are of the ordinary uncirculated cupro-nickel crown-size coins. Many of these coins are also produced in other metals, including silver, gold and platinum in non proof and proof form and in 1984 some were also issued in silver clad cupro-nickel in proof form.

DATE

1970 Manx Cat
1972 Royal Silver Wedding
1974 Centenary of Churchill's birth£15
1975 Manx Cat
1976 Bi-Centenary of American Independence
1976 Centenary of the Horse Drawn Tram
1977 Silver Jubilee
1977 Silver Jubilee Appeal
1978 25th Anniversary of the Coronation
1979 300th Anniversary of Manx Coinage
1979 Millennium of Tynwald (5 coins)
1980 Winter Olympics
1980 Derby Bicentennial
1980 22nd Olympics (3 coins)
1980 80th Birthday of Queen Mother
1981 Duke of Edinburgh Award Scheme (4 coins)
1981 Year of Disabled (4 coins)
1981 Prince of Wales' Wedding (2 coins)
1982 12th World Cup—Spain (4 coins)
1982 Maritime Heritage (4 coins)
1983 Manned Flight (4 coins)
1984 23rd Olympics (4 coins)
1984 Quincentenary of College of Arms (4 coins)
1984 Commonwealth Parliamentary Conference (4 coins)
1985 Queen Mother (6 coins)
1986 13th World Cup—Mexico (6 coins)
1986 Prince Andrew Wedding (2 coins)
1987 200th Anniversary of the United States Constitution

DATE

1987 America's Cup Races (5 coins)
1988 Bicentenary of Steam Navigation (6 coins)
1988 Australia Bicentennial (6 coins)
1988 Manx Cat
1989 Royal Visit
1989 Bicentenary of the Mutiny on the Bounty (4 coins)
1989 Persian Cat
1989 Bicentenary of Washington's Inauguration (4 coins)
1990 150th Anniversary of the Penny Black
1990 World Cup—Italy (4 coins)
1990 25th Anniversary of Churchill's Death (2 coins)
1990 Alley Cat
1990 Queen Mother's 90th Birthday
1991 Norwegian Forest Cat
1991 Centenary of the American Numismatic Association
1991 1992 America's Cup
1991 10th Anniversary of Prince of Wales' Wedding (2 coins)
1992 Discovery of America (4 coins)
1992 Siamese Cat
1992 1992 America's Cup
1993 Maine Coon Cat
1993 Preserve Planet Earth—Dinosaurs (2 coins)
1994 Preserve Planet Earth—Mammoth
1994 Year of the Dog
1994 World Football Cup (6 coins)
1994 Japanese Bobtail Cat
1994 Normandy Landings (8 coins)
1994 Preserve Planet Earth—Endangered Animals (3 coins)
1995 Man in Flight—Series i (8 coins)
1995 Man in Flight—Series ii (8 coins)
1995 Queen Mother's 95th Birthday
1995 Year of the Pig
1995 Turkish Cat
1995 Preserve Planet Earth—Egret and Otter
1995 America's Cup
1995 Aircraft of World War II (19 coins)
1995 Famous World Inventions—Series i (12 coins)
1996 Year of the Rat
1996 70th Birthday of HM the Queen
1996 The Flower Fairies—Series i (4 coins)
1996 Famous World Inventions—Series ii (6 coins)
1996 Olympic Games (6 coins)
1996 Preserve Planet Earth—Killer Whale and Razorbill
1996 Burmese Cat
1996 Robert Burns (4 coins)
1996 King Arthur & the Knights of the Round Table (5 coins)
1996 European Football Championships (8 coins)
1996 Football Championships Winner
1996 Explorers (2 coins)
1997 Year of the Ox
1997 The Flower Fairies—Series ii (4 coins)
1997 Royal Golden Wedding (2 coins)
1997 Explorers—Eriksson and Nansen (2 coins)
1997 Long-haired Smoke Cat
1997 10th Anniversary of the "Cats on Coins" series (silver only)
1997 90th Anniversary of the TT Races (4 coins)
1998 The Millennium (16 coins issued over 3 years)
1998 Year of the Tiger
1998 FIFA World Cup (4 coins)
1998 Birman Cat
1998 The Flower Fairies—Series iii (4 coins)
1998 18th Winter Olympics, Nagano (4 coins)
1998 Explorers—Vasco da Gama and Marco Polo (2 coins)
1998 125th Anniversary of Steam Railway (8 coins)
1998 International Year of the Oceans (4 coins)
1999 50th Birthday of HRH the Prince of Wales
1999 Year of the Rabbit

DATE

1999 27th Olympics in Sydney (5 coins)
1999 Rugby World Cup (6 coins)
1999 Wedding of HRH Prince Edward and Sophie Rhys-Jones
1999 Queen Mother's 100th Birthday (4 coins)
1999 The Millennium (4 coins)
1999 Titanium Millennium crown
2000 Year of the Dragon
2000 Scottish Fold cat
2000 Millennium—own a piece of time
2000 Explorers, Francisco Piarro and Wilem Brents (2 coins)
2000 Life and times of the Queen Mother (4 coins)
2000 Queen Mother's 100th Birthday
2000 60th Anniversary of the Battle of Britain
2000 BT Global Challenge
2000 18th Birthday of HRH Prince William
2001 Year of the Snake
2001 The Somali cat
2001 Life and times of the Queen Mother (2 coins)
2001 Explorers, Martin Frobisher and Roald Amundsen (2 coins)
2001 75th Birthday of HM the Queen
2001 Joey Dunlop
2001 Harry Potter (6 coins)
2002 Year of the Horse
2002 The XIX Winter Olympiad, Salt Lake City (2 coins)
2002 World Cup 2002 in Japan/Korea (4 coins)
2002 The Bengal Cat
2002 The Queen's Golden Jubilee—i (1 coin)
2002 Introduction of the Euro
2002 The Queen's Golden Jubilee—ii (4 coins)
2002 A Tribute to Diana Princess of Wales—5 years on
2003 Year of the Goat
2003 The Balinese Cat
2003 Anniversary of the "Star of India"
2003 Lord of the Rings (5 coins)
2004 Olympics (4 coins)
2004 100 Years of Powered Flight (2 coins)
2005 Lord of the Rings: The Return of the King
2005 Manx Hero Lt. John Quilliam and the Battle of Trafalgar (2 coins)
2005 The Himalayan Cat with kittens
2005 Bicentenary of the Battle of Trafalgar (6 coins)
2005 60th Anniversary of D-Day (6 coins)
2005 60th Anniversary of Victory in Europe
2005 200th Anniversary of the Battle of Trafalgar
2005 400th Anniversary of the Gun Powder Plot (2 coins)
2005 Bicentenary of the Battle of Trafalgar and Death of Nelson
2005 Italy and the Isle of Man TT races (2 coins)
2005 Harry Potter and the Goblet of Fire (4 coins)
2006 100 Years of Norwegian Independence
2006 80th Birthday of Her Majesty the Queen (4 coins)
2006 The Battles that Changed the World—Part II (6 coins)
2006 150th Anniversary of the Victoria Cross (2 coins)
2006 30th Anniversary of the first Translantic Flight
2007 The Ragdoll Cat
2007 Fairy Tales—Sleeping Beauty, The Three Little Pigs (2 coins)
2007 The Graceful Swan
2007 The Royal Diamond Wedding Anniversary
2007 The Centenary of the TT races
2007 The Centenary of the Scouting
2008 50th Anniversary of Paddington Bear
2008 Prince Charles 60th Birthday
2008 Centenary of the Olympics
2008 Burmilla Cat
2008 Year of Planet Earth
2008 The Adorable Snowman
2008 UEFA European Football Championships
2008 The Return of Tutankhamun

DATE

2008 The Olympic Collection—The Olympics coming to London
2009 Winter Olympics (2 coins)
2009 The Chinchilla Cat
2009 40th Anniversary of the 1st Concorde Test Flight
2009 50 Years of Championship Racing
2009 Fifa World Cup South Africa 2010
2010 50 Years of racing by the Suzuki Racing Team
2010 Abyssinian Cat and her Kitten
2010 Celebrating 15 Years of the Gold Noble
2010 25th Anniversary of the Gold Angel coin
2011 Year of the Rabbit coloured coin
2011 Engagement of HRH Prince William to Catherine Middleton
2011 Royal Wedding of HRH Prince William and Catherine Middleton
2011 Buckingham Palace
2011 A Lifetime of Service—Queen Elizabeth II and Prince Philip
2011 The Turkish Angora Cat
2011 Donatello's famous Chellini Madonna
2011 TT Races
2012 European Football Championships (4 coins)
2012 Manx Cat Coin
2012 Centenary of RMS *Titanic*
2012 Juno Moneta Coin
2012 Petra Coin
2012 River Thames Diamond Jubilee Pageant
2012 Olympics (6 coins).
2013 St. Patrick Commemorative
2013 Kermode Bear
2013 Anniversary of Queen Victoria and Queen Elizabeth II Coronations
2013 Siberian Cat
2013 Winter Olympic (4 coins)
2013 Lifetime of Service—Queen Elizabeth II and Prince Philip
2014 Centenary of WWI
2014 200th Anniversary of Matthew Flinders
2014 Snowshoe Cat
2014 The Snowman & Snowdog Christmas crown (+coloured issue)
2014 70th Anniversary of D-Day (poppies picked out in red)
2015 75th Anniversary of the Battle of Britain (search lights in yellow)
2015 200th Anniversary of the Battle of Waterloo—Napoleon
2015 200th Anniversary of the Battle of Waterloo—Wellington
2015 Sir Winston Churchill
2015 Selkirk Rex Cat
2015 175th Anniversary of the Penny Black Stamp (issued in a pack)
2015 Paddington Bear
2015 Her Majesty the Queen Elizabeth II Longest reigning Monarch
2016 Tobacco Brown Cat

The regular attractive issues from the Isle of Man are popular with many thematic collectors and can make a superb display.

GUERNSEY

DATE	F	VF	EF	UNC
TEN SHILLINGS				
1966..	—	£5	£9	£15
1966 Proof..	—	—	—	£25
THREEPENCE				
1956..	£1	£4	£8	£10
1956 Proof..	—	—	—	£15
1959..	£1	£4	£8	£15
1966 Proof..	—	—	—	£15
EIGHT DOUBLES				
1834..	£10	£15	£50	£175
1858 5 berries.....................................	£6	£10	£50	£150
1858 4 berries.....................................	£6	£10	£50	£160
1864 1 stalk..	£6	£10	£40	£70
1864 3 stalks	£6	£10	£30	£65
1868..	£6	£10	£30	£65
1874..	£4	£6	£15	£50
1885H..	£4	£6	£15	£45
1889H..	£3	£4	£15	£40
1893H small date	£3	£4	£15	£40
1893H large date	£3	£4	£15	£40
1902H..	£3	£4	£15	£40
1903H..	£3	£4	£15	£40
1910..	£3	£4	£15	£40
1911H..	£3	£4	£15	£45
1914H..	£1	£3	£10	£30
1918H..	£1	£3	£8	£25
1920H..	£1	£3	£8	£25
1934H..	£1	£3	£10	£35
1934H Proof	—	—	—	£200
1938H..	£1	£3	£10	£25
1945H..	£1	£2	£8	£15
1947H..	£1	£2	£8	£15
1949H..	—	£2	£9	£15
1956..	—	£1	£7	£15
1956..	—	£1	£5	£15
1959..	—	£1	£5	£15
1966 Proof..	—	—	—	£35
FOUR DOUBLES				
1830..	£4	£9	£50	£125
1830 Mule with obv. St Helena 1/2d	—	£850	—	—
1858..	£6	£12	£50	£135
1864 Single stalk	£2	£6	£20	£60
1864 3 stalks	£2	£6	£25	£65
1868..	£3	£7	£22	£75
1874..	£2	£6	£22	£75
1885H..	£2	£6	£20	£45
1889H..	£2	£3	£15	£35
1893H..	£2	£3	£15	£35
1902H..	£2	£3	£10	£30
1903H..	£2	£3	£13	£30
1906H..	£2	£3	£10	£25
1908H..	£2	£3	£10	£25
1910H..	£2	£3	£10	£25
1911H..	£2	£3	£8	£25
1914H..	£2	£3	£13	£45
1918H..	£2	£3	£12	£35
1920H..	£2	£3	£10	£35
1945H..	£2	£3	£10	£35
1949H..	£2	£3	£12	£35
1956..	£1	£2	£8	£15
1966 Proof..	—	—	—	£20

DATE	F	VF	EF	UNC
TWO DOUBLES				
1858	£6	£10	£50	£200
1868 Single stick	£6	£12	£55	£200
1868 3 stalks	£7	£15	£85	£225
1874	£4	£10	£50	£150
1885H	£3	£6	£20	£35
1889H	£3	£5	£20	£35
1899H	£3	£5	£25	£50
1902H	£3	£5	£20	£35
1903H	£3	£5	£20	£35
1906H	£3	£5	£20	£35
1908H	£3	£5	£20	£35
1911H	£3	£5	£25	£45
1914H	£3	£5	£25	£45
1917H	£7	£20	£85	£225
1918H	£3	£5	£15	£30
1920H	£3	£5	£15	£30
1929H	£2	£3	£12	£20

	F	VF	EF	UNC
ONE DOUBLE				
1830	£3	£4	£22	£45
1868	£4	£10	£35	£120
1868/30	£5	£7	£27	£85
1885H	£2	£3	£8	£20
1889H	£1	£2	£6	£20
1893H	£1	£2	£6	£20
1899H	£1	£2	£6	£20
1902	£1	£2	£6	£20
1903H	£1	£2	£6	£20
1911H	£1	£2	£8	£20
1911 (new shield)	£1	£2	£6	£20
1914H	£1	£2	£8	£20
1929H	£1	£2	£6	£20
1933H	£1	£2	£6	£20
1938H	£1	£2	£6	£20

DECIMAL COINAGE

Ordinary circulating coinage from 1986 onwards is usually available in uncirculated condition at a small premium above face value thus it is not listed here. The coins listed are cupro-nickel unless otherwise stated.

	UNC
ONE HUNDRED POUNDS	
1994 50th Anniversary of Normandy Landings. Gold proof	£1500
1995 Anniversary of the Liberation. Gold proof	£1500
FIFTY POUNDS	
1994 50th Anniversary of Normandy Landings. Gold proof	£950
1995 Anniversary of the Liberation. Gold proof	£950
1998 Queen Elizabeth and Queen Mother Gold proof	£1000
1999 Queen Elizabeth and Queen Mother Gold	£900
2004 Anniversary of D-Day. Gold	£1100
2013 70th Anniversary of the Dambuster Raid. Silver proof 10oz	£600
TWENTY-FIVE POUNDS	
1994 50th Anniversary of Normandy Landings. Gold	£ 420
1994 — Gold proof	£ 420
1995 Anniversary of the Liberation. Gold proof	£ 420
1995 Queen Mothers 95th Birthday. Gold	£ 420
1996 European Football Championships. Gold proof	£ 420
1997 Royal Golden Wedding. Gold proof	£ 420
1998 Royal Air Force. Gold proof	£ 420
2000 Queen Mother 100th Birthday. Gold proof	£ 420
2001 Queen Victoria centennial Gold proof	£ 420
2001 Queen Victoria gold proof	£ 420
2001 HM the Queen's 75th Birthday. Gold proof	£425
2002 Princess Diana memorial. Gold proof	£ 420
2002 Duke of Wellington. Gold proof	£ 420

DATE	UNC
2002 Golden Jubilee. Gold proof	£ 420
2002 Queen Mother. Gold proof	£ 420
2003 Golden Jubilee. Gold proof	£ 420
2003 Golden Hind. Gold proof	£ 420
2004 Anniversary of D-Day. Gold proof	£ 420
2004 Age of Steam—Truro. Gold proof	£ 420
2004 Age of Steam—Mallard. Gold proof	£ 420
2004 HMS Invincible. Gold proof	£ 420
2005 HMS Ark Royal. Gold proof	£ 420
2006 FIFA World Cup. Gold proof	£ 420

TEN POUNDS

1994 50th Anniversary of Normandy Landings. Gold proof	£225
1995 Anniversary of the Liberation. Gold proof	£225
2000 Century of Monarchy. Silver proof	£150
2000 Guernsey Gold proof 'Nugget'	£250
2001 19th Century Monarchy. Silver proof	£150
2002 18th Century Monarchy. Silver proof	£150
2004 Anniversary of D-Day. Silver proof	£150
2012 Diamond Jubilee. 5 oz Silver proof	£250
2013 Coronation Jubilee 5 oz Silver proof	£250

FIVE POUNDS

1995 Queen Mother's 95th birthday	£25
1995 — Silver proof	£55
1995 — Small size gold	£250
1996 HM the Queen's 70th birthday	£18
1996 — Silver proof	£55
1996 European Football Championships	£35
1996 — Silver proof	£55
1997 Royal Golden Wedding	£25
1997 — Silver proof	£55
1997 — Small size gold. BU	£250
1997 Castles of the British Isles—Castle Cornet, Guernsey	£20
1997 — Silver proof	£65
1997 Castles of the British Isles—Caernarfon Castle. Silver proof	£75
1997 Castles of the British Isles—Leeds Castle. Silver proof	£75
1998 Royal Air Force.	£15
1998 Royal Air Force. Silver proof	£70
1999 Millennium. Brass	£25
1999 — Silver proof	£55
1999 Wedding of HRH Prince Edward and Sophie Rhys-Jones	£25
1999 — Silver proof	£55
1999 Queen Mother	£25
1999 — Silver proof	£80
1999 Winston Churchill	£15
1999 — Gold	£1000
2000 Queen Mother's 100th Birthday	£10
2000 — Silver proof	£85
2000 — Small size gold. proof	£200
2000 Centuries of the British Monarchy	£45
2000 — Silver proof	£85
2000 — Small size gold. proof	£200
2001 The Reign of Queen Victoria	£20
2001 — Gold proof	£300
2001 — proof	£60
2001 — Silver proof	£60
2001 HM the Queen's 75th Birthday	£15
2001 — Silver proof	£60
2001 — Small size gold. proof	£200
2001 19th Century Monarchy	£20
2001 — Silver proof	£60
2001 — Small size gold. proof	£200
2002 Golden Jubilee (two types)	£15
2002 — Silver proof	£65
2002 Princess Diana Memorial	£15
2002 — proof	£60
2002 — Gold proof	£1000

DATE	UNC
2002 Century of Monarchy	£15
2002 — Silver proof	£60
2002 — Small size gold. proof	£200
2002 Queen Mother Memoriam	£20
2002 — proof	£25
2002 — Silver proof	£65
2002 — Small size gold proof	£200
2002 — Large size gold proof	£1000
2003 Duke of Wellington	£15
2003 — Silver proof	£50
2003 — Small size gold proof	£200
2003 — Large size gold proof	£1000
2003 Prince William	£20
2003 — Silver proof	£60
2003 — Gold proof	£1000
2003 Golden Hind	£20
2003 17th Century Monarchy	£25
2003 History of the Royal Navy, Nelson	£20
2003 — Nelson with coloured flag. proof	£30
2004 — Invincible. Silver proof	£50
2004 16th Century monarchs	£15
2004 History of the Railways, Mallard	£12
2004 — City of Truro	£15
2004 — The Boat Train	£12
2004 — The Train Spotter	£15
2004 History of the Royal Navy, Henry VIII	£15
2004 — Invincible	£15
2004 Anniversary of D-Day	£12
2004 — Silver proof	£50
2004 — Gold proof	£1000
2004 Anniversary of the Crimean War. Plain	£12
2004 — with colour	£15
2004 — Silver proof	£55
2004 — Gold proof with colour	£1250
2005 200th Anniversary of the Battle of Trafalgar	£25
2005 60th Anniversary of the Liberation of the Channel Islands	£25
2005 End of World War II. Silver proof	£55
2005 — Gold proof	£1250
2005 Anniversary of Liberation. Gold proof	£1250
2006 Royal 80th Birthday. Silver proof	£55
2006 FIFA World Cup. Silver proof	£55
2006 Great Britons—Sir Winston Churchill Silver. Issued as part of set	£60
2006 80th Birthday of Her Majesty the Queen	£25
2007 History of the Royal Navy—Henry VIII, The Golden Hind (2 coins)	£65
2007 Royal Diamond Wedding	£25
2008 90th Anniversary of the RAF (10 different designs in silver proof) ea.	£35
2009 British warships (6 different designs in silver proof) ea.	£35
2009 Anniversary of Apollo Moon landings. Cu-ni	£5
2009 — Silver proof	£35
2010 Charles II Unite. Gold proof	£1500
2010 Florence Nightingale. Gold proof	£1500
2011 350th Anniversary of the Crown Jewels. Silver proof	£95
2011 90th Anniversary of the British Legion (gold-plated copper)	£45
2011 — Silver proof	£95
2011 40th Anniversary of decimalisation, proof	£20
2011 Anniversary of the sinking of the *Titanic*	£20
2011 — Silver proof	£55
2011 30th Birthday of Duke of Cambridge	£20
2011 — Silver proof	£55
2011 Wedding of Prince William and Kate Middleton	£25
2011 — Silver proof	£55
2011 400th Anniversary of the King James Bible	£25
2012 Diamond Jubilee £5	£25
2012 — Gold proof	£1500
2012 The Tribute to the British Army. Gold proof	£2000
2013 70th Anniversary of the Dambuster Raid.	£20
2013 — Silver proof	£65
2013 — Gold proof	£2000
2013 Coronation Jubilee	£25

DATE	UNC
2013 — Silver proof..	£55
2013 — Gold proof..	£2000
2013 200th Guinea Anniv.	£25
2013 — Silver proof..	£55
2013 — Gold proof..	£2000
2014 Centenary of the First World War. Silver proof	£85
2014 — 5oz Silver proof..	£450
2014 — Gold proof..	£2500
2016 Battle of the Somme proof..	—
2016 90th Birthday of HM the Queen. Silver proof	—

TWO POUNDS

1985 40th anniversary of Liberation..	£10
1985 — proof	£30
1985 — Silver proof..	£55
1986 Commonwealth Games, in plastic case......................................	£12
1986 — in special folder..	£12
1986 — .500 Silver...	£45
1986 — .925 Silver proof..	£55
1987 900th Anniv. of death of William the Conqueror, in folder..............	£15
1987 — Silver proof..	£55
1987 — Gold proof..	£1300
1988 William II, in presentation folder	£15
1988 — Silver proof..	£55
1989 Henry I, in presentation folder	£15
1989 — Silver proof..	£55
1989 Royal Visit...	£15
1989 — Silver proof..	£55
1990 Queen Mother's 90th birthday..	£15
1990 — Silver proof..	£55
1991 Henry II, in presentation folder	£15
1991 — Silver proof..	£55
1993 40th Anniversary of the Coronation..	£15
1993 — Silver proof..	£60
1994 Anniversary of the Normandy Landings.......................................	£15
1994 — Silver proof..	£55
1995 50th Anniversary of Liberation	£154
1995 — Silver proof..	£55
1995 — Silver Piedfort proof...	£100
1997 Conserving Nature i..	£12
1997 — Silver proof..	£55
1997 Bimetallic Latent image..	£8
1997 — proof	£10
1998 Conserving Nature ii...	£10
1998 Bimetallic Latent image..	£6
2003 —	£6
2006 —	£8
2011 Prince Philip's 90th Birthday (conjoined portraits)	£6
2011 — Silver proof..	£50

ONE POUND

1981	£10
1981 Gold proof	£145
1981 Gold piedfort	£345
1983 New specification, new reverse..	£10
1985 New design (in folder)..	£10
1995 Queen Mother's 95th Birthday. Silver proof	£50
1996 Queen's 70th Birthday. Silver proof..	£55
1997 Royal Golden Wedding. Silver BU...	£20
1997 — Silver proof..	£55
1997 Castles of the British Isles—Tower of London. Silver proof only ...	£35
1998 Royal Air Force. Silver proof...	£45
1999 Wedding of Prince Edward. Silver proof	£55
1999 Queen Mother. Silver proof...	£55
1999 Winston Churchill. Silver proof	£55
2000 Millennium. Silver proof (gold plated)...	£65
2000 Queen Mother's 100th Birthday. Silver proof	£45
2001	£2
2001 HM the Queen's 75th Birthday. Silver proof................................	£45

DATE	UNC
2002 William of Normandy. Silver	£20
2003	£2
2006	£2

FIFTY PENCE

1969	£4
1970	£6
1971 proof	£9
1981	£4
1982	£4
1985 New design	£4
2000 60th Anniversary of the Battle of Britain.	£4
2000 — Silver proof	£55
2000 — Silver piedfort	£55
2000 — Gold proof	£365
2003	£2
2006	£2
2008	£2
2012 The Diamond Jubilee (coloured portrait)	£10
2013 The RAF 617 Squadron Gold-Plated coin	£25
2013 50th Anniversary of the Flying Scotsman's retirement in 1963	£25
2014 New Queen Elizabeth II	£45
2016 90th Birthday of Queen Elizabeth II (two round crown-size coloured coins)	—

TWENTY-FIVE PENCE

1972 Royal Silver Wedding	£12
1972 — Silver proof	£45
1977 Royal Silver Jubilee	£10
1977 — Silver proof	£45
1978 Royal Visit	£10
1978 — Silver proof	£45
1980 Queen Mother's 80th birthday	£10
1980 — Silver proof	£45
1981 Royal Wedding	£10
1981 — Silver proof	£45

Since the introduction of decimal coinage a number of companies have been involved in marketing the coins of the Channel Islands. As a consequence many special limited edition commemorative coins have been issued in a wide variety of sizes, metals and finishes. These are very numerous with some issues being produced in very small numbers and many are omitted from our listings. These issues are generally outside of the scope of this catologue but we intend to cover them more fully in a future edition.

JERSEY

DATE	F	VF	EF	UNC

FIVE SHILLINGS

	F	VF	EF	UNC
1966	—	£3	£7	£15
1966 Proof	—	£3	£9	£25

ONE QUARTER OF A SHILLING

	F	VF	EF	UNC
1957	—	£2	£5	£10
1960 Proof	—	—	£5	£15
1964	—	—	£4	£10
1966	—	—	£4	£10

ONE TWELFTH OF A SHILLING

	F	VF	EF	UNC
1877H	£2	£3	£18	£60
1877H Proof in nickel	—	—	—	£1275
1877 Proof only	—	—	—	£475
1877 Proof in nickel	—	—	—	£1275
1881	£3	£3	£15	£60
1888	£2	£3	£15	£50
1894	£2	£3	£20	£50
1909	£2	£3	£15	£35
1911	£2	£3	£10	£30
1913	£2	£3	£10	£30
1923 Spade shield	£2	£3	£10	£30
1923 Square shield	£2	£3	£10	£30
1926	£2	£3	£12	£45
1931	£2	£3	£8	£15
1933	£2	£3	£8	£15
1935	£2	£3	£8	£15
1937	£2	£3	£8	£15
1946	£2	£3	£8	£15
1947	—	£3	£8	£15
"1945" GVI	—	—	£2	£10
"1945" QE2	—	—	£2	£8
1957	—	—	£2	£7
1960 1660–1960 300th anniversary	—	—	£2	£7
1960 Mule	—	—	—	£150
1964	—	£2	£3	£10
1966 "1066–1966"	—	—	£1	£8

ONE THIRTEENTH OF A SHILLING

	F	VF	EF	UNC
1841	£4	£8	£40	£200
1844	£4	£9	£40	£200
1851	£5	£12	£60	£250
1858	£4	£9	£45	£200
1861	£5	£13	£60	£175
1865 Proof only	—	—	—	£750
1866 with LCW	£2	£5	£95	£150
1866 without LCW Proof only	—	—	—	£400
1870	£4	£8	£40	£125
1871	£4	£8	£42	£125

ONE TWENTY-FOURTH OF A SHILLING

	F	VF	EF	UNC
1877H	£3	£4	£15	£60
1877 Proof only	—	—	—	£300
1888	£3	£4	£15	£45
1894	£3	£4	£15	£45
1909	£3	£4	£15	£45
1911	£2	£3	£10	£45

DATE	F	VF	EF	UNC
1913	£2	£3	£10	£45
1923 Spade shield	£2	£3	£10	£35
1923 Square shield	£2	£3	£8	£35
1926	£2	£3	£10	£25
1931	£2	£3	£10	£25
1933	£2	£3	£10	£25
1935	£2	£3	£10	£25
1937	£1	£2	£6	£20
1946	£1	£2	£6	£20
1947	£1	£2	£6	£20

ONE TWENTY-SIXTH OF A SHILLING

	F	VF	EF	UNC
1841	£4	£7	£30	£100
1844	£4	£7	£25	£100
1851	£3	£6	£25	£100
1858	£4	£11	£50	£200
1861	£3	£6	£25	£65
1866	£3	£6	£30	£85
1870	£3	£6	£20	£55
1871	£3	£6	£20	£55

ONE FORTY-EIGHTH OF A SHILLING

	F	VF	EF	UNC
1877H	£6	£12	£60	£150
1877 Proof only	—	—	—	£450

ONE FIFTY-SECOND OF A SHILLING

	F	VF	EF	UNC
1841	£9	£25	£60	£200
1861 Proof only	—	—	—	£650

DECIMAL COINAGE

Ordinary circulating coinage from 1986 onwards is usually available in uncirculated condition at a small premium above face value thus it is not listed here.

ONE HUNDRED POUNDS

1990 50th Anniversary of the Battle of Britain. Gold Proof.	£1000
1995 50th Anniversary of Liberation. Gold proof	£1000

FIFTY POUNDS

1972 Silver Wedding. Gold proof	£850
1990 50th Anniversary of the Battle of Britain. Gold proof	£850
1995 50th Anniversary of Liberation. Gold proof	£850
2003 Golden Jubilee. Silver Proof (100mm)	£650
2013 RMS Titanic Centenary. 10oz Silver Proof	£600

TWENTY-FIVE POUNDS

1972 25th Royal Wedding anniversary. Gold	£300
1972 — Gold proof	£375
1990 50th Anniversary of Battle of Britain. Gold proof	£350
1995 50th Anniversary of Liberation. Gold proof	£350
2002 Princess Diana memorial. Gold proof	£350
2002 Queen Mother. Gold proof	£350
2002 Golden Jubilee. Gold proof	£350
2002 Duke of Wellington. Gold proof	£350
2003 Golden Jubilee. Gold proof	£350
2003 History of the Royal Navy. Naval Commanders	£350
2003 — Francis Drake	£350
2003 — Sovereign of the Seas	£350
2004 60th Anniversary of D-Day. Gold proof	£350
2004 Charge of the Light Brigade. Gold proof	£350
2004 HMS Victory. Gold proof	£350
2004 John Fisher 1841–1920 Gold proof	£350
2004 The Coronation Scot. Gold proof	£350
2004 The Flying Scotsman. Gold proof	£350
2004 Golden Arrow. Gold proof	£350

DATE	UNC
2004 Rocket and Evening Star. Gold proof	£350
2005 Andrew Cunningham. Gold proof	£350
2005 HMS Conqueror. Gold Proof	£350
2005 200th Anniversary of Nelson. Gold proof	£350
2009 500th Anniversary of Accession. Gold proof	£350

TWENTY POUNDS
1972 Royal Wedding. The Ormer. Gold	£300
1972 — Gold proof	£300

TEN POUNDS
1972 25th Royal Wedding anniversary. Gold	£75
1972 — Gold proof	£180
1990 50th Anniversary of the Battle of Britain. Gold proof	£180
1995 50th Anniversary of Liberation. Gold proof	£140
2003 Coronation Anniversary. Gold/silver proof	£50
2004 Crimea. Silver proof	£20
2205 Trafalgar. Silver proof	£20
2005 — Silver/gold proof	£110
2005 End of World War II. Silver proof	£25
2007 Diamond Wedding. Platinum proof	£280
2008 History of RAF. Silver proof	£25
2008 — Silver/Gold proof	£110
2011 Royal Wedding of HRH Prince William & Catherine Middleton, silver (65mm)	£395
2012 Poppy. 5oz Silver Proof	£350
2013 Flying Scotsman. 5oz Silver Proof	£350

(Enlarged)

FIVE POUNDS
1972 Gold proof	£65
1990 50th Anniversary of the Battle of Britain. Silver Proof (5 ounces)	£180
1997 Royal Golden Wedding	£10
1997 — Silver proof	£25
2000 Millennium. Silver proof	£35
2002 Princess Diana memorial	£12
2002 — Silver proof	£30
2002 — Gold proof	£800
2002 Royal Golden Jubilee	£25
2003 Golden Jubilee	£20
2003 — Silver proof	£55
2003 — Gold proof	£1000
2003 Prince William 21st Birthday	£15
2003 — Silver Proof	£55
2003 —Gold proof	£1000
2003 Naval Commanders	£15
2003 — Silver proof	£55
2003 — Gold proof	£1000
2003 Francis Drake	£15
2003 — Silver proof	£55
2003 — Gold proof	£1000
2003 Sovereign of the Seas	£15
2003 — Silver proof	£55
2003 — Gold proof	£1000
2004 60th Anniversary of 'D' Day	£15
2004 — Silver proof	£55
2004 — Gold proof	£1000
2004 Charge of the Light Brigade	£15
2004 — Silver proof	£50
2004 — Gold proof	£1000
2004 HMS Victory	£15
2004 — Silver proof	£55
2004 — Gold proof	£1000
2004 John Fisher 1841–1920	£15
2004 — Silver proof	£55

(Reduced)

(Enlarged)

DATE	UNC
2004 —Gold proof	£1000
2004 The Coronation Scot	£15
2004 — Silver proof	£55
2004 — Gold proof	£1000
2004 The Flying Scotsman	£15
2004 — Silver proof	£55
2004 — Silver/Gold proof	£500
2004 — Gold proof	£1000
2004 Golden Arrow	£15
2004 — Silver proof	£55
2004 — Gold proof	£1000
2005 Driver and Fireman	£15
2005 — Silver proof	£45
2005 — Gold proof	£1000
2005 Box Tunnel and King Loco	£15
2005 — Silver Proof	£45
2005 — Gold Proof	£1000
2005 Rocket and Evening Star	£15
2005 — Silver proof	£45
2005 — Silver/Gold proof	£500
2005 — Gold proof	£1000
2005 200th Anniversary of the Battle of Trafalgar	£30
2005 Andrew Cunningham	£20
2005 — Silver proof	£65
2005 — Gold proof	£1000
2005 HMS Conqueror	£15
2005 — Silver proof	£20
2005 — Gold proof	£1000
2005 Battle of Trafalgar	£15
2005 — Silver proof	£45
2005 — Gold proof (9mm)	£500
2005 — Gold proof (38.6mm)	£1000
2005 Returning Evacuees	£15
2005 — Silver proof	£45
2005 — Gold proof	£1000
2005 Searchlights and Big Ben	£15
2005 — Silver proof	£45
2005 — Gold proof	£1000
2006 60th Anniversary of the Liberation of the Channel Islands	£30
2006 80th Birthday of Her Majesty the Queen (3-coin set)	—
2006 Sir Winston Churchill	£15
2006 — Silver proof	£45
2006 — Gold proof	£1000
2006 Charles Darwin	£15
2006 — Silver proof	£45
2006 — Gold proof	£1000
2006 Bobby Moore	£20
2006 — Silver Proof	£55
2006 — Gold Proof	£1150
2006 Florence Nightingale	£20
2006 — Silver proof	£55
2006 — Gold proof	£1000
2006 Queen Mother	£20
2006 — Silver proof	£55
2006 — Gold proof	£1000
2006 Henry VIII	£15
2006 — Silver proof	£55
2006 — Gold proof	£1000
2006 Princess Diana	£20
2006 — Silver Proof	£60
2006 — Gold Proof	£1250
2006 Sir Christopher Wren	£15
2006 — Silver proof	£55
2006 — Gold proof	£1000
2006 HM the Queen's 80th Birthday—Streamers	£15
2006 — Silver proof	£60

DATE	UNC
2006 — Gold proof	£1000
2006 HM the Queen's 80th Birthday—Trooping colour	£25
2006 — Proof	£60
2006 — Silver proof	£1000
2006 — Silver/Gold proof	£650
2006 — Gold proof	£1150
2006 HM the Queen's 80th Birthday—Wembley Stadium	£20
2006 — Silver proof	£55
2006 — Gold proof	£1150
2006 Guy Gibson	£15
2006 — Silver proof	£55
2006 — Gold proof	£1150
2006 Eric James Nicholson	£15
2006 — Silver proof	£55
2006 — Gold proof	£1150
2006 Hook, Chard and Bromhead	£15
2006 — Silver proof	£55
2006 — Gold proof	£1150
2006 1st Lancs Fusiliers	£15
2006 — Silver proof	£55
2006 — Gold proof	£1150
2006 Noel Chavasse	£15
2006 — Silver proof	£55
2006 — Gold proof	£1150
2006 David Mackay	£15
2006 — Silver proof	£55
2006 — Gold proof	£1150
2006 Coronation Scot. Silver proof	£60
2006 Flying Scotsman. Silver proof	£60
2006 Fireman and Driver. Silver proof	£60
2006 Box Tunnel. Silver proof	£60
2007 Diamond Wedding balcony scene waving	£15
2007 — Silver proof	£60
2007 Diamond Wedding cake	£15
2007 — Silver proof	£60
2007 Diamond Wedding balcony scene waving	£15
2007 — Silver proof	£60
2007 Diamond Wedding HM the Queen and Prince Philip	£20
2007 — Silver proof	£60
2007 Diamond Wedding arrival at Abbey	£20
2007 — Silver proof	£55
2007 — Gold proof	£1150
2008 George & Dragon	£20
2008 Dambusters, Wallis, Chadwick, Gibson	£15
2008 — Silver/Copper proof	£30
2008 — Silver proof	£55
2008 Frank Whittle	£15
2008 — Silver proof	£55
2008 — Gold proof	£1150
2008 R. J. Mitchell	£15
2008 — Silver proof	£55
2008 — Gold proof	£1150
2008 Maj. Gen. Sir Hugh Trenchard	£15
2008 — Silver proof	£55
2008 — Gold proof	£1150
2008 Bomber Command	£15
2008 — Silver proof	£55
2008 — Gold proof	£1150
2008 Coastal Command	£20
2008 — Silver proof	£60
2008 — Gold proof	£1200
2008 Fighter Command	£20
2008 — Silver proof	£60
2008 — Gold proof	£1200
2008 Battle of Britain	£20
2008 — Silver proof	£60
2008 — Gold proof	£1200

DATE	UNC
2008 RBL Poppy	£20
2008 — Silver proof	£60
2008 — Gold proof	£1200
2008 Flying Legends	£15
2008 — Silver proof	£55
2008 — Gold proof	£1150
2009 George & Dragon. Silver proof	£50
2009 Battle of Agincourt. Silver proof	£55
2009 Battle of the Somme. Silver proof	£55
2009 Capt. Cook and *Endeavour.* Silver proof	£55
2009 500th Anniversary of Accession of Henry VIII. Silver proof	£55
2011 Landmark birthdays of HM the Queen & Prince Philip	£15
2011 90th Anniversary of the British Legion (poppy-shaped)	£40
2011 — Silver proof	£95
2011 — 5oz silver	£500
2011 — Gold proof	£2500
2011 30th Birthday of the Duke of Cambridge. Silver proof	£50
2011 Wedding of Prince William and Kate Middleton. Silver proof	£50
2011 —Gold proof	£1500
2011 Spirit of the Nation (4 coins). Silver proof, each	£50
2012 HM the Queen's Diamond Jubilee. Gold proof	£2000
2012 Poppy. Silver Proof	£65
2012 — Gold Proof	£2000
2012 RMS *Titanic* Centenary	£15
2012 — Silver Proof	£65
2013 Coronation Jubilee. Silver proof	£65
2013 — Gold Proof	£2000
2013 The Flying Scotsman. Silver proof	£65
2013 350th Guinea Anniversary. Silver proof	£55
2013 — Gold Proof	£2000
2013 Poppy Coin. Silver proof	£95
2014 70th Anniversary of D-Day. Silver proof	£85
2014 — Gold Proof	£2500
2014 The Red Arrows 50th Display Season. Silver proof	£95
2014 William Shakespeare—450th Birthday. Silver proof	£80
2016 90th Birthday of Queen Elizabeth II	—

TWO POUNDS FIFTY PENCE

1972 Royal Silver Wedding	£25
1972 — Silver proof	£35

TWO POUNDS
(note all modern Proof coins have frosted relief)

1972 Royal Silver Wedding. Silver	£25
1972 — Silver proof	£35
1981 Royal Wedding, nickel silver (crown size)	£5
1981 — in presentation pack	£8
1981 — Silver proof	£20
1981 — Gold proof	£450
1985 40th Anniversary of Liberation (crown size)	£5
1985 — in presentation pack	£12
1985 — Silver proof	£20
1985 — Gold proof	£1150
1986 Commonwealth Games	£6
1986 — in presentation case	£8
1986 — .500 silver	£12
1986 — .925 silver proof	£20
1987 World Wildlife Fund 25th Anniversary	£80
1987 — Silver proof	£25
1989 Royal Visit	£15
1989 — Silver proof	£25
1990 Queen Mother's 90th Birthday	£15
1990 — Silver proof	£25
1990 — Gold proof	£600

DATE	UNC
1990 50th Anniversary of the Battle of Britain, silver proof	£30
1993 40th Anniversary of the Coronation	£15
1993 — Silver proof	£20
1993 — Gold proof	£600
1995 50th Anniversary of Liberation	£15
1995 — Silver Proof	£25
1995 — — Piedfort	£75
1996 HM the Queen's 70th Birthday	£15
1996 — Silver proof	£25
1997 Bi-metal	£5
1997 — Silver proof	£50
1997 — new portrait	£5
1998 —	£5
2003 —	£5
2005 —	£5
2006 —	£5
2007 —	£5
2011 Prince Philip's 90th Birthday	£12
2012 HM the Queen's Diamond Jubilee. Gold proof	£1000

ONE POUND

1972 Royal Silver Wedding	£15
1972 — Silver proof	£20
1981	£15
1981 Silver proof	£15
1981 Gold proof	£320
1983 New designs and specifications on presentation card (St Helier)	£5
1983 — Silver proof	£18
1983 — Gold proof	£395
1984 Presentation wallet (St Saviour)	£21
1984 — Silver proof	£45
1984 — Gold proof	£450
1984 Presentation wallet (St Brelade)	£20
1984 — Silver proof	£45
1984 — Gold proof	£495
1985 Presentation wallet (St Clement)	£25
1985 — Silver proof	£45
1985 — Gold proof	£490
1985 Presentation wallet (St Lawrence)	£25
1985 — Silver proof	£40
1985 — Gold proof	£490
1986 Presentation wallet (St Peter)	£15
1986 — Silver proof	£35
1986 — Gold proof	£495
1986 Presentation wallet (Grouville)	£18
1986 — Silver proof	£40
1986 — Gold proof	£490
1987 Presentation wallet (St Martin)	£18
1987 — Silver proof	£40
1987 — Gold proof	£490
1987 Presentation wallet (St Ouen)	£12
1987 — Silver proof	£40
1987 — Gold proof	£495
1988 Presentation wallet (Trinity)	£15
1988 — Silver proof	£40
1988 — Gold proof	£495
1988 Presentation wallet (St John)	£15
1988 — Silver proof	£40
1988 — Gold proof	£490
1989 Presentation wallet (St Mary)	£15
1989 — Silver proof	£40
1989 — Gold proof	£490

DATE   UNC

1991 Ship Building in Jersey Series

1991 "Tickler". Nickel-brass	£5
1991 "Tickler". Silver proof	£25
1991 — Gold proof Piedfort	£495
1991 "Percy Douglas". Nickel-brass	£5
1991 "Percy Douglas". Silver proof	£25
1991 — Gold proof Piedfort	£450
1992 "The Hebe". Nickel-brass	£5
1992 "The Hebe". Silver proof	£25
1992 — Gold proof Piedfort	£490
1992 "Coat of Arms". Nickel-brass	£5
1992 "Coat of Arms". Silver proof	£25
1992 — Gold proof Piedfort	£450
1993 "The Gemini". Nickel-brass	£5
1993 "The Gemini". Silver proof	£25
1993 — Gold proof Piedfort	£490
1993 "The Century". Nickel-brass	£5
1993 "The Century". Silver proof	£25
1993 — Gold proof Piedfort	£495
1994 "Resolute". Nickel-brass	£5
1994 "Resolute". Silver proof	£25
1994 — Gold proof Piedfort	£495
1997 — Nickel-brass	£5
1998 — — Nickel-brass	£5
2003 — — Nickel-brass	£5
2005 — — Nickel-brass	£5
2006 — — Nickel-brass	£5
2007 Diana Commem. Gold proof	£280
2012 Diamond Jubilee. Gold Proof £1	£400
2012 Anniversary of the *Titanic*	—
2013 Coronation Jubilee. Gold Proof	£600

FIFTY PENCE

1969	£10
1972 Royal Silver Wedding. Silver	£12
1972 — Silver proof	£12
1980 —	£1
1980 Arms	£2
1980 — Proof	£5
1981 —	£1
1981 —	£5
1981 — Proof	£5
1983 Grosnez Castle	£10
1983 — Silver proof	£12
1984 —	£2
1985 40th Anniversary of Liberation	£3
1986	£5
1986	£5
1987	£5
1988	£5
1989	£5
1990	£5
1992	£5
1994	£5
1997	£5
1997 Smaller size	£4
1998 —	£3
2003	£3
2003 Coronation Anniversary (4 types)	£4
2003 — 4 types. Silver proof	£15
2005	£4
2006	£4

DATE	UNC
2009	£5
2011 Diamond Jubilee (full colour reverse, gold-plated)............................	£15
2013 Coronation Jubilee	£25

TWENTY-FIVE PENCE

1977 Royal Jubilee..	£3
1977 — Silver proof...	£20

TWENTY PENCE

1982 Corbiere Lighthouse (cased)	£8
1982 — Silver proof piedfort	£35
1983 — Obv. with date, rev. no date on rocks	£5
1983 — — Silver proof	£15
1984 —	£1
1986 —	£1
1987 —	£1
1989 —	£1
1992 —	£1
1994 —	£1
1996 —	£1
1997 —	£1
1998 —	£1
2002 —	£1
2003 —	£1
2005 —	£1
2006 —	£1
2007 —	£1
2009 —	£1

SOVEREIGN—Gold sovereign size

1999 The Millennium. King William on Throne	£250
1999 — Gold proof...	£300

TEN PENCE

1968 Arms	£1
1975 Arms	£1
1979 (dated 1975 on thick flan)...	£2
1980 —	£1
1980 — Proof	£5
1981 -	£1
1981 — Proof	£5
1983 L'Hermitage	£1
1983 — Silver proof..	£5
1984 —	£1
1985 —	£1
1986 —	£1
1987 —	£1
1988 —	£1
1989 —	£1
1990 —	£1
1992 —	£1
1997 —	£1
2002 —	£1
2003 —	£1
2005 —	£1
2006 —	£1
2007 —	£1

FIVE PENCE

1968 Arms..	£1
1980 —	£1
1981 —	£1

DATE	UNC
1981 — Proof	£2
1983 Seymour Towers	£1
1983 — Silver proof	£5
1984 —	£1
1985 —	£1
1986 —	£1
1987 —	£2
1988 —	£1
1990 —	£1
1991 —	£1
1992 —	£5
1993 —	£1
1997 —	£4
1998 —	£1
2002 —	£1
2003 —	£1
2005 —	£5
2006 —	£1
2008 —	£1

Other denominations are generally available at face value or a small premium above.

Since the introduction of decimal coinage a number of companies have been involved in marketing the coins of the Channel Islands. As a consequence many special limited edition commemorative coins have been issued in a wide variety of sizes, metals and finishes. These are very numerous with some issues being produced in very small numbers and many are omitted from our listings. These issues are generally outside of the scope of this catologue but we intend to cover them more fully in a future edition.

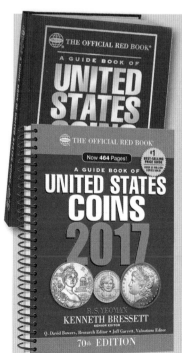

ALDERNEY

DATE	UNC

ONE THOUSAND POUNDS
2003 Concorde. Gold proof.. —
2004 D-Day Anniversary. Gold proof.. —
2011 Royal Wedding of Prince William and Catherine Middleton.............. —

ONE HUNDRED POUNDS
1994 50th Anniversary of D-Day Landings. Gold proof £285
2003 Prince Wiliam. Gold proof (100mm) .... —
2005 Trafalgar Anniversary. Gold proof (100mm) .... —

FIFTY POUNDS
1994 50th Anniversary of D–Day Landing. Gold proof............................. £500
2003 Anniversay of Coronation (4 types). Silver proof ea. (100mm) £500
2003 Prince William. Silver proof (100mm)................................... £500
2004 Anniversary of D-Day. Silver proof (100mm) £500
2005 200th Anniversary of the Battle of Trafalgar. Silver proof (100mm) ... £500

TWENTY FIVE POUNDS
1993 40th Anniversary of Coronation. Gold proof...................... £200
1994 50th Anniversary of D-Day Landings. Gold proof £200
1997 Royal Golden Wedding. Gold proof £295
1997 — Silver proof.. £40
1999 Winston Churcill. Gold proof £350
2000 Queen Mother. Gold proof... £325
2000 60th Anniversary of the Battle of Britain. Gold proof £275
2001 Royal Birthday. Gold proof £300
2002 Golden Jubilee. Gold proof £295
2002 Princess Diana. Gold proof £295
2002 Duke of Wellington. Gold proof £300
2003 Prince William. Gold proof £300
2003 HMS Mary Rose. Gold proof £300
2004 D-Day Anniversary. Gold proof................................... £395
2004 The Rocket. Gold proof.. £295
2004 Merchant Navy Class Locomotive. Gold proof £295
2005 Battle of Saints Passage. Gold proof £295
2006 World Cup 2006 (4 Coins). Gold ea............................... £350

TEN POUNDS
1994 50th Anniversary of D–Day Landing. Gold proof............................. £150
2003 Concorde. Silver proof (65mm) £280
2005 60th Anniversary of the Liberation of the Channel Islands (65mm)... £250
2007 80th Birthday of Her Majesty the Queen (65mm)............................. £180
2008 Concorde. Silver proof £180
2008 90th Anniversary of the end of WWI. Silver Proof £180
2009 50th Anniversary of the Mini—Silver with colour............................. £180
2012 Prince William's 30th Birthday .... —

FIVE POUNDS
1995 Queen Mother £15
1995 — Silver proof.. £50
1995 — Silver piedfort... £155
1995 — Gold proof... £900
1996 HM the Queen's 70th Birthday £20
1996 — Silver proof.. £60
1996 — Silver piedfort... £150
1996 — Gold proof... £1000
1999 Eclipse of the Sun £25
1999 — Silver proof with colour centre................................... £55
1999 Winston Churchill. Gold proof £1000
2000 60th Anniversary of the Battle of Britain.......................... £25
2000 — Silver proof.. £55

DATE	UNC
2000 Queen Mother. 100th Birthday. Silver proof	£50
2000 Millennium. Silver proof	£35
2001 HM Queen's 75th Birthday.	£15
2001 — Silver proof	£45
2002 Golden Jubilee. Silver proof	£50
2002 50 Years of Reign.	£15
2002 — Silver proof	£50
2002 Diana memorial	£15
2002 — Silver proof	£45
2002 — Gold proof	£900
2002 Duke of Wellington	£20
2002 — Silver proof	£50
2002 — Gold proof	£900
2003 Prince William	£20
2003 — Silver proof	£50
2003 — Gold proof	£900
2003 Mary Rose	£20
2003 — Silver proof	£120
2003 Alfred the Great. Silver proof	£150
2003 — Gold proof	£1000
2003 Last Flight of Concorde	£25
2003 — Silver proof	£150
2003 — Gold proof	£1000
2004 Anniversary of D-Day	£20
2004 — Silver proof	£75
2004 — Gold proof	£1000
2004 Florence Nightingale	320
2004 — Silver proof	£45
2004 150th Anniversary of the Crimean War	£20
2004 — Silver proof	£45
2004 — Gold proof	£1000
2004 The Rocket	£20
2004 — Silver proof	£45
2004 — Gold proof	£900
2004 Royal Scot	£20
2004 — Silver proof	£45
2004 Merchant Navy Class Locomotive	£20
2004 — Silver proof	£45
2005 End of WWII. Silver proof	£45
2005 — Gold proof	£900
2005 200th Anniversary of the Battle of Trafalgar	£16
2005 — Silver proof	£50
2005 History of the Royal Navy. John Woodward. Silver proof	£30
2005 Anniversary of Liberation. Gold proof	£1000
2005 Anniversary of the Battle of Saints Passage	£15
2005 — Silver proof	£45
2005 HMS Revenge 1591	£15
2005 — Silver proof	£45
2006 80th Birthday of Her Majesty the Queen (3-coin set) ea	£20
2006 Gold plated portraits of Her Majesty the Queen	—
2006 80th Birthday of Her Majesty the Queen (3-coin set) ea	£16
2007 History of the Royal Navy—*Mary Rose* (2 coins) ea	£16
2007 150th Anniversary of the Victoria Cross (18 coin set). Silver proof	£250
2007 Monarchs of England (12 coin set). Gold plated	£150
2008 90th Anniversary of the end of WWI (3 coins). Gold proof	£2500
2008 Classic British Motorcars (18 coin set). Silver proof.	£250
2008 Concorde. Gold proof	£1000
2009 50th Anniversary of the Mini (4 coins). Silver proof ea.	£50
2011 Royal Engagement gold proof	£1000
2011 — Gold plated silver proof	£150
2011 — Silver proof	£55
2011 — Cupro Nickel	£15
2011 John Lennon Silver proof	£55
2011 Battle of Britain 70th Anniversary silver proof	£55
2012 RMS *Titanic*	£15

DATE	UNC
2012 Remembrance Day (Re-issued 2013)..	£25
2014 70th Anniversary of D-Day	£15
2014 — Silver proof...	£25
2014 — Gold proof..	£1000
2014 Destiny to Dynasty. Silver proof	£25
2014 300th Anniversary of the Coronation of King George I......................	£20
2014 — Silver proof...	£25
2014 — Gold proof..	£1000
2014 Centenary of the birth of poet Dylan Thomas	£15
2014 — Silver proof...	£45
2014 — Gold proof..	£1000
2015 Churchill Quotations (4-coin set)	£40
2015 — Silver proof (4-coin)..	£250
2015 70th Anniversary of VE Day	£15
2015 — Silver proof...	£45
2015 — Silver proof piedfort	£75
2015 150th Anniversary of the Salvation Army	£10
2015 — Silver proof...	£45
2016 The FIFA World Cup	£15
2016 — Silver proof...	£45
2016 — Gold proof..	£1000

TWO POUNDS

1989 Royal Visit	£12
1989 — Silver proof...	£25
1989 — Silver piedfort...	£45
1989 — Gold proof..	£1000
1990 Queen Mother's 90th Birthday	£12
1990 — Silver proof...	£25
1990 — Silver piedfort...	£45
1990 — Gold proof..	£1000
1992 40th Anniversary of Accession...	£15
1992 — Silver proof...	£35
1992 — Silver piedfort...	£50
1992 — Gold proof..	£1000
1993 40th Anniversary of Coronation..	£15
1993 — Silver proof...	£35
1993 — Silver piedfort...	£50
1994 50th Anniversary of D-Day Landings...	£15
1994 — Silver proof...	£35
1994 — Silver piedfort...	£50
1995 50th Anniversary of Return of Islanders	£15
1995 — Silver proof...	£35
1995 — Silver piedfort...	£50
1995 — Gold proof..	£1000
1997 WWF Puffin..	£18
1997 — Silver proof...	£35
1997 Royal Golden Wedding..	£20
1997 — Silver proof...	£50
1999 Eclipse of the Sun. Silver..	£20
1999 — Silver proof...	£50
1999 — Gold proof..	£1250
2000 Millennium. Silver proof	£50

ONE POUND

1993 40th Anniversary of Coronation Silver proof	£50
1995 50th Anniversary of VE Day Silver proof...	£45
1995 — Gold proof..	£500
2008 Concorde. Gold proof..	£275
2009 50th Anniversary of the Mini. Gold proof..	£375

IRELAND

As in the English hammered section (q.v.) the prices given here are for the most common coins in the series. For a more specialised listing the reader is referred to Coincraft's *Standard Catalogue of Scotland, Ireland, Channel Islands & Isle of Man*, or other specialised publications. Collectors should be aware that with most of the coins of the Irish series there are many varieties struck at different mints. The coins listed are all silver unless mentioned otherwise. Another important factor to consider when collecting early Irish coins is that few examples exist in high grades.

	F	VF

HIBERNO-NORSE ISSUES (995–1155)

	F	VF
Penny, imitating English silver pennies, many various types	£250	£550

JOHN, Lord of Ireland (1185–99)

	F	VF
Halfpenny, profile		Extremely rare
Halfpenny, facing	£100	£350
Farthing	£350	£1200

Hiberno-Norse phase II example.

JOHN de COURCY, Lord of Ulster (1177–1205)

	F	VF
Halfpenny		Extremely rare
Farthing	£700	£3000

JOHN as King of England and Lord of Ireland (c. 1199–1216)

	F	VF
Penny	£70	£300
Halfpenny	£160	£450
Farthing	£650	£2300

John Lord of Ireland penny.

HENRY III (1216–72)

	F	VF
Penny	£150	£500

EDWARD I (1272–1307)

	F	VF
Penny	£75	£150
Halfpenny	£75	£150
Farthing	£150	£400

Henry III penny.

No Irish coins were struck for Edward II (1307–27).

EDWARD III (1327–77)

Halfpenny	Extremely rare

No Irish coins were struck for Richard II (1377–99), Henry IV (1399–1413) or Henry V (1413–22).

HENRY VI (1422–61)

Penny	Extremely rare

Edward I penny.

	F	VF

EDWARD IV (1461–83)

	F	VF
"Anonymous crown" groat	£650	£13000
— penny..............................	£1200	—
"Titled crown" groat	£1600	—
— halfgroat.............................		Extremely rare
— penny..............................		Extremely rare
Cross on rose/Sun groat	£1850	—
Bust/Rose on sun double groat	£2250	£7000
— groat................................	£2250	—
— halfgroat.............................		Extremely rare
— penny..............................		Extremely rare
Bust/Cross & pellets groat—First issue	£150	£550
— halfgroat.............................	£600	£1500
— penny..............................	£100	£350
— halfpenny		Extremely rare
— Second (light) issue..........................	£120	£450
— halfgroat.............................	£650	£1650
— penny..............................	£100	
£250— halfpenny		Extremely rare
Bust/Rose on cross groat.....................	£570	£1400
— penny..............................	£80	£225
Billon/Copper issues		
Small crown/Cross farthing (1460–61) ..	£1700	—
— half farthing ("Patrick").....................	£1100	—
Large crown/Cross farthing (1462)........		Extremely rare
Patricius/Salvator farthing (1463–65)	£350	£2000
— half farthing.................................		Extremely rare
Shield/Rose on sun farthing..................	£200	£900

Edward IV groat. "Anonymous crown" issue.

Edward IV penny struck in Dublin.

RICHARD III (1483–85)

	F	VF
Bust/Rose on cross groat......................	£1100	£3850
— halfgroat...........................		Unique
— penny..............................		Unique
Bust/Cross and pellets penny	£100	£3000
Shield/Three-crowns groat....................	£650	£2850

HENRY VII (1485–1509)

Early issues (1483–90)

	F	VF
Shield/Three crowns groat	£170	£500
— halfgroat.............................	£250	£550
— penny..............................	£650	£2500
— halfpenny		Extremely rare

Later issues (1488–90)

	F	VF
Shield/Three crowns groat	£100	£370
— halfgroat.............................	£200	£600
— penny..............................	£500	£1300
Facing bust groat (1496–1505).............	£150	£400
— halfgroat.............................	£1100	—
— penny.................................	£950	—

Richard III bust/rose on cross groat.

LAMBERT SIMNEL
(as EDWARD VI, Pretender, 1487)

	F	VF
Shield/Three crowns groat	£1250	£4250

Henry VII groat.

	F	VF

HENRY VIII (1509–47)

"Harp" groat	£100	£350
— halfgroat	£500	£2500

The "Harp" coins have crowned initials either side of the reverse harp, e.g. HR (Henricus Rex), HA (Henry and Anne Boleyn), HI (Henry and Jane Seymour), HK (Henry and Katherine Howard).

Posthumous (Portrait) issues

Sixpence	£150	£500
Threepence	£150	£550
Threehalfpence	£500	£1750
Threefarthings	£650	£2000

Henry VIII Posthumous portrait issues threepence.

EDWARD VI (1547–53)

Shilling (base silver) 1552 (MDLII)	£1000	£3500
Brass contemporary copy	£100	£350

MARY (1553–54)

Shilling 1553 (MDLIII)	£850	£3300
Shilling 1554 (MDLIIII)		Extremely rare
Groat		Extremely rare
Halfgroat		Extremely rare
Penny		Extremely rare

PHILIP & MARY (1554–58)

Shilling	£350	£1400
Groat	£150	£450
Penny		Extremely rare

ELIZABETH I (1558–1603)

Base silver portrait coinage

Shilling	£350	£1500
Groat	£200	£700

Philip & Mary shilling

Fine silver, portrait coinage (1561)

Shilling	£300	£1000
Groat	£350	£1100

Third (base silver) shield coinage

Shilling	£250	£700
Sixpence	£200	£500

Copper

Threepence	£250	£700
Penny	£50	£200
Halfpenny	£100	£300

JAMES I (1603–25)

Shilling	£100	£400
Sixpence	£100	£250

Coins struck under Royal Licence from 1613

"Harrington" farthing (small size)	£50	£250
"Harrington" farthing (large size)	£50	£200
"Lennox" farthing	£50	£200

Elizabeth I "fine" shilling of 1561.

CHARLES I (1625–49)

During the reign of Charles I and the Great Rebellion many coins were struck under unusual circumstances, making the series a difficult but fascinating area for study. Many of the "coins" were simply made from odd-shaped pieces of plate struck with the weight or value.

	F	VF
Coins struck under Royal Licence from 1625		
"Richmond" farthing	£50	£200
"Maltravers" farthing	£50	£200
"Rose" farthing	£50	£200

Siege money of the Irish Rebellion, 1642–49

	F	VF
"Inchiquin" Money (1642)		
Crown	£2200	£6000
Halfcrown	£2000	£5000
Shilling		Extremely rare
Ninepence		Extremely rare
Sixpence		Extremely rare
Groat		Extremely rare
"Dublin" Money (1643)		
Crown	£900	£3500
Halfcrown	£600	£2500
"Ormonde" Money (1643–44)		
Crown	£500	£1500
Halfcrown	£350	£1000
Shilling	£150	£450
Sixpence	£150	£450
Groat	£120	£350
Threepence	£120	£300
Twopence	£500	£1500
"Ormonde" gold coinage (1646)		
Double pistole. 2 known (both in museums)		Extremely rare
Pistole. 10 known (only 1 in private ownership		Extremely rare
"Ormonde" Money (1649)		
Crown		Extremely rare
Halfcrown	£1200	£3750
Dublin Money 1649		
Crown	£2800	£7850
Halfcrown	£2200	£4750

Charles I "Ormonde" crown.

Issues of the Confederated Catholics

	F	VF
Kilkenny issues (1642–43)		
Halfpenny	£300	£900
Farthing	£400	£1100
Rebel Money (1643–44)		
Crown	£2500	£5500
Halfcrown	£3000	£5500
"Blacksmith's" Money (16??)		
Imitation of English Tower halfcrown	£700	£3000

A rare Charles I "Rebel" halfcrown.

	F	VF

Local Town issues of "Cities of Refuge"

Bandon
Farthing (copper) .... | | Extremely rare

Cork
Shilling		Extremely rare
Sixpence	£750	£1300
Halfpenny (copper)		Extremely rare
Farthing (copper)	£600	—

Kinsale
Farthing (copper) .... | £400 | —

Youghal
Farthing (copper) .... | £500 | £2000

CHARLES II (1660–85)

	Fair	F	VF	EF
"Armstrong" coinage				
Farthing (1660–61)	£65	£250	—	—
"St Patrick's" coinage				
Halfpenny	£225	£475	—	—
Farthing	£75	£200	£500	£1500
Legg's Regal coinage				
Halfpennies				
1680 large lettering	£35	£100	£275	—
1681 large lettering	—	£200	£675	—
1681 small lettering			Extremely rare	
1682 small lettering	—	£200	£650	—
1683 small lettering	£30	£45	£400	
1684 small lettering	£40	£125	£650	—

Halfpenny of Charles I.

JAMES II (1685–88)

REGAL COINAGE

Halfpennies				
1685	£25	£75	£300	£700
1686	£25	£60	£200	£600
1687			Extremely rare	
1688	£25	£100	£300	£1300

"St Patrick" farthing of Charles II.

Our grateful thanks to Del Parker, specialist in Irish rarities, for supplying the images for this section. An impressive and extensive range of Irish coins can be viewed and purchased at his website at www.irishcoins.com.

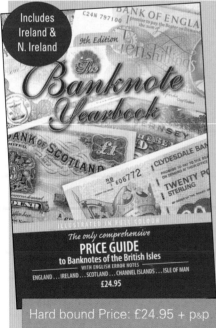

	Fair	F	VF	EF

EMERGENCY COINAGE

GUN MONEY
Most of these coins were struck in gun metal but a few rare specimens are also known struck in gold and in silver

Crowns
1690 (many varieties)......................from £45 £60 £600 —

Large halfcrowns
Dated July 1689–May 1690
....from £35 £65 £200 —

Small halfcrowns
Dated April–October1690
....from £35 £60 £220 —

Large shillings
Dated from July 1689–April 1690
....from £35 £65 £120 £485

Small shillings
Dated from April–September 1690
....from £25 £35 £120 £400

"Gun Money" crown.

Sixpences
Dated from June 1689–October 1690
....from £35 £60 £275 —

PEWTER MONEY (1689–90)
Crown....................................... £700 £1100 £3000 —
Groat....................................... Extremely rare
Penny large bust..................................... £230 £650 — —
— small bust .... £165 £485 £1350 —
Halfpenny large bust .... £130 £325 £795 —
— small bust .... £110 £235 £675 —

LIMERICK MONEY (1690–91)
Halfpenny, reversed N in HIBERNIA...... £35 £75 £250 —
Farthing, reversed N in HIBERNIA........ £35 £75 £250 —
— normal N .... £45 £125 £300 —

WILLIAM & MARY (1689–94)
Halfpennies
1692... £15 £50 £100 £650
1693... £15 £50 £85 £650
1694... £20 £75 £125 £700

WILLIAM III (1694–1702)
1696 Halfpenny draped bust................ £35 £75 £250 —
1696 — crude undraped bust .... £45 £275 £875 —

William & Mary half-penny of 1693.

No Irish coins were struck during the reign of Queen Anne (1706–11).

DATE	F	VF	EF	UNC

GEORGE I (1714–27)

Farthings

	F	VF	EF	UNC
1722 D.G. REX Harp to left (Pattern)	£650	£1550	£2350	—
1723 D.G. REX Harp to right	£120	£225	£500	—
1723 DEI GRATIA REX Harp to right	£35	£65	£250	£600
1723 — Silver Proof	—	—	—	£2500
1724 DEI GRATIA REX Harp to right	£60	£150	£350	£850

Halfpennies

	F	VF	EF	UNC
1722 Holding Harp left	£55	£130	£385	£1000
1722 Holding Harp right	£45	£110	£350	£795
1723/2 Harp right	£50	£150	£350	£795
1723 Harp right	£25	£65	£200	£550
1723 Silver Proof	—	—	—	£3500
1723 Obv. Rs altered from Bs	£35	£100	£275	—
1723 No stop after date	£25	£80	£275	£500
1724 Rev. legend divided	£40	£100	£300	—
1724 Rev. legend continuous	£40	£110	£385	—

GEORGE II (1727–60)

Farthings

	F	VF	EF	UNC
1737	£35	£60	£175	£475
1737 Proof	—	—	—	£500
1737 Silver Proof	—	—	—	£1200
1738	£35	£65	£165	£475
1744	£35	£65	£165	£475
1760	£30	£50	£100	£375

Halfpenny of George II

Halfpennies

	F	VF	EF	UNC
1736	£25	£60	£225	£600
1736 Proof	—	—	—	£650
1736 Silver Proof	—	—	—	£1350
1737	£25	£50	£200	—
1738	£30	£60	£200	—
1741	£30	£60	£200	—
1742	£30	£60	£200	—
1743	£30	£60	£180	—
1744/3	£30	£60	£185	—
1744	£30	£60	£350	—
1746	£30	£60	£350	—
1747	£30	£60	£225	—
1748	£30	£60	£225	—
1749	£30	£60	£225	—
1750	£30	£60	£225	—
1751	£30	£60	£225	—
1752	£30	£60	£225	—
1753	£30	£60	£250	—
1755	£30	£100	£350	—
*1760	£30	£60	£250	—

GEORGE III (1760–1820)

All copper unless otherwise stated

Pennies

	F	VF	EF	UNC
1805	£20	£40	£190	£475
1805 Proof	—	—	—	£575
1805 in Bronze Proof	—	—	—	£575
1805 in Copper Gilt Proof	—	—	—	£575
1805 in Silver Proof (restrike)	—	—	—	£3250

George III proof penny 1805

DATE	F	VF	EF	UNC
Halfpennies				
1766	£30	£55	£165	—
1769	£30	£55	£165	—
1769 Longer bust	£40	£75	£250	£650
1774 Pattern only Proof	—	—	—	£2000
1775	£30	£55	£200	£450
1775 Proof	—	—	—	£650
1776	£55	£140	£400	—
1781	£45	£60	£165	£400
1782	£45	£60	£165	£400
1805	£18	£45	£120	£400
1805 Copper Proof	—	—	—	£400
1805 in Bronze	—	—	—	£295
1805 in Gilt Copper	—	—	—	£450
1805 in Silver (restrike)	—	—	—	£1800
Farthings				
1806	£20	£35	£100	£200
1806 Copper Proof	—	—	—	£375
1806 Bronzed Copper Proof	—	—	—	£265
1806 Copper Gilt Proof	—	—	—	£350
1806 Silver Proof (restrike)	—	—	—	£1150

One of the scarcer dates, a 1776 George III halfpenny.

GEORGE IV (1820–30)

Pennies	F	VF	EF	UNC
1822	£20	£40	£180	£400
1822 Proof	—	—	—	£575
1823	£12	£25	£150	£400
1823 Proof	—	—	—	£600

DATE	F	VF	EF	UNC
Halfpennies				
1822...	£20	£40	£120	£400
1822 Proof.....................................	—	—	—	£600
1823...	£20	£40	£120	£400
1823 Proof.....................................	—	—	—	£650

NB Prooflike Uncirculated Pennies and Halfpennies of 1822/23 are often mis-described as Proofs. The true Proofs are rare. Some are on heavier, thicker flans.

Farthings				
1822 (Pattern) Proof	—	—	—	£1800

TOKEN ISSUES BY THE BANK OF IRELAND

Five Pence in Silver				
1805...	£30	£45	£75	£350
1806...	£30	£65	£150	£375
1806/5..	£60	£145	£450	£1400

Ten Pence in Silver				
1805...	£20	£35	£95	£250
1806...	£20	£65	£150	£275
1813...	£20	£35	£90	£300
1813 Proof.....................................	—	—	—	£450

Thirty Pence in Silver				
1808...	£45	£100	£250	£650

1804 six shillings.

Six Shillings				
1804 in Silver................................	£100	£250	£450	£1850
1804 Proof.....................................	—	—	—	£1775
1804 in Copper (restrike)..................	—	—	—	£750
1804 Copper Gilt............................	—	—	—	£1700
1804 in Gilt Silver	—	—	—	£3000

In this series fully struck specimens, with sharp hair curls, etc., are worth appreciably more than the prices quoted.

IRISH FREE STATE/EIRE

DATE	F	VF	EF	UNC
TEN SHILLINGS				
1966 Easter Rising	—	£12	£18	£40
1966 Cased Proof	—	—	—	£42
1966 special double case	—	—	—	£75

HALF CROWNS				
Silver				
1928	£7	£12	£40	£75
1928 Proof	—	—	—	£85
1930	£12	£35	£175	£550
1931	£12	£35	£175	£525
1933	£12	£25	£175	£550
1934	£12	£12	£55	£255
1937	£60	£200	£650	£1850
Modified obverse: Eire				
1938				Unique
1939	£7	£17	£30	£75
1939 Proof	—	—	—	£645
1940	£8	£18	£35	£90
1941	£7	£17	£35	£90
1942	£7	£20	£35	£85
1943	£85	£300	£975	£3350
Cupro-nickel				
1951	£2	£3	£20	£55
1951 Proof	—	—	—	£500
1954	£2	£3	£15	£85
1954 Proof	—	—	—	£520
1955	£2	£3	£15	£45
1955	—	—	—	£595
1959	£2	£3	£12	£45
1961	£2	£3	£25	£55
1961 Obv as 1928, rev. as 1951	£30	£75	£325	£750
1962	£2	£3	£6	£35
1963	£2	£3	£6	£35
1964	£2	£3	£6	£35
1966	£2	£3	£6	£35
1967	£2	£3	£6	£35

FLORINS				
Silver				
1928	£3	£6	£25	£60
1928 Proof	—	—	—	£75
1930	£5	£20	£150	£450
1930 Proof				Unique
1931	£5	£20	£175	£450
1933	£5	£18	£140	£450
1934	£15	£125	£275	£750
1934 Proof	—	—	—	£3000
1935	£5	£18	£65	£195
1937	£6	£25	£140	£410
Modified obverse: Eire				
1939	£2	£6	£35	£80
1939 Proof	—	—	—	£675
1940	£3	£6	£30	£80
1941	£3	£6	£35	£75
1941 Proof	—	—	—	£850
1942	£6	£15	£30	£75
1943	£3000	£5500	£10000	£22500

Beware of fake 1943 florins.

DATE	F	VF	EF	UNC
Cupro-nickel				
1951	60p	£2	£12	£45
1951 Proof	—	—	—	£480
1954	60p	£2	£10	£42
1954 Proof	—	—	—	£400
1955	—	£2	£6	£45
1955 Proof	—	—	—	£550
1959	40p	£2	£6	£40
1961	60p	£3	£15	£55
1962	40p	£2	£6	£30
1963	30p	£2	£6	£30
1964	30p	£2	£6	£30
1965	30p	£2	£6	£30
1966	30p	£2	£6	£30
1968	30p	£2	£6	£30

SHILLINGS
Silver

	F	VF	EF	UNC
1928	£2	£6	£18	£45
1928 Proof	—	—	—	£75
1930	£6	£25	£100	£455
1930 Proof	—	—	—	£855
1931	£3	£17	£95	£450
1933	£3	£17	£95	£450
1935	£3	£13	£50	£150
1937	£10	£75	£250	£1250
1939	£2	£6	£25	£65
1939 Proof	—	—	—	£750
1940	£2	£6	£17	£55
1941	£2	£5	£17	£55
1942	£2	£5	£12	£50

Cupro-nickel

	F	VF	EF	UNC
1951	£1	£2	£6	£25
1951 Proof	—	—	—	£450
1954	£1	£2	£6	£25
1954 Proof	—	—	—	£500
1955	£1	£2	£6	£25
1959	£1	£2	£6	£35
1962	50p	£2	£3	£22
1963	50p	£2	£3	£15
1964	50p	£2	£3	£15
1966	50p	£2	£3	£15
1968	50p	£2	£3	£15

SIXPENCES
Nickel

	F	VF	EF	UNC
1928	£1	£5	£15	£50
1928 Proof	—	—	—	£65
1934	£1	£3	£18	£100
1935	£1	£3	£25	£130
Modified obverse: Eire				
1939	£1	£2	£10	£55
1939 Proof	—	—	—	£650
1940	£1	£2	£6	£55
Cupro-nickel				
1942	£1	£2	£9	£65
1945	£3	£12	£35	£100
1946	£5	£10	£100	£400
1947	£2	£2	£25	£90
1948	£1	£3	£15	£75
1949	£1	£2	£10	£50
1950	£2	£3	£25	£100
1952	£1	£2	£5	£25

DATE	F	VF	EF	UNC
1953	£1	£2	£5	£25
1953 Proof	—	—	—	£120
1955	£1	£2	£4	£25
1956	£1	£2	£3	£25
1956 Proof	—	—	—	£168
1958	£2	£3	£12	£68
1958 Proof	—	—	—	£380
1959	50p	60p	£3	£20
1960	50p	60p	£2	£20
1961	—	£2	£3	£25
1962	£2	£6	£35	£75
1963	£1	£3	£6	£20
1964	£1	£2	£5	£12
1966	£1	£2	£5	£12
1967	£1	£2	£2	£10
1968	£1	£2	£2	£10
1969	£2	£3	£6	£20

THREEPENCES
Nickel

	F	VF	EF	UNC
1928	£2	£3	£10	£35
1928 Proof	—	—	—	£42
1933	£3	£13	£75	£375
1934	£1	£3	£15	£80

Modified obverse: Eire

	F	VF	EF	UNC
1935	£2	£4	£30	£230
1939	£3	£7	£60	£375
1939 Proof	—	—	—	£1000
1940	£2	£3	£13	£65

Cupro-nickel

	F	VF	EF	UNC
1942	—	£2	£6	£50
1942 Proof	—	—	—	£500
1943	£2	£3	£15	£78
1946	£2	£5	£10	£50
1946 Proof	—	—	—	£500
1948	£2	£3	£25	£80
1949	—	£2	£6	£40
1950	—	£2	£6	£25
1950 Proof	—	—	—	£550
1953	—	£2	£4	£18
1956	—	£2	£3	£10
1961	—	60p	£2	£5
1962	—	60p	£2	£10
1963	—	60p	£2	£10
1964	—	60p	£2	£5
1965	—	60p	£2	£5
1966	—	60p	£2	£5
1967	—	60p	£2	£5
1968	—	—	£2	£5

PENNIES

	F	VF	EF	UNC
1928	£2	£3	£12	£50
1928 Proof	—	—	—	£60
1931	£2	£4	£35	£120
1931 Proof	—	—	—	£1000
1933	£2	£5	£50	£250
1935	£1	£2	£25	£75
1937	£1	£2	£35	£125
1937 Proof	—	—	—	£1000

Modified obverse: Eire

	F	VF	EF	UNC
1938		Only two known		
1940	£10	£50	£175	£750
1941	£1	£2	£10	£35
1942	—	£1	£5	£20
1943	—	£2	£6	£35

DATE	F	VF	EF	UNC
1946	—	£2	£4	£20
1948	—	£2	£4	£20
1949	—	£2	£4	£20
1949 Proof	—	—	—	£500
1950	—	£2	£6	£32
1952	—	£2	£4	£12
1962	—	£2	£4	£15
1962 Proof	—	—	—	£200
1963	—	—	£2	£12
1963 Proof	—	—	—	£200
1964	—	—	£2	£10
1964 Proof	—	—	—	£500
1965	—	—	£1	£5
1966	—	—	£1	£5
1967	—	—	£1	£5
1968	—	—	£1	£5
1968 Proof	—	—	—	£300

HALFPENNIES

	F	VF	EF	UNC
1928	£2	£3	£12	£35
1928 Proof	—	—	—	£45
1933	£6	£20	£100	£500
1935	£5	£10	£50	£200
1937	£2	£5	£15	£50

Modified obverse: Eire

	F	VF	EF	UNC
1939	£5	£10	£50	£200
1939 Proof	—	—	—	£875
1940	£2	£4	£50	£185
1941	£1	£2	£6	£25
1942	£1	£2	£6	£25
1943	£1	£2	£8	£35
1946	£2	£5	£20	£100
1949	£1	£2	£6	£25
1953	—	£2	£3	£12
1953 Proof	—	—	—	£500
1964	—	—	£1	£5
1965	—	—	£1	£6
1966	—	—	£1	£4
1967	—	—	£1	£4

FARTHINGS

	F	VF	EF	UNC
1928	£3	£4	£10	£20
1928 Proof	—	—	—	£45
1930	£3	£4	£10	£32
1931	£4	£6	£15	£35
1931 Proof	—	—	—	£850
1932	£4	£6	£18	£45
1933	£3	£4	£12	£32
1935	£4	£6	£18	£35
1936	£4	£6	£18	£35
1937	£3	£4	£12	£32

Modified obverse: Eire

	F	VF	EF	UNC
1939	£3	£4	£10	£18
1939 Proof	—	—	—	£600
1940	£4	£5	£10	£25
1941	£3	£4	£6	£12
1943	£3	£4	£6	£12
1944	£3	£4	£6	£12
1946	£3	£4	£6	£12
1949	£4	£6	£8	£25
1949 Proof	—	—	—	£465
1953	£3	£4	£5	10
1953 Proof	—	—	—	£320
1959	£3	£4	£5	£13
1966	£3	£4	£5	£13

For the 1928–50 copper issues it is worth noting that UNC means UNC with some lustre. BU examples with full lustre are extremely elusive and are worth much more than the quoted prices.

IRISH DECIMAL COINAGE

DATE	MINTAGE	BU
HALF PENCE		
1971	100,500,000	£5
1975	10,500,000	£6
1976	5,500,000	£6
1978	20,300,000	£5
1980	20,600,000	£4
1982	9,700,000	£4
1985	2,800,000	Rare
1986. Only issued in the 1986 set	19,750,000	£100

ONE PENNY

1971	100,500,000	£3
1974	10,000,000	£10
1975	10,000,000	£15
1976	38,200,000	£5
1978	25,700,000	£8
1979	21,800,000	£12
1980	86,700,000	£3
1982	54,200,000	£5
1985	19,200,000	£8
1986	36,600,000	£5
1988	56,800,000	£5
1990	65,100,000	£5
1992	25,600,000	£6
1993	10,000,000	£6
1994	45,800,000	£5
1995	70,800,000	£3
1996	190,100,000	£1
1998	40,700,000	£1
2000	Unknown	£1

TWO PENCE

1971	75,500,000	£3
1975	20,000,000	£8
1976	5400,000	£12
1978	12,000,000	£12
1979	32,400,000	£8
1980	59,800,000	£6
1982	30,400,000	£5
1985	14,500,000	£6
1986	23,900,000	£6
1988	35,900,000	£5
1990	34,300,000	£5
1992	10,200,000	£8

DATE	MINTAGE	BU
1995	55,500,000	£5
1996	69,300,000	£2
1998	33,700,000	£2
2000	Unknown	£1

FIVE PENCE

1969 Toned	5,000,000	£5
1970	10,000,000	£5
1971	8,000,000	£6
1974	7,000,000	£10
1975	10,000,000	£10
1976	20,600,000	£5
1978	28,500,000	£5
1980	22,200,000	£5
1982	24,400,000	£4
1985	4,200,000	£8
1986	15,300,000	£5
1990	7,500,000	£5
Size reduced to 18.4mm		
1992	74,500,000	£5
1993	89,100,000	£5
1994	31,100,000	£5
1995	12,000,000	£5
1996	14,700,000	£2
1998	158,500,000	£1
2000	Unknown	£1

TEN PENCE

1969	27,000,000	£10
1971	4,000,000	£10
1973	2,500,000	£16
1974	7,500,000	£12
1975	15,000,000	£12
1976	9,400,000	£12
1978	30,900,000	£10
1980	44,600,000	£7
1982	7,400,000	£7
1985	4,100,000	£8
1986. Only issued in the 1986 set	11,280	£275
Size reduced to 22mm		
1992	2 known	—
1993	80,100,000	£5
1994	58,500,000	£5

DATE	MINTAGE	BU	DATE	MINTAGE	BU

DATE	MINTAGE	BU
1995	16,100,000	£5
1996	18,400,000	£3
1997	10,000,000	£3
1998	10,000,000	£3
1999	24,500,000	£3
2000	Unknown	£2

TWENTY PENCE

DATE	MINTAGE	BU
1985. Only 600 minted and 556 melted down, only 3 known	Extremely rare	
1986	50,400,000	£6
1988	20,700,000	£6
1992	14,800,000	£5
1994	11,100,000	£5
1995	18,200,000	£5
1996	29,300,000	£5
1998	25,000,000	£3
1999	11,000,000	£3
2000	Unknown	£2

FIFTY PENCE

DATE	MINTAGE	BU
1970	9,000,000	£8
1971	650,000	£7
1974	1,000,000	£55
1975	2,000,000	£55
1976	3,000,000	£45
1977	4,800,000	£55
1978	4,500,000	£45
1979	4,000,000	£45
1981	6,000,000	£25
1982	2,000,000	£25
1983	7,000,000	£25
1986. Only issued in the 1986 set	10,000	£300
1988	7,000,000	£5
1988 Dublin Millennium	5,000,000	£5
1988 — Proof	50,000	£25
1996	6,000,000	£7
1997	6,000,000	£7
1998	13,800,000	£5
1999	7,000,000	£4
2000	Unknown	£4

ONE POUND

DATE	MINTAGE	BU
1990	42,300,000	£5
1990 Proof	50,000	£25
1994	14,900,000	£5
1995	9,200,000	£5
1995 UN silver proof in case of issue	2,850	£175
1996	9,200,000	£5
1998	22,960,000	£4
1999	10,000,000	£5
2000	4,000,000	£5

	MINTAGE	BU
2000 Millennium	5,000,000	£5
2000 – Silver Proof Piedfort	90,000	£35

OFFICIAL COIN SETS ISSUED BY THE CENTRAL BANK

1971 Specimen set in green wallet. 6 coins	£20
1975 6 coin set	£55
1978 6 coin set	£55
1978 6 coin set. Black cover, scarce	£75
1982 6 coin set. Black cover	£75
1986 Specimen set in card folder 1/2p to 50p, 7 coins. Very scarce. Most sets have glue problems	£650
1996 7 coin set	£60
1998 7 coin set	£50
2000 Millennium set. Last decimal set	£125
2000 — With 1999 instead of the 2000 £1 coin	£250

Dublin Millennium 50p

It is probably a strong love of history, rather than the strict disciplines of coin collecting that make collectors turn to commemorative medals. The link between the two is intertwined, and it is to be hoped that collectors will be encouraged to venture into the wider world of medallions, encouraged by this brief guide, originally supplied by Daniel Fearon (author of the *Catalogue of British Commemorative Medals)* and kindly updated again this year by Charles Riley.

DATE	VF	EF
JAMES I		
1603 Coronation (possibly by C. Anthony), 29mm, Silver	£1200	£1800
QUEEN ANNE		
1603 Coronation, 29mm, AR	£800	£1500
CHARLES I		
1626 Coronation (by N. Briot), 30mm, Silver	£650	£1000
1633 Scottish Coronation (by N. Briot), 28mm, Silver	£450	£750
1649 Memorial (by J. Roettier). Struck after the Restoration, 50mm, Bronze	£120	£250
CROMWELL		
1653 Lord Protector (by T. Simon), 38mm, Silver	£700	£1700
— Cast examples	£350	£600
CHARLES II		
1651 Scottish Coronation, in exile (from design by Sir J. Balfour), 32mm, Silver	£1300	£2200
CHARLES II		
1661 Coronation (by T. Simon), 29mm		
— Gold	£1800	£3200
— Silver	£350	£550
1685 Death (by N. Roettier), 39mm, Bronze	£150	£325

James I Coronation, 1603

Charles II Coronation, 1661

329

DATE	VF	EF

JAMES II
1685 Coronation (by J. Roettier), 34mm
— Gold £2000 £3600
— Silver £350 £800

MARY
1685 Coronation (by J. Roettier), 34mm
— Gold £1500 £3000
— Silver £300 £600

WILLIAM & MARY
1689 Coronation (by J. Roettier), 32mm
— Gold £1750 £3000
— Silver £350 £525
1689 Coronation,"Perseus" (by G. Bower),
   38mm, Gold £1750 £3000

MARY
1694 Death (by N. Roettier), 39mm, Bronze........ £95 £235

WILLIAM III
1697 "The State of Britain" (by J. Croker), 69mm,
   Silver £850 £1400

Queen Anne, 1702–1713.

ANNE
1702 Accession, "Entirely English" (by J. Croker), 34mm
— Gold £1500 £2750
— Silver £150 £295
1702 Coronation (by J. Croker), 36mm
— Gold £1800 £3200
— Silver £225 £300
1707 Union with Scotland (by J. Croker, rev. by S. Bull), 34mm
— Gold £1500 £2800
— Silver £200 £300
1713 Peace of Utrecht (by J. Croker—issued in gold to Members
of Parliament), 34mm
— Gold £850 £1500
— Silver £150 £275

GEORGE I
1714 Coronation (by J. Croker), 34mm
— Gold £1250 £1750
— Silver £150 £250
1727 Death (by J. Dassier), 31mm, Silver £150 £275

GEORGE II
1727 Coronation (by J. Croker), 34mm
— Gold £1500 £3200
— Silver £175 £350

George I Coronation, 1714.

QUEEN CAROLINE
1727 Coronation (by J. Croker), 34mm
— Gold £1750 £3000
— Silver £185 £350
1732 The Royal Family (by J. Croker), 70mm
— Silver £1500 £3000
— Bronze.. £400 £700

DATE	VF	EF

GEORGE III
1761 Coronation (by L. Natter), 34mm
— Gold	£2750	£4250
— Silver	£350	£550
— Bronze	£150	£250

QUEEN CHARLOTTE
1761 Coronation (by L. Natter), 34mm
— Gold	£1850	£3500
— Silver	£375	£600
— Bronze	£150	£295
1810 Golden Jubilee, "Frogmore", 48mm, Silver	£130	£275
— Bronze	£95	£175

GEORGE IV
1821 Coronation (by B. Pistrucci), 35mm
— Gold	£900	£1600
— Silver	£200	£325
— Bronze	£65	£110

WILLIAM IV
1831 Coronation (by W. Wyon; rev.shows
Queen Adelaide), 33mm
— Gold	£1150	£2250
— Silver	£175	£325
— Bronze	£65	£100

QUEEN VICTORIA
1838 Coronation (by B. Pistrucci), 37mm
— Gold	£1000	£1500
— Silver	£185	£320
— Bronze	£45	£95

George III, Coronation, 1761

Queen Victoria Coronation, 1838

Queen Victoria Diamond Jubilee 1897

DATE	VF	EF
1887 Golden Jubilee (by J. E. Boehm, rev. by Lord Leighton)		
— Gold, 58mm	£2750	£4250
— Silver, 78mm	£250	£500
— Bronze, 78mm	£95	£180
1897 Diamond Jubilee (by G. de Saulles),		
— Gold, 56mm	£2750	£4250
— Silver, 56mm	£95	£125
— Bronze, 56mm	£35	£60
— Gold, 25mm	£450	£600
— Silver, 25mm	£20	£35

EDWARD VII
1902 Coronation (August 9) (by G. W. de Saulles)

	VF	EF
— Gold, 56mm	£3250	£3750
— Silver, 56mm	£95	£135
— Bronze, 56mm	£30	£55
— Gold, 31mm	£450	£600
— Silver, 31mm	£20	£30

Some rare examples of the official medal show the date as June 26, the original date set for the Coronation which was postponed because the King developed appendicitis.

George V Silver Jubilee, 1935

GEORGE V
1911 Coronation (by B. Mackennal)

	VF	EF
— Gold, 51mm	£3250	£3750
— Silver, 51mm	£95	£250
— Bronze, 51mm	£30	£65
— Gold, 31mm	£450	£600
— Silver, 31mm	£20	£35

1935 Silver Jubilee (by P. Metcalfe)

	VF	EF
— Gold, 58mm	£3500	£4250
— Silver, 58mm	£100	£150
— Gold, 32mm	£450	£650
— Silver, 32mm	£20	£30

PRINCE EDWARD
1911 Investiture as Prince of Wales (by W. Goscombe John)

	VF	EF
— Gold, 31mm	£1000	£1950
— Silver, 31mm	£45	£75

Edward, Prince of Wales, 1911

EDWARD VIII
1936 Abdication (by L. E. Pinches), 35mm

	VF	EF
— Gold	£750	£1200
— Silver	£45	£65
— Bronze	£20	£35

GEORGE VI
1937 Coronation (by P. Metcalfe)

	VF	EF
— Gold, 58mm	£3500	£4000
— Silver, 58mm	£65	£95
— Gold, 32mm	£550	£650
— Silver, 32mm	£25	£35
— Bronze, 32mm	£12	£15

Edward VIII, Abdication, 1936.

ELIZABETH II
1953 Coronation (by Spink & Son)—illustrated

	VF	EF
— Gold, 57mm	£3000	£3500
— Silver, 57mm	£65	£125
— Bronze, 57mm	£35	£65
— Gold, 32mm	£300	£400
— Silver, 32mm	£20	£35
— Bronze, 32mm	£12	£15

1977 Silver Jubilee (by A. Machin)

	VF	EF
— Silver, 57mm	—	£70
— Silver, 44mm	—	£40

*The gold medals are priced for 18ct—they can also be found as
22ct and 9ct, and prices should be adjusted accordingly.*

PRINCE CHARLES
1969 Investiture as Prince of Wales (by M. Rizello)

	VF	EF
— Silver, 57mm	—	£65
— Bronze gilt, 57mm	—	£40
— Silver, 45mm	—	£35
— Gold, 32mm	—	£450
— Silver, 32mm	—	£35
— Bronze, 32mm	—	£8

QUEEN ELIZABETH THE QUEEN MOTHER
1980 80th Birthday (by L. Durbin)

	VF	EF
— Silver, 57mm	—	£55
— Silver, 38mm	—	£38
— Bronze, 38mm	—	£25

N.B.—Official Medals usually command a premium when still in
their original case of issue.

Prince Charles, Prince of Wales 1969.

The Royal Mint Museum contains a charming group of medallic portraits of seven of the
children of Queen Victoria and Prince Albert. They appear to have been made in 1850 and
therefore do not include the two children who were born after that date. The skilfully-
executed portraits are the work of Leonard Wyon, a member of the extremely talented
family of engravers whose name is so well known to numismatists. The son of William
Wyon, he was actually born in the Royal Mint in 1826. These particular portraits were not
commissioned by the Mint and little is known about the circumstances in which they were
prepared, but for some reason the dies have survived in the Royal Mint Museum, along
with single-sided bronze impressions roughly the size of a half-crown.

Images and information courtesy of Dr Kevin Clancy, The Royal Mint.

DIRECTORY *section*

O N the following pages will be found the most useful names and addresses needed by the coin collector.

At the time of going to press with this edition of the YEARBOOK the information is correct, as far as we have been able to ascertain. However, people move and establishments change, so it is always advisable to make contact with the person or organisation listed before travelling any distance, to ensure that the journey is not wasted.

Should any of the information in this section not be correct we would very much appreciate being advised in good time for the preparation of the next edition of the COIN YEARBOOK.

Dealers who display this symbol are Members of the

British Numismatic Trade Association

Buy in confidence from members of the British Numismatic Trade Association—an association formed to promote the very highest standards of professionalism in all matters involving members of the public in the sale or purchase of numismatic items.

BNTA MEMBERS IN COUNTY ORDER

LONDON AREA
*A.H. Baldwin & Sons Ltd · www.baldwin.co.uk
*ArtAncient Ltd · www.artancient.com
ATS Bullion Ltd · www.atsbullion.com
Beaver Coin Room · www.beaverhotel.co.uk
Jon Blyth · www.jonblyth.com
Bonhams incorporating Glendining's
· www.bonhams.com
Arthur Bryant Coins Ltd · www.bryantcoins.com
Keith Chapman · www.anglosaxoncoins.com
*Classical Numismatic Group Inc / Seaby Coins
· www.cngcoins.com
*Philip Cohen Numismatics · www.coinheritage.co.uk
Coin Invest Direct.com · www.coininvestdirect.com
Andre de Clermont · www.declermont.com
*Dix Noonan Webb · www.dnw.co.uk
Christopher Eimer · www.christophereimer.co.uk

Harrow Coin & Stamp Centre
*Knightsbridge Coins
C. J. Martin (Coins) Ltd · www.antiquities.co.uk
Nigel Mills · www.nigelmills.net
Morton & Eden Ltd · www.mortonandeden.com
Moruzzi Ltd · www.moruzzi.co.uk
Numismatica Ars Classica · www.arsclassicacoins.com
Physical Gold Ltd · www.physicalgold.co.uk
Predecimal.com incorporating
Rotographic Publications · www.predecimal.com
Roma Numismatics Ltd · www.romanumismatics.com
Simmons Gallery · www.simmonsgallery.co.uk
*Sovereign Rarities Ltd
*Spink & Son Ltd · www.spink.com
Surena Ancient Art & Numismatic
The London Coin Company Ltd
· www.thelondoncoincompany.com

The BNTA is a member of the International Numismatic Commission.

AVON
Saltford Coins • www.saltfordcoins.com

BEDFORDSHIRE
Simon Monks • www.simonmonks.co.uk

BERKSHIRE
*Douglas Saville Numismatic Books
• www.douglassaville.com

BUCKINGHAMSHIRE
Charles Riley • www.charlesriley.co.uk

CAMBRIDGESHIRE
*Dave Allen Collectables
• www.daveallencollectables.co.uk
Den of Antiquity International Ltd
• www.denofantiquity.co.uk

CHESHIRE
Colin Cooke • www.colincooke.com

CORNWALL
Richard W Jeffery

DEVON
Glenn S Ogden • www.glennogdencoins.com

DORSET
*Dorset Coin Co. Ltd • www.dorsetcoincompany.co.uk

ESSEX
Time Line Originals • www.time-lines.co.uk

GLOUCESTERSHIRE
Silbury Coins Ltd • www.silburycoins.com

HAMPSHIRE
*SPM Jewellers • www.spmjewellers.co.uk
Studio Coins • www.studiocoins.net
*Victory Coins
West Essex Coin Investments

HERTFORDSHIRE
Michael Dickinson
DRG Coins and Antiquities
• www.drgcoinsantiquities.com
K B Coins • www.kbcoins.com
David Miller
David Seaman • www.davidseamancoins.co.uk

KENT
London Coins • www.londoncoins.co.uk
*Peter Morris • www.petermorris.co.uk
Wilkes & Curtis Ltd • www.wilkesandcurtis.com

MONMOUTHSHIRE
Anthony M. Halse • www.coinsandtokens.com

NORFOLK
BucksCoins • www.westminsterauctions.com
*Roderick Richardson • www.roderickrichardson.com
Chris Rudd • www.celticcoins.com

NOTTINGHAMSHIRE
History in Coins • www.historyincoins.com

OXFORDSHIRE
*Richard Gladdle • Gladdle@plumpudding.org

SHROPSHIRE
M. Veissid & Co • www.veissid.com

SUFFOLK
*Lockdale Coins Ltd • www.lockdales.com
Mike R. Vosper Coins • www.vosper4coins.co.uk

SURREY
Daniel Fearon • www.danielfearon.com
M. J. Hughes • www.gbgoldcoins.co.uk
Kingston Coin Company
• www.kingstoncoincompany.co.uk
KMCC Ltd
Mark Rasmussen Numismatist • www.rascoins.com

SUSSEX
John Newman Coins • www.johnnewmancoins.com

TYNE AND WEAR
*Corbitts Ltd • www.corbitts.com

WARWICKSHIRE
*Peter Viola
*Warwick & Warwick Ltd
• www.warwickandwarwick.com

WEST MIDLANDS
*Atkinsons Coins and Bullion
• www.atkinsonsbullion.com
*Birmingham Coins
David Craddock
Paul Davis Birmingham Ltd
*Format of Birmingham Ltd

YORKSHIRE
Airedale Coins • www.airedalecoins.co.uk
AMR Coins • www.amrcoins.com
Paul Clayton
Paul Davies Ltd
*Paul Dawson York Ltd
*Weighton Coin Wonders • www.weightoncoin.co.uk

WALES
Lloyd Bennett • www.coinsofbritain.com
*North Wales Coins Ltd
Colin Rumney

SCOTLAND
*Scotmint Ltd • www.scotmint.com

IRELAND
Ormonde Coins • www.ormondecoins.com

(Those members with a retail premises are indicated with an *)

MUSEUMS *& libraries*

Listed below are the Museums and Libraries in the UK which have coins or items of numismatic interest on display or available to the general public.

A

• Anthropological Museum, University of Aberdeen, Broad Street, **Aberdeen,** AB9 1AS (01224 272014).

• Curtis Museum (1855), High Street, **Alton,** Hants (01420 82802). *General collection of British coins.*

• Ashburton Museum, 1 West Street, **Ashburton,** Devon, TQ13 7DT (01364 653595) *Ancient British and Roman antiquities including local coin finds.*

• Ashwell Village Museum (1930), Swan Street, **Ashwell,** Baldock, Herts. SG7 5NY (01462 742956) *Roman coins from local finds, local trade tokens, Anglo-Gallic coins and jetons.*

• Buckinghamshire County Museum (1862), Church Street, **Aylesbury,** Bucks HP20 2QP (01296 331441). *Roman and medieval English coins found locally, 17th/18th century Buckinghamshire tokens, commemorative medals.*

B

• Banbury Museum, Spiceball Park Road, **Banbury,** Oxon OX16 2PQ (01295 753752). *Wrexlin Hoard of Roman coins.*

• Museum of North Devon (1931), The Square, **Barnstaple,** EX32 8LN (01271 346747). *General coin and medal collection, including local finds. Medals of the Royal Devonshire Yeomanry.*

• Roman Baths Museum, Abbey Church Yard, Stall St, **Bath,** Avon BA1 1LZ (01225 477785). *Comprehensive collection of Roman coins from local finds.*

• Bagshaw Museum and Art Gallery (1911), Wilton Park, **Batley,** West Yorkshire WF17 0AS (01924 326155). *Roman, Scottish, Irish, English hammered, British and foreign coins, local traders' tokens, political medalets, campaign medals and decorations.*

• Bedford Museum (1961), Castle Lane, **Bedford** MK40 3XD (01234 718618). *Collections of the Bedford Library and Scientific Institute, the Beds Archaeological Society and Bedford Modern School (Pritchard Memorial) Museum.*

• Ulster Museum (1928), Botanic Gardens, **Belfast** BT9 5AB (0845 608 0000). *Irish, English and British coins and commemorative medals.*

• Berwick Borough Museum (1867), The Clock Block, Berwick Barracks, Ravensdowne, **Berwick**. TD15 1DQ (01289 301869). *Roman, Scottish and medieval coins.*

• Public Library, Art Gallery and Museum (1910), Champney Road, **Beverley,** Humberside (01482 393939). *Beverley trade tokens, Roman, English, British and foreign coins.*

• Bignor Roman Villa (1811), **Bignor,** nr Pulborough, West Sussex RH20 1PH (01798 869259). *Roman coins found locally.*

• City Museum and Art Gallery (1861), Chamberlain Square, **Birmingham** B3 3DH (0121 303 2834). *Coins, medals and tokens (special emphasis on the products of the Soho, Heaton, Birmingham and Watt mints.*

• Blackburn Museum, Museum Street, **Blackburn,** Lancs BB1 7AJ (01254 667130). *Incorporates the Hart (5,000 Greek, Roman and early English) and Hornby (500 English coins) collections, as well as the museum's own collection of British and Commonwealth coins.*

• Museum Collection, 25 – 27 West Street, **Bognor Regis,** West Sussex PO21 1XA (01243 865636) *Roman, English and British coins and trade tokens.*

• Museum and Art Gallery,(1893), Le Mans Crescent, **Bolton,** Lancashire BL1 1SE (01204 332211). *General collection of about 3000 British and foreign coins, and over 500 British medals. Numismatic library.*

• Art Gallery and Museum, Central Library, Oriel Road, **Bootle,** Lancs. *Greek, Roman, English, British and some foreign coins, local trade tokens.*

• Roman Town and Museum (1949) Main Street, **Boroughbridge,** N. Yorks. YO2 3PH (01423 322768). *Roman coins.*

• The Museum (1929), South Street, **Boston,** Lincs PE21 6HT (01205 365954). *Small collection of English coins.*

• Natural Science Society Museum (1903), 39 Christchurch Road, **Bournemouth,** Dorset BH1 3NS (01202 553525). *Greek, Roman and English hammered coins (including the Hengistbury Hoard), local trade tokens.*

• Bolling Hall Museum (1915), Bolling Hall Road, **Bradford,** West Yorkshire BD4 7LP (01274 431814). *Some 2,000 coins and tokens, mostly 18th–20th centuries.*

• Cartwright Hall Museum and Art Gallery (1904), Lister Park, **Bradford,** West Yorkshire BD9 4NS (01274 431212). *Roman coins found locally.*

• Museum and Art Gallery (1932), South Street, **Bridport,** Dorset (01308 458703). *Roman coins, mainly from excavations at Claudian Fort.*

• The City Museum (1820), Queen's Road, **Bristol** BS8 1RL (0117 922 3571). *Ancient British, Roman (mainly from local hoards), English hammered coins, especially from the Bristol mint, and several hundred local trade tokens.*

• District Library and Museum (1891), Terrace Road, **Buxton,** Derbyshire SK17 6DA (01629 533540). *English and British coins, tokens and commemorative medals. Numismatic library.*

C

• Segontium Museum (1928), Beddgelert Road, **Caernarfon,** Gwynedd (01286 675625) *Roman coins and artifacts excavated from the fort.*

• Fitzwilliam Museum (1816), Department of Coins and Medals, Trumpington Street, **Cambridge** CB2 1RB (01223 332900). *Ancient, English, medieval European, oriental coins, medals, plaques, seals and cameos.*

• National Museum & Galleries of Wales, Cathays Park, **Cardiff** CF10 3NP (029 2057 3000). *Greek, Celtic, Roman and British coins and tokens with the emphasis on Welsh interest. Also military, civilian and comm. medals.*

• Guildhall Museum (1979), Market Street, **Carlisle,** Cumbria CA3 8JE (01228 618718). *General collection of coins and medals.*

• Tullie House (1877), Castle Street, **Carlisle,** Cumbria CA3 8TP (01228 618718). *Roman, medieval and later coins from local finds, including medieval counterfeiter's coin-moulds.*

• Gough's Cave Museum (1904), The Cliffs, **Cheddar,** Somerset BS27 3QF (01934 742343). *Roman coins.*

• Chelmsford and Essex Museum (1835), Oaklands Park, Moulsham Street, **Chelmsford,** Essex CM2 9AQ (01245 605700). *Ancient British, Roman, medieval and later coins mainly from local finds, local medals.*

• Town Gate Museum (1949), **Chepstow,** Gwent. (01291) 625981 *Local coins and trade tokens.*

• Grosvenor Museum (1886), Grosvenor Street, **Chester** CH1 2DD (01244 972197). *Roman coins from the fortress site, Anglo-Saxon, English medieval and post-medieval coins of the Chester and Rhuddlan mints, trade tokens of Chester and Cheshire, English and British milled coins.*

• Public Library (1879), Corporation Street, **Chesterfield,** Derbyshire (01246 2047). *Roman coins from local finds, Derbyshire trade tokens, medals, seals and railway passes. Numismatic library and publications.*

• Red House Museum (1919), Quay Road, **Christchurch,** Dorset (01202 482860). *Coins of archaeological significance from Hampshire and Dorset, notably the South Hants Hoard, ancient British, Armorican, Gallo-Belgic, Celtic and Roman coins, local trade tokens and medals.*

• Corinium Museum (1856), Park Street, **Cirencester,** Glos (01285 655611). *Roman coins.*

• Colchester and Essex Museum (1860), The Castle, **Colchester,** Essex (01206 712931/2). *Ancient British and Roman coins from local finds, medieval coins (especially the Colchester Hoard), later English coins and Essex trade tokens, commemorative medals.*

D

• Public Library, Museum and Art Gallery (1921), Crown Street, **Darlington,** Co Durham DL1 1ND (01325 462034). *Coins, medals and tokens.*

• Borough Museum (1908), Central Park, **Dartford,** Kent (01322 224739). *Roman, medieval and later English hammered coins, trade tokens and commemorative medals.*

• Dartmouth Museum (1953), The Butterwalk, **Dartmouth,** Devon TQ6 9PZ (01803 832923). *Coins and medals of a historical and maritime nature.*

• Museum and Art Gallery (1878), The Strand, **Derby** DE1 1BS (01332 641901). *Roman coins, English silver and copper regal coins, Derbyshire tradesmen's tokens, British campaign medals and decorations of the Derbyshire Yeomanry and the 9/12 Royal Lancers.*

• Museum and Art Gallery (1909), Chequer Road, **Doncaster,** South Yorkshire DN1 2AE (01302 734293). *General collection of English and foreign silver and bronze coins. Representative collection of Roman imperial silver and bronze coins, including a number from local hoards. English trade tokens, principally of local issues, medals.*

• Dorset County Museum (1846), High West Street, **Dorchester,** Dorset DT1 1XA (01305 262735). *British, Roman, medieval and later coins of local interest.*

• Central Museum (1884), Central Library, St James's Road, **Dudley,** West Midlands DY1 1HU (01384 815575). *Small general collection of coins, medals and tokens.*

• Burgh Museum (1835), The Observatory, Corberry Hill, **Dumfries** (01387 53374). *Greek, Roman, Anglo-Saxon, medieval English and Scottish coins, especially from local hoards. Numismatic library.*

• Dundee Art Galleries and Museums (1873). Albert Square, **Dundee** DD1 1DA ()1382 307200). *Coins and medals of local interest.*

• The Cathedral Treasury (995 AD), The College, **Durham** DH1 3EH (0191 386 4266). *Greek and Roman coins bequeathed by Canon Sir George Wheeler (1724), Renaissance to modern medals, medieval English coins, especially those struck at the Durham ecclesiastical mint.*

• Durham Heritage Centre, St Mary le Bow, North Bailey, **Durham** DH1 3ET (0191 384 5589). *Roman, medieval and later coins, mainly from local finds.*

E

• National Museum of Scotland (1781), Chambers Street, **Edinburgh** EH1 1JF (0300 123 6789). *Roman, Anglo-Saxon, Englsh and Scottish coins, trade tokens, commemorative medals and communion tokens. Numismatic library. Publications.*

• Royal Albert Memorial Museum (1868), Queen Street, **Exeter** EX4 3RX (01392 265858). *Roman and medieval. Coins of the Exeter Mint.*

G

• Hunterian Museum (1807), Gilbert Scott Building, University Of Glasgow, University Avenue, **Glasgow** G12 8QQ (0141 330 4221). *Greek, Roman, Byzantine, Scottish, English and Irish coins, Papal and other European medals, Indian and Oriental coins, trade and communion tokens.*

• Art Gallery and Museum (1888), Kelvingrove, **Glasgow** G3 (0141 357 3929). *General collection of coins, trade tokens, communion tokens, commemorative and military medals.*

• Museum of Transport (1974), Riverside Museum, 100 Pointhouse Place **Glasgow** G3 8RS (0141 357 3929). *Transport tokens and passes, commemorative medals, badges and insignia of railway companies and shipping lines.*

• City Museum and Art Gallery (1859), Brunswick Road, **Gloucester** (01452 524131). *Ancient British, Roman, Anglo-Saxon (from local finds), early medieval (from local mints), Gloucestershire trade tokens.*

• Guernsey Museum and Art Gallery, St Peter Port, **Guernsey** (01481 726518). *Armorican, Roman, medieval and later coins, including the coins, medals, tokens and paper money of Guernsey.*

• Guildford Museum (1898), Castle Arch, **Guildford,** Surrey GU1 3SX (01483 444750). *Roman and medieval coins and later medals.*

H

• Gray Museum and Art Gallery, Clarence Road, **Hartlepool,** Cleveland (01429 268916). *General collection, including coins from local finds.*

• Public Museum and Art Gallery (1890), John's Place, Cambridge Road, **Hastings,** East Sussex (01424 721952). *General collection of English coins, collection of Anglo-Saxon coins from Sussex mints.*

• City Museum (1874), Broad Street, **Hereford** (01432 268121 ext 207). *Coins from the Hereford mint and local finds, Herefordshire trade tokens, general collection of later coins and medals.*

• Hertford Museum (1902), 18 Bull Plain, **Hertford** (01992 582686). *British, Roman, medieval and later English coins and medals.*

• Honiton and Allhallows Public Museum (1946), High Street, **Honiton,** Devon (01404 44966). *Small general collection, including coins from local finds.*

• Museum and Art Gallery (1891), 19 New Church Road, **Hove,** East Sussex (01273 779410). *English coins, Sussex trade tokens and hop tallies, campaign medals, orders and decorations, comm. medals.*

• Tolson Memorial Museum (1920), Ravensknowle Park, **Huddersfield,** West Yorkshire (01484 541455). *Representative collection of British coins and tokens, Roman and medieval coins, mainly from local finds.*

• Hull and East Riding Museum (1928), 36 High Street, **Hull** (01482 593902). *Celtic, Roman and medieval coins and artifacts from local finds. Some later coins including tradesmen's tokens.*

I

• The Manx Museum, Douglas, **Isle of Man** (01624 675522). *Roman, Celtic, Hiberno-Norse, Viking, medieval English and Scottish coins, mainly from local finds, Manx traders' tokens from the 17th to 19th centuries, Manx coins from 1709 to the present day.*

J

• Jersey Museum, Weighbridge, St Helier, **Jersey** (01534 30511). *Armorican, Gallo-Belgic, Roman, medieval English and French coins, coins, paper money and tokens of Jersey.*

K

• Dick Institute Museum and Art Gallery (1893), Elmbank Avenue, **Kilmarnock,** Ayrshire (01563 26401). *General collection of coins and medals, and the Hunter-Selkirk collection of communion tokens.*

L

• City Museum (1923), Old Town Hall, Market Square, **Lancaster** (01524 64637). *Roman, Anglo-Saxon, medieval English coins, provincial trade tokens, medals of the King's Own Royal Lancashire Regiment.*

• City Museum (1820), Municipal Buildings, The Headrow, **Leeds,** West Yorkshire (01532 478279). *Greek, Roman, Anglo-Saxon, English medieval, Scottish, Irish, British, Commonwealth and foreign coins. Several Roman and Saxon hoards. The Backhouse collection of Yorkshire banknotes, the Thornton collection of Yorkshire tokens, British and foreign commemorative medals.*

• Leicester Museum and Art Gallery (1849), New Walk, **Leicester** (01533 554100). *Roman, medieval and later coins, mainly from local finds, tokens, commemorative medals, campaign medals and decorations.*

• Pennington Hall Museum and Art Gallery, **Leigh,** Lancashire. *Roman and British coins and medals.*

• Museum and Art Gallery (1914), Broadway, **Letchworth,** Herts (01462 65647). *Ancient British coins minted at Camulodunum, Roman, medieval and English coins, Hertfordshire trade tokens, commemorative and campaign medals.*

• City Library, Art Gallery and Museum (1859), Bird Street, **Lichfield,** Staffs (01543 2177). *Roman, medieval and later English coins, Staffordshire trade tokens and commemorative medals.*

• Liverpool Museum(1851), William Brown Street, **Liverpool** L3 8EN (0151 207 0001). *General collection of Roman, medievaland later British coins, tokens.*

• Bank of England Museum, Threadneedle Street, **London** EC2 (020-7601 5545). *Exhibits relating to gold bullion, coins, tokens and medals, the design and manufacture of banknotes, and a comprehensive collection of bank notes dating from the 17th century to the present day.*

• British Museum(1752), HSBC Coin Gallery, Great Russell Street, **London** WC1 (020-7636 1555). *Almost a million coins, medals, tokens and badges of all period from Lydia, 7th century BC to the present time. Extensive library of books and periodicals.*

• British Numismatic Society (1903), Warburg Institute, Woburn Square, **London** WC1. *Library containing over 5,000 volumes, including sale catalogues, periodicals and pamphlets. Open to members only.*

• Cuming Museum (1906), Walworth Road, **London** SE17 (020-7703 3324/5529). *Some 8,000 items, including Greek, Roman, medieval English and modern British coins, English tokens and commemorative medals.*

• Gunnersbury Park Museum (1927), Acton, **London** W3. *Ancient British, Greek, Roman, medieval English, British and some foreign coins, tradesmen's tokens and commemorative medals, including local finds.*

• Horniman Museum and Library (1890), London Road, Forest Hill, **London** SE23 (020-7699 2339). *General collection, primitive currency, some tokens.*

• Imperial War Museum, Lambeth Road, **London** SE1 6HZ (020-7416 5000). *Emergency coinage of two world wars, occupation and invasion money, extensive collection of German Notgeld, commemorative, propaganda and military medals, badges and insignia.*

• Sir John Soane's Museum (1833), 13 Lincoln's Inn Fields, **London** WC2 (020-7405 2107). *Napoleonic medals and medallic series of the late 18th and early 19th centuries.*

• National Maritime Museum, Romney Road, Greenwich, **London** SE10 (020-8858 4422). *Commemorative medals with a nautical or maritime theme, naval medals and decorations.*

• Victoria and Albert Museum (1852), South Kensington, **London** SW7 (020-7938 8441). *Byzantine gold and medieval Hispano-Mauresque coins (Department of Metalwork), large collection of Renaissance and later medals (Department of Architecture and Sculpture). Numismatic books.*

• Ludlow Museum (1833). The Assembly Rooms. Castle Square, **Ludlow** (01584 873857). *Roman and medieval coins from local finds.*

• Luton Museum and Art Gallery (1927), Wardown Park, **Luton**, Beds (01582 36941). *Coins, tokens and medals.*

M

• Museum and Art Gallery (1858), **Maidstone**, Kent (01622 754497). *Ancient British, Roman, Anglo-Saxon and medieval coins found in Kent, modern British coins, Kent trade tokens, banknotes, hop tallies and primitive currency, collections of Kent Numismatic Society.*

• The Manchester Museum (1868), The University, **Manchester** M13 (0161-275 2634). *Very fine collections of Greek and Roman coins, comprehensive collections of English, European and Oriental coins, over 30,000 in all.*

• Margate Museum (1923), The Old Town Hall, Market Place, **Margate**, Kent (01843 225511 ext 2520). *Small collection of coins, including Roman from local finds.*

• Montrose Museum and Art Gallery (1836). Panmure Place, **Montrose**, Angus DD10 8HE (01674 73232). *Scottish and British coins.*

N

• Newark-on-Trent Museum (1912), Appleton Gate, **Newark**, Notts (01636 702358). *Siege pieces, trade tokens and coins from local finds and hoards.*

• Newbury District Museum, The Wharf, **Newbury**, Berkshire (01635 30511). *Ancient British, Roman and medieval coins and artifacts, later coins and tokens.*

• The Greek Museum, Percy Building, **Newcastle-upon-Tyne** (0191 2226000 ext 7966). *Ancient coins.*

O

• Heberden Coin Room, Ashmolean Museum (1683), **Oxford** (01865 278000). *Extensive collections of all periods, notably Greek, Roman, English and Oriental coins, Renaissance portrait and later medals, tokens and paper money. Large library. Numerous publications.*

P

• Peterborough Museum (1881), Priestgate, **Peterborough**, Cambs (01733 340 3329). *Roman (mainly from local hoards and finds), Anglo-Saxon, medieval English, British and modern European coins, English and British commemorative medals and tokens.*

• City Museum and Art Gallery (1897), Drake Circus, **Plymouth**, Devon (01752 264878). *General collections of British and Commonwealth coins and tokens, Devon trade tokens and Plymouth tradesmen's checks, Ancient British and Roman coins from local sites.*

• Waterfront Museum, 4 High Street, **Poole**, Dorset (01202 683138). *General collection of British and foreign coins, medals and tokens (view by appointment).*

• City Museum (1972), Museum Road, Old **Portsmouth** PO1 (023 80827261). *Roman, medieval and later coins mainly from local finds and archaeological excavation, British coins, trade tokens of Hampshire, commemorative medals.*

• Harris Museum and Art Gallery (1893), Market Square, **Preston**, Lancashire (01772 58248). *English and British coins, tokens and medals.*

R

• The Museum of Reading (1883), Blagrave Street, **Reading**, Berks (0118 939 9800). *British, Roman and medieval English coins, many from local finds, tradesmen's tokens and commemorative medals.*

• Rochdale Museum (1905), Sparrow Hill, **Rochdale**, Lancs (01706 41085). *Roman and medieval coins from local finds, Rochdale trade tokens, miscellaneous British and foreign coins and medals.*

• Municipal Museum and Art Gallery (1893), Clifton Park, **Rotherham** (01709 382121). *Collection includes Roman coins from Templeborough Forts, medieval English coins from local hoards and a general collection of British coins.*

S

• Saffron Walden Museum (1832) (1939), Museum Street, **Saffron** Walden, Essex (01799 522494). *Ancient British, Roman, medieval and later coins, mainly from local finds and archaeological excavation, trade tokens and commemorative medals.*

• Verulamium Museum, St Michael's, **St Albans**, Herts (01727 819339). *Coins and artifacts excavated from the Roman town.*

• Salisbury and South Wiltshire Museum (1861), The Cathedral Close, **Salisbury,** Wilts (01722 332151). *Collection of coins minted or found locally, including finds of Iron Age, Roman, Saxon and medieval coins, as well as 18th and 19th century tradesmen's tokens.*

• Richborough Castle Museum (1930), **Sandwich,** Kent (0304 612013). *Roman coins of 1st–5th centuries from excavations of the Richborough site.*

• Scarborough Museum (1829), The Rotunda, Vernon Road, **Scarborough**, North Yorkshire (01723 374839). *Collection of over 4,000 Roman coins, 1,500 English and 600 coins from local finds, siege pieces and trade tokens.*

• Shaftesbury and Dorset Local History Museum (1946), 1 Gold Hill, **Shaftesbury**, Dorset (01747 52157). *Hoard of Saxon coins.*

• City Museum (1875), Weston Park, **Sheffield** (0114 2 768588). *Over 5,000 coins of all periods, but mainly English and modern British. European coins, imperial Roman (including three hoards of about 500 coins each), Yorkshire trade tokens, British historical medals, campaign medals. Library.*

• Rowley's House Museum, Barker Street, **Shrewsbury**, Salop (01743 361196). *Coins minted at Shrewsbury 925-1180, Civil War coinage of 1642, Shropshire tradesmen's tokens, English coins and medals.*

• Museum of Archaeology (1951), God's House Tower, Town Quay, **Southampton**, Hants (023 8022 0007). *Main emphasis lies in Ancient British, Roman and medieval English coins from local archaeological excavations. General collection of later coins and medals.*

• Atkinson Art Gallery (1878), Lord Street, **Southport**, Lancs (01704 533133). *Roman coins.*

• Botanic Gardens Museum, Churchtown, **Southport**, Lancs (01704 87547). *English and British coins and medals, military medals and decorations.*

• Southwold Museum (1933), St Bartholomew's Green, **Southwold**, Suffolk (01502 722375). *General collection of coins, specialised Suffolk trade tokens.*

• Stamford Museum (1961), Broad Street, **Stamford**, Lincs (01780 66317). *General collection of coins, medals and tokens, including a selection from the Stamford mint.*

• Municipal Museum (1860), Vernon Park, Turncroft Lane, **Stockport**, Cheshire (0161 474 4460) *Miscellaneous collection of coins, tokens and medals.*

• Stroud Museum (1899), Lansdown, **Stroud**, Glos (01453 376394). *Ancient British, Roman, Saxon, Norman, later medieval English, British coins and Gloucestershire trade tokens.*

• Museum and Art Gallery (1846), Borough Road, **Sunderland,** Tyne & Wear (0191 514 1235). *Roman imperial, medieval and later English, including examples of the pennies minted at Durham, modern British and foreign coins, 17th-19th century tradesmen's tokens, local medallions and campaign medals.*

• Swansea Museum (1835), Victoria Road, **Swansea**, W. Glamorgan, SA1 1SN (0792 653765). *Coins and medals of local interest.*

T

• Tamworth Castle and Museum (1899), The Holloway, **Tamworth**, Staffs (01827 63563). *Anglo-Saxon coins, medieval English including coins of the Tamworth mint, later English and British coins, tokens, commemorative medallions and medals.*

• Somerset County Museum, Taunton Castle, **Taunton**, Somerset (01823 255510/320200). *Celtic, Roman, Anglo-Saxon, early Medieval, tokens, medallions and banknotes. Strong emphasis on locally-found items.*

• Thurrock Local History Museum (1956), Civic Square, **Tilbury**, Essex (01375 390000 ext 2414). *Roman coins.*

• Royal Cornwall Museum (1818), River Street, **Truro,** Cornwall (01872 72205). *Coins, tokens and medals pertaining principally to the county of Cornwall.*

W

• Wakefield Museum (1919), Wood Street, **Wakefield,** West Yorkshire (01924 295351). *Roman and medieval English silver and copper coins.*

• Epping Forest District Museum, 39/41 Sun Street, **Waltham Abbey**, Essex EN 9. *Ancient British, Roman and medieval coins, Essex tradesmen's tokens of local interest.*

• Warrington Museum and Art Gallery (1848). Bold Street, **Warrington**, Cheshire, WA1 1JG (01925 30550). *Coins, medals and tokens.*

• Worcester City Museum (1833), Foregate Street, **Worcester** (01905 25371). *Roman, medieval and later coins and tokens. Coins of the Worcester mint.*

• Wells Museum (18903), 8 Cathedral Green, **Wells,** Somerset (01749 3477). *Ancient and modern British and world coins, local trade tokens and medals.*

• Municipal Museum and Art Gallery (1878), Station Road, **Wigan**, Lancashire. *British, Commonwealth and foreign coins from about 1660 to the present. Roman coins from local sites, commemorative medals.*

• City Museum (1851), The Square, **Winchester**, Hants (01962 848269). *Roman and medieval coins chiefly from local hoards and finds. Hampshire tradesmen's tokens and commemorative medals. Small reference library.*

• Wisbech and Fenland Museum (1835), Museum Square, **Wisbech**, Cambridgeshire (01945 583817), *British Roman, medieval and later coins, medals and tokens.*

Y

• The Museum of South Somerset (1928), Hendford, **Yeovil**, Somerset (01935 24774). *Roman coins from local sites, medieval English, modern British coins and medals and a fine collection of tokens (particularly 17th century Somerset).*

• Castle Museum (1938), **York** (01904 653611). *English and British coins, campaign medals, orders and decorations, commemorative medals.*

• Jorvik Viking Centre (1984), Coppergate, **York** (01904 643211). *Coins and artefacts pertaining to the Viking occupation of York.*

• The Yorkshire Museum (1823), **York** (01904 629745). *Roman imperial, medieval English and later coins, about 12,000 in all.*

CLUB *directory*

Details given here are the names of Numismatic Clubs and Societies, their date of foundation, and their usual venues, days and times of meetings. Meetings are monthly unless otherwise stated. Finally, the telephone number of the club secretary is given; the names and addresses of club secretaries are withheld for security reasons, but full details may be obtained by writing to the Secretary of the British Association of Numismatic Societies, Keith Sugden, Honorary Curatorial Assistant, Department of Numismatics, Manchester Museum, Oxford Road, Manchester M13 9PL or visiting the website at www.coinclubs.freeserve.co.uk.

Banbury & District NS (1967). St John's Social Club, St John's Church, Oxford Road, Banbury 2nd Mon (exc Jul & Aug), 19.45. (01295 275128).

Bath & Bristol Numismatic Society (1950). Fry's Club, Keynsham, Bristol. 2nd Thu, 19.30. (0117 968 7259).

Bedfordshire Numismatic Society (1966). 2nd Thu. Dave Allen, Secretary (01234 870645).

Bexley Coin Club (1968). St Martin's Church Hall, Erith Road, Barnehurst, Bexleyheath, Kent. 1st Mon (exc Jan & Aug), 19.30. (020 8303 0510).

Birmingham Numismatic Society (1964). Friend's Meeting House, Bull Street. (0121 308 1616).

Matthew Boulton Society (1994). PO Box 395, Bir-mingham B31 2TB (0121 781 6558 fax 0121 781 6574).

Bradford & District Numismatic Society (1967). East Bowling Unity Club, Leicester Street, Bradford, West Yorkshire. 3rd Mon, 19.00. (01532 677151).

British Cheque Collectors' Society (1980). John Purser, 71 Mile Lane, Cheylesmore, Coventry, West Midlands CV3 5GB.

British Numismatic Society (1903). Warburg Institute, Woburn Square, London WC1H 0AB. Monthly meetings (exc Aug & Dec), 18.00. (020 7323 8585)

Cambridgeshire Numismatic Society (1946). Friends' Meeting House, 12 Jesus Lane (entrance in Park Street), Cambridge, CB5 8BA. 3rd Mon, Sept–June, 19.30. (01480 210992).

Chester & North Wales Coin & Banknote Society (1996). Liver Hotel, 110 Brook Street, Chester. 4th Tue, 20.00. (0151 478 4293)

Crewe & District NS. Memorial Hall, Church Lane, Wistaston, Crewe. 2nd Tue, 19.30 (exc Jan & July). (01270 569836)

Derbyshire NS The Friends Meeting House, St Helen's Street, Derby. (01283 223893)

Devon & Exeter NS, Courtenay Room, The St James Centre, Stadium Way, Exeter. 3rd Wed. (01395 568830)

Essex Numismatic Society (1966). Chelmsford Museum, Moulsham Street, Chelmsford, Essex. 4th Fri (exc Dec), 20.00. (01277 656627).

Glasgow & West of Scotland NS (1947). Woodside Halls, 26 Glenfarg Street, Glasgow, G3. 2nd Thu, Oct–May, 19.30. (0141 9424776).

Harrow Coin Club (1968). The Scout Building, off Walton Road, Wealdstone, Harrow. 2nd and 4th Mon, 19.30. (01923 826392).

Havering Numismatic Society (1967). Fairkytes Arts Centre, Billet Lane, Hornchurch, Essex. 1st Tue, 19.30. (07910 124549).

Horncastle & District Coin Club (1963). Bull Hotel, Bull Ring, Horncastle, Lincs. 2nd Thu (exc Aug), 19.30. (01754 2706).

Huddersfield Numismatic Society (1947). The Albert Hotel, Victoria Lane, Huddersfield. 1st Mon (exc Jul & Aug), 19.30. (01484 866814).

Hull & District Numismatic Society (1967). The Young People's Institute, George Street, Hull. Monthly (exc Aug & Dec), 19.30. (01482 441933).

International Bank Note Society (1961). Victory Services Club, 63–79 Seymour Street, London W1. Website: www.ibns.org.uk. Last Thu (exc Dec), 18.00. (www.ibnslondon.org.uk).

Ipswich NS, The Golden Hind, 470 Nacton Road, Ipswich, IP3 9NF. (email: administrator@ipnumsoc. org.uk).

International Bank Note Society (East Midlands Branch), Wollaton Park Community Association, Wollaton Park, Nottingham. (0115 928 9720).

International Bank Note Society, Scottish Chapter (1995). West End Hotel, Palmerston Place, Edinburgh. Last Sat (exc Dec), 14.30.

Ireland, Numismatic Society of (Northern Branch). Denman International, Clandeboye Road, Bangor or Shaws Bridge Sports Assoc.123 Milltown Road, Belfast. 1st Fri 19.30. (028 9146 6743)

Ireland, Numismatic Society of. (Southern Branch). Ely House, 8 Ely Place, Dublin. Third Fri, 20.00. (0035 3 283 2027).

Ipswich Numismatic Society (1966). Ipswich Citizens Advice Bureau, 19 Tower Street, Ipswich, Suffolk. Monthly meetings, 19.30. (01473 728653).

Kent Towns Numismatic Society (1913). (Mr. R. Josland, 01634 721187).

Kingston Numismatic Society (1966). St Paul's Parish Hall, 280 Hook Road, Chessington, Surrey. Meetings 3rd Thu (exc Dec & Jan), 19.30. (020-8397 6944).

Lancashire & Cheshire Numismatic Society (1933). Reception Room, 2nd Floor, Manchester Central Library, St Peter's Square, Manchester. Monthly, Sep-June, Sat (14.00). Manchester Museum (May & Dec only). (0161 275 2661).

Lincolnshire Numismatic Society (1932). Grimsby Bridge Club, Bargate, Grimsby, South Humberside. 4th Wed (exc Aug), 19.30.

London Numismatic Club (1947). Warburg Institute, Woburn Square, London WC1H 0AB. First Tuesday of month (except January and August), 1830. (01223 332918).

Loughborough Coin & Search Society (1964). Wallace Humphry Room, Shelthorpe Community Centre, Loughborough, Leics. 1st Thu, 19.30. (01509 261352).

Mid Lanark Coin Circle (1969). Hospitality Room, The Civic Centre, Motherwell, Lanarkshire. 4th Thu, Sep–Apr (exc Dec), 19.30. (0141-552 2083).

Newbury Coin & Medal Club (1971). Monthly, 20.00. (01635 41233).

Northampton Numismatic Society (1969). Old Scouts RFC, Rushmere Road, Northampton.
Norwich Coin & Medal Society, The White Horse, Trowse, Norwich. (01603 408393).

Norwich Numismatic Society (1967). Assembly House, Theatre Street, Norwich, Norfolk. 3rd Mon, 19.30. (01603 408393).

NS of Nottinghamshire (1948). Highfields Fire Station, Hassocks Lane, Beeston, Nottingham. 2nd Tue (Sep-Apr), 18.45. (0115 9257674).

Nuneaton & District Coin Club (1968). United Reformed Church Room, Coton Road, Nuneaton, Warwickshire. 2nd Tue, 19.30. (01203 371556).

Orders & Medals Research Society (1942). National Army Museum, Royal Hospital Road, Chelsea, London SW3. Monthly, 14.30 (020-8680 2701).

Ormskirk & West Lancashire Numismatic Society (1970). The Eagle & Child, Maltkiln Lane, Bispham Green L40 1SN. 1st Thu, 20.15. (01704 531266).

Peterborough & District Numismatic Society (1967). Belsize Community Centre, Celta Road Peter-borough, Cambs. 4th Tue (exc July & Aug), 19.30. (01733 562768 or 567763).

Plymouth Numismatics Society (1970). Mutley Conservative Club, Mutley Plain, Plymouth, Devon. Meetings on second Wed (exc Dec), 19.30. (01752 490 394).

Reading Coin Club (1964). Abbey Baptist Church, Abbey Square, Reading. 1st Mon, 20.00. (01753 516390).

Romsey Numismatic Society (1969). Romsey WM Conservative Club, Market Place, Romsey, Hants SO5 8NA. 4th Fri (exc Dec), 19.30. (01703 253921).

Rotherham & District Coin Club (1982). Rotherham Art Centre, Rotherham, South Yorkshire. 1st Wed, 19.00. (01709 528179).

Royal Mint Coin Club, PO Box 500, Cardiff CF1 1HA (01443 222111).

Royal Numismatic Society (1836). Warburg Institute, Woburn Square, London, WC1H 0AB. (some meetings held at British Museum). Third Thursday of monthly (Oct-June), 18.00. Joe Cribb, Coins and Medals, British Museum, London WC1B 3DG (020-7323 8175).

Rye Coin Club (1955). Rye Further Education Centre, Lion Street, Rye, East Sussex. 2nd Thu (Oct-Dec, Feb-May), 19.30. (01424 422974).

St Albans & Hertfordshire Numismatic Society (1948). St Michael's Parish Centre, Museum Entrance, Verulamium Park, St Albans, Herts AL3 4SL. 2nd Tue (exc Aug), 19.30. (01727 824434).

Southampton and District Numismatic Society (1953). Central Baptist Church, Devonshire Road, Polygon, Southampton SO15 2GY. Contact T. Winsborough, (02380 556648).

South East Hants Numismatic Society. The Langstone Conservative Club, Havant. Second Fri. Contact: Tony Matthews, (01292 389419)

South Manchester Numismatic Society (1967). Nursery Inn, Green Lane, Heaton Mersey, Stockport. 1st & 3rd Mondays of each month (excl. Public hols), 20.15. (0161-476 3184).

South Wales & Monmouthshire Numismatic Society (1958). 1st Mon (except Bank Holidays when 2nd Mon, 19.30. (For location tel: 029 20561564).

Thurrock Numismatic Society (1970). Stanley Lazell Hall, Dell Road, Grays, Essex. 3rd Wed, 19.00.

Tyneside Numismatic Society (1954). RAFA Club, Eric Nelson House, 16 Berwick Road, Gateshead, Tyne & Wear. Meetings on second Wed, 19.30. (01661 825824).

Wessex NS (1948). Edward Wright Room, Beaufort Community Centre, Southbourne, Bournemouth, Dorset. 2nd Thurs (exc Aug), 20.00. (020 7731 1702).

Wiltshire Numismatic Society (1965). The Raven Inn, Poulshot, Nr. Devizes, Wiltshire. 3rd Wednesday, March–Dec, 20.00. (01380 828453).

Worthing & District Numismatic Society (1967). The Chatsworth Hotel, Worthing, BN11 3DU. 3rd Thu, 20.00. (www.worthingnumismatics.co.uk).

Yorkshire Numismatic Society (1909). Swarthmore Institute, Woodhouse Square, Leeds. 1st Sat (exc Jan, Aug & Dec) (0113 3910848).

Important Notice to Club Secretaries:

If your details as listed are incorrect please let us know in time for the next edition of the **COIN YEARBOOK.**
Amendments can be sent via post
or email to: fiona@tokenpublishing.com

IMPORTANT ORGANISATIONS

ADA
The Antiquities
Dealers Association
Secretary: Susan Hadida, Duke's Court, 32 Duke Street, London SW1Y 6DU

ANA
The American
Numismatic Association
818 North Cascade Avenue, Colorado Springs, CO 80903-3279, USA

BNTA
The British Numismatic
Trade Association
Ema Šikié, The Gallery, Trent Park Equestrian Centre, Bramley Rd, London N14 4UW

IAPN
International Association of
Professional Numismatists
Secretary: Jean-Luc Van der Schueren, 14 Rue de la Bourse, B–1000, Brussels.

IBNS
International
Bank Note Society
Membership Secretary:
David Hunt, PO Box 412, Halifax
W. Yorks HX3 5YD

RNS
Royal Numismatic Society
Dept of Coins & Medals, British Museum, London WC1B 3DG.

BAMS
British Art Medal Society
Philip Attwood, Dept of Coins & Medals, British Museum, London WC1B 3DG.

BNS
British Numismatic Society
Dr K. Clancy, The Royal Mint,
Llantrisant, Pontyclun,
Mid Glamorgan CF72 8YT

Society activities are featured every month in the "Diary Section" of COIN NEWS— available from all good newsagents or on subscription.
Telephone 01404 46972 for more details or log onto www.tokenpublishing.com

DIRECTORY *of auctioneers*

Listed here are the major auction houses which handle coins, medals, banknotes and other items of numismatic interest. Many of them hold regular public auctions, whilst others handle numismatic material infrequently. A number of coin companies also hold regular Postal Auctions—these are marked with a ℗

Auction World Company Ltd
Mori Bldg 2F,1-27-8 Hamamatsucho,Minato-ku, Tokyo, 105-0013 Japan (www.auction-world.co)

Baldwin's Auctions Ltd
399 The Strand, London WC2R 0LX. (020 7930 6879, fax 020 7930 9450, coins@baldwin.co.uk, www.baldwin.co.uk).

Biddle & Webb
Ladywood, Middleway, Birmingham, B16 0PP. (0121 455 8042, www.biddleandwebb.com)

Blyth & Co
7/9 Market Square, Ely, Cambs, CB7 4NP. (01353 668320, auctions@fenlord.com).

Bonhams (incorporating Glendinings)
Montpelier Street, Knightsbridge, London SW7 1HH. (020 7393 3914, www.bonhams.com).

BSA Auctions
Units 1/2, Cantilupe Court, Cantilupe Road, Ross on Wye, Herefordshire HR9 7AN . (01989 769529, bids@birmauctions.co.uk, www.birmauctions.co.uk).

Bushey Auctions
(020 8386 2552, enquiries@busheyauctions. com, www.busheyauctions.com).

cgb.fr
36, Rue Vivienne, 75002, Paris, France. (contact@cgb.fr, www.cgbfr.com).

Christie, Manson & Wood Ltd
8 King Street, St James's, London SW1Y 6QT. (020 7839 9060).

Classical Numismatic Group Inc (Seaby Coins)
14 Old Bond Street, London W1X 4JL. (020 7495 1888 fax 020 7499 5916, cng@historicalcoins.com, www.historicalcoins.com). ℗

The Coin Cabinet
On-line auctions at www.thecoincabinet.co.uk

Corbitts
5 Moseley Sreet, Newcastle upon Tyne NE11YE. (0191-232 7268, fax 0191-261 4130).

Croydon Coin Auctions
PO Box 201, Croydon, CR9 7AQ. (020 8656 4583, www.croydoncoinauctions.co.uk).

Davissons Ltd.
PO Box 323, Cold Spring, MN 56320 USA. ((001) 320 6853835, www.davcoin.com).

Dix Noonan Webb (IAPN)
16 Bolton Street, Piccadilly, London. (020 7016 1700, auctions@dnw.co.uk, www.dnw.co.uk).

Duke's
Brewery Square, Dorchester, Dorset DT1 1GA. (01305 265080, www.dukes-auctions.com)

Edinburgh Coin Shop
11 West Crosscauseway, Edinburgh EH8 9JW. (0131 668 2928 fax 0131 668 2926). ℗

English Coin Auctions
West Court Lodge, West Street, Scarborough YO11 2QL. (01723 364760, www.englishcoinauctions.com)

Jean Elsen & ses Fils s.a.
Avenue de Tervueren 65, B–1040, Brussels. (0032 2 7346356, www.elsen.eu).

Fellows & Sons
Augusta House, 19 Augusta Street, Hockley, Birmingham B18 6JA. (0121-212 2131, www.fellows.co.uk).

B. Frank & Son
3 South Avenue, Ryton, Tyne & Wear NE40 3LD. (0191 413 8749, mobile: 07806 658011) www.bfrankandson.com).

Gadoury
57, rue Grimaldi, MC98000 - MONACO. (0 377 93 25 12 96, www.gadoury.com).

Goldberg Coins & Collectibles
350 South Beverly Drive, Ste. 350, Beverly
Hills CA 90212. (001 310.432.6688,
www.goldbergcoins.com).

Heritage World Coin Auctions
3500 Maple Avenue, 17th Floor, Dallas, Texas
75219–3941, USA. (001 214 528 3500,
www.heritagecoins.com).

**Horizon Coin Auctions (in association with Steve
Album Rare Coins)**
c/o Wilkes & Curtis PO Box 566, Tonbridge, Kent
TN9 9LR (07535 383321, www.horizon.auction)

International Coin Exchange
Charter House, 5 Pembroke Row, Dublin 2.
(+353 (1) 6768775, email: auctionice@gmail.
com, www.ice-auction.com).

Kleeford Coin Auctions
22 Peak Avenue, Riddings, Alfreton, Derbyshire,
DE55 4AR. (01773 528743 or 07969 645952,
www.kleefordcoins.webs.com, kleeford@
btinternet.com). **P**

Fritz Rudolf Künker
Nobbenburger, Strasse 4A, 49076, Osnabrüeck,
Germany. (0049 541 9620224, fax: 0049 541 96
20222, www.kuenker.com).

Lawrence Fine Art Auctioneers
South Street, Crewkerne, Somerset TA18 8AB.
(01460 73041).

Lockdale Coins
52 Barrack Square, Martlesham Heath, Ipswich,
Suffolk, IP5 3RF37. (01473 627110,
www.lockdales.com).

London Coins
4–6 Upper Street South, New Ash Green, Kent
DA3 8JJ. (01474 871464,
www.londoncoins.co.uk).

Morton & Eden Ltd
45 Maddox Street, London W1S 2PE.
(020 7493 5344 fax 020 7495 6325,
info@mortonandeden.com,
www.mortonandeden.com).

Mowbray Collectables
Private Bag 63000, Wellington New Zealand.
(+64 6 364 8270,
www.mowbraycollectables.co.nz).

Noble Numismatics
169 Macquire Street, Sydney, Australia. (+61 2
9223 4578, www.noble.com.au).

Numismatica Ars Classica NAC AG
3rd Floor, Genavco House, 17 Waterloo Place,
London SW1Y 4AR (020 783 97270,
email: info@arsclassicacoins.com).

Numis-Or
4, Rue des Barques 1207, Geneva Switzerland
(0041 (0) 22 7359255, www.numisor.ch).

Pacific Rim Online Auction
P O Box 847, North Sydney, NSW 2060,
Australia. (+61 2 9588 7111,
www.pacificrimonlineauctions.com)
Online coin auction.

Penrith, Farmers' & Kids PLC
Skirsgill Saleroom, Penrith, Cumbria, CA11 0DN.
(01768 890781, www.pfkauctions.co.uk)

Chris A. Rudd (IAPN, BNTA)
PO Box 222, Aylsham, Norfolk, NR11 6TY.
(01263 735007, www.celticcoins.com)

Simmons Gallery
PO Box 104, Leytonstone, London. (Tel: 0207
8989 8097. info@simmonsgallery.co.uk, www.
simmonsgallery.co.uk). **P**

Smiths of Newent
The Old Chapel, Culver Street, Newent, GL18
1DB. (Tel: 01531 821776. info@smithsauction-
room.co.uk, www.smithsnewentauctions.co.uk).

Spink & Son Ltd
69 Southampton Row, Bloomsbury, London
WC1B 4ET. (020 7563 4000, fax 020 7563 4066,
info@spink.com, www.spink.com).

Stacks, Bowers and Ponterio
118061 Fitch, Irvine, California 92614, USA.
(001 949 253 0916, www.stacksbowers.com

St James's Auctions
10 Charles II Street, London SW1Y 4AA.
(020 7930 7888, www.sixbid.com).

Tennants Auctioneers
The Auction Centre, Leyburn, North Yorkshire
DL8 5SG. (01969 623780, www.tennants.co.uk).

The-saleroom.com
115 Shaftesbury Avenue, London WC2H 8AF.
Live bidding in real-time auctions from around
the world. (www.the-saleroom.com).

Thomson Roddick & Metcalf
Coleridge House, Shaddongate, Carlisle
CA2 5TU. (01228 528939,
www.thomsonroddick.com).

Thomson Roddick Scottish Auctions
The Auction Centre,118 Carnethie Street,
Rosewell. Edinburgh EH24 9AL (0131 440 2448).

Timeline Auctions
The Court House, 363 Main Road, Harwich,
Essex CO12 4DN (01277 815121,
www.timelineauctions.com).

Mavin International
20 Kramat Lane, #01-04/05 United House,
Singapore 228773. (+65 6238 7177)
mail@mavininternational.com).

Warwick & Warwick
Chalon House, Scarbank, Millers Road, Warwick
CV34 5DB. (01926 499031 fax 01926 491906,
richard.beale@warwickandwarwick.com,
www.warwickandwarwick.com).

Whyte's Auctions
38 Molesworth Street, Dublin2, Ireland.
(+00 3531 676 2888, www.whytes.com).

WIlkes & Curtis
PO Box 566, Tonbridge, Kent TN9 9LR
(07535 383321, www.wilkesandcurtis.com).)

Woolley & Wallis
51-61 Castle Street, Salisbury, Wiltshire SP1 3SU.
(01722 424594, www.woolleyandwallis.co.uk)

DIRECTORY *of fairs*

Listed below are the names of the fair organisers, their venue details where known along with contact telephone numbers. Please call the organisers direct for information on dates etc.

Aberdeen
Jarvis Amatola Hotel, Great Western Road, also venues in **Glenrothes** and **Glasgow.** *Cornucopia Collectors Fairs (01382 224946).*

Altrincham
Crest Court Hotel, Church Street, Town Centre. *Nationwide Collectors Fairs (01484 866777).*

Birmingham
National Motor Cycle Museum, Bickenhill, Birmingham. *Midland Stamp & Coin Fair (01694 731781, www.coinfairs.co.uk).*

Birmingham
Collingwood Centre, Collingwood Drive, Great Barr, Birmingham. *Dave Burnett Fairs (0776 5792998).*

Bristol
Patchway Community College, Hempton Lane, Almondsbury, Bristol. *Minster Stamps (01522 857343,).*

Britannia Medal Fair
Carisbrooke Hall, The Victory Services Club, 63/79 Seymour Street, London W2 2HF. *Coin & Medal Fairs Ltd (01694 731781).*

Colchester
Stanway Football Club, New Farm Road, Colchester. *ClickCollect Fairs (01485 578117).*

Cardiff
City Hall, Cardiff. *M. J. Promotions. (01792 415293).*

Cheltenham
The Regency Hotel, Gloucester Road. *Mark Grimsley (0117 9623203).*

Dublin
Serpentine Hall, RDS, Ballsbridge, Dublin 4. *Mike Kelly (00353 86 87 14 880).*

East Grinstead
Sackville School, Bourg-De-Peague Avenue, East Grinstead, RH19 3TY. *John Terry Fairs (01342 326317).*

Ely
The Maltings, Ship Lane, Ely. *ClickCollect (01485 578117).*

Exeter
The America Hall, De La Rue Way, Pinhoe, Exeter. *Michael Hale Collectors Fairs (01761 414304).*

Harrogate
Old Swan Hotel, Swan Road, Harrogate HG1 2SR. *Simon Monks (01234 270260).*

Lichfield
Civic Hall, Castle Dyke, City Centre. *C. S. Fairs (01562 710424).*

London
Holiday Inn, Coram St., Bloomsbury, London WC1. *London Coin Fair. (01694 731781).*

London
Jury's Hotel, 16-22 Great Russell Street, London WC1 3NN. *Bloomsbury Fairs (01694 731781).*

Plymouth
Lower Guildhall. *Bruce Stamps (01749 813324).*

Southport
Royal Clifton Hotel, the Promenade. *Nationwide Collectors Fairs (01484 866777).*

Stowmarket
Stowmarket Football Club, Bury Road, Stowmarket. *ClickCollect (01485 578117).*

Suttton Coldfield
Fellowship Hall, South Parade. *C. S. Fairs (01562 710424).*

Wakefield
Cedar Court Hotel, Denby Dale Road, Calder Grove, Wakefield *Eddie Smith (01552 684681).*

West Bromwich
Town Hall, High Street. *C. S. Fairs (01562 710424).*

Weston-super-Mare
Victoria Methodist Church Hall, Station Road. BS23 1XU. *Michael Hale (01749 677669).*

York
The Grandstand, York Race Course. *York Coin Fair (01793 513431, 020 8946 4489 or 01425 656459).*

Information correct at time of going to press

COIN, MEDAL & BANKNOTE FAIRS

THE LONDON COIN FAIR
HOLIDAY INN
London, Bloomsbury, Coram Street, WC1N 1HT
2016 dates: 5th November
2017 dates: 4th February, 3rd June, 4th November

THE MIDLAND COIN FAIR
NATIONAL MOTORCYCLE MUSEUM
Bickenhill, Birmingham, B92 0EJ
(Opposite the NEC on the M42/A45 junction)
2016 dates: 9th October, 13th November, 11th December
2017 dates: 8th January, 12th February, 12th March, 9th April,
14th May, 11th June, 9th July, 13th August, 10th September,
8th October, 12th November, 10th December

BRITANNIA MEDAL FAIR
CARISBROOKE HALL
The Victory Service Club,
63/79 Seymour Street, London W2 2HF
2016 date: 20th November
2017 date: 19th March, 19th November

For more information please contact:
Lu Veissid, Hobsley House, Frodesley, Shrewsbury SY5 7HD
Tel: 01694 731781   Email: l.veissid@btinternet.com

www.coinfairs.co.uk

Like us on facebook **f** @ coin and medal fairs
Follow us on twitter **y** @coinmedalfairs

DEALERS *directory*

The dealers listed below have comprehensive stocks of coins and medals, unless otherwise stated. Specialities, where known, are noted. Many of those listed are postal dealers only, so to avoid disappointment always make contact by telephone or mail in the first instance, particularly before travelling any distance.

Abbreviations:
ADA— — Antiquities Dealers Association
ANA — American Numismatic Association
BADA — British Antique Dealers Association
BNTA — British Numismatic Trade Association
IAPN — International Association of Professional
        Numismatists
IBNS — International Bank Note Society
🅟 — — Postal only
🅛 — — Publishes regular lists

ABC Coins & Tokens
PO Box 52, Alnwick, Northumberland NE66 1YE. (01665 603851, email: d–stuart@d–stuart.demon. co.uk, www.abccoinsandtokens.com).

A. Ackroyd (IBNS)
62 Albert Road, Parkstone, Poole, Dorset BH12 2DB. (Tel/fax 01202 739039, www.AAnotes.com). 🅟 🅛 *Banknotes and cheques*

Airedale Coins (ANA, BNTA)
PO Box 392, Guiseley, Leeds LS19 9JG. (01943 876221, email: info@airedalecoins.com, www.airedalecoins.co.uk). 🅟 🅛 *British and modern coins of the world.*

Joan Allen Electronics Ltd
190 Main Road, Biggin Hill, Kent TN16 3BB. (01959 571255). Mon–Sat 09.00–17.00. *Metal detectors.*

Allgold of Sevenoaks
P.O Box 260, Wallington, SM5 4H. (0844 5447952, email: sales@allgoldcoins.co.uk, www.allgoldcoins. co.uk). *Quality Sovereigns.*

A. J. W. Coins
Taunton, Somerset. (0845 680 7087, email: andrewwide@ajw-coins.co.uk, www.ajw-coins. co.uk). 🅟 *Sovereigns and CGS-UK specialist.*

Dave Allen Collectables
Shop 1: 52 High Street, Biggleswade SG18 0LJ. Shop 2: Antiques Emporium, 13 Fishers Yard, St NEOTS, PE19 2AG. (07541 461021. Email: coinsandmedals@outlook.com, www.daveallencollectables.co.uk). *Coins, medals, banknotes, bullion and jewellery.*

AMR COINS
(07527 569308, www.amrcoins.com). *Quality English coins specialising in rare hammered and milled coins of exceptional quality.*

Ancient & Gothic
PO Box 5390, Bournemouth, BH7 6XR. (01202 431721).🅟 🅛*Greek, Roman, Celtic and Biblical coins. English hammered coins & antiquities.*

Otavio Anze
Avenida Oaula Ferreira, 2159 Vila Bonilha. Pirtuba. Sao Paulo. SP. Brazil. *Coins, Antiques and collectables.*

Argentum Coins
PO Box 130, Peterlee, Co Durham SR8 9BE (07720769005, email: john.stephenson815@sky. com, www.argentumandcoins.co.uk). *British milled coins from 1662 to date.*

Arghans
Unit 9, Callington Business Park, Tinners Way Moss side, Callington PL17 7SH. (01579 382405, email: keithp44@waitrose.com). *British banknotes.*

ARL Collectables
(www.litherlandcollectables.com). *Coins, banknotes, medallions and paper emphemera.*

S P Asimi
Cabinet at The Emporium, 112 High Street, Hungerford, Berkshire RG17 0NB. (01488 686959) *British milled coins.*

Athens Numismatic Gallery
Akadimias 39, Athens 10672, Greece. (0030 210 3648386, www.athensnumismaticgallery.com). *Rare & common sovereigns. British & world coins.*

Atlas Numismatics
10 Jay Street, Suite 706, Brooklyn, NY 11201 USA. (www.atlasnumismatics.com) *Ancient, world and US coinage*

ATS Bullion (BNTA)
2, Savoy Court, Strand. London WC2R 0EZ. (020 7240 4040, email: bullion@atslimited.fsnet. co.uk). *Bullion and modern coins.*

Keith Austin (IBNS)
10A-12-2 Pearl View Condo, Jalan Bunga Pudak,
1200, Tanjang Bunga, Penang, Malaysia.
email: kaustin2368@gmail.com).
Ⓛ *Banknotes.*

Mark Bailey
120 Sterte Court, Sterte Close, Poole, Dorset
BH15 2AY. (01202 674936). **ⓅⓁ***Ancient,
modern, world coins and antiquities.*

A. H. Baldwin & Sons Ltd (ANA, BADA, BNTA, IAPN)
399 The Strand, London WC2R 0LX.
09.00–17.00 weekdays.
(email: coins@baldwin.co.uk) *Coins, tokens,
numismatic books.*

Bath Stamp and Coin Shop
Pulteney Bridge, Bath, Avon BA2 4AY.
(01225 463073). Mon–Sat 09.30–17.30. *British.*

Michael Beaumont
PO Box 8, Carlton, Notts NG4 4QZ. (0115 9878361).
Ⓟ *Gold & Silver English/Foreign Coins.*

Beaver Coin Room (BNTA)
57 Philbeach Gardens, London SW5 9ED.
(020 7373 4553). **Ⓟ** *European coins and medals.*

R. P. & P. J. Beckett
Maesyderw, Capel Dewi, Llandyssul, Dyfed
SA44 4PJ. (Fax only 01559 395631, email:
becket@xin.co.uk). **Ⓟ** *Coin sets and banknotes.*

Lloyd Bennett (BNTA)
PO Box 2, Monmouth, Gwent NP25 3YR. (01600
890634). *English hammered and milled coins.*

Berkshire Coin Centre
35 Castle Street, Reading, Berkshire RG1 7SB.
(0118 957 5593). 0630–15.00 W, Th, Fri & Sat.
Sat. *British British and world coins and militaria.*

Stephen J. Betts
4 Victoria Street, Narborough, Leics LE9 5DP.
(0116 2864434).**ⓅⓁ***Medieval and modern coins,
counters, jetons, tokens and countermarks.*

Bigbury Mint
River Park, Ermington Mill, Ivybridge, Devon
PL21 9NT. (01548 830717. *Specialists in
reproduction hammered coins*

Jon Blyth
Office 63, 2 Lansdowne Row, Mayfair, London
W1J 6HL . (07919 307645. *Specialists in
quality British coins*

Barry Boswell and Kate Bouvier
24 Townsend Lane, Upper Boddington, Daventry,
Northants NN11 6DR. (01327 261877, fax 01327
261391, email: Barry.Boswell@btinternet.com).
ⓅⓁ*British and world banknotes.*

James & C. Brett
17 Dale Road, Lewes, East Sussex BN7 1LH.
ⓅⓁ*British and world coins.*

J. Bridgeman Coins
129a Blackburn Road, Accrington, Lancs
(01254 384757). 09.30–17.00 (closed Wednesday).
British & World coins.

Britaly Coins Ltd
1 Lumley Street, Mayfair, London W1K 6TT
(07479 862432, www.britalycoins.co.uk)
British and world Coins.

Arthur Bryant Coins
PO Box 67499, London, NW3 3SN (07768 645686
email: abcoins@live.co.uk, website: www.bryancoins.
com). *British Coins and Medals.*

BRM Coins
3 Minshull Street, Knutsford, Cheshire WA16 6HG.
(01565 651480 and 0606 74522). Mon–Fri 11.00–
15.00, Sat 11.00–1.00 or by appt. *British coins.*

Bucks Coins
St Mary's House, Duke Street, Norwich. Callers by
appointment only. (01603 927020). *English milled
coins, Celtic and Roman.*

Iain Burn
2 Compton Gardens, 53 Park Road, Camberley,
Surrey GU15 2SP. (01276 23304).
Bank of England & Treasury notes.

Cambridgeshire Coins
355 Newmarket Road, Cambridge CB5 8JG.
(01223 503073, info@cambridgeshirecoins.com,
www.cambridgeshirecoins.com).
Coins, banknotes and accessories.

Cambridge Stamp Centre Ltd
9 Sussex Street, Cambridge CB4 4HU.
(01223 63980). Mon–Sat 09.00–17.30.
British coins.

Castle Galleries
81 Castle Street, Salisbury, Wiltshire SP1 3SP.
(01722 333734). Tue, Thu Fri 09.00–17.00,
Sat 09.30–16.00. *British coins, medals and tokens.*

Cathedral Coins
23 Kirkgate, Ripon, North Yorkshire HG4 1PB.
(01765 701400). Mon–Sat 10.00–17.00.

Cathedral Court Medals
First Floor Office, 30A Market Place, West Ripon,
North Yorks HG4 1BN. (01765 601400). *Coin and
medal sales. Medal mounting and framing.*

Central Bank of Ireland
Currency Centre, Sandyford Road, Dublin 16,
Ireland. *Issuer of new coin and banknote issues of
Ireland.*

C. G. S.
4-6 Upper Street South, New Ash Green, Longfield,
Kent DA3 8JJ. (01474 874895, email: info@cgs-uk.
biz). *Coin grading service.*

Lance Chaplin
17 Wanstead Lane, Ilford, Essex IG1 3SB.
(020 8554 7154. www.shaftesburycoins.com).
ⓅⓁ*Roman, Greek, Celtic, hammered coins and
antiquities.*

Chard (BNTA)
Gold & Foreign Exchange: 521 Lytham Road,
Blackpool, Lancs FY4 1RJ. (01253 473931)
Main Showroom: 32-36 Harrowside, Blackpool,
FY4 1RJ. (01253 843525). (www.chards.co.uk,
Mon–Sat 09.00–17.00. *British and world coins.*

Jeremy Cheek Coins Ltd
(01923 450385/07773 872686,
jeremycoins@aol.com). *Advice, valuation and
representation at auctions.*

Nigel A. Clark
28 Ulundi Road, Blackheath, London SE3 7UG. (020
8858 4020, email: nigel.a.clark@btinternet.com).**ⓅⓁ**
Tokens (Mainly 17th century) and British Farthings.

Classical Numismatic Group (IAPN)
20 Bloomsbury Street, London, WC1B 3QA.
(020 7495 1888, email cng@cngcoins.com,
www.cngcoins.com). ⓟ *Ancient and world coins.
Publishers of the Classical Numismatic Review.
Regular high quality auctions of ancient coins.*

Paul Clayton (BNTA)
PO Box 21, Wetherby, West Yorkshire LS22 5JY.
(01937 724441). *Modern gold coins.*

André de Clermont (BNTA)
PO Box 3615, London, SW10 0YD. (020 7351 5727,
Fax 020 7352 8127). *World coins, especially Islamic.*

M. Coeshaw
PO Box 115, Leicester LE3 8JJ. (0116 287 3808). ⓟ
Coins, banknotes, coin albums and cases.

Philip Cohen Numismatics (ANA, BNTA)
20 Cecil Court, Charing Cross Road, London
WC2N 4HE. (020 7379 0615). Mon–Sat 11.00–17.30.

Coin & Collectors Centre
PO Box 22, Pontefract, West Yorkshire WF8
1YT. (01977 704112, email sales@coincentre.co.uk,
www.coincentre.co.uk). ⓟ*British coins.*

Coinage of England
51 Arnhem Wharf, 2 Arnhem Place, Canary Wharf,
London, E1 3RU. (020 7538 5686,
www.coinageofengland.co.uk). *Fine and rare English
Coins.*

Coincraft (ANA, IBNS)
45 Great Russell Street, London, WC1B 3JL.
(020 7636 1188 and 020 7637 8785 fax 020
7323 2860, email: info@coincraft.com). Mon–
Fri 09.30–17.00, Sat 10.00–14.30. ⓛ(newspaper
format). *Coins and banknotes.*

Coinote
74 Elwick Road, Hartlepool TS26 9AP. Tel: 01429
890894. www.coinnote.co.uk. Coins, Medals, ,
Banknotes and accessories.

Coinswap.co.uk
Swap, sell or trade coins.

Coins of Beeston
PO Box 19, Beeston, Notts BG9 2NE.ⓟ ⓛ
Tokens, medals and paranumismatics.

Coins of Canterbury
PO Box 47, Faversham, Kent ME13 7HX.
(01795 531980). ⓟ *English coins.*

Collectors' World (Mark Ray)
188 Wollaton Road, Wollaton, Nottingham NG8 1HJ.
(01159 280347). *Coins, Banknotes, Accessories.*

Constantia CB
15 Church Road, Northwood, Middlesex
HA6 1AR. ⓟ *Roman and medieval hammered coins.*

Colin Cooke
P.O. Box 602, Altrincham, WA14 5UN. (0161
927 9524 fax 0161 927 9540, email coins@colin
cooke.com, www.colincooke.com).
ⓛ*British coins.*

Colonial Coins & Medals
218 Adelaide Street, Brisbane, QLD 4001.
(Email:coinshop@bigpond.net.au).
Auctions of World coins

Copperbark Ltd
Suite 35, 37, St Andrew's Street, Norwich NR2 4TP
(07834 434780, www.copperbark.com). *English,
Russian and 17th century tokens.*

Corbitts (BNTA)
5 Mosley Street, Newcastle Upon Tyne NE1 1YE.
(0191 232 7268 fax: 0191 261 4130). *Dealers and
auctioneers of all coins and medals.*

David Craddock
PO Box 3785, Camp Hill, Birmingham B11 2NF.
(0121 733 2259) ⓛ*Crown to farthings. Copper and
bronze specialist. Some foreign.*

Roy Cudworth
8 Park Avenue, Clayton West, Huddersfield HD8
9PT. *British and world coins.*

Paul Dawson
47 The Shambles, York, YO1 7XL, (01904 654769
email: pauldawsonyork@hotmail.com, www.
historycoin.com. *Ancient and British coins.*

Mark Davidson
PO Box 197, South Croydon, Surrey, CR3 0ZD.
(020 8651 3890). *Ancient, hammered coinage.*

Paul Davis
PO Box 418, Birmingham, B17 0RZ.
(0121 427 7179). *British and World Coins.*

R. Davis
(01332 862755 days/740828 evenings). *Maker of
traditional coin cabinets.*

Paul Davies Ltd (ANA, BNTA, IAPN)
PO Box 17, Ilkley, West Yorkshire LS29 8TZ.
(01943 603116 fax 01943 816326). ⓟ
World coins.

Ian Davison
PO Box 256, Durham DH1 2GW (0191 3750808).ⓛ
English hammered and milled coins 1066–1910.

Dei Gratia
PO Box 3568, Buckingham MK18 4ZS (01280
848000).ⓟ ⓛ *Pre–Roman to modern coins,
antiquities, banknotes.*

Den of Antiquity
(01223 863002, www.denof antiquity.co.uk.)
Ancient and medieval coins.

Clive Dennett (BNTA)
66 St Benedicts Street, Norwich, Norfolk NR2 4AR.
(01603 624315). Mon–Fri 09.00–17.30, Sat 09.00–
16.00 (closed 1.00–2.00 & Thu).ⓛ *Specialising in
paper money.*

C. J. Denton (ANA, BNTA, FRNS)
PO Box 25, Orpington, Kent BR6 8PU (01689
873690).ⓟ *Irish coins.*

Detecnicks
3 Orchard Crescent, Arundel Road, Fontwell. West
Sussex BN18 0SA. (01243 545060 fax 01243
545922) *Retail shop. Wide range of detectors.*

Michael Dickinson (ANA, BNTA)
Ramsay House, 025 High Road Finchley, London
N12 8UB. (0181 441 7175).ⓟ
British and world coins.

Douglassaville.com
(0118 918 7628). *Out of print, second-hand and rare
coin and medal books.*

Drake Sterling Numismatics Pty Ltd
GPO Box 2913, Sydney 2001, Australia (UK callers:
020 7097 178, www.drakesterling.uk), *Ancient, milled
and world gold and silver coins.*

Eagle Coins
Winterhaven, Mourneabbey, Mallow, Co. Cork,
Ireland. (010 35322 29385).ⓟ ⓛ *Irish coins.*

Edinburgh Coin Shop (ANA)
11 West Crosscauseway, Edinburgh EH8 9JW.
(0131 668 2928 fax 0131 668 2926). Mon–Sat
10.00–17.30. ⓛ *World coins and medals.* .

Educational Coin Company
Box 892, Highland, New York 12528, USA.
(+ 845 691 6100.) *World banknotes.*

Christopher Eimer (ANA, BNTA, IAPN)
PO Box 352 London NW11 7RF. (020 8458 9933
email: art@christophereimer.co.uk). ⓟ
Commemorative medals.

Malcolm Ellis Coins
Petworth Road, Witley, Surrey, GU8 5LX. (01428
685566, www.malcolmelliscoins.co.uk). *Collectors
and dealers of British and foreign coins*

Elm Hill Stamps & Coins
27 Elm Hill, Norwich, Norfolk NR3 1HN. (01603
627413). Mon. 09.00–17.00, Tues–Wed. 09.00–
17.00, Thur. 0900–13.00, Sat. 09.30–15.00. *Mainly
stamps, occasionally coins.*

Europa Numismatics (ANA, BNTA)
PO Box 119, High Wycombe, Bucks HP11 1QL.
(01494 437307). ⓟ *European coins.*

Evesham Stamp & Coin Centre
Magpie Antiques, Paris House, 61 High Street,
Evesham, Worcs WR11 4DA (01386 41631).
Mon–Sat 09.00–17.30. *British coins.*

Michael E. Ewins
Meyrick Heights, 20 Meyrick Park Crescent,
Bournemouth, Dorset BH3 7AQ. (01202 290674).ⓟ
World coins.

Robin Finnegan Stamp Shop
83 Skinnergate, Darlington, Co Durham DL3 7LX.
(01325 489820/357674). Mon–Sat 10.00–17.30
(closed Wed). *World coins.*

David Fletcher (Mint Coins) (ANA, BNTA)
PO Box 64, Coventry, Warwickshire CV1 5YR.
(024 7671 5425, Fax 024 7601 0300). ⓟ
World new issues.

Format of Birmingham Ltd (ANA, BNTA, IAPN, IBNS)
2nd Floor, Burlington Court, Lower Temple Street,
Birmingham, B2 4JD. (0121 643 2058 fax 0121 643
2210). Mon–Fri 09.30–7.00. ⓛ *Coins, tokens
and medals.*

B. Frank & Son (ANA, IBNS)
3 South Avenue, Ryton, Tyne & Wear NE40 3LD.
(0191 413 8749. www.bfrankandson.com). ⓟⓛ
Coins, banknotes and cheques.

Galata Coins Ltd (ANA)
The Old White Lion, Market Street, Llanfylin,
Powys SY22 5BX. (01691 648 765).ⓟ*British and
world coins.*

G. Gant
Glazenwood, 37 Augustus Way, Witham, Essex
CM8 1HH. ⓟ*British and Commonwealth coins.*

A. & S. Gillis
59 Roykilner Way, Wombwell, Barnsley,
South Yorkshire S73 8DY. (01226 750371,
email: catalogues@gilliscoins.com. www.gilliscoins.
com). ⓟ ⓛ*Ancient coins and antiquities.*

Richard Gladdle – Northamptonshire
(01327 858511, email: gladdle@plumpudding.org).
Tokens. ⓟ ⓛ

Glance Back Books
17 Upper Street, Chepstow, Gwent NP6 5EX.
(01291 626562). 10.30–17.30. *Coins, banknotes.*

Glendining's (Bonhams) (ANA, BNTA)
101 New Bond Street, London W1Y 9LG (020 7493
2445). Mon–Fri 08.30–17.00, Sat 08.30–13.00.
Auctioneers.

GM Coins
(01242 701144, email: gmcoins@blueyonder.co.uk,
www.gmonlinecoins.co.uk/gmcoins). *Hammered
and milled coins.*

Adrian Gorka Bond
(email: sales@ 1stsovereign.co.uk, website
www.1stsovereign.co.uk). *Coins bought and sold.*

Goulborn
4 Sussex Street, Rhyl LL18 1SG. (Tel: 01745
338112). *English Coins and Medallions.*

Ian Gradon
PO Box 359, Durham DH7 6WZ. (0191 3719 700,
email: igradon960@aol.com, www.worldnotes.
co.uk). ⓛ *World banknotes.*

Eric Green—Agent in UK for Ronald J. Gillio Inc
1013 State Street, Santa Barbara, California, USA
93101. (020 8907 0015, Mobile 0468 454948).
Gold coins, medals and paper money of the world.

Philip Green
Suite 207, 792 Wilmslow Road, Didsbury,
Manchester M20 6UG. (0161 440 0685). *Gold coins.*

Gurnhills of Leicester
8 Nothampton Street, Leicester, LE1 1PA (0116
2556633). *British and World Coins and Banknotes.*

Hallmark Coins Ltd
PO Box 69991, I Canada Square, Canary Warf,
London (0800 612 7327 email: info@hallmarkcoins.
co.uk, www.hallmarkcoins.co.uk). British *Coins.*

Anthony Halse
PO Box 1856, Newport, Gwent NP6 2JN. (01633
413238).ⓟ ⓛ*English and foreign coins and tokens.*

A. D. Hamilton & Co (ANA)
7 St Vincent Place, Glasgow G1 5JA. (0141 2215423,
email: jefffineman@hotmail.com, www.adhamilton.
co.uk). Mon, Wed & Fri 10am–5pm; Tues, Thurs &
Sat 10am–4pm. *British and World coins.*

Peter Hancock
40–41 West Street, Chichester, West Sussex
PO19 1RP. (01243 786173). Tues–Sat. *World coins,
medals and banknotes.*

Munthandel G. Henzen
PO Box 42, NL – 3958ZT, Amerogngen, Netherlands.
(0031 343 430564 fax 0031 343 430542,
email: info@henzen.org, www.henzen.org).
ⓛ*Ancients, Dutch and foreign coins.*

History In Coins.com
(01949 836988, www.historyincoins.com).
World coins.

Craig Holmes
6 Marlborough Drive, Bangor, Co Down BT19 1HB.
P L *Low cost banknotes of the world.*

R. G. Holmes
11 Cross Park, Ilfracombe, Devon EX34 8BJ. (01271 864474). **P L**
Coins, world crowns and banknotes.

HTSM Coins
26 Dosk Avenue, Glasgow G13 4LQ. **P L**
British and foreign coins and banknotes.

M. J. Hughes Coins
27 Market Street, Alton, Hampshire, GU34 1HA.
(07917 160308). *World coins and bullion.*

T. A. Hull
15 Tangmere Crescent, Hornchurch, Essex RM12 5PL. **P L** *British coins, farthings to crowns, tokens.*

J. Hume
107 Halsbury Road East, Northolt, Middlesex UB5 4PY. (020 8864 1731). **P L** *Chinese coins.*

D. A. Hunter
(Email: coins@dahunter.co.uk, www.dahunter.co.uk/coins). **P L** *UK and World Coins.*

D. D. & A. Ingle
380 Carlton Hill, Nottingham. (0115 9873325).
Mon–Sat 09.30–17.00. *World coins.*

R. Ingram Coins
206 Honeysuckle Road, Bassett, Southampton, Hants SO16 3BU. (023 8032 4258, email: info@ringramcoins.com, www.ringramcoins.com). **P L**
Dealers in UK coins.

Isle of Wight Mint
PO Box 195, Cowes, Isle of Wight, PO30 9DP. (www.iowmint.org). *Producer of Isle of Wight bullion.*

F. J. Jeffery & Son Ltd
Haines Croft, Corsham Road, Whitley, Melksham, Wilts SN12 8QF. (01225 703143). **P**
British, Commonwealth and foreign coins.

Richard W. Jeffery
Trebehor, Porthcurno, Penzance, Cornwall TR19 6LS. (01736 871263). **P** *British and world coins. Banknotes.*

JN Coins
(07916 145038): ,
www.jncoins.co.uk).
British coins from Celtic to modern.

Kates Paper Money
Kate Gibson, PO Box 819, Camberley, Surrey, GU16 6ZU. email: kate@katespapemoney.co.uk, www.katespapermoney.co.uk). *Banknotes.*

KB Coins (BNTA)
PO BOX 499, Stevenage, Herts, SG1 9JT. (01438 312661, fax 01438 311990).
09.00–18.00 by appointment only. www.kbcoins.com
L *Mainly British coins.*

Kleeford Coins
22 Peak Avenue, Riddings, Alfreton, Derbyshire, DE55 4AR. (01773 528743 or 07969 645952, www.kleefordcoins.webs.com, kleeford@btinternet.com). **P** *Monthly Auctions of coins, banknotes, tokens & medals.*

K&M Coins
PO Box 3662, Wolverhampton WV10 6ZW. (0771 2381880/07971 9 50246, email: M_Bagguley@hotmail.com). *English milled coins.*

Knightsbridge Coins (ANA, BNTA, IAPN, PNG)
43 Duke Street, St James's, London SW1Y 6DD. (020 7930 8215/7597 Fax 020 7930 8214). Mon–Fri 10.00–17.30. *Quality coins of the world.*

Lancashire Coin & Medal Co
31 Adelaide Street, Fleetwood, Lancs FY7 6AD . (01253 779308). **P** *British coins and medals.*

Lighthouse Publications (Duncannon Partnership)
4 Beaufort Road, Reigate, Surrey RH2 9DJ (01737 244222 www.duncannon.co.uk). **L** *Coin albums, cabinets and numismatic accessories.*

Liberty Coins and Bullion
17g Vyse Street, Birmingham, B18 6LE. (0121 554 4432, wwwlibertycoinsbullion.co.uk) *Coins and precious metals.*

Lindner Publications Ltd
3a Hayle Industrial Park, Hayle, Cornwall TR27 5JR. (01736 751914 fax: 01736 751911, email lindner@prinz.co.uk). Mon–Fri 09.00–13.00.
L *Manufacturers of coin albums, cabinets and accessories.*

Jan Lis (BNTA)
Beaver Coin Room, 57 Philbeach Gardens, London SW5 9ED. (020 7373 4553 fax 020 7373 4555).
By appointment only. *European coins.*

Keith Lloyd
45 Bramblewood, The Beeches, Ipswich, Suffolk IP8 3RS. (01473 603067). **P L** *Ancient coins.*

Lockdale Coins (BNTA)
52 Barrack Square, Martlesham Heath, Ipswich, Suffolk, IP5 3RF. (01473 627110) www.lockdales.com). **L** *World coins, medals and banknotes*

Stephen Lockett (BNTA)
4–6 Upper Street, New Ash Green, Kent, DA3 8JJ. (01474 871464). *British and world coins.*

The London Coin Company
PO Box 495, Stanmore, Greater London, HA7 9HS (0800 085 2933, 020 8343 2231, www.thelondoncoincomany.com).
Modern gold and silver coins.

Mike Longfield Detectors
83 Station Road, Balsall Common, nr Coventry, Warwickshire CV7 7FN. (01676 533274).
Mon–Sat 09.30–17.00. *Metal detectors.*

MA Shops
(www.mashops.com). On-line coin mall. *Coins, medals, banknotes and accessories.*

Mannin Collections Ltd
5 Castle Street, Peel, Isle of Man, IM5 1AN. (01624 843897, email: manncoll@advsys.co.uk). Mon–Sat 10.00–16.00. Closed Thu. *IOM coins, tokens, etc.*

Manston Coins of Bath
8 Bartletts St. Antique Centre, Bath. (01225 487888). *Coins, tokens and medals.*

I. Markovits
1–3 Cobbold Mews, London W12 9LB. (020 8749 3000). *Enamelled coins.*

C. J. Martin Coins (BNTA)
The Gallery, Trent Park Equestrian Centre, Eastpole Farm House, Bramley Road, Oakwood, N14 4UW. (020 8364 4565, www.ancientart.co.uk). **P L** Bi-monthly catalogue. *Greek, Roman & English hammered coins.*

Maverick Numismatics
(07403 111843, www.mavericknumismatics.com).
Coin and currency design.

M. G. Coins & Antiquities
12 Mansfield, High Wych, Herts CM21 0JT. (01279
721719). ⓛ*Ancient and hammered coins, antiquities.*

M&H Coins
PO Box 10985, Brentwood, CM14 9JB. (07504
804019, www.mhcoins.co.uk). ⓛ *British hammered
and milled coins.*

Michael Coins
6 Hillgate Street, London W8 7SR. (020 7727 1518).
Mon–Fri 10.00–17.00. *World coins and banknotes.*

David Miller Coins & Antiquities (ANA, BNTA)
PO Box 711, Hemel Hempstead, HP2 4UH. (Tel/fax
01442 251492). *Ancient,hammered English coins.*

Timothy Millett
PO Box 20851, London SE22 0YN.
www.historicmedals.com). ⓛ *Historical medals.*

Nigelmills.net
(020 8504 2569. email: nigelmills@onetel.com,
www.nigelmills.net). *Coins and antiquities.*

Graeme & Linda Monk (ANA, BNTA)
PO Box 201, Croydon, Surrey, CR9 7AQ.
(020 8656 4583 fax 020 8656 4583). Ⓟ .

Moore Antiquities
Unit 12, Ford Lane Industrial Estate, Ford, nr.
Arundel, West Sussex BN18 0AA. (01243 824 232,
email moore.antiquities@virgin.net).
Coins and artefacts up to the 18th Century.

Mike Morey
19 Elmtrees, Long Crendon, Bucks HP18 9DG.Ⓟⓛ
British coins, halfcrowns to farthings.

Peter Morris (BNTA, IBNS)
1 Station Concourse, Bromley North Station,
Bromley, BR1 1NN or PO Box 223, Bromley,
BR1 4EQ (020 8313 3410 fax 020 8466 8502,
email: info@petermorris.co.uk, www.petermorris.
co.uk). Mon–Fri 10.00–18.00, Sat 0900–14.00 or
by appointment. ⓛ *British and world coins, proof
sets and numismatic books.*

N3 Coins—London
(07768 795575, email: mail@n3coins.com,
www.n3coins.com). *Roman and Ancient coins.*

Colin Narbeth & Son Ltd (ANA, IBNS)
20 Cecil Court, Leicester Square, London WC2N.
4HE (020 7379 6975 fax 01727 811 244,
www.colin–narbeth.com). Mon–Sat 10.30–17.00.
World banknotes.

John Newman Coins
(01903 239867, email: john@newmancoins.co.uk,
www.johnnewmancoins.co.uk). *English hammered
coins, British milled coins and British tokens.*

Peter Nichols Cabinet Makers
(0115 922 4149, email: orders@coincabinets.com,
www.coincabinets.com). *Manufacturers of bespoke
mahogany coin and medal cabinets.*

Wayne Nicholls
PO Box 44, Bilston, West Midlands. (01543 45476).
ⓛ *Choice English coins.*

North Wales Coins Ltd (BNTA)
1b Penrhyn Road, Colwyn Bay, Clwyd. (01492
533023/532129). Mon–Sat (closed Wed) 09.30–
17.30. *British coins.*

NP Collectables
9 Main Street, Gedney Dyke, Spalding, Lincs PE12
0AJ. (01406 365211Ireland (010 35322 29385).Ⓟⓛ
English Hammered and Milled coins.

Notability Notes (IBNS)
(Email: info@notability-banknotes.com,
www.notability-banknotes.com). *British,
Commonwealth and world notes.*

Oddysey Antiquities
PO Box 61, Southport PR9 0PZ.(01704 232494).
Classical antiquities, ancient and hammered coins.

Glenn S. Ogden
(01626 859350 or 07971 709427,
www.glennogdencoins.com).
Ⓟⓛ *English milled coinage.*

John Ogden Coins
Hodge Clough Cottage, Moorside, Oldham OL1
4JW. (0161 678 0709)Ⓟ ⓛ*Ancient and hammered.*

Don Oliver Gold Coins
Stanford House, 23 Market Street, Stourbridge,
West Midlands DY8 1AB. (01384 877901).
Mon–Fri 10.00–17.00. *British gold coins.*

Ongar Coins
14 Longfields, Marden Ash, Ongar, Essex IG7 6DS.
Ⓟ *World coins.*

Roger Outing
PO Box 123, Huddersfield HD8 9WY. (01484
60415, email: rogerandlizbanknotes4u.co.uk,
www.chequemate4collectors.co.uk). *World
banknotes.*

Tim Owen Coins
63 Allerton Grange Rise, Leeds 17, West Yorkshire.
Ⓟ ⓛ *Quality hammered coins.*

P&D Medallions
PO Box 269, Berkhampstead, Herts HP4 3FT.
(01442 865127, www.pdmedallions.co.uk). Ⓟ
Historical and Commemorative medals.

Del Parker
PO Box 7568, Dallas, TX 75209, USA.
(+ 1 214 352 1475. Email: Irishcoins2000@
hotmail.com, www.irishcoins.com). *Irish, American
Coins. Irish Art medals and banknotes.* ⓛ

Pavlos S. Pavlou
Stand L17, Grays Antique Market, 1–7 Davies
Mews, Mayfair, London W1Y 2LP. (020 7629 9449,
email: pspavlou@hotmail.com). *Ancient to Modern*

PCGS
(+33 (0) 140200994, email:info@pcgsglobal.com,
www.pcgs.com). *Coin grading and authentication.*

www.pennycrowncoins.co.uk
Specialising in British milled coins 1662–1970.

Penrith Coin & Stamp Centre
37 King Street, Penrith, Cumbria CA11 7AY. (01768
64185). Mon–Sat 09.00–17.30. *World coins.*

Pentland Coins (IBNS)
Pentland House, 92 High Street, Wick, Caithness
KW14 L5. Ⓟ *British and world coins and banknotes.*

John Phillimore
The Old Post Office, Northwood, Shropshire SY4
5NN. ⓛ *Foreign coins 1600–1950.*

B. C. Pickard
1 Treeside, Christchurch, Dorset BH23 4PF. (01425
275763, email: bcpickard@fsmail.net). Ⓟ *Stone Age,
Greek, Roman items (inc. coins) for sale.*

Pobjoy Mint Ltd (ANA)
Millennium House, Kingswood Park, Bonsor
Drive, Kingswood, Surrey KT20 6AY. (01737 818181
fax 01737 818199). Mon–Fri 09.00–17.00. Europe's
largest private mint. *New issues.*
David Pratchett
UCCE, PO Box 57648, Mill Hill, London NW7
0FE. (07831 662594, fax 020 7930 1152, email:
uccedcp@aol.com, www.coinsonline.co.uk). Mon–
Fri 10.00–7.30. *Gold and silver world coins.*
Pykerleys Collectables
PO Box 649, Whitley Bay NE26 9AF. (Email:
pykereley@yahoo.co.uk, www.pykerley.worldonline.
co.uk). *Western European and US coins.*
George Rankin Coin Co Ltd (ANA)
325 Bethnal Green Road, London E2 6AH. (020 7729
1280 fax 020 7729 5023). Mon–Sat 10.00–18.00
(half-day Thu). *World coins.*
Mark Rasmussen (BNTA, IAPN)
PO Box 42, Betchworth RH3 7YR. (01737 84100,
Email: mark.rasmussen@rascoins.com, www.
rascoins.com). **L** *Quality hammered, milled coins.*
Mark T. Ray (see Collectors World)
Rhyl Coin Shop
12 Sussex Street, Rhyl, Clwyd. (01745 338112).
Mon–Sat 10.00–17.30. *World coins and banknotes.*
Chris Rigby
PO Box 181, Worcester WR1 1YE. (01905 28028).
P L*Modern British coins.*
Roderick Richardson (BNTA)
The Old Granary Antiques Centre, King's Staithe
Lane, King's Lynn, Norfolk. (01553 670833, www.
roderickrichardson.com) **L** *English, Hammered and
early milled coins.*
Charles Riley (BNTA)
PO Box 733, Aylesbury HP22 9AX. (01296 747598,
charlesrileycoins@gmail.com,
www.charlesriley.co.uk). *Coins and medallions.*
Robin–on–Acle Coins
Parkeston House, Parkeston Quay, Harwich, Essex
CO12 4PJ. (01255 554440, email: enquiries@robin–
on–acle–coins.co.uk). *Ancient to modern coins and
paper money.*
Roma Numismatics
20 Hanover Square, London, W1S 1JY.
(020 3178 2874, www.romanumismatics.com).
Dealers and Auctioneers of fine ancient coins.
S. J. Rood & Co Ltd
52–53 Burlington Arcade, London W1V 9AE. (0171
493 0739). Mon–Sat 09.30–17.00. *World gold coins.*
Royal Australian Mint
(www.ramint.gov.au) *New coin issues.*
Royal Gold
PO Box 123, Saxonwold, 2132, South Africa,
(+27 11 483 0161, email: royalg@iafrica.com, www.
royalgold.co.za). *Gold coins.*
Royal Mint Coin Club
PO Box 500, Cardiff CF1 1YY. (01443 623456).**P**
*Updates and special offers of new issues struck by
the Royal Mint.*
Colin de Rouffignac (BNTA)
57, Wigan Lane, Wigan, Lancs WN1 2LF. (01942
237927). P. *English and Scottish hammered.*

R. P. Coins
PO Box 367, Prestwich, Manchester, M25 9ZH.
(07802 713444, www.rpcoins.co.uk).
Coins, books, catalogues and accessories.
Chris A. Rudd (IAPN, BNTA)
PO Box 222, Aylsham, Norfolk, NR11 6TY.
(01263 735007 fax 01263 731777, www.celticcoins.
com).**P L** *Celtic coins.*
Colin Rumney (BNTA)
PO Box 34, Denbighshire, North Wales, LL16 4YQ.
(01745 890621). *All world including ancients.*
R & J Coins
21b Alexandra Street, Southend-on-Sea, Essex, SS1
1DA. (01702 345995). *World coins.*
Safe Albums (UK) Ltd
16 Falcon Business Park, 38 Ivanhoe Road,
Finchampstead, Berkshire RG40 4QQ. (0118 932
8976 fax 0118 932 8612). *Accessories.*
Saltford Coins
Harcourt, Bath Road, Saltford, Bristol, Avon BS31
3DQ. (01225 873512, email: info@saltfordcoins.com,
www.saltfordcoins.com). **P***British, Commonwealth
and world coins.*
Satin Coins
PO Box 63, Stockport, Cheshire SK4 5BU.
(07940 393583 answer machine).
Scotmint Ltd
68 Sandgate, Ayr, Scotland KA7 1BX
(01292 268244), email: rob@scotmint.com,
www.scotmint.com. *Coins, medals and banknotes.*
David Seaman
PO Box 449, Waltham Cross EN9 3WZ. (01992
719723, email: davidseamancoins@outlook.com).
P L *Hammered, Milled, Maundy.*
Patrick Semmens
3 Hospital Road, Half Key, Malvern, Worcs WR14
1UZ. (0886 33123). **P** *European and British coins.*
Mark Senior
553 Falmer Road, Woodingdean, Brighton, Sussex
(01273 309359). By appointment only.
P L*Saxon, Norman and English hammered.*
S. E. Sewell
Cronin, Westhorpe Road, Finningham, Stowmarket,
Suffolk, IP14 4TN. (01449 782185 or 07739 071822,
email: sewellmedals@hotmail.com,
www.sewellmedals.co.uk). *Mainly British milled.*
Sharps Pixley
64, St James's Street, London SW1A 1JT (0207871
0532, www.sharpspixley.com). *Safe deposit boxes in
St James's, buying and selling gold bullion.*
Silbury Coins
PO Box 281, Cirencester, Gloucs GL7 9ET (info@
silburycoins.com, www.silburycoins.com). *Iron Age,
Roman, Saxon, Viking, medieval coins and later.*
Simmons Gallery (ANA, BNTA, IBNS)
PO Box 104, Leytonstone, London E11 1ND (020
8989 8097, www.simmonsgallery.co.uk). **L** *Coins,
tokens and medals.*
E. Smith (ANA, IBNS)
PO Box 348, Lincoln LN6 0TX (01522 684681 fax
01522 689528). Organiser of the Wakefield (formally
known as Leeds) monthly coin fair. **P** *World coins
and paper money.*

Neil Smith
PO Box 774, Lincoln LN4 2WX. (01522 522772 fax 01522 689528). *GB and World Gold coins 1816 to date, including modern proof issues.*

Jim Smythe
PO Box 6970, Birmingham B23 7WD. (Email: Jimdens@aol.com).**P L** *19th/20th century British and world coins.*

Sovereign Rarities Ltd (BNTA)
32, St George Street, London W1S 2EA (0203 019 1185, www.sovereignrrrities.com). *Quality British and world coins.*

Spink & Son Ltd (ANA, BNTA, IAPN, IBNS)
69 Southampton Row, Bloomsbury, London. WC1B 4ET. (020 7563 4000, fax 020 7563 4066, email: info@spinkandson.com, www.spink.com). *Ancient to modern world coins, medals, banknotes.*

SPM Jewellers (BNTA)
112 East Street, Southampton, Hants SO14 3HD. (023 80 223255/020 80 227923, fax 023 80 335634, email: user@spm.in2home.co.uk, www.spm goldcoins.co.uk). Tue–Sat 09.15–17.00, Sat 09.15–16.00. *World coins and medals.*

Stamford Coins
65–67 Stamford Street, Bradford, West Yorkshire BD4 8SD. (07791 873595, email: stamfordcoins@ hotmail.co.uk.

Stamp & Collectors Centre
404 York Town Road, College Town, Camberley, Surrey GU15 4PR. (01276 32587 fax 01276 32505). *World coins and medals.*

St Edmunds Coins & Banknotes
PO Box 118, Bury St Edmunds IP33 2NE. (01284 761894).

Sterling Coins & Medals
2 Somerset Road, Boscombe, Bournemouth, Dorset BH7 6JH. (01202 423881). Mon–Sat 09.30–16.30 (closed Wed). *World coins and medals.*

Studio Coins (ANA, BNTA)
Studio 111, 80 High Street, Winchester, Hants SO23 9AT. (01962 853156 email: stephenmitchell13@ bttconnect.com). **P** *English coins.*

The Coin House
01935 824 878), email: thecoinhouse@ btinternet.com. *Quality investment coins and silver bars.*

Time Line Originals
PO Box 193, Upminster, RM14 3WH. (01708 222384/ 07775 651218, email: sales@time–lines. co.uk).

Stuart J. Timmins
Smallwood Lodge Bookshop, Newport, Salop. (01952 813232). *Numismatic literature.*

R. Tims
39 Villiers Road, Watford, Herts WD1 4AL.**P L** *Uncirculated world banknotes.*

Token Publishing Ltd
40, Southernhay East, Exeter, Devon EX1 1PE, (01404 46972, email info@tokenpublishing.com, www.tokenpublishing.com)
Publishers of COIN NEWS, COIN YEARBOOK, MEDAL YEARBOOK and suppliers of numismatic titles and coin accessories..

Michael Trenerry
PO Box 55, Truro, Cornwall TR1 2YQ. (01872 277977, email veryfinecoins@aol. com). By appointment only. **L** *Roman, Celtic and English hammered coins and tokens.*

Vera Trinder Ltd
Unit 3a, Hayle Ind Park, Hayle, Cornwall TR27 5JR. (01736 751 910, email: richardvtrinder@aol.com www.veratrinder.co.uk). **L** *Coin accessories.*

Robert Tye
7–9 Clifford Street, York, YO1 9RA. (0845 4 900 724, email: orders@earlyworlscoins.com. **P***European and Oriental hammered coins.*

Universal Currency Coin Exhange
PO Box 57648, Mill Hill, London, NW7 0FE. (07831 662594, email: uccedcp@aol.com.) *German, Canadian and American Coins. Accumulations.*

Vale (ADA)
21 Tranquil Vale, Blackheath, London SE3 0BU. (01322 405911. *British coins and medals.*

Van der Schueren, John-Luc (IAPN)
14 Rue de la Borse, 1,000 Bussels, Belgium. (Email: iapnsecret@compuserve.com, www.coins.be.) Mon–Fri 1100–1800 hrs. *Coins and tokens of the world and of the low countries.*

Tony Vaughan Collectables
PO Box 364, Wolverhampton, WV3 9PW. (01902 27351). **P L** *World coins and medals.*

Victory Coins (BNTA)
184 Chichester Road, North End, Portsmouth, Hants PO2 0AX. (023 92 751908/663450). Thurs–Sat 09.00–17.00. *British and world coins.*

Mark J. Vincenzi (BNTA)
Rylands, Earls Colne, Essex CO6 2LE. (01787 222555). **P** *Greek, Roman, Hammered.*

Mike Vosper
PO Box 32, Hockwold, Brandon IP26 4HX. (01842 828292, email: mikevosper@vosper4coins.co.uk, www.vosper4coins.co.uk). *Roman, Hammered.*

Weighton Collectables
50 Market Place, Market Weighton, York, Y043 3AL, (01430 879740, www.weightoncoin.co.uk). *Modern gold, silver proofs and sets.*

John Welsh
PO Box 150, Burton–on–Trent, Staffs DE13 7LB. (01543 473073 fax 0543 473234).**P L***British coins.*

Wessex Coins
(023 8184 8560, 07788 253345, www.wessexcoins. co.uk). *Ancient Greek, Roman, English hammered coins and antiquities, also shipwreck treasure.*

Pam West (IBNS, BNTA)
PO Box 257, Sutton, Surrey SM3 9WW. (020 8641 3224, email: pamwestbritnotes@aol.com, www. brishnotes.co.uk,).**P L** *English banknotes*

West Essex Coin Investments (BNTA, IBNS)
Croft Cottage, Station Road, Alderholt, Fordingbridge, Hants SP6 3AZ. (01425 656 459). *British and World coins and paper money.*

West Wicklow Coins
Blessington, Co Wicklow, Ireland. (00353 45 858767, email: westwicklowcoins@hotmail.com). *Irish and World coins.*

Simon Willis Coins
(07908 240978, swcoins@simonwilliscoins.com,
www.simonwilliscoins.com). *Quality hammered and
early milled British coins.*

Worldwide Coins (IBNS)
PO Box 11, Wavertree, Liverpool L15 0FG. (Email:
sales@worldwidecoins.co.uk,www.worldwidecoins.
co.uk. *World coins and paper money.*

World Treasure Books
PO Box 5, Newport, Isle of Wight PO30 5QE. (01983
740712). **L** *Coins, books, metal detectors.*

Barry Wright
54 Dooley Drive, Bootle, Merseyside. L3O 8RT.**P L**
World banknotes.

I. S. Wright (Australia Numismatic Co)
208 Sturt Street, Ballarat, Vic. Australia 3350.
(0061 3 5332 3856 fax 0061 3 5331 6426,
email: ausnumis@netconnect.comau). **P** *Coins,
banknotes, medallions, tokens.*

D. Yapp
PO Box 4718, Shrewsbury Mail Centre SY1 9EA.
(01743 232557, www.david-yapp.com).**L**
World and British Banknotes.

York Coins
PO Box 160, Red Hook, New York 12571. (Tel/fax:
(718) 544 0120 email: antony@yorkcoins.com).
Ancient coins.

York Coin and Stamp Centre
Cavendish Antique & Collectors Centre, 44 Stone
gate, York, YO1 8AS.
Retail shop. Coins and medals.

Information included in this Directory is correct
at the time of going to press. An extensive range
of dealers can also be found on our website at
www.tokenpublishing.com

*Coin dealers also take the
opportunity to catch up with
each other at the many coin
fairs held up and down the
country (details of monthly
events are featured every
month in COIN NEWS).*

Fairs are a great place to meet your favourite dealer and see some exceptional coins.

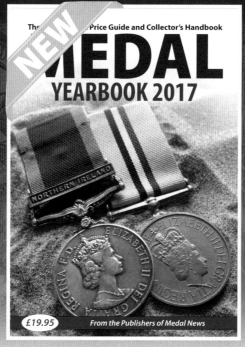

Banks, Mints and Numismatic

BUREAUX *of the World*

Many national banks and mints operate numismatic bureaux and sales agencies from which coins, medals and other numismatic products may be obtained direct. The conditions under which purchases may be made vary considerably. In many cases at the present time bureaux will accept orders from overseas customers quoting their credit card number and its expiry date; but in others payment can only be made by certified bank cheque, or international money order, or by girobank. Cash is seldom, if ever, acceptable. It is best to write in the first instance to enquire about methods of payment.

A

National Mint, Baghe Arg, Kabul, Afghanistan

Bank Mille Afghan, Kabul, Afghanistan

Banque d'Algerie, Sucursale d'Alger, 8 Boulevard Carnot, Alger, Algeria

Banco de Angola, Luanda, Daroal, Angola

Casa de Moneda de la Nacion, Avenida Antartica, Buenos Aires, BA, Argentina

Royal Australian Mint, Department of the Treasury, Canberra, ACT, Australia

GoldCorp Australia, Perth Mint Buildings, GPO Box M924, Perth, Western Australia 6001

Oesterreichsiches Hauptmunzamt, Am Heumarkt 1, A-1031 Wien, Postfach 225, Austria

Oesterreichische Nationalbank, A-1090 Wien, Otto Wagner-platz 3, Austria

B

Treasury Department, PO Box 557, Nassau, Bahamas (coins)

Ministry of Finance, PO Box 300, Nassau, Bahamas (banknotes)

Bank of Bahrain, PO Box 106, Manama, Bahrain

Eastern Bank, PO Box 29, Manama, Bahrain

Monnaie Royale de Belgique, Avenue de Pacheco 32, B-1000 Bruxelles, Belgium

Banque Nationale de Belgique SA, Caisse Centrale, Bruxelles, Belgium

Banque de Bruxelles SA, 2 Rue de la Regence, Bruxelles 1, Belgium

Casa de la Moneda, Potosi, BoliviaBanco Central de Bolivia, La Paz, Bolivia

Casa da Moeda, Praca da Republica 173, Rio de Janeiro, Brazil

Hemus FTO, 7 Vasil Levski Street, Sofia C-1, Bulgaria

Banque de la Republique, Bujumbura, Burundi

C

Banque Centrale, Douala, Boite Postale 5.445, Cameroun

Royal Canadian Mint, 320 Sussex Drive, Ottawa 2, Ontario, Canada K1A 0G8

Casa de Moneda, Quinta Normal, Santiago, Chile

Casa de Moneda, Calle 11 no 4-93, Bogota, Colombia

Numismatic Section, The Treasury, Avarua, Rarotonga, Cook Islands

Banco Centrale de Costa Rica, Departamento de Contabilidad, San Jose, Costa Rica, CA

Central Bank of Cyprus, PO Box 1087, Nicosia, Cyprus

Artia, Ve Smekach 30, PO Box 790, Praha 1, Czech Republic

D

Den Kongelige Mønt, Amager Boulevard 115, København S, Denmark

Danmarks Nationalbank, Holmens Kanal 17, 1060 København K, Denmark

Banco Central de Santo Domingo, Santo Domingo, Dominican Republic

E

Banco Central, Quito, Ecuador

Mint House, Abbassia, Cairo, Egyptian Arab Republic

Exchange Control Department, National Bank of Egypt, Cairo, Egyptian Arab Republic

Banco Central de la Republica, Santa Isabel, Equatorial Guinea

Commercial Bank of Ethiopia, Foreign Branch, PO Box 255, Addis Ababa, Ethiopia

F

Currency Board, Victoria Parade, Suva, Fiji

Suomen Rahapaja, Katajanokanlaituri 3, Helsinki 16, Finland

Suomen Pankki, PO Box 10160, Helsinki 10, Finland

Hotel de Monnaie, 11 Quai de Conti, 75-Paris 6e, France

G

Banque Centrale Libreville, Boite Postale 112, Gabon

Verkaufstelle fur Sammlermunzen, D-638 Bad Homburg vdH, Bahnhofstrasse 16–18, Germany

Staatliche Munze Karlsruhe, Stephanienstrasse 28a, 75 Karlsruhe, Germany

Staatliche Munze Cannstatt, Taubenheimerstrasse 77, 7 Stuttgart-Bad, Germany

Bayerisches Hauptmunzamt, Hofgraben 4, 8 Munich, Germany

Hamburgische Munze, Norderstrasse 66, 2 Hamburg 1, Germany

Bank of Ghana, PO Box 2674, Accra, Ghana

Pobjoy Mint, Millennia House, Kingswood Park, Bonsor Drive, Kingswood, Surrey KT20 6AY

Royal Mint, Llantrisant, Mid Glamorgan, Wales, CF7 8YT

Royal Mint Coin Club, PO Box 500, Cardiff, CF1 1HA

Bank of Greece, Treasury Department, Cash, Delivery & Despatch Division, PO Box 105, Athens, Greece

Casa Nacional de Moneda, 6a Calle 4-28, Zona 1, Ciudad Guatemala, Republica de Guatemala CA

States Treasury, St Peter Port, Guernsey, Channel Islands

Bank of Guyana, PO Box 658, Georgetown, Guyana

H

Banque Nationale de la Republique d'Haiti, Rue Americaine et Rue Fereu, Port-au-Prince, Haiti

Banco Central de Honduras, Tegucigalpa DC, Honduras CA

State Mint, Ulloi utca 102, Budapest VIII, Hungary

Artex, PO Box 167, Budapest 62, Hungary

Magyar Nemzeti Bank, Board of Exchange, Budapest 54, Hungary

I

Sedlabanki Islands, Reykjavik, Iceland

Indian Government Mint, Bombay 1, India

Arthie Vasa, Keabajoran Baru, Djakarta, Indonesia

Perum Peruri, Djakarta, Indonesia

National Mint, Tehran, Iran

Bank Markazi Iran, Tehran, IranCentral Bank of Iraq, PO Box 64, Baghdad, Iraq

Central Bank of Ireland, Dublin 2, Republic of Ireland

The Treasury, Government Buildings, Prospect Hill, Douglas, Isle of Man

Israel Stamp and Coin Gallery, 4 Maze Street, Tel Aviv, Israel

Istituto Poligraphico e Zecca dello Stato, Via Principe Umberto, Roma, Italy

J

Decimal Currency Board, PO Box 8000, Kingston, Jamaica

Mint Bureau, 1 Shinkawasakicho, Kita-ku, Osaka 530, Japan

Numismatic Section, Treasury Department, St Helier, Jersey

Central Bank of Jordan, Amman, Jordan

Banque Nationale du Liban, Rue Masraf Loubnan, Beirut, Lebanon

K

Central Bank, PO Box 526, Kuwait

L

Bank of LatviaK. Valdemara iela 2A, LV-1050, Riga, Latvia

Bank of Lithuania, Cash Department, Gedimino av. 6, 2001 Vilius, Lithuania

Caisse Generale de l'Etat, 5 Rue Goethe, Luxembourg-Ville, Grande Duche de Luxembourg

M

Institut d'Emission Malgache, Boite Postale 205, Tananarive, Madagascar

Central Bank of Malta, Valletta 1, Malta

Casa de Moneda, Calle del Apartado no 13, Mexico 1, DF, Mexico

Le Tresorier General des Finances, Monte Carlo, Principaute de Monaco

Banque de l'Etat du Maroc, Rabat, Morocco

Banco Nacional Ultramarino, Maputo, Republica de Mocambique

British Bank of the Middle East, Muscat

N

Royal Mint, Dharahara, Katmandu, Nepal

Nepal Rastra Bank, Katmandu, Nepal

Rijks Munt, Leidseweg 90, Utrecht, Netherlands

Hollandsche Bank-Unie NV, Willemstad, Breedestraat 1, Curacao, Netherlands Antilles

Central Bank of Curacao, Willemstad, Curacao, Netherlands Antilles

New Zealand Post Stamps Centre, Private Bag 3001, Wanganui 4540, New Zealand

Banco de Nicaragua, Departamento de Emison, La Tresoria, Apartada 2252, Managua, Nicaragua

Nigerian Security Printing and Minting Corporation, Ahmadu Bello Road, Victoria Island, Lagos, Nigeria

Central Bank of Nigeria, Tinubu Square LB, Lagos, Nigeria

Norges Bank, Oslo, Norway

Den Kongelige Mynt, Hyttegaten, Konigsberg, Norway

P

Pakistan State Mint, Baghban Pura, Lahore 9, Pakistan

National Development Bank, Asuncion, Paraguay

Casa Nacional de Moneda, Calle Junin 791, Lima, Peru

Central Bank of the Philippines, Manila, Philippines

Bank Handlowy w Warszawie, Ul. Romuald Traugutta 7, Warsaw, Poland

Desa Foreign Trade Department, Al. Jerozolimskie 2, Warszawa, Poland

Casa da Moeda, Avenida Dr Antonio Jose de Almeida, Lisbon 1, Portugal

R

Cartimex, 14-18 Aristide Briand St, PO Box 134-135, Bucharest, Roumania

Bank of Foreign Trade, Commercial Department, Moscow K 16, Neglinnaja 12, Russian Federation

Banque Nationale du Rwanda, Boite Postale 351, Kigali, Republique Rwandaise

S

Numismatic Section, Box 194, GPO, Apia, Samoa

Azienda Autonoma di Stato Filatelica-Numismatica, Casalla Postale 1, 47031 Repubblica di San Marino

Banque Internationale pour le Commerce, 2 Avenue Roume, Dakar, Senegal

Bank of Yugoslavia, PO Box 1010, Belgrade, Serbia

The Treasury, PO Box 59, Victoria, Seychelles

Bank of Sierra Leone, PO Box 30, Freetown, Sierra Leone

The Singapore Mint, 20 Teban Gardens Crescent, Singapore 608928

South African Mint, PO Box 464, Pretoria, South Africa

Government Printing Agency, 93 Bukchang Dong, Chungku, Seoul, Republic of South Korea

Fabrica Nacional de Moneda y Timbre, Jorge Juan 106, Madrid 9, Spain

Bank of Sri Lanka, PO Box 241, Colombo, Sri Lanka

Hong Kong and Shanghai Banking Corporation, PO Box 73, Colombo 1, Sri Lanka

Sudan Mint, PO Box 43, Khartoum, Sudan

Bank of Sudan, PO Box 313, Khartoum, Sudan

Bank of Paramaribo, Paramaribo, Suriname

Kungelige Mynt och Justeringsverket, Box 22055, Stockholm 22, Sweden

Eidgenossische Staatskasse, Bundesgasse 14, CH-3003, Berne, Switzerland

Central Bank of Syria, Damascus, Syrian Arab Republic

T

Central Mint of China, 44 Chiu Chuan Street, Taipei, Taiwan, ROC

Royal Thai Mint, 4 Chao Fah Road, Bangkok, Thailand

Numismatic Section, The Treasury, Nuku'alofa, Tonga

Central Bank of Trinidad and Tobago, PO Box 1250, Port of Spain, Trinidad

Banque Centrale de Tunisie, Tunis, Tunisia

State Mint, Maliye Bakanligi Darphane Mudurlugu, Istanbul, Turkey

U

Bank of Uganda, PO Box 7120, Kampala, Uganda

Numismatic Service, US Assay Office, 350 Duboce Avenue, San Francisco, CA, 94102, USA

Office of the Director of the Mint, Treasury Department, Washington, DC, 20220, USA

Philadelphia Mint, 16th and Spring Garden Streets, Philadelphia, PA, 19130, USA

Franklin Mint, Franklin Center, Pennsylvania, 19063, USA

Banco Central del Uruguay, Cerrito 351, Montevideo, RO del Uruguay

V

Ufficio Numismatico, Governatorato dello Stato della Citta de Vaticano, Italy

Banco Central de Venezuela, Caracas, Venezuela

Y

Yemen Bank, Sana'a, Yemen.

Z

Bank of Zambia, PO Box 80, Lusaka, Zambia

Chief Cashier, Reserve Bank, PO Box 1283, Harare, Zimbabwe

TREASURE and the law

Until the introduction of the new Treasure Act, the legal position regarding articles of gold, silver or bullion, found long after they were hidden or abandoned, was not as simple and straightforward as it might be supposed. Furthermore, this was a case where the law in England and Wales differed fundamentally from that in Scotland.

Treasure Trove was one of the most ancient rights of the Crown, deriving from the age-old right of the monarch to gold, silver or bullion treasure whose owner was not known. In England and Wales, the law applied only to objects made of, or containing, gold or silver, whether in the form of coin, jewellery, plate or bullion. Moreover, the object had to be shown to have been deliberately hidden with intent to retrieve and the owner could not be readily found. The English law therefore excluded precious stones and jewels set in base metals or alloys such as bronze or pewter. It also took no account of artifacts in pottery, stone, bone, wood or glass which might be of immense antiquarian value.

In recent years, as a result of the rise in metal-detecting as a hobby, the archaeological lobby brought pressure to bear on Parliament to change the law and bring it into line with Scotland where the rules on Treasure Trove were far more rigorously interpreted. In Scotland the Crown is entitled to *all* abandoned property, even if it has not been hidden and is of little value. This applies even to objects dumped in skips on the pavement. Strictly speaking you would be committing a criminal offence if you removed an old chair from a skip without the owner's permission, although in practice such helping oneself rarely proceeds to a prosecution. In 1958 an archaeological expedition from Aberdeen University found several valuable

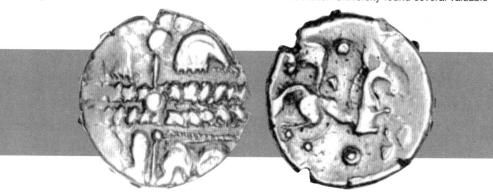

The discovery of hoards is not a new phenomenon. This early Whaddon Chase, Rounded Wing type, gold stater (ABC 2433) is from the William Robinson collection (1915–26) and it more than likely came from the Whaddon Chase Hoard discovered in 1849. (Image kindly supplied by Chris Rudd.)

artifacts on St Ninian's Isle, Shetland. These included silver vessels and ornaments, as well as a porpoise bone which had incised decoration on it. The archaeologists challenged the rights of the Crown to this treasure, arguing that the Crown would have to prove that the articles had been deliberately hidden, and that a porpoise bone was in any case not valuable enough to count as treasure. The High Court, however, decided that as long as the property had been abandoned, it belonged automatically to the Crown. Its value, intrinsic or otherwise, or whether or not it was hidden, did not make any difference. Since then, as a result of this decision in case law, the criteria for Treasure Trove have been very strictly applied in Scotland. It would have only required a similar test case in England or Wales to result in a similar tightening of the rules. This has been resisted, mainly by the detectorist lobby, but inevitably the government considered legislation to control the use of metal detectors, if not to ban them altogether.

In England and Wales a find of gold or silver coins, artifacts or ornaments, or objects which contain some of these metals, which appears to have been concealed by the original owner, was deemed to be Treasure Trove. It was not even necessary for the articles to be buried in the ground; objects concealed in thatched roofs or under the floorboards of buildings have been judged to be Treasure Trove. Such finds had to be notified immediately to the police who then informed the district coroner. He then convened an inquest which decided whether all or part of the find was Treasure Trove. Establishing the gold or silver content was straightforward, but

the coroner's inquest had to decide whether the material was hidden deliberately and not just lost or abandoned, and that the owner could not be located. A gold coin found on or near a country footpath might reasonably have been dropped by the original possessor through a hole in pocket or purse and in such cases it was very unlikely that it would be deemed Treasure Trove, even if the coin turned out to be very rare. In this instance the coroner would then have had to determine who was the lawful owner of the find: the actual finder, the owner of the land where it was found or even the tenant of the land. As a rule, however, it was left to the finder and landowner to decide between them who the owner of the coin should be, and in some cases the matter could only be resolved by referring to a civil court. For this reason it was vital that metal detectorists should secure permission *in writing* from landowners before going on to their land, defining rights and obligations on both sides, in order to determine the disposal or share-out of any finds or proceeds from the sale of finds, *beforehand*.

If the coroner decided that the articles were deliberately concealed, and declared them to be Treasure Trove, the find automatically reverted to the Crown. In practice the find was considered by the Treasure Trove Reviewing Committee of the Treasury. They might decide that although the articles, *invariably coins,* were gold or silver, they were so common that they were not required by the British Museum or one of the other great national collections, and would return them to the finder to dispose of at their discretion. If some or

A number of American coins have turned up recently, including this one found by Neil Chauntrey while detecting a soggy field just outside the Nottingham area in early 2016. The dime is one of the very first minted, dated 1796, and despite the unfortunate hole, will still prove of great interest to US collectors. This find was hot on the heels of a rare "Pine Tree" coin found in the same area causing much speculation as to how and why they ended up in the UK.

Treasure, of course, can be found even when you are not looking for it, as was the case in Switzerland in Spring 2015. As work began on a new cherry orchard, a molehill was spotted with some shimmering green coins on it. Upon further investigation it turned out to be a hoard of almost mint-state Roman coins. An archaeological excavation yielded a haul of 4,166 Roman coins which were unearthed in only a few square metres of ground. This is one of the biggest coin hoards ever discovered in Switzerland.

all of the coins were deemed vital for inclusion in a national collection the finder was recompensed with the full market value of the material. On the other hand, if someone found gold or silver which might be Treasure Trove and failed to declare it at the time, that person was liable to prosecution under the Theft Act 1968 should the find subsequently come to light. Not only could they face a heavy fine but the articles would be forfeit to the Crown, and of course no reward or recompense was then payable either.

The anomalies and inconsistencies of existing law on Treasure Trove were eliminated and the position considerably tightened up by the passage, on July 5, 1996, of the Treasure Act.

Announcing that the Treasure Act had received the Royal Assent, Lord Inglewood, National Heritage Minister, said, "This represents the first legislation on Treasure Trove to be passed in England and Wales and will replace Common Law precedents and practices dating back to the Middle Ages. The Act, which offers a clearer definition of treasure and simplified procedures for dealing with finds, will come into force after a code of practice has been drawn up and agreed by both Houses of Parliament". The Act came into force in England, Wales and Northern Ireland on September 24, 1997, replacing the Common Law of Treasure Trove.

The act was introduced as a Private Member's Bill by Sir Anthony Grant, after the failure of an earlier attempt by Lord Perth. For the first time, it would be a criminal offence to fail to report within 14 days the discovery of an item which could be declared Treasure Trove. Finders will continue to be rewarded for reporting their discoveries promptly,

while landowners and occupiers will also be eligible for rewards for the first time.

The Treasure Act covers man-made objects and defines treasure as objects other than coins which are at least 300 years old and contain at least 10 per cent by weight of gold or silver; coins more than 300 years old which are found in hoards (a minimum of two coins if the precious metal content is more than 10 per cent, and a minimum of 10 coins if the precious metal content is below 10 per cent). The act also embraces all objects found in clear archaeological association with items which are treasure under the above definitions. It also covers any object which would have been Treasure Trove under the previous definitions (e.g. hoards of 19th century gold or silver coins).

An extension to The Act from January 1992 provides that groups of prehistoric bronze implements are also deemed to be Treasure.

The maximum penalty for failing to report the discovery of treasure within 14 days will be a fine of £5,000 or three months imprisonment, or both.

In Scotland the police pass the goods on to the procurator fiscal who acts as the local representative of the Queen's and Lord Treasurer's Remembrancer. If the articles are of little value, historically or intrinsically, the finder will usually be allowed to keep them. If they are retained for the appropriate national collection then a reward equal to the market value is payable.

A favourite haunt of metal-detectorists these days is the beach, and many hobbyists make quite a lucrative living by sweeping the beaches especially just after a Bank Holiday. It's surprising how much loose change gets lost from pockets and handbags over a holiday weekend. Technically the

coins recovered from the beach are lost property, in which case they ought to be surrendered to the police, otherwise the finder may be guilty of theft. In practice, however, the law turns a blind eye to coins, on the sensible grounds that it would be impossible to prove ownership. On the other hand, banknotes are treated as lost property since someone could in theory at least identify a note as his by citing the serial number.

In the case of other objects, such as watches and jewellery, of course the law governing lost property is enforced, and the old adage of "finders keepers" does not apply. Any object of value, identifiable as belonging to someone, that is washed up on the foreshore or found in territorial waters is known technically as "wreck". This includes not just a wrecked ship, but any cargo that was being carried by a ship.

If wreck is not claimed by its owner, it falls to the Crown. In this case it is not necessary to prove deliberate concealment, as in the case of Treasure Trove. This law has a specific numismatic application in the case of the gold and silver coins washed up after storms around our shores, from Shetland to the Scillies. Such coins, emanating from wrecks of Spanish treasure ships and Dutch East Indiamen in particular, are well documented, and any such finds ought to be reported immediately to the police.

Stray finds of coins, as well as other objects of value, on public places, such as the street, a public park or a sports ground, are also subject to law. In this case the finder must take all reasonable steps to locate the owner. Anyone who keeps a coin without making reasonable effort to find the owner could be prosecuted for theft. As with the beach, however, such "reasonable effort" would clearly be impractical. Finding coins on private premises is another matter. In this case large bodies, such as the Post Office, British Rail, the British Airports Authority, bus companies, municipal authorities, hospitals, the owners of department stores, theatre and cinema proprietors and the like, may have bye-laws, rules and regulations for dealing with lost property found within their precincts, or in their vehicles. If you found a purse or wallet on a bus or train, or in a telephone kiosk or a shop, common sense (and your conscience) would tell you to hand it over to the driver, conductor, shopkeeper or official in charge.

As a rule, unclaimed lost property reverts eventually to the finder, but not always; British Rail and some other organisations have a rule that in such cases the property reverts to the organisation. In any event, failure to disclose the find immediately might render you liable to prosecution for stealing by finding.

The Leominster Hoard was found by work colleagues and detecting partners Jeremy Daw and Martin Fulloway in July 2015. The hoard comprised 518 mixed copper coins struck in the second half of the 3rd century AD. Pictured above, the happy finders of the hoard, both with a member of their family— back row, Jeremy Daw and his granddaughter, front row, Martin Fulloway and his daughter. (Courtesy the British Museum's Portable Antiquities Scheme.)

ADVERTISERS *Directory*

See our website at tokenpublishing.com for up-to-date dealer entries, with hyperlinks taking you directly to their websites.

Second Edition

The Dynamics
of Law

Second Edition
The Dynamics of Law

George W. Spiro
University of Massachusetts, Boston

James L. Houghteling, Jr.
Boston College Law School

HARCOURT BRACE JOVANOVICH, INC.
New York   San Diego   Chicago   San Francisco   Atlanta
London   Sydney   Toronto

Cover photo: Bill Call

Printed in the United States of America

Library of Congress Catalog Card Number: 80-83554
ISBN: 0-15-518513-6

Preface

The Dynamics of Law, Second Edition, is, like the First Edition, designed for use in various social science and business administration courses that concern themselves with our legal environment. I have always admired Professor Houghteling's ability in the First Edition to present a subject as complex as law with such clarity and precision. I have therefore attempted to maintain as much of his basic style as possible in this edition.

Some changes in the book, however, will be evident. Many new cases have been added and older ones discarded where it seemed appropriate. In addition, I have tried to enhance the text by adding study problems and review questions to each chapter. Most chapter problems are excerpts from articles, books, or other materials that I have found useful in stimulating classroom discussion.

I wish to express my appreciation to Susan Bennett for all her useful comments and suggestions. Thanks also go to Steven Dowling and Susan Clark, both of Harcourt Brace Jovanovich, Inc., who were so helpful to me during the preparation of this manuscript. I appreciate the generosity of those authors who have permitted me to quote from their materials. Finally, thanks to my wife for her understanding and support.

George Spiro
Boston, Massachusetts

Contents

3
The Trial Stage   42

4
Judicial Lawmaking I:
Law Built on Precedents   71

5
Lawmaking by Legislatures   105

6
Judicial Lawmaking II:
The Interpretation of Statutes   121

7
Judicial Lawmaking III:
Interpreting the Constitution   141

8

Lawmaking and Adjudication
by Administrative Agencies 167

9

Private Contributions
to the Legal System 192

10

Law in Society:
A Conclusion 216

A Bibliographical Note 219

Index of Cases 222

Index 223

1

The Nature
and Function
of Law

Law is an important part of our lives. Therefore, many people have a vague feeling that they ought to know more than they do about the law. They suspect that knowledge of legal rules might help them in their jobs or keep them out of trouble.

You could make no greater mistake, however, than to convince yourself that by simply memorizing legal rules from a book, you will gain the knowledge you need to handle your own legal problems. Such rote learning is a waste of time, even for lawyers, for several reasons:

1. There are simply too many rules.
2. The same rules are not applied in all states. We can make a good many generalizations that will hold true for most states, but without investigation we can never be sure that a particular generalization is true for any one state.
3. Rules are constantly being modified by legislators, by judges, and by administrative agencies.
4. Most rules are not simple and categorical. To state a legal rule with accuracy is likely to require a surprising number of qualifications and exceptions. We shall find that many situations in which people become involved are not neatly covered by any single rule. Indeed, a lawyer—that is, an expert on legal rules—can often do no better than venture a prediction of what rule a court of law will apply in a given situation.

The proposition that underlies this book is that law must be viewed not as a body of static rules but as a *dynamic process by which rules are constantly being changed, created, and molded to fit particular situations.* We shall describe and analyze the processes of the law in the belief that no one can truly understand legal rules without understanding the processes from which they emerge. This analysis will include a study of the interaction between private activities (planned and unplanned) and the activities of judges, legislators, and administrative officials.

Why Do We Need
A System of Rules?

All of us have grown up in a world in which there are established guides for social behavior. As children, our parents made rules that we were expected to obey; as we grew older, more was expected of us, and we had to follow more rules that regulated our behavior. The vast majority of these rules are not rules of law but rather norms of conduct. It is impolite, for example, to speak while you are eating, but although you might be considered crude for doing so, you would never be convicted as a criminal for violating this norm.

Some forms of social behavior are more necessary and some are more socially desirable than others. For this reason, a system for establishing priorities among them is needed. Conceivably, a society could allow considerations of sheer power—physical, economic, social, and political—to determine which form of social behavior should be enforced. But most civilized societies have rejected private power as the primary criterion for establishing priorities and have substituted, instead, such criteria as "justice" and "social utility." A major task of governments is to create and enforce rules of law based on these criteria.

What are rules of law? *Legal rules are guides to human conduct in society, established and enforced by public officials.* In our nation, these laws are designed to achieve a balance among the diverse interests in our society; and they are enforced by officials acting on behalf of the whole community. But rules are not, and can never be, unchanging. In societies in which new problems keep emerging, new rules are continually needed. So it is less important to know the rules than it is to understand the processes by which rules are created and applied. This is why we suggested above that it is best to think of "law" not as a body of rules but as a dynamic process—a system of regularized, institutionalized procedures for the orderly decision of social questions, including the settlement of disputes.

Private Rules
for Social Ordering

Law establishes the framework within which private decision making takes place. For example, we all know that there is a law stating that you may not travel faster than 55 m.p.h. on our major highways. As an individual you make a private decision either to observe this law or to disregard it and risk the possibility of being ticketed. The decision is yours; the law merely gives you guidance.

Although the legal system is the most powerful mechanism for the exercise of social control (since public officials can, if necessary, apply methods of enforcement not available to private persons), there are other sources of guidance. Nongovernmental entities such as families, churches, educational institutions, social clubs, professional associations, business enterprises, and labor unions are encouraged to manage their own internal affairs within the legal framework. These private organizations are often as effective as the legal system itself in ordering our society.

In situations where the distinctions between right and wrong are particularly subtle, where the facts are hard to obtain, or where rapid remedies (damage awards, court orders, and criminal penalties) are not readily applicable, the law is effectively helpless. Courts and judges can do little to make people kinder to their spouses, to prevent students from cheating on examinations, or to induce people to be more devoted or more truthful. Consequently, most social control in these areas must be exercised privately or not at all.

There is, then, a clear need that is filled by private groups. These groups create rules that in many ways resemble laws passed by the state or federal government. Your college or university, for example, probably has a students' rights document that outlines the rules concerning student discipline. The only real distinctions between these rules and those that we call laws are that the college rules govern a relatively small society (the students in the school) and they are not enforced by public officials, but rather by officials of the school.

Many contemporary scholars would argue that our earlier definition of law is too narrow. They would object to limiting law to those rules that are enforced by public officials. Why do we need the force of the state to have "law"? Why not define law as a guide to human conduct in society established and enforced by "any" official, thereby including rules created by private organizations?

While it is possible to define law that broadly, the vast majority of legal scholars take a narrower view. Both for this reason and because this

text will be looking at the U.S. legal system as a model, we shall use the narrower definition. In a later chapter, however, we shall see the direct and important link between private organizations' rules and those of the formal U.S. legal system.

Customs and Morals
Versus Law

Legal rules are distinguished from other rules by the fact that public officials create them and are supposed to enforce them. Behind legal rules stands the authority of the state. Although many of a community's customs and moral rules eventually become law, a custom or moral rule is not in itself a rule of law; it does not become one unless acknowledged as such by officials who have the power to create legal rules.

Morality encompasses an individual's ability to distinguish right from wrong and to act accordingly. The ideas of right and wrong, good and bad, are value judgments as determined and generally accepted by some reference group. Moral behavior may or may not coincide with a legal rule. It may, for example, be morally right to respect your parents, but it is not a legal necessity.

PROBLEM
Elderly and infirm Aunt Sadie is quite poor and hungry. She is so desperate that she steals a loaf of bread from a local store. The store owner is quite well-to-do, but he has had a rash of shoplifting cases in the past few weeks and has vowed to "get revenge." Aunt Sadie is caught, and the owner insists on pressing charges.

Do you see any moral problems in this case? Are there any value conflicts? How would you handle this problem if you were the judge trying Aunt Sadie's case?

The problems faced by Aunt Sadie's judge are typical of those that intrigue philosophers and bedevil policy makers. Although it is obviously necessary to have a law against stealing, it may seem unfair to apply the law in the same way to Aunt Sadie as to someone who is well-off and shoplifts just for the fun of it. Aunt Sadie has broken the law, but it is a matter of argument whether she has also "done wrong." In order to be a good citizen, should one obey the law, no matter how much sacrifice that entails? Conversely, should one do as one thinks is right under the circumstance, even if it means breaking the law? Perhaps the important thing is that any person considering these questions must un-

derstand the consequences, both legal and moral, of following each course of action.

You will notice in our problem that the question of moral judgment is made quite obvious by the use of value-laden words. Aunt Sadie is "poor," "hungry," "elderly," and "infirm," while the shopkeeper is described as "well-to-do." Words like these influence the argument. In analyzing cases throughout this text, you should make every attempt to analyze conflicting values and to recognize value-laden words.

Custom, like moral behavior, may or may not coincide with legal behavior; yet custom is different from morality. It is custom to eat lunch at noon, but eating lunch at eleven cannot be said to be immoral. (The law makes no statement about when one can eat lunch.) A custom is a course of action that people have chosen to repeat when faced with a particular circumstance; it is usually enforced only by the private method of social approval and disapproval. Sometimes, though, a custom can become a law, as, for example, when the custom of closing businesses on Sundays was made a law by some states.

The Various Perspectives of Law

In the attempt to resolve such problems as finding the proper relation between law, custom, and morality, many people have spent a great deal of time trying to find one perfect legal theory. Scholars such as Aristotle, Kant, and Kelsen have spent lifetimes refining legal theories. Such an exercise is frustrating and ultimately not very useful for students. It is best for students to keep their minds open to as many theories as possible. None of the theories you learn should prevent you from thinking of another: Each can provide a useful insight into law and can illuminate a particular problem.

You might want to read some of the works of the scholars mentioned above in order to see how legal theory has evolved and profited from the legal thinkers of the past. For example, Aristotle refined a definition of law suggesting that society is organized by *cosmic* or *natural law*. This cosmic law is an ideal form of law, higher than that made by mortals. Another theory, refined by Friedrich Karl von Savigny, is known as the *historical school of jurisprudence*. Von Savigny believed that law developed out of a particular nation's history, and that legal experts merely interpreted the historical drift of a nation.

New models of law are constantly being developed and tested in the hope that they will help to clarify the significant societal institution we

call law. As you advance in your study of law, and as you face particular legal problems, you should ask yourself which of the many theories would be most useful to you in resolving your particular concern. Right now, your job is to learn about our legal system and the interaction of its elements.

Some Requirements for an Effective Legal System

Once you have a reasonable definition of law, your next job is to begin to assemble a legal system that operates effectively. As you can imagine, there are an infinite number of ways in which a legal system can be put together. Every nation in the world has a slightly different legal system. In fact, Karl Llewellyn, a legal scholar, developed the concept of a law-government continuum to illustrate just that point.[1]

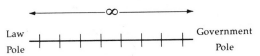

The *government pole* of the continuum represents a legal system in which all decisions are left to the judgment of a leader of the system. For example, Iran under the leadership of Ayatollah Ruhollah Khomeini is near the government pole. The *law pole* represents the opposite situation. In such a system the set of rules is so complete that human judgment is unnecessary: Every conceivable contingency is covered by specific laws. While no legal system exemplifies the law pole completely, the U.S. legal system is closer to it than most. Obviously, societies merely approach the extreme positions. It is entirely possible to conceive of a viable legal system at any point along this continuum. Our own legal system is but one model among many; it contrasts in varying degrees with the others. Since it is closer to the law pole than to the government pole, it contrasts most sharply with a highly autocratic system, such as monarchy, which is nearer to the government pole.

Whatever legal system is adopted, there are certain requirements for it to be effective. First, *most rules must be obeyed voluntarily*. One objective of a legal system is to set forth guides for human conduct that will cause people to behave by choice as society wants them to behave. This is the

---

[1] Richard Hartzler, *Justice, Legal Systems and Social Structure* (Port Washington, N.Y.: Kennikat Press, 1976), page 58.

preventive function of law. The most important legal rules (sometimes known as the *primary rules*) are those designed to channel the conduct of private persons and groups into patterns that will keep conflict to a minimum. Without a large measure of voluntary compliance with the primary rules, social life would be impossible: No community can afford to employ a large enough number of officials to compel everyone to obey the law.

Inevitably, though, some people do not comply, either deliberately or through carelessness or ignorance. So a legal system must have officials such as police and judges to apply the *secondary*, or *remedial, rules.* These are the rules that determine what happens to people who have violated the primary rules. But again, recourse to officials and to remedial rules must always be the exception if a legal system is to be effective. Most people, most of the time, must observe the speed limits, live up to their contractual obligations, pay their taxes, and in other ways comply with the law if the law enforcement system is not to be overburdened.

Next, *the rules must seem just and reasonable.* Why do most people comply with the rules most of the time? To be sure, the remedial rules are partly responsible: People do not want any trouble with the officials. They do not want to be arrested and prosecuted or to be sued; they do not want to be punished or to have to pay damages to somebody they have harmed. But we probably tend to overestimate the importance of these fears. Most people obey legal rules both out of force of habit and because they feel, at least dimly, that doing so is right.

It does not follow from this that people will accept just any set of rules. They must believe that rules are relatively fair and reasonable. A rule that any considerable part of the community finds unjust or unreasonable will be difficult to enforce.

Circumstances sometimes arise, of course, in which it is desirable to establish a rule even though many people may not like it: The anti-discrimination laws adopted in many communities may well be examples. Such laws are designed to raise the prevailing moral standards of the community. It is nonetheless true that a law disapproved by many people is likely to be hard to enforce; it may even cause harm that outweighs any possible good that the law itself might have accomplished. Prohibition during the 1920s and most of our current gambling laws are often cited as evidence to support this proposition.

Third, *the rules must be flexible.* Since the material circumstances of community life, and thus the values and attitudes of the community, are continually changing, the system of rules under which the community lives must be flexible and adaptable. There must be ways to bend existing rules to meet new situations, and ways to make more substantial

changes in the rules when such changes seem necessary. In our legal system, the task of bending the rules to meet new situations has traditionally been assigned to the courts, while the more substantial changes are usually made by legislative bodies.

Fourth, *the rules must be knowable* if the community expects its members to comply with the legal rules. It is obviously not necessary for every citizen to know all the rules, but the experts in the rules—the lawyers—must be able to advise their clients on the probable legal consequences of their acts, and citizens must have a general idea of the most important laws. As a famous judge, Benjamin N. Cardozo, once said: "Law as a guide to conduct is reduced to the level of mere futility if it is unknown and unknowable."

Under some circumstances, though, the requirement that laws must be knowable may conflict with other requirements. The most certain and knowable rules tend to be those that are relatively simple and categorical and that have no qualification or exceptions ("Thou shalt not kill"). To make a rule seem reasonable and just, however, qualifications and exceptions have to be added. Thus, killing in self-defense is permitted in some circumstances, as is killing in times of war. Conversely, flexible and changing rules are less certain in their application, and less knowable, than inflexible and unchanging rules. One of the hardest tasks for lawmakers is to balance these competing requirements.

The Creation and Application of Law: Some Introductory Remarks

We have stated that this book will deal with the processes and institutions by which legal rules are created and applied in particular cases. Following is a brief overview of how these subjects will be covered.

When we speak of applying rules in particular cases, we are referring primarily to the process known as *adjudication*. Adjudication involves deciding exactly what happened—what the facts were in the particular case—and then deciding what legal rules should be applied to those facts. This process will be considered in Chapters 2 and 3.

When we speak of creating and modifying rules—of *lawmaking*—we are referring to several processes. The best known of these is *legislative lawmaking*, a term that refers first and foremost to the enactment of "legislation" (that is, statutes) by popularly elected legislative bodies. Many people are aware of no other kind of lawmaking; indeed, to most of us a "law" means a legislative act.

The other great lawmaking process is *decisional lawmaking*. The no-

tion that judges (and other case deciders) "make law" is much less familiar than the concept of legislative lawmaking. Nonetheless, it is true that law is made in the course of adjudicating cases. Whenever a question arises about the proper rule of law to apply in a particular case, the answering of that question by the judges is a creative act—an act of lawmaking. The judges make law for the future, because their decisions become potential precedents that are likely to influence the deciding of future cases involving similar fact-situations. Law created by judicial decisions is variously called decisional law, case law, and judge-made law.

Chapter 4 describes how judges create new rules out of old ones by building on precedent. Chapter 5 discusses the manner in which legislators make law. Then, Chapters 6 and 7 return to judicial lawmaking: Chapter 6 describes how judges interpret statutes in the course of applying them in particular cases, and Chapter 7 describes how judges interpret the federal Constitution.

Legislators and judges have been making law and adjudicating cases for hundreds of years, but the last seventy-five years have seen a vast increase in the role of administrators in the legal system. Today, administrative officials and agencies both adjudicate cases and make law. Their lawmaking[2] is in part decisional (when they decide cases) and in part legislative (when they exercise powers delegated to them by legislatures to issue regulations that have the force of law). In Chapter 8 we shall consider the role of administrators in the legal system.

We have defined legal rules to refer only to rules created by officials. However, private persons and groups make important contributions to official lawmaking and, in addition, create rules of their own that supplement the rules of law. This contribution will be the subject of Chapter 9.

Chapter Problem

A significant question currently being debated by concerned groups of parents and representatives of the cereal and toy industries is the amount and form of advertising that is directed toward children. The parents feel that such advertising is extremely deceptive. They argue that youngsters

---

[2] Since we speak continually of the creation of rules, it could be argued that we might better use the term *rulemaking*. But because *lawmaking* is more familiar and seems more natural, and because *rulemaking* has a somewhat special connotation among lawyers, we shall use the term *lawmaking*.

---

are unable to make informed judgments about the things they see on television, and thus they are really helpless victims of corporate giants. The corporate executives disagree with this analysis. On January 22, 1979, the following article appeared in *Advertising Age.*

> *FCC KID HEARINGS OPEN:*
> *GF ATTACKS MORE RULES*

Washington—Advertisers acted on a second front in the children's ad debate last week as General Foods and others urged the Federal Communications Commission to resist demands that it tighten its regulations.

The question for FCC is whether it should go beyond its 1974 children's TV policy statement, which endorsed as a ceiling on allowable commercialization an industry standard of 9½ commercial minutes per hour on weekend kid shows and 12 commercial minutes per hour for weekday programs.

The Commission also barred using hosts of children's shows to sell products and warned against weaving mention of a product into the context of children's shows. But it stopped short of adopting another consumerist request—specific requirements compelling broadcasters to air certain amounts of children's programming.

The 1974 FCC said it preferred to rely on industry self-regulation, but claimed it had the authority to further restrict, or even eliminate, advertising from children's shows.

General Foods and Kellogg, in separate filings last week, argued that FCC's power to ban advertising is on shaky ground because of the Supreme Court decisions since 1974 that established limited First Amendment protections for advertising.

GF went further and specifically rejected practically all activist demands for tighter rules as unwarranted and inflationary.

Questions

1.   Do you think that television advertising should be regulated? Why or why not?

2.   In your opinion, is law the appropriate device for solving problems such as the one described above?

3.   What other alternatives are available to consumerists?

4.   What value judgments underlie the premises of the various parties?

Questions for Review

1.   One possible definition of law is: "Law is what the strongest person says it is." Evaluate this statement. What would be a better definition of law? Why?

2.   Can you think of an example of a custom that later became law? Of a custom that you believe *should* become law?

3.   The city council wants to induce landlords to raise the standards of safety, sanitation, and overall habitability of apartment houses. One way of dealing with this problem would be to pass a law stating that any landlord who lets a building fall below certain minimum standards would be subject to a fine. What other approaches are open to the council? What are the pros and cons of each?

4.   One of the requirements of a legal system is that the rules must seem just and reasonable. One law states that the sanction for murder is that the murderer will be put to death. Is this law just and reasonable? Must *all* laws be just and reasonable?

5.   It was stated in this chapter that laws must be flexible. Does this mean that there should be different standards for different people?

2
The Courts
and the Process
of Adjudication

Only a tiny fraction of the innumerable social transactions that take place every day in our society ever come before courts of law. But the few cases that do are of particular importance to the legal system and to the student of law. For one thing, these cases furnish the best documentation we have of the legal system at work. Even more important, they provide the occasions on which judges make authoritative restatements of the scope and content of legal rules.

When courts decide cases, they perform two distinct, though interrelated, functions. First, they settle the controversy between the parties: They determine what the facts were and apply the appropriate rules to those facts. This is the function commonly known as *adjudication*. But whenever there is any question about what rules to apply, the courts also perform a second function: They decide what the appropriate rules are and how they fit the particular case. Deciding what rules are applicable often requires the courts to reformulate and modify the scope of existing rules. Some of these reformulations become precedents that determine the future scope and content of the rules. This second function is sometimes referred to as *judicial lawmaking*.[1] In this chapter and the next, we

---

[1] One significant result of the precedent-creating activity of courts is to keep many disputes from coming before the courts at all. The position a court takes in one case often makes possible a relatively reliable prediction of how it would view a similar case, if that second case were to come before it. This predictability may deter the parties in the second case from taking the time and trouble to bring their case to court.

are concerned with the first of these functions. We shall examine the second function in later chapters.

This chapter begins by briefly distinguishing between civil and criminal law. Next, attention is turned toward the categories of courts that make up a court system and the limits that are placed on their jurisdiction. Finally, we trace the sequence of steps that make up the adjudicative process. Chapter 3 will be devoted entirely to one of those steps: the trial.

Criminal Law and Civil Law

The classification of legal rules and court proceedings as either criminal or civil is very basic and familiar. Yet it is so confusing to so many people that the distinction should be clarified at once.

If somebody has performed an act that probably violates some rule of law and you want to make a preliminary guess as to whether the violation is criminal or civil, ask yourself this question: What is likely to happen to the wrongdoer? If you decide that she is probably subject to official punishment—to a fine or imprisonment, for instance—then she has probably violated a criminal rule. If, on the other hand, you think that she will probably be sued and ordered to pay damages to whomever she has harmed, or ordered to do or desist from doing some act, then she has probably violated a civil rule.

This is only a rule of thumb, however; we need some definitions.

Rules of *criminal law* impose duties on people (and sometimes on associations of people) and specify that any violation of those duties is a wrong, not merely to the individuals who are harmed, but to the community at large. Since the whole community has been wronged, public officials take the initiative in bringing the wrongdoer to justice, prosecuting him before a court, and urging the judge and jury to convict and punish him. Any redress received by the individuals wronged as a result of a criminal proceeding is purely incidental. Criminal wrongs are classed as either felonies or misdemeanors, depending on their gravity. To give two examples at opposite extremes, a murder is a felony, while a simple assault is a misdemeanor.

Rules of *civil law* also impose duties on people and associations of people. (In addition, they establish liberties and powers; however, in distinguishing civil from criminal rules, we are only concerned with the civil rules that impose duties.) Violation of a duty created by a civil rule is, of course, a wrong; it differs from a criminal wrong, however, in that

it does *not* constitute a wrong against the community at large. When a wrongful act is merely a civil wrong, therefore, public officials will not take the initiative in prosecuting and punishing the wrongdoer; instead, the injured person must bring a civil suit against the wrongdoer. All civil wrongs except breaches of contract are more commonly known as *torts* (from the French word meaning "wrong"). Torts with which you are doubtless familiar in a general way are trespass, libel, and negligence.

The problem of definition is made more difficult because, as you may have guessed by now, a particular act may be both a criminal wrong and a civil wrong. For example, if SPEEDER, while driving recklessly and in violation of the speed limit, sideswipes CAREFUL DRIVER and damages the latter's car, she is guilty of both a crime and a tort. The state is likely to prosecute SPEEDER for her criminal conduct, and CAREFUL DRIVER may sue her for the tort, asking payment for the damage done. (Under the U.S. legal system, a criminal prosecution and a civil suit cannot be combined, even though both are based on the same act.)

Many wrongful acts, however, are *only* criminal wrongs. For instance, if SPEEDER drives recklessly and too fast, but harms no one, she is guilty only of a crime. By the same token, many wrongful acts are *only* civil wrongs, simply because the lawmakers have decided that they do not endanger the public welfare. For example, if HOMEOWNER carelessly leaves a rollerskate on his front porch and VISITOR steps on it and falls, injuring her back, HOMEOWNER will probably not be subject to prosecution by the state, because such negligence is usually considered tortious, not criminal. Similarly, if BUYER refuses to go through with his contract to purchase SELLER's lawnmower, he will not be prosecuted, since breach of contract is not a crime. But VISITOR and SELLER probably have grounds for bringing civil suits.

There is, unfortunately, no basis for wholly reliable prediction as to whether a particular act that appears wrongful is a crime or a civil wrong or both. This is because lawmakers are free (within the broad limits imposed by constitutions) to make almost any sort of act a criminal or civil wrong, just as they can "legalize" acts that have in the past been legal wrongs. For instance, nothing prevents a legislature from passing a law tomorrow declaring that failure to keep a front porch safe for visitors in certain respects will henceforth be a misdemeanor punishable by a fine.

To recapitulate, some wrongful acts violate both criminal and civil rules of law and may result in either criminal prosecution or civil proceedings or both. Some wrongful acts violate only criminal rules, usually because no private person can claim to have been harmed, while other wrongful acts violate only civil rules, because, they are not considered to

affect the public interest.[2] In this book we shall be primarily concerned with civil rules of law. Our generalized discussion of courts will not cover criminal courts or proceedings, important as they are. Needless to say, though, everybody is subject to criminal law and thus should be familiar with the distinctions discussed above.

Court Systems: Organization and Jurisdiction

People outside the legal profession have no need for a detailed knowledge of the numerous types of courts that make up the court system of any given state, but a general familiarity with the structure of a typical court system is indispensable to an understanding of the cases that will be presented in this book.

Each of the fifty states of the United States has its own court system, and, in addition, there is the federal court system. No two systems are alike. Indeed, the differences in both the functions and the labels given to U.S. courts are many and bewildering, and no generalization is absolutely reliable for all states. Court systems have rarely been the product of long-range planning; nearly all represent a series of patchwork accommodations to changing needs.

We will not deal in this chapter with the many administrative agencies and tribunals—worker's compensation boards, for example—that perform court-like functions; these will be discussed in Chapter 8.

At the outset, it is necessary to recognize a basic distinction that prevails in all court systems: the distinction between trial courts and appellate courts. *Trial courts* are the courts in which cases are first heard and decided; here the opposing parties present evidence on the facts and arguments on the law. Ordinarily, a single judge hears any given trial-court proceeding. (But since many trial courts are manned by more than one judge, each of whom can preside over a case, several proceedings may take place simultaneously.)

The great majority of cases go no further than the trial court. But if one of the parties is dissatisfied with the outcome of the trial, the law usually allows that party to take an appeal—that is, to ask an *appellate*

---

2 Once a wrongful act has come before a court, the character of the court action can usually be identified by the label given to the proceeding. If it is something like "STATE (or PEOPLE) versus SPEEDER," it is usually criminal. But if it is "CAREFUL DRIVER versus SPEEDER," it is civil.

court (a court of appeal) to review the rulings of the trial court. An appellate court consists of a number of judges, several or all of whom hear each appeal.

The State Court Systems

The typical state court system consists of a considerable number of trial courts of limited jurisdiction, a smaller number of general trial courts, and a single appellate court for the whole state. (See Figure 1 showing the hierarchy of the state courts in Massachusetts.)

TRIAL COURTS OF LIMITED JURISDICTION   The vast majority of cases that come to our courts are tried by trial courts of limited jurisdiction. These cases are usually routine in character and of little importance except to the parties involved. The trial courts of limited jurisdiction fall into three classes: minor courts, intermediate courts, and specialized courts.

The Minor Courts   This lowest tier of trial courts, which are also referred to as local, petty, or inferior courts, are those manned by rural justices of

FIGURE 1
The State Court System of Massachusetts

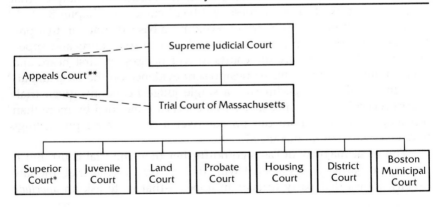

Source: Chart reprinted by permission of *Massachusetts Lawyers Weekly*, Vol. 6, No. 43 (July 24, 1978).
*The plaintiff can bring a civil action seeking money damages in either the District or Superior Court. If he brings it in the District Court, he has waived his trial by jury and, generally speaking, cannot claim a retrial in the Superior Court.
**In Massachusetts, not all cases must pass through the Appeals Court on their way to the Supreme Judicial Court.

the peace and their urban counterparts, often known as aldermen or magistrates. The "J.P." is heir to centuries of tradition, dating back to English knights and country squires who were commissioned by the Crown to keep the peace in rural areas. The modern namesakes of these knights and squires have authority to try petty criminal offenses and to hear civil cases involving claims not exceeding a few hundred dollars. Remuneration for the J.P.'s consists of fees received for each case tried, and they usually have some other source of income—for example, from selling insurance. J.P.'s are elected to the office; few have had legal training. The traditional minor courts are often criticized for the incompetence and bias of their magistrates. On their behalf, it may be said that the justice they dispense is readily accessible, speedy, and relatively inexpensive.

Many states have replaced the numerous J.P. courts and their urban counterparts with a smaller number of courts manned by full-time, salaried, professionally trained judges. Even where this change has not occurred on a statewide basis, one often finds that it has taken place in the larger towns and cities, or that at least part of the original authority of the petty magistrates has been assigned to courts with full-time, legally trained judges. In the criminal sphere, the traffic and police courts are examples of the modernized minor courts. Courts that hear civil cases (or both civil and criminal cases) often bear such labels as city, town, municipal, or district courts.

In many ways, these modernized minor courts resemble the intermediate-type trial courts (to be discussed) more closely than they do the older type of minor court. But the trial courts in the minor-court classification do have some features in common. One is that, with occasional exceptions, they do not provide for a trial before a jury. Another is that appeals from their decisions are taken to the general trial courts (or occasionally to special courts of appeal) rather than to the regular appellate courts. Furthermore, such "appeals" often consist of complete new trials rather than mere reviews of the errors alleged to have been made in the original trial.

Intermediate Trial Courts   In those states in which the modernization of the minor courts has proved constitutionally or politically impossible, an intermediate tier of trial courts has sometimes been established (particularly in urban areas) between the J.P.'s and the general trial courts. These intermediate courts are often called county courts. As one might expect, they usually perform the same functions as the modernized minor courts. They try the less serious criminal cases, and civil cases involving claims not in excess of a few thousand dollars. But their sphere of authority is much greater than that of the J.P.'s. Most of these intermediate

courts were created to take over part of the work formerly done by the general trial courts. They provide jury trials, and appeals from their decisions go to the regular appellate courts.

Specialized Courts On the whole, there is strikingly little subject-matter specialization in the American court system. But a few subject-matter fields are frequently (particularly in urban areas) assigned to special courts.

A number of cities, for instance, have special juvenile and domestic-relations courts. Perhaps the specialized courts with the longest tradition are those that deal with such matters as the disposition of property left by deceased persons, and with guardianships and adoptions. These are variously called probate, orphans', and surrogate courts.

Why have certain kinds of cases been taken away from the regular courts and assigned to specialized courts? Usually the reason has been that handling those cases requires judges to perform functions markedly different from the trial judge's ordinary function of adjudication. Probate court judges, for instance, spend much of their time supervising the distribution (by executors and administrators) of property left by deceased persons—a task that involves adjudicating disputes only in exceptional cases. A major responsibility of the juvenile-court judge, after ascertaining that a wrongful act has been done, is to search for a means of preventing the young offender from becoming a hardened criminal. An important part of the job of a domestic-relations judge is to see whether it is possible to keep estranged couples from dissolving their marriage. Performing these tasks requires knowledge and skills quite different from those required for adjudication. Hence there are important advantages to assigning such cases to judges who have, or can attain, a special competence, and whose courts can be staffed with specialized personnel, such as accountants, psychiatrists, and social workers.

GENERAL TRIAL COURTS The most important cases—those involving major crimes and large sums of money—are tried in the general trial courts, also called courts of general jurisdiction. The cases you will read in this book virtually all began in general trial courts. When we speak of trial courts hereafter, we shall be referring to these courts unless we state otherwise. These courts are labeled *general* because they have authority to hear all types of cases not specifically assigned to the courts of limited jurisdiction. Some of the smaller states have only one general trial court for the whole state, though that court usually consists of several judges who sit separately and hear cases in different cities in the state. Most states, however, are divided into a number of judicial districts, each con-

sisting of one or more counties, and each district has its own general trial court.

General trial courts bear such varied labels as circuit, district, and common pleas courts. But labels can be deceptive: These same titles are used in some states to designate courts of limited jurisdiction or even appellate courts. New York State's general trial courts are called supreme courts, although this is the title usually given to final courts of appeal.

APPELLATE COURTS   All states have at least one appellate court, usually known as the supreme court. This is the "court of last resort"; it hears appeals from all trial-court decisions, criminal and civil, except those of minor courts. In a few states, however, the volume of appeals is so great that one or more intermediate appellate courts have been established to hear appeals in less important cases. Alternatively, the single appellate court may be subdivided into several "divisions" that hear appeals as if they were separate courts.

The Federal Court System

The federal court hierarchy (shown in Figure 2) is comparatively simple. The basic unit of jurisdiction is the *district*. Each district has a U.S. District Court. These are the general trial courts of the federal system. (The system has no minor courts.) There are ninety district courts in the fifty states, plus courts in the District of Columbia, Puerto Rico, Guam, and the Virgin Islands. Many of the states constitute a single district, but some states are divided into two, three, or four districts. Pennsylvania, for instance, has three districts; the court for the Western District, sitting in Pittsburgh and Erie, has eight district judges. Each district (with one exception[3]) forms part of a larger judicial area known as a *circuit*. There are eleven circuits, each served by a U.S. Court of Appeals. A major responsibility of each court of appeals is to hear appeals from the decisions of the district courts in its circuit.

The Court of Claims, established in 1855, was generally designed to take jurisdiction over claims against the United States. Typical of the cases it hears are claims against the United States for the taking of property or claims that grow out of construction contracts. The U.S. Customs Court and the Court of Customs and Patent Appeals exert jurisdiction,

---

[3] The exceptional district is the District of Columbia, which not only has its own district court but also comprises the eleventh circuit and so has its own court of appeals. This arrangement is made necessary by the large number of cases originating in the federal administrative agencies.

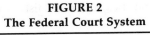

FIGURE 2
The Federal Court System

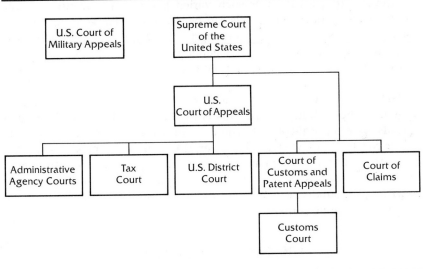

both original and appellate, over civil actions arising under the tariff laws.

The Tax Court enters into cases in which the Commissioner of Internal Revenue has determined that there is a discrepancy. The court, under the Tax Reform Act of 1969 (83 Stat. 733), may have final jurisdiction over cases involving less than $5,000 in any disputed year. Lastly, the U.S. Court of Military Appeals, which is independent of the rest of the court system, is the final appellate court in which individuals may review court-martial proceedings.

The nation's highest appellate court is the Supreme Court of the United States, whose nine justices sit in Washington. Contrary to a widespread belief, the national Supreme Court is not available as a court of last resort for any appellant with the perseverance to take a case "all the way to the top." The truth is that the Supreme Court considers only a limited number of cases that are considered to be particularly important to the legal system.

Limitations on Jurisdiction

We have already said quite a bit about the jurisdiction of courts, but we have not really defined *jurisdiction*. Although this term is used in several

different ways, the root concept has to do with the boundaries of a court's authority to hear and decide cases.

SUBJECT–MATTER JURISDICTION No court has unlimited jurisdiction to hear and decide all kinds of cases. One type of limitation on jurisdiction is based either on the subject matter of the controversy or on the nature of the parties. For example, as we discussed earlier, probate courts deal only with cases involving property left by deceased persons, and juvenile courts handle only those cases in which children are involved.

TERRITORIAL JURISDICTION Every court serves some specified geographical area, which is known as its *territory of jurisdiction*. The territorial jurisdiction of the Supreme Court of the United States, the Court of Appeals of New York, or the Boston Municipal Court, for instance, is indicated in the official title of each court. If the judges on a court are elected, the residents of the territory of jurisdiction vote to elect them. If the court is empowered to grant jury trials, the jurors are selected from among persons living within the territory. The past decisions of the court are in a sense "law" within the territory, and the cases brought before the court ordinarily have some connection with the territory.

This geographical connotation of jurisdiction accounts for the common practice of speaking of a jurisdiction as if it were a particular area. When we say, for instance, that a decision of the Massachusetts Supreme Judicial Court is a binding precedent "throughout the jurisdiction," we mean that it is binding throughout Massachusetts or, more literally, throughout the territory of jurisdiction of the Massachusetts Supreme Judicial Court. In general, the states are the most significant territorial units of jurisdiction in the U.S. legal system.

JURISDICTION OVER PARTICULAR PERSONS AND PROPERTY Let us suppose that BUYER institutes a lawsuit against SELLER in the Superior Court of Massachusetts, asking for $10,000 in damages for breach of contract. Let us suppose, too, that the Superior Court has jurisdiction over this type of controversy, and that BUYER and SELLER signed the contract now at issue in Suffolk County in Massachusetts. It is still quite possible that the court may not have jurisdiction to try BUYER's lawsuit.

This is because another rule on jurisdiction requires that a court have jurisdiction over the person of the defendant who is being sued or over some of his or her property. This is, first, a matter of the court's ability to exercise some control over the defendant. The officials who serve a state court never have power to act outside the state, and frequently they even

lack power to act outside the court's judicial district. Hence the court wants to be shown, before it hears the case and renders a decision, that there is some chance of its being able to make its decision effective. It is also important to make sure that the defendant knows that he or she is being sued. (The plaintiff's efforts to prove that the court has jurisdiction will most likely make the defendant aware of what is happening.)

How can BUYER demonstrate to the court that it has jurisdiction over SELLER? The most common procedure is for her to ask the court clerk to issue a *summons* (a document notifying SELLER that BUYER is suing him), and then to arrange to have the summons "served" on SELLER. There are a number of alternative methods for serving SELLER with a summons, but ordinarily it is delivered to him in person or, if he is a resident of the district, to his residence or place of business. Summonses cannot be served outside the state in which they are issued (except under limited circumstances that we need not consider here). If BUYER succeeds in having a summons validly served on SELLER, the court will assume that a sufficient connection has been established between SELLER and the court's territory of jurisdiction to warrant it in proceeding to hear the case.

If BUYER were suing SELLER in connection with property owned by SELLER located in Suffolk County, it might under some circumstances be sufficient for BUYER to prove to the court that it has jurisdiction over the property. In that event, the court could make a decision affecting the property even though it never asserted its jurisdiction over SELLER's person.

STATE VERSUS FEDERAL JURISDICTION   The great majority of cases can be tried only in state courts, since they do not involve subject matter or parties that would bring them within the jurisdiction of the federal courts. A much smaller number of cases fall exclusively within the jurisdiction of the federal courts. And between these two groups is a sizable class of cases for which jurisdiction of the state and federal courts overlaps.

Most of the cases over which the federal courts have jurisdiction fall into one of two categories:

1. *Cases involving "diversity of citizenship."* A large proportion of the cases in the federal district courts are there solely because the respective parties are citizens of different states. The Founding Fathers, apprehensive of state-court bias against out-of-state parties, gave Congress authority to allow such cases to be brought to the federal courts. Congress has decided that when the parties in a lawsuit are citizens of different states and when the amount in controversy exceeds $10,000, the

parties may bring their case to the federal courts. All such cases may also be tried in state courts but for various reasons, including the impression that federal judges are more competent and broader in their views than their state counterparts, one party or the other in a lawsuit often chooses to take advantage of this privilege.

2. *Cases involving "federal questions."* There are a number of subjects over which Congress has decided the federal courts should have *exclusive* jurisdiction. Their jurisdiction is exerted even if diversity of citizenship does not exist and the amount in controversy does not exceed the $10,000 level. Trademarks, copyrights, patents, bankruptcy, and admiralty actions are all examples of the sort of cases over which federal courts exert their exclusive jurisdiction. There are, however, many federal questions that have not been categorized as exclusively the domain of federal courts, and these may routinely be heard in state courts.

Conflict of Laws

Once a court has decided that it has authority to hear a case, it may also have to decide whether to apply the local rules of law or those of some other jurisdiction.[4] Many people take it for granted that the courts of State X always apply the legal rules of State X in deciding cases, but this is not necessarily true. Let us suppose, for instance, that BUYER and SELLER make a contract in Illinois in which they agree that SELLER will sell to BUYER some machinery located in Indiana and that the machinery will be delivered to BUYER's plant in that state. Instead, SELLER sells the machinery to someone else, and BUYER is now preparing to sue her for breach of contract. SELLER currently lives in Pittsburgh, Pennsylvania, and BUYER decides that it will be simplest to bring his suit in the Allegheny County Court of Common Pleas.

Assume that Illinois, Indiana, and Pennsylvania have slightly different rules with respect to sales contracts. Which state's rules should be applied in this case? Although the Allegheny County Court ordinarily applies Pennsylvania rules, there are perhaps reasons for not applying them in this particular case. For one thing, it seems likely that BUYER and SELLER (if they gave the matter any thought at all when they entered into the contract) contemplated that the law of Illinois (where the contract was made) or of Indiana (where it was to be performed) would apply.

For us to examine here the principles by which problems of this sort

---

[4] *Jurisdiction* is used here—as it will be frequently throughout this book—to refer to a territory of jurisdiction (see page 20).

are solved would carry us far afield. The body of legal principles governing such situations is known as *conflict of laws*.

Federal courts also have problems in deciding what set of rules to
apply to a case. Suppose that since BUYER is not a citizen of Pennsylvania
but of Illinois, and since his claim exceeds $10,000, he exercises his right
to sue SELLER in the federal district court in Pittsburgh. What rules of
contract law will the federal court apply? Will it apply Pennsylvania,
Illinois, or Indiana rules, or will it apply some sort of federal rule? In
general, the federal court in Pittsburgh will try to apply the same contract rules as the state court in Pittsburgh would have applied if the case
had been brought before it.

The Process
of Adjudication

Now that we know something about the courts and their jurisdiction, we
can begin to discuss the process by which a civil suit is adjudicated in the
courts.[5] First, however, we must distinguish between two classes of issue
that the courts are called upon to resolve.

The Distinction Between Issues of Fact
and Issues of Law

The basic tasks of courts in adjudication are (a) to appraise the *evidence*
presented by the parties to support their allegations about the facts, and
(b) to appraise the *arguments* presented by the parties to support their
assertions about what rules of law should be applied to the facts. Conflicting evidence creates *questions* (or *issues*) *of fact*; conflicting arguments
create *questions* (or *issues*) *of law*.[6]

Three kinds of cases come before the courts. First are cases in which

---

[5] Again, *adjudication* refers to the proceedings in which a controversy (which may be
either a civil case or a criminal prosecution) is judged. When the focus is not on the
judging but on the contest between parties, we speak of *litigation*. The parties are often
called *litigants*. This part of the chapter might equally well have been titled "The Process
of Litigation."

[6] One way of looking at the process of deciding cases is in terms of the syllogism.
The major premise is supplied by answering the question(s) of law, the minor premise by
answering the question(s) of fact. To use a very simple example:

All who drive over 60 m.p.h. are guilty of speeding. (*Rule.*)
John drove over 60 m.p.h. (*Fact.*)
Therefore John is guilty of speeding. (*Decision.*)

there is no doubt about what rules to apply once the facts have been established. Second are cases in which there is no dispute over the facts but a very real dispute over the proper rules to apply to those facts. Third are cases in which there is disagreement about both the facts and the applicable rules.

At first blush, the distinction between questions of fact and questions of law seems perfectly obvious. A question of *fact* concerns what happened (or, in some cases, what is happening or will happen). To be more precise, it may involve an event, a relationship, a condition, or a state of mind. In the BUYER–SELLER example above, such factual questions as these might arise: What words did BUYER address to SELLER? (Event.) Had BUYER and SELLER previously been on friendly terms? (Relationship.) Was BUYER over twenty-one years old? (Condition.) Was BUYER speaking seriously when he made his proposal? (State of mind.) To answer a pure question of fact should require no knowledge of the law.

A question of *law* involves determining what legal rule to apply to a given set of facts. Answering it clearly requires a knowledge of the law. A convenient way of formulating a question of law is: "Given this combination of facts, what is the applicable rule?"

How a court answers a question of law is important not only to the parties concerned but to the legal system as a whole, because the court's ruling may become a precedent affecting the decision of similar cases in the future. Answers to questions of fact have no such significance.

All this seems simple and straightforward. Unfortunately, however, some of the questions that arise in cases cannot be classified neatly as pure questions of fact or pure questions of law. Consider, for instance, these questions: "Was DRIVER driving negligently?" "Is HUSBAND still married to WIFE?" "Did BUYER make SELLER a valid offer?"

None of these questions can be characterized as purely factual or purely legal. Each contains both an element of "what happened?" and an element of "what are the rules?" Moreover, the elements must be considered together: To try to isolate out a pure question of fact would simply not be worthwhile, for in each case the factual element is stated in terms of legal concepts. We must know something about the law (of negligence, marriage, and contract) to know what facts matter. When the rule is that "all who drive over 60 m.p.h. are guilty of the offense of speeding," then the question to be answered is one of pure fact: "Was John driving over 60 m.p.h.?" No knowledge of law is needed to answer this. But when the rule is that "all who drive negligently may be liable for the harm they do," the question "Was DRIVER driving negligently?" can be answered only by someone who knows what legal negligence is. Further, we cannot transform this into a pure question of fact by substituting for the

definition of negligence. For instance, we cannot answer the question "Was DRIVER driving with less care than a reasonably prudent person would have shown under the same circumstances?" unless we know how a court goes about measuring DRIVER's conduct against that of "the reasonably prudent person."

Similarly, the question "Are HUSBAND and WIFE still married?" cannot be answered without reference to the legal rules about the formation and dissolution of marriages. Nor can we say whether BUYER made SELLER a valid offer without knowing something about the various combinations of circumstances that the law says may constitute a valid offer, and against which the circumstances of BUYER's proposal must be compared.

In short, the factual and legal elements in these questions are inextricably intertwined. Consequently, writers about the law recognize a class of questions that they call *mixed questions of law and fact.*

You may ask why it matters how a particular question is classified. It matters because questions of fact and questions of law are handled quite differently in the courts. As we shall see in Chapter 3, when a case is tried before a judge and jury, the jury's basic function is to find the facts. Doing so is supposed to require no knowledge of law. The trial judge, on the other hand, rules on the issues of law. Moreover, courts of appeal normally accept the trial jury's findings of fact as conclusive, and they review only the answers that the trial court has given to questions of law. But no special provision is made for mixed questions. Over the years, judges have put some questions that were really "mixed" into the "fact" category and others into the "law" category. Their classification has depended on tradition and on policy judgments (judgments as to what juries and judges do best, for instance) rather than on logic. The question of whether DRIVER was driving negligently is normally treated as a question of fact; in other words, it is answered by a jury whenever a jury is hearing the case. The legal component of the question is dealt with by the judge when explaining to the jurors what the rules of negligence are and then instructing them to apply those rules to the facts they find. The classification of the question of whether BUYER made a valid offer to SELLER may depend on whether the proposal was oral or written. If BUYER simply made an informal oral proposal, the question of whether he intended his words to be a legal offer is usually treated as a question of fact. But if BUYER wrote SELLER a letter, the question of whether he made an offer is much more likely to be treated as a question of law. This difference in the treatment given to oral utterances and to written communications seems to be largely a matter of policy, representing perhaps a decision that jurors are well qualified to decide what a person meant by

spoken words, in light of evidence as to tone and demeanor, whereas judges should be left to interpret the more calculated intent behind a letter.

Defining and Resolving the Issues

Using an actual case for illustration, we shall now trace the steps that make up the process of adjudication.

The official report of this case begins as follows:[7]

George v. *Jordan Marsh Company et al.*

Supreme Judicial Court of Massachusetts, Middlesex
359 Mass. 244, 268 N.E.2d 915

> Argued Nov. 5, 1970. Decided April 12, 1971. . . . Joseph Stashio, Natick, for plaintiff. Joseph P. Warner, Boston, for defendants. Before TAURO, C. J., and SPAULDING, REARDON and QUIRICO, J. J.   <

Irene George, Jr., and Jordan Marsh Company et al. were, of course, the *adversaries*. Irene George, Jr., was the *plaintiff* (the party who sued) in the lower courts of Massachusetts, while Jordan Marsh Company and some of its employees were the *defendants* (the people who were being sued). The plaintiff's name is not always listed first, however. The first name is often that of the person who loses in the trial courts and appeals—the *appellant*. This person may originally have been either the plaintiff or the defendant. The opposing party is called the *appellee*.

The decision here is that of the Supreme Judicial Court of Massachusetts. (Nearly all the decisions you will read in this book are decisions of appellate courts, for reasons that will be explained shortly.) The report of the decision is taken from an official reporter, the report that each state publishes of its supreme court. In addition, these reports are published by West Publishing Co., which has organized its "National Reporter System" by regions. Massachusetts is in the northeastern region.

The remainder of the report consists of the opinion written by Justice Quirico. An *opinion* not only announces the court's decision but presents a justification of it.

---

[7] The symbol > is used to signal the beginning of a case quotation, and the symbol < to signal the end of a case quotation. These symbols also appear at the top of pages that carry continuing case quotations.

> This is an action of tort to recover damages for mental anguish and emotional distress resulting in two heart attacks, all allegedly caused by the defendants in attempting to collect from the plaintiff on a debt incurred by her emancipated son. The counts are identical except for the fact that the first count names Jordan Marsh Company (Jordan Marsh), and each of the second and third counts names an employee of the company, as the defendants. The case is before us on the plaintiff's appeal . . ., from an order of a judge of the Superior Court sustaining the defendants' demurrer to each of the three counts.

We summarize the allegations contained in the three counts of the declaration. Each count alleged that Jordan Marsh sold goods on credit to the plaintiff's emancipated son, and that thereafter each defendant (Jordan Marsh acting through the individual defendants as its agents, servants and employees) did the following: They alleged that the plaintiff had guaranteed in writing to pay her son's debt, and that they knew that she had not given such a guaranty. With the intent to cause the plaintiff emotional distress and in an attempt to intimidate the plaintiff into paying the debt which she did not owe or guarantee, they badgered and harassed her (a) by telephone calls during late evening hours, (b) by repeating mailing bills to her marked "account referred to law and collection department," (c) by letters to her stating that her credit was revoked, that the debt was charged to her personal account, and that late charges were being added to the debt, and (d) by "numerous other dunning tactics." These acts allegedly caused the plaintiff "great mental anguish and emotional distress as intended by the defendant(s)," and as a result her health deteriorated and she suffered a heart attack. The plaintiff's attorney requested that the "harassing tactics be discontinued" because the plaintiff did not owe the debt and because the tactics were adversely affecting her health. The defendants persisted in their "above mentioned harassing tactics," and as a result thereof the plaintiff suffered greater emotional distress resulting in a second heart attack. All of this has allegedly prevented the plaintiff from engaging in gainful employment and she has incurred expenses for medicine, medical attendance and nursing. . . .

. . . The defendants argue that "there is no authority under existing Massachusetts law for the proposition that the intentional infliction of mental or emotional distress provides a separate and distinct basis of tort liability." That is true only because the precise question has never been presented to this court for decision. That argument is therefore no more valid than would be an argument by the plaintiff that there is no record of any Massachusetts law denying recovery on such facts. No litigant is automatically denied relief solely because he presents a question on

which there is no Massachusetts judicial precedent. It would indeed be unfortunate, and perhaps disastrous, if we were required to conclude that at some unknown point in the dim and distant past the law solidified in a manner and to an extent which makes it impossible now to answer a question which had not arisen and been answered prior to that point. The courts must, and do, have the continuing power and competence to answer novel questions of law arising under ever changing conditions of the society which the law is intended to serve.

The defendants also argue that "this Court has heretofore allowed recovery for these items of damages (mental or emotional distress) only in the cases where the defendant has committed an independent and separate tort recognized at common law." This, if true, is basically the same argument, or a subsidiary of the same argument, discussed and disposed of in the preceding paragraph. The right to recover for these items of damages should not be denied just because they do not fit in any of the existing niches in the ancient walls surrounding the law of torts. . . .

Despite the absence of any controlling judicial precedent on this subject in this Commonwealth, there have been many persuasive decisions thereon in other jurisdictions. These decisions, particularly those within the last forty years, show a considerable change by way of a departure from the former position limiting recovery for emotional distress to cases where it resulted from the commission of a recognized common law tort. The development in the law on this subject has been reflected in changing statements in succeeding editions of the Restatement of the Law and in scholarly treatises by recognized authorities on the law of torts. . . . (I)t may be sufficient to give the following summary of the statements illustrating the developments in this field of law.

. . . In 1936 Professor Calvert Magruder (later Judge Magruder), writing on "Mental and Emotional Disturbance in the Law of Torts" in 49 Harv. L. Rev. 1033, said at p. 1067: "No longer is it even approximately true that the law does not pretend to redress mental pain and anguish 'when the unlawful act complained of causes that alone.' If a consistent pattern cannot yet be clearly discerned in the cases, this but indicates that the law on this subject is in a process of growth."

. . . In the 1948 Supplement to the Restatement: Torts, §46 was changed to provide that "one who, without a privilege to do so, intentionally causes severe emotional distress to another is liable (a) for such emotional distress, and (b) for bodily harm resulting from it."

. . . When Restatement 2d: Torts, was published in 1965, § was again revised so that the part applicable to the case before us now reads as follows: "(1) One who by extreme and outrageous conduct intentionally or recklessly causes severe emotional distress to another is subject to lia-

bility for such emotional distress, and if bodily harm to the other results from it, for such bodily harm." ...

Although the change in the law in this area has been extensive in a relatively short span of time, there has never been any holding or even suggestion that the law should permit recovery by every person whose feelings have been hurt even though the hurt be inflicted intentionally. In his 1936 article, Professor Magruder cautioned against opening up "a wide vista of litigation in the field of bad manners, where relatively minor annoyances had better be dealt with by instruments of social control other than the law." He added: "Of course there is danger of getting into the realm of the trivial in this matter of insulting language. No pressing social need requires that every abusive outburst be converted into a tort. . . ." 49 Harv. L. Rev. 1033, 1035, 1053.

It is now obvious that the cautionary comments and limitations suggested by Professor Magruder in 1936 were followed and incorporated in the law as it developed. The rule most recently stated in 1965 in Restatement 2d: Torts, §46, bases liability for emotional distress and any bodily harm resulting therefrom on the concurrence of (a) intentional or reckless conduct which is "*extreme and outrageous*," and (b) resulting "*severe emotional distress*" (emphasis supplied).

The meaning of the words "extreme and outrageous" as used in §46 is discussed in comment of the reporter's notes to the section. It says in part that "(l)iability has been found only where the conduct has been so outrageous in character, and so extreme in degree, as to go beyond all possible bounds of decency, and to be regarded as atrocious, and utterly intolerable in a civilized community." Comment f deals with a defendant's knowledge as bearing on the issue whether his conduct is extreme and outrageous. It says in part: "The extreme and outrageous character of the conduct may arise from the actor's knowledge that the other is peculiarly susceptible to emotional distress, by reason of some physical or mental condition or peculiarity. The conduct may become heartless, flagrant, and outrageous when the actor proceeds in the face of such knowledge, where it would not be so if he did not know." This comment has particular significance in the case before us because of the plaintiff's allegation that the defendants continued their alleged "harassing tactics" after being informed that the plaintiff did not owe the bill in question and that the tactics were affecting her health adversely. Comment j, in discussing the meaning of the words "severe emotional distress," says in part that "(t)he law intervenes only where the distress inflicted is so severe that no reasonable man could be expected to endure it."

... Considering the weight of judicial authority as reflected in the most recent statement of the law in Restatement 2d: Torts, §46, and limiting ourselves to the allegations contained in the declaration before us, we

hold that the law of this Commonwealth should be, and is, that one who, without a privilege to do so, by extreme and outrageous conduct intentionally causes severe emotional distress to another, with bodily harm resulting from such distress, is subject to liability for such emotional distress and bodily harm even though he has committed no heretofore recognized common law tort. Because of the allegations in the declaration before us, we are not required to rule, and do not rule, on the legal sufficiency of allegations of negligent, grossly negligent, wanton or reckless conduct causing severe emotional distress resulting in bodily injury, or on the legal sufficiency of allegations of distress without resulting bodily injury. . . .

. . . Testing the plaintiff's declaration by the rules stated above, we hold that each count thereof states a cause of action and is therefore legally sufficient. The plaintiff is entitled to an opportunity to prove the allegations which she has made. The demurrer should have been overruled. The order sustaining the demurrer is therefore reversed as to each count of the declaration.

So ordered.

COMMENT AND QUESTION
Though you may not understand every word and phrase in this opinion, the question of law facing the court, and the court's answer to that question, should be clear enough. Try to state them in your own words.

The answer to a question of law is sometimes referred to as the *rule of the case*, since it is likely to affect the decision of future cases. As we shall learn in Chapter 4, however, the precise content and breadth of such a "rule" become clear only as later cases arise and the courts decide them.

PRETRIAL EFFORTS TO DEFINE THE ISSUES   The first stage of *George* v. *Jordan Marsh* took place in the trial court. What happened there? The answer to this question is nearly always to be found near the beginning of the appellate-court report. Judge Quirico's opinion tells us that the court sustained "the defendants' demurrer to each of the three counts." The meaning of these words will become clear as we consider the steps in a lawsuit that precede the trial.

When the plaintiff (George) first decided to bring suit, she had her lawyer send the defendant (Jordan Marsh) a legal document known as a *complaint*.[8] This consisted of a brief summary of George's version of what

---

[8] Procedural practices and nomenclature vary somewhat from one jurisdiction to another. The practices described and the terms used here are those encountered in most jurisdictions.

had happened and stated what remedies she was asking. The complaint normally accompanies the summons, which we discussed a few pages back. Once Jordan Marsh had received the summons and the complaint, they were obliged either to make some sort of response or else to lose the suit by default.

A defendant's response to a complaint may take several forms:

1.   *The answer.* If the defendant thinks he can contest the plaintiff's version of the facts, he will send the plaintiff a document known as an *answer.* In his answer he may deny all the plaintiff's important allegations of fact. (For instance, Jordan Marsh might simply have denied that they had harassed Mrs. George at all.) Denying an allegation in the complaint immediately raises an issue of fact; the court will have to decide whose allegation is correct. Alternatively, the defendant may admit some of the plaintiff's allegations but go on to allege additional facts that throw a new light on the situation. (For instance, Jordan Marsh might have admitted that they did call Mrs. George, but then they might have gone on to explain that she asked to be called about bills.)

If the defendant alleges new facts, the plaintiff sometimes responds with a document known as a *reply.* If the reply denies the defendant's allegations, further exchanges, or amendments to the original documents, may be called for.

2.   *The counterclaim.* The defendant may respond to the plaintiff's complaint by entering a *counterclaim;* in other words, he may make a claim of his own for damages against the plaintiff. (For instance, in addition to justifying their calls to Mrs. George, Jordan Marsh might have claimed that one of their collection agents was harassed by her.) A counterclaim may raise issues of fact or issues of law or both.

3.   *The demurrer.* Finally, the defendant's response may say, in effect, "Even if all the plaintiff has alleged were true, it would still not provide the basis for a legal claim." This is what is known as a *demurrer* (or a *motion to dismiss*). A demurrer raises an issue of law.[9]

In the *George* case, the defendant demurred. This action is in no sense an admission that all the charges made against them by the plain-

---

[9] For the sake of completeness, we should note that the plaintiff may demur to the defendant's answer, or a portion of it, and that the defendant may likewise demur to the plaintiff's reply. In each instance the demurrer says, "Even if that were true, you would not have a legally effective claim or defense."

To carry one step further the analogy to syllogistic responding proposed in footnote 6 on page 24, one might say that a demurrer challenges the major premise underlying the opposing party's position, while a denial in an answer or reply challenges the opponent's minor premise.

tiff were true. A demurrer admits allegations only for the purpose of argument. It merely says, "Even if these allegations *were* true, they would not constitute a basis for legal action." (Indeed, if Jordan Marsh's demurrer had been overruled by the trial court, it would at that point have been permitted to present an answer.) If, however, the defendant is confident that the complaint states no basis for legal action, a demurrer is the simplest way to dispose of the whole matter.

The documents exchanged by the plaintiff and the defendant—the plaintiff's complaint; the defendant's answer, demurrer, or counterclaim; and, if necessary, the plaintiff's reply—are known collectively as the *pleadings.* They have three purposes: to narrow the issues to those really in dispute; to let the parties know beforehand what issues they must be prepared to deal with; and to inform the trial judge (who receives copies) what the case is about before the trial begins.

For many years the exchange of pleadings was the only means used to narrow the issues in dispute prior to the trial. Yet the pleadings were often too brief to reveal all the details of the charges and countercharges that the parties intended to make against one another in the trial. Delays were often caused, and injustice sometimes done, when some element of the allegations of fact or of the legal arguments presented by one party caught the other party by surprise during the trial. Today most courts rely on various procedures, known as *discovery procedures,* to eliminate the element of surprise from the trial of a lawsuit. One of these procedures, for instance, calls for the use of *depositions*—sworn statements made by parties or witnesses before a court officer in response to questions put by the attorneys of the opposing parties. Still another procedure for clarifying the issues before the trial is the *pretrial conference,* at which the opposing lawyers review in the judge's presence their legal arguments and the evidence they propose to produce. In many courts this procedure has proved remarkably effective not only in narrowing the issues but in bringing about out-of-court settlements before any trial takes place.

THE TRIAL STAGE[10]   A surprisingly large proportion of the lawsuits initiated actually do get settled out of court. But what does the trial court do with those cases that come to trial?

How a case is handled in the trial court depends in part on whether

---

[10] The actual procedure of the court trial is described in some detail in Chapter 3. This section serves merely to indicate the place of the trial in the whole adjudicative process.

the facts are in dispute. In cases like *George* v. *Jordan Marsh*, where the only issues in dispute are issues of law raised by demurrers and other types of *motions* (for instance, motions challenging the court's jurisdiction), a relatively simple procedure can be used. No jury is needed (since jurors, being lay persons, have nothing to do with interpreting the law), and no witnesses have to be heard. The judge, who has read the lawyers' written arguments about the applicable rules (known as *briefs*), conducts what is often known as a *hearing on motions*, in which he or she listens to oral arguments and sometimes asks questions. At the conclusion, or at a later date if the problem is difficult, the judge hands down a decision either granting or denying the motion. This decision is often accompanied by a short opinion (though these opinions, unlike those of appellate judges, are usually not published). Cases that may be disposed of on the basis of pretrial motions are generally heard and decided expeditiously.

When there are disputed questions of fact in a case, however, a full-dress trial must be held to give the parties a chance to present evidence in support of their respective versions of the facts. Sometimes trials are held before a judge alone, in which event the judge decides both the legal and the factual issues. But cases involving claims for damages must ordinarily be tried before a jury if either party so desires.

As we have mentioned, the jury's task is to "find the facts"—that is, to decide from the evidence presented which party's version of the facts is, on the whole, more convincing. (This is not because jurors are regarded as expert fact-finders; indeed, most jurors have had no previous experience in weighing the conflicting evidence introduced in a trial. Rather, it is because jurors are ordinary citizens who are presumed capable of making common-sense judgments.) In most trials the jury is also responsible for applying the rules, as outlined by the judge, to the facts it has found. (For more on the jury system, see pp. 42–43.)

The judge's task in a trial is to rule on the motions made by the opposing attorneys during the proceedings. Each motion raises an issue of law. An attorney may contend, for instance, that there has been an irregularity in the conduct of the trial; or that a particular item of evidence that the opposing attorney wishes to present should be excluded; or that the judge's instructions to the jury are incorrect; or that since the opposing side has failed to present a case that could conceivably be regarded as convincing, a verdict should be entered for the attorney's client at once. (Each of these motions will be considered further in Chapter 3.)

THE APPELLATE STAGE   Most of the cases that come before a trial court are never appealed. But if one of the parties is dissatisfied with the outcome, he or she has the right to take an appeal within a specified time.

Why is an appeal allowed? There are two reasons. First, since trial judges often have to decide questions of law rapidly and with little time for reflection, they inevitably make mistakes. So it is only fair to give the loser a chance to ask an appellate court, which is under less pressure, to review the rulings of the trial judge. If the appellate court finds an error serious enough so that it may have affected the outcome of the trial, it will reverse the decision of the trial court and send the case back to that court with instructions to take further action in accordance with the appellate decision.

The second reason is that in most jurisdictions there is more than one trial court, and different trial courts faced with cases raising essentially the same question of law may give different answers to that question. This means that the same rules are not being applied throughout the jurisdiction, a situation that is hardly conducive to public confidence. When confusion of this sort arises, an appellate court can produce uniformity by deciding once and for all what the "correct" rule is.

What does the appellate court review? It reviews the trial court's disposition of issues of law, some of which are raised by the types of motions that the lawyers may make before and during the trial.

The appellate court does *not* try to reevaluate the evidence itself. An appellate review is not a new trial. Appellate judges do not sit with juries, nor do they rehear the testimony. All they know about the evidence is what they can read in the transcript of the trial that is submitted to them. Consequently, they are in no position to decide whether the trial court has drawn the right conclusions from the evidence. The only question about the facts that appellate judges feel at liberty to ask themselves is whether there is sufficient evidence in the record to make it possible for a reasonable person to reach the conclusion that the trial jury (or judge) actually reached. Once in a while, it is fairly obvious to an appellate court that a trial court has been wrong in its finding on the facts (perhaps because the jury had a strong prejudice against one of the parties). Reversals on such grounds are rare, however, and appellate courts nearly always accept as conclusive the trial court's finding on the facts.

Each appeal is heard by several appellate judges sitting together. The opposing lawyers submit written briefs spelling out their arguments and then usually supplement these briefs with oral arguments before the court. The judges may, in turn, question the lawyers. The courtroom atmosphere is quite different from that at a trial: With no witnesses and no jurors, it is usually quiet and undramatic. Unlike trial judges, appellate judges are not acting as referees in a close-fought tactical contest; their function is to decide close legal questions in the light of past decisions, scholarly writings, and their own perceptions of the law's ultimate objec-

tives. After they have arrived at a decision, they do what most trial judges have no time to do: They write opinions spelling out at length their reasons for deciding as they have the issues of law brought before them.

Unless the parties in the case can obtain a rehearing, which is rarely granted, they are obliged to accept the appellate decision as the last word. The so-called principle of *res judicata* ("the matter having already been judged") prevents the loser from bringing a new suit against the winner on the same set of facts, either in the same court or in another court. Even if the appellate court later comes to believe that its own decision on the issues in the case was wrong, and, indeed even if it reverses its position on the legal issue involved in the course of deciding a similar case later on, the original decision will not be reviewed or overturned.

Appellate decisions are, of course, important to the parties involved, but they are even more important to the legal system itself. Because these decisions represent the fruits of extensive judicial study and reflection, they assume great authority as declarations of the scope and meaning of legal rules. Their usefulness as precedents is particularly enhanced by the opinions that accompany them, for in these the appellate judges try to explain and justify their decisions to the judges and lawyers who may in the future be confronted with similar cases.[11]

Appendix:
How to Read and Abstract
an Appellate Decision

Why should anyone who is not a lawyer or training to become one read judicial decisions? The lawyer reads them partly to be able to prophesy for a client what the courts are likely to do, and partly to try to influence judges by citing precedents in support of the arguments he or she presents to them. Law-school students, for whom reading cases is both an intellectual exercise and a means of learning about legal rules and the judicial process, spend a great deal of their time in an exhaustive analysis and comparison of decisions involving closely related issues of law. But even for the student who is not studying to become a lawyer, there is no better way of learning about legal rules and the judicial process than by seeing how rules emerge from the decisions of courts in actual cases.

---

[11] Trial-court decisions on legal issues lack the finality of appellate decisions and are only occasionally accompanied by published opinions, so they are seldom cited as precedents. The reputation of the particular trial judge or the cogency of the judge's reasoning may give some of these decisions considerable influence; officially, however, their authority as precedents does not extend beyond the court in which they originate.

(One general observation must be made at the outset. As you read the judicial decisions in this book, you will encounter many unfamiliar words and phrases. Those that are essential to your understanding of the case are explained, either in footnotes or parenthetical insertions or in the text. But the language of judges contains so many technical words that if you tried to understand every one of them before proceeding, the flow of your reading and your understanding of the whole would be needlessly impeded.)

Probably the best way to understand a case is to prepare an *abstract* of it. An abstract of a case is simply a brief summary stating what were the irreducibly essential facts, what happened in the trial court, what was the question of law that the appellate court faced, how it answered that question, and how it justified its answer. If an abstract is well prepared, anyone who reads it should be able to get a clear and accurate idea of what the case was all about without having to refer back to the original report.

There is no one "right" way to abstract a case, but the outline below suggests a useful approach.

Suggested Outline of an Abstract
Title Of Case
Name of appellate court, year of decision

1. *Facts.* What were the events leading up to this lawsuit? Leave out nonessentials. For instance, P and D are usually sufficient designations for Plaintiff and Defendant, and place names can usually be omitted. Be sure, though, that you have included every fact essential to an understanding of the legal problem.

(*Important note:* The facts included in the appellate court's report do not necessarily represent what *really happened*. They are merely the facts that the appellate court has *assumed* to be true. If the appeal is based on the trial judge's ruling on the defendant's demurrer, for instance, then the facts before the appellate court are merely those that the plaintiff *alleged* in his or her complaint, since a demurrer says, in effect, "Even if these alleged facts were true, they would not be a basis for legal action." In disposing of the legal question that a demurrer raises, the trial judge and the appellate court must treat the alleged facts *as if* they were true. Appellate courts also act on the assumption that a jury's findings on the facts are correct, even though the jury might very well have misinterpreted the facts. It makes no difference; though they may not be the true facts, these are the facts on which the appellate court based its decision, and the ones that must be summarized.)

The final sentence in this first section of the abstract should indicate what remedy the plaintiff is seeking. For instance, "P then sued D to recover damages for breach of contract."

2.   *What happened in the courts below this one?* What rulings were made on motions? Was there a jury verdict?

3.   *Question(s) of law raised on appeal.* This is the most difficult and important item in the abstract. Here are some suggestions: (a) Always frame the questions in such a way that they can be answered yes or no. (The appellate court itself must formulate the issues in this way in order to deal with them.) (b) Don't include any questions that the court did not have to answer in order to dispose of the case. (c) Be sure you have not inadvertently included questions about the facts. (d) Don't frame the question too broadly. For instance, "Did P and D make a contract?" usually does not narrow the issue sufficiently. "Did D's letter constitute a valid offer?" would probably be more useful. It is normally best to word the question so that it refers to the parties. "Must a contract be in writing?" is unlikely to be as useful as "Was the agreement between P and D invalid because not in writing?"

4.   *Appellate court's answer to these questions, and its reasons.* Give the court's answer to each question asked. The first word of each answer should be yes or no, followed by a brief summary, in your own words, of the court's reasoning. This paragraph should, in short, contain a statement of the rule of law that emerges from the case.

You may wish to add one more item:

5.   *Personal observations on this decision.* Ask yourself: All things considered, does this decision seem to produce "justice"? Does the court's reasoning seem sound? Does the decision seem to fit in with related rules and decisions with which you are familiar? Does the decision seem likely to provide a useful precedent on which courts faced with similar cases can build, or is it more likely to create difficulties? Is there any reason to believe that factors not revealed in the case report—for instance, the personal beliefs of the judge, or unmentioned economic facts—may provide the best explanation for the decision?

Here is a sample abstract of the decision in *George* v. *Jordan Marsh:*

George v. *Jordan Marsh*

Supreme Judicial Court of Massachusetts, 1971, 359 Mass. 244

1.   *Facts:* Mrs. George claims to have suffered two heart attacks because of defendant's attempts to collect from her a debt incurred by her

son. This is a tort action against Jordan Marsh to recover damages for mental anguish and emotional distress. (Actually, there are three counts: one against Jordan Marsh and two more against employees of the company.)

2. *In court below:* The Superior Court sustained Jordan Marsh's demurrer to each of the three counts, since there was no previous law on this subject in Massachusetts.

3. *Question(s) of law raised on appeal:* Is intentional infliction of emotional or mental distress a separate and distinct basis for tort liability, even though there is no authority under existing Massachusetts law for the proposition?

4. *Resolution:* Yes. No person is automatically denied recovery solely because he or she presents a question on which there is no Massachusetts judicial precedent. Decisions in other jurisdictions show a development in law toward treating the infliction of emotional distress as a distinct basis for liability. The demurrer is therefore reversed as to each count.

Chapter Problem

Roscoe Pound said,

A ... problem is to make adequate provision for petty litigation, to provide for disposing quickly, inexpensively, and justly of the litigation of the poor, for the collection of debts in a shifting population, and for the great volume of small controversies which a busy, crowded population, diversified in race and language, necessarily engenders. It is here that the administration of justice touches the greatest number of people.[12]

One of the ways of handling these claims in our society is through small-claims courts. In an interesting article in the *University of Michigan Journal of Law Reform* Vol. 9, 1975–1976), Alexander Romanakis included a Model Small Claims Court Act, outlined on the next page.

PROBLEM SOURCE: Alexander Romanakis, *University of Michigan Journal of Law Reform*, Vol. 9 (1975–1976), p. 590. © 1976 by the University of Michigan Law School.

[12] "The Administration of Justice in the Modern City," *Harvard Law Review*, Vol. 26 (1913), pp. 302, 315. See also *University of Michigan Journal of Law Reform*, Vol. 9, p. 590.

MODEL SMALL CLAIMS COURT ACT

Section 1 *Small claims division; judges*

A small claims division is established in each (district) as a division of the (district court). Judges of the (district court) are the judges of the small claims division.

Section 2 *Jurisdiction*

The jurisdiction of the small claims court shall extend to all civil actions, other than actions for injunctive relief, brought by any person(, association, corporation, or other legal entity) where the amount involved, exclusive of costs does not exceed ($500–$1,000). . . .

Section 5 *Pleadings; service of process*

a. No formal pleadings shall be necessary. A claimant must prepare a complaint which adequately informs the defendant of the nature of the claim.

b. Service of the complaint upon the defendant shall be by registered or certified mail with return receipt requested from the addressee. If return receipt shows that there has not been effective service, the court may direct that service on the defendant be completed by personal service. . . .

Section 7 *Time for appearance; order for plaintiff to appear*

The date for the appearance of the defendant shall not be more than 30 days or less than 10 days from the date of filing. If the complaint is not served upon the defendant at least 5 days prior to the appearance date, the clerk shall set a new date for the appearance of the defendant which shall be not more than 30 days or less than 10 days from the date of the issuance of the new notice and the clerk shall inform both parties thereof. When the date for appearance is fixed, the plaintiff shall be informed of said date and ordered to appear.

Section 8 *Fees*

Fees shall be levied for filing and service of process. (The fees charged will be the same as those in the district court.) The judge may waive prepayment or payment of fees upon the plaintiff's sworn statement or evidence of the inability to pay fees.

Section 9 *No trial by jury*

There shall be no trial by jury in the small claims division. Trial by jury may be had on appeal.

Section 10 *No attorney to take part*

No attorney at law or other person than the plaintiff and defendant shall take any part in the prosecution or defense of litigation in the small claims division. Either party may present witnesses at any small claims proceeding.

Questions

1. How does this model compare to your area's technique for handling small claims?

2. Is there any reporter system in your area that indexes small-claims reports?

3. What is the jurisdiction of the small-claims court of your area?

4. Can one appeal the decision of your area's small-claims court? If so, to which court?

Questions for Review

1. What is the difference between civil and criminal law?

2. What type of courts exist, and what type of cases does each handle?

3. Describe and diagram the court system of your state. Also diagram the federal court system.

4. Why do we define the boundaries of courts' authority to hear and decide cases? What are some of these boundaries?

5. What is the difference between an issue of fact and an issue of law?

6. In the United States, we have a dual system of courts, that is, courts at both the state and federal levels. Is this system a necessary condition for the efficient administration of justice? Describe some pros and cons of the dual system.

7. What are the pretrial pleadings, and what is their purpose?

8. Why do we need appellate courts? Why not let trial courts act as the court of last resort?

9. Assume that a party loses a case based on some principle of law that is later changed. May the decision then be appealed?

3

The
Trial
Stage

In the last chapter we reviewed the whole adjudicative process, starting with the exchange of pleadings and ending with the disposition of the final appeal. In this chapter we shall focus on the trial, which, from the viewpoint of the litigants, is by far the most important stage in the adjudicative process.

The first part of the chapter consists of a step-by-step description of a civil trial before a jury.[1] The second part consists of a critical appraisal of some problem areas in the trial process.

Trial Procedure in a Civil Case Before a Jury

The following is a generalized description of the sequence of events in a trial, from the selection of the jury to the recording of a judgment. It is generalized because there are many variations in the details of procedure from one court to another.

---

[1] Many civil cases are tried without a jury—for instance, cases that involve the rules of equity (see pages 72–73), and any case in which the parties have agreed to waive their right to a jury trial. But a trial without a jury is not sufficiently different from a jury trial to warrant a separate description. The principal difference is that in a trial without a jury, the judge is both the formulator of the legal rules (including the rules of trial procedure) and the finder of the facts.

The Jury Is Selected

As you will remember from Chapter 2, every trial court serves a judicial district. (The district of a state trial court is often a county; a federal district court may serve an entire state.) Officials in each district maintain a list of residents who are available for jury duty. Periodically, the names of enough jurors to meet the trial court's needs for its current session are chosen by lot from this list, and the prospective jurors are then summoned to the courthouse. Some of them may be excused if they have a good reason, but the rest must report to the courthouse every day for several weeks, standing ready to serve if they are assigned to a case.

When the case is ready for trial, twelve of the prospective jurors are chosen by lot to fill the jury box.[2] They are then questioned—collectively or individually, by the judge or by the lawyers, according to the local practice—on whether they have any connection with any of the participants in the trial (parties, lawyers, or witnesses) or any biases on the issues involved. (For instance, in an accident case the prospective jurors may be asked whether they have ever been involved in an accident suit.)

The lawyers may demand the exclusion of any prospective juror for a specified cause. They may also make a limited number of *peremptory challenges,* exclusions made without giving any reason. This privilege enables a lawyer to exclude jurors who, he feels intuitively, may be unfriendly to his client's cause. For example, he may have a hunch that farmers, or plumbers, would be hostile to his client, and therefore challenge any prospective jurors in these categories. The rejected jurors go back to the jury room to await assignment to other cases. Their places are taken by other prospective jurors, chosen by lot, who are also questioned. In a case that has aroused strong public interest or emotions, selecting a jury may take days or even weeks. Lawyers may even call upon experts from other disciplines (such as psychologists) to help them decide upon the best jurors.

The Plaintiff's Case Is Presented

The lawyer representing the plaintiff[3] now makes her opening statement to the court. She outlines the version of the facts that she expects to prove and makes clear what she is asking the court to do for her client. Next

---

[2] Often as many as fourteen are chosen; two of these are alternate jurors who hear the whole case and are available to replace jurors who become incapacitated during the trial.

[3] Hereafter, we shall use P in referring to the plaintiff's lawyer, and D in referring to the defendant's lawyer.

she presents her evidence in whatever order she thinks best. She calls each of her witnesses to the stand and subjects them to "direct examination," phrasing questions in a way that will elicit answers favorable to her client's case. (She will almost certainly have interviewed these witnesses beforehand in an effort to prepare them for the witness stand, but efforts to have witnesses "memorize their lines" usually backfire.) D has the right to object to any of P's questions, or to any answer from P's witnesses, on the ground that the question or answer is improper under the rules of evidence; the judge must either accept or reject D's objections.

When P has finished her direct examination of each witness, D may, if he wishes, "cross-examine" the witness. D may try to bring out facts that P has preferred not to touch upon, or he may try to cast doubt on testimony by revealing the witness to be confused, forgetful, misled, self-contradictory, deliberately untruthful—or, if worst comes to worst, simply ridiculous. Cross-examination at its best is a high art.

After D's cross-examination of each witness, P has another chance to question the witness. This "redirect examination" gives P an opportunity to try to repair any weakening of the witness's original testimony caused by the cross-examination.

When P is finished presenting her evidence, she "rests her case." At this point, D is likely to move that P's suit be thrown out, on the grounds that even if all P's evidence were true and even if it were interpreted as favorably to P's position as possible, P has still failed to prove her case. (This is known as a motion for a "directed verdict" or for a "nonsuit.") If the judge accepts D's contention, P's suit is thrown out and the trial is over. Of course, P probably would not have brought her suit to court in the first place unless she had some basis for believing that she could establish the elements of a case; hence, the chances are that D's motion will be denied. But occasionally a plaintiff's witnesses fail to give the testimony expected, or else their testimony is completely discredited on cross-examination. Then the plaintiff's case may simply collapse, and D's motion may be granted. If, however, it it denied, the trial continues.

The Rules of Evidence

Before we go on with our trial, let us look for a moment at the rules that govern the admissibility of evidence.

Why are there restraints placed on what lawyers may introduce in evidence and on what witnesses may say? Would it not be better to let the judge and jury "get the whole story," including every bit of evidence that any participant might possibly consider relevant?

The answer is clear: First, such a procedure could mean that the trial

of even a fairly simple case might drag on for weeks. And second, no "finder of fact"—least of all a jury—should have to extract the truth from the tangle of irrelevant, misleading, and unreliable evidence that such a freewheeling procedure would produce.

Our rules of evidence have been largely shaped with the jury in mind. Most jurors have little experience in analyzing evidence objectively, and many of them have prejudices that are not easy to suppress. They are apt to become confused, forgetful, and, in a long trial, bored and inattentive. The rules of evidence are designed to keep the jury from hearing items of evidence that are (a) irrelevant and immaterial to the questions of fact at issue, (b) repetitious of evidence already admitted, (c) of a sort shown by experience to be of dubious reliability, (d) not readily testable by cross-examination, and (e) in violation of certain confidential relationships.

The rules of evidence have been developed piecemeal over the years, mostly by judges faced with novel problems of proof. They are numerous and complex, and we shall do no more than touch on a few of them to give some idea of their purpose and operation.

Suppose that BUMPED is suing TRUCKER (a small furniture-moving company) for damage resulting from an accident in which BUMPER, a truckdriver employed by TRUCKER, collided with BUMPED's automobile. BUMPED's lawyer starts to introduce evidence designed to show that BUMPER was involved in another accident three years before, and TRUCKER's lawyer immediately objects to the evidence. The question that the judge must decide is whether a showing that BUMPER had an earlier accident would increase the probability that he is at fault in the accident with BUMPED, thus justifying admission of the evidence. Most courts have answered no to this question, holding that the evidence is not really relevant and that there is a risk that some jurors will jump to the unwarranted conclusion that a driver with one past accident must be "accident-prone" and therefore at fault in the present case. So the judge will probably rule that BUMPED's lawyer may not present this evidence.

May BUMPED's lawyer mention before the jury that TRUCKER carries liability insurance? Carrying insurance makes TRUCKER neither more nor less responsible for the accident, but knowledge of that fact might lead some jurors to favor passing the repair bills along to the rich insurance company, regardless of who was at fault. So the evidence is excluded. (Plaintiffs' lawyers have, however, discovered various ways of hinting to the jury that the defendant is insured.)

Should the court admit testimony from a seven-year-old boy about what he saw of the accident? The answer used to be no, but in many courts now the judge will admit the testimony if he has satisfied himself,

by questioning the boy outside the courtroom, that the boy is a competent witness: that he has the ability to observe, recollect, and communicate, and that he understands the importance of telling the truth.

Should a witness be allowed to express her opinion about whether BUMPER was driving carelessly when the accident occurred? Probably not. Unless a witness is an acknowledged expert on some subject that demands expertise, the court wants to hear only her factual observations, and not the inferences she has drawn from those observations. The task of drawing inferences, and of forming opinions, is for the jury.

How about the testimony of someone who did not see the accident himself but who was told about it by an eyewitness? If the eyewitness is not available to testify, should the court hear his account at second hand? Such "hearsay" is normally excluded, because the eyewitness, whose perception of the accident is what really matters, cannot be put under oath or subjected to the acid test of cross-examination. (The reliability of the eyewitness's perception of the event cannot be tested by cross-examining the person to whom he described it.) Since a great deal of valuable evidence would be lost if the courts excluded all hearsay, however, numerous exceptions to this exclusionary rule have been made to cover particular situations in which the hearsay evidence is likely to be trustworthy.

Finally, suppose that BUMPED's lawyer has reason to believe that BUMPER told his physician shortly after the accident that he had had one of his dizzy spells at the moment the accident occurred. May the lawyer insist that BUMPER's doctor take the stand and reveal what BUMPER told her? No, unless BUMPER consents. Confidential communications of patient to doctor, client to lawyer, confessant to confessor, and spouse to spouse, and in a few other relationships, are "privileged"; the person to whom the communication was made cannot be compelled to testify as to its contents if the communicator raises an objection.

The Defendant's Case Is Presented

Now to return to our trial. P has rested her case, and D now makes his opening statement, outlining what he intends to prove. He then presents his evidence. D may concentrate on rebutting the implications of P's evidence, or he may introduce new facts that alter the legal significance of what P has proved. In BUMPED's suit against TRUCKER, for instance, TRUCKER's lawyer may try to show that BUMPER was *not* driving negligently; or that even if he was, his negligent driving did not cause the accident; or that BUMPED was also negligent (since "contributory negligence" by the plaintiff will usually prevent his recovering damages). The

examination of D's witnesses follows the usual sequence: Direct examination by D, cross-examination by P, and redirect examination by D if desired.

The Plaintiff's Rebuttal
Is Presented

After D has rested his case, P is permitted to introduce further evidence in order to rebut D's evidence.

At this point, D may once again move for a directed verdict; that is, he may ask that P's suit be thrown out on the ground that P has failed to establish a case that the jury could decide otherwise than for the defendant. P may make a similar motion, contending that she has so clearly established her client's right to a judgment that no jury could reasonably decide otherwise. Once in a great while the judge will grant one of these motions, thus taking the case away from the jury. But even if the judge himself thinks that P has failed to prove her case or D his defense, he will often let the case go to the jury.

The Lawyers Make
Their Closing Statements

The lawyers (usually D first and then P) now sum up. Each reviews the evidence, stressing the strong points of his own case and the weaknesses of his adversary's case. These closing statements can be extremely important, for they may be what the jurors remember best when they retire to decide on a verdict.

The Judge Instructs the Jury

The judge's most important moment in the trial comes when he instructs the jury. He usually starts by spelling out the questions of fact that the jury must answer on the basis of the evidence presented. In the federal courts and the courts of some states, the judge may give the jury his own evaluation of the various items of evidence, but in most state trial courts the judge is not permitted to do this.

Ordinarily, the jury is instructed to decide what the facts are, to apply the rules to those facts, and to come up with a "general verdict"— that is, a decision in favor of one party or the other. If it decides for the plaintiff, its verdict will include an award of damages in a specified amount. In order for the jury to arrive at a general verdict, the judge must, of course, first explain the rules that would apply to alternative

findings of fact. In our auto accident case, for instance, he would have to explain to the jury what is meant by negligence, what would be the consequence of a finding of contributory negligence, and (in case the jury finds for the plaintiff) how damages are measured under the law.[4]

After the judge has given his instructions, the lawyers may challenge their correctness or may ask him to give the jury certain additional instructions. The judge then has to decide whether these proposed instructions correctly state the law and whether a useful purpose will be served in repeating them to the jury.

The Jury Deliberates and Brings in a Verdict

The jurors' deliberations in the jury room are secret. There is no officially sanctioned way of finding out, during or after the trial, how they went about performing their task. This means, of course, that jurors may willfully ignore the judge's instructions; they may even decide the case by flipping a coin. (All evidence indicates, however, that most juries are conscientious and do the best job they can.)

The judge has told the jury that under the law of the jurisdiction all twelve jurors, or some majority of them, must agree on the verdict. He has urged them to make every effort to reach agreement. But sometimes the jurors are unable to agree, even after many hours of deliberation. Then a jury is said to be "hung." A mistrial is declared and the whole case must be tried again.

If the jurors reach a verdict, they return to the courtroom and report their decision. At this point the loser may move that the court award him a "judgment notwithstanding the verdict" (on the ground that no *reasonable* jury could have decided as this jury did), or that a new trial be granted because of some alleged irregularity in the trial just completed or because the verdict is "contrary to the manifest weight of the evidence." And if the plaintiff has won a verdict for damages, the alleged excessive-

---

4 Under certain circumstances, the judge instructs the jury to bring in a set of answers to the questions of fact that he formulates for them. This is known as a *special verdict*. The judge himself then applies the rules to the facts found and assesses the damages.

In a trial without a jury, there is, of course, no need for instructions. But if the judge prepares a formal opinion, it usually contains a separate statement of his "Findings of Fact" and of his "Conclusions of Law." This facilitates the task of the appellate court, which normally accepts his findings on the facts but must review his conclusions concerning the proper rules to apply.

ness or insufficiency of the amount awarded may warrant a motion for a new trial.

A Judgment Is Entered
on the Record

Unless the judge grants a motion for a new trial, he now orders that a *judgment* be entered on the record. In most cases this judgment is, in effect, a formal confirmation and recording of the jury's verdict.

A dissatisfied party has a certain number of days in which to appeal. If no appeal is taken, or if the appellate court affirms the trial court's judgment, that judgment stands on the record as the final disposition of the case. Under the rule of *res judicata* (see page 36), the matter may not be brought again before any court.

The Judgment Is Executed

Winning a judgment for damages is not always the end of the road for the plaintiff. If the defendant does not pay up voluntarily, the plaintiff must go to the sheriff to get her judgment "executed." The sheriff has no power to act against the defendant's person to enforce an award of damages; in order to satisfy the judgment he must seize some of the defendant's property, if any can be found within the jurisdiction. As a result, valid judgments often prove impossible to execute. However, a judgment does remain on the record and may provide the basis for a later suit in another court.

If instead of a judgment for money damages, the plaintiff has won an equity judgment—if the judge had granted her an injunction, for instance—she would probably have much less difficulty in enforcing it. Equity judgments (or *decrees,* as they are usually called) are addressed to the defendant personally; they order him to do something, or to stop doing something. If he fails to comply with such an order, he may be held in "contempt of court" and have to pay a fine or even go to prison.

The Adversary System

At the heart of the adjudicative process are two basic principles. The first is the belief that both sides to a controversy must have a chance to be heard—that each party must have "his day in court." Closely related to this is a second belief: that the best way to find the truth and "do justice"

in a case is to make the parties themselves responsible for most of what happens at the trial. In U.S. trials, the judge is little more than a referee throughout most of the proceedings, while the jury merely observes and listens. The parties (acting through their lawyers) must plan and execute their own strategies, must find and present their own evidence and arguments. We call this the *adversary system.*

What are the practical implications of this system?

1.   The facts on which a trial court bases its decision are those that the parties assert and substantiate with evidence. Important witnesses may go unheard and important items of evidence remain unrevealed simply because the parties did not discover them or chose not to introduce them. Moreover, the evidence that is presented may fail to influence the outcome, even though it is important, simply because it is ineptly presented. The court, in short, does not really base its decision on "all the true and relevant facts," but merely on those facts discovered and effectively presented to it.

Although we tend to take the concept of the party presentation of evidence for granted, there are alternative methods. For instance, the court could have a staff of its own investigate the facts and report its findings to the judge. And the judge and jurors could take a much more active part in initiating inquiries and in asking questions of the witnesses. But underlying our adversary system is a conviction that the court is more likely to learn all the facts it needs to know and to make a balanced appraisal of them if the initiative for producing them is left with the adversaries.

2.   It is up to the parties' lawyers to object whenever they believe that an irregularity in the proceedings has occurred or is about to occur. Suppose one party tries to introduce evidence that falls into one of the categories of evidence considered inadmissable under the exclusionary rules of evidence (see pages 44–46). Although the judge would readily exclude such evidence if the other party objected to it, ordinarily she will not exclude it if no objection is made. Moreover, a lawyer who fails to object at the time the evidence is introduced, loses the right to object to it later in appealing an unfavorable decision.

3.   Although many trial judges have had years of experience in evaluating evidence, a majority of U.S. courts do not allow a judge to comment on the evidence when she makes her charge to the jury. Even in those jurisdictions in which judges may comment on the evidence, their discretion in doing so is more restricted than in the courts of many other countries.

4.   In deciding what rules of law apply to a particular case, the

trial judges rely heavily on the briefs and oral arguments of the lawyers. Ordinarily trial judges simply do not have time to search out, on their own, past decisions, statutes, or relevant passages in scholarly treatises; they are obliged to rely on the citations brought to their attention by the lawyers. (Although they are less pressed, appellate judges also tend to choose from among the arguments made and the precedents cited by the lawyers.)

The Trial Process:
Some Problem Areas

A major theme of this book is that a litigant often cannot be sure what rules of law govern her case until an appellate court has finally decided it. But we shall have little to say hereafter about another form of uncertainty that is just as unsettling for the litigant: Can she actually prove her version of the facts in the trial court?

Critics of U.S. trials and trial courts claim that the hazards of litigation are greater than they need be. They complain that the adversary system puts the trial lawyer under too great a temptation to mislead the court, that juries of untrained citizens are too easily misled, that our methods of recruiting judges too often discourage the best candidates, and that the delays in securing justice in many of our trial courts constitute a denial of justice.

Let us consider briefly each of these problem areas in the administration of justice in the United States.

The Role of the Lawyer

As we suggested in the preceding section, under the adversary system every trial is a contest. The contestants are the lawyers—experts in the art of *advocacy* (that is, in preparing and presenting evidence and arguments). The rules of the game are enforced by a referee—the judge. The jury (or the judge when there is no jury) decides who wins.

The lawyer's role is thus of crucial importance. The French novelist Balzac once described the jury as "twelve men chosen to decide who has the better lawyer." And it is true that the performance of a skilled lawyer often has a greater effect on the jury than the testimony of witnesses or even the instructions of the judge.

Behind the adversary system is a presupposition that each lawyer will do his or her best to win. The expectation is usually justified. But not all lawyers are equally skillful, and the party with the stronger case, with

"justice" on his side, does not necessarily have the better lawyer. Litigants with strong cases have lost because their lawyers were inept; apparently hopeless causes have been saved by brilliant advocacy.

There is no obvious way to eliminate this distortion from the administration of justice. Some critics have suggested that the advantage enjoyed by a superior lawyer could be offset by assigning a more active role to the judge, allowing her more freedom to put questions to the witnesses and to comment critically to the jury on the evidence.[5]

In the case that follows, the Supreme Court of Colorado concluded that the plaintiff's attorney had failed to provide adequate representation for his client. They went on to say that incompetence or neglect of counsel will, under some circumstances, entitle the litigant to a new trial. Few would argue that this plaintiff was entitled to a new trial, but where would you draw the line between incompetence and "less skill"?

Garrett v. Osborn

[John M. GARRETT, Plaintiff in Error, v. William S. OSBORN, Mrs. Carl R. Osborn, and O. G. Cattle Co., a partnership in which John M. Garrett, William S. Osborn, and Mrs. Carl R. Osborn do business as co-partners, Defendants in Error.]

Supreme Court of Colorado, 1967
431 P.2d 1012
> Calkins, Kramer, Grimshaw and Carpenter, Richard L. Harring, Denver, for plaintiff in error.
 Young & Young, Colorado Springs, for defendants in error.
 MOORE, Chief Justice.

Plaintiff in error Garrett was the plaintiff in the trial court, and the defendants in error occupy the same relative position they now have in this court. The trial was to the court without a jury.

Garrett sought to recover a balance of $37,000 he claimed to be due

---

[5] What we say in this section about the role of lawyers in the trial court obviously has some application to their role in the appellate court. But appellate judges, free from the tensions and time pressures of the trial court, are better able than trial judges to prevent the unequal abilities of the two lawyers from distorting the outcome. Appellate judges also have the time to do their own research if they wish, which makes such tactics as misinterpretation or suppression of precedents less rewarding for the unethical lawyer.

from the total of $72,000 he had advanced and paid to the individuals, the corporation, and the co-partnership named as defendants. . . .

After a two-day trial involving the introduction into evidence of approximately one hundred group and individual exhibits; hearing extended evidence by the defendants; and considering the brief filed by counsel for defendants; the court below decided the case (for the defendants). . . .

Plaintiff through his present counsel, who did not participate in the trial, filed and argued a motion for a new trial, one of the grounds of which was that plaintiff was denied a fair trial by reason of inadequacy of legal representation. The motion was denied and final judgment entered. This writ of error challenges the judgment of the trial court by four assignments of error, one of which was the above stated lack of adequate representation.

In the judgment complained of in this writ of error, the trial court entered findings which included the following:

"2.   The Court has had no assistance from counsel for the plaintiff in this case. At no time during the trial nor at the pre-trial conference or the other hearings has counsel offered any argument or discussion of the issues. Quite obviously, whatever the reason, plaintiff has not been adequately represented in this litigation.

"3.   Trial was held on June 18th and 19th, 1964, and respective counsel were granted time to file briefs. Counsel for defendants have done so. Plaintiff's counsel, although the time for his brief has expired, has filed none. He has excused his failure to offer discussion or argument or even statement of the issues, by the non-cooperation of his client. However that may be, it does not maintain as to his failure to file brief."

. . . Examination of the full record shows conclusively that the lawyer purporting to represent Garrett utterly failed to adequately represent his interest in the controversy, and the above quoted findings of the trial court were overwhelmingly supported by the record. The shortcomings in the conduct of counsel for Garrett are so flagrant and so numerous that a fair trial of the case was denied his client. When lack of adequate representation was made a ground for granting a motion for a new trial, and the court found as a fact that Garrett's case was not adequately presented, a new trial should have been granted.

. . . There can be no doubt that the substantive rights of Garrett were adversely affected by the palpable malfeasance, misfeasance and nonfeasance of his counsel. We take judicial notice of the fact that for reasons other than conduct involved in this case, Garrett's trial attorney has been

disbarred. The common law recognized that incompetence or neglect of counsel, under some circumstances, will entitle a litigant to a new trial. . . .

The judgment is reversed and the cause remanded for a new trial. $<$

The adversary system raises another problem: It subjects lawyers to conflicting loyalties. On the one hand they are expected to fight to win. In presenting a client's case, a lawyer must be one-sided and partisan, not neutral and objective. Not only is this the presupposition behind the system, it is also what the client who pays a lawyer expects her to do. And lawyers, being human, want to win. They know that their reputation and future income depend on victories.[6]

On the other hand, lawyers can never forget that they are participating in a process that has as its object the doing of justice. Lawyers are often described as "officers of the court," a reflection of the degree to which the court must depend on them. And yet some of the steps they may take in order to win may defeat the law's objective of arriving at a just decision.

A body of rules and principles has been developed to help lawyers reconcile these conflicting pressures. Some are official rules, enforceable with the aid of such sanctions as judicial reprimand, forfeiture of the lawyer's case, fine or imprisonment for contempt of court, and suspension or revocation of the lawyer's license to practice. (The latter penalty is known as *disbarment*.) But some of the most important rules are nonofficial and only persuasive in their force. Most of these latter rules, called canons, are embodied in "The Code of Professional Responsibility and Code of Judicial Conduct" of the American Bar Association.[7]

The canons are couched in general terms. Their tone and spirit are illustrated by the following excerpts, which have to do with the conflicting loyalties just discussed.

> Canon 7. *A lawyer should represent a client zealously and within the bounds of the law.*
>
> 7-3 Where the bounds of the law are uncertain, the action of a lawyer may depend on whether he is serving as advocate or ad-

---

6 This is most nakedly evident when lawyers take cases on a "contingency" basis: They will be paid an agreed percentage of any damages they win—and nothing if they lose.

7 The original thirty-two canons were adopted by the American Bar Association in 1908. They have been taken over in their entirety or in substance by most of the state bar associations and have even been enacted into law in several states. Since 1908 the canons have been significantly revised and enlarged.

viser. A lawyer may serve simultaneously as both advocate and adviser, but the two roles are essentially different. In asserting a position on behalf of his client, an advocate for the most part deals with past conduct and must take the facts as he finds them. By contrast, a lawyer serving as adviser primarily assists his client in determining the course of future conduct and relationships. While serving as advocate, a lawyer should resolve in favor of his client's doubts as to the bounds of the law. In serving a client as adviser, a lawyer in appropriate circumstances should give his professional opinion as to what the ultimate decisions of the courts would likely be as to the applicable law.

7–27 Because it interferes with the proper administration of justice, a lawyer should not suppress evidence that he or his client has a legal obligation to reveal or produce. In like manner, a lawyer should not advise or cause a person to secrete himself or to leave the jurisdiction of a tribunal for the purpose of making him unavailable as a witness therein.

The Role of the Jury

We would have far less cause to worry about the courtroom tactics of lawyers if the finders of fact in most civil cases were trained judges, rather than untrained, easily misled jurors. U.S. courts try a much higher proportion of cases before juries than do the courts of any other country. Most countries that use juries limit their use to major criminal cases. Only the United States uses them extensively in civil cases.

Even in this country, as we have seen, not all civil cases go before juries: Most minor-court trials and most equity cases are heard by a judge alone. But either party in an ordinary suit for damages normally has a right to insist on a jury trial. For the federal courts, this right is protected by the Constitution of the United States, and some form of jury-trial right is guaranteed, constitutionally or by statute, in all the states.[8]

The reasons for this loyalty to the jury system are primarily historical. The right to a trial "by a jury of one's peers"—particularly in criminal cases—was one of the hard-won victories of the long struggle against abuses of power by the monarchs of England. On a number of notable occasions in the colonial period, juries stood up to oppressive royal judges. When our early constitutions were framed, therefore, the right to

---

[8] The U.S. Constitution, Seventh Amendment, provides: "In suits at common law [see page 72, footnote 1], where the value in controversy shall exceed twenty dollars, the right of trial by jury shall be preserved. . . ." The Constitution of Pennsylvania, Article I, Section 6, says simply: "Trial by jury shall be as heretofore, and the right thereof remain inviolate."

trial by jury was considered extremely important. In the nineteenth century, during the Jacksonian era and again later in the century, public confidence in the jury was further strengthened by the concept of "popular sovereignty," which stressed popular participation in government and discounted the importance of training and expertise (such as that possessed by judges) in government service.

The average American probably continues to think favorably of trial by jury. But among students of our legal system, the institution has been a subject of controversy for years. Here are some of the criticisms often made of it, and some answers to those criticisms:

1.   Most jurors, say the critics, are not trained to draw objective conclusions from a body of factual evidence. They are all too often at the mercy of their emotions and prejudices. Except in very short trials, they tend to become confused, bored, inattentive, and forgetful. Eager to finish the job, they are often willing to abandon personal convictions, or even to resort to the toss of a coin, in order to reach agreement. These well-known frailties encourage the lawyer to "put on a show" for the jury—to appeal to their emotions and biases—instead of presenting the case in an orderly, logical manner as he or she would if a judge were trying it. Finally, if the plaintiff's lawyer (in an accident case, for instance) can win the jury's sympathy, the jury is likely to grant inordinately generous damages.

The defenders of the jury insist that these allegations are greatly exaggerated, and that most juries are conscientious, serious, sensible, and sometimes even rather stingy in their awards. They point to the testimony of a number of trial judges who have written about the high proportion of cases in which jury awards have been very close to what the judges would have awarded had they been sitting alone.

2.   Jurors, the critics go on, are particularly ill-qualified to "apply the law to the facts." To be sure, this is not necessarily their fault. The judge is supposed to explain the relevant rules in language jurors can understand. But judges learn from bitter experience that appellate courts scrutinize their instructions to make sure that they have stated the law correctly, and they know that if they make any significant error the appellate courts will reverse their judgments. Faced with the choice of either addressing the jury in simple, everyday language or of being impeccably correct in technical language, many judges play it safe and use well-worn verbal formulas that they know will be acceptable to the appellate court—even though by so doing they may make their instructions virtually incomprehensible to the jurors.

Once again the defenders of the jury system charge exaggeration. In

the great majority of cases—and notably in the personal-injury cases that take up so much of the time of our trial courts—the real controversy is over the facts; the rules are simple, and jurors ordinarily have no trouble understanding them.

The defenders admit, however, that in the more complex cases involving business arrangements and transactions, trial by jury does not always work particularly well. In these cases, in fact, more and more litigants are waiving their right to a jury trial.

The jury's defenders may even concede to the critics that our courts should make greater use of the "special" rather than the "general" verdict (pages 47–48). When a judge asks the jury for a special verdict, he requires it to give yes-or-no answers to the questions of fact he has formulated. Then he applies the law to the jury's answers. The jury does not need to understand the rules of law that the judge will apply to its findings of fact.

3. Even when jurors understand the rules that the judge explains, retort the critics, they sometimes choose to ignore them. Take the "contributory-negligence" rule, for example. Some states still adhere to the common-law rule that contributory negligence prevents the plaintiff from recovering any damages. In an auto accident suit, for instance, even though the defendant was obviously driving carelessly, the plaintiff will not be awarded damages if she is shown to have been in the least bit careless herself. Where the defendant was driving very carelessly and the plaintiff was only a little bit careless, applying the rule is apt to seem grossly unfair, and in many verdicts it is clear that the jury has chosen to ignore it. This is easy to do when only a general verdict is required; the jurors have only to announce to the court that they find for the plaintiff and award her so much in damages. They are not required to specify—as they would in a special verdict—that they found the plaintiff to have been wholly without negligence. In effect, the jurors are thus able to defy the judge.[9]

The defenders of the jury contend that the jury's power to alter the law in particular cases is a *virtue* of the system. The jury, they say, blunts the law's sharp edges and brings to the trial process the average person's sympathy with human frailty and sense of what is "reasonable" conduct. Judges are trained professionals, in the upper-income brackets, and are

---

[9] If the judge were sure that the jury had disobeyed her instruction, she could overturn the verdict. But proof of defiance is rarely available, and most judges are reluctant to overturn jury verdicts on the ground that they are contrary to the evidence. Furthermore, it seems probable that judges often tacitly approve of the jury's refusal to apply the contributory-negligence rule.

likely to be somewhat insulated from the harsher realities of life; hence they are usually less qualified than the jurors to apply the community's standards of what is justifiable. Moreover, there are twelve jurors to one judge: When the task is to appraise the credibility of evidence and apply vague standards, such as the "reasonable-care" standard of negligence law, the consensus of twelve persons of diverse origins and temperaments may be more valid than the decision of one person.

The judge, the defenders point out, cannot make exceptions to the rule in the "hard" cases, because her interpretations of the law create precedents. Juries can make exceptions by interpreting the facts in order to reach the desired result, because their verdicts do *not* create precedents.

The critics of the jury system concede some merit to this argument, but they point out that it raises serious questions: Can juries always be counted on to bend the law in the right direction? Are they not capable of being shortsighted, irrational, and even vindictive? And what happens to the goals of predictability and "equality before the law" if different juries apply a rule differently in similar cases? Finally, when a rule is really unsatisfactory, isn't public pressure on the legislature (rather than a jury's defiance of the judge's instructions) the proper way to get it changed?[10]

4. The critics argue that jury trials take too long and cost too much. As we shall see later in this chapter, the long delays in obtaining justice pose a serious problem, particularly in metropolitan areas. And it is true that trials before a jury take longer than trials held before a judge alone. No time is wasted in selecting the jury and instructing it, and presenting the facts to a trained judge normally takes considerably less time than presenting them to a jury. In short, reducing the proportion of jury trials would save time and would help eliminate the delays that now plague the administration of justice. It would also lower the costs of litigation (for the state as well as for the litigant, who pays "court costs" covering part of the actual costs), both because each trial would take less time and because jurors' fees would be eliminated.

The defenders of the jury reply, first, that if the jury system has other virtues, as they contend, the extra time and money it entails are worth putting up with. They also remind us that pairs of litigants who wish to have their case tried more speedily and at less cost may waive their right to a jury trial.

---

10 It is interesting to note that, perhaps partly because of juries' widespread defiance of instructions, many state legislatures have substituted a rule of "comparative negligence" for the strict "contributory-negligence-bars-liability" rule described above.

Ian

5.   The defenders of the jury have one further argument: Jury service, they insist, gives the people a chance to participate in government; it is "education in citizenship"; it increases respect for the judicial process and the law; and it makes the public share responsibility for decisions that may be difficult and unpopular.

One could be more enthusiastic about all this, retort the critics, if the obligation to serve were more rationally distributed. The lists of eligibles from which jury lists are made up are rarely complete; members of many occupational groups are automatically exempt, not always for good reasons; and many people who prefer not to serve can get excused. And unfortunately, those exempted or excused are often those who would make the best jurors.

This controversy over the merits of the jury system has been going on for a long time and will doubtless continue. The pressure for change may lead to greater use of the special verdict, and possibly to greater popularity for the "blue-ribbon jury" (drawn from a restricted list of citizens who have achieved a certain level of education) in certain kinds of cases. More promising, perhaps, are the efforts being made in many communities to speed up trials by inducing litigants to forgo their right to a jury trial. (More will be said about these efforts later in this chapter.) But in view of the continued popularity of the jury system and the ample constitutional protection it enjoys, it is not likely to disappear.

The Recruitment of Trial Judges

Another controversy centers on our methods of recruiting trial judges. Many students of our legal system are convinced that we could do far more to secure the services of the best possible people for our trial bench.

What qualities should trial judges possess? They must have technical competence, a broad knowledge of many fields of law. Most important, probably, is their familiarity with the rules of trial procedure and evidence; hence some prior experience as a trial lawyer is invaluable. They must have a "judicial temperament": Not only must they be capable of rigorous objectivity, but they must be firm, patient, and not easily flustered.

Trial judges must also be capable of independence of judgment. Central to the democratic tradition is the principle that judges should be immune to improper pressures both from private-interest groups and from other officials. In principle, the only influences that may be brought to bear on a judge are those exerted in the courtroom by the presentation of evidence and argument. But other influences are always in the back-

ground. Every judge has friends and former associates; every judge belongs to a variety of organizations; every judge knows that certain officials and party leaders played a part in placing him on the bench; every judge knows that certain acts will enhance his popularity, while others will diminish it. A judge must resist the temptation to take these influences into account in arriving at decisions.

This is not to say that a judge should be insulated from the currents of popular opinion—if, indeed, that was possible. As we shall see in later chapters, the judge frequently finds that no rule of law is clearly applicable to the case before her. She must make a choice, and her beliefs about what is "just" or what is best for the community inevitably affect her decision. If her personal philosophy and convictions are too different from those held by the community, her decisions will provoke conflict and frustration. In the 1920s, for example, antilabor judges freely granted injunctions against strikes and picketing at a time when public sympathy was swinging toward labor. The result was the Norris-LaGuardia Act, and its state counterparts, which prohibited all labor injunctions. But to say that judges must share the dominant beliefs and aspirations of their time is not to say that they must court popularity by responding to every popular whim and sentiment.

QUALIFICATIONS FOR ELIGIBILITY   In most European countries, the judiciary is a career service. Young law-school graduates who want to become judges take a special set of examinations; if they pass them, they enter the service and work their way up the ladder. Each promotion is decided upon by senior judges and other civil servants. In Great Britain, all trial judgeships (except in the minor courts) are filled by appointment from among the elite group of specialized trial lawyers known as *barristers*. In the United States, the only requirement is that the would-be judge be trained in the law—and even that is not necessary for some minor judgeships.

PROCESSES OF SELECTION   In the early decades of the Republic most judges were appointed. Then came the era of "Jacksonian Democracy," with its distrust of appointed officials and its tendency to minimize the importance of special competence and security of tenure for public officials. From then on, nearly all the new states entering the Union adopted the practice of having judges elected by the voters. Today judges are elected in about two-thirds of our states. In most of the remaining states, and in the federal system, judges are appointed by the chief executive, usually with the concurrence of one house of the legislature. A few states have variants or combinations of these methods.

COMPENSATION   Compensation has a lot to do with who does, and who does not, decide to become a judge. Few jurisdictions today offer salaries as inadequate as those commonly offered in earlier days, but no judge earns an income comparable to those received by highly successful private practitioners. Prestige, a sense of power, and the opportunity for public service, rather than the level of compensation, account for the willingness of able lawyers to become judges.

TENURE   The length of the term of office also affects the attractiveness of a judicial position. A lawyer will hesitate to abandon a flourishing private practice for a judgeship if, after a few years, she does not stand a good chance of being returned to office.

Federal judges and the judges in a few states enjoy life tenure. Most judges, however, have limited terms, frequently as short as four or six years. But in some states in recent decades, terms have been lengthened; in others, reappointment or renomination has become more or less automatic for any judge who has served honorably. And under the so-called "sitting-judge" tradition that is followed in some states, a judge who has once stood for election is able to run for reelection without opposition (in other words, she is the nominee of both parties).

One reason for the reluctance of some states to grant judges extended tenure is that there is still no effective way of getting rid of bad judges. In principle, judges can be impeached, and some states provide for their removal by popular vote, but these procedures are rarely invoked and then only in extreme cases. Judges whose conduct on the bench is unworthy—because they are tyrannical, arbitrary, abusive, bigoted, or even drunk—are usually hard to get rid of and are subject to no effective discipline from the higher courts.

APPOINTMENT VERSUS ELECTION   The respective merits of appointment and election are a subject of continuing debate. Some observers believe that in a democracy the people should play a direct part in choosing their judges; others are convinced that the best people cannot be persuaded to become judges if they have to act like politicians and campaign for office.

But the elective and appointive systems are not really as different as they seem, and there is no evidence that states using one system have better judges than those using the other. The truth is that under both systems the selection of judges falls pretty much to local political leaders. In filling an appointive post, the president or governor almost invariably takes the advice of the local chieftains of his or her party in the jurisdiction where the judge will serve. When the position is elective, party lead-

ers pick the candidates who will appear on the party ticket. (Their choice rarely fails to be ratified in the primary or by the party convention.) Since voters are notoriously unable to appraise the professional qualifications of opposing judicial candidates, they vote by party label, and the winners are swept into office along with the rest of the ticket.

In any case, campaigning for judicial office is no longer so distasteful a chore as it once was. In jurisdictions with a sitting-judge tradition, for example, the would-be judges know that they will not have to wage much of a campaign when they run, unopposed, for reelection. And even where there is a real contest, most communities no longer expect of judicial candidates the aggressive, partisan, "pie-in-the-sky" campaign that they expect of other candidates. Furthermore, the lengthening of judicial terms in many states has meant that campaigns are less frequent. Longer terms have also meant more midterm vacancies, created by the death or retirement of incumbents, to be filled by interim appointments. Appointees must, of course, run for the office in the next election, but by that time their names are often well enough known to give them a clear advantage in the campaign.

POLITICS AND THE JUDICIARY   What part should partisan politics play in the recruitment of judges? Are we unwise to leave the selection of judges to the political parties, as we do under both the elective and the appointive systems? Or does party politics play a necessary and desirable role in the process of selecting judges?

The judiciary must be taken out of politics, says one group. Party leaders must not be permitted to choose the appointees and the candidates, because politicians are less concerned with finding the best man than they are with using judgeships as inducements to party loyalty and as rewards for those who have worked for the party or contributed to its treasury. These critics point out that lawyers who have stayed out of politics or who are affiliated with the party out of power stand almost no chance of becoming judges, no matter how well-qualified they are.

Judges who owe their position to a political party, continue the critics, come to the bench with an indebtedness that may imperil their independence. Of course, they cannot openly serve the interests of that party or favor the lawyers who belong to it, but they are able to perform a host of small favors. They can help pay their political debts, for example, by choosing party regulars when they select some of the court's regular employees. And they have the power to make appointments to a variety of temporary jobs: receivers, trustees in bankruptcy, referees in foreclosure proceedings, administrators of estates, and special guardians, for instance. Some of these posts are quite lucrative. No judge is likely to appoint a

dishonest or incompetent person, but it is customary to distribute these jobs on a "patronage" basis—that is, to give them to people who have worked for the party in power.

Those who seek to take the judiciary out of politics have suggested several reforms. One is the so-called "nonpartisan" election of judges, in which candidates run in special elections without party labels. Whether calling an election nonpartisan makes it nonpolitical is open to doubt, however. Candidates nearly always have backers—either parties or private-interest groups—and the nonpartisan election may simply conceal from the voters who those backers are.

Another proposed reform is the *Missouri Plan*—so called because it was first used in choosing some of the judges in that state. Whenever a judicial vacancy occurs, a nonpartisan nominating commission—made up of appellate judges, representatives of the bar association, and lay persons—selects a panel of three candidates to fill it. The governor is obliged to appoint one of the three. The appointee serves for a year's probationary period and then stands for election to a much longer term, running unopposed on his or her record. (The only question before the voters is whether Judge X shall be retained in office.) This plan combines nonpartisanship, the appointive principle, and the elective principle.

Opposed to this whole approach are those who insist that since judges are not merely technicians but wielders of power and makers of rules, their recruitment simply cannot be taken out of politics. Politics, they say, is the struggle to obtain and exercise power, and judgeships are bound to be prizes in that struggle. Efforts to make the selection process nonpolitical are doomed to failure. Whatever group chooses the appointees or candidates for judgeships will become the focus of political pressure. If the bar associations make the choice, they will be dragged into the arena of political struggle. If nominating commissions do it, pressure will be exerted on those who name the commissioners and then on the commissioners themselves. Since political influences are bound to affect the selection of judges, it is better to have those influences operate through the established political parties. Voters give their support to the party that comes nearest to standing for what they believe in, knowing that if that party wins, it will probably bring into office judges who share its general attitudes and philosophy. The public can hold the party responsible.

Those who defend present methods of recruitment recognize that each has its shortcomings. But these shortcomings have been lessened, they insist, by the adoption of longer terms and the sitting-judge tradition.

All the evidence shows that the great majority of U.S. trial judges are

competent, conscientious, and incorruptible. And so they will remain as
long as the bar and the public hold them to a high standard of conduct—
higher than that to which most other officials are held. True, voters are
often confused and indifferent when they have to choose between competing candidates at the polls. But they know that they want judges of
high caliber, and they are prepared to punish any party whose choices
for the bench prove unsatisfactory. In addition, party leaders are not
likely to risk having their selections for judgeships denied endorsement,
or censured, by the local bar association.

The same forces operate on the judges themselves. The high standards that the public and the bar have set for the judiciary, together with
the judges' natural self-esteem and their respect for the judicial office and
the tradition surrounding it, impel nearly all new judges to do the best
job they can—regardless of how they were chosen for the office.

Delay in the Courts

Certainly the greatest source of dissatisfaction with our trial courts is the
long delay that frequently occurs between a litigant's decision to bring
suit and the entry of a judgment.

Fortunately, most of the disputes in our society do not have to be
settled in the courts; if they did, the burden on our courts would be
intolerable. Only a tiny percentage of disputes end up in lawsuits, and
only a very small percentage of the suits initiated ever go to trial. The
great majority are settled out of court, often "on the courthouse steps," as
the saying goes.[11]

Even so, the number of cases that do reach the trial stage is so great
that many of our trial courts are unable to keep up with them. This is
particularly true of courts serving large metropolitan areas, where there
are sometimes delays of two or more years between the time a lawsuit is
initiated and the time it is disposed of by a trial court. Recently, some of
these courts have taken drastic measures that promise gradually to bring
them up to date (or at least to keep the backlog constant), but others are
still permitting new cases to pile up on the court calendar more rapidly
than they can dispose of old ones.

Some delay between the date a lawsuit is filed and the date it comes
to trial is probably desirable, because it gives time for strong feelings to
subside and affords the lawyers a chance to sound out the possibilities of

---

11 Moreover, of the suits that do go to trial and on which a judgment is entered,
only a small percentage are appealed.

settlement. Delays of a few months are not serious, but delays of one or more years are. The truth of the maxim "Justice delayed is justice denied" is most dramatically illustrated by the accident victim who is deprived of her earning power by the negligence of another but who must wait several years before a court awards her damages; during that time she may exhaust her savings and be forced to go on relief. But there are other unfortunate consequences. For one thing, the longer the delay, the higher the costs of litigation become. Moreover, long delays often penalize one or both parties by depriving them of the testimony of witnesses who cease to be available. It is sometimes possible to obtain sworn statements from such witnesses while they can still be heard. But sworn statements are likely to be less effective than live testimony, just as testimony based on fresh recollection is likely to be more persuasive than testimony relating to incidents dimly remembered from several years back.

The prospect of extended delays may, it is true, encourage the parties to reach a settlement out of court. But some can better afford to wait than others. The party who finally gives in and accepts a settlement may be a plaintiff who deserved to receive more than he settled for—or a defendant, fighting a frivolous suit, who would in all likelihood have won in court had she felt she could hold out. Delays encourage the defendant with a weak defense, or the claimant with a frivolous claim, to bluff in the hope of achieving an ill-deserved settlement. It may be that the prospect of long delays serves to discourage people from bringing lawsuits, but, assuming this to be true, how do we know that those who are discouraged are not precisely those who most deserve aid from the courts?

In the ensuing paragraphs we shall mention some proposals for dealing with delays. The proposals are based on some of the factors that are believed to cause delay. But let us note here one partial explanation. Although the volume of civil litigation has not risen as fast as the country's population, it has grown faster than the number of courts and judges available to handle it. The most striking increase is in personal-injury claims (particularly claims arising from automobile accidents), which have long been our greatest source of litigation. Not only are there more personal injuries today than there used to be, but the proportion of such injuries that lead to lawsuits is rising—perhaps because of the widespread impression that juries are prone to award very generous damages to personal-injury claimants.

MEASURES TO DEAL WITH DELAYS   One way of cutting down on delays would be to increase the number of courts, or at least the number of judges, and many jurisdictions are adopting this solution. But officials hesitate to propose an increase in the number of judges, until they are

satisfied that nothing else can be done to speed up the disposition of cases. Here are some of the corrective measures that are being tried or considered.

Improvements in the Management of Court Systems   The efficiency of the court system would probably be improved if all the general trial courts in a state were brought into an integrated and centrally administered system. This would allow judges with relatively light loads to be assigned temporarily to help out in overloaded courts. The federal court system has set the example here: Its central administrative office compiles statistics comparing the caseloads of the various federal districts. These comparisons help the presiding judges of the higher federal courts to exercise their authority in assigning district judges to temporary duty in districts other than their own. A few states have begun to follow this example.

Another way of relieving congestion in the general trial courts would be to transfer part of their caseload down to the minor courts; this could be done by raising the maximum amount that may be sued for in the minor courts. Some states have made this change. In others, though, the quality of justice dispensed by the minor courts is so poor—particularly in courts manned by nonprofessional, part-time justices of the peace—that the legislatures hesitate to increase their responsibilities.

More Efficient Judges   Trial judges are sometimes criticized for not working long enough or hard enough. As a generalization, the charge is certainly unjustified, but it is probably fair in some instances. Therefore, some critics feel that the appellate courts should have power to supervise the performance of trial judges. A related problem is that of retirement: How can judges with failing intellectual powers be eased from the bench with dignity and compassion? Some states have a compulsory retirement age, though such arbitrary arrangements inevitably deprive our courts of the services of some judges who are still at the height of their powers.

More Efficient Trial Lawyers   Many trial lawyers take on more cases than they can handle and then have to ask the courts for repeated postponements. By its very nature, the operation of a trial court entails some time wasting—by lawyers, litigants, witnesses, prospective jurors, and even judges. Thus, no court can plan a daily schedule with precision, because it is impossible to predict exactly how long it will take to dispose of each case. (In fact, some cases will not be tried at all: One of the participants may become ill, or there may be a last-minute settlement.) But many of the postponements requested by poorly organized lawyers could be

avoided if judges were more willing to be stern and deny their requests. Also, many trials could be shortened if the judge were willing to keep a tighter rein on the proceedings—to be more strict in excluding irrelevancies, repetition, and mere showmanship.

Better Training of Trial Attorneys   In recent years the judiciary has become more vocal about its dissatisfaction with the training of lawyers for trial work. They argue that the courts would operate more efficiently and provide more rapid service if the lawyers appearing before them all demonstrated at least a minimum level of competence in the special skills required for courtroom defense. In fact, some federal courts now require lawyers who wish to practice in their courts to demonstrate their competence by showing proof that they have taken a list of specialized courses. In effect, they have established more rigorous licensing requirements for lawyers who wish to practice in their courts.

Wider Use of Pretrial Techniques   Earlier we noted the value of the various "discovery" techniques and of the pretrial conference. Narrowing the issues to the true areas of controversy, and letting each side know exactly what the other side expects to prove and what its evidence will be, make it more likely that the trial will be a rapid and efficient proceeding. These techniques also improve the chances of pretrial settlement.

Shorter Trials   It has already been explained that trial judges can shorten trials by keeping a tighter rein on the proceedings. But certainly the best way to reduce the number of courtroom hours spent on each case is to curtail the proportion of cases tried before a jury.

As we have seen, a party in a suit for damages has a constitutionally protected right to a jury trial in the federal courts and in the courts of many states. In order to induce litigants to forgo that right voluntarily, some states require that a case be heard in a minor court or before a special tribunal before a jury trial can be demanded.[12] Others set the court costs charged for a nonjury trial much lower than the costs charged for a jury trial, in the hope that the parties will accept the nonjury trial. But as long as plaintiffs in accident cases believe that a jury will treat them more generously than a judge will, they will probably insist on their constitutional right.

---

[12] In some parts of Pennsylvania, for instance, plaintiffs with small claims must first have them heard by a panel of three lawyers. Parties who are dissatisfied with the panels' awards, however, and who are prepared to pay the additional costs may insist on regular jury trials.

Trial judges can reduce the time they must devote to nonjury trials by appointing members of the bar to serve as their special fact-finders, thus relieving themselves of the time-consuming task of hearing evidence. These special fact-finders are variously referred to as "masters," "auditors," and "referees." A master takes testimony at a formal hearing, not unlike an ordinary trial, and then prepares a report to the judge in which the evidence is summarized and a finding of fact is made on each factual issue the master has been asked to examine. If the entire case has been turned over to a master, he may also recommend how the case should be decided. Although the final judgment is the responsibility of the judge, she rarely inquires further into the factual issues examined by the master.

Adjudicating Cases Outside the Court System   Certain kinds of cases have been removed from the regular courts for reasons unconnected with court congestion, but this practice has served incidentally to relieve that congestion. For example, special administrative tribunals[13] have been set up to handle the claims of employees against their employers in connection with on-the-job injuries. Every state now has one or more tribunals of this sort (often called worker's compensation boards). They resemble ordinary courts in many ways, but they follow simplified procedures and apply quite different rules in determining and measuring liability. It has been suggested that the automobile accident cases that now swamp our courts might be tried before tribunals modeled on these worker's compensation boards. But since the suggestion has provoked a great deal of opposition from lawyers' organizations, it is not likely to be adopted in the near future.

Many business firms include an "arbitration clause" in their commercial contracts, specifying that if a dispute should arise under the contract, it will be settled by arbitration rather than in the courts. Arbitration is likely to be speedier and less expensive than litigation. Moreover, the dispute can be settled by arbitrators who have expert knowledge of the subject matter of the disputed contract—a knowledge that trial judges are unlikely to possess.

These, then, are some of the measures that are being taken, or proposed, to lessen the delays in our courts. Although some jurisdictions are making progress, the problem of court congestion remains a serious one.

---

13 Administrative tribunals will be discussed in Chapter 8.

Chapter Problem

T.V. OR NOT T.V.:
TELEVISED AND PHOTOGRAPHIC COVERAGE OF TRIALS

Since the advent of the modern news media, with their ability to report news events to large portions of the population, there has been a search . . . for an appropriate relationship between the new mass media and judicial proceedings. . . .

The modern controversy can be traced to the trial of Bruno Hauptmann for kidnapping of the Lindbergh baby in 1934.[14] In that trial the court's lack of experience in controlling the press personnel in the courtroom and the press' inexperience in covering courtroom proceedings resulted in a "carnival atmosphere" which detracted from the essential dignity of the courtroom.

As a response to the threat to the dignity of the court proceeding (and not in response to any perceived violation to a defendant's right to due process under the 14th amendment) the American Bar Association adopted Canon 35 of the Code of Professional and Judicial Ethics in 1937. The Canon, as amended in 1952 and 1963, stated:

> "The taking of photographs in the courtroom, during sessions of the court or recesses between sessions, and the broadcasting or televising of courtroom proceedings are calculated to detract from the essential dignity of the proceedings, distract the witness in giving his testimony, degrade the court and create misconceptions with respect thereto in the mind of the public and should not be permitted."

Questions

1. Evaluate the canon quoted above. This particular canon does not have the force of law. Should this be changed? What is the force of a canon, and why are all canons not made laws?

2. Should television and radio coverage of important trials be permitted? Why or why not?

3. Do you think that television coverage of courtroom proceedings would increase the efficiency or effectiveness of the judicial process?

4. Would your feelings about televised courtroom proceedings change if you were one of the defendants in a criminal trial? One of the witnesses? If you were the prosecuting attorney?

PROBLEM SOURCE: *Mercer Law Review*, Vol. 29 (1978), p. 1119.
[14] 296 U.S. 649 (1935).

Questions for Review

1. The text argues that it is reasonable to place certain restraints on what lawyers may introduce in evidence. Despite these arguments, would it not be better to let the judge and jury receive all evidence that any participant might want to present?

2. What is the adversary system? What are its practical implications for courtroom procedure?

3. Lawyers are supposed to be advocates for their clients. Are there any clients for whom you would find it difficult to provide a defense? Can you think of any fair way of handling the defense of a client you disliked?

4. Discuss briefly some of the advantages and disadvantages of trial by jury.

5. As our society becomes more complex, the subjects that are litigated also become increasingly complex. Would you be in favor of a law that would allow judges to appoint blue-ribbon juries (that is, juries composed of experts in the particular case being litigated) when they believe that such appointments would speed trials? Do you feel that such appointments would affect the quality of justice dispensed? In what way?

6. How do you feel about efforts to reform the judiciary by making judgeships appointive, rather than elective, offices?

7. Federal judges enjoy life tenure in their jobs. Do you believe that this benefit leads to better decision making? Why or why not?

8. Contact a local court clerk and find out what the typical delay is for civil cases. What is the delay in criminal cases? Have any reforms been proposed to ease the backlog of cases in that particular court?

9. Lawyers must pass a bar examination before being admitted to the practice of law. Would you be in favor of periodic reexamination of lawyers? Why or why not?

4
Judicial Lawmaking I:
Law Built
on Precedents

W hen do judges "make law"? They do so every time they decide a case that no existing rule quite fits. They make law when in order to determine what rule applies to a case, they interpret a statute or a constitutional provision. (We shall discuss these forms of judicial lawmaking in Chapters 6 and 7.) They also make law when in the absence of either an applicable legislative rule or a directly controlling precedent, they have to create a rule by building on the precedents established in analogous cases. The present chapter is about judicial lawmaking by building on precedents.

Nowadays most of the major innovations in legal rules are introduced by legislatures, and much of the work of judges is interpreting legislative rules. But this has not always been so. In the early centuries of the legal tradition we share with England, legislative lawmaking was comparatively unimportant; most lawmaking was the work of judges building on precedents. Indeed, in some fields—contracts, for instance— the rules even to this day are primarily of judicial origin.

The Common-Law Tradition

English Origins

When the Normans conquered England in the eleventh century, they found a land with no nationwide, systematized body of law. Such law as existed was essentially a formalization of local custom. In an effort to

unite the country under their rule, the early Norman kings sent royal judges out into the land to adjudicate the disputes and accusations brought before them by the people. The royal justice dispensed by these judges was firm but fair, inexpensive, and expeditious. By the beginning of the thirteenth century, it had wholly displaced the patchwork of Anglo-Saxon institutions that had prevailed before the Norman Conquest.

Since the royal judges had no body of generally accepted rules on which to base their decisions, they had to create rules as they went along. Understandably, they drew heavily on the traditions, customs, business usages, and moral standards of the people. But they also relied on their own judgment, their "sense of justice," and their notions of the community's needs. The body of rules that thus evolved came to be known as the *common law*—"common" simply because it was common to all of England. For well over a century, the process of judicial lawmaking provided England with virtually all its legal rules for the channeling of private conduct; it was not until the late thirteenth century that enacted law—first royal edicts and then acts of Parliament—became a significant element in English law.

The Emergence of Equity

By the fourteenth century, certain deficiencies had begun to appear in the justice that was being dispensed by the royal courts. Would-be plaintiffs found themselves increasingly baffled and thwarted by the rigidly and highly technical procedural requirements. Moreover, the royal courts tended to confine themselves to redressing wrongs by awarding money damages to the person wronged. Little by little, plaintiffs dissatisfied with the treatment they received from the royal courts began to petition the king for some other form of redress. The king adopted the practice of turning these petitions over to the Lord Chancellor, a high official in the king's court. By the latter part of the fifteenth century, this practice had become institutionalized, and the Chancellor (now presiding over a new Court of Chancery) was issuing decrees on his own authority. The body of principles and remedies developed by the Court of Chancery came to be known as *equity* (from the Latin *aequitas*, meaning "justice" or "fairness").

In effect, England now had two bodies of judge-made law—the traditional common law[1] of the older courts, and the newer equity. Equity

---

1 The term *common law*, you will discover, is used in several slightly different senses:
   a. Most broadly, it is used to designate the Anglo-American legal tradition, which also prevails in most other English-speaking countries. This tradition is often contrasted

brought to English law some important new principles. One such principle, for example, held that a plaintiff must come to equity "with clean hands"—meaning that the plaintiff's own role in the affair at issue must have been wholly without fault.[2] Perhaps even more important were equity's new remedies. If a plaintiff could show that the common-law remedy of money damages would not be adequate in his case, he might persuade the Court of Chancery to grant him an injunction or a decree of specific performance. These are two kinds of orders addressed to the defendant. On pain of a fine or imprisonment for contempt of court, the decree requires a defendant to do, and the injunction requires him to refrain from doing, specified acts.

The English Legal Tradition in North America

When the English colonists settled in North America, they established a legal system modeled on what they had known in England. Though the demands of a new society in a new environment called for some changes in the old system, many English legal principles and institutions had become firmly rooted in the colonies by 1776. Despite the strong anti-British revulsion that followed the Revolution, the states of the new nation preserved intact a large part of their legal heritage. Furthermore, the new states that were admitted to the Union as the years passed borrowed heavily from the same tradition.[3] Only Louisiana had a legal system that

---

with the civil-law tradition, which derives from Roman law and prevails today in the countries of continental Europe and some others.

    b. "Common law" is used, as here, to distinguish the body of rules originally administered by the royal courts of law from the rules of equity, administered by the Court of Chancery. (Sometimes the word *law* alone is also used in this sense.)

    c. "Common law" is often used to refer to all judge-made rules built on precedents, as distinguished from legislative enactments and the decisions in which these enactments are interpreted. One often encounters the phrase, "At common law, the rule was that . . ."; here the reference is to the decisional rule that prevailed before the passage of some statute.

    d. Lastly, "common law" occasionally refers to the body of English rules that was transplanted to the American colonies and was in force in 1776 when the colonies claimed their independence.

    2 See William Zelermyer, *The Legal System in Operation: A Case Study from Procedural Beginning to Judicial Conclusion* (San Francisco: West Publishing Co., 1977), especially pages 228–285, "Along the Clean Hands Trail."

    3 A number of states have consitutional provisions or statutes incorporating the English common law into their legal systems. The following Arkansas Statutory provision is representative: "The common law of England, so far as the same is applicable and of a general nature, and all the statutes of the British Parliament in aid of [it] . . . made prior to the fourth year of James the First [1607] that are applicable to our form of government, of a general nature and not local to that kingdom, and not inconsistent with the Constitution and laws of the United States or . . . of this State, shall be the rule of decision in this State unless altered or repealed by the General Assembly. . . ."

was not based on the common-law traditions; its legal institutions were inherited from France and Spain, both of which belonged to the civil-law tradition.[4]

The Fusion of the Law Courts and the Equity Courts

Among the legal institutions transplanted to the American colonies were the rules and procedures of equity. In some colonies (and later in some of the states), separate courts of equity were established; in others, equity was administered by the regular courts of law. In the nineteenth century, however, movements to reform court systems and to simplify judicial procedures led to the elimination of most separate equity courts. Today only five states have such courts; in the others, original jurisdiction over equity cases is in the trial courts of general jurisdiction,[5] and appeals go to the regular appellate courts.

Although the two court systems have been fused, there is still a significant distinction between a "law" case and an "equity" case. In some states, for instance, a plaintiff must indicate at the outset whether he or she is bringing an "action at law" or a "suit in equity." Even when no such designation is required, the judge may have to classify the case if one of the parties asks for a trial by jury. This is because the constitutional guarantees of a jury trial extend only to those cases that are essentially "legal" in character. (A plaintiff seeking an injunction or a decree of divorce cannot claim the right to a jury trial.) The procedures in the two kinds of cases are essentially the same, but some of the terms used are different: A "complaint" at law is sometimes still called a "bill" in equity, and a "judgment" is called a "decree."

The fusion of courts has, on the other hand, had some important consequences for litigants. It is now possible, for instance, for a litigant in an action at law to introduce arguments based on equity principles, and vice versa.

Over the centuries, equitable principles and remedies have undergone gradual change as judges have had to decide new cases involving novel situations. In addition, legislatures from time to time have broadened the scope and flexibility of equitable remedies and have even created some new remedies modeled on the traditional ones.

---

[4] The most significant difference between the civil-law tradition and our own is that in civil-law countries, comprehensive legislative enactments known as *codes* have always been the main repository of legal rules. (The first code, on which all modern codes are based, was drawn up under the Roman emperor Justinian.) Judicial lawmaking built on precedent has thus never been a part of the civil-law tradition.

[5] See Document #74, *Law and Equity Organization of the American Courts*, American Jurisprudence 2d Desk Book (Rochester, N.Y.: 1962, rev. 1978), p. 199.

The Role of Precedents

Stare Decisis:
The Doctrine and Its Rationale

The power of judges to formulate legal rules in dealing with the cases brought before them is limited by the duty, imposed on them by our legal tradition, to seek guidance by looking back at past decisions in similar cases. The principle that judges should build on the precedents established by past decisions is known as the doctrine of *stare decisis* (from the Latin phrase, *stare decisis et non quieta movere*, which means "to adhere to precedents and not unsettle things that are settled").

Observance of *stare decisis* is more than a deeply rooted tradition, however; it is a logical way for judges to act. Following precedents is often much easier and less time-consuming than working out all over again solutions to problems that have already been faced. It enables the judge to take advantage of the accumulated wisdom of successive generations. It conforms to the community's instinctive belief that "like wrongs deserve like remedies," and to the desire for "equal justice under law." But above all, the practice of following precedents enables citizens (with the expert assistance of lawyers) to plan their conduct in the expectation that past decisions will be honored in the future. Certainty, predictability, and continuity are not the only objectives of law, but they are important ones. Many disputes are avoided, and others are settled without litigation, simply because people have a good notion of how the courts will respond to certain types of behavior.

Precedents: The Range of Their Influence

In Chapter 2, we examined the case of *George* v. *Jordan Marsh*, which, you will remember, was decided in 1971 by the Supreme Judicial Court of Massachusetts. There the court held that "one who, without privilege to do so, by extreme and outrageous conduct, intentionally causes severe emotional distress to another, with bodily harm resulting from such distress, is subject to liability."

Let us assume that the *George* decision has not been overturned by the courts or superseded by statute. What precisely is its influence in determining the outcome of a later case involving closely similar facts?

First, suppose that such a case were to come before a Massachusetts trial court any time after 1971. The answer here is clear: The Massachusetts trial judge would be obliged under the *stare decisis* principle to apply the rule laid down in *George*, no matter what he himself thought

of that rule. Within each jurisdiction, lower courts must follow the precedents established by higher courts.

But suppose that the unsuccessful plaintiff in this case was dissatisfied with the trial-court judgment against her and decided to take an appeal to the Massachusetts Supreme Court. Under the *stare decisis* principle, the appellate judges would normally feel obliged to follow the court's own earlier decision, even though they themselves might have doubts concerning its correctness and wisdom. From time to time, however, appellate courts do overrule their past decisions. (We shall have more to say on this point later in the chapter.)

Finally, suppose a case very similar to *George* were to come before a trial or appellate court in another jurisdiction—in Illinois, let us say. The Illinois court would be under no obligation to follow the rule laid down in *George*. Properly speaking, *George* is only an interpretation of the decisional and statutory law of Massachusetts and has no controlling effect on courts in other states. But judges normally do give consideration to decisions from other jurisdictions. If the Massachusetts judges found no Massachusetts decisions covering the point at issue, they would almost certainly look at cases decided elsewhere. In fact, if you will refer back to the *George* case, you will see Justice Quirico doing precisely that. After all, the American states—and, for that matter, Great Britain and the British Commonwealth—share a common legal tradition; moreover, their institutions and the problems they face are often similar. So it is sometimes said that decisions from other jurisdictions, though not binding, are persuasive. The persuasiveness of a given decision depends on such factors as the cogency of the supporting opinion, the prestige of the deciding court, and the unanimity of the judges. And any given decision will obviously have greater weight as a precedent if it coincides with decisions in other jurisdictions.

Building on Precedents

By simply describing our fictitious case in the preceding section as "closely similar" to *George* v. *Jordan Marsh*, we put off answering some difficult questions: How similar must earlier Case A be to later Case B before it is considered a precedent? (After all, no two cases are identical.) And once the requisite similarity has been established, how do judges go about determining precisely what rule Case A stands for and just how that rule applies to Case B?

If a Massachusetts court were faced with a case that was exactly like *George* v. *Jordan Marsh* except that the parties' names and the date and locale of the events were different, the *George* decision would certainly be controlling. Any competent and scrupulous Massachusetts lawyer would

tell a would-be plaintiff in such a controversy that his chances of winning were good enough to justify his bringing suit.

Litigation occurs because either the facts or the applicable legal rule is in dispute. When a court finds itself faced with a case in which *George* is cited by one of the parties as a precedent, it is pretty sure to be a case resembling *George* only in some respects, so that while one party is insisting on the similarities, the other party is emphasizing the dissimilarities. Imagine, for instance, a case arising in Massachusetts in which a cashier at a local department store yells and gestures at one of the patrons for some alleged wrongdoing. Further assume that the patron suffers a mild heart attack. The patron's lawyer might argue that the case is analogous to the *George* v. *Jordan Marsh* case. How does the court go about deciding whether *George* has established a precedent that must be followed?

Actually, the court has three questions to answer: First, is the earlier case essentially similar in its significant facts to the later one? Second, if it is found to be similar, what legal rule is inherent in the earlier case? Third, how does that rule apply to the later case?

Shortly, in the famous case of *MacPherson* v. *Buick Motor Co.*, we shall see how a new rule is built on old decisions. But a few preliminary observations will help you understand what the judges who wrote the opinions in that case were doing.

First of all, remember what we said in Chapter 3 about the role of lawyers under the adversary system. The judges depend heavily on the lawyers not only to identify the relevant prior cases but also to present arguments demonstrating the similarity or dissimilarity of those earlier cases to the current one. In a very real sense, therefore, the skill (or lack of skill) of the opposing lawyers plays a role in shaping the law.[6]

Next, remember that the judges who decided each earlier case now being cited as a precedent were preoccupied with disposing of the case before them; they were only secondarily concerned with the future influence of their decision. No appellate judges are unaware that their decisions are likely to become precedents. But they can foresee only to a very limited extent what sorts of future cases their decisions will influence. Knowing that their opinions will probably be read by judges and lawyers for years to come, they still must concern themselves primarily with justifying the courts' decisions to the litigants and their attorneys.

The most important implication of the forgoing observation is that

---

[6] The litigants themselves also help shape the law. People who bring lawsuits are not always well thought of in our society, but we should recall that if there had not been plaintiffs in the past ready to assert their rights, and defendants ready to resist those assertions, many of the decisional rules that today protect us would not exist.

what the judges said in their opinions in Case A does not crystallize for
eternity the significance of that case. They could not have foreseen all the
problems that would later arise in somewhat similar cases, such as Case
B; hence the judges who must decide Case B should feel free to reevaluate
the facts in Case A when they review it as a possible precedent. A fact to
which the earlier judges attached little importance may very well strike
the later judges as crucially significant. Their reevaluation of Case A may
lead them, for instance, to conclude that the rule inherent in it is much
narrower in scope than the earlier judges seemed to think, and therefore
that it would not apply to Case B. On the other hand they may see similarities between Cases A and B that the earlier judges would never have
acknowledged; in other words, they may find a broader rule in Case A
than the earlier judges had in mind. Nor does this reevaluation occur
only once: Each time Case A is reexamined in the course of deciding a
later case, its significance as a precedent is likely to undergo some modi-
fications.

The point of all this is not that judicial opinions are of no importance. On the contrary, they are enormously valuable. An opinion is essentially a brief essay—or sometimes several brief essays—in which
judges discuss the relevance of the principles and doctrines gleaned from
earlier opinions and from scholarly treatises and other writings. What
the judges say in their opinions is extremely useful to other judges and to
lawyers; the words reveal the thinking of the decision makers. But these
opinions are not in themselves binding and final interpretations of the
decisions they accompany. Later judges are likely to rely heavily on what
the earlier judges have written, but nonetheless they are free to find new
meanings in the old cases—meanings not envisaged by the earlier
judges.[7]

Clearly, then, the act of the appellate judge in building on precedents
involves much more than following the rules of logic. Indeed, whenever
we speak (as we repeatedly do in this book) of "applying rules to cases,"
we must remember that the phrase does not mean that the rules are all
fixed and ready to be applied. The truth is that rules emerge during the
process of deciding a case, and the judges have a considerable range of
discretion in determining which rules emerge. They can find that Case A
contains either a rule broad enough to cover Case B or a rule narrow
enough to exclude it. The Massachusetts judges would probably hold either that the *George* rule did or did not cover the case before them. And
their decision would probably be influenced less by the reasoning that

---

[7] The doctrine of precedent, after all, is known as *stare decisis*, not *stare opinionibus*. It
is what the earlier court *did*, not what it *said*, that is a precedent for the later court.

produced the *George* rule than by their own views on whether applying that rule in the later case would produce a just result.[8]

Often the appellate court must fit cases into classifications whose boundary lines are ill defined. Here the exercise of discretion—the creative act of lawmaking—is unavoidable. Consider, for instance, this problem in the law of agency: Under what circumstances should an employer be held liable for harm caused by an employee who has an accident while driving a vehicle belonging to the employer? Is the employer relieved of liability if the employee has departed from the route that he or she was ordered to take? Broadly stated, the applicable principle is that if the employee is on a mere "detour," the employer is probably liable for any harm caused, but that if the employee is on a "frolic," the employer is not liable. So far, so good. But the real problem lies in deciding whether a particular employee in a particular case is on a detour or on a frolic. There are no rules of thumb for classifying the borderline case. The judges have to reexamine past decisions and decide whether the case before them is on the whole more like the detour cases or the frolic cases. If the case is close to the line, however, they must also redefine a portion of the line itself. If they do a good job of explaining their decision, they may make the distinction between detours and frolics a little clearer. But the chances are slight that they will arrive at a formulation so durable that the task of classification will be easy for all future judges.

This brings us to our last point. There are two reasons why few formulations of legal rules are ever final. The first is that the number of possible fact-combinations that may occur is infinite. The formulator of rules, whether judge or scholar, is forever being surprised by unforeseen cases. The second reason is that our society is constantly producing new problems, new needs, and new community attitudes and values. Not only are truck drivers continually becoming involved in slightly different kinds of accident, but our community attitudes on the proper legal relationships between employers, employees, and injured third parties are continually changing.

Many of the major changes that must take place in our law are made by legislatures. Most of the minor adjustments, though, are made by judges as they decide cases over the years. Judges owe a duty to the concept of certainty in the law, a duty that they fulfill by relating each new decision to what has gone before and by providing in their opinions a

---

[8] You may be a little shocked by the thought that judges have such latitude in using precedents. What is to prevent judges from simply making up their minds on the results they wish to arrive at and then manipulating precedents to justify those results? We shall consider this important question in the final section of this chapter.

justification of each new decision based on established principles. But that duty does not oblige them to maintain fixed and unchanging rules. Rather, it obliges them to preserve continuity—to see to it that change takes place by gradual steps, with each step rationally related to preceding steps so that no single decision will ever come as a total surprise to lawyers who have studied the pattern of the judges' decisions.

An Illustrative Case:
MacPherson v. *Buick Motor Co.*

Now let us look at a notable example of judicial lawmaking in action. The case that follows is a classic among judicial decisions, partly because the rule that emerged from it was an important one, but also because superb judicial craftsmanship was exhibited by the great judge who wrote the majority opinion.[9]

MacPherson v. *Buick Motor Co.* involved injuries suffered by an automobile owner when his car broke down because of a defective wheel. The trial jury, in awarding the plaintiff $5,000 in damages, had determined that the accident was caused by the defective wheel. It had also determined that the defendant, the Buick Motor Co., had been negligent in failing to test sufficiently the wheel it put on the car. But a major issue of law remained: *To whom* did Buick owe a duty to test the wheel? It was reasonably clear that Buick had violated a duty of care that it owed to the dealer to whom it sold the car. It was also probable that the dealer was liable to MacPherson for a breach of warranty. But had Buick violated any duty of care owed to MacPherson? There had been no dealings between them; indeed, Buick had never heard of MacPherson until he brought the suit. Throughout the nineteenth century, the courts had held, with only a few exceptions, that manufacturers were liable solely to those with whom they had contractual relations. The decisions involving vehicles seemed wholly unfavorable to MacPherson, from the leading case of *Winterbottom* v. *Wright* in 1842 right down to a 1915 case decided in a federal court the year before *MacPherson* came before the New York Court of Appeals.

This case is particularly useful for our purposes because the majority opinion and the dissenting opinion review the same group of cases but

---

9 Benjamin Nathan Cardozo (1870–1938). Cardozo was named to the United States Supreme Court in 1932, after serving for eighteen years on the Court of Appeals of New York, the highest court of that state, which decided the case given here. A book by Cardozo, *The Nature of the Judicial Process,* is still widely regarded as the best description ever written of how appellate judges decide cases.

interpret them quite differently. The writer of each opinion is thus able to establish a reasoned justification for his conclusions by basing them on established precedents and principles. But the majority opinion seeks to justify a new rule, a step forward in response to new needs, while the dissent argues that the new rule favored by the majority entails an unwarranted break with the past.

(Both opinions are quite long, and each has been abridged. To point up the techniques of analysis used by the two opinion-writers, we have interpolated a few explanatory notes and italicized certain key passages.)

MacPherson v. *Buick Motor Co.*

Court of Appeals of New York, 1916
217 N.Y. 382, 111 N.E. 1050

> Appeal, by permission, from a judgment of the Appellate Division of the Supreme Court affirming a judgment in favor of plaintiff entered upon a verdict.

CARDOZO, J. The defendant is a manufacturer of automobiles. It sold an automobile to a retail dealer. The retail dealer resold to the plaintiff. While the plaintiff was in the car, it suddenly collapsed. He was thrown out and injured. One of the wheels was made of defective wood, and its spokes crumbled into fragments. The wheel was not made by the defendant; it was bought from another manufacturer. There is evidence, however, that its defects could have been discovered by reasonable inspection, and that inspection was omitted. There is no claim that the defendant knew of the defect and wilfully concealed it. The case, in other words, is not brought within the rule of Kuelling v. Lean Mfg. Co., 183 N.Y. 78. The charge is one, not of fraud, but of negligence. The question to be determined is whether the defendant owed a duty of care and vigilance to any one but the immediate purchaser.

[Here Judge Cardozo introduces the "leading case" in New York on the manufacturer's liability to persons other than the immediate purchaser.]

The foundations of this branch of the law, at least in this state, were laid in Thomas v. Winchester, 6 N.Y. 397 [1853]. A poison was falsely labeled. The sale was made to a druggist, who in turn sold to a customer. The customer recovered damages from the seller who affixed the label. "The defendant's negligence," it was said, "put human life in imminent danger." A poison falsely labeled is likely to injure any one who gets it. Because the danger is to be foreseen, there is a duty to avoid the injury. Cases were cited by way of illustration in which manufacturers were not

subject to any duty irrespective of contract. The distinction was said to be that their conduct, though negligent, was not likely to result in injury to any one except the purchaser. We are not required to say whether the chance of injury was always as remote as the distinction assumes. Some of the illustrations might be rejected today. The principle of the distinction is for present purposes the important thing.

[Cardozo now goes on to discuss some later New York cases. The first two seemed to set narrow limits to manufacturers' liability, but two later decisions extended the scope of what might be called "the Thomas rule." The opinion points out certain factors that might account for the different results in the two groups of cases.]

Thomas v. Winchester became quickly a landmark of the law. *In the application of its principle there may at times have been uncertainty or even error. There has never in this state been doubt or disavowal of the principle itself. The chief cases are well known,* yet to recall some of them will be helpful. Loop v. Litchfield, 42 N.Y. 351 [1870], is the earliest. It was the case of a defect in a small balance wheel used on a circular saw. The manufacturer pointed out the defect to the buyer, who wished a cheap article and was ready to assume the risk. The risk can hardly have been an imminent one, for the wheel lasted five years before it broke. In the meanwhile the buyer had made a lease of the machinery. It was held that the manufacturer was not answerable to the lessee. Loop v. Litchfield was followed in Losee v. Clute, 51 N.Y. 494 [1873], the case of the explosion of a steam boiler. That decision has been criticised (Thompson on Negligence, 233; Shearman & Redfield on Negligence, 117); but *it must be confined to its special facts. It was put upon the ground* that the risk of injury was too remote. The buyer in that case had not only accepted the boiler, but had tested it. The manufacturer knew that his own test was not the final one. The finality of the test has a bearing on the measure of diligence owing to persons other than the purchaser.

These early cases suggest a narrow construction of the rule. Later cases, however, evince a more liberal spirit. First in importance is Devlin v. Smith, 89 N.Y. 470 [1882]. The defendant, a contractor, built a scaffold for a painter. The painter's servants were injured. The contractor was held liable. He knew that the scaffold, if improperly constructed, was a most dangerous trap. He knew that it was to be used by the workmen. He was building it for that very purpose. Building it for their use, he owed them a duty, irrespective of his contract with their master, to build it with care.

From Devlin v. Smith we pass over intermediate cases and turn to the latest case in this court in which Thomas v. Winchester was followed. That case is Statler v. Ray Mfg. Co., 195 N.Y. 478 [1909]. The defendant manufactured a large coffee urn. It was installed in a restaurant. When

heated the urn exploded and injured the plaintiff. We held that the manufacturer was liable. We said that the urn "was of such a character inherently that, when applied to the purposes for which it was designed, it
was liable to become a source of great danger to many people if not carefully and properly constructed."

It may be that Devlin v. Smith and Statler v. Ray Mfg. Co. have
extended the rule of Thomas v. Winchester. *If so, this court is committed to
the extension.* The defendant argues that things imminently dangerous to
life are poisons, explosives, deadly weapons—things whose normal function it is to injure or destroy. *But whatever the rule in Thomas v. Winchester
may once have been, it has no longer that restricted meaning.* A scaffold is not
inherently a destructive instrument. It becomes destructive only if im-
perfectly constructed. A large coffee urn may have within itself, if negligently made, the potency of danger, yet no one thinks of it as an
implement whose normal function is destruction. What is true of the
coffee urn is equally true of bottles of aerated water, Torgeson v. Schultz,
192 N.Y. 156 [1908]. . . .

[Judge Cardozo then quotes with approval the opinion of an English
judge in a case similar to *Devlin* decided by the Court of Appeals of England in 1883. He sums up:]

What was said by Lord Esher in that case did not command the full
assent of his associates. It may not be an accurate exposition of the law of
England. Perhaps it may need some qualification even in our own state.
*Like most attempts at comprehensive definition, it may involve errors of inclu-
sion and of exclusion. But its tests and standards, at least in their underlying
principles, with whatever qualification may be called for as they are applied to
varying conditions, are the tests and standards of our law.*

[The *Thomas* v. *Winchester* "principle" is now reformulated.]

We hold, then, that *the principle of Thomas v. Winchester is not limited
to poisons, explosives, and things of like nature,* to things which in their
normal operation are implements of destruction. If the nature of a thing
is such that it is reasonably certain to place life and limb in peril when
negligently made, it is then a thing of danger. Its nature gives warning of
the consequences to be expected. If to the element of danger there is
added knowledge that the thing will be used by persons other than the
purchaser, and used without new tests, then, irrespective of contract, the
manufacturer of this thing of danger is under a duty to make it carefully.
That is as far as we are required to go for the decision of this case. There
must be knowledge of a danger, not merely possible, but probable. It is
possible to use almost anything in a way that will make it dangerous if
defective. That is not enough to charge the manufacturer with a duty
independent of his contract. Whether a given thing is dangerous may be

sometimes a question for the court and sometimes a question for the jury. There must also be knowledge that in the usual course of events the danger will be shared by others than the buyer. . . . We are not required at this time to say that it is legitimate to go back of the manufacturer of the finished product and hold the manufacturer of the component parts. . . . *We leave that question open. We shall have to deal with it when it arises.* The difficulty which it suggests is not present in this case. . . .

[The rule as reformulated is now applied to automobiles.]

From this survey of the decisions, *there thus emerges a definition of the duty of a manufacturer which enables us to measure this defendant's liability.* Beyond all question, the nature of an automobile gives warning of probable danger if its construction is defective. This automobile was designed to go fifty miles an hour. Unless its wheels were sound and strong, injury was almost certain. It was as much a thing of danger as a defective engine for a railroad. The defendant knew the danger. It knew also that the car would be used by persons other than the buyer. This was apparent from its size; there were seats for three persons. It was apparent also from the fact that the buyer was a dealer in cars who bought to resell. The maker of this car supplied it for the use of purchasers from the dealer just as plainly as the contractor in Delvin v. Smith supplied the scaffold for use by the servant of the owner. The dealer was indeed the one person of whom it might be said with some approach to certainty that by him the car would *not* be used. Yet the defendant would have us say that he was the one person whom it was under a legal duty to protect. The law does not lead us to so inconsequent a conclusion. *Precedents drawn from the days of travel by stagecoach do not fit the conditions of travel today. The principle that the danger must be imminent does not change, but the things subject to the principle do change. They are whatever the needs of life in a developing civilization require them to be.*

[Contrary decisions from other jurisdictions are noted.]

In reaching this conclusion, *we do not ignore the decisions to the contrary in other jurisdictions.* It was held in Cadillac M. C. Co. v. Johnson, 221 F. 801 [1915], that an automobile is not within the rule of Thomas v. Winchester. There was, however, a vigorous dissent. Opposed to that decision is one of the Court of Appeals of Kentucky. Olds Motor Works v. Shaffer, 145 Ky. 616 [1911]. The earlier cases are summarized by Judge Sanborn in Huset v. J. I. Case Threshing Machine Co., 120 F. 865 [1903]. *Some of them, at first sight inconsistent with our conclusion, may be reconciled* upon the ground that the negligence was too remote, and that another cause had intervened. *But even when they cannot be reconciled, the difference is rather in the application of the principle than in the principle itself.* Judge Sanborn says, for example, that the contractor who builds a bridge, or the

manufacturer who builds a car, cannot ordinarily foresee injury to other persons than the owner as a probable result. We take a different view. We think that injury to others is to be foreseen not merely as a possible, but as an almost inevitable result. Indeed, Judge Sanborn concedes that his view is not to be reconciled with our decision in Devlin v. Smith. *The doctrine of that decision has now become the settled law of this state, and we have no desire to depart from it.*

[Judge Cardozo goes on to discuss the principal English cases. Some of these he finds "distinguishable"; in others, he finds statements of principle that he views as supporting his formulation of the rule. In the final paragraphs of his opinion, he notes an analogous rule in the law governing the duties of landlords to tenants, discusses the issues raised by the trial judge's instructions to the jury, and rules that the defendant was not absolved from its duty to inspect merely because it had brought the defective wheel from a reputable wheel manufacturer.

[One judge dissented. In his dissenting opinion, Chief Judge Willard Bartlett reviews most of the cases already discussed by Cardozo. But he finds no justification in them for Cardozo's view that "the *Thomas* rule" had been broadened so that it covered articles not "inherently" dangerous, such as automobiles.

[Bartlett's opinion, excerpts from which follow, leans heavily on *Winterbottom* v. *Wright*, the English case decided in 1842, which Cardozo mentions only briefly. The relevance of *Winterbottom* lies partly in the fact that it involved an injury occurring in a defectively constructed stagecoach. (The defendant was not, however, the maker of the coach, as Cardozo's opinion points out.) Wrote Bartlett:]

The *doctrine of that decision* [*Winterbottom*] was recognized as the *law of this state by the leading New York case* of Thomas v. Winchester, which, however, involved an exception to the general rule. . . .

The case of Devlin v. Smith is cited as an *authority in conflict with the view* that the liability of the manufacturer and vendor extends to third parties only when the article manufactured and sold is inherently dangerous. . . . It is said that the scaffold, if properly constructed, was not inherently dangerous, and hence that this decision affirms the existence of liability in the case of an article not dangerous in itself, but made so only in consequence of negligent construction. Whatever logical force there may be in this view it seems to me clear from the language of Judge Rapallo, who wrote the opinion of the court, that the scaffold was deemed to be an inherently dangerous structure, and that the case was decided as it was because the court entertained that view. Otherwise he would hardly have said, as he did, that the circumstances *seemed to bring the case fairly within the principle of* Thomas v. Winchester.

I do not see how we can uphold the judgment in the present case *without overruling what has been so often said by this court and other courts of like authority* in reference to the absence of any liability for negligence on the part of the original vendor of an ordinary carriage to any one except his immediate vendee. The absence of such liability was the very point decided in the English case of Winterbottom v. Wright. . . . In the case at bar, the defective wheel on an automobile, moving only eight miles an hour, was not any more dangerous to the occupants of the car than a similarly defective wheel would be to the occupants of a carriage drawn by a horse at the same speed, and yet, unless the courts have been all wrong on this question up to the present time, there would be no liability to strangers to the original sale in the case of the horse-drawn carriage.

The rule upon which, in my judgment, the determination of this case depends, and the recognized exceptions thereto, were discussed by Circuit Judge Sanborn, of the United States Circuit Court of Appeals in the Eighth Circuit, in Huset v. J. I. Case Threshing Machine Co., in an opinion which reviews all the leading American and English decisions on the subject up to the time when it was rendered (1903). I have already discussed the leading New York cases, but as to the rest I feel that I can add nothing to the learning of that opinion or the cogency of its reasoning. I have examined the cases to which Judge Sanborn refers, but if I were to discuss them at length, I should be forced merely to paraphrase his language, as a study of the authorities he cites has led me to the same conclusions; and the *repetition of what has already been so well said would contribute nothing to the advantage of the bench, the bar, or the individual litigants whose case is before us.*

A few cases decided since his opinion was written, however, may be noticed. In Earl v. Lubbock, the Court of Appeal [of England] in 1904 considered and approved the *propositions of law* laid down by the Court of Exchequer in Winterbottom v. Wright, declaring that the decision in that case, since the year 1842, *had stood the test of repeated discussion.* The Master of the Rolls approved the principles laid down by Lord Abinger as based upon sound reasoning; and all the members of the court agreed that his decision was a *controlling authority which must be followed.* That the federal courts still adhere to the general rule, as I have stated it, appears by the decision of the Circuit Court of Appeal in the Second Circuit, in March, 1915, in the case of Cadillac Motor Car Co. v. Johnson. That case, like this, was an action by a subvendee against a manufacturer of automobiles for negligence in failing to discover that one of its wheels was defective, the court holding that such an action could not be maintained. It is true there was a dissenting opinion in that case, *but it was*

based chiefly upon the proposition that rules applicable to stagecoaches are archaic when applied to automobiles, and that if the law did not afford a remedy to strangers to the contract, the law should be changed. If this be true, the change should be effected by the Legislature and not by the courts. A perusal of the opinion in that case and in the Huset Case will disclose *how uniformly the courts throughout this country have adhered to the rule and how consistently they have refused to broaden the scope of the exceptions.* I think we should *adhere to it in the case at bar,* and therefore, I vote for a reversal of this judgment.

HISCOCK, CHASE, and CUDDEBACK, JJ., concur with CARDOZO, J., and HOGAN, J., concurs in result. WILLARD BARTLETT, C. J., reads dissenting opinion. POUND, J., not voting.

Judgment affirmed. <

It has been suggested that legal standards—such as the "inherently dangerous" test for manufacturers' liability discussed in *MacPherson*—have a life span marked by three stages. In the first stage, the courts are groping toward a new verbal formula that will aid them in their task of drawing fine distinctions. Eventually they arrive at a standard that seems to do the job. In the second stage, the standard is fairly well accepted, though it is still being tested and refined. In the third stage, cases are arising that show that the standard is no longer satisfactory. Eventually it crumbles, whereupon the search begins for a new standard. The *MacPherson* case marked the decline and fall of the "inherently dangerous" standard. As a result of the decision, what had once been an exception to the general rule (that manufacturers were liable only to those who purchased from them) swallowed the rule itself. Today manufacturers are normally held liable for foreseeable harm resulting from defects in their products.

Deciding Truly Novel Cases

What happens, you may wonder, when a case arises for which there simply are no precedents, a case that is in no way similar to anything that can be found in the court reports?

During the centuries after the Norman Conquest of England, when the common-law tradition was being established, courts frequently had to cope with just this problem. As we have seen, the judges of those days drew heavily for their rules on prevailing customs, traditions, business usages, and moral standards, as well as on their own "sense of justice." These extralegal sources of social rules continue to influence the growth of law today. But as more and more cases are decided over the years, and as more and more laws are enacted, the network of legal rules becomes

ever more closely woven. An increasing number of fact-situations have been directly ruled upon by the courts, and many other situations are sufficiently similar to decided cases to make it possible to predict the probable rule with some assurance. Moreover, legal scholars are continually publishing treatises, articles, and "restatements" of the law full of speculative generalizations about the probable rules governing situations not yet ruled upon. These writings do not have the authority of judicial opinions, but they are nonetheless of great value to judges and lawyers dealing with difficult cases.

In short, the truly novel case is harder to find than one might think. Indeed, it is impossible to imagine a case for which no precedents or established principles would have any relevance whatever. However, cases do arise for which there are no close and obvious analogies in previous decisions.

Consider, for example, a problem that judges first had to face during the 1920s, when farmers began to complain that airplanes were disturbing the peace and frightening livestock by flying over their land. For a while, there were no statutes concerning the respective rights and duties of landowners and of persons who flew over their land, nor were there any precedents. Yet the courts could not simply tell the plaintiff to come back later; some decisions on their complaints had to be reached. What the judge in our illustrative case did, essentially, was to reach back to some of the *fundamental concepts* that underlie the particular subjects of law. He attempted to see whether any logical inferences could be drawn from conceptual underpinnings.

Hinman et al. v. Pacific Air Transport
Same v. United Air Lines Transport Corporation

Circuit Court of Appeals, Ninth Circuit, 1936
84 F.(2d) 755
> HANEY, Circuit Judge.

From decrees sustaining motions to dismiss filed by defendants in two suits, appellants appeal and bring for review by this court the rights of a landowner in connection with the flight of aircraft above his land. . . .

It is . . . alleged that defendants are engaged in the business of operating a commercial air line, and that at all times "after the month of May, 1929, defendants daily, repeatedly, and upon numerous occasions have disturbed, invaded and trespassed upon the ownership and possession of

plaintiff's tract"; that at said times defendants have operated aircraft in, across, and through said airspace at altitudes less than 100 feet above the surface; that plaintiffs notified defendants to desist from trespassing on said airspace; and that defendants have disregarded said notice, unlawfully and against the will of plaintiffs, and continue and threaten to continue such trespasses. . . .

The prayer asks an injunction restraining the operation of the aircraft through the airspace over plaintiffs' property and for $90,000 damages in each of the cases.

. . . Appellees contend that it is settled law in California that the owner of land has no property rights in superjacent airspace, either by code enactments or by judicial decrees and that the ad coelum [up to the sky] doctrine does not apply in California. We have examined the statutes of California . . . , but we find nothing therein to negative the ad coelum formula. Furthermore, if we should adopt this formula as being the law, there might be serious doubt as to whether a state statute could change it without running counter to the Fourteenth Amendment to the Constitution of the United States. If we could accept and literally construe the ad coelum doctrine, it would simplify the solution of this case; however, we reject that doctrine. We think it is not the law, and that it never was the law.

This formula "from the center of the earth to the sky" was invented at some remote time in the past when the use of space above land actual or conceivable was confined to narrow limits, and simply meant that the owner of the land could use the overlying space to such an extent as he was able, and that no one could ever interfere with that use.

This formula was never taken literally, but was a figurative phrase to express the full and complete ownership of land and the right to whatever superjacent airspace was necessary or convenient to the enjoyment of the land.

In applying a rule of law, or construing a statute or constitutional provision, we cannot shut our eyes to common knowledge, the progress of civilization, or the experience of mankind. A literal construction of this formula will bring about an absurdity. The sky has no definite location. It is that which presents itself to the eye when looking upward; as we approach it, it recedes. There can be no ownership of infinity, nor can equity prevent a supposed violation of an abstract conception.

The appellants' case, then, rests upon the assumption that as owners of the soil they have an absolute and present title to all the space above the earth's surface, owned by them, to such a height as is, or may become, useful to the enjoyment of their land. This height, the appellants assert in the bill, is of indefinite distance, but not less than 150 feet.

If the appellants are correct in this premise, it would seem that they would have such a title to the airspace claimed, as an incident to their ownership of the land, that they could protect such a title as if it were an ordinary interest in real property. Let us then examine the appellants' premise. They do not seek to maintain that the ownership of the land actually extends by absolute and exclusive title upward to the sky and downward to the center of the earth. They recognize that the space claimed must have some use, either present or contemplated, and connected with the enjoyment of the land itself.

Title to the airspace unconnected with the use of land is inconceivable. Such a right has never been asserted. It is a thing not known to the law. [Emphasis added.]

Since, therefore, appellants must confine their claim to 150 feet of the airspace above the land, to the use of the space as related to the enjoyment of their land, to what extent, then, is this use necessary to perfect their title to the airspace? Must the use be actual, as when the owner claims the space above the earth occupied by a building constructed thereon; or does it suffice if appellants establish merely that they may reasonably expect to use the airspace now or at some indefinite future time?

This, then, is appellants' premise, and upon this proposition they rest their case. Such an inquiry was never pursued in the history of jurisprudence until the occasion is furnished by the common use of vehicles of the air.

... We believe, and hold, that appellants' premise is unsound. The question presented is applied to a new status and little aid can be found in actual precedent. The solution is found in the application of elementary legal principles. The first and foremost of these principles is that the very essence and origin of the legal right of property is dominion over it. Property must have been reclaimed from the general mass of the earth, and it must be capable by its nature of exclusive possession. Without possession, no right in it can be maintained.

... The air, like the sea, is by its nature incapable of private ownership, except in so far as one may actually use it. This principle was announced long ago by Justinian. It is in fact the basis upon which practically all of our so-called water codes are based. ...

... When it is said that man owns, or may own, to the heavens, that merely means that no one can acquire a right to the space above him that will limit him in whatever use he can make of it as a part of his enjoyment of the land. To this extent his title to the air is paramount. No other person can acquire any title or exclusive right to any space above him.

Any use of such air or space by others which is injurious to his land, or which constitutes an actual interference with his possession or his beneficial use thereof, would be a trespass for which he would have remedy. But any claim of the landowner beyond this cannot find a precedent in law, nor support in reason.

It would be, and is, utterly impracticable and would lead to endless confusion, if the law should uphold attempts of landowners to stake out, or assert claims to definite, unused spaces in the air in order to protect some contemplated future use of it. . . .

We cannot shut our eyes to the practical result of legal recognition of the asserted claims of appellants herein, for it leads to a legal implication to the effect that any use of airspace above the surface owned on land, without his consent, would be a trespass either by the operator of an airplane or a radio operator. We will not foist any such chimerical property rights upon the jurisprudence of this country. . . .

The decree of the District Court is affirmed. MATHEWS, Circuit Judge, dissents. <

There are other ways of approaching such situations. The judges could have (and often did) searched through the property-law cases for any analogies that seemed suggestive. For example, were a landowner's rights with respect to overlying planes similar to the rights that enabled her to prohibit people from shooting bullets or stringing wires over her land? Or were they more like the rights of the beachowner who objects to boats passing in front of her property? Since a landowner can do much more about wires and bullets passing over her property than she can about boats sailing past her beach, the judges' choice of an analogy would have a great deal to do with how much relief the landowners would get from the airplane nuisance.

This power to choose between competing analogies, neither of which is very close to the case at hand, is obviously an instance of the judicial freedom of choice that we discussed in the preceding section. The question before the judges is not really "Which of these analogies is the closer?" but rather "Which analogy will lead to the more desirable result?" Judge Cardozo's opinion in the *MacPherson* case makes it clear that he believed the public interest would best be served by holding automobile manufacturers liable to final purchasers who were injured because of defects in the cars they bought. Nor is there any doubt that the judges who decided that farmers had no legal right to forbid all plane flights over their land did so after reflecting that to grant such a right would probably strangle the infant aviation industry. Although judges

traditionally stress in their opinions the foundations of precedent and
principle more heavily than they stress considerations of public policy,
the latter unquestionably play an important part in their thinking.[10]

In *Hinman* v. *United*, the court had no real precedents on which to
build. In *Williams* v. *Walker Thomas Furniture Company*, which follows,
the court's problem was quite different: Although the U.S. Circuit Court
of Appeals, District of Columbia Circuit, found no District of Columbia
precedents, there was an abundance of precedents from other states.

Williams v. Walker-Thomas Furniture Company

U.S. Circuit Court of Appeals, D.C. Circuit, 1965
350 F. 2d 445

> J. SKELLY WRIGHT, Circuit Judge.

Appellee, Walker-Thomas Furniture Company, operates a retail furniture store in the District of Columbia. During the period from 1957 to
1962 each appellant in these cases purchased a number of household
items from Walker-Thomas, for which payment was to be made in in-
stallments. The terms of each purchase were contained in a printed form
contract which set forth the value of the purchased item and purported
to lease the item to appellant for a stipulated monthly rent payment. The
contract then provided, in substance, that title would remain in Walker-
Thomas until the total of all the monthly payments made equaled the
stated value of the item, at which time appellants could take title. In the
event of a default in the payment of any monthly installment, Walker-
Thomas could repossess the item.

The contract further provided that "the amount of each periodical
installment payment to be made by [purchaser] to the Company under
this present lease shall be inclusive of and not in addition to the amount
of each installment payment to be made by [purchaser] under such prior
leases, bills or accounts; and *all payments now and hereafter made by
[purchaser] shall be credited pro rata on all outstanding leases, bills and accounts*
due the Company by [purchaser] at the time each such payment is
made." The effect of this rather obscure provision was to keep a balance

---

10 Note how the two types of consideration are combined in Cardozo's words in
MacPherson: "Precedents drawn from the days of travel by stagecoach do not fit the conditions of travel today. The principle that the danger must be imminent does not change,
but the things subject to the principle do change. They are whatever the needs of life in a
developing civilization require them to be."

due on every item purchased until the balance due on all items, whenever purchased, was liquidated. As a result, the debt incurred at the time of purchase of each item was secured by the right to repossess all the items previously purchased by the same purchaser, and each new item purchased automatically became subject to a security interest arising out of the previous dealings.

On May 12, 1962, appellant Thorne purchased an item described as a Daveno, three tables, and two lamps, having total stated value of $391.10. Shortly thereafter, he defaulted on his monthly payments and appellee sought to replevy all the items purchased since the first transaction in 1958. Similarly, on April 17, 1962, appellant Williams bought a stereo set of stated value of $514.95. She too defaulted shortly thereafter, and appellee sought to replevy all the items purchased since December, 1957. The Court of General Sessions granted judgment for appellee. The District of Columbia Court of Appeals affirmed, and we granted appellants' motion for leave to appeal to this court.

Appellants' principal contention, rejected by both the trial and the appellate courts below, is that these contracts, or at least some of them, are unconscionable and, hence, not enforceable. In its opinion in Williams v. Walker-Thomas Furniture Company, 198 A.2d 914, 916 (1964), the District of Columbia Court of Appeals explained its rejection of this contention as follows:

> "Appellant's second argument presents a more serious question. The record reveals that prior to the last purchase appellant had reduced the balance in her account to $164. The last purchase, a stereo set, raised the balance due to $678. Significantly, at the time of this and the preceding purchases, appellee was aware of appellant's financial position. The reverse side of the stereo contract listed the name of appellant's social worker and her $218 monthly stipend from the government. Nevertheless, with full knowledge that appellant had to feed, clothe and support both herself and seven children on this amount, appellee sold her a $514 stereo set.
>
> "We cannot condemn too strongly appellee's conduct. It raises serious questions of sharp practice and irresponsible business dealings. A review of the legislation in the District of Columbia affecting retail sales and the pertinent decisions of the highest court in this jurisdiction disclose, however, no ground upon which this court can declare the contracts in question contrary to public policy. We note that were the Maryland Retail Installment Sales Act, Art. 83 §§128–153, or its equivalent, in force in the District of Columbia, we could grant appellant appropriate relief. We think Congress should consider corrective legislation to

protect the public from such exploitive contracts as were utilized in the case at bar."

We do not agree that the court lacked the power to refuse enforcement to contracts found to be unconscionable. In other jurisdictions, it has been held as a matter of common law that unconscionable contracts are not enforceable. While no decision of this court so holding has been found, the notion that an unconscionable bargain should not be given full enforcement is by no means novel. [Emphasis added.] In Scott v. United States, 79 U.S. (12 Wall.) 443, 445, 20 L.Ed. 438 (1870), the Supreme Court stated:

> "... If a contract be unreasonable and unconscionable, but not void for fraud, a court of law will give to the party who sues for its breach damages, not according to its letter, but only such as he is equitably entitled to. ..."

Since we have never adopted or rejected such a rule, the question here presented is actually one of first impression. [Emphasis added.]

... Congress has recently enacted the Uniform Commercial Code, which specifically provides that the court may refuse to enforce a contract which it finds to be unconscionable at the time it was made. ... The enactment of this section, which occurred subsequent to the contracts here in suit, does not mean that the common law of the District of Columbia was otherwise at the time of enactment, nor does it preclude the court from adopting a similar rule in the exercise of its powers to develop the common law for the District of Columbia. In fact, in view of the absence of prior authority on the point, we consider the congressional adoption of §2-302 persuasive authority for following the rationale of the cases from which the section is explicitly derived. Accordingly, we hold that where the element of unconscionability is present at the time a contract is made, the contract should not be enforced.

... Unconscionability has generally been recognized to include an absence of meaningful choice on the part of one of the parties together with contract terms which are unreasonably favorable to the other party. Whether a meaningful choice is present in a particular case can only be determined by consideration of all the circumstances surrounding the transaction. In many cases the meaningfulness of the choice is negated by a gross inequality of bargaining power. The manner in which the contract was entered is also relevant to this consideration. Did each party to the contract, considering his obvious education or lack of it, have a reasonable opportunity to understand the terms of the contract, or were the important terms hidden in a maze of fine print and minimized by

deceptive sales practices? Ordinarily, one who signs an agreement without full knowledge of its terms might be held to assume the risk that he has entered a one-sided bargain. But when a party of little bargaining power, and hence little real choice, signs a commercially unreasonable contract with little or no knowledge of its terms, it is hardly likely that his consent, or even an objective manifestation of his consent, was ever given to all the terms. In such a case the usual rule that the terms of the agreement are not to be questioned should be abandoned and the court should consider whether the terms of the contract are so unfair that enforcement should be withheld.

. . . Because the trial court and the appellate court did not feel that enforcement could be refused, no findings were made on the possible unconscionability of the contracts in these cases. Since the record is not sufficient for our deciding the issue as a matter of law, the cases must be remanded to the trial court for further proceedings.

So ordered.   <

Refusal to Follow Precedents

Some decisions withstand the test of time better than others. Some become valuable precedents on which judges can build; others become barriers to progress.

Let us suppose that the highest court of State X, in trying to decide a case, comes upon its own decision in an earlier case entitled *"Smith* v. *Jones."* Although *"Smith* v. *Jones"* appears to be a controlling precedent, the court is reluctant to follow it. Perhaps the court perceives that the reasoning in the opinion is faulty. Perhaps it realizes that the facts in the case were peculiar—not really typical of the fact-combinations usually found in such cases. But the judges who decided it did not recognize this peculiarity and therefore stated "the rule of the case" in too broad a form, giving it a scope that made it appear to cover future situations for which it was ill suited. Or perhaps the present court realizes that since the time when *"Smith* v. *Jones"* was decided, changes in social arrangements or in community attitudes have undermined the appropriateness of the rule of this case for cases with apparently similar facts.

Cardozo's *MacPherson* opinion has shown us a number of ways in which the inconvenient precedent can be dealt with. It is often possible, for instance, to emphasize dissimilarities between the previous case and the present one, sometimes relying on facts in the earlier case to which the earlier judges attached little importance. This is known as *distinguishing* the earlier case or *reconciling* the two decisions.

But this technique has its limits. Some precedents are so obviously

relevant that it would be intellectually dishonest to distinguish them or
to ignore them. In such a situation, judges usually feel obliged to follow
the precedent. They may justify doing so with words like these: "The
decision in 'Smith v. Jones' is at variance with what now seems to be the
more reasonable view. If the question that the present case raises were
now before us for the first time, we might well answer it differently. But
'Smith v. Jones' has long been a part of our law, and under the principle
of stare decisis we have no alternative but to follow it." They may go on to
point out that, after all, primary responsibility for making changes in the
law belongs to the legislature.[11]

As we have seen, there are excellent reasons for following precedents. Occasionally, though, courts find themselves faced with cases in
which the value of continuity is clearly outweighed by the injustice, or
the plain absurdity, of blindly following the old rule. In such cases, the
possibility that the legislature may someday take note of the undesirable
effects of the rule does not seem to justify doing a present injustice, and
the court concludes that the precedent must be swept out of the way
once and for all. Such overrulings must be exceptional, of course, or stare
decisis would become meaningless. In some of the fields of law in which
continuity and predictability are particularly important—in property
law, for instance—precedents are almost never overruled. But in other
fields, decisional rules can be changed by new decisions with less danger
of defeating legitimate expectations.

Consider, for instance, the situation that prevailed in those states in
which judge-made rules once held that the driver of a vehicle had a duty
to dismount and look up and down the railroad tracks before proceeding
over a grade crossing. If he failed to do so and was hit by a train, his
contributory negligence prevented him from recovering damages. As the
normal speeds of trains and automobiles increased, the obligation to dismount became absurd. In the states in which the rule had not already
been changed by statute, the courts usually felt free to overrule the early
cases.

Let us now examine another New York case in which Judge Cardozo
spoke for the majority. In Hynes v. New York Central Railroad Co., the
court's problem was not whether it had to follow a particular precedent,
but whether it had to apply literally the traditional definition of a legal
concept. In four lower-court decisions in this case (two by trial judges,
each of which was appealed to the intermediate appellate court), judges

---

11 We shall consider the relation between decisional lawmaking and legislative lawmaking in Chapter 5.

had ruled that since the plaintiff's son was a "trespasser" when the defendant's negligence caused his death, the mother could not recover damages. But the result was a harsh one. The Hynes boy had trespassed only in a technical sense; his act did not fall within the reason for the rule holding that no duty of care is owed by a property owner to a trespasser on his or her property. Could the highest court arrive at a result that would be just and yet would not create doubt and confusion about the continuing validity of established principles? Judge Cardozo was able to persuade only three of the six other judges who heard the case to join in his bold—and superbly written—opinion.

Hynes v. *New York Central Railroad Co.*

Court of Appeals of New York, 1921
231 N.Y. 229, 131 N.E. 898

> Appeal from a judgment of the Appellate Division of the Supreme Court in the second judicial department, entered January 12, 1920, affirming a judgment in favor of defendant entered upon a dismissal of the complaint by the court at a Trial Term.

CARDOZO, J. On July 8, 1916, Harvey Hynes, a lad of sixteen, swam with two companions from the Manhattan to the Bronx side of the Harlem River or United States Ship Canal, a navigable stream. Along the Bronx side of the river was the right of way of the defendant, the New York Central Railroad, which operated its trains at that point by high tension wires, strung on poles and crossarms. Projecting from the defendant's bulkhead above the waters of the river was a plank or springboard from which boys of the neighborhood used to dive. One end of the board had been placed under a rock on the defendant's land, and nails had been driven at its point of contact with the bulkhead. Measured from this point of contact the length behind was five feet; the length in front eleven. The bulkhead itself was about three and half feet back of the pier line as located by the government. From this it follows that for seven and a half feet the springboard was beyond the line of the defendant's property, and above the public waterway. Its height measured from the stream was three feet at the bulkhead, and five feet at its outermost extremity. For more than five years swimmers had used it as a diving board without protest or obstruction.

On this day Hynes and his companions climbed on top of the bulkhead intending to leap into the water. One of them made the plunge in safety. Hynes followed to the front of the springboard, and stood poised for his dive. At that moment a crossarm with electric wires fell from the

defendant's pole. The wires struck the diver, flung him from the shattered board, and plunged him to his death below. His mother, suing as administratrix, brings this action for her damages. Thus far the courts have held that Hynes at the end of the springboard above the public waters was a trespasser on the defendant's land. They have thought it immaterial that the board itself was a trespass, an encroachment on the public ways. They have thought it of no significance that Hynes would have met the same fate if he had been below the board and not above it. The board, they have said, was annexed to the defendant's bulkhead. By force of such annexation, it was to be reckoned as a fixture, and thus constructively, if not actually, an extension of the land. The defendant was under a duty to use reasonable care that bathers swimming or standing in the water should not be electrocuted by wires falling from its right of way. But to bathers diving from the springboard, there was no duty, we are told, unless the injury was the product of mere willfulness or wantonness, no duty of active vigilance to safeguard the impending structure. Without wrong to them, crossarms might be left to rot; wires highly charged with electricity might sweep them from their stand, and bury them in the subjacent waters. In climbing on the board, they became trespassers and outlaws. The conclusion is defended with much subtlety of reasoning, with much insistence upon its inevitableness as a merely logical deduction. A majority of the court are unable to accept it as the conclusion of the law.

We assume, without deciding, that the springboard was a fixture, a permanent improvement of the defendant's right of way. Much might be said in favor of another view. We do not press the inquiry, for we are persuaded that the rights of bathers do not depend upon these nice distinctions. Liability would not be doubtful, we are told, had the boy been diving from a pole, if the pole had been vertical. The diver in such a situation would have been separated from the defendant's freehold. Liability, it is said, has been escaped because the pole was horizontal. The plank when projected lengthwise was an extension of the soil. We are to concentrate our gaze on the private ownership of the board. We are to ignore the public ownership of the circumambient spaces of water and of air. Jumping from a boat or a barrel, the boy would have been a bather in the river. Jumping from the end of a springboard, he was no longer, it is said, a bather, but a trespasser on a right of way.

Rights and duties in systems of living law are not built upon such quicksands.

Bathers in the Harlem River on the day of this disaster were in the enjoyment of a public highway, entitled to reasonable protection against

destruction by the defendant's wires. They did not cease to be bathers entitled to the same protection while they were diving from encroaching objects or engaging in the sports that are common among swimmers. Such acts were not equivalent to an abandonment of the highway, a departure from its proper uses, a withdrawal from the waters, and an entry upon land. A plane of private right had been interposed between the river and the air, but public ownership was unchanged in the space below it and above. The defendant does not deny that it would have owed a duty to this boy if he had been leaning against the springboard with his feet upon the ground. He is said to have forfeited protection as he put his feet upon the plank. Presumably the same result would follow if the plank had been a few inches above the surface of the water instead of a few feet. Duties are thus supposed to arise and to be extinguished in alternate zones or strata. Two boys walking in the country or swimming in a river stop to rest for a moment along the side of the road or the margin of the stream. One of them throws himself beneath the overhanging branches of a tree. The other perches himself on a bough a foot or so above the ground. Both are killed by falling wires. The defendant would have us say that there is a remedy for the representatives of one, and none for the representatives of the other. We may be permitted to distrust the logic that leads to such conditions.

The truth is that every act of Hynes, from his first plunge into the river until the moment of his death, was in the enjoyment of the public waters, and under cover of the protection which his presence in those waters gave him. The use of the springboard was not an abandonment of his rights as bather. It was a mere by-play, an incident, subordinate and ancillary to the execution of his primary purpose, the enjoyment of the highway. The by-play, the incident, was not the cause of the disaster. Hynes would have gone to his death if he had been below the springboard or beside it. The wires were not stayed by the presence of the plank. They followed the boy in his fall, and overwhelmed him in the waters. The defendant assumes that the identification of ownership of a fixture with ownership of land is complete in every incident. But there are important elements of difference. Title to the fixture, unlike title to the land, does not carry with it rights of ownership *usque ad coelum* [up to the sky]. There will hardly be denial that a cause of action would have arisen if the wires had fallen on an aeroplane proceeding above the river, though the location of the impact could be identified as the space above the springboard. The most that the defendant can fairly ask is exemption from liability where the use of the fixture is itself the efficient peril. That would be the situation, for example, if the weight of the boy upon the

board had caused it to break and thereby throw him into the river. There was no such causal connection here between his position and his injuries. We think there was no moment when he was beyond the pale of the defendant's duty—the duty of care and vigilance in the storage of destructive forces.

This case is a striking instance of the dangers of "a jurisprudence of conceptions" (Pound, Mechanical Jurisprudence, 8 *Columbia Law Review* 605, 608, 610), the extension of a maxim or a definition with relentless disregard of consequences to a "dryly logical extreme." The approximate and relative become the definite and absolute. Landowners *are* bound to regulate their conduct in contemplation of the presence of trespassers intruding upon private structures. Landowners *are* bound to regulate their conduct in contemplation of the presence of trouble in marking off the field of exemption and immunity from that of liability and duty. Here structures and ways are so united and commingled, super-imposed upon each other, that the fields are brought together. In such circumstances, there is little help in pursuing general maxims to ultimate conclusions. They have been framed *alio intuitu* [from another point of view]. They must be reformulated and readapted to meet exceptional conditions. Rules appropriate to spheres which are conceived of as separate and distinct cannot, both, be enforced when the spheres become concentric. There must then be readjustment or collision. In one sense, and that a highly technical and artificial one, the diver at the end of the springboard is an intruder on the adjoining lands. In another sense, and one that realists will accept more readily, he is still on public waters in the exercise of public rights. The law must say whether it will subject him to the rule of the one field or of the other, of this sphere or of that. We think that considerations of analogy, of convenience, of policy, and of justice, exclude him from the field of the defendant's immunity and exemption, and place him in the field of liability and duty.

The judgment of the Appellate Division and that of the Trial Term should be reversed, and a new trial granted, with costs to abide the event.

HOGAN, POUND and CRANE, JJ., concur; HISCOCK, C. J., CHASE and McLAUGHLIN, JJ., dissent [without opinion].

Judgments reversed, etc.   <

QUESTIONS
If you had been one of the judges hearing this case, would you have joined in the majority opinion? Do you think Cardozo avoided creating doubt and confusion about established legal principles?

Restraints
on Judicial Lawmaking

Whenever appellate judges make a choice among alternative rules in deciding a case, they are making law. They are also making a decision about public policy. In every case we have studied in this chapter, the judges took into account not only legal precedents and principles but the community's changing needs, desires, and notions of what is fair.

Students of the law used to be reluctant to acknowledge the influence of such considerations on judicial decisions. The writings of Oliver Wendell Holmes, one-time law teacher, state appellate judge, and finally Justice of the Supreme Court of the United States from 1902 to 1932, helped bring about a more realistic understanding of the things judges consider when they decide cases. At the beginning of his book, *The Common Law* (1881), he said:

> The life of the law has not been logic: it has been experience. The felt necessities of the time, the prevalent moral and political theories, intuitions of public policy, avowed or unconscious, even the prejudices which judges share with their fellowmen, have had a good deal more to do than the syllogism in determining the rules by which men should be governed.

Some years later, Holmes wrote:

> . . . [T]he logical method and form flatter that longing for certainty and for repose which is in every human mind. But certainty generally is illusion, and repose is not the destiny of man. Behind the logical form lies a judgment as to the relative worth and importance of competing legislative grounds. . . . I think that the judges themselves have failed adequately to recognize their duty of weighing considerations of social advantage. . . .

The notion that judges weigh "considerations of social advantage" inevitably raises a question: What is to prevent them from simply deciding cases in accordance with their whims and prejudices and with what they conceive to be the best interests of their social class, political party, or religious group?

This question can perhaps best be answered by recalling three pertinent facts. First, appellate judges do not sit singly; three or more judges hear each appeal. Thus each judge's peculiar biases are to some extent canceled out by those of his or her colleagues. Second, appellate judges have no power to create the situations in which they make law; they must decide the cases brought before them. Nor can they ignore the legal contentions presented by the lawyers for each party. Third, they must

explain their decisions in carefully reasoned opinions, which are subsequently published. These obligations—to convince their colleagues on the bench, to decide each case on the basis of the facts and of the contentions in the lawyers' briefs and oral arguments, and finally to explain to the world in a published opinion how they arrived at their decision—impose important constraints on judges.

But the most important constraint on the freedom of judges is a more subtle one. Judges are heirs to a judicial tradition of individual self-restraint and objectivity that goes back to the twelfth century, a tradition that stresses the continuity of the law and requires that each new decision be related to established principles and precedents. However prone to bias, however ardent a partisan a person may have been before becoming a judge, he or she is likely to find it well-nigh impossible to violate this tradition.

In one of his opinions, Justice Holmes made this comment on the limits of judicial thinking:

> Judges do and must legislate, but they do so only interstitially. . . .
> A common-law judge could not say, "I think the doctrine of consideration a bit of historical nonsense and shall not enforce it in my court."

Here is how Canon 20 of the Canons of Judicial Ethics drawn up by the American Bar Association states the argument against unrestricted judicial lawmaking:

> . . . [O]urs is a government of laws and not of men, and [the judge] violates his duty as a minister of justice under such a system if he seeks to do what he may personally consider substantial justice in a particular case and disregards the general law as he knows it to be binding on him. Such action may become a precedent unsettling accepted principles and may have detrimental results beyond the immediate controversy.

The evidence is plentiful that judges, with rare exceptions, accept the restraints imposed by the judicial tradition. If anything, they are perhaps too cautious at times. Deciding where justice and the public interest lie is often difficult. Criteria are likely to be few and uncertain. Moreover, cases rarely present whole problems; they tend rather to present fragments of problems. Judges are therefore hesitant to build bold new rules on the inadequate base provided by a single case; they tend rather to stick pretty close to the rules indicated by established precedents and principles whenever these can be found. They make choices between what Holmes candidly called "competing legislative grounds" only

when precedents and clearly relevant analogies are absent. Moreover, when they do make such choices, they do their best to maintain continuity with the past and to articulate not their own views but the "felt necessities of the time"—the shared purposes of the community.

Chapter Problem

Judge Roger Traynor offered the following comments on the judicial process:

> The very caution of the judicial process offers the best of reasons for confidence in the recurring reformation of judicial rules. A decision that has not suffered premature birth has a reduced risk of premature death. Insofar as a court remains uncommitted to unduly wide implications of a decision, it gains time to inform itself further through succeeding cases. It is then better situated to retreat or advance with little disturbance to the evolutionary course of the law and to those who act in reliance upon judicial decisions.
>
> After a generation of experience, I believe that the primary obligation of a judge, at once conservative and creative, is to keep the inevitable evolution of the law on a rational course. Twenty years ago I wrote that the danger was not that judges would exceed their power, but that they would fall short of their obligation. Better the active pilot, sensitive to the currents of the river, than an armchair captain hidebound to a dated rulebook. The pilot who knows the river, however, must above all know the moorings well. If he disengages his bark from one, he must be certain he can reach another.
>
> So constant a responsibility, involving such active thought, resists inclusion within so befuddled a term as activism. Given reason and not merely the rulebook as the soul of law, I would also voice a cautionary note that the reasoning judge, the pilot on the *qui vive* [keeping a sharp lookout], is not one indifferent to rulebooks. He takes care to keep them up-to-date, reading more than ever to do so, with a critical eye for words that wear poorly and a discriminating sense for those that wear well. If he is on guard against mechanical incantations of obsolescent rules in the name of ancestral loyalty, he is also on guard against mechanical rejections of sturdy rules in the name of social justice. The complacent captain in the armchair is not more of a danger than the

PROBLEM SOURCE: Roger J. Traynor, "The Limits of Judicial Creativity," *Hastings Law Journal*, Vol. 29 (May 1978), pp. 1032–1033, © Hastings College of Law, 1978. First appeared in *Iowa Law Review*, Vol. 63 © 1977 by the University of Iowa.

pilot who would navigate with a clenched fist in the air instead of at the helm.

In sum, the thinking judge might reexamine the rules that had been preserving the status quo of Marie Antoinette, but he would not join those who would repudiate the spirit of the law so that they could proceed to behead her.

Questions

1.   Judge Traynor states elsewhere in his article: "There are even a few lawyers who still believe that it is for a judge to state, restate, occasionally expand or even contort established precedents, but that he cannot properly create new ones." Would you agree with that argument? Explain.

2.   The argument above "then goes that innovation today rests with the legislators by virtue of their unique sensitivity to public moods, or what is sometimes called an ear to the ground." What assumptions are involved in using the "ear to the ground" method to create law? Do you agree that legislators are the best lawmakers?

3.   Do you feel that judges have fallen short of their obligation to keep law on a rational course? Can you think of any examples in which judicial lawmaking has resulted in *more* rather than *less* confusion?

Questions for Review

1.   Based upon what you now know of the judges' role in lawmaking, how do you believe judges should be appointed to their positions (election or political appointment)?

2. ╱ How can one detect personal bias in a judge's decision? What recourse, if any, should the public have against judges whose decisions seem to reflect more personal bias than precedent?

3.   Do you believe that a judge should first research the law on a case and then come to a decision? Or do you believe that a judge should first decide what is right and then find cases to support his view? Defend your position.

4.   Are there a sufficient number of restraints on judicial lawmaking?

5.   If equity is such an important part of the law, why do you think there has been a merger of most courts of equity and law?

6.   Using the concepts developed in this chapter, especially the role of precedent, how would a case be decided concerning possession of land on the moon?

5
Lawmaking by Legislatures

In the last chapter we saw how courts create new legal rules by building on judge-made precedents and principles. This was once the only type of lawmaking, and it remains extremely important. In the past century or so, however, legislatures have become the primary makers of new law. And in the field of business law, even the long-standing rules that were originally established by courts have now been embodied in statutes.[1]

In this discussion of legislative lawmaking, we shall first see how statutes are enacted. Then we shall examine some of the differences between statute law and decisional law. Finally, we shall consider some of the problems that must be faced in deciding what to put into statutes.

The Legislative Process

Before a draft proposal for legislation can be enacted into law, it must clear a series of hurdles. Some have been erected by federal or state constitutions; others have been set up by the legislatures themselves, either by rule or tradition. Although the legislative process is not the same in

---

[1] We shall use the word *statutes* as a generic term; it covers, for instance, the acts of Congress and the ordinances of local governments. The common characteristic is that all are enacted by elected legislative bodies.

every legislature, the following brief description of how a bill moves through the U.S. Congress will give you a good idea of the procedures followed in most of the state legislatures.

Preparation and Introduction of the Bill

A *draft proposal*, or *bill*, must first be introduced in one house of the legislature.[2] Let us assume that our bill is introduced in the House of Representatives. Although the bill must be presented by a member of Congress, it may have been conceived and drafted by someone else: by the legislator's staff, by the staff of one of the House committees, by the House's Office of the Legislative Counsel, by a bureau in the executive branch, or by a private-interest group.

The Committee Stage

Once the bill has been introduced, it is referred to one of the standing committees of the House. Most bills never get any further. It is almost impossible to compel a committee to send a bill back to the House, and many proposals simply die in committee. If, however, the committee chair, whose power is great, decides that a bill is worthy of consideration, he or she usually schedules a public hearing at which interested groups and individuals have an opportunity to testify on it. The committee may end up by approving the bill as originally written, amending it, completely redrafting it, or declining to act favorably on it.

Modern legislative bodies are faced with such onerous workloads that they are obliged to rely heavily on their committees. No legislator can hope to become familiar with more than a fraction of the legislative proposals that are introduced. Each legislator must trust the judgment of committee members, many of whom have become intimately familiar with a particular subject and have studied hundreds of bills related to it. So when the majority of a committee refuse to act favorably on a bill, the other lawmakers can rarely be induced to override the committee's decision. Nor are they likely to oppose the revisions that the committee has suggested or to propose further amendments of their own.

In a very real sense, then, the committees determine what bills become law and what the content of those bills will be. This is why special-interest groups, in their efforts to push a bill, try so hard to influence committee members. It is also why the committee's report on a bill, and

---

2 The U.S. Congress and the legislatures of all the states except Nebraska consist of two houses.

the committee chair's remarks on the bill when it comes up for debate, are taken as the most authoritative interpretation of what the final enactment is intended to accomplish. We shall see that when judges attempt to interpret a statute, they often rely on these items of "legislative history" in their search for the legislative intent; the assumption is that the purposes that motivated the legislature as a whole to enact a law are likely to be the same as those that prompted the committee to recommend passage. For the great majority of bills, then, the House does little more than review and ratify the decisions of its committees.

Action by the Whole House

Responsibility for deciding when each of the bills reported out of committee should be brought before the House of Representatives rests with the House Rules Committee. This practice gives the Rules Committee almost a life-or-death power over the fate of each bill, and makes it probably the most influential committee of the House.

Some of the House members usually want to speak on the floor about a newly introduced bill. In the House (unlike the Senate) the total time allowed for discussion on any bill is severely restricted, and members who wish to speak must arrange for speaking time with the leaders of their party. Often the purpose of these speeches is to impress the members' constituents at home rather than to influence the other legislators.

While most of the bills that pass the House are little changed from the versions recommended by the committees, amendments are sometimes offered. The supporters of a bill must then decide whether to resist each proposed amendment. If opposition to the bill is strong, they may decide to accept certain amendments in the hope of assuring the bill's adoption.

Passage Through the Other House

After a bill has been passed by the House of Representatives, it must clear a similar set of hurdles in the Senate. If the Senate fails to approve it before the current two-year term of Congress comes to an end, the bill is dead. Then the process must start all over again with a new Congress.

Reconciliation of Differences

If the Senate passes a bill whose text is identical to that passed by the House, the bill goes at once to the President for signature. If the versions are different, however, further action is necessary to secure agreement on

a version acceptable to both houses. Sometimes the house that first passed the bill will accept the changes later made by the other house. At other times, a conference committee made up of representatives of each house will try to work out a compromise version, which each house must then approve. But bills that have cleared all the earlier stages have failed to be passed even at this late stage.

Action by the President

Before a bill can become law, it must be brought before the chief executive, the President of the United States, who has the choice of signing the bill, letting it become law without signing it, or vetoing it. A veto can be overridden by a two-thirds vote in each house, but vetoes are seldom overridden.

When a bill has passed through all these stages, it becomes a law of the United States and an act of Congress, and in due course it is published in several compilations of federal statutes.

Differences Between Decisional and Legislative Lawmaking

The two lawmaking processes, and the two forms of law that they produce, are obviously quite different. Let us consider exactly what some of the differences are.

Big Steps and Little Ones

We saw in the last chapter that the judicial tradition sharply restricts the freedom of courts to create new legal rules. Judges do make law, but since they must build on principles and precedents, they are essentially limited to "interstitial" lawmaking, that is, to filling gaps and making small adjustments in the rules. Rarely do they take bold strides. When they do, it is usually because a truly novel case has come before them for decision, though occasionally they bring about an abrupt shift in legal rules by overruling (either explicitly or implicitly) a well-established but outmoded precedent.

Legislators are much less confined. They are quite free, for instance, to repeal tomorrow a law that they passed today. They can, and quite often do, pass laws that annul long-established decisional rules. They and they alone can establish those arbitrary dividing lines so essential to any system of laws. For example, a legislature can pass a law stating that contracts to sell personal property for a price exceeding $500 are enforce-

able only if certain formal prerequisites can be shown to have been met. Judges can apply such a rule, of course, but they could not have originated it. The rules that judges make must be reasoned extensions of established principles, and an arbitrary dividing line like $500, however useful, cannot be justified in terms of principle. Finally, legislators have the power to establish new government agencies and to alter the authority of existing ones. This makes possible the adoption of far-reaching legal solutions that no court could attempt, since judges have no comparable power to create and alter institutional arrangements.

This is not to say, of course, that legislatures can do anything they choose. For one thing, constitutions impose various limitations on legislative action, some of which we shall discuss in Chapter 7. More important, the need to reconcile change with continuity, progress with tradition, limits legislatures just as it does the courts. It is true that legislators have no formal obligation to relate what they do to what has gone before. Nonetheless, considerations of what is politically prudent and administratively feasible effectively prevent bold innovations most of the time. More often than not, legislation is a belated and insufficient response to needs that have finally become too urgent to ignore. And when legislators do take action, even when they are dealing with a really new problem (such as that raised by the advent of jet propulsion), they are likely to build on existing rules, to adapt old and tested models to new uses, or to copy effective solutions worked out in other jurisdictions. Legislators are like judges, then, in preferring small steps to large ones.

Yet the difference remains: Legislatures have much more freedom to make major changes and innovations in the law than do the courts. Most people would agree, moreover, that this is both inevitable and desirable. The accumulation of precedents and the growth of an ever more complex body of principles have inevitably narrowed the scope of judicial innovation. Meanwhile, with the strengthening of democratic traditions and institutions, legislatures have become the governmental bodies most immediately responsive to the popular will and hence the most appropriate makers of major changes in the law. Finally, and perhaps most important, the swift social, economic, and technological changes of the last hundred years have necessitated the creation of new rules and new techniques of regulation at a rate that the slow judicial process of case-by-case accretion simply could not achieve.

General Problems and Particular Instances

One reason for limiting the freedom of judges to make bold policy innovations is that they do not encounter problems whole but in fragments. The first responsibility of a court is to decide the case before it. A court is

well equipped to fit rules to cases, to fill in the gaps, and to adjust existing rules; the opposing lawyers can normally be counted on to supply the needed information. The court, of course, cannot ignore the significance of its decision for future cases, but its perception of the future situations that its decision will affect must always be imperfect. The court has limited means of investigating the broader problem area of which the case before it is a part. It has neither a mandate nor the apparatus for conducting a general investigation.[3]

A legislature, on the other hand, spends far more time dealing with problem areas, with whole classes of related situations, than with particular instances. Sometimes the legislature's attention is drawn to a problem by a particular incident, but the law it eventually passes is designed for general applicability. Thus, when the members of Congress passed the federal kidnapping law of 1932, the kidnapping and death of the Lindbergh baby were fresh in their minds; however, the law they enacted was designed to deal with a whole class of possible occurrences. This is not to deny that legislatures often base their efforts on what proves to be a distorted and fragmentary picture of the problem area, but at least their attention is focused on the general problem rather than on the single case. And their traditionally broad investigatory powers enable them to make a much more thorough study of the problem than can the courts.

The Opportunity and the Obligation to Act

What we have been saying suggests a relatively simple division of functions. The legislators, we might conclude, are solely responsible for formulating broad new rules and for creating and revising the institutions necessary to put them into effect. The judges, limited to the function of disposing of the cases that others have brought before them, decide how the rules apply to the cases, and in the course of doing so, they make such interstitial adjustments in the rules as are needed to meet new situations.

---

3 Appellate judges are not, of course, wholly unable to inform themselves concerning the legislative facts (that is, the background facts needed for lawmaking, as distinguished from the adjudicative facts concerning the events in the particular case). The opposing lawyers may include legislative facts—statistical data, for instance—in the briefs and oral argument, and the judges may do a certain amount of research on their own. Before deciding the famous school desegregation cases in 1954, for example, the Supreme Court of the United States received an enormous amount of evidence on the social and psychological consequences of school segregation. Still, nobody would seriously contend that a court is as well equipped as a legislature to undertake extensive investigations.

In practice, the division of functions is not so neat. For while legislatures are certainly in a better position than judges to take major steps—to deal with whole problems—it does not follow that they always assume responsibility for doing so. When a court is presented with a case that falls within its jurisdiction, it must make some decision.[4] That decision may be bold and creative or it may be narrowly confined. Legislatures also may choose between broad and restricted action, but they have a third alternative: They may refrain from acting at all.

The statute books are full of outmoded laws that are no longer appropriate to the situations they were designed to cover, but that are still in force because legislatures have not amended or repealed them. And all states have numerous outmoded decisional rules that their courts feel compelled to apply because legislatures have not got around to passing laws superseding them.

Nearly all legislatures have more work than they can handle during their regular sessions. Only a small fraction of their time is spent in enacting laws affecting private transactions and relationships. Legislators spend much more time, for instance, in discharging their responsibility for the operation and financing of government, and in keeping in touch with their constituents. If they are to be induced to revise an existing rule, strong, persuasive, and articulate pressure must be exerted on them. If those who favor change are unable to organize and give voice to their views, or if any strong opposition to the change is expressed, busy legislators are likely to avoid taking any action.

Some fifty years ago Judge Cardozo wrote an article proposing, as a means of counteracting this inertia, that each state should establish a commission for law revision. These commissions, manned by experts, would have no power of their own. They would simply carry on a continuing study of the state's legal rules, both decisional and statutory, and from time to time would submit to the state legislature draft proposals embodying needed changes in the law. New York adopted this proposal, and its commission has done valuable work. The need for revision and modernization in most states is too great, however, for any commission, even if it works with the most conscientious and energetic of legislatures, to do much more than scratch the surface.

Under the *stare decisis* principle, primary responsibility for changing well-established but unsatisfactory decisional rules may be said to lie with the legislatures, not with the courts. But the persistent failure of

---

4 There are a few exceptions to this: The Supreme Court of the United States and some other top appellate courts have the power to choose which cases they will hear; when these courts refuse to hear a case, the decision of the lower court of appeals is final.

legislatures to meet this responsibility puts the courts under pressure to change the unsatisfactory rules themselves by overruling the offending precedents. Some critics believe that the courts have not been sufficiently willing to take this responsibility for keeping decisional rules up to date.

Influencing the Lawmakers

The forgoing remarks about legislative inertia suggest another difference between the two types of lawmaking: the difference in the methods by which private persons seek to influence judges and legislators.

Assume for the moment that you are a member of a group in Massachusetts that is extremely dissatisfied with the rule laid down by the Massachusetts Supreme Judicial Court in *George* v. *Jordan Marsh*.[5] Your group wants to get the rule changed. What can it do?

One possibility is to arrange for a lawsuit in the Massachusetts courts in which the issues of the *George* case will again be raised. Arranging for such a *test case* is not always easy, but let us assume it can be done. Presumably the lower court will feel obliged to follow the *George* precedent and thus will decide against the party your group is backing.

Knowing how reluctant courts are to overrule their earlier decisions, your group may ask itself whether it could supplement the briefs and oral arguments of the appellant's lawyer by bringing other pressures to bear on the judges. For instance, could it send a delegation to explain to the judges why the *George* rule is so bad? Could it persuade as many citizens as possible to write letters to the judges urging them to overrule *George*? If other pressures seemed insufficient, could it send pickets with placards to parade around the courthouse?

As you know, these are not proper ways to influence judges. Picketing a court is illegal in many states, and the other proposed methods, if tried, would certainly be ignored or rebuffed by the judges. The only permissible method for trying to influence a judicial decision is through the formal presentation of evidence and arguments, with each party having an opportunity to refute the evidence and arguments of the other. This is the essence of the adversary system.

Judges are supposed to be immune to private pressures of the sort traditionally exerted on political leaders. Their decisions should not be affected by concern for their personal popularity and career advancement. Moreover, their religious beliefs, personal associations, and politi-

---

[5] Refer back to pages 27–31. The court held that a person who causes severe emotional distress to another is subject to liability (as defined in the case).

cal affiliations should not determine their decisions. This is not to say, of course, that improper pressures, biases, and calculations of advantage have never been known to affect a judge's decision. Such influences, however, are repugnant to the whole judicial tradition. Certainly no competent attorney would even hint at such considerations in his or her argument.

Suppose now that your group decides that the chances of persuading the Massachusetts Supreme Judicial Court to overrule *George* are slim. The alternative, of course, is to try to persuade the Massachusetts legislature to pass a law superseding and modifying the *George* rule.

Influencing a legislature is completely different from influencing a court. The freedom of choice of legislators, as we have seen, is relatively unconfined; no adversary principle limits the permissible methods of influencing them. Legislators are openly and avowedly makers of policy decisions, and consequently the legislatures are the main arena of debate over policy. Indeed, the pressure of interest groups has always been an essential part of the legislative process. Where legislation affecting private transactions and relationships is concerned, legislators have more often been arbiters between competing groups than originators of law. In short, a group of Massachusetts citizens who wished to persuade Massachusetts legislators to change the *George* rule could expect at least a respectful hearing from them.

Moreover, the legislators would be willing to listen to arguments that could not be presented to a court. The legislators would want to know whether the change would be popular, whether it would please more voters than it would displease. The citizens' group could quite openly argue that the change would bring about social and economic advantages for the community, a type of persuasion that would not be of primary importance in arguments presented to a court.

"Written" Versus "Unwritten" Law

Up to this point we have been talking about differences between two *processes* of lawmaking. There is also a difference between the *products*. Laws passed by legislatures are often referred to as "written" law, in contrast to the "unwritten" decisional law produced by courts. Actually, of course, the decisions that embody decisional rules are reported and published. The distinction is that statutes and other enactments—constitutions, executive orders, and administrative regulations—are "written" in the sense that they have an exclusive, official text; decisional rules, on the other hand, are "unwritten" in the sense that although they can be extracted from what happened in decided cases, they have no official text.

While the words of a statute often have to be interpreted, the words themselves may not be ignored. The words *are* the law. As we shall see in Chapter 6, they set limits to the meanings that can be attributed to the statute. For instance, if a law provides that no male under the age of sixteen may marry, no amount of interpreting will make it permissible for a boy of fifteen to get married.

The language of the opinion that accompanies a judicial decision has no comparable force. As we saw in Chapter 4, the precedent is established by what the court does, not by what it says. An opinion is an authoritative discussion of rules relating to the problem at hand, but it is not the official text of a rule or rules. To put it differently, an opinion announcing an appellate decision could be phrased in a number of different ways without changing the rule of the case.

Convenience, Uniformity, and Codification

A final basis of comparison concerns the relative convenience of the decisional and statutory forms of law for the lawyers and judges who have to work with them. On the whole, it is easier to determine the applicable rule in a particular case when the basic rules are statutory than when they are purely decisional. Even with all the modern aids to case research—treatises, digests, encyclopedias, and the like[6]—finding controlling precedents is usually a much more arduous task than finding relevant statutory provisions.[7]

The greater convenience of working with statutes is one of several reasons why, over the past century, our legislatures have enacted a considerable part of U.S. decisional law into statutory form. The process of assembling scattered decisional rules into an orderly statutory code is known as *codification*. Sometimes the transformation has taken place

---

[6] In recent years there has been a development of great interest to legal researchers. That development is the increasing capacity of computers to assist in searching for legal reference matter. A number of law libraries and law firms now have computer terminals that will, among other things, provide a lawyer with many current case citations on particular topics. Students interested in this development can obtain more information about it by contacting a law librarian or *Lexis* (200 Park Avenue, New York, N.Y. 10017).

[7] The searcher's work is not always finished, however, when the statute is found; it may still be necessary to look up cases. This is because the statute is likely to include concepts and subordinate rules taken from decisional law. To understand these, it may be necessary to look up cases antedating the statute. Moreover, once a statute has been applied and interpreted by a court, the court's interpretation becomes in effect a part of the statute; in the future, lawyers and judges must look at the interpretation as well as the statute itself. This is why many statute books are annotated: Following each provision is a brief summary of the decisions interpreting it.

without change in the rules themselves; sometimes the codification has been in response to pressure for substantive change, and the legislators have modified the rules in the course of codifying them.

Much of the stimulus for codification has arisen from the need for greater uniformity among the rules of the several states. This has been particularly true in the field of commercial law, where conflicting state decisional rules have often interfered seriously with the conduct of interstate business. In 1890 the states set up a Conference of Commissioners on Uniform State Laws. The commissioners, appointed by their state governors, were to be specialists in the various fields of law under study. Over the years the conference has drafted a number of legislative proposals for submission to the state legislatures. Some of these proposals—most notably the Uniform Commercial Code—have been adopted by all or most of the states; others have been less well received.

The extent to which decisional law has been codified differs from state to state. Many states have codified their criminal law and now have no purely common-law crimes (that is, acts made criminal solely by judicial decision). There is, however, still a great deal of uncodified decisional law in every one of the states; nowhere do we find the comprehensive codification that characterizes the civil-law tradition.

Some Problems of Legislative Drafting

Some day you may be asked to collaborate with a lawyer in preparing a draft proposal for legislation in some field in which you are an expert. It is more likely, however, that your contacts with legislation will be confined to figuring out with a lawyer how some already-enacted statute affects transactions that concern you. Thus, even if you never have anything to do with the actual drafting of legislation, you will find it useful to have some conception of the problems involved in this process.

Before setting to work, the drafter of a statute must decide the answers to certain broad questions.

What Technique of Channeling Conduct Is Most Likely to Achieve the Desired Results?

As an example, imagine that the framer's object is to limit the actions that a debt collector may take in collecting money from a debtor. Should the law be written to limit these actions sharply no matter what form they take? Or should debt collectors be restrained only from acting out-

rageously? What penalties should be imposed on the erring debt collector? Should collectors treat consumers who routinely evade their bills differently from those who have failed to pay due to temporary financial difficulties? Perhaps the Consumer Protection Division of the State Attorney General's Office should launch a major educational campaign to inform consumers of the pitfalls of failing to pay their bills.

Nowadays the drafter of legislation is likely to be not a legislator but a trained specialist. Although answering the forgoing questions requires the making of policy decisions that are probably beyond the authority of the drafter, he or she must be familiar with the alternative techniques of channeling private conduct and with the experiences that different jurisdictions have had in applying these techniques to similar problems in the past. Only then will the drafter be able to outline the alternatives and suggest what their respective advantages and disadvantages are likely to be.

How Precise and Detailed Should the Statute Be?

How far should the legislative drafter go in trying to devise specific provisions to cover future situations? The ideal statute would specify all the possible situations to which it should apply. In addition, its words would convey precisely the same meaning to everyone who read them. Obviously, no statute writer could ever realize these goals. Since human foresight is limited, a drafter could never hope to anticipate all the possible situations to which the statute might conceivably apply. And words are at best imperfect symbols for communicating intent.

Most people believe that while perfect clarity and precision are impossible, they must always be the ideals toward which the statute writer should strive. There are circumstances, however, in which the framers of a statute are justified in being *deliberately imprecise*. Sometimes legislators realize that some sort of action must be taken to deal with a certain problem, but they also realize that the scope of the problem and of the remedies needed are not yet clear and will be revealed only as the future unfolds. They may therefore decide to enact a statute that merely identifies the problem, outlines in relatively broad terms the primary and remedial rules to be applied, and leaves the details to be filled in through successive applications of the statute to particular cases.

This is, of course, the typical approach of the framers of constitutional provisions, for they realize that constitutions must last a long time and usually are hard to amend. What phrase could be more deliberately imprecise, for instance, than "No State shall . . . deprive any person of life, liberty, or property, without due process of law"?

The key provision of the Sherman Antitrust Act of 1890 is embodied in a single sentence: "Every contract, combination in the form of trust or otherwise, or conspiracy, in restraint of trade or commerce among the several states or with foreign nations, is hereby declared to be illegal." Another sentence of about equal length and imprecision makes it illegal to "monopolize or attempt to monopolize." The rest of the brief statute consists of remedial provisions. No attempt is made to define the broad terms used in the key sentence.[8]

A statute is a sort of communication, addressed to the various categories of people who will be affected by its enactment. It requires (or forbids or permits or enables) private persons to do certain things; it tells enforcement officials what they must or may do; and it provides judges with a new set of rules to apply and interpret in disposing of cases. In effect, a broad, general statute "passes the buck" to the addressees; it delegates to them the task of elaborating its meaning, progressively, case by case. A private person is likely to be the first to test the statute, by doing something that causes another private person, or an official, to react. Each of them is "interpreting" the statute. The ultimate and authoritative interpretation, however, must come from the courts, when controversies engendered by conduct with which the statute is concerned are brought before them.[9]

A broad, general statute starts out, then, as a somewhat cryptic communication. It takes on precision as its addressees test it out by adopting their successive interpretations. The uncertainty produced initially by an imprecise law is often preferable to the crippling certainty of a highly specific law that is ill adapted to the situations that arise after its enactment. Premature, excessive precision may deny enforcement officials and judges all latitude of interpretation and may make it impossible for them to administer justice in an orderly and reasonable way. When a "hard" case arises, of a sort not foreseen by the lawmakers, the judge who must decide it is left with no choice but to apply a rule that he or she knows will produce an inappropriate result.

We must not make too strong a case for vagueness and imprecision in statute writing, however. More often than not, imprecision is inap-

---

[8] Terms like *contract, combination, conspiracy, restraint of trade,* and *monopolize* are not quite so empty of specific content as they may seem to the layperson. They had been used before 1890 in judicial opinions and statutes and had taken on meaning from such uses. Even so, judges have had a large measure of freedom to create law when they apply the Sherman Act provisions to particular cases.

[9] We traditionally employ the word *interpret* to describe what a court does when it applies a statute. This is true even though it is obvious, when the statute is deliberately imprecise, that the judges are doing much more than determining what the words of the statute mean. We shall say more about this in the next chapter.

propriate and troublesome. Statute writers usually fall into vague language not because they decide to do so, but because their thinking is fuzzy or because they are in a hurry. Sometimes, too, vague words are used with the hope of lulling potentially antagonistic legislators into voting for what seems to be a harmless bill.

What Vocabulary Is Appropriate?

The legislative drafter must first try to identify the sort of people who will probably be reading the statute, and then choose a vocabulary that will be appropriate to them. Such questions as these are appropriate: Are the private addressees members of the general public, or are they a restricted group familiar with a technical vocabulary (for example, the vocabulary of pharmacology)? Are the officials who must read the statute likely to be familiar with a technical vocabulary? Must the statute be made understandable to persons without legal training?

Anyone who has read statutes must realize that the typical drafter assumes that the principal readers will be lawyers, experienced administrative officials, and judges. Little effort is made to use language intelligible to persons outside the legal profession. The usual aim is to avoid ambiguity at all costs, and so a drafter tends to choose words and phrases with sharply delimited meanings familiar to persons trained in the law. This accounts for the unlovely style sometimes known as "legal English," which many people assume is designed to confuse and mystify them. Among its characteristics are the repetition of the same words or phrases, strings of near-synonyms, and awkward words like "aforesaid" and "heretofore."[10] Inelegant though they may seem, such words and phrases often have a relatively precise scope and content established by judicial interpretation. Under most circumstances, drafters are justified in their decision to concentrate on speaking clearly and unambiguously to the reader trained in law.

As you can see, the legislative drafter faces an extremely difficult task when drafting a document. The problem of balancing precision and clarity is often quite troublesome.

---

10 A sample: "Be it enacted . . . that from and after the passage of this act it shall be unlawful for any person, company, partnership or corporation, in any manner whatsoever, to prepay the transportation, or in any way assist or encourage the immigration or migration of any alien or aliens, any foreigner or foreigners, into the United States, its Territories, or the District of Columbia, under contract or agreement, parol or special, express or implied, made previous to the importation or migration of such alien or aliens, foreigner or foreigners, to perform labor or service of any kind in the United States, its Territories, or the District of Columbia."

Chapter Problem

Suppose that a group of citizens from the state of Massachusetts decides that it would like to draft a statute to help people like Mrs. George in *George* v. *Jordan Marsh*. Their plan is to present a draft proposal to the state legislature. They are convinced that nobody should be harassed by a credit bureau, but they have not thought the whole problem through. They want you to do that for them, and to embody your conclusions in a draft statute that they will discuss at their next meeting.

Prepare a short draft statute for them, together with notes explaining your inclusions and exclusions. As a starting point, consider the following section of the U.S. Fair Debt Collection Practices Act (15 USCA §1692d).

§1692d. Harassment or abuse

A debt collector may not engage in any conduct the natural consequence of which is to harass, oppress, or abuse any person in connection with the collection of a debt. Without limiting the general application of the foregoing, the following conduct is a violation of this section:

(1)   The use or threat of use of violence or other criminal means to harm the physical person, reputation, or property of any person.

(2)   The use of obscene or profane language or language the natural consequence of which is to abuse the hearer or reader.

(3)   The publication of a list of consumers who allegedly refuse to pay debts, except to a consumer reporting agency or to persons meeting the requirements of section 1681a(f) or 1681b(3) of this title.

(4)   The advertisement for sale of any debt to coerce payment of the debt.

(5)   Causing a telephone to ring or engaging any person in telephone conversation repeatedly or continuously with intent to annoy, abuse, or harass any person at the called number.

(6)   Except as provided in section 1692b of this title, the placement of telephone calls without meaningful disclosure of the caller's identity.

Questions for Review

1.   How does a draft proposal become law?

2.   Judging from the description of the process by which legislation is enacted, what do you think would be the most appropriate stage

at which an interest group might seek to influence the shaping of a particular legislative proposal? Why?

3. The pressure of interest groups has always been an intrinsic part of the legislative process. But if a legislature responds only to the interest groups that apply the most pressure, will the laws that it makes be unjust? Explain your answer.

4. Explain how the House Rules Committee has life-or-death power over the fate of each bill. Do you feel that it is right for the committee to have this power?

5. What are some of the differences between the lawmaking role of a judge (decisional lawmaking) and that of a member of one of the committees of a house of the legislature (legislative lawmaking)?

6. Explain the statement made earlier in this chapter: "An opinion announcing an appellate decision could be phrased in a number of different ways without changing the rule of the case."

7. What is the purpose of codification?

8. What are some important considerations that must be made before a draft proposal for legislation is written?

6
Judicial Lawmaking II: The Interpretation of Statutes

The meaning of a statutory provision and the types of situations it does or does not cover are matters that are ultimately determined by the courts. Citizens who wish to understand their legal environment should know something about this process of interpretation and application, which is called, *statutory construction*. They do not, of course, need a detailed knowledge of the many rules of statutory construction that judges have developed, but they should have some idea of the main problems that judges encounter.

In the vast majority of cases, the courts have no trouble determining how a statute applies. But a significant minority of cases do present problems of application.

Difficulties of interpretation are created in several ways. Some statutes contain unintentional errors and ambiguities because they were poorly drafted. Other statutes are unclear because those who pushed them through the legislature sought to avoid opposition by being vague or silent on potentially controversial matters. But the most important reason for the lack of absolute clarity and preciseness in many statutes is that their framers were not able to foresee and to provide for all possible future situations. Realizing their inability to do this, the wisest legislators have usually preferred to be deliberately imprecise, and by the generality of their language, they have necessarily delegated to others the task of filling in the details. The principal recipients of this task are administrative officials[1] and judges. The more imprecise the statute is, the greater

---

[1] For a discussion of the lawmaking and adjudicative functions of administrators, see Chapter 8.

the delegated authority must be. With a very broad and general statute like the Sherman Act, the "interpreter" becomes, in effect, the true lawmaker.

Problems of statutory interpretation typically fall into one of the following categories:

1. A legislature passes a statute that states that it applies to a designated class of persons or objects but that fails to specify the precise boundaries of the class. For example, in a statute that applies to "vehicles," the question is whether "vehicles" as a class includes, for instance, an airplane, a tricycle, and an ancient carriage mounted on a pedestal. Or a statute may refer to "persons," and a case arises involving a corporation: Is a corporation a "person"?

2. From its language alone, a statute seems to apply to a particular situation, but common sense suggests that it really should not. For example, a federal statute makes it a crime to detain a postal employee while on duty. Does this statute apply to a local sheriff who serves an arrest warrant on a mail carrier charged with murder?

3. From its language alone, a statute does *not* seem to apply to a particular situation, but common sense suggests that it really should. For example, an old act of Congress providing for the sale of public land at a low price to settlers specified the amount of land that single men and married men might buy. A widow sought to buy some land. Was she a "single man" or a "married man," or was she not qualified under the law to buy land?

4. An old statute remains on the books long after the immediate problems it was designed to deal with have changed. For example, a statute passed in 1880 refers to "vehicles." A case arising in 1962 involves an automobile. Since automobiles were unknown in 1880, does the statute apply? Is it reasonable to assume that any vehicle unknown to the statute writers in 1880 should be excluded from its coverage? Or should any object to which the designation "vehicle" could reasonably be applied at any later date automatically be covered? Or is some intermediate interpretation preferable?

The Intention
of the Legislature

When writing an opinion in a case requiring statutory construction, a judge usually says at the outset that the court's object is to carry out as best it can the intention of the legislature. There is no disagreement over

this objective, but difficulties arise in trying to achieve it. Some of these difficulties are discussed in the following sections.

Finding a Collective Intention

Determining what a group of legislators "intended" when they voted for a bill is not easy. Although they all voted for the same set of words, it does not follow that they all did so with the same intention. What they thought is, indeed, largely unrecorded, but we can be sure that they did not all favor the law for precisely the same reasons or with the same expectations as to what it would accomplish. Many of them unquestionably voted for it merely because they trusted or were beholden to its sponsors. Others voted for it because they expected those sponsors to reciprocate on some later occasion, and still others were pressed to vote for it by the leaders of their party. Some legislators, particularly the bill's sponsors and the members of the committees that worked on it, certainly had definite views on what the bill was designed to accomplish. As we have already suggested, it is usually assumed that in voting for a bill, the legislative majorities are in effect ratifying the policies enunciated by their committees. Although this assumption is usually justified, one of the reasons for adopting it is the impossibility of making any better generalization about the legislative intention.

Finding an Intention
with Respect to Specific Situations

Hard as it is to identify a general legislative intention, it is harder still to surmise what the legislature "intended" with respect to particular situations not explicitly provided for. Few legislators give much thought to the detailed application of a statute. Even those who are most concerned with its passage inevitably fail to foresee some of the situations that later arise; consequently, its applicability to these situations is uncertain. In short, talking about the legislative intent with reference to specific fact-situations is likely to be wholly unrealistic.

Finding an Underlying Purpose

Judges have tended to conclude that the only sensible solution to this problem of identifying the intention of the legislature is not to look for a specific intent shared by all those who voted for the law but to search instead for the broad purposes and policies that probably motivated those who actively favored the bill. The judges ask themselves such ques-

tions as these: What were the legal rules channeling conduct in this area of activity before this statute was enacted? How does the statute seem to have changed those rules? What seem to have been the ills that the statute was designed to cure? Then, having identified as best they can the general purposes underlying the statute, the judges ask themselves one final question: What interpretation of the specific statutory provisions that are apparently applicable to the fact-situation before us will best serve the purposes of the statute as a whole?

Not only is this the only realistic way to use the legislative intent, but it is also the way in which legislators almost certainly expect judges to behave. Having done their best to embody their collective objectives in a final enactment, legislators do not expect judges to try to figure out precisely what their thoughts were with respect to particular fact-situations, or what their thoughts *would have been* if the situations had occurred to them. Legislators are aware that the applicability of their statute to particular cases will not always be clear. They expect judges to decide cases by accepting the authority delegated to them to elaborate the statute's meanings—that is, to work out sensible applications of the statute's identified purposes. And by accepting this authority, judges exercise the limited power to make law that our legal system bestows upon them.

The case of *Wolverton* v. *Stanwood* provides an excellent illustration of the difficulties faced by judges in interpreting ambiguous statutes.

Kirk Wolverton v. Martin H. Stanwood et al.

Supreme Court of Oregon, 1977
Or. 563 P. 2d 1203

> HOWELL, Justice.

Plaintiff filed an action for damages under the Unlawful Trade Practices Act.... A jury returned a verdict for plaintiff for $500 general damages and $500 punitive damages. The trial court granted defendant's motion for a judgment n.o.v.[2] Plaintiff appeals.

... The primary issue on appeal is whether the Act applies to the facts in the instant case....

Defendants, as a partnership, operate a Texaco service station known as B. & M. Texaco. Plaintiff answered an advertisement placed in a newspaper by the defendants for the sale of a 427 cubic inch Chevrolet en-

---

2 Authors' note: *non obstante veredicto*. If the jury clearly makes a grievously wrong decision, the court may enter a verdict for the plaintiff even though the jury held for the defendant (or vice versa).

gine. While inspecting the engine, he was again orally assured that it was a 427. However, after purchasing the engine, plaintiff discovered it was a 400 cubic inch engine, rather than a 427. According to plaintiff, defendants also represented the engine to be in good running condition and that it had only about 18,000 miles on it. Plaintiff contends that each of these representations was false, and there was evidence to support this contention.

ORS 646.608(1) provides:

"A person engages in a practice hereby declared to be unlawful when in the course of his business, vocation or occupation he:

"... (g) Represents that real estate, goods or services are of a particular standard, quality, or grade, or that real estate or goods are of a particular style or model, if they are of another; ..."

... Because of the jury's verdict for plaintiff, we must assume that the engine was sold by the B. & M. Texaco partnership and that the "standard, quality, or grade" of the engine was not as represented, although there was conflicting evidence on these issues. The only remaining issue is whether the engine was sold "in the course of (the partnership's) business, vocation or occupation." Ordinarily, this, too, is a question for the jury, but it is the duty of the court to determine whether there is any substantial evidence to support that finding. When, as in this case, the wording of the statute is ambiguous, the court must first interpret the statute so that the evidence can be reviewed against an objective and meaningful background.

Although the statutory language in question was taken from Section 2 of the Uniform Deceptive Trade Practices Act, 7 ULA 836 and 354, we have been unable to discover any previous judicial interpretation of that language or any legislative history which would explain its intended meaning. Moreover, the wording of similar provisions in analogous statutes is so different that it is of little or no assistance in defining the meaning of this provision. ...

It could be argued that the phrase "in the course of his business, vocation or occupation" should be construed so as to apply to all unlawful practices except those which arise out of strictly private transactions and which are totally unconnected with the business or employment of the defendant. On the other hand, the statute could be interpreted to apply only to those unlawful practices which arise out of the ordinary, everyday activities of the defendant's business or occupation. *The former construction could be justified on the basis of a broad reading of the general*

policy of the statute to discourage deceptive trade practices and to provide a viable remedy for consumers who are damaged by such conduct. The latter construction could be supported by a broad reading of the limitation which restricts the application of the statute to those unlawful practices that arise out of the course of the defendant's business. [Emphasis added.] Such an interpretation would reflect a presumption that this restriction was intended to limit the application of the statute to those situations which tend to present a continuing, and therefore more serious, threat to the general public.

... In the absence of any guidance as to which of these policies the legislature would have intended to prevail, we have determined to seek a middle ground. We believe that the statute should be applied only to those unlawful practices which arise out of transactions which are at least indirectly connected with the ordinary and usual course of defendant's business, vocation or occupation.

... Applying that construction to this case, we believe that the jury could have reasonably found that the sale of the automobile engine was at least indirectly connected with the ordinary business of defendants' automotive service station. Moreover, there was testimony that on at least one previous occasion the defendants had procured an engine for another customer and installed it in his car. Therefore, we believe that the entry of a judgment for defendants notwithstanding the jury's verdict was in error.

Reversed and remanded with directions to reinstate the judgment for plaintiff.   <

The Meaning and Context
of a Statute's Words

Justice Howell's opinion suggest two other important principles of statutory interpretation.

The first is that words rarely have only a single meaning. A few words have perfectly specific referents, but most words have a range of meanings. Indeed, they have a slightly different meaning each time they are used in a new sentence. The proper question to ask about a word, then, is not just "What does it mean?" but "What can it mean?" and "What are the limits of permissible meaning that can be attributed to it?"

"A word," Justice Holmes once wrote, "is not a crystal, transparent and unchanged; it is the skin of a living thought and may vary greatly in color and content according to the circumstances and time in which it is used." Note in *Wolverton* v. *Stanwood* how Justice Howell plays with the

meaning of the phrase "in the course of his business, vocation or occupation."

Second, words cannot really be understood apart from their contexts. Context first of all means textual context. *Textual context* includes not only the sentence in which the word or phrase appears but also the successively larger units into which the statute is divided: the paragraph, section, chapter or article, and the whole statute.

Much broader than textual context is what is sometimes called *circumstantial context*. The circumstantial context of a statutory provision embraces such relevant matters as the sources of dissatisfaction that gave rise to the new act and the legal rules in effect prior to its enactment. Circumstantial context may even include relevant social, economic, and technological circumstances that prevailed at the time the statute was passed.

A consideration of a statute's circumstantial context is indispensable to a search for purpose. To discover what legislators intended to include under the concept "vehicle" in a statute passed in 1880, a judge will probably want to know what types of vehicles existed in 1880.[3] He will also want to identify the particular problem to which the legislators were addressing themselves. Whether the term "vehicles" in an 1880 statute should be construed today to cover automobiles and airplanes depends on what the statute was meant to accomplish. If it concerns safety on the roads, for instance, it presumably covers automobiles (even though they did not exist in 1880) but not airplanes. If, on the other hand, it is a tax statute designed to offset local government expenditures in aid of transportation, perhaps airplanes are also covered. Similarly, whether a statute referring to "persons" covers corporations depends on the reasons that led to its enactment. If it was designed to regulate marriages, obviously corporations are not "persons"; but if its purpose was to regulate the use of property, perhaps they are.

It is important for you to understand that we are *not* saying that judges are free to give to statutory words a meaning outside their range of etymologically permissible meanings just to produce a more reasonable result in a particular case. Judges have no authority to rewrite statutes merely because they think that the indicated meaning of the language will lead to an undesirable result, or because they suspect that the legislators overlooked some important policy consideration. The words used *do* limit the judges' freedom of interpretation; judges may not

---

[3] On the other hand, it is not necessarily true that the legislators intended to limit the scope of their enactment to vehicles they knew about; they may have intended that the legislation should cover new types of vehicles as they were developed.

assign a wholly unnatural meaning to words in order to carry out some surmised purpose.[4]

What we *are* saying is that when using an apparently clear meaning would produce a surprising result, a judge should look again to see whether the meaning is really as clear as it seems. She should make sure that she has read the provision in relation to its underlying purpose as indicated by the textual and circumstantial contexts. If after doing this, however, she remains convinced that no other meaning can reasonably be attributed to the words, then she must use that meaning and leave to the legislature the responsibility for amending the statute if it so desires.

Suppose, for instance, that a legislature has passed a law saying that certain occupational categories are subject to a special tax, but it has inadvertently omitted one category from the list. That category could not be made subject to the tax no matter how overwhelming the evidence that it should have been included. Or suppose a law specifies that "no male under the age of sixteen may marry." No judge could so construe the provision as to permit the marriage of a particular fifteen-year-old boy, whatever the peculiar circumstances of the case or the evidence that the legislature had overlooked the need for exceptions to this rule.

The Use
of Legislative History

Since the text of a statute is the final, official embodiment of the legislature's efforts, it is obviously the first place that judges must look in their search for purpose. More often than not, they can find the purpose or policy behind the statute by reading it, bearing in mind what they know of its circumstantial context. But sometimes this is not enough; sometimes the most careful reading of the language reveals no underlying purpose that is readily applicable to the problem before the court. Faced with this situation, judges may turn to other sources of evidence of the

---

4 We have been stressing the importance of carrying out the legislature's purpose. Another reason for limiting the freedom of judges to interpret is that private addressees of a statute may have assumed that the statutory words mean what they appear to mean. If judges are too free to interpret, they may defeat the legitimate expectations of these addressees.

The courts are particularly careful in construing criminal statutes to make sure that those who are subject to them have had fair warning. Such statutes are construed strictly: Courts try not to attribute to their words any but the clearest and most obvious meanings, lest the charge be made that a defendant was not given fair warning and has therefore been denied due process of law.

legislative purpose. Of these, the most important is the statute's *legislative history*—the proceedings in the legislature that led to its enactment.

As we have already suggested, the most significant items of evidence in the legislative history are undoubtedly the reports of the committees that worked on the bill and the statements made for the record by the heads of those committees. This is because legislatures ordinarily accept the work of their committees on matters of detail and merely vote to ratify the purposes that the committees have announced. Where different bills have been voted by the two houses and have had to be reconciled (see page 108), the reports of the members of the conference committee to their respective houses are valuable, too. Also consulted, though less reliable, are speeches made during debate on the bill, testimony received in committee hearings, and recorded votes on amendments.

Judges have not always been willing to hear evidence of a statute's legislative history; indeed, in many jurisdictions such evidence is not considered even today. In many states the use of legislative history is effectively prevented by the absence or inadequacy of records of legislative proceedings.

For many years the Supreme Court of the United States was reluctant to consider evidence of legislative history. The Court would only consider such evidence if the language of the statute before it was "of doubtful meaning and susceptible on its face of two constructions" (to quote one of its opinions). If the language was plain, the Court would look no further, even though the result produced by applying the "plain meaning" might seem questionable. In 1940, however, a majority of the Court joined in expressing a much more receptive view: Whenever there could be any doubt about the legislature's purpose—even though the literal meaning of the language was clear—a consideration of legislative history might be appropriate. This 1940 opinion is worth quoting at some length, since it probably represents the present position of members of the Supreme Court and of many other judges.

> There is, of course, no more persuasive evidence of the purpose of a statute than the words by which the legislature undertook to give expression to its wishes. Often these words are sufficient in and of themselves to determine the purpose of the legislation. In such cases we have followed their plain meaning. When that meaning has led to absurd or futile results, however, this Court has looked beyond the words to the purpose of the act. Frequently, however, even when the plain meaning did not produce absurd results but merely an unreasonable one "plainly at variance with the policy of the legislation as a whole" this Court has

followed that purpose, rather than the literal words. When aid to construction of the meaning of words, as used in the statute, is available, there certainly can be no "rule of law" which forbids its use, however clear the words may appear on "superficial examination." The interpretation of the meaning of statutes, as applied to justiciable controversies, is exclusively a judicial function. This duty requires one body of public servants, the judges, to construe the meaning of what another body, the legislators, has said. Obviously there is danger that the courts' conclusion as to legislative purpose will be unconsciously influenced by the judges' own views or by factors not considered by the enacting body. A lively appreciation of the danger is the best assurance of escape from its threat but hardly justifies an acceptance of a literal interpretation dogma which withholds from the courts available information for reaching a correct conclusion. . . .[5]

Many judges are still reluctant, however, to open the door to legislative history. This is not just a sign of judicial conservatism. The evidence provided by legislative history is often meager, contradictory, and hard to appraise. Much of what legislators say and do while they are acting on a bill cannot be trusted as an indication of the collective intention. Moreover, now that legislators know that courts will look at the legislative record, they are occasionally tempted to try to "manufacture" legislative history.[6] Finally, the practice of reviewing evidence of legislative history may be burdensome for litigants. Once they know that the courts will look at this kind of evidence, lawyers may feel that in all cases involving problems of statutory interpretation, they must pore over the legislative records for evidence to put in their briefs. But often these records are not readily accessible in local law libraries, and searching through them is a time-consuming job that may prove a waste of time in the end.

To illustrate the courts' use of legislative history, we have chosen the case of *United Steelworkers of America* v. *Weber*, which was decided by the

---

[5] *United States* v. *American Trucking Associations*, 310 U.S. 534 [1940].

[6] Take the hypothetical case of Senator Mugwump, who represents a widget-manufacturing community. He rises during debate on a tax bill to remark: "Naturally the excise tax that this bill establishes does not fall on widgets." Nobody contradicts him—possibly because nobody is listening. Later, when the widget manufacturers are claiming exemption from the tax, they point to Senator Mugwump's uncontradicted statement as evidence of the legislative purpose. (Competent judges would presumably not accept this assertion by a single legislator as proof of a legislative intention to exempt widgets.)

We are not suggesting that statements inserted into the record for the purpose of creating evidence of legislative intention are always unreliable. Normally, committee reports and statements by committee members are prompted, at least in part, by a desire to help addressees to interpret a piece of legislation.

Supreme Court of the United States in 1979. The issue of interpretation in this case was relatively complex, and a few background facts are necessary to help you understand it.

The Civil Rights Act of 1964 is one of the most significant pieces of legislation passed in the last twenty years. Title VII of the act specifically forbids employers from discrimination in employment practices on the basis of color, religion, race, sex, or national origin. This rather broad statement is qualified by allowing discrimination where religion, sex, or national origin could be considered a "bona fide occupational qualification."

Personnel managers and labor relations executives have made significant attempts to improve their hiring, training, and promotion strategies in line with the mandate of Title VII. In fact, many major employers have instituted affirmative action plans to improve the situation. These plans mean that organizations *actively* move in the direction of finding, hiring, training, and rewarding individuals who have previously been the targets of discrimination. But not all employees react to affirmative action plans in the same way. While some employees are pleased with the results of the plans, others feel that the plans do not create equal employment opportunities for all, but rather discriminate against those who are not specifically the targets of affirmative action. Kaiser Aluminum and Chemical Corporation recently had its affirmative action plan tested for precisely that reason. Brian Weber, a white male, brought a class-action suit against Kaiser, complaining that he had been discriminated against in violation of his own Title VII rights when Kaiser implemented its affirmative action plan, which reserved 50 percent of the in-plant training openings for black employees.

Mr. Weber's case recently came before the Supreme Court, presenting it with a difficult problem: On the one hand, the Court wanted to make sure that *all people* are treated equally; on the other hand, it wanted to help groups that have been hurt in the past. The Court also wanted to be certain, by acquainting itself with the history of the legislation, that it did not contradict the purpose of the Civil Rights Act.

United Steelworkers of America v. *Brian F. Weber*

Supreme Court of the United States, 1979

> MR. JUSTICE BRENNAN delivered the opinion of the Court.

... Challenged here is the legality of an affirmative action plan—collectively bargained by an employer and a union—that reserves for black employees 50% of the openings in an in-plant craft training pro-

gram until the percentage of black craft workers in the plant is commensurate with the percentage of blacks in the local labor force. The question for decision is whether Congress, in Title VII of the Civil Rights Act of 1964 as amended, left employers and unions in the private sector free to take such race-conscious steps to eliminate manifest racial imbalances in traditionally segregated job categories. We hold that Title VII does not prohibit such race-conscious affirmative action plans.

I

In 1974 petitioner United Steelworkers of America (USWA) and petitioner Kaiser Aluminum & Chemical Corporation (Kaiser) entered into a master collective-bargaining agreement covering terms and conditions of employment at 15 Kaiser plants. The agreement contained, inter alia, an affirmative action plan designed to eliminate conspicuous racial imbalances in Kaiser's then almost exclusively white craft work forces. Black craft hiring goals were set for each Kaiser plant equal to the percentage of blacks in the respective local labor forces. To enable plants to meet these goals, on-the-job training programs were established to teach unskilled production workers—black and white—the skills necessary to become craft workers. The plan reserved for black employees 50% of the openings in these newly created in-plant training programs.

. . . This case arose from the operation of the plan at Kaiser's plant in Gramercy, La. Until 1974 Kaiser hired as craft workers for that plant only persons who had had prior craft experience. Because blacks had long been excluded from craft unions, few were able to present such credentials. As a consequence, prior to 1974 only 1.83% (five out of 273) of the skilled craft workers at the Gramercy plant were black, even though the work force in the Gramercy area was approximately 39% black.

Pursuant to the national agreement Kaiser altered its craft hiring practice in the Gramercy plant. Rather than hiring already trained outsiders, Kaiser established a training program to train its production workers to fill craft openings. Selection of craft trainees was made on the basis of seniority, with the proviso that at least 50% of the new trainees were to be black until the percentage of black skilled craft workers in the Gramercy plant approximated the percentage of blacks in the local labor force. . . .

During 1974, the first year of the operation of the Kaiser-USWA affirmative action plan, 13 craft trainees were selected from Gramercy's production work force. Of these, 7 were black and 6 white. The most junior black selected into the program had less seniority than several white production workers whose bids for admission were rejected. Thereafter one of those white production workers, respondent Brian Weber, instituted

this class action in the United States District Court for the Eastern District of Louisiana.

The complaint alleged that the filling of craft trainee positions at the Gramercy plant pursuant to the affirmative action program had resulted in junior black employees receiving training in preference to more senior white employees, thus discriminating against respondent and other similarly situated white employees in violation of §§703(a) and (d) of Title VII. The District Court held that the plan violated Title VII, entered a judgment in favor of the plaintiff class, and granted a permanent injunction prohibiting Kaiser and the USWA "from denying plaintiffs, Brian F. Weber and all other members of the class, access to on-the-job training programs on the basis of race." 415 F Supp 761 (1976). A divided panel of the Court of Appeals for the Fifth Circuit affirmed, holding that all employment preferences based upon race, including those preferences incidental to bona fide affirmative action plans, violated Title VII's prohibition against racial discrimination in employment. . . .

II

We emphasize at the outset the narrowness of our inquiry. Since the Kaiser-USWA plan does not involve state action, this case does not present an alleged violation of the Equal Protection Clause of the Constitution. Further, since the Kaiser-USWA plan was adopted voluntarily, we are not concerned with what Title VII requires or with what a court might order to remedy a past proven violation of the Act. The only question before us is the narrow statutory issue of whether Title VII forbids private employers and unions from voluntarily agreeing upon bona fide affirmative action plans that accord racial preferences in the manner and for the purpose provided in the Kaiser-USWA plan. That question was expressly left open in McDonald v. Santa Fe Trail Trans. Co., 427 US 273 (1976), which held, in a case not involving affirmative action, that Title VII protects whites as well as blacks from certain forms of racial discrimination.

Respondent argues that Congress intended in Title VII to prohibit all race-conscious affirmative action plans. Respondent's argument rests upon a literal interpretation of §§703(a) and (d) of the Act. Those sections make it unlawful to "discriminate . . . because of . . . race" in hiring and in the selection of apprentices for training programs. Since, the argument runs, McDonald v. Santa Fe Trans. Co., supra, settled that Title VII *forbids* discrimination against whites as well as blacks, and since the Kaiser-USWA affirmative action plan operates to discriminate against white employees solely because they are white, it follows that the Kaiser-USWA plan violates Title VII.

... Respondent's argument is not without force. But it overlooks the significance of the fact that the Kaiser-USWA plan is an affirmative action plan voluntarily adopted by private parties to eliminate traditional patterns of racial segregation. In this context respondent's reliance upon a literal construction of §§703(a) and (d) and upon McDonald is misplaced. The prohibition against racial discrimination ... *must therefore be read against the background of the legislative history of Title VII and the historical context from which the Act arose.* [Emphasis added.] ...

Congress's primary concern in enacting the prohibition against racial discrimination in Title VII of the Civil Rights Act of 1964 was with "the plight of the Negro in our economy." 110 Cong Rec 6548 (remarks of Sen. Humphrey). Before 1964, blacks were largely relegated to "unskilled and semi-skilled jobs." Id., at 6548 (remarks of Sen. Humphrey). . . . Because of automation the number of such jobs was rapidly decreasing. See 110 Cong Rec, at 6548 (remarks of Sen. Humphrey); id., at 7204 (remarks of Sen. Clark). As a consequence "the relative position of the Negro worker (was) steadily worsening. In 1947 the non-white unemployment rate was only 64 percent higher than the white rate; in 1962 it was 124 percent higher." Id., at 6547 (remarks of Sen. Humphrey). . . . Congress considered this a serious social problem. . . .

Congress feared that the goals of the Civil Rights Act—the integration of blacks into the mainstream of American society—could not be achieved unless this trend were reversed. And Congress recognized that that would not be possible unless blacks were able to secure jobs "which have a future." Id., at 7204 (remarks to Sen. Clark). . . . As Senator Humphrey explained to the Senate:

> "What good does it do a Negro to be able to eat in a fine restaurant if he cannot afford to pay the bill? What good does it do him to be accepted in a hotel that is too expensive for his modest income? How can a Negro child be motivated to take full advantage of integrated educational facilities if he has no hope of getting a job where he can use that education?" Id., at 6547. . . .

. . .[I]t was clear to Congress that "the crux of the problem (was) to open employment opportunities for Negroes in occupations which have been traditionally closed to them," id., at 6548 (remarks of Sen. Humphrey), and it was to this problem that Title VII's prohibition against racial discrimination in employment was primarily addressed. . . .

Given this legislative history, we cannot agree with respondent that Congress intended to prohibit the private sector from taking effective steps to accomplish the goal that Congress designed Title VII to achieve. [Emphasis added.] ... It would be ironic indeed if a law triggered by a Nation's concern over centuries of racial injustice and intended to improve the lot

of those who had "been excluded from the American dream for so long," 110 Cong Rec, at 6552 (remarks of Sen. Humphrey), constituted the first legislative prohibition of all voluntary, private, race-conscious efforts to abolish traditional patterns of racial segregation and hierarchy.

. . . Our conclusion is further reinforced by examination of the language and legislative history of §703(j) of Title VII. Opponents of Title VII raised two related arguments against the bill. First, they argued that the Act would be interpreted to *require* employers with racially imbalanced work forces to grant preferential treatment to racial minorities in order to integrate. Second, they argued that employers with racially imbalanced work forces would grant preferential treatment to racial minorities, even if not required to do so by the Act. See 110 Cong Rec (remarks of Sen. Sparkman). Had Congress meant to prohibit all race-conscious affirmative action, as respondent urges, it easily could have answered both objections by providing that Title VII would not require or *permit* racially preferential integration efforts. But Congress did not choose such a course. Rather Congress added §703(j) which addresses only the first objection. The section provides that nothing contained in Title VII "shall be interpreted to *require* any employer . . . to grant preferential treatment . . . to any group because of the race . . . of such . . . group on account of" a de facto racial imbalance in the employer's work force. The section does *not* state that "nothing in Title VII shall be interpreted to *permit*" voluntary affirmative efforts to correct racial imbalances. The natural inference is that Congress chose not to forbid all voluntary race-conscious affirmative action.

The reasons for this choice are evident from the legislative record. Title VII could not have been enacted into law without substantial support from legislators in both Houses who traditionally resisted federal regulation of private business. Those legislators demanded as a price for their support that "management prerogatives and union freedoms . . . be left undisturbed to the greatest extent possible." HR Re No. 914, 88th Cong, 1st Sess, Pt 2 (1963), at 29. Section 703(j) was proposed by Senator Dirksen to allay any fears that the Act might be interpreted in such a way as to upset this compromise. The section was designed to prevent §703 of Title VII from being interpreted in such a way as to lead to undue "Federal Government interference with private businesses because of some Federal employee's ideas about racial balance or imbalance." 110 Cong Rec, at 14314. . . . In view of this legislative history and in view of Congress' desire to avoid undue federal regulation of private businesses, use of the word "require" rather than the phrase "require or permit" in §703(j) fortifies the conclusion that Congress did not intend to limit traditional business freedom to such a degree as to prohibit all voluntary, race-conscious affirmative action.

... We therefore hold that Title VII's prohibition in §§703(a) and (d) against racial discrimination does not condemn all private, voluntary, race-conscious affirmative action plans.

III

We need not today define in detail the line of demarcation between permissible and impermissible affirmative action plans. It suffices to hold that the challenged Kaiser-USWA affirmative action plan falls on the permissible side of the line. The purposes of the plan mirror those of the statute. . . .

... At the same time the plan does not unnecessarily trammel the interests of the white employees. The plan does not require the discharge of white workers and their replacement with new black hires. . . . Nor does the plan create an absolute bar to the advancement of white employees; half of those trained in the program will be white. Moreover, the plan is a temporary measure; it is not intended to maintain racial balance, but simply to eliminate a manifest racial imbalance. . . .

We conclude, therefore, that the adoption of the Kaiser-USWA plan for the Gramercy plant falls within the area of discretion left by Title VII to the private sector voluntarily to adopt affirmative action plans designed to eliminate conspicuous racial imbalance in traditionally segregated job categories. Accordingly, the judgment of the Court of Appeals for the Fifth Circuit is reversed.

MR. JUSTICE POWELL and MR. JUSTICE STEVENS took no part in the consideration or decision of this case.   <

QUESTIONS
   1.   How did the Supreme Court use legislative history to support its decision?
   2.   Would it have been possible for the Supreme Court to arrive at its decision without the use of legislative history? Why or why not?

Other Aids
to Statutory Interpretation

Private and Administrative Interpretations

We have said that when the courts cannot discover the purpose underlying a statutory provision by examining the statute itself, they may turn to other sources of evidence. Since it is the legislature's purpose that they are seeking, the most important of these sources is the legislative history

of the statute. Judges are aware, however, that legislatures often count on the primary addressees of a statute, both private and official, to fill in some of the gaps themselves. Hence they may sometimes be influenced by the interpretations that these addressees adopt.

Private persons and organizations have to work out their own tentative interpretations of a new statute long before any case arising under it comes before the courts. If their interpretations seem to be relatively uniform and to be motivated by a desire to comply with the law rather than by a search for loopholes in it they may influence the interpretations adopted by the court. Likewise, the interpretations that administrative officials adopt in the course of administering a statute may be taken into account by the judges who later must work out a definitive interpretation. The administrators usually have specialized experience in the area regulated, and their interpretations are likely to be molded to fit the practical problems of administration. Judges should normally hesitate to adopt an interpretation at variance with a well-established administrative interpretation.[7]

Prior Judicial Interpretations

When a court must apply a statutory provision in a case, what weight should it give to earlier judicial interpretations of the provision? Does the *stare decisis* principle oblige a court to follow prior interpretations even if they seem wrong? Or is the court free to return to the language and legislative history of the statute in search of a better interpretation?

One view is that when a court is convinced that an earlier interpretation is wrong, it should adopt a new interpretation in order to give proper effect to the legislative purpose. This is particularly necessary, it is argued, because legislatures so often fail to exercise their power to pass new laws correcting erroneous interpretations. If courts are unwilling to get rid of bad interpretations, the interpretations are likely to remain in effect indefinitely.

The prevailing view, probably, is that decisions interpreting statutes should exert approximately the same control over the future as do decisions interpreting common-law rules, and for essentially the same reason. People should be able to plan their conduct on the assumption that once an appellate court has interpreted a statutory provision, it will normally adhere to that interpretation in later cases. Most judges refuse to

---

[7] We are speaking here of the less formal interpretations adopted by administrators, not of the regulations that some agencies issue under authority expressly delegated to them by legislatures. These formal, published regulations are treated by the courts as having the force of law. (See Chapter 8.)

accept the view that the inability of legislatures to review and revise decisional rules is sufficient reason for courts to ignore the precedents they have established.

The Occasional Need
for Creative Judicial Lawmaking

In a large majority of cases involving the application of statutory provisions, the meaning of the statute is so clear that no real problems of interpretation arise. In a smaller number of cases, interpretation is more difficult. Even in most of these, though, the judges can reach a satisfactory solution by examining the language of the statutory provision in its textual and circumstantial context. Occasionally they find it useful to look also at the legislative history or at private or administrative interpretations. Sometimes the provision has already been interpreted by a court.

Once in a while, however, judges find that all their efforts to discover the legislative purpose of a statute are in vain. It simply is not clear how the statute applies to the case before them. In those cases the judges must do just what they do when faced with a case for which there are no precedents: They must perform a creative act of lawmaking. In all likelihood this is exactly what the legislature, unwilling to prescribe details for an unknown future, counted on them to do. It is the duty of judges to infer a purpose that is applicable to a particular case from what they know of the legislature's broader purposes and of the shared purposes and aims of the community. As long as they forward these broad purposes and not private purposes of their own, the judges are acting within the limits of the judicial function.

Chapter Problem

Suppose a state legislature has recently enacted a statute to prohibit price-fixing agreements among sellers of goods and services. The provisions of the new law cover business firms and "all self-employed persons engaged in business or trade."

Now suppose that somebody brings a lawsuit under the new act against several physicians whom, he says, have caused him injury by their price-fixing activities. The defendants demur: Regardless of whether the facts alleged are true, the law does not apply to them, they say, because they are not "engaged in business or trade." The trial judge's

decision overruling this demurrer has been appealed to the state Supreme Court.

Several years earlier, the state legislature adopted a statute imposing a special tax on certain classes of persons and organizations, but specifically exempting (presumably because they were thought to be sufficiently taxed under existing levies) "all self-employed persons engaged in business or trade." *Thus, the phrases of the two statutes were identical.* For understandable reasons, physicians were eager to be classified as persons "engaged in business or trade" under this earlier statute, and they rejoiced when the state Supreme Court so classified them in a case in which it interpreted the provision.

The state Supreme Court must now deal with the apparent conflict between the two statutes and the resulting impact on physicians. In particular, the court must determine whether its decision that physicians were "engaged in business or trade" under the earlier statute *obliges* it to classify them similarly under the price-fixing law.

Questions

1. Sketch the arguments for both sides of the question: Is the court now obliged to apply its earlier classification of physicians to the price-fixing statute, or is it not? What are the premises of each argument?

2. What is your opinion as to the proper resolution? Explain your reasoning.

Questions for Review

1. What are the major categories of problems in interpreting statutes?

2. "When judges must apply a statutory provision to a particular case, the best way for them to understand the statute is to look up the key words in the dictionary. Having done that, they will usually have no further difficulty." Comment on this statement.

3. To what sources might a judge turn when trying to interpret an imprecise statute?

4. What is the difference between legislative intent and legislative purpose?

5. If you were a judge, how much weight would you give to materials other than the statute itself in interpreting a statute? Would you give the same weight to committee reports as to materials that appear in

the Congressional Record? Would you take into consideration private interpretations? Explain your answer.

6. It has been suggested that a statement of general purpose should be appended to each future law. Would such a statement be useful? Would it be workable from a political point of view? Why or why not?

7. Comment on the following statement by Justice Frankfurter: "The Court no doubt must listen to the voice of Congress. But often Congress cannot be heard clearly because its voice is muffled." ["Some Reflections on the Reading of Statutes," 2 Record of NYC BA 234 (1947).]

7
Judicial Lawmaking III: Interpreting the Constitution

In the last five chapters we have discussed how the courts and legislatures make and apply the rules that channel private conduct. We have taken for granted the authority of those bodies to make and apply legal rules. But think for a moment of citizens who find their activities thwarted by statutes or decisions or administrative rulings that they consider outrageous. These citizens might well begin to wonder about the source of the authority that is being exercised by those whose actions have proved so annoying. If they explored the matter, they would learn that the ultimate sources of all official authority in the U.S. legal system are the constitutions, and that the rules about official authority stated in those constitutions or developed through judicial interpretation are known collectively as *constitutional law*.

Chapter 7 will describe how constitutional rules are created and how they evolve as new cases involving constitutional issues are decided. Although the United States has fifty-one constitutions, we shall speak only about the federal Constitution, since it is far more important in the lives of most of us than any of the fifty state constitutions. Much of what we have to say about the federal Constitution, however, is applicable to the state constitutions as well.

Some Examples
of Constitutional Issues

Here are a few examples of constitutional controversies, based on actual cases that have been brought before the Supreme Court of the United States by parties challenging as unconstitutional the action of governmental officials or bodies:

1. Seeking to avert a threatened strike, the President of the United States orders federal officials to seize and operate the nation's steel mills. The steel companies challenge his power to do so under Article II of the Constitution, which deals with the powers and duties of the President.

2. Congress enacts a heavy tax on the sale of colored oleomargarine and a much lighter tax on uncolored oleomargarine, with the avowed goal of restricting the sale of oleomargarine that has been colored to resemble butter. A dealer refuses to pay the tax, claiming that Congress's power to tax under Article I cannot be used to achieve a regulatory objective unrelated to the raising of revenue.

3. An overzealous sheriff in a small town breaks into the offices of a business firm and searches for evidence of illegal sales, even though he has no search warrant. When the firm's owners are brought to trial for unlawful operations, they challenge the admission of the evidence offered against them on the grounds that it has been illegally obtained and that admitting it would violate the due-process clause of the Fourteenth Amendment, which is supposed to protect individuals from irregular official procedures.

4. A state legislature enacts a privilege tax on all persons or corporations not regularly doing business in the state who display samples in hotel rooms for the purpose of securing retail orders. An out-of-state firm pays the tax under protest and then sues for a refund, contending that the tax, by discriminating in favor of intrastate firms, places an unconstitutional burden on interstate commerce.

5. A group of homeowners sign an agreement that none of them will sell a home to persons "not of the Caucasian race." When one of the signers later sells his home to a black citizen, another signer asks a court for an injunction restraining the buyer from taking possession and divesting him of his title. The buyer resists on the ground that for a court to lend its coercive power to the enforcement of a restrictive agreement based on race would be a denial of the "equal protection of the laws" guaranteed by the Fourteenth Amendment.

U.S. Constitutions

When Americans think of a constitution, they think of a written document adopted by some sort of representative body.[1] The fifty states and the federal Union each have such a document. Constitutions typically perform three functions: (1) They prescribe the structure, organization, and major duties of the legislative, executive, and judicial branches of government. (2) They allocate power between the respective levels of government—that is, between the central and local authorities. (3) Having established and allocated power, constitutions place restrictions on the exercise of that power, specifying what governments may *not* do.

New constitutions, and major revisions of existing ones, are usually *adopted* initially by constitutional conventions—representative bodies especially convened for that purpose. Ordinarily, the convention writes into the constitution a procedure under which the constitution must be *ratified* after being adopted by the convention. Ratification is either by popular vote or by the vote of designated representative bodies.[2]

Constitutional *amendments* are normally adopted by legislatures; then they must be ratified.[3] The amendment process is customarily made rather cumbersome in order to discourage frequent and ill considered tampering with the fundamental law.

As we shall see, though, the process of formal amendment is not the most important means by which our constitutional law is modified. The federal Constitution has been in effect for almost 175 years. In that time—during which the infant nation of 1789 was transformed into the enormously powerful and wealthy giant of today—only twenty-five amendments have been added to the Constitution. Moreover, ten of these—the so-called Bill of Rights—were adopted by the first Congress in 1789, so that realistically they must be considered as a part of the original Constitution. Some of the amendments have been important, but certainly no more important than the many changes that Americans have

---

[1] In contrast, when the English speak of their constitution, they have no single document in mind; they are referring to the sum of the basic laws and traditions that determine the form and functioning of their government. The difference, however, is more apparent than real, since U.S. constitutional law is by no means limited to the rules explicitly enunciated in constitutional documents.

[2] The federal Constitution provided that ratification by conventions in nine of the original thirteen states would be sufficient to bring it into effect. Eleven of the states had ratified it before it went into effect in March 1789.

[3] A two-thirds vote by each house of Congress, followed by ratification by the legislatures of three-quarters of the states, is required for amendments to the federal Constitution. (See Article V of the Constitution.)

made in their constitutional rules without bothering to amend the Constitution. Sometimes institutions have been created or modified in order to bring about these changes: Witness the development of the two-party system and of the powerful congressional committees, and the greatly reduced importance of the Electoral College. Many changes, however, are the result of the Supreme Court's reinterpretation of key constitutional phrases.

The Supreme Court as the Final Constitutional Arbiter

Challenges to the constitutionality of an official act may be raised either in a state court or in a lower federal court. Although these courts must rule on such challenges, their decisions have weight only as tentative interpretations, for the definitive interpretations of the Constitution are made by the Supreme Court of the United States.

This is not to say that the Supreme Court hears only cases that raise constitutional issues. Many of its decisions, for instance, involve the interpretation of federal statutes. (The Weber case in the preceding chapter is an example.) But the Court's best-known and, on the whole, most-important cases have involved constitutional questions.

The Supreme Court of the United States differs from most other appellate courts in one important respect: It has extremely wide discretion in deciding which cases it will hear. For most types of cases, the only way to secure a hearing before the Court is to persuade it to grant a *writ of certiorari*.[4] Out of the great number of cases that are urged upon it, it accepts only a hundred or so a year for a full hearing. For the cases it refuses to hear, the decision of the lower court becomes final. This arrangement enables the Court to focus its attention on cases that raise novel and important legal issues.

One might expect that interpreting the words of a constitution would not be too different from interpreting a statute. But the two processes are actually quite different, mainly because of the generality of constitutional language. We have spoken of the deliberate imprecision of some statutory provisions, but few statutes are as imprecise as the key phrases in the federal Constitution. Since the Constitution was designed to endure for centuries, the framers found it advisable to enunciate broad

---

4 A writ of certiorari is an order from a higher court to a lower court directing it to send up the record of a case for review.

directives in terse and general terms. In effect, the framers delegated to the Supreme Court the responsibility for giving meaning to these provisions by relating them to the particular situations that come before it. Justice Felix Frankfurter has commented that the major constitutional phrases have been "purposely left to gather meaning from experience." Chief Justice Charles Evans Hughes once put the matter even more baldly: "The Constitution is what the Judges say it is."

Take, for instance, the power granted to Congress in Article I to "regulate commerce . . . among the several states." Again and again the Court has had to interpret this broad and imprecise provision. What is the scope of the power to "regulate"? What is "commerce"? What brings an activity into the category of "among the several states"? At different times the Court has given different answers to each of these questions. There have been periods when the Court has acted as if the commerce clause granted almost unlimited regulatory power to the federal government. During other periods it has interpreted the clause restrictively, invalidating federal statutes for exceeding the power granted to Congress.

The two most important clauses in the Fourteenth Amendment are equally imprecise: ". . . [N]or shall any State deprive any person of life, liberty, or property, without due process of law; nor deny to any person within its jurisdiction the equal protection of the laws." The framers of the amendment probably intended the words "due process of law" as a guarantee of fair treatment in police, prosecuting, and trial procedures. But between the 1890s and the early 1930s, the justices of the Supreme Court used the due-process clause to strike down various state statutes regulating business that they considered arbitrary and unreasonable. During the three decades following, however, the Court abandoned this broad interpretation of the due-process clause. Similarly, for many years the Court held that the clause guaranteeing "equal protection of the laws" did not stand in the way of officially ordained segregation of the races, as long as the minority races were provided "equal" (though separate) facilities. But more recently the Court has held that the equal-protection clause makes such segregation unconstitutional.

Examples could be multiplied indefinitely. What is important to recognize is that the Court, guided by its own perception of society's changing needs and values, has been able to forge vague constitutional phrases into effective instruments for expanding or limiting official power. This arrangement imposes a heavy responsibility on the justices, but on the whole they have discharged it admirably. With comparatively few amendments, the Constitution has served as our organic law throughout an era that has seen changes in the nation's size, wealth, and world position, in the conditions of living, and in the role of government that have

far exceeded anything the Founding Fathers could possibly have foreseen.[5]

The Power of Judicial Review

The Supreme Court's power to decide constitutional issues includes the power to decide whether or not the act of another agency of government is permitted by the Constitution. This is often called the power of *judicial review*.

Suppose that an administrative official at the federal, state, or local level performs an act that is challenged in court as being in violation of the federal Constitution. Or suppose that a state court renders a decision that is challenged as being in conflict with the federal Constitution. Or suppose that Congress or a state or local legislative body passes a law that is said to be unconstitutional. In all these situations, the Supreme Court of the United States has jurisdiction and may be called upon to decide on the constitutionality of the act, decision, or law in question. If it is found to be unconstitutional, it is invalid.

In a federal system of government like ours, there must be some way of assuring that the officials, courts, and legislatures of the states do not exceed the powers permitted by the federal Constitution. The constitutional compact that the original states adopted in 1787 makes it clear that if the act of any branch of a state or local government ever comes into conflict with the federal Constitution (or with any federal statute or treaty), the latter shall prevail. In the words of Article VI:

> This Constitution, and the laws of the United States which shall be made in pursuance thereof; and all treaties made, or which shall be made, under the authority of the United States, shall be the supreme law of the land; and the judges in every state shall be bound thereby, any thing in the Constitution or laws of any state to the contrary notwithstanding.

Although the state courts and lower federal courts have authority to decide constitutional issues, their decisions are not necessarily final. Ever

---

[5] Some of our state constitutions provide excellent examples of what happens when constitutional documents are *not* deliberately imprecise. These constitutions are lengthy and detailed; often they contain provisions concerning matters too transitory in importance to justify inclusion in a constitution at all. Constitutional provisions that are detailed and specific cannot readily be reinterpreted by a court as the need for change becomes apparent. The needed change is therefore thwarted unless it is possible to amend the constitution. As a result, these state constitutions have needed to be amended much more often than has the federal Constitution, but since the amendment process is usually difficult, many desirable amendments have come about slowly or not at all.

since the Judiciary Act of 1789, the Supreme Court of the United States has had the ultimate authority to decide whether or not the act of a state official or agency is constitutional. The Supreme Court has exercised this power over state acts since the early days of the Republic, and few people today seriously question its legitimacy, although particular exercises of that power have aroused great resentment and hostility to the Court.

The constitutional underpinnings of the Court's power to invalidate the acts of the other two branches of the federal government—that is, of Congress and the President—are somewhat less firm. Nowhere does the Constitution state that the Supreme Court has the final say in deciding what limits the Constitution imposes on Congress or the President. There is some evidence to suggest that most of the Founding Fathers assumed that if in the course of deciding a case duly brought before it, the Court believed that an act of one of the other branches was contrary to the Constitution, it could deny legal effect to that act. But if this is indeed what the framers had in mind, they never spelled it out.

The argument that each branch of the federal government should be the final interpreter of its own powers is not without merit; it is the position taken in a number of other countries. But the issue was settled otherwise in 1803, when Chief Justice John Marshall declared in the famous case of *Marbury* v. *Madison*, that the Court was empowered under the Constitution to invalidate an act of Congress. The Court has continued to exercise this power (and the related power to invalidate acts of the President). It has used the power sparingly and, on the whole, with a wise caution. On a few occasions, however, it has seriously impaired its own prestige and effectiveness by unwise invalidations of acts of Congress. The *Dred Scott* decision of 1857, for instance, unquestionably hurt the Court, as did the striking down of much of the New Deal legislation in 1935 and 1936.

It is clear today that conflicts over the extent and limits of governmental power were bound to arise, both between federal and state authorities and between the respective branches of the federal government. These conflicts have had to be resolved somehow, and the Supreme Court is probably better able to do the job than any other agency. Judges have always had to interpret and apply the provisions of legal documents; interpreting constitutional provisions differs from other tasks of interpretation performed by appellate courts principally in the remarkably broad discretion granted to the judges and in the unusual importance of the issues at stake.

In one respect the Supreme Court is uniquely suited to act as final arbiter on constitutional issues. In our democratic system, Congress and the President are elected by popular majorities and can be expected to

respond to majority desires. But one of the unspoken premises of the Constitution is that the majority must not be allowed to deprive racial, religious, ideological, and other minority groups of their rights. Since Supreme Court justices are appointed for life, they are relatively insulated from majority pressures. Consequently, they are in a relatively good position to withstand popular opposition when they strike down arbitrary, undemocratic legislation designed to curb or penalize minority groups.

Restraints on the Exercise of Judicial Review

The power to invalidate the legislative and executive acts of popularly elected officials, lodged in the hands of nine justices who are neither chosen by nor subject to removal by the people, would be intolerable if it were not subject to restraints. In the absence of restraints, nothing would prevent the Court from striking down legislation or executive acts simply because a majority of the justices considered them unfair or unwise.

The restraints are of two sorts: (1) external restraints, imposed by the political environment in which the Court operates; and (2) internal restraints, which the justices have traditionally imposed upon themselves.

THE EXTERNAL RESTRAINTS   The effectiveness of the Court's authority depends in large measure on how much prestige it enjoys in the eyes of the American people. In recent years, the Court's prestige has been remarkably high, even when the Court was under strong attack from certain quarters. But there have been periods when its prestige was low: in the years before 1800, for instance, and in the period following the disastrous *Dred Scott* decision of 1857. The Court has no enforcement arm of its own, and the effectiveness of its decisions depends primarily on the voluntary compliance of the officials concerned, although the executive branch may, if it is willing, aid in their enforcement. A highly unpopular decision may be resisted or ignored. This has not happened often in our history, but on a number of occasions compliance has been far from complete, and the Court's prestige has suffered. So, although the justices have no obligation to respond to every shift in popular sentiment, they cannot afford to get too far out of step with the nation's mood and desires.

Congress has certain powers that could be used to influence or restrict the Court. For example, it has the power to impeach, and it might impeach a justice of whose philosophy it violently disapproved. No justice has ever been removed by impeachment, however (though an attempt was made in 1804), and the prospect of its ever happening seems

remote. But a sharp decline in the Court's prestige might bring this extreme measure within the realm of possibility.

Congress also has the power to decide what types of cases the Court may hear on appeal. If the Court's decisions became irksome to enough legislators, Congress might be induced to curtail its jurisdiction in certain areas. Indeed, several bills designed to exclude the Court from hearing certain kinds of cases have been introduced in Congress within the past dozen years; however, the Court's prestige is currently high enough so that the passage of such legislation seems unlikely. But it has happened before,[6] and it could happen again.

Congress also has the power to increase the number of seats on the Court, and if it became sufficiently dissatisfied with the Court's performance, it could authorize the President to appoint enough additional justices to assure a more favorable line of decisions. Since 1869, however, Congress has left the Court's number of justices at nine. In 1937, President Franklin D. Roosevelt proposed that the Court be enlarged. In the preceding two years, the justices had struck down a dozen major New Deal laws, and Roosevelt, fresh from his overwhelming reelection in 1936, was convinced that the justices were using the Constitution to thwart policies that the nation needed and wanted. The Roosevelt "court-packing plan," as it was called, aroused violent opposition, however, and in the end was soundly defeated in Congress.

Yet it is worth noting that even though President Roosevelt's proposal was defeated, the Court from 1937 on stopped declaring federal economic legislation unconstitutional. One explanation may be that Chief Justice Hughes and Justice Roberts, one or both of whom had voted to strike down each of the invalidated New Deal laws, came to realize that the Court had put itself in the untenable position of standing in the way of policies and programs that most Americans favored, and for that reason changed sides. Within the following few years, too, retirement and death removed three of the justices most firmly opposed to the New Deal philosophy of government, and the President was able to replace them with justices more sympathetic to his policies.

THE INTERNAL RESTRAINTS   More important than these external restraints are the internal restraints imposed by the judicial tradition in

---

6 In 1868—when the Court's prestige was still at a low ebb following the *Dred Scott* decision—Congress, fearful lest the Court in deciding on the appeal of one McCardle should invalidate some Reconstruction legislation, passed a law that in effect withdrew the Court's appellate jurisdiction in cases such as McCardle's. Although the justices had already heard arguments in the *McCardle* case, they held (in *Ex parte McCardle*, 1869) that they no longer had jurisdiction to decide the case.

general, and by the Supreme Court's own tradition in particular. It was to this tradition that Justice (later Chief Justice) Harlan Fiske Stone was alluding in 1936 when he said, in a dissenting opinion: ". . . [W]hile unconstitutional exercise of power by the executive and legislative branches of the government is subject to judicial restraint, the only check upon our exercise of power is our own sense of self-restraint."

The Traditional Restraints on Judicial Lawmaking   Much of what we have said in Chapters 4 and 6 about judicial lawmaking is relevant here. The Constitution is a special sort of enactment, and, as we saw in Chapter 6, judges have rules about how enactments should be interpreted. Many constitutional rules are today embodied in decisional precedents, and, as we saw in Chapter 4, judges have rules about building on—and occasionally overruling—precedents.

One of the most basic rules of interpretation is that statutory words whose meaning is plain cannot be ignored. For example, the Constitution provides that "the Senate of the United States shall be composed of two Senators from each State," regardless of the state's size. Under no circumstance could the Court allow a state to elect a third senator.

But the constitutional phrases around which most controversies have turned are not so precise. Phrases like "due process of law" do not *in themselves* give the Court much guidance; consequently they impose no real restraint on the justices' freedom to interpret.

Another basic rule of interpretation is that courts must try to ascertain what those who adopted an enactment meant by the language they used—what general purposes they had in mind. When we study Supreme Court opinions, we find that the Court has tried to answer these questions whenever it could. In many opinions the justices have referred back to the recorded deliberations of the Constitutional Convention of 1787 or to the deliberations of the Congress that adopted the various amendments.

The older a constitutional provision becomes, however, the less useful is the guidance provided by its legislative history. Those who adopted and ratified a provision a century or more ago did not and could not have anticipated our modern problems. It seems reasonable to assume that they intended the officials, judges, and lawyers of future generations to accept responsibility for giving the original words a new and more precise meaning suited to current needs.

Thus, neither the actual words of constitutional provisions nor the context of circumstances surrounding their enactment is usually the most important source of restraint on the Court's freedom of interpretation. Far more important are the restraints imposed by previous Court deci-

sions interpreting the provision in question, for these decisions are precedents, and the Court normally feels constrained to follow its own precedents. All the important constitutional phrases have by now been interpreted in many cases, and most modern Supreme Court opinions are discussions, not of the meaning of the constitutional phrases or of the framers' presumed intention, but of the scope and applicability of prior decisions.

As we saw in Chapter 4, no appellate court always adheres to precedents, and the Supreme Court is no exception. The Court, in fact, has felt freer to reverse itself in constitutional cases than would a court applying common-law rules or judicial interpretations of statutes. After all, when an ordinary appellate decision proves to be unwise or becomes outmoded, the legislature can supersede it by passing a statute. But unless the Supreme Court is willing to overrule itself, the only way to nullify a constitutional decision is by the long and uncertain process of constitutional amendment.

Nevertheless, the Supreme Court avoids overruling its precedents directly whenever it can. It prefers to narrow the scope of the unsatisfactory decisions gradually by "distinguishing" later cases. As it holds that more and more later cases are not covered by the rule of a particular decision, that decision eventually ceases to be significant as a precedent. And when the court does announce that it is overruling an earlier decision, the reversal is rarely unexpected; investigation will usually reveal that the Court has given warning in one or more earlier opinions that it is moving away from the original decision.

As an illustration, let us look at the overruling of *Hammer* v. *Dagenhart*. This was a 1918 case in which the Court held that Congress had no power to prohibit the use of child labor in the manufacture of goods to be sold in interstate commerce. It was one of a number of decisions in which the Court restricted the power of legislatures to enact economic regulations. After 1937, the year of President Roosevelt's court-packing proposal, this trend came to an end, and in the next few years an unusually large number of precedents were overruled. The decision that explicitly overruled *Hammer* v. *Dagenhart* was *United States* v. *Darby* (1941), which involved a challenge to the constitutionality of the Fair Labor Standards Act of 1938. Speaking for a unanimous Court in the *Darby* case, Justice Stone said:

> . . . The motive and purpose of a regulation of interstate commerce are matters for the legislative judgment upon the exercise of which the Constitution places no restriction and over which the courts are given no control. . . .

... [T]hese principles of constitutional interpretation have been so long and repeatedly recognized by this Court as applicable to the Commerce Clause that there would be little occasion for repeating them now were it not for the decision of this Court twenty-two years ago in *Hammer* v. *Dagenhart*, 247 U.S. 251. In that case it was held by a bare majority of the Court over the powerful and now classic dissent of Mr. Justice Holmes setting forth the fundamental issues involved, that Congress was without power to exclude the products of child labor from interstate commerce. The reasoning and conclusion of the Court's opinion there cannot be reconciled with the conclusion which we have reached. . . .

Hammer v. *Dagenhart* has not been followed. The distinction on which the decision was rested . . . a distinction which was novel when made and unsupported by any provision of the Constitution—has long since been abandoned. . . .

The conclusion is inescapable that *Hammer* v. *Dagenhart* was a departure from the principles which have prevailed in the interpretation of the Commerce Clause both before and since the decision and that such vitality, as a precedent, as it then had has long since been exhausted. It should be and now is overruled.[7]

As we have remarked before, judicial lawmaking provides both for a degree of certainty and for the possibility of change when change becomes necessary. The Court's normal adherence to precedent creates a large measure of predictability. The more closely woven the web of interpretations becomes, the more unlikely it is that the Court will adopt bold new interpretations. Yet the Court retains the power to distinguish and, if necessary, to overrule undesirable precedents if that proves to be the only way to achieve essential changes in the law.

Other Internal Restraints In addition to the traditional restraints acting on all appellate judges, there are certain special restraints that the Supreme Court has imposed upon itself in dealing with constitutional issues.

In the first place, the Court has supplemented the constitutional and statutory rules defining its jurisdiction with some self-limiting jurisdictional rules of its own. For example, to implement the constitutional declaration in Article III that the Court's jurisdiction extends to "cases" and "controversies," the justices have spelled out specific standards designed

---

7 *United States* v. *Darby*, 312 U.S. 100 (1941)

to assure that the cases it hears are true contests between parties, with each having a genuine interest to protect.

The Court has also refused to decide certain cases that present "political questions." It has used this term to describe questions that it considers to be within the special competence of the elected branches of the government, questions that judges are not particularly well equipped to decide or that might bring the Court into open conflict with the other branches. The Court was once asked, for instance, to rule that one of the states did not have "a republican form of government," as required by the Constitution. It ruled instead that the question was one that only the executive and legislative branches could decide, that no judicial intervention was warranted. Until 1962 the Court took a similar position in refusing to rule on the persistent failure of many state legislatures to redraw the boundaries of legislative districts to reflect population shifts, but in that year it ruled that courts may adjudicate such cases. More than once in its history, the Court has lost prestige by rashly involving itself in controversies that brought it into conflict with the other branches of government, and so it has learned to shun situations in which it can perform no useful function.

Sometimes the Court avoids deciding a constitutional issue by disposing of the case before it on nonconstitutional grounds. This practice often disappoints lawyers who hope to get a definitive answer to an unresolved constitutional problem. The Court, however, has nearly always taken the position that when a case turns on several questions of law, the constitutional questions must be decided last—or not at all, if the case can be disposed of on other grounds.

Suppose, for instance, that an administrative official notifies John Jones that he must pay a certain tax. Jones takes the matter to court, arguing that he is exempt from the tax and, moreover, that if the relevant provision in the tax statute were construed to cover him, the provision would be unconstitutional. The justices believe that Jones is probably right: If they interpret the provision broadly enough to make Jones taxable, the statute would probably then be unconstitutional. If, however, they interpret it narrowly enough to exclude Jones, it will pass muster. In such a situation, even if the broad interpretation seems more natural and is probably the one that the legislature intended, the Court is likely to adopt the narrow interpretation in order to avoid invalidating the provision. So the Court rules that the official has misinterpreted the tax law and that it does not apply to Jones. What the justices have done, in effect, is to refer the question of the statute's meaning back to the legislature, with this implicit message: "We, the Supreme Court, presume that you, the legislature, intended to write a constitutionally valid statute. If we

were to give this provision a broad interpretation, its constitutionality
would be doubtful. To avoid the possibility of having to declare it unconstitutional, we have decided to interpret it narrowly. Now this may not
be what you had in mind, but it is up to you either to let our interpretation stand or else to amend the provision to achieve your purpose. If you
amend it, we will decide any constitutional issues raised by your amendment when and if they are brought before us."

Even when the Court is willing to consider a constitutional question,
it starts from a strong presumption that the challenged official action is
constitutional and throws the burden of demonstrating its unconstitu-
tionality on the challenging party. And when the Court does feel compelled to invalidate an official act, it usually does so on the narrowest
possible grounds. If, for instance, it can dispose of a case by invalidating
only a single statutory section, it will normally say nothing at all about
the constitutionality of the other sections.

The Supreme Court
as Policy Maker

When, in the early days of the Republic, Chief Justice Marshall had to
interpret the scope of the federal power to regulate interstate commerce,
he found little guidance in the sixteen words of the Constitution that
make up the commerce clause. Essentially, he had to make a policy decision: Would a broad or narrow interpretation of the federal power best
suit the needs of the country? When the Court today has to decide
whether the conduct of a certain sheriff or police officer or jailer meets
the requirement of due process of law, the constitutional phrase in itself
is of no use as a standard of measurement. Past decisions may be of some
use in suggesting criteria against which the official's conduct can be measured, but the Court's job is essentially to decide whether the official's
conduct was within the limits of what is "fair" or "just" under the standards we set for an agent of government in our democratic society.[8] *This
is a policy-making, lawmaking function.*

Sometimes an official act seems valid with reference to one constitutional principle but invalid with reference to another. Then the Court is

---

[8] According to Justice Frankfurter, the concept of due process in matters of procedure "expresses a demand for civilized standards of law. It is thus not a stagnant formulation of what has been achieved in the past but a standard for judgment in the
progressive evolution of the institutions of society." The judgment "must move within
the limits of accepted notions of justice." The Court, then, must decide what the currently
accepted notions of justice are.

compelled to establish a priority between the two principles. Some of the statutes designed to restrict picketing by labor unions have raised this problem. Viewed as a potential interference with property rights, picketing would seem to be subject to regulation under the states' "police power"; viewed as an exercise of free speech by the unions, however, it would seem to be protected from legislative interference by the First and Fourteenth Amendments (which together restrict the power of the states to interfere with freedom of expression). Sometimes the Court has given priority to one of these competing values, and sometimes to the other, depending on the form of regulation and the purpose of the picketing. It should be clear that the Court can take no position on a question of this sort without making a *policy decision*—without, that is, making a choice between conflicting social aims and values.

But when acting as a policy maker, a Supreme Court justice must display infinitely more objectivity and self-restraint than is demanded of legislative or executive policy makers. No matter how broad the discretion granted, the justice's task is never to ask: How do *I* feel about the wisdom of this statute or the fairness of this official act? It is only to ask: Is this official act—however unwise it may seem to me—within the limits of what the Constitution permits? And since, as we have seen, the words of the Constitution usually provide no direct answer, the task is to interpret the *spirit* of the Constitution and to relate that spirit to the changing needs and values of an evolving society. Finally, the justice may have to explain and justify the decision in a written opinion that, when published, should clarify and illuminate the constitutional principles in question.

Needless to say, the justices of the Supreme Court have not always practiced such perfect self-restraint. On occasion, both "conservative" and "liberal" members of the Court have confused their personal convictions with the law of the land. But some of our greatest justices have resisted this temptation. In the first half of the present century, Justices Holmes and Stone stood as outstanding examples of judicial self-restraint. Neither was enthusiastic about many of the laws regulating business that came before the Court during his tenure, yet each dissented again and again when his colleagues voted to strike down those laws. Although they each believed that many of the enactments were ill conceived and futile, they could find nothing in the Constitution to justify the assumption that judges were better qualified than the people's elected representatives to decide what was good for a state or for the nation. Unless a legislature has clearly exceeded the express or implied powers granted to it by the Constitution, they insisted, the Court must not override its enactments, however unwise they may seem. As Justice Stone once put it:

> For the removal of unwise laws from the statute books, appeal lies
> not to the courts but to the ballot and to the processes of demo-
> cratic government. . . . Courts are not the only agency of govern-
> ment that must be assumed to have capacity to govern.

From time to time the Court has misused its power by acting as a
sort of superlegislature. But not every attack made on the Court for abuse
of power has been justified. The underlying cause of most of the attacks
on the Court has been acute disappointment over the outcome of particular cases. It is not surprising that in 1935–1936, when so many of the New
Deal programs were being struck down, the Court's most vocal critics
tended to be those who favored the New Deal programs. Today a different set of issues is being brought before the Court, and now many of
the groups that in the 1930s deplored the Court's decisions are its most
ardent defenders, while its former friends are among its critics.

Like other democratic institutions, the Supreme Court is not exempt
from criticism, and constructive criticism (as distinguished from personal
attacks on particular justices) can serve a useful purpose. Even the intem-
perate attacks on the Court made during the late 1950s may have encouraged people to reflect on the values and limitations of the Court as a U.S.
political institution, and on the moral issues implicit in the cases it was
deciding. Indeed, the Court's decisions on such major issues as equal
rights for minorities, limits of free speech, and separation of church and
state do not achieve their fullest effect until they have been studied and
understood by the nation's citizens. Only when they have been accepted,
not just as "the law," but as just and right, are they truly effective.

The Justices

So far we have mostly spoken of the Supreme Court as a unit. We must
never forget, however, that the Court is made up of justices who die or
retire and are replaced by others, who have personal philosophies and
prejudices, religious affiliations, and political, social, and economic back-
grounds that inevitably influence their appraisals of "the felt necessities
of the time."

Vacancies on the Court are filled by the President "with the advice
and consent of the Senate." Understandably, he is likely to appoint persons whose political and economic views are not too different from his
own. He is certain to nominate individuals with legal training, but there
is no tradition requiring that the appointees have prior judicial experience, and some of our greatest justices had never previously been judges.

Once appointed, a justice has indefinite tenure and is virtually irremovable. As we have noted, this immunity insulates the justices from direct political pressure[9] and enables them to hand down decisions that they know will be unpopular in some quarters. Immunity has its disadvantages as well. Some justices have remained on the bench long after their intellectual powers have declined or their ability to accept new ideas has vanished. But for every justice who has sought to stand in the way of change, there have been others who have kept their judicial philosophies superbly attuned to the needs of the times. Some of the most memorable justices have been persistent dissenters from the majority view in their time, only to have history prove them right; thus their dissenting views have later become the law of the land.

The Protection of Due Process in Academia: An Example of a Constitutional Question and Judicial Decision Making

The Fourteenth Amendment to the Constitution of the United States reads in part:

> Section 1—All persons born or naturalized in the United States, and subject to the jurisdiction thereof, are citizens of the United States and of the State wherein they reside. No state shall make or enforce any law which shall abridge the privileges or immunities of citizens of the United States; nor shall any State deprive any person of life, liberty, or property, without due process of law; nor deny to any person within its jurisdiction the equal protection of the laws.

This amendment is designed to protect some of the most treasured aspects of life in the United States. Part of what many people consider their liberty is the right to choose and pursue an appropriate career, and for many the most reasonable way to train for a particular occupation is to attend a state university. It could be argued, then, that dismissal from a state university substantially reduces opportunities to acquire the appropriate training and so impairs one's liberty. Therefore, dismissal should involve a certain amount of due process.

---

[9] Their immunity is accompanied by a disability, however: Tradition bars justices from defending themselves publicly against criticism, however misguided and unfair it may be.

In the case that follows, a student at the University of Missouri—
Kansas City Medical School was dismissed during her final year. Understandably upset, she appealed her dismissal to the courts. The decision
reprinted below is an excellent example of the Supreme Court's analysis
of an important constitutional issue.

Board of Curators of the University of Missouri et al. v. Charlotte Horowitz

Supreme Court of the United States, 1978
55 L Ed 2d

> MR. JUSTICE REHNQUIST delivered the opinion of the Court.
    . . . Respondent, a student at the University of Missouri—Kansas City
Medical School, was dismissed by petitioner officials of the school during
her final year of study for failure to meet academic standards. Respondent sued petitioners under 42 USC §1983 . . . in the United States
District Court for the Western District of Missouri alleging, among other
constitutional violations, that petitioners had not accorded her procedural due process prior to her dismissal. The District Court, after conducting a full trial, concluded that respondent had been afforded all of
the rights guaranteed her by the Fourteenth Amendment to the United
States Constitution and dismissed her complaint. The Court of Appeals
for the Eighth Circuit reversed . . . and a petition for rehearing en banc
was denied by a divided court . . . 542 F2d 1335 (1976). We granted certiorari, 430 US 964, 52 L Ed 2d 355, 97 S Ct 1642, to consider what procedures must be accorded to a student at a state educational institution
whose dismissal may constitute a deprivation of "liberty" or "property"
within the meaning of the Fourteenth Amendment. We reverse the judgment of the Court of Appeals.

I

Respondent was admitted with advanced standing to the Medical School
in the fall of 1971. During the final years of a student's education at the
school, the student is required to pursue in "rotational units" academic
and clinical studies pertaining to various medical disciplines such as
obstetrics-gynecology, pediatrics, and surgery. Each student's academic
performance at the school is evaluated on a periodic basis by the Council
on Evaluation, a body composed of both faculty and students, which can
recommend various actions including probation and dismissal. The rec-

ommendations of the Council are reviewed by the Coordinating Committee, a body composed solely of faculty members, and must ultimately be approved by the Dean. Students are not typically allowed to appear before either the Council or the Coordinating Committee on the occasion of their review of the student's academic performance.

In the spring of respondent's first year of study, several faculty members expressed dissatisfaction with her clinical performance during a pediatrics rotation. The faculty members noted that respondent's "performance was below that of her peers in all clinical patient-oriented settings," that she was erratic in her attendance at clinical sessions, and that she lacked a critical concern for personal hygiene. Upon the recommendation of the Council on Evaluation, respondent was advanced to her second and final year on a probationary basis.

Faculty dissatisfaction with respondent's clinical performance continued during the following year. For example, respondent's docent, or faculty adviser, rated her clinical skills as "unsatisfactory." In the middle of the year, the Council again reviewed respondent's academic progress and concluded that respondent would not be considered for graduation in June of that year; furthermore, the Council recommended that, absent "radical improvement," respondent be dropped from the school.

Respondent was permitted to take a set of oral and practical examinations as an "appeal" of the decision not to permit her to graduate. Pursuant to this "appeal," respondent spent a substantial portion of time with seven practicing physicians in the area who enjoyed a good reputation among their peers. The physicians were asked to recommend whether respondent should be allowed to graduate on schedule and, if not, whether she should be dropped immediately or allowed to remain on probation. Only two of the doctors recommended that respondent be graduated on schedule. Of the other five, two recommended that she be immediately dropped from the school. The remaining three recommended that she not be allowed to graduate in June and be continued on probation pending further reports on her clinical progress. Upon receipt of these recommendations, the Council on Evaluation reaffirmed its prior position.

The Council met again in mid-May to consider whether respondent should be allowed to remain in school beyond June of that year. Noting that the report on respondent's recent surgery rotation rated her performance as "low-satisfactory," the Council unanimously recommended that "barring receipt of any reports that Miss Horowitz has improved radically, [she] not be allowed to re-enroll in the . . . School of Medicine." [Brackets in original.] The Council delayed making its recommendation official until receiving reports on other rotations; when a report on re-

spondent's emergency rotation also turned out to be negative, the Council unanimously reaffirmed its recommendation that respondent be dropped from the school. The Coordinating Committee and the Dean approved the recommendation and notified respondent, who appealed the decision in writing to the University's Provost for Health Sciences. The Provost sustained the school's actions after reviewing the record compiled during the earlier proceedings.

II

A

... To be entitled to the procedural protections of the Fourteenth Amendment, respondent must in a case such as this demonstrate that her dismissal from the school deprived her of either a "liberty" or a "property" interest. Respondent has never alleged that she was deprived of a property interest. Because property interests are creatures of state law ..., respondent would have been required to show at trial that her seat at the Medical School was a "property" interest recognized by Missouri state law. Instead, respondent argued that her dismissal deprived her of "liberty" by substantially impairing her opportunities to continue her medical education or to return to employment in a medically related field.

The Court of Appeals agreed, citing this Court's opinion in Board of Regents v. Roth, 408 US 564. . . . In that we held that the State had not deprived a teacher of any liberty or property interest in dismissing the teacher from a nontenured position, but noted:

> "[T]here is no suggestion that the State, in declining to re-employ the respondent, imposed on him a stigma or other disability that foreclosed his freedom to take advantage of other employment opportunities. The State, for example, did not invoke any regulations to bar the respondent from all other public employment in state universities." Id., at 573, 33 L Ed 2d 548, 92 S Ct 2701. [Brackets in original.]

We have recently had an opportunity to elaborate upon the circumstances under which an employment termination might infringe a protected liberty interest. In Bishop v. Wood, 426 US 341, 48 L Ed 2d 684, 96 S Ct 2074 (1976), we upheld the dismissal of a policeman without a hearing; we rejected the theory that the mere fact of dismissal, absent some publicizing of the reasons for the action, could amount to a stigma infringing one's liberty. . . .

B

... We need not decide, however, whether respondent's dismissal deprived her of a liberty interest in pursuing a medical career. Nor need we decide whether respondent's dismissal infringed any other interest constitutionally protected against deprivation without procedural due process. Assuming the existence of a liberty or property interest, respondent has been awarded at least as much due process as the Fourteenth Amendment requires. The school fully informed respondent of the faculty's dissatisfaction with her clinical progress and the danger that this posed to timely graduation and continued enrollment. The ultimate decision to dismiss respondent was careful and deliberate. These procedures were sufficient under the Due Process Clause of the Fourteenth Amendment. We agree with the District Court that respondent:

> "was afforded full procedural due process by the [school]. In fact, the Court is of the opinion, and so finds, that the school went beyond [constitutionally required] procedural due process by affording [respondent] the opportunity to be examined by seven independent physicians in order to be absolutely certain that their grading of the (respondent) in her medical skills was correct." App 47. [Brackets in original.]

... In Goss v. Lopez, 419 US 565 (1975), we held that due process requires, in connection with the suspension of a student from public school for disciplinary reasons, "that the student be given oral or written notice of the charges against him and, if he denies them, an explanation of the evidence the authorities have and an opportunity to present his side of the story." Id., at 581. . . . The Court of Appeals apparently read Goss as requiring some type of formal hearing at which respondent could defend her academic ability and performance. All that Goss required was an "informal give-and-take" between the student and the administrative body dismissing him that would, at least, give the student "the opportunity to characterize his conduct and put it in what he deems the proper context." Id., at 584. . . . But we have frequently emphasized that "[t]he very nature of due process negates any concept of inflexible procedures universally applicable to every imaginable situation." [Brackets in original.] Cafeteria Workers v. McElroy, 367 US 886, 895 (1961). The need for flexibility is well illustrated by the significant difference between the failure of a student to meet academic standards and the violation by a student of valid rules of conduct. This difference calls for far less stringent procedural requirements in the case of an academic dismissal.

Since the issue first arose 50 years ago state and lower federal courts have recognized that there are distinct differences between decisions to suspend or dismiss a student for disciplinary purposes and similar actions taken for academic reasons which may call for hearings in connection with the former but not the latter. Thus, in Barnard v. Inhabitants of Shelburne, 216 Mass 19, 102 NE 1095 (1913), the Supreme Judicial Court of Massachusetts rejected an argument, based on several earlier decisions requiring a hearing in disciplinary contexts, that school officials must also grant a hearing before excluding a student on academic grounds. According to the court, disciplinary cases have

> "no application. . . . Misconduct is a very different matter from failure to attain a standard of excellence in studies. A determination as to the fact involves investigation of a quite different kind. A public hearing may be regarded as helpful to the ascertainment of misconduct and useless or harmful in finding out the truth as to scholarship." Id., at 22–23, 102 NE. at 1097. . . .

. . . [P]rior decisions of state and federal courts, over a period of 60 years, unanimously holding that formal hearings before decisionmaking bodies need not be held in the case of academic dismissals, cannot be rejected lightly. . . .

Reason, furthermore, clearly supports the perception of these decisions. A school is an academic institution, not a courtroom or administrative hearing room. In Goss, this Court felt that suspensions of students for disciplinary reasons have a sufficient resemblance to traditional judicial and administrative factfinding to call for a "hearing" before the relevant school authority. . . . Even in the context of a school disciplinary proceeding, however, the Court stopped short of requiring a *formal* hearing since "further formalizing the suspension process and escalating its formality and adversary nature may not only make it too costly as a regular disciplinary tool but also destroy its effectiveness as a part of the teaching process." Id., at 583, 42 L Ed 2d 725, 95 S Ct 729.

Academic evaluations of a student, in contrast to disciplinary determinations, bear little resemblance to the judicial and administrative factfinding proceedings to which we have traditionally attached a full-hearing requirement. In Goss, the school's decision to suspend the students rested on factual conclusions that the individual students had participated in demonstrations that had disrupted classes, attacked a police officer, or caused physical damage to school property. The requirement of a hearing, where the student could present his side of the factual issue, could under such circumstances "provide a meaningful hedge against

erroneous action." Ibid. The decision to dismiss respondent, by comparison, rested on the academic judgment of school officials that she did not have the necessary clinical ability to perform adequately as a medical doctor and was making insufficient progress toward that goal. Such a judgment is by its nature more subjective and evaluative than the typical factual questions presented in the average disciplinary decision. Like the decision of an individual professor as to the proper grade for a student in his course, the determination whether to dismiss a student for academic reasons requires an expert evaluation of cumulative information and is not readily adapted to the procedural tools of judicial or administrative decisionmaking.

Under such circumstances, we decline to ignore the historic judgment of educators and thereby formalize the academic dismissal process by requiring a hearing. The educational process is not by nature adversary; instead it centers around a continuing relationship between faculty and students, "one in which the teacher must occupy many roles—educator, adviser, friend, and, at times, parent-substitute." Goss v. Lopez, 419 US, at 594, 42 L Ed 2d 725, 95 S Ct 729. . . . We decline to further enlarge the judicial presence in the academic community and thereby risk deterioration of many beneficial aspects of the faculty-student relationship. We recognize, as did the Massachusetts Supreme Judicial Court over 60 years ago, that a hearing may be "useless or harmful in finding out the truth as to scholarship." Barnard v. Inhabitants of Shelburne, 216 Mass, at 23, 102 NE, at 1097.

"Judicial interposition in the operation of the public school system of the Nation raises problems requiring care and restraint. . . . By and large, public education in our Nation is committed to the control of state and local authorities." Epperson v. Arkansas, 393 US 97, 104, 21 L Ed 2d 228, 89 S Ct 266 (1968). We see no reason to intrude on that historic control in this case.

III

. . . In reversing the District Court on procedural due process grounds, the Court of Appeals expressly failed to "reach the substantive due process ground advanced by Horowitz." 538 F2d, at 1321 n. 5. Respondent urges that we remand the cause to the Court of Appeals for consideration of this additional claim. In this regard, a number of lower courts have implied in dictum that academic dismissals from state institutions can be enjoined if "shown to be clearly arbitrary or capricious." Mahavong-sanan v. Hall, 529 F2d at 449. . . . Even assuming that the courts can re-

view under such a standard an academic decision of a public educational institution, we agree with the District Court that no showing of arbitrariness or capriciousness has been made in this case. Courts are particularly ill-equipped to evaluate academic performance. The factors discussed in Part II with respect to procedural due process speak a fortiori here and warn against any such judicial intrusion into academic decisionmaking.

The judgment of the Court of Appeals is therefore reversed. $<$

QUESTIONS

1.   Briefly outline the court's reasoning. Are there any points with which you disagree? Why?

2.   Do you believe that judges should become involved in making decisions about academic performance? Why or why not?

3.   Should the final word concerning academic disputes remain with the university?

Chapter Problem

ARE WE READY FOR TRUTH IN JUDGING?

The constant reader of constitutional cases soon comes to know that many of the important decisions of the Supreme Court of the United States are not based on law, in the popular sense of that term.

The Court endeavors to identify constitutional clauses on which to hang its pronouncements, but some key words and phrases in the Constitution are so highly indeterminate that they cannot qualify as law in any usual sense. They are semantic blanks—verbal vacuums that may be filled readily with any one of many possible meanings. It should not be surprising that different judges over a period of time, as well as at the same time, choose to fill them with their own meanings. . . .

In the present scheme of things, the Supreme Court's nature is not primarily that of a court. Its role and function are more closely akin to that of a legislative body or of an executive oligarchy. Perhaps it is our central committee. The search for analogues is an interesting one. But comparatists tell me there is no exact copy—now or in political history.

. . . But note well that it is not an act of condemnation or disapproval to say that the institution is not primarily a court. It is a

PROBLEM SOURCE: "Are We Ready for Truth in Judging?" *American Bar Association Journal*, Vol. 63 (September 1977), pp. 1212 and 1216. Excerpted with permission from *American Bar Association Journal*.

matter of healthy recognition that a new kind of governmental institution has evolved—one probably unique in the history of governmental institutions. It is an institution that has thus far been highly successful as an instrument of political action despite the fact that in combining legislative, judicial, and executive powers it has contradicted the basic warnings of the doctrine of separation of powers, and the apprehensions against concentrated power expressed by the framers of the Constitution.

By honestly and accurately identifying what we have wrought through the development of this singular institution, the American people may more wisely evaluate and observe its workings in the exercise of great and concentrated power. That power, vast as it has become, is still contained within a proved system of checks and balances and within a working structure of constitutional government that vest the ultimate power of choice and direction in the American people.

The merit of our Legiscourt in our democratic framework is worthy of further straightforward analysis and evaluation, particularly in relation to long-range effects. The maintenance of this body as the designated protector of minorities against the will of the majority is a strong point in its favor. But the tendency of the body to venture into other areas of government, where the necessity to safeguard minorities is not present or ambiguous, may be less favorable. There is much to study and to think about. But the first thing to do is to identify and reveal the true nature of the institution.

Questions

1. What does the author of this article mean by the term *Legiscourt*?

2. How is the Supreme Court acting like a new kind of governmental institution? Can you give an example?

3. Do you agree with the author of this article that the Supreme Court exercises "great and concentrated power"? Why or why not?

Questions for Review

1. To better understand the process of constitutional amendment, research the history and progress of the Equal Rights Amendment. How has its history differed from that of other constitutional amendments?

2. How does the Supreme Court decide which cases to hear among all those that are sent to it for consideration?

3.   The text suggests that the Supreme Court is uniquely suited to act as final arbiter on constitutional issues. Do you agree with this? Why or why not?

4.   Why do you suppose the Supreme Court has nearly always taken the position that when a case turns on several questions of law, the constitutional questions must be decided last—or not at all, if the case can be disposed of on other grounds?

5.   What types of restraints are imposed on the actions of the Supreme Court?

6.   Do you agree with the notion that Supreme Court justices should have indefinite tenure and should be virtually unremovable from office? Explain your answer.

8
Lawmaking and Adjudication by Administrative Agencies

To many Americans, the influence of administrative officials[1] seems far more pervasive than that of judges and legislators. Not only do these officials execute the laws; together they create more legal rules than all the legislatures and try more cases than all the courts. The body of law that controls their activity is known as *administrative law*. We shall consider some of the principles of administrative law in this chapter.

Administrators perform such a great variety of functions that it would be impossible to enumerate them all. The following examples of their rulemaking and adjudicative functions, however, will suggest the sorts of activities with which this chapter is concerned.

1.   Administrators assess the value of our taxable property. They review our declarations of our taxable incomes. They issue regulations defining the categories of income that must be included in our income declarations. They negotiate disputes over tax liability with particular

---

[1] When we speak of administrative officials in this chapter, we are referring to officials in the executive branch of the government. While this category includes the President, state governors, mayors, and other elective officials, we shall be mostly concerned with the activities of nonelective officials: cabinet members; heads of departments, bureaus, and offices; and the innumerable officials subordinate to them. The category specifically includes those who staff the so-called regulatory commissions, even though these agencies are sometimes classified as being outside the executive branch. In short, these administrative officials are the bureaucrats.

taxpayers. They staff a special federal tax court that adjudicates controversies over liability when negotiation has failed.

2. Administrators grant (and may deny, suspend, or revoke) a great variety of licenses, permits, franchises, charters, and patents.

3. Administrators establish the rates charged by transportation, communications, and public utility companies and supervise the services these companies provide.

4. Administrators serve as both judges and prosecutors in proceedings to determine whether laws prohibiting unfair competition, unfair labor practices, and racial discrimination in housing and employment have been violated. They also rule on alleged violations of laws setting standards for wages and hours and for the quality of food and drugs.

5. Administrators determine whether certain persons should be excluded from government or defense-industry jobs, and whether others should be deported from the country.

6. Administrators hear and rule on the claims of employees who have suffered injuries while at work.

The Emergence
of the Modern Administrative Agency

There have always been administrators, but they have not always had the breadth of discretionary power that many of them have today. How has it happened that nonelective officials now make rules governing our conduct and that officials outside the judicial tradition hear and decide cases?

The power of modern administrators is a product of economic developments that began in the latter part of the last century. In the years following the Civil War, the United States was transformed with remarkable speed from a farming and trading nation into an industrial nation. A vigorous generation of entrepreneurs created great manufacturing, railroad, and financial empires. The resulting concentration of power in private hands brought widespread abuses, which, in turn, provoked a popular demand for government regulation of business practices deemed harmful to the general interest.

Traditionally, when a legislature decided to lay down a new set of rules regulating private conduct, it simply adopted a statute setting up standards in terms as specific or as general as the circumstances warranted. The courts were left to fill in the gaps in the law as cases—criminal prosecutions or civil suits, depending on the remedies provided by the statute—were brought before them. This was the pattern of lawmak-

ing set in 1890, for example, with the enactment of the Sherman Act (see page 117). Our body of federal antimonopoly rules has been the joint creation of Congress and the federal courts.[2]

But this traditional lawmaking technique proved inadequate in providing the complex system of regulation that Americans felt it necessary to inaugurate during the past eighty years. Legislatures came to realize that lawmaking under the new regulatory programs would not be a "one-shot" affair: It would require continuous attention and enough flexibility to allow lawmakers to readily change the rules as new problems (including new techniques of evasion) emerged. It soon became clear that legislatures had neither the time nor the knowledge to undertake this large and continuing responsibility for making and modifying the rules. Equally important, it became clear that the courts could not be saddled with primary responsibility for filling in the gaps in the new regulatory statutes. The judges were little better equipped than the legislators to acquire the knowledge and experience, and to give the continuous attention, necessary for dealing with complex and rapidly changing problems.

Hence a new pattern of regulation emerged. Administrative officials began to receive much larger discretionary powers and to perform a variety of functions previously reserved for the legislatures and the courts.

The new pattern emerged at the federal level in 1887 with the enactment of the Interstate Commerce Act. The original purpose of this statute was to eliminate inequities in rate setting and other practices in interstate rail transportation. It resembled the Sherman Act in that it provided for criminal prosecutions and civil suits against practices declared to be unlawful. But it also established a new agency, the Interstate Commerce Commission, and gave it general responsibility for making day-to-day policy decisions pertaining to the regulation of railroads. The Commission had authority, among other things, to investigate complaints by shippers against the railroads, to hold hearings at which witnesses could be compelled to testify, and, if necessary, to issue formal orders that the courts were expected to enforce.

For almost twenty years, hostile courts interpreted the assigned powers of the new agency so restrictively as to deny it any real authority. For a while, the state railway commissions, created at about the same time for similar purposes, were blocked by similar obstacles. Eventually, however, these obstacles were overcome, by new legislation designed to strengthen the ICC and by an abatement of judicial hostility. Thereafter

---

[2] A third participant was the Antitrust Division of the Department of Justice, which influenced the growth of antitrust law by deciding which violators to prosecute and by choosing which legal arguments to present to the judges. In this limited sense, administrators participated in lawmaking even under the traditional arrangements.

the new technique of regulating economic activities by administrative agencies came to be relied on more and more at both the federal and state levels. Among the best known of the federal regulatory agencies, all created in the twentieth century, are the Federal Trade Commission, the Federal Power Commission, the Federal Communications Commission, the Securities and Exchange Commission, the Civil Aeronautics Board, and the National Labor Relations Board.[3] Perhaps the best-known state regulatory agencies are the public utilities commissions.

The powers of modern regulatory agencies tend to be greater than those of nineteenth-century administrators in three respects:

1.   Their purely executive powers are greater. They have broader authority to investigate, to insist that private concerns keep certain kinds of records, to negotiate settlements with regulated parties, and to initiate enforcement action.

2.   Many of them have expressly delegated authority to issue regulations that serve to elaborate the meaning of statutes couched in general terms. Many of the enabling statutes do no more than indicate a policy objective, define a set of abuses to be dealt with, and prescribe in broad terms the standards against which private or official acts are to be measured. In these circumstances, the agency is the real lawmaker.

3.   Many of the agencies have authority to hold trial-like hearings to determine the facts in particular controversies. The decisions that result from these hearings are subject to review by a court, but the scope of that review is limited; it is more like an appeal than a new trial.

It is these last two types of authority that will be the subject of the rest of this chapter.

Legislative Rulemaking by Administrators

In Chapter 1 we mentioned that legal rules are either *legislative* or *decisional* in origin. A legislative rule, you will remember, is embodied in an authoritative, official text. A decisional rule is a precedent, the by-product of the decision handed down in a particular case.

---

3 These agencies, along with a few others, are sometimes called the independent regulatory commissions, since they are in some ways less subject to the President's control than the agencies that make up the executive branch. The reasons for this limited grant of independence are as much historical as functional, and a number of agencies in the executive branch perform functions much like those performed by the independent commissions.

The statutes passed by legislatures are the most familiar embodiments of legislative rules. But the executive orders issued by Presidents and governors and the detailed regulations issued by administrative agencies are also examples of legislative rules. The most familiar decisional rules are the precedents established by appellate courts, but the decisions of administrative agencies adjudicating cases also establish precedents and hence are decisional rules.

Let us first consider the process of legislative rulemaking by agencies. An administrative agency supplements the general policies enunciated in the statutes it administers by issuing a variety of pronouncements of its own. The most formal and important of these are usually known as *regulations*. If an agency has explicit authority to issue such regulations, and if it exercises that authority in a valid manner, its regulations are just as much "law," just as likely to be honored in the courts, as any statute.

Regulations are normally published, so that affected parties (or at least their lawyers) may have an opportunity to learn about them. The agency is free to amend its regulations after publishing them, of course, but they remain binding so long as they have not been formally amended.[4]

Challenges to the Validity of Regulations

Under what circumstances might a court hold a regulation to be invalid and hence not entitled to enforcement?

Judges do not ask themselves whether they consider the regulation wise, fair, and likely to produce the desired result. Doing that would make the judges the ultimate legislators. Legislative power has been delegated to the administrators, presumably because of their technical knowledge and specialized experience. Therefore, their exercise of judgment is no more an issue before the court than would be the judgment of the legislature in passing a statute.

The first question the judges must ask in deciding on the validity of a regulation is whether the authority delegated to the agency is broad enough to cover the particular regulation. Has the agency done what it was told to do? Is there a reasonable correspondence between the regula-

---

[4] To have legal force, all regulations of federal agencies must be published in a daily journal called the *Federal Register* (which also publishes presidential proclamations and executive orders, as well as certain other documents). Periodically, federal regulations are codified and republished in the *Code of Federal Regulations*. A number of states have similar arrangements.

tion and the policies and standards enunciated in the statute? If the answer to these questions is negative, then the agency has acted *ultra vires* (beyond its powers), and its act is invalid.

The degree of discretion delegated to administrators varies; as we have already remarked, enabling statutes frequently state policies and prescribe standards in extremely general terms. Often, for instance, the legislature will instruct an agency to establish standards that are "fair and equitable" or "in the public interest," or that "serve the public convenience and necessity," or that "effectuate the purposes of this Act." Obviously such general phrases leave great discretion to the agency.

These broad delegations of authority raise a constitutional issue. After all, U.S. constitutions assign to the legislative branch the basic responsibility for legislating. (The federal Constitution says: "All legislative Powers herein granted shall be vested in a Congress of the United States. . . .") Are there no limits to the power of legislatures to delegate this responsibility?

A few judicial decisions, mostly by state courts, have invalidated executive and administrative acts on the ground that they were based on delegations of authority deemed to be excessive. The best-known federal decision of this sort is the one that struck down the New Deal's National Industrial Recovery Act in 1935. But most courts today seem willing to uphold laws that contain extremely general statements of policy and standards.

One of the issues in the case of *Yakus* v. *United States* was whether Congress had made an unconstitutional delegation of power to a federal administrative agency. The following excerpts from the Supreme Court's majority opinion are worth reading with care, for the opinion is both a statement of the Court's position on the delegation-of-authority issue and an example of the modern regulatory statute and the type of regulations that are often issued under it.

Under wartime laws designed to check inflation, the Office of Price Administration was empowered to set maximum price levels for specified commodities and services. When administrators fix maximum prices or rates they are making rules, because they are establishing standards, enforceable by the courts, for the future conduct of a class of persons. Unlike some regulatory statutes, the price-control law did not provide for administrative adjudication of alleged violations; instead, those charged with violations were criminally prosecuted. The defendents in *Yakus* were tried and convicted of selling beef at prices above the levels prescribed in the OPA's regulations. In their appeal to the Supreme Court of the United States, they challenged the constitutionality of the basic statute.

Yakus v. *United States*

Supreme Court of the United States, 1944
321 U.S. 414, 64 S.Ct. 660
> MR. CHIEF JUSTICE STONE delivered the opinion of the Court. . . .

[The Chief Justice first identified the basic statutes and the policies underlying them.]

The Emergency Price Control Act provides for the establishment of the Office of Price Administration under the direction of a Price Administrator appointed by the President, and sets up a comprehensive scheme for the promulgation by the Administrator of regulations or orders fixing such maximum prices of commodities and rents as will effectuate the purpose of the Act and conform to the standards which it prescribes. The Act was adopted as a temporary wartime measure and provides in §1(b) for its termination on June 30, 1943, unless sooner terminated by Presidential proclamation or concurrent resolution of Congress. By the amendatory act of October 2, 1942, it was extended to June 30, 1944.

Section 1(a) declares that the Act is "in the interest of the national defense and security and necessary to the effective prosecution of the present war," and that its purposes are:

"to stabilize prices and to prevent speculative, unwarranted, and abnormal increases in prices and rents; to eliminate and prevent profiteering, hoarding, manipulation, speculation, and other disruptive practices resulting from abnormal market conditions or scarcities caused by or contributing to the national emergency; to assure that defense appropriations are not dissipated by excessive prices; to protect persons with relatively fixed and limited incomes, consumers, wage earners, investors, and persons dependent on life insurance, annuities, and pensions, from undue impairment of their standard of living; to prevent hardships to persons engaged in business, . . . and to the Federal, State, and local governments, which would result from abnormal increases in prices; to assist in securing adequate production of commodities and facilities; to prevent a post-emergency collapse of values. . . ."

[The Court then identified the standards prescribed in the two statutes and in a presidential executive order.]

The standards which are to guide the Administrator's exercise of his authority to fix prices, so far as now relevant, are prescribed by §2(a) and by §1 of the amendatory Act of October 2, 1942, and Executive Order

9250. . . . By §2(a) the Administrator is authorized, after consultation with representative members of the industry so far as practicable, to promulgate regulations fixing prices of commodities which "in his judgment will be generally fair and equitable and will effectuate the purposes of this Act" when, in his judgment, their prices "have risen or threaten to rise to an extent or in a manner inconsistent with the purposes of this Act."

This section also directs that

> "So far as practicable, in establishing any maximum price, the Administrator shall ascertain and give due consideration to the prices prevailing between October 1 and October 15, 1941 (or if, in the case of any commodity, there are no prevailing prices between such dates, or the prevailing prices between such dates are not generally representative because of abnormal or seasonal market conditions or other cause, then to the prices prevailing during the nearest two-week period in which, in the judgment of the Administrator, the prices for such commodity are generally representative) . . . and shall make adjustments for such relevant factors as he may determine and deem to be of general applicability, including . . . [s]peculative fluctuations, general increases or decreases in costs of production, distribution, and transportation, and general increases or decreases in profits earned by sellers of the commodity or commodities, during and subsequent to the year ended October 1, 1941."

By the Act of October 2, 1942, the President is directed to stabilize prices, wages and salaries "so far as practicable" on the basis of the levels which existed on September 15, 1942, except as otherwise provided in the Act. By Title I, §4 of Executive Order No. 9250, he has directed "all departments and agencies of the Government . . . to stabilize the cost of living in accordance with the Act of October 2, 1942."

[The relevant administrative regulation was then summarized.]

Revised Maximum Price Regulation No. 169 was issued December 10, 1942, under authority of the Emergency Price Control Act as amended and Executive Order No. 9250. The Regulation established specific maximum prices for the sale at wholesale of specified cuts of beef and veal. As is required by §2(a) of the Act, it was accompanied by a "statement of the considerations involved" in prescribing it. From the preamble to the Regulation and from the Statement of Considerations accompanying it, it appears that the prices fixed for sales at wholesale were slightly in excess of those prevailing between March 16 and March 28, 1942, and approximated those prevailing on September 15, 1942. Findings that the Regula-

tion was necessary, that the prices which it fixed were fair and equitable, and that it otherwise conformed to the standards prescribed by the Act, appear in the Statement of Considerations. . . .

[The Court then explained why the delegation of legislative power to the agency was not unconstitutional.]

Congress enacted the Emergency Price Control Act in pursuance of a defined policy and required that the prices fixed by the Administrator should further that policy and conform to standards prescribed by the Act. The boundaries of the field of the Administrator's permissible action are marked by the statute. It directs that the prices fixed shall effectuate the declared policy of the Act to stabilize commodity prices so as to prevent war-time inflation and its enumerated disruptive causes and effects. In addition the prices established must be fair and equitable, and in fixing them the Administrator is directed to give due consideration, so far as practicable, to prevailing prices during the designated base period, with prescribed administrative adjustments to compensate for enumerated disturbing factors affecting prices. . . .

The Act is thus an exercise by Congress of its legislative power. In it Congress has stated the legislative objective, has prescribed the method of achieving that objective—maximum price fixing—and has laid down standards to guide the administrative determination of both the occasions for the exercise of the price-fixing power, and the particular prices to be established. . . .

The Constitution as a continuously operative charter of government does not demand the impossible or the impracticable. It does not require that Congress find for itself every fact upon which it desires to base legislative action [emphasis added], or that it make for itself detailed determinations which it has declared to be prerequisite to the application of the legislative policy to particular facts and circumstances impossible for Congress itself properly to investigate. *The essentials of the legislative function are the determination of the legislative policy and its formulation and promulgation as a defined and binding rule of conduct* [emphasis added]—here the rule, with penal sanctions, that prices shall not be greater than those fixed by maximum price regulations which conform to standards and will tend to further the policy which Congress has established. These essentials are preserved when Congress has specified the basic conditions of fact upon whose existence or occurrence, ascertained from relevant data by a designated administrative agency, it directs that its statutory command shall be effective. It is no objection that the determination of facts and the inferences to be drawn from them in the light of the statutory standards and declaration of policy call for the exercise of judgment, and for the formulation of subsidiary administrative policy within the prescribed statutory framework. . . .

Nor does the doctrine of separation of powers deny to Congress power to direct that an administrative officer properly designated for that purpose have ample latitude within which he is to ascertain the conditions which Congress has made prerequisite to the operation of its legislative command. Acting within its constitutional power to fix prices, it is for Congress to say whether the data on the basis of which prices are to be fixed are to be confined within a narrow or a broad range. In either case the only concern of courts is to ascertain whether the will of Congress has been obeyed. . . .

. . . Congress is not confined to that method of executing its policy which involves the least possible delegation of discretion to administrative officers. . . . It is free to avoid the rigidity of such a system, which might well result in serious hardship, and to choose instead the flexibility attainable by the use of less restrictive standards. . . . *Only if we could say that there is an absence of standards for the guidance of the Administrator's action, so that it would be impossible in a proper proceeding to ascertain whether the will of Congress has been obeyed, would we be justified in overriding its choice of means for effecting its declared purpose of preventing inflation* [emphasis added].

[Finally, the Court compared the standards of the price-control statutes with those prescribed in other laws which had been upheld by the Court in earlier decisions.]

The standards prescribed by the present Act, with the aid of the "statement of the considerations" required to be made by the Administrator, are sufficiently definite and precise to enable Congress, the courts and the public to ascertain whether the Administrator, in fixing the designated prices, has conformed to those standards. . . . Hence we are unable to find in them an unauthorized delegation of legislative power. The authority to fix prices only when prices have risen or threaten to rise to an extent or in a manner inconsistent with the purpose of the Act to prevent inflation is no broader than the authority to fix maximum prices when deemed necessary to protect consumers against unreasonably high prices . . . or the authority to take possession of and operate telegraph lines whenever deemed necessary for the national security or defense . . . or the authority to suspend tariff provisions upon findings that the duties imposed by a foreign state are "reciprocally unequal and unreasonable." . . .

The directions that the prices fixed shall be fair and equitable, that in addition they shall tend to promote the purposes of the Act, and that in promulgating them consideration shall be given to prices prevailing in a stated base period, confer no greater reach for administrative determination than the power to fix just and reasonable rates . . . or the power to approve consolidations in the "public interest" . . . or the power to regu-

late radio stations engaged in chain broadcasting "as public interest, convenience or necessity requires" ... or the power to prohibit "unfair methods of competition" not defined or forbidden by the common law ... or the direction that in allotting marketing quotas among states and producers due consideration be given to a variety of economic factors ... or the similar direction that in adjusting tariffs to meet differences in costs of production the President "take into consideration" "in so far as he finds practicable" a variety of economic matters ... or the similar authority, in making classifications within an industry, to consider various named and unnamed "relevant factors" and determine the respective weights attributable to each....

Affirmed.   <

Although the courts rarely invalidate administrative regulations on the ground that they have been issued under unconstitutional delegations of power, regulations are sometimes invalidated because they fail to satisfy other constitutional standards. Regardless of how much authority the legislature grants to an agency, the agency is not permitted to issue a regulation that represents an unconstitutional exercise of government power. For example, a federal agency whose regulatory authority is constitutionally based on the commerce clause may not attempt to regulate purely *intrastate* commerce. Nor may any agency issue a regulation that serves to "deprive any person of life, liberty, or property without due process of law." Several early efforts by railroad commissions to establish rates foundered on the due-process restriction in the Fourteenth Amendment; the Supreme Court decided that the rates set were so low that they deprived the railroads of property without due process. Similarly, an administrative rule establishing a discriminatory classification might be invalidated under the Fourteenth Amendment's equal-protection clause.

Finally, in deciding on the validity of administrative regulations, the courts ask whether the agency has followed proper procedures in adopting the regulations. A major purpose of procedural requirements is to assure fair treatment to the private persons who are likely to be affected by the agency's rules. Are such persons entitled, for example, to receive notice that a new rule is under consideration and to have an opportunity to express themselves on its contents? Ordinarily, an agency's failure to give notice and to hold a hearing before issuing a regulation is not considered a denial of constitutional rights.[5] Still, many of the statutes under which administrative agencies operate require the agency to publish

---

[5] Similarly, legislatures are not constitutionally required to give advance notice and to hold a hearing when they are studying a legislative proposal, but most of them try to give affected parties a chance to be heard.

notice of the proposed regulations and to give interested parties an opportunity to express their views.

Less Formal
Administrative Pronouncements

Administrative agencies issue a variety of pronouncements, less formal
and binding than their legislative regulations, that are designed to clarify
the laws they are administering. Some of these pronouncements are described as "interpretive regulations." Others, issued in response to inquiries, are advisory "rulings" that interpret the law with reference to
particular types of situations. In addition, some agencies also publish instructions, guides, explanatory pamphlets, and so forth.

   In approaching federal income tax problems, for instance, lawyers
will look first at the Internal Revenue Code and at the voluminous regulations of the Treasury Department and the Internal Revenue Service.
But they will also look at the other interpretations and guides that the
IRS publishes. These have some of the qualities of legal rules. They indicate how the agency interprets the law it is administering, and hence
they form a basis for predicting its position in particular cases. The
courts, too, accord considerable respect to these informal pronouncements, particularly if they seem to be reasonable elaborations of the policies and standards of the statute.

Adjudication[6]
and Decisional Rulemaking
by Administrators

So far we have been talking about how administrators *create* rules, that
is, directives designed to influence the future conduct of whole categories
of persons. Now let us consider how administrators *apply* rules to particular cases.[7]

---

   [6] Used broadly, *adjudication* refers to any proceeding in which, after an examination
of evidence and arguments, a finding of facts is made and a decision is reached by applying rules to the facts found. The court trial is the best-known example.

   [7] Often the distinction between making general rules and deciding particular cases
is merely a matter of degree. For example, when an administrative agency prescribes the
freight rate to be charged by a particular railroad for transporting a particular commodity
between two named points, is it establishing a rule or dealing with a particular case?
Since it channels future conduct, rate setting is classified as rulemaking, but since the
setting of a particular rate usually affects only a few private parties, it closely resembles
case deciding. Consequently, the parties affected usually get the same sort of hearing
they would have if their rights were being adjudicated.

Administrative Adjudication

Administrators have always engaged in fact-finding. In order to determine whether a law was being complied with, for example, or whether an applicant was entitled to a license or a franchise, they have always had to investigate, inspect, ask questions, and insist that their questions be answered. But only with the emergence of the modern regulatory agency has the trial-like hearing, at which testimony and documents may be presented and challenged with the aid of counsel, come into widespread use.

One of the most important categories of administrative adjudication is the so-called *enforcement proceeding.* This is a proceeding to adjudicate charges that the standards established by a particular law have not been complied with. The National Labor Relations Roard, for example, conducts enforcement proceedings to determine whether an unfair labor practice has been committed. And the state fair employment practices commissions hold enforcement proceedings to determine whether an employer's hiring and promoting practices have involved racial or religious discrimination.

The agency's enforcement officials, acting either on their own initiative or in response to a private complaint (depending on what the statute provides), inquire into possible violations. If they find evidence of wrongdoing, they usually try first to negotiate a settlement with the violator under which he or she agrees to comply with the law. Many violations are brought to an end by negotiation, and administrative intervention goes no further. But if negotiation proves fruitless, the agency files a formal complaint and holds a public hearing.

Many of the procedures of the court trial have been taken over for the administrative hearing (perhaps partly because the officials who participate in the hearings are usually lawyers). But one difference is noteworthy: In administrative hearings the functions of both prosecutor and judge are normally performed by officials of the same agency, and occasionally by the same official. In the larger agencies cases are generally heard by a trial examiner, whose decision is later reviewed by the top officials of the agency (usually referred to collectively as the commission or the board).[8] If the commission sustains the enforcement official's con-

---

[8] This combination of the functions of prosecutor and judge has long been an object of criticism. After years of controversy, a compromise between the proponents and the critics of the "integrated" agency was incorporated into the federal Administrative Procedure Act of 1946. Proposals for a completely autonomous corps of trial examiners and for a special administrative court were rejected. Briefly, the objects of the provisions adopted were as follows: (1) to insulate trial examiners from intra-agency pressures by

tentions, it usually issues an agency order to the accused party. If this order is not voluntarily obeyed, the agency must obtain a court order to enforce it.

Other types of administrative hearings are held to determine whether a license should be revoked, or which of several parties should be awarded a franchise, or whether a person accused of past wrongdoing should be discharged from government service or deported from the country. Some hearings, in which one private party presses a claim against another, are very similar to civil proceedings—as, for example, when an employee comes before a worker's compensation board to claim damages from his or her employer for an injury sustained while at work.

Judicial Review

Administrative decisions affecting named individuals or organizations are often made after a hearing, but this is not always required or necessary. (For instance, a registrar of motor vehicles should not have to hold a hearing before it can grant or deny a driver's license to a new applicant.) Regardless of whether the agency has acted on the basis of an administrative hearing, the law normally gives to affected persons the right to contest the agency's action in the courts. (This is another aspect of the power of judicial review already discussed; see page 146.) The court may be asked to rule on such issues as the statute's constitutionality, the agency's jurisdiction, or the regularity of the procedures followed in reaching a decision. And individuals can always persuade the courts to reverse an administrative decision if they can prove prejudice or corruption. To cut the private party off from this access to the courts might well be a denial of constitutional due process.

Over the centuries, judges and legislators have devised a variety of procedures by which the individual may challenge administrative acts in the courts. (We need not enumerate them here.) It is not always necessary, moreover, for the individual to take the initiative. Since, with a few exceptions, administrators have no power to enforce their own decisions (that is, to compel private persons to obey their orders or to punish them

---

giving the Civil Service Commission a special role in decisions concerning their salary and tenure; (2) to prevent trial examiners from discussing any case before them with outsiders or with other agency officials unless all interested parties could take part in the discussions; and (3) to deny the enforcement officials of an agency any role in making the final agency decision. In 1947 Congress responded to criticisms of the National Labor Relations Board by going one step further: It took the board's Office of General Counsel completely out of the agency, making it an independent entity charged with investigating complaints and acting as prosecutor in enforcement proceedings heard by the board.

for not complying), the individual is often able to contest a decision simply by defying it and forcing the administrator to take the case to court.

Having the right to an administrative hearing does not deprive a
person of the right to judicial review, but as administrative fact-finding
procedures have improved, the scope of judicial review has narrowed. As
legislators and judges have gained confidence in the fairness of administrative procedures, they have abandoned their earlier insistence on a
judicial reexamination of the agency's findings of fact. The reviewing
court may be either a trial court or an appellate court (depending on
what the relevant statute provides), but in either event the review proceeding ordinarily resembles an appeal rather than a new trial. The court
does not rehear the evidence; it merely reviews the record of the agency
proceedings, and if there appears to be "substantial evidence in the
whole record" to support the agency's finding, the judges do not reject it
even though they might have drawn different conclusions from the evidence if they themselves had heard the case. The judges do, of course,
review all the agency's conclusions of law, but they often acknowledge
that the agency, through its knowledge and experience, is far better
equipped than they to work out the implications of the statutory policy.
Hence, if an agency's conclusions of law seem to be a reasoned and reasonable elaboration of the statute's objectives, most courts are inclined to
accept them.

The availability of judicial review undoubtedly makes administrators
less arbitrary in their decisions and more careful in construing their legal
powers. This is so, although only a small percentage of each year's administrative decisions are actually reviewed in the courts; the administrator's decision is almost always the final decision.

Decisional Rulemaking by Administrators

To decide cases, agencies must interpret the law as well as determine the
facts. Their interpretations appear in the opinions that accompany
agency decisions, many of which are published. Most agencies, though
they do not feel rigidly bound by *stare decisis*, still tend to follow their
own precedents, for the same reasons that courts do. Hence adjudicative
decisions give interested parties a fairly reliable basis for predicting an
agency's future position. Of course, an agency ruling ceases to be controlling once it is appealed and a court reverses it. As we have just seen,
though, most agency decisions are not appealed, and, of those few that
are, most are upheld.

In short, agency decisions become in effect decisional rules: They

channel future conduct. If, for instance, a company wishes to know how far it must go in bargaining with a union in order to satisfy the statutory requirement of "bargaining in good faith," it can do no better than to study the National Labor Relations Board's decisions (plus the relatively few court decisions) in which the requirement has been interpreted.

Since many agencies have both the power to issue regulations and the power to adjudicate cases, they can choose between these two methods of rulemaking. When an agency believes that the time has come to formulate a policy decision in an official text, it can draft and issue a regulation. But when an agency prefers to wait until the contours of a problem become clearer, it can continue to deal with the problem on a case-by-case basis, formulating a series of decisional rules couched in terms that insure continuing flexibility. Furthermore, an agency, unlike a court, does not have to wait passively for cases to be brought before it. Its enforcement officials can go out looking for cases that will raise the issues on which its adjudicating officials want to rule. And since the agency can pretty much decide for itself what enforcement proceedings to initiate, it can choose cases that present the issues in such a way that the courts will be likely to uphold the agency's ruling if an appeal is taken.

An Illustrative Case

The case of *Warner-Lambert Company* v. *Federal Trade Commission* was first decided by the commission and then appealed to the U.S. Court of Appeals of the District of Columbia Circuit. It exemplifies judicial restraint in reviewing decisions of administrative agencies.

Warner-Lambert Company v. *Federal Trade Commission*

U.S. Court of Appeals, District of Columbia Circuit, 1977
562 F.2d 749 (1977)
> J. SKELLY WRIGHT, Circuit Judge:

The Warner-Lambert Company petitions for review of an order of the Federal Trade Commission requiring it to cease and desist from advertising that its product, Listerine Antiseptic mouthwash, prevents, cures, or alleviates the common cold. The FTC order further requires Warner-Lambert to disclose in future Listerine advertisements that: "Contrary to prior advertising, Listerine will not help prevent colds or

sore throats or lessen their severity." We affirm but modify the order to delete from the required disclosure the phrase "Contrary to prior advertising."

I. BACKGROUND

The order under review represents the culmination of a proceeding begun in 1972, when the FTC issued a complaint charging petitioner with violation of Section 5(a)(1) of the Federal Trade Commission Act by misrepresenting the efficacy of Listerine against the common cold.

Listerine has been on the market since 1879. Its formula has never been changed. Ever since its introduction it has been represented as being beneficial in certain respects for colds, cold syptoms, and sore throats. Direct advertising to the consumer, including the cold claims as well as others, began in 1921.

Following the 1972 complaint, hearings were held before an administrative law judge (ALJ). The hearings consumed over four months and produced an evidentiary record consisting of approximately 4,000 pages of documentary exhibits and the testimony of 46 witnesses. In 1974 the ALJ issued an initial decision sustaining the allegations of the complaint. Petitioner appealed this decision to the Commission. On December 9, 1975 the Commission issued its decision essentially affirming the ALJ's findings. It concluded that petitioner had made the challenged representations that Listerine will ameliorate, prevent, and cure colds and sore throats, and that these representations were false. Therefore the Commission ordered petitioner to:

    1.   cease and desist from representing that Listerine will cure colds or sore throats, prevent colds or sore throats, or that users of Listerine will have fewer colds than non-users;

    2.   cease and desist from representing that Listerine is a treatment for, or will lessen the severity of, colds or sore throats; that it will have any significant beneficial effect on the symptoms of sore throats or any beneficial effect on symptoms of colds; or that the ability of Listerine to kill germs is of medical significance in the treatment of colds or sore throats or their symptoms;

    3.   cease and desist from disseminating any advertisement for Listerine unless it is clearly and conspicuously disclosed in each such advertisement, in the exact language below, that: "Contrary to prior advertising, Listerine will not help prevent colds or sore throats or lessen

their severity." This requirement extends only to the next ten million dollars of Listerine advertising.

Petitioner seeks review of this order.

II. SUBSTANTIAL EVIDENCE

. . . The first issue on appeal is whether the Commission's conclusion that Listerine is not beneficial for colds or sore throats is supported by the evidence. The Commission's findings must be sustained if they are supported by substantial evidence on the record viewed as a whole. We conclude that they are.

Both the ALJ and the Commission carefully analyzed the evidence. They gave full consideration to the studies submitted by petitioner. The ultimate conclusion that Listerine is not an effective cold remedy was based on six specific findings of fact.

First, the Commission found that the ingredients of Listerine are not present in sufficient quantities to have any therapeutic effect. This was the testimony of two leading pharmacologists called by Commission counsel. The Commission was justified in concluding that the testimony of Listerine's experts was not sufficiently persuasive to counter this testimony.

Second, the Commission found that in the process of gargling it is impossible for Listerine to reach the critical areas of the body in medically significant concentration. The liquid is confined to the mouth chamber. Such vapors as might reach the nasal passage would not be in therapeutic concentration. Petitioner did not offer any evidence that vapors reached the affected areas in significant concentration.

Third, the Commission found that even if significant quantities of the active ingredients of Listerine were to reach the critical sites where cold viruses enter and infect the body, they could not interfere with the activities of the virus because they could not penetrate the tissue cells.

Fourth, the Commission discounted the results of a clinical study conducted by petitioner on which petitioner heavily relies. Petitioner contends that in a four-year study schoolchildren who gargled with Listerine had fewer colds and cold symptoms than those who did not gargle with Listerine. The Commission found that the design and execution of the "St. Barnabas study" made its results unreliable. For the first two years of the four-year test no placebo was given to the control group. For the last two years the placebo was inadequate: the control group was given colored water which did not resemble Listerine in smell or taste. There was also evidence that the physician who examined the test sub-

jects was not blinded from knowing which children were using Listerine and which were not, that his evaluation of the cold symptoms of each child each day may have been imprecise, and that he necessarily relied on the non-blinded child's subjective reporting. Both the ALJ and the Commission analyzed the St. Barnabas study and the expert testimony about it in depth and were justified in concluding that its results are unreliable.

Fifth, the Commission found that the ability of Listerine to kill germs by millions on contact is of no medical significance in the treatment of colds or sore throats. Expert testimony showed that bacteria in the oral cavity, the "germs" which Listerine purports to kill, do not cause colds and play no role in cold symptoms. Colds are caused by viruses. Further, "while Listerine kills millions of bacteria in the mouth, it also leaves millions. It is impossible to sterilize any area of the mouth, let alone the entire mouth."

Sixth, the Commission found that Listerine has no significant beneficial effect on the symptoms of sore throat. The Commission recognized that gargling with Listerine could provide temporary relief from a sore throat by removing accumulated debris irritating the throat. But this type of relief can also be obtained by gargling with salt water or even warm water. The Commission found that this is not the significant relief promised by petitioner's advertisements. It was reasonable to conclude that "such temporary relief does not 'lessen the severity' of a sore throat any more than expectorating or blowing one's nose 'lessens the severity' of a cold."

... In its attack on the Commission's findings, petitioner relies heavily on a recent study of over-the-counter cold remedies by the Food and Drug Administration.... [But w]e conclude that ... the FDA study does not, to any significant degree, contradict the Commission's findings....

III. THE COMMISSION'S POWER

Petitioner contends that even if its advertising claims in the past were false, the portion of the Commission's order requiring "corrective advertising" exceeds the Commission's statutory power. The argument is based upon a literal reading of Section 5 of the Federal Trade Commission Act, which authorizes the Commission to issue "cease and desist" orders against violators and does not expressly mention any other remedies. The Commission's position on the other hand, is that the affirmative disclosure that Listerine will not prevent colds or lessen their severity is absolutely necessary to give effect to the prospective cease and desist order; a hundred years of false cold claims have built up a large reservoir

of erroneous consumer belief that would persist, unless corrected, long after petitioner ceased making the claims.

... The need for the corrective advertising remedy and its appropriateness in this case are important issues which we will explore *infra*. But the threshold question is whether the Commission has the authority to issue an order. We hold that it does.

Petitioner's narrow reading of Section 5 was at one time shared by the Supreme Court. In *FTC* v. *Eastman Kodak Co.* the Court held that the Commission's authority did not exceed that expressly conferred by statute. The Commission has not, the Court said, "been delegated the authority of a court of equity."

But the modern view is very different. In 1963 the Court ruled that the Civil Aeronautics Board has authority to order divestiture in addition to ordering cessation of unfair methods of competition by air carriers. The CAB statute, like Section 5, spoke only of the authority to issue cease and desist orders, but the Court said, "We do not read the Act so restrictively.... [Where] the problem lies within the purview of the Board, ... Congress must have intended to give it authority that was ample to deal with the evil at hand." The Court continued, "Authority to mold administrative decrees is indeed like the authority of courts to frame injunctive decrees.... [The] power to order divestiture need not be explicitly included in the powers of an administrative agency to be part of its arsenal of authority...." [Brackets in original.] ...

Thus it is clear that the Commission has the power to shape remedies which go beyond the simple cease and desist order....

... According to petitioner, "The first reference to corrective advertising in Commission decisions occurred in 1970, nearly fifty years and untold numbers of false advertising cases after passage of the Act." In petitioner's view, the late emergence of this "newly discovered" remedy is itself evidence that it is beyond the Commission's authority. This argument fails on two counts. First the fact that an agency has not asserted a power over a period of years is not proof that the agency lacks such power. Second, and more importantly, we are not convinced that the corrective advertising remedy is really such an innovation. The label may be newly coined, but the concept is well established. It is simply that under certain circumstances an advertiser may be required to make affirmative disclosure of unfavorable facts.

One such circumstance is when an advertisement that did not contain the disclosure would be misleading. For example, the Commission has ordered the sellers of treatments for baldness to disclose that the vast majority of cases of thinning hair and baldness are attributable to heredity, age, and endocrine balance (so-called "male pattern baldness") and

that their treatment would have no effect whatever on this type of baldness. It has ordered the promoters of a device for stopping bedwetting to disclose that the device would not be of value in cases caused by organic defects or diseases. And it has ordered the makers of Geritol, an iron supplement, to disclose that Geritol will relieve symptoms of tiredness only in persons who suffer from iron deficiency anemia, and that the vast majority of people who experience such symptoms do not have such a deficiency.

Each of these orders was approved on appeal over objections that it exceeded the Commission's statutory authority. The decisions reflect a recognition that, as the Supreme Court has stated,

> If the Commission is to attain the objectives Congress envisioned, it cannot be required to confine its road block to the narrow lane the transgressor has traveled; it must be allowed effectively to close all roads to the prohibited goal, so that is order may not be by-passed with impunity.

. . .

IV. THE REMEDY

. . . Having established that the Commission does have the power to order corrective advertising in appropriate cases, it remains to consider whether use of the remedy against Listerine is warranted and equitable. We have concluded that part 3 of the order should be modified to delete the phrase "Contrary to prior advertising." With that modification, we approve the order.

. . . Our role in reviewing the remedy is limited. The Supreme Court has set for the standard:

> The Commission is the expert body to determine what remedy is necessary to eliminate the unfair or deceptive trade practices which have been disclosed. It has wide latitude for judgment and the courts will not interfere except where the remedy selected has no reasonable relation to the unlawful practices found to exist.

The Commission has adopted the following standard for the imposition of corrective advertising:

> [I]f a deceptive advertisement has played a substantial role in creating or reinforcing in the public's mind a false and material belief which lives on after the false advertising ceases, there is

clear and continuing injury to competition and to the consuming
public as consumers continue to make purchasing decisions based
on the false belief. Since this injury cannot be averted by merely
requiring respondent to cease disseminating the advertisement,
we may appropriately order repondent to take affirmative action
designed to terminate the otherwise continuing ill effects of the
advertisement. [Brackets in original.]

We think this standard is entirely reasonable. It dictates two factual inquiries: (1) did Listerine's advertisements play a substantial role in creating or reinforcing in the public's mind a false belief about the product?
and (2) would this belief linger on after the false advertising ceases? It
strikes us that if the answer to both questions is not yes, companies
everywhere may be wasting their massive advertising budgets. Indeed, it
is more than a little peculiar to hear petitioner assert that its commercials
really have no effect on consumer belief. . . .
    We turn next to the specific disclosure required: "Contrary to prior
advertising, Listerine will not help prevent colds or sore throats or lessen
their severity." Petitioner is ordered to include this statement in every
future advertisement for Listerine for a defined period. In printed advertisements it must be displayed in type size at least as large as that in
which the principal portion of the text of the advertisement appears and
it must be separated from the text so that it can be readily noticed. In
television commercials the disclosure must be presented simultaneously
in both audio and visual portions. During the audio portion of the disclosure in television and radio advertisements, no other sounds, including music, may occur.
    . . . These specifications are well calculated to assure that the dis-
closure will reach the public. It will necessarily attract the notice of readers, viewers, and listeners, and be plainly conveyed. Given these
safeguards, we believe the preamble "Contrary to prior advertising" is
not necessary. It can serve only two purposes: either to attract attention
that a correction follows or to humiliate the advertiser. The Commission
claims only the first purpose for it, and this we think is obviated by the
other terms of the order. The second purpose, if it were intended, might
be called for in an egregious case of deliberate deception, but this is not
one. While we do not decide whether petitioner proffered its cold claims
in good faith or bad, the record compiled could support a finding of good
faith. On these facts, the confessional preamble to the disclosure is not
warranted.
    . . . Finally, petitioner challenges the duration of the disclosure re-
quirement. By its terms it continues until respondent has expended on

Listerine advertising a sum equal to the average annual Listerine advertising budget for the period April 1962 to March 1972. That is approximately ten million dollars. Thus if petitioner continues to advertise normally the corrective advertising will be required for about one year. We cannot say that is an unreasonably long time in which to correct a hundred years of cold claims. . . . The Commission concluded that correction was required and that a duration of a fixed period of time might not accomplish that task, since petitioner could evade the order by choosing not to advertise at all. The formula settled upon by the Commission is reasonably related to the violation it found.

Accordingly, the order, as modified, is affirmed.   <

Achievements
and Disappointments

When the decision was made to create a large number of specialized administrative agencies, they were given broader powers than administrators had traditionally exercised. These included the power to issue regulations having the force of law and the power to hear and decide cases—powers that had previously been reserved to the legislatures and the courts.

It was recognized that the granting of these powers held some dangers. The bureaucrats who received the new rulemaking power did not have to face the salutary test of standing for election every few years, and the new adjudicators were not heirs to a long and honorable professional tradition. But various safeguards existed—particularly judicial review, which, it was hoped, would curb arbitrariness, oppression, and corruption on the part of officials.

The regulatory agencies have had a mixed record of performance. Some of the hopes of those who framed the early legislation have been disappointed. For one thing, too few of the regulatory agencies have become effective formulators of long-range policy. We have learned that establishing a specialized agency with broad authority to create new rules is only a beginning. The agency must be staffed by officials who are bold and imaginative, farsighted in their planning and yet ready to renounce policy formulations that have been made obsolete by changing economic conditions, and capable of running an efficient agency without letting daily routine obscure the needs of the future. Such administrators have always been in short supply, and their absence has made the agencies only partially effective.

Over the past twenty-five years, the criticisms leveled against admin-

istrative agencies have changed. In the 1940s, when some of the most important agencies were still young, critics complained that the administrators were high-handed zealots, often suspicious or downright hostile toward the economic group whose practices they were supposed to regulate. In those days the main focus of criticism was on the assignment to some agencies of both enforcement and adjudicative functions. Some of these earlier criticisms have been met over the years. But a new generation of critics complains that today's administrators too often lack zeal, and are mediocre and inefficient; that they have often become so sympathetic with the problems of the groups they regulate that they have lost sight of the broader public interest; and, finally, that too many administrators have been shown to be susceptible to improper and even corrupt influences. Yet another group of critics argue that we have created both too many and too specialized administrative agencies. These agencies are challenged as being extremely costly to the consumer and are even accused of having counterproductive tendencies.[9]

In conclusion, however, we must acknowledge that although some expectations have been disappointed, many have been realized. And it is difficult to see how more of the original objectives could have been achieved, within the limitations imposed by our democratic principles, the federal system, and long-standing constitutional arrangements, by any governmental arrangement substantially different from the one that was adopted.

Chapter Problem

John J. McCloy, chairman of the American Bar Association Commission on Law and the Economy, recently wrote a useful and interesting article concerning the development of federal regulatory agencies. In the article he stated:

> A principal theme of the commission's report, which now has been issued in final form, is that congressional and administrative consideration of government intervention has been undertaken all too often without adequate analysis and evaluation of the po-

---

[9] See American Bar Association, *Roads to Reform*, report of the Commission on Law and the Economy, cited in John J. McCloy, "Federal Regulation: Roads to Reform," *American Bar Association Journal*, Vol. 66 (April 1980), p. 461.

PROBLEM SOURCE: "Federal Regulation: Roads to Reform," *American Bar Association Journal*, Vol. 66 (April 1980), pp. 461–464, at 462.

tentially adverse economic impact of the various forms of intervention, both by increasing the cost of goods and services and by impeding private initiatives. As a result, some forms of intervention have been demonstrably counterproductive; others have made progress toward their objectives but at unnecessarily high cost.

The commission concluded that in view of these facts, it would be wise to draw on the analogy of the law's "burden of proof" principle. The precept would be that those who would seek the establishment of a new agency, or the expansion of an old agency that has been identified for reexamination after a certain period of existence, would carry the burden of proving that the advantages to be gained by so doing outweigh the advantages of permitting the free-market or private-enterprise system to cope with whatever economic or social objectives are involved.

Questions

1. Pick a regulatory agency and see if you think that it meets the burden of proof noted above.
2. Can you think of any alternatives to regulatory rules?
3. Do you think that administrative agencies have as a general rule overstepped their authority?

Questions for Review

1. How does Congress justify its decision to delegate legislative power to administrative agencies?
2. What power do the courts have to review administrative decisions? Should the courts have greater or lesser powers than they currently have?
3. Can you see any potential for conflicts of interest in adminstrative agencies? Keep in mind that agencies often act as judge, jury, and prosecutor.
4. Individuals now have the right to be represented by counsel at administrative hearings. Do you believe this should be changed? Explain.
5. How have opponents of administrative agencies changed the grounds of their criticism over the past twenty-five years? Do you believe that the form and function of these agencies is likely to change in the future?

9
Private Contributions to the Legal System

In this book, *law* is defined to include only those guides to conduct that are created by officials; hence *lawmaking* is defined to cover only the creation of rules by officials. Some scholars use a broader definition that includes "private lawmaking." They point out that many of the arrangements that private individuals and groups work out among themselves have the same effect as legal rules.

Our narrower definition of lawmaking corresponds more closely to what most people understand by the term. But we cannot on that account ignore the contributions made by private persons to the legal system. These contributions are discussed in this chapter. First, we shall consider very briefly the contributions of private persons and groups to the legal fabric that is continuously being woven by legislators, judges, and administrators. Then we shall consider at much greater length the contributions that private groups make to social ordering by creating their own systems of private rules. As an example of such a system, we shall study the "government under law" that has been developed in industry by employers and organized labor under collective-bargaining agreements.

Private Contributions to Lawmaking

In a democratic society, the major aim of government and law is to provide a setting in which individuals can pursue their own objectives. For

example, we continue to rely to a great extent on the decisions of private producers and consumers to determine what gets produced, how, and by whom. Law establishes the framework within which such private decision making takes place. But the reverse relationship is equally important: Patterns of private conduct play a part in forming law. What the rules permit largely determines what people do, but what people do (and aspire to do) largely determines the problems with which officials must deal, and thus the content of the rules they make.

How, specifically, does private conduct affect the content of legal rules?

1. *Private controversies produce decisional rules.* Those who prosecute cases in the courts or in administrative hearings influence the shaping of decisional rules by their choice of which cases to bring and of which legal arguments to present in those cases. The character of the decisions that emerge from court and agency adjudications is largely determined by the way in which the legal issues are presented for decision, which in turn depends on the facts of the particular case and the arguments advanced by the parties. In short, how private persons go about settling their disputes plays a part in creating law.

2. *Group pressures produce legislative rules.* Legislative rules are enacted because of a felt need for legislative action. This felt need is usually stimulated by the actions of private persons and the political pressures of organized interest groups. In a free society such pressures are inevitable and desirable. Often an interest group will not only point out the need but propose a remedy. It may even come up with a draft bill for enactment, and where the subject matter is technical, legislators tend to rely heavily on such drafts. Clearly, what private groups do about creating the need for legislative action and then pushing for specific enactments plays a part in creating law.

3. *Private arrangements become legal standards.* In the eighteenth century the privately enforced rules and usages that merchants had been developing ever since the Middle Ages were absorbed into English law. English judges had long been willing to accept evidence of merchants' usages as aids in interpreting commercial contracts, but the eighteenth-century judges went further and declared these nonofficial arrangements to be a part of the law of England. Many of our modern rules of commercial law thus had their origins in a privately developed body of rules.

This process continues in modern times. Suppose a woman wishes to exercise a legal power in such a way as to secure certain results while avoiding certain other results. (Perhaps she wants to complete a certain transaction while incurring the minimum possible tax liability. Or she may want to make an airtight contract with someone she does not

wholly trust. Or she may want to create an ownership interest in a business with only a limited right of control.) She goes to a lawyer and presents her problem. The lawyer discovers that none of the standard tools in his kit is exactly what is needed. So he invents a solution: a new arrangement, a new type of document, or a new combination of words especially designed to achieve the desired result. His invention may eventually be challenged and tested in a court. If it survives, and if it is shown to accomplish what the client wanted, other lawyers will learn of it and copy it. Before long the new device is likely to be given a standardized form and a label. Judges will acknowledge it as an approved method of exercising a legal power. Drafters of legislation—of tax laws, for example—will take it into account and make provisions for it. And finally it will take its place among the tools in the kit of every competent lawyer.

The terms of standardized sales contracts, deeds, mortgages, leases, and corporate charters and bylaws were largely created by lawyers, as were such arrangements of relatively recent origin as the employee pension trust and the stock option for corporate executives.[1]

Private Supplements to Lawmaking

When a power is exercised by private persons in such a way as to determine the rights and duties of a large number of people, the process has much in common with lawmaking as we have defined it; hence, we can say that such an exercise of power creates private supplements to law. Take, for example, the Major League Agreement that controls the activities of the baseball teams forming the two major leagues. In form, this agreement is a contract drawn up by the club owners and subscribed to by all the major-league players. But it might also be described as the constitution of a system of private self-government in which the club owners are the legislators, the league presidents the executives, and the commissioner of baseball the judge. (The actual division of functions is not quite so neat, of course. Yet it is interesting to note that the first commissioner of baseball was a former federal judge.)

It would be most undesirable, if not impossible, for the state to try to prescribe all the rules governing private conduct. Our innumerable pri-

---

1 It should be noted here that many customs and usages that have no status as authoritative rules are regularly taken into account by courts in deciding cases. A trade practice may illuminate the probable intentions of the parties to a commerical contract, for instance. Moreover, when a court must decide whether a business or professional person has acted with "due care," it has to measure that person's act against the traditional standards and practices of the trade or profession.

vate associations—corporations, labor unions, clubs, schools, churches, and families, to name only a few—all have their own rules, and the state relies on these private rules to channel much of the conduct of its citizens. Essentially, the legal system provides a framework, a backstop, for the operation of these private rules.

A particularly interesting illustration of a supplementary legal system is the labor-management relationship established under a collective-bargaining agreement. Such agreements have some of the characteristics of contracts, but in many ways they resemble constitutions. When the United Steelworkers of America and the major steel companies sign an agreement, their act puts into effect a set of basic rules governing the relationship of hundreds of thousands of employees with their employers. The agreement contains not only rules governing the conduct of the parties, but also rules establishing institutions and procedures under which disputes arising between the parties will be handled while the agreement is in force. This type of supplementary system will be the subject of the remainder of this chapter.

Industrial Self-Government Within the Legal Framework

The relations between an employer and his or her organized employees are carried on under a system of rules that they themselves have created, acting within the framework provided by the law. The *collective-bargaining agreement* (of which more than 150,000 are now in operation in the United States) might be described as the "constitution" of an industrial community. Such communities have other "legislative" rules, too, some of them laid down by the employer alone, but most of them the product of negotiations carried on under provisions of the agreement. The agreement also establishes a procedure for settling disputes between employer and employees. The final stage in that procedure is usually *arbitration*, a form of adjudication. Arbitration produces decisions that come to have some of the quality of decisional rules for the industrial community.

Let us first consider the bargaining that leads up to the collective agreement, and then the agreement itself and the arrangements established under it.

The Conditions and Products of Collective Bargaining

What conditions are essential to effective bargaining? Remember that a bargain is an exchange. First, each party must have something that the

other wants, so that it will be to their mutual advantage if they can come to terms. Second, each party must be in a position to exercise the alternative of *not* exchanging what he or she has if the terms offered are too unfavorable. When a party lacks either one of these prerequisites, he or she has no bargaining power, and there can be no real bargaining.

Bargaining between management and labor boils down to the exchange of work opportunities for workers. The employer may make jobs available or may close down the plant (an act known as a *lockout*). Organized workers may do the employer's work, or they may refuse as a group to go on working (an act known as a *strike*). Although choosing the second alternative in both cases entails short-run sacrifices, this alternative in the long run is essential to each party's bargaining position. In the days when most employees had to negotiate singly with their employers the workers usually found that they were not really able to bargain at all. Their individual services were rarely indispensable to the employer, since the supply of labor for most types of work was relatively abundant. And even if they possessed skills that were in short supply, they could afford to quit only if they could start at once on another job, since they normally had little or no savings, and there was no union strike fund standing ready to aid them. It was only when they joined a union that they could bargain, because then others would join them in refusing to work if their terms were not met. And even a union would be unable to bargain effectively if the law prevented it from going out on strike or using other means of pressure on the employer.

To promote bargaining, modern labor law has tried to lessen the inequalities between the parties and to bring them together around the bargaining table. But it also permits employees to strike and employers to close down their plants. Both rights are subject to limitations, however, as are the other weapons in the industrial struggle: labor's picketing and boycotts, and the various techniques that management has developed to resist union pressures. The collective-bargaining agreements negotiated by employers and unions usually contain self-imposed limitations on the right of the parties to use coercive pressures on each other during the life of the agreement, and these limitations, too, are backed up by law.

The law has, of course, never sought to assure that the bargaining parties would be of exactly equal strength. To do so would be quite impossible, for the outcome of any negotiation depends on subtle and shifting factors, including the skill of the negotiating representatives and the external circumstances at the time of the negotiation. A union's bargaining position is obviously stronger, for instance, in a period when the demand for the company's product is strong and workers are scarce than in a period of slack demand and widespread unemployment.

The first step in the bargaining process is to secure an agreement. Then, since agreements must be renewed periodically, there will be further bargaining when revisions in the agreement are proposed by one party or the other. Bargaining goes on even while an agreement is in operation: New problems may appear in the production process, and disputes may arise over the meaning and application of the agreement. Contrary to the impression given by news reports, however, the orderly settlement of differences at all these stages is the rule, and resort to economic warfare the exception.

The Contents
of a Collective-Bargaining Agreement

What matters do collective bargaining agreements cover? The agreements have no standard form, of course. Those negotiated in small establishments are likely to be much briefer than those negotiated in giant firms, and relatively weak unions are often unable to win the commitments from management that strong unions can secure. In an insightful article, however, Edwin Beal[2] suggested that almost all agreements have four major sections: (1) management rights and union security; (2) the wage and effort bargain; (3) individual security; and (4) administration.

MANAGEMENT RIGHTS AND UNION SECURITY   A basic term of any agreement, whether or not it is made explicit, is the principle that the employer is responsible for managing the enterprise and directing the labor force. Many agreements contain a section specifying that management is responsible for scheduling production, making work assignments, hiring, demoting, transferring, discharging, classifying, and disciplining personnel for just cause. In all these matters, management has the initiative. Most of the other terms of the agreement may be viewed as voluntarily accepted limitations on the fundamental prerogatives of management. As an example, the employer's power to lay off workers during a period of reduced production may be qualified by seniority provisions in the agreement, which specify the criteria to be used in deciding who is laid off first and rehired last. As a further example, the employer's power to discharge workers for disciplinary reasons may be qualified by a provision that disciplinary discharges must be for

---

[2] See *Personnel* (September–October 1962). This article outlines a complete guide for analyzing labor contracts, upon which the following paragraphs rely. This guide was later developed at length in Edwin F. Beal et al., *The Practice of Collective Bargaining*, 5th ed. (Irwin, 1976), p. 251. Students interested in more detail should consult this book.

"just cause." (This allows the union to file a grievance and have the case fully aired if it believes that an employee has been fired without just cause.)

Every union is understandably anxious to hold on to its members, to collect members' dues regularly, and to make members of as many employees as it can. Many employers actually help the unions to do these things, usually on the ground that if the union feels secure, it is more likely to be reasonable and responsible. Unless prohibited by the law of the state in which a plant is located, the employer has the right under federal legislation to agree to a "union shop" clause, in which the employer promises to discharge any employee who fails to join the union within a set period of time (usually thirty days) after being employed or who fails to continue as a member thereafter.

THE WAGE AND EFFORT BARGAIN   Many people consider this section of the labor contract to be the most important of all. It deals with the total amount of compensation paid by the employer to the employees. In addition to information about standard rates of pay, this section of the contract provides employees with explanations of their extra benefits, premium pay, and holidays.

INDIVIDUAL SECURITY   The individual-security section of the contract deals with an employee's ability to keep his or her job. One standard technique employed by unions to establish individual security is job seniority. This system guarantees that in the event of a work shortage, the least senior individual will be required to leave first and the most senior person to leave last.

The individual-security section of the contract also contains information about the company's grievance procedure, which is used to resolve disputes that regularly occur on the job. In addition to spelling out the procedure for resolving disputes, some contracts contain information about sanctions for particular forms of misbehavior. Shortly, we shall discuss in detail how disputes are settled under an agreement, so as to clarify how private legal systems perform judicial functions.

ADMINISTRATION   The final section of the contract deals with the procedures for implementing the other parts of the agreement. For example, it states which agency will be hired to carry out any arbitration work that might be needed. It also specifies the powers that people such as shop stewards (the elected employee who speaks for the union in the basic production unit) have in resolving contract questions.

The Handling of Disputes
Arising Under the Agreement

No matter how good relations are between a company and its employees, events are bound to occur that produce disagreements. For example, Brown is discharged for misconduct on the job and claims that he did not do what he is accused of, that it was not misconduct, or that discharge is too severe a penalty. Or Jones is promoted, whereupon Smith says that the promotion should have been his because he has been with the company longer than Jones. Or management lowers the classification and wage rate on a certain job because a newly installed machine has made the job less hazardous; the affected workers protest.

One of the major pieces of federal labor law, the Taft-Hartley Act, makes it clear that the legal obligation to negotiate with management continues after an agreement has been signed. The act established a Federal Mediation and Conciliation Service to aid companies and unions in settling their disputes, but Section 203(d) clearly indicates that Congress wants them to settle their disputes in their own way whenever possible. The act states:

> Final adjustment by a method agreed upon by the parties is hereby declared to be the desirable method for settlement of grievance disputes arising over the application or interpretation of an existing collective-bargaining agreement.

As has already been noted, nearly all agreements make some provision for a grievance procedure. In principle, employees, the union, and management all have the right to file grievances, but the procedures are usually based on the assumption that virtually all grievances will be filed by employees, with the support of their union representatives. Management will probably take the position that in running the plant it may make any decision it sees fit, subject only to its commitments under the agreement, and that any employee who believes that any management decision violates the agreement must file a grievance. This throws the initiative for filing a grievance on the employees, though of course the employer can indirectly take the initiative by doing something that forces the union to file a grievance.

We have spoken of the grievance procedure as an alternative to industrial strife, as indeed it is. We must recognize, however, that the handling of grievances is far from being an easy process; indeed, it is better thought of as an extension of the hardheaded bargaining that produced

the agreement. In negotiating the agreement, the employer probably fought to define as narrowly as possible the area falling under the grievance procedure, because there is a strategic advantage to keeping the area of unrestricted management discretion as broad as possible. For opposite reasons, the union probably fought to have the grievance area broadly defined.[3] The outcome is to some degree a reflection of the bargaining power and skill of the two parties. Once the grievance machinery is in operation, the volume of complaints at any given time is likely to be a function not merely of what happens in the plant but of union tactics: Is this a good time to press hard, or should it ease up? Whether management adopts a hard or a conciliatory position on complaints filed by the union is likely to be influenced by similar tactical considerations.

Grievance settlements contribute to the "law of the plant." The outcome of a grievance proceeding (particularly if the final stage, arbitration, is reached) has a significance for the law of the industrial community roughly comparable to the significance of a judicial or administrative decision. The precedent it establishes has no binding effect, but under many circumstances it will influence patterns of future conduct. The parties are well aware of this. When the negotiators of an agreement cannot agree on the wording of a provision, they often put in some vague words, counting on the grievance procedure to help fill in the gap as the area of dispute is illuminated by actual cases. The rule that grows out of the grievance settlement may, indeed, prove so satisfactory to both parties that they will formalize it as a new provision in the next revision of the agreement.

In agreements negotiated with larger companies, the grievance procedure consists of a series of meetings between union and management representatives at successively higher levels of authority in the company. The first step is usually for the shop steward to present the grievance to the shop foreman immediately concerned. If no settlement can be reached at that level, the union's elected grievance committee presents the grievance to the divisional superintendent. If this does not produce a settlement, one or more further appeals are carried to managers at higher levels; the final appeal is to a representative of top management. For each step (after the first) there is usually a deadline both for filing and for responding to the appeal, so that a succession of appeals up to the top-management level ordinarily does not take more than a few weeks at most.

---

[3] A closely related source of dispute is the breadth of the arbitration clause, which will be considered in the next section.

Most grievances are disposed of (or abandoned) at one of these stages. But in a small minority of cases a final stage is reached: The union asks that the grievance be submitted to a neutral third party for arbitration.

Arbitration

WHAT IS IT? When two parties submit a dispute to arbitration, they are asking one or more nonofficial outsiders to hear and judge the controversy, on the understanding that they will accept whatever decision is reached. Arbitration is thus a special form of adjudication. Its procedures, and such law as exists concerning it (mostly on the enforceability of agreements to arbitrate and of arbitral awards), have developed largely as a result of its widespread use under commercial contracts. Employers making such contracts often include a provision binding themselves to arbitrate any dispute that may arise under the contract, in the belief that arbitration is cheaper, speedier, and more "private" than litigation in the courts. Arbitration has also been used in settling certain kinds of international disputes.

Arbitration, as a form of adjudication, is to be distinguished from mediation and conciliation. *Arbitrators* are called upon to suggest a solution to a particular problem. The parties agree ahead of time to be bound by the arbitrator's decision. In both mediation and conciliation, however, the disagreeing parties are not bound to a third-party decision.

A *mediator* is a neutral called in by the disputants who is asked to suggest a solution to a problem; the parties may choose either to accept or to reject the suggestion. A *conciliator*, on the other hand, is called in by the aggrieved parties to act as a catalyst, to try to keep the parties talking to one another. The conciliator may offer solutions to problems or may simply play the role of an active listener, suggesting alternative strategies for resolving the dispute.[4]

Various methods have been devised for selecting an arbitrator accept-

---

[4] The conceptual distinction between arbitration and mediation is important, but in practice arbitrators sometimes act as mediators. The same is true of judges; perhaps the best example is the judge in a domestic relations court who makes a practice of trying to help married couples patch up their differences before considering a petition for divorce. Judges who conduct pretrial conferences also act as mediators on occasion.

Although some mediating by adjudicators is probably inevitable, many students of our legal institutions feel that the combining of roles should be kept to a minimum. They argue that the possibility of performing both functions may cause confusion and prevent the adjudicator from performing either one properly.

able to both parties. One method is to invite an outside agency to submit a list of three or five names to the parties, who then take turns at eliminating a name until only one is left. Lists of persons available and qualified to serve as labor arbitrators are maintained by the Federal Mediation and Conciliation Service (a government agency) and the American Arbitration Association (a private, nonprofit organization).

Most labor arbitrators are chosen to hear only a single case (although an arbitrator whose work satisfies the parties may be chosen again by them). But a large company faced with a substantial flow of grievance cases often joins with the union representing its employees in hiring one or more arbitrators on a continuing basis. Sometimes arrangement is made for *tripartite arbitration*: Each party names one arbitrator and then both parties jointly name a third, who heads the group. Under all these arrangements the costs of arbitration are shared equally by the parties.

SPECIAL PROBLEMS OF THE LABOR ARBITRATOR   Although labor arbitrators perform functions that in many ways resemble those of both the commercial arbitrator and the trial judge, their role is unique in a number of respects.

Labor arbitrators, unlike judges, are not public officials whose authority is imposed on the parties by the state and whose decision will be enforced by other officials. They are hired and paid by the parties to the agreement (who may discharge them if they become dissatisfied with their performance). Their assigned task is not to "do justice" in any general sense, but to perform a function in the system of self-government the parties have created, to apply the rules established by their agreement.

The job of labor arbitrators is different from that of commercial arbitrators because collective-bargaining agreements are not like ordinary commercial contracts, in which the parties have normally come together only to carry out a single transaction. Management and labor are bound together by the strongest of ties. However bitter their occasional differences may be, each needs the other, and each has the same ultimate concern for maintaining the flow of production. Under these circum-

---

5 We are confining ourselves here to grievance arbitration. Sometimes an employer and a union that have been unable in their negotiations to resolve their differences over a particular term of the agreement finally decide to "leave it to arbitration." This substitution of arbitration for the negotiation of terms is quite different from the arbitration of grievances under an agreement. Indeed, some commentators insist that it is properly a job for a mediator rather than an arbitrator, since there is ordinarily no body of principles on which an arbitrator can base a decision.

stances, the task of adjudicating one of their disputes[5] often requires rare skill. It may be particularly challenging for the temporary, one-time arbitrator, who somehow must rapidly acquire an awareness of the total relationship between the parties. If, failing to acquire such an awareness, the arbitrator comes up with a decision that is formally impeccable but leaves one side bitter and relations tenser than ever, the arbitration can hardly be deemed a success. After all, a major aim of the grievance procedure is to eliminate causes of tension. "Let justice be done though the heavens fall" is not an appropriate slogan for a labor arbitrator.

Labor arbitrators must also bear in mind that arbitration is the last step in a settlement procedure, to be taken only after all attempts at negotiated settlement have failed. If a commercial arbitrator cannot render a satisfactory decision, the dispute can be carried to the courts. But litigation is not a practical alternative to grievance arbitration. True, the law provides that parties to a collective agreement may sue in the courts for alleged breaches of contract. But such suits are, and must always be, exceptional. There are too many grievances, and litigation is too costly. Prompt settlement of most grievances is imperative, and litigation is slow. Finally, courts, being courts of *law*, have to apply doctrines of law when they are relevant, but some of these doctrines may be quite inappropriate for the handling of grievances. Labor arbitrators can never forget, then, that the alternative to an acceptable award is likely to be not a lawsuit but a strike.[6]

IDENTIFYING THE RULES TO APPLY   Perhaps the greatest difference between labor arbitration and other forms of adjudication stems from the unique character of the "body of principle" on which labor arbitrators must base their decisions.

The arbitration clause in a collective-bargaining agreement usually specifies that arbitrators are authorized to settle only those grievances that are related to "the interpretation and application of this Agreement," and that they may not add to, subtract from, or modify the agreement. But if these words make the arbitrators' job of identifying the rules to apply sound easy, they are deceptive.

We have already compared collective-bargaining agreements with constitutions. Like most other constitutional documents, agreements tend

---

[6] A party is sometimes able to take a dispute arising under an agreement to the National Labor Relations Board by complaining that the other party is guilty of an unfair labor practice (for instance, refusing to bargain in good faith). But constant resort to administrative adjudication is no more a practical alternative to grievance proceedings than constant resort to the courts would be.

to be notably imprecise and incomplete. They are usually pounded out by negotiators working against a deadline—the expiration date of the current contract. The temptation is always strong, when accord on a particular issue seems remote as the deadline draws near, to say nothing about the issue at all, or else to include a fuzzy provision that satisfies both sides because it means so little. Nor is the agreement couched in the carefully chosen "legalistic" words characteristic of commercial contracts. (Sometimes, indeed, lawyers play no part in the drafting.) A major aim of the negotiators is to produce a relatively brief document that can be distributed to the employees with some expectation of their understanding it. Finally, even where the negotiators try to be precise, they may still stumble into the traps presented to all drafters by the undetected ambiguity of words and by the impossibility of predicting the future.

As a consequence, arbitrators have a wide measure of discretion. Although they cannot alter the words of the agreement, they are often able to choose from among a variety of possible meanings. For instance, when a case raises the question of whether the disciplinary discharge of a certain employee was for "just cause," an arbitrator will not get very far by simply trying to define the words "just cause." Instead, it is necessary to give meaning to this empty phrase by formulating a standard against which the particular discharge can be measured.

When the agreement is not clear, where do arbitrators look for help in setting up such a standard? If they have had legal training, they may turn to relevant legal doctrines. They may also try to find out what other arbitrators have done in similar cases in the past. Though there is no tradition that arbitral precedents must be followed, arbitrators are understandably prone to strive for some degree of consistency in the "interpretation" of a particular agreement, and the absence of a *stare decisis* rule does not deter arbitrators from looking for ideas in the records of earlier awards.[7] Even more important than such precedents, however, may be relevant circumstances in the "legislative history" of the negotiations that produced the agreement, and relevant practices within the enterprise (sometimes referred to as the "common law of the plant"). Arbitrators are also influenced by their own views on what is consistent with sound industrial practice and with the national labor policy, and by their own notions of what is just and reasonable.

ARBITRABILITY   Occasionally one of the parties resists the submission of a grievance to arbitration. This party usually argues that under the ar-

---

[7] Note, however, that only a minority of arbitral awards are published. Indeed, awards are often not accompanied by written opinions.

bitration clause of the agreement, the arbitrator can only hear grievances involving the interpretation and application of the agreement, and that the grievance in question is not covered by any provision. To contest the "arbitrability" of a grievance in this way is somewhat like contesting the jurisdiction of a court to hear a case.

To take an example, an agreement contains no provision on the company's right to subcontract work out to other firms. (Either it has never occurred to the parties that a dispute might arise over subcontracting or else they tried but were unable to agree on a formula.) Even though some of its own employees are working only part time, the company subcontracts some work that might have been done in the plant.

The union files a grievance. It claims that subcontracting is a violation of the *implied* terms of the agreement. It points out that the agreement recognizes the union as the representative of *all* the company's production and maintenance workers, and it contends that the provisions concerning layoffs and part-time labor constitute an implied promise that work will not be turned over to outsiders while employees are idle.

The company retorts that the union's arguments are farfetched, that making decisions about subcontracting is clearly management's prerogative and that the union has nothing to say about them. The company goes on to insist that since the contract is silent about subcontracting, the arbitrator has no authority over the matter under the terms of the arbitration clause. After all, concludes the company, when we agreed to this arbitration procedure we did not agree to having every little gripe the union comes up with submitted to arbitration.

Most arbitrators are reluctant to refuse to arbitrate. After all, the result of a refusal to arbitrate is that the dispute goes back to the parties, who have already found that they could not settle it in the earlier stages of the grievance procedure. Moreover, a refusal to arbitrate usually has the effect of a decision against the grievant. If, however, the arbitrators feel that the union's attempt to relate the dispute to some provision in the agreement is completely farfetched, or if they get the impression— from the general tone of the agreement or from what they know of its legislative history—that this agreement should be interpreted literally rather than liberally, they probably will refuse to arbitrate.

If one party feels strongly enough that a dispute is not arbitrable, it can try to prevent arbitration by simply refusing to participate in the hearing. The law now provides, however, that the party desiring arbitration may ask a court to order the other to submit to arbitration, on the ground that the refusal to do so is a breach of the contract.

One might think that such a suit would compel the court to decide

whether the matter in dispute was covered by the agreement. But in three cases decided in 1960 the Supreme Court of the United States made it clear that the role of the federal courts, at least, would be much more modest. The Court held that unless the arbitration clause of an agreement makes it perfectly clear that a particular dispute could not under any possible interpretation be covered by the agreement, the lower court must order that the dispute be submitted to arbitration, thus letting the arbitrators decide whether to arbitrate. Nor can the lower court refuse to order a reluctant party to submit to arbitration merely because it feels that the grievance in question is frivolous and certain to be rejected. The Court also ruled that when a party that has submitted to arbitration under protest later refuses to comply with the award and the other party asks a lower court to order compliance, the court may not refuse to do so merely because it disagrees with the arbitrators' interpretation of the contract; if their interpretation has any possible justification, the court must accept it. The parties, the Court pointed out, bargained for the arbitrators' interpretation of the contract, not for a judge's interpretation. The prestige and usefulness of labor arbitrators were unquestionably enhanced by these decisions.

A SAMPLE ARBITRATION CASE   The arbitrator's opinion in *J. R. Simplot Company and Oil, Chemical and Atomic Workers, Local 2-632*, which follows, provides an interesting illustration of an arbitrator's justification of his award. The case involves the application of a typically vague clause regulating employee conduct.

J. R. Simplot Company and Oil, Chemical and Atomic Workers, Local 2-632

FMCS Case No. 76K/22606, October 14, 1976
> Arbitrator: RONALD L. WIGGINS, selected by parties through procedures of Federal Mediation & Conciliation Service

IRRESPONSIBLE BEHAVIOR

Statement of Case
Wiggins, Arbitrator:—A storekeeper testified that, on the day in question, employee S— came to the counter and asked for a can to hold a snake he had captured and also asked that holes be punched in the top— apparently, the top or lid of the can. The storekeeper punched holes as requested and handed the can to S— over the counter; he stated that he

did not see the snake. Thereafter, the storekeeper serviced another employee at the counter.

S— asked another storekeeper to let him through the locked door into the main stores area, and this was done. S— stated he wanted to poke more holes into the top of the can and knew there were tools in the Tool Repair Room, inside the locked area, where a suitable punch could be found. . . . S— was holding the snake in one hand and punching holes in the can with the other when the incident involving employee B— occurred.

S— testified that he had asked if B— was in the Tool Repair Room at the time he requested entry through the locked door. S— further stated he would not have entered if B— had been there, knowing that B— was afraid of snakes and had a heart condition. [Employee] H— testified he did not enter through the locked door with S— but stayed in the vestibule issuance area. H— apparently saw B— enter the stores area and testified that B— "came out in a hurry."

B— testified he had been out in the plant, and was returning to his work station. He unlocked and opened the locked door, entered, and had partially closed that door when he saw the snake. . . . As B— stated on cross-examination, he was "scared to death of snakes" so that he left in a hurry upon seeing the snake; this included pushing someone out of his way in his haste to leave the area. B— left the building and stayed outside for 3–5 minutes, until S— and H— came out, S— carrying a can with the snake in it. B— stated that S— did not attempt to frighten him with the snake, that S— explained his intent to take the snake home, and that he, B—, did not experience heart palpitations as a result of his scare in the Stores area. . . .

These events took place mid-morning on the Friday indicated. Apparently, there was an investigation. On Wednesday, July 14, 1976, S— was discharged under a Company rule for his part in the events.

Issue

The parties stipulated the issue to be: Was the termination of (Employee S—) by the J. R. Simplot Company, on July 14, 1976, a fair and just termination? If not, what shall be the remedy?

Opinion

Article V of the Agreement, Rights of Management, recites the rights to "discipline" and to "discharge for cause." Article XII contains specifications and requirements relative to "DISCHARGE/SUSPENSION." Section 1 thereof is quoted as follows: "The Company shall not discharge an

employee without just cause and shall give at least one (1) warning
notice of any complaint, in writing, to the employee affected and the
Union, except that no warning notice need be given to an employee before he is discharged if a violation of the Company's rules and the severity of the offense is the cause for discharge."

Employee S— was discharged under Rule 9 for irresponsible behavior. Since, at a minimum, employee B— could have suffered heart
damage from the unexpected sight of a snake in the shop, it cannot be
said that the Company was in error in concluding that S— 's behavior
was in violation of Rule 9. . . .

The Union's argument was that S—'s actions to capture and contain
the snake were not contrary to Company rules and not inconsistent with
what others, including a foreman, had done. A Company witness did say
an effort was made to discourage the practice because it took time away
from work. By the argument, S—'s behavior was not punishable or was,
at least, excusable. Had the containment been a straightforward and un-
demonstrative securing of the reptile until the end of the shift, this argument would have prevailed.

The Company conceded that horseplay and practical joking had existed prior to January, 1976. It argued and established through testimony
that the horseplay/practical joking incidents involving supervisors had
all occurred prior to January, 1976; in fact, the supervisory capture and
containment of animals brought out in testimony had also occurred prior
to January 1976.

It was developed through testimony that the Company directed a
vigorous campaign against horseplay and practical joking, after the incident on January, 1976.

The Union elicited testimony from a supervisor that some horseplay
occurred, subsequent to the campaign against it, but the witness did say
it was mostly minor. He did, however, state he had heard about an "acet-
ylene bomb joke"; it appeared that this was planned, not executed. The
Company argument was that horseplay or practical joking would not be
tolerated, with emphasis on the potentially dangerous "bomb." With respect to the main argument, it was not established that any supervisor
had engaged in horseplay subsequent to the January crackdown by management.

The final argument by the Union was that no evidence of malice by
employee S— had been shown. The arguments were that S— had at no
time attempted to scare any employee with the snake, had not flaunted it
at B— or any other employee, and had inquired if B— was in the store-
room before entering because he knew of B—'s fear of snakes. The argu-

ment is valid; there was no evidence of malice. However, irresponsible behavior does not require malicious intent.

There is another argument implicit in the record, which was not developed. This is the indication of some supervisory tolerance for non-work activities by employees, contrary to Company Rule 5 which prohibits "ignoring the job," among other things....

The Company tolerance of capture and containment of animals and the somewhat casual approach to employee non-work activities together pose a critical issue in causation. By analogy to the law, was the Company's approach to these matters the approximate cause producing the potential injury or harm to employees in the plant? I believe not....

The general point is that employee S—'s pride in his capture of the snake resulted in the showy parade which, because of S—'s indifference, carried the potential for injury or harm to other employees. In the specified case of employee B—, the potential was realized to the extent, at least, of a thorough fright....

More important is the real potential that B— could have suffered a serious or possibly fatal heart attack from the unexpected sight of the snake occurring, as it did, at a busy work location which is possibly the last place an individual frightened of snakes would expect to encounter one. It was fortuitous that the more serious consequences did not occur since, otherwise, in addition to the remorse and contriteness which would have been experienced by all concerned, both S— and the Company could have faced liability claims.

It is in the context of the real potential for injury or harm arising from the snake incident, that the Company decision must be evaluated. And that decision should be made in the light of an earlier, fire-extinguisher incident. There, as here, it was the indifference or disregard of the potential for injury or harm to other employees which is critical. The indifference or lack of consideration in the earlier case arose from the excesses of horseplay and, to that extent, differs from the present case.

Otherwise, I believe that the two cases are closely interrelated. S— was discharged in both cases for irresponsible behavior under Rule 9. The irresponsible behavior in the first case was the excesses of horseplay while the showy parade was the irresponsible behavior in the instant case. The interrelationship and cumulative effect of the two incidents is in the irresponsible behavior, not what gave rise to the behavior.

Employee S— showed by his actions in this case that he was not willing to adhere to an appropriate standard of conduct. That standard is not difficult to attain or to describe; it is no more than the reasonable behavior of a responsible adult. There is no question, in my opinion, that

S— was capable of understanding this, and that he did so. But, in fact, he verified his contrary view by the opinion, expressed at the hearing, that the 12-day suspension without pay, as a substitute for discharge in the fire-extinguisher case, was excessive. His concern was with the discipline, not with what gave rise to the discipline.

It may be that a disciplinary layoff without pay for a substantial time period (six months, for example) would be effective to convince S— that he is required as an employee to adhere to the responsible standard of conduct required of all employees. Such action, if effective, would preserve the job of an employee with ten years of service with the Company. There was not, unfortunately, anything in S—'s behavior nor in his expressed attitudes to forecast success for such an action.

Finally, there were no substantial reasons in the record to indicate that equity is better served by a remedy such as a more severe disciplinary suspension. Accordingly, I follow the general rule that an arbitrator will not substitute his judgment for that of management simply because he would have done something different in the circumstances.

On the record as a whole and the analysis in this Opinion, it is concluded that the discharge was for just cause and equitable in the circumstances.

Award
The termination of Employee S— by the J. R. Simplot Company, on July 14, 1976, was a fair and just termination.   <

Collective Bargaining and National Policy

The national policy on labor-management relations is to allow employers and employees to work out for themselves the rules and procedures under which their relations will be carried on. The principal aim of the legal rules in this area is to foster conditions favorable to the negotiation of collective-bargaining agreements and to the settlement of disputes arising under them. There are also legal rules that restrict the use of economic weapons and the terms the parties may agree to, and each party is given the right to seek assistance in the courts if the other party breaches the agreement. Within this legal framework, labor and management are expected to work out the details of their relationship in each industrial "community."

CASE SOURCE: Labor Arbitration Reports BNA 1978 Washington, D.C., and 67 LA 645.

Underlying the national policy is the presupposition that in a free society it is ordinarily desirable for private individuals and groups to work out their own contractual arrangements. They will be better citizens if they have to bear this responsibility themselves, and they will probably devise more imaginative and flexible rules and procedures to govern their affairs than would even the wisest of public officials. (This is our policy not only for labor-management relations but also for the internal affairs of such private associations as corporations, unions, churches, educational institutions, and clubs; legal rules merely establish a framework within which the complex of voluntary private relationships take their course.)

On the whole, we can say that the record of labor-management industrial communities in the past quarter-century in setting up and operating their own systems of self-government has justified our national presupposition. Thousands of arrangements have been negotiated, and under them large numbers of grievances are settled year after year. Strikes, lockouts, picketing, and boycotts are resorted to in only a tiny minority of instances in which contract negotiations or grievance procedures have failed. In many industries it is clear that labor-management relations are no longer marked by the bitterness that characterized the era before collective bargaining was introduced.

Underlying the national policy on industrial relations is another presupposition: that the occasional results of the bargaining process that seem contrary to "the public interest" are a price worth paying for industrial self-government. From time to time negotiations are bound to break down and to produce work stoppages that are often inconvenient to the public and harmful to the economy. From time to time a company and a union will sign an agreement containing provisions (most often relating to wages) that seem likely to interfere with such national goals as price stability and rapid growth. The presupposition of our national policy is that, at least in time of peace, such occurrences are worth enduring for the sake of preserving the system of collective bargaining.

Some of the strikes and inflationary wage settlements in basic U.S. industries in recent years have raised questions about this second presupposition. A balancing of values is involved, and some people wonder whether the government should not have more effective means to prevent these undesirable occurrences, even though government intervention would lessen the freedom to bargain collectively.

A further exploration of the issues raised by recent proposals for an expanded government role in industrial relations would carry us far beyond the subject of this chapter. But this proposed increase in government intervention in certain industries does raise some important

questions: What would be the effect of such intervention (either to prevent a work stoppage or to prevent adoption of a particular term in a
collective agreement) on the persistence with which bargaining—both
agreement negotiation and dispute settlement—would be pursued? For
instance, is there a danger that when the parties know that the government may step in to prevent a strike, they will stop doing their utmost to
settle the differences between them? And if the possibility of government intervention *does* weaken the bargaining processes in a particular
industry, may not this result be *more* undesirable in the long run than
the misfortunes that government intervention was designed to prevent?
We should give serious thought to these questions before making any
radical changes in our national policies regarding labor-management relations.

Chapter Problem

UNIVERSITY OF NORTH DAKOTA RULES
AND PROCEDURES

Academic Honesty

Each student is expected to be honest in his academic work. Dishonesty
in examinations, papers, or other work is considered an extremely serious offense by the faculty and students.

Financial Obligation of the Student

It is the responsibility of the student to make satisfactory arrangements
for the settling of accounts with the University.

Failure to settle a University account will result either in cancellation
of the student's enrollment or the placing of a "hold" on the student's
official records and future registration.

The intentional passing of worthless checks to the University or the
failure to redeem promptly a worthless check passed unintentionally to
the University is considered sufficient cause for stringent disciplinary action.

PROBLEM SOURCE: This material was extracted from the rules and procedures of
the University of North Dakota as they appeared in Grace Holmes, ed., *Law and Discipline
on Campus* (Ann Arbor, Mich.: The Institute of Continuing Legal Education, 1971) pp.
289-292. Reprinted with permission from the Michigan Institute of Continuing Legal
Education, Ann Arbor, Michigan.

Solicitation

All solicitation on University property must have the approval of the responsible University administrator or student group.... If approved, the solicitation in residence halls, fraternity houses, or sorority houses must be confined to the public areas of the hall or house; solicitors are not to enter the living quarters of an individual student. Door-to-door solicitation in University family housing projects is not permitted.

Falsification of Documents

The falsification, defacing, altering, or mutilating of any official University document—I.D. card, receipt, transcript, etc.—or the withholding or falsification of information on an admissions application, subjects the student to cancellation of registration.

Keys

The possession of keys to University buildings by students who have not been authorized to use such keys is strictly forbidden. The duplication of a key issued to a student by the University is prohibited.

Hazing

Hazing is prohibited on- or off-campus. Hazing is defined to include any actions, activities, or situation intentionally created to produce unnecessary or undue mental or physical discomfort, embarrassment, harrassment, ridicule, excessive fatigue, interference with scholarship or personal lives, or exposure to situations wherein one's physical or mental well-being may be endangered.

Drugs

The University unequivocally disapproves of, and will not condone, the illegal possession or professionally unsupervised use of hallucinogenic or narcotic drugs by any member of the University community. It is considered an especially serious offense to sell, provide, share, or distribute such drugs illegally.

Disorderly Behavior

Behavior which is disturbing or disorderly, e.g., physical or verbal abuse of another person, obscene language or actions, disrespect for the rights or privileges of others, or drunkenness, detracts from the academic environment and is therefore contrary to the best interests of the University community.

Disorderly behavior by students or non-students at public events on-

campus, e.g., athletic contests, or University Center programs, subjects the violator(s) to arrest and referral to civil authorities.

Telephone Abuse

Students who defraud the University and the telephone company by failing to give correct information on long distance calls or on charge numbers are subject to disciplinary action, as are individuals who use unauthorized attachments or extensions to telephones.

Cheating or Plagiarism

These words refer to the use of unauthorized books or notes or otherwise securing help in a test; copying tests, assignments, reports or term papers; or being in unauthorized places like offices, buildings after hours, or a professor's office without his permission. These forms of dishonesty are very serious matters in a University.

In cases of cheating or plagiarism, the instructor shall refer the case to his academic dean. After meeting with the instructor and student involved, the academic dean shall have the authority to act.

A student has the right to appeal the academic dean's action to the Student Relations Committee. The student's appeal is initiated with his academic dean.

Questions

1. Does this code constitute a complete legal system for the University of North Dakota? Explain. (It will help to refer back to the materials covered in Chapter 2 concerning the elements of a legal system.)

2. Suppose that Jim, a student, slips and falls at an athletic event and in the process shouts an obscenity. May he be punished for disorderly behavior? Describe at least four other situations for which the university's code provides no clear sanctions.

3. Design a list of sanctions for these situations. Be prepared to justify your list.

Questions for Review

1. State an example of an interaction between a private legal system and the public legal system.

2. Examine your university's legal system. Does it have a clear statement of rules and procedures? If you find it to be unclear, give three examples of this lack of clarity.

3.   Define the term *collective bargaining*. Is collective bargaining an adequate tool for maintaining industrial peace? Why or why not?

4.   Discuss the four major sections found in most collective-bargaining agreements.

5.   What is a grievance procedure? Can you think of any examples of how a grievance procedure might be used other than for labor disputes?

6.   What is the difference between arbitration, mediation, and conciliation? Do you believe that these processes should ever be merged?

7.   Earlier in this chapter (on page 211), recent proposals to expand the government's role in industrial relations were discussed. There is an abundance of experience from World War II to guide us here. What effect did the restrictions on strikes and wage increases imposed during that war have on the process of bargaining? (If necessary, research the answer to this question in your school library.)

10
Law in Society: A Conclusion

The emphasis throughout this book has been on the processes and institutions of the law, rather than on the aims and policies that law seeks to implement. But it is important to remember that the legal system is not a machine that runs for its own sake. It exists to serve the purposes of the community. Law is not a set of restrictions imposed on the community by some external power; it is a system of rules, institutions, and procedures that the community itself has established as a means of achieving its many and varying objectives.

This is not to say, of course, that every member of the community likes and approves of every legal rule that restricts his or her freedom. But experience shows that in a democratic community a rule is rarely effective unless a substantial majority of those affected are willing, however reluctantly, to accept the restraints that the rule imposes. Persistent disobedience has nullified many a law, and political pressures have brought about the repeal of many others. The rules that remain in effect are accepted because most people feel that they are necessary or acknowledge the difficulties involved in devising or enforcing better ones.

We should also not forget that while some rules command and prohibit, many rules merely permit us to do certain things, and others provide means to enable us to achieve our objectives. Rules that create liberties merely say: "If you choose to act in this way, public officials will not interefere with you." Rules that create powers say: "If you choose to

216

act in this way, you can alter your legal position; you can create for yourself and others new rights and duties—provided only that you follow the prescribed procedures."

We are most aware of the legal system when it is dealing with breakdowns in normal social relations: when it is providing for the punishment of wrongdoers, for the compensation of those who have been wronged or the enjoining of further wrongdoing, or for the settlement of disputes. And these are important functions of the law. Even more important, however, is its function of channeling conduct in such a way that most clashes of competing interests will be resolved without resort to the coercive powers of the system. In a well-ordered community, the adjustment of differences without resort to litigation and prosecution is the normal pattern of life; disruptions requiring remedial action are the rare exception.

Moreover, while the legal system is a powerful mechanism for the exercise of social control, it is certainly not the only system. In Chapter 9, we looked at labor relations as an example of a social control mechanism in the workplace. Families, churches, and social organizations all exercise private control where official intervention would be undesirable or futile.

A perpetual problem of any legal system is how to reconcile the need for certainty, predictability, and stability with the inevitable need for continuing social change. We have stressed again and again that a legal system cannot serve as an effective instrument of social control unless people can be sure that, under most circumstances, yesterday's rules still apply today. Without some stability in the law, people would have no way of foreseeing the legal consequences of their acts. Nonetheless, continual changes in legal rules are inevitable. Some of these may be relatively minor adjustments to take account of new combinations of facts, but some of them will be major innovations made necessary by changes in the social, economic, and technological environment and in the attitudes and values of a dynamic society. Chapters 4 through 9 all dealt with the means by which the legal system maximizes certainty wherever possible and yet makes possible the continuous modification of the law as the need for change arises.

As legal rules impinge upon our lives, we may be able to understand them better if we understand the workings of the interacting processes and institutions from which they emerge; if we recognize the difficulties of combining a maximum of individual freedom and private self-government with an indispensable element of coercive public control, and of reconciling the need for stability and the need for change; and, finally, if we recognize that the legal system is a *process*—a never-ending, trial-and-

error process of distilling the community's shared purposes from its many competing purposes, and of translating those purposes into effective guides to human conduct.

Chapter Problem

As a final problem, consider the following controversial statement made by Bayless Manning in *Business Lawyer*.

TOO MUCH LAW: OUR NATIONAL DISEASE

By any index or measure that you might choose to apply, our law is exploding. We are innundated by waves of new regulations, by judicial decision, by legislation. Whole new areas of the law have sprung out of the ground overnight—environmental regulation is an example—and familiar areas like good old fashioned property law have undergone a process of infinite fission. We have increasing numbers of statutory codes that are becoming increasingly particularistic: commercial law and taxation are two examples. The truth is we are simply drowning in law.

All this law is irritating, annoying, and a nuisance. But I would like to suggest that it is much more serious than that and that a great deal more is at stake than the irritations we all feel as citizens and as lawyers in wrestling with this mass of material.

Questions

1. How would you respond to Manning's statement?
2. Should more power be turned over to private organizations, such as churches and social clubs? Do you believe that these organizations could satisfactorily replace the public legal system in many areas? Why or why not?

PROBLEM SOURCE: *Business Lawyer*, Vol. 33 (1977–1978), p. 435. Reprinted with permission from *The Business Lawyer*, a publication of the ABA Section of Corporation, Banking and Business Law, 1155 E. 60th Street, Chicago, Illinois 60637.

A
Bibliographical
Note

The body of literature about legal processes and institutions is enormous. The purpose of this note is merely to list a very limited number of works that will be particularly useful to the student wishing to inquire further into the subjects treated in the text. (*The books available in paperback editions are marked with an asterisk, and the paperback series is listed.*)

First, there are some books concerned with the nature of law and its role in society that are worthy of mention. In *Social Control Through Law* (Yale University Press, 1942), Roscoe Pound, the former dean of the Harvard Law School, discourses on this broad subject. Of the many books written to introduce the beginning law student to the nature of law, perhaps the most penetrating is Karl N. Llewellyn's *The Bramble Bush* (Oceana Publications, 1960). *The Nature and Functions of Law*, 5th ed. (Foundation Press, 1980) by Harold J. Berman and William R. Greiner is an interesting collection of cases and other materials designed for use in general legal-studies courses. Professor Berman is also the editor of a small volume of seventeen short talks about U.S. law (each by a Harvard Law School professor) that were broadcast to foreign audiences over the Voice of America; this book is titled *Talks on American Law** (Vintage Books, 1961).

Next to be recommended are some books in which all or most of the legal processes and institutions examined throughout the text are discussed. The revised edition of Lewis Mayers' *The American Legal System* (Harper & Row, 1964) describes "the administration of justice by judicial,

administrative, and arbitral tribunals." *The Law in America: A History* by
Bernard Schwartz (McGraw-Hill, 1974) considers the evolution of U.S.
legal institutions from 1790 to today. Also helpful are two books of cases
and other materials designed to introduce students to the legal processes.
The first—*The Legal Process* (Chandler, 1961) by Carl A. Auerbach, Lloyd
K. Garrison, Willard Hurst, and Samuel Mermin—was compiled primarily for students not training to become lawyers. The second—*Introduction to Law: Legal Process and Procedure* (West Publishing, 1977) by
Cornelius Murphy—was prepared for first-year law students. A political
scientist has written about the law with zest in C. Gordon Post's *An Introduction to Law** (Spectrum, 1963). Also interesting are Frederick J. Kem-
pin, Jr.'s, *Legal History: Law and Change* (Prentice-Hall, 1963), and Richard
Hartzler's *Justice, Legal Systems, and Social Structure* (Kennikat Press, 1976).

Among the many books about the judicial process, *The Nature of the
Judicial Process** (Yale University Press, 1921) by Benjamin N. Cardozo is a
classic. Its author was one of the United States' greatest judges and legal
scholars. Justice Cardozo was also the author of two of the essays, mostly
reprinted from the pages of *Harvard Law Review*, that the *Review's* editors
brought together in a valuable collection under the title *An Introduction to
Law** (Harvard University Press, 1957); among the authors represented
are eight who were (or later became) distinguished judges. A penetrating
analysis of the reasoning process by which appellate judges arrive at decisions is found in Edward H. Levi's *An Introduction to Legal Reasoning**
(University of Chicago Press, 1949). On this subject see also William
Zelermyer's *The Legal System in Operation** (West Publishing, 1977). In *A
Judge Takes the Stand* (Knopf, 1933), Joseph N. Ulman considers the judicial process from the viewpoint of a trial judge. Jerome Frank's *Courts on
Trial** (Atheneum, 1949) is a brilliant critical analysis of the trial process,
with particular stress on the jury system. Frank's classic *Law and the Mod-
ern Mind** (Anchor, 1930) is also about the judicial process. Stuart Nagel's
Improving the Legal Process (Lexington Books, 1975) contains a useful contemporary study of this issue and others.

A useful book dealing with modern problems of judicial administration is *The Courts, the Public, and the Law Explosion** (Spectrum, 1965), edited by Harry W. Jones. Judicial administration is also the theme of *An
Introduction to the Courts and the General Process* by Lewis Merlin (Prentice-Hall, 1978). On the judicial process discussed from the litigant's viewpoint, see Delmar Karlen's *The Citizen in Court** (Holt, Rinehart &
Winston, 1964). And general note should be taken of the useful collections of readings on law brought together by social scientists; a good one
is *Law and the Behavioral Sciences*, 2nd ed. (Bobbs-Merrill, 1977) by L.
Friedman and S. Macaulay.

We come finally to a few works on special topics that were considered in this book. On the role of the lawyer, see Albert P. Blaustein and Charles O. Porter's *The American Lawyer* (University of Chicago Press, 1954), which summarizes a survey of the legal profession, and *Law and Lawyers in the United States* (Harvard University Press, 1964) by Erwin N. Griswold, who was dean of the Harvard Law School. One of the best descriptions of a lawyer's practice is to be found in Louis Nizer's *My Life in Court** (Pyramid, 1961). For an unusually fine short treatment of some problems of ethics and law, see Eugene Rostow, *The Ideal in Law* (University of Chicago Press, 1978). Perhaps the most fascinating of the many books for the layperson about the Supreme Court is Anthony Lewis's *Gideon's Trumpet** (Vintage, 1964). For a short historical interpretation, see Robert McCloskey, *The American Supreme Court** (University of Chiago Press, 1960). On administrative law, see *Administrative Law Cases: Text Problems*, 6th ed. (West Publishing, 1977) by Kenneth C. Davis. And on the law of labor-management relations, see Julius G. Getman, *Labor Relations: Law Practice and Policy* (Foundation Press, 1978).

Index
of Cases

Index

C

D